APR - - 2004

Stine, Scott Aaron,
 The Gorehound's Guide to splatter fi
the 1980s
R 791.4361 STI

The Gorehound's Guide to
Splatter Films of the 1980s

D1558959

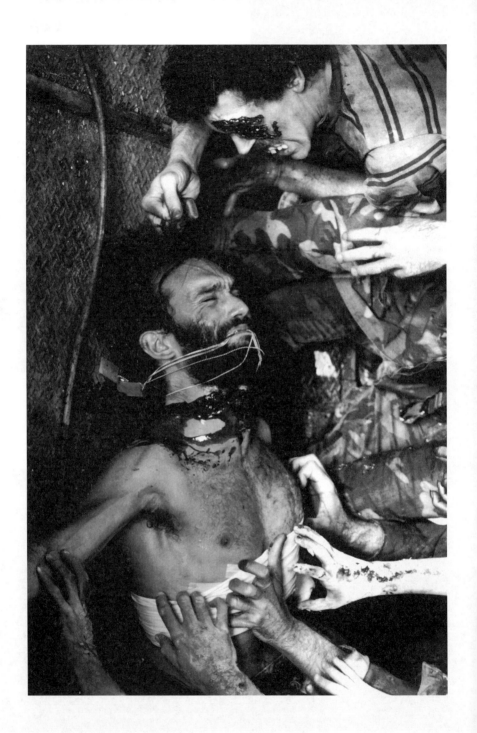

R
791.4361
STI

The Gorehound's Guide to Splatter Films of the 1980s

by SCOTT AARON STINE

McFarland & Company, Inc., Publishers
Jefferson, North Carolina, and London

ALSO BY SCOTT AARON STINE

*The Gorehound's Guide to
Splatter Films of the 1960s and 1970s*
(McFarland, 2001)

Frontispiece: Miguel (Antonie di Leo) sacrifices himself
to a horde of ravenous zombies in George A. Romero's
Day of the Dead (1985).

LIBRARY OF CONGRESS CATALOGUING-IN-PUBLICATION DATA

Stine, Scott Aaron, 1968–
    The gorehound's guide to splatter films of the 1980s / by Scott
Aaron Stine.
        p.   cm.
    Includes bibliographical references and index.

    ISBN 0-7864-1532-0 (softcover : 50# alkaline paper) ∞

    1. Horror films—Catalogs.   2. Horror films—History and
criticism.   I. Title.
PN1995.9.H6S77   2003
016.79143'6164—dc21   2003004649

British Library cataloguing data are available

©2003 Scott Aaron Stine. All rights reserved

*No part of this book may be reproduced or transmitted in any form
or by any means, electronic or mechanical, including photocopying
or recording, or by any information storage and retrieval system,
without permission in writing from the publisher.*

Front cover design by Scott Aaron Stine

Manufactured in the United States of America

*McFarland & Company, Inc., Publishers
    Box 611, Jefferson, North Carolina 28640
        www.mcfarlandpub.com*

FRANKLIN TOWNSHIP PUBLIC LIBRARY
485 De MOTT LANE
SOMERSET, NJ 08873
732-873-8700

Acknowledgments

The following sources were helpful in compiling this book:

The Amazing Herschell Gordon Lewis, Asian Trash Cinema, Asian Cult Cinema, Bizarre Sinema!, Brutarian, Cannibal Holocaust, Carnage, Castle of Frankenstein, Cinefantastique, Cinema: A Critical Dictionary, Creature Features Movie Guide, Cult Movie Stars, Cult Movies, Deep Reed, The Deep Red Horror Handbook, Delirium, Demonique, Dracula—The Vampire Legend on Film, Draculina, Ecco, L'Ecran Fantastique, The Encyclopedia of Science Fiction Movies, Eros in Hell, European Trash Cinema, Eyeball, Famous Monsters of Filmland, Fangoria, Fantastic Cinema Subject Guide, Fatal Visions, Fear, Film Directors: A Complete Guide, Film Threat, Film Threat Video Guide, The Film Yearbook, Filmfax, Filthy Habits, Flesh & Blood, For One Week Only, Foreign Affairs, Fragments of Fear, G.A.S.P., GICK! The Journal of Horror, Splatter & Exploitation Films, Giallo Pages, Gore Creatures, The Gore Gazette, The Gore Score, Gorezone, Grindhouse, Guilty Pleasures, Headpress Magazine, Highball, Horror Fan, Horror Holocaust, House of Horror, International Movie Database, Imagi-Movies, Immoral Tales, Is It ... Uncut?, Japanese Cinema—The Essential Handbook, Japanese Cinema Encyclopedia, Killing for Culture, Knights of Terror, Little Shoppe of Horrors, Magick Theatre, Meat Is Murder, Memoirs of a Wolfman, Midnight Marquee, Midnight Movies, Mondo Macabro, Monster International, Movie Fantastic, Naked! Screaming! Terror!, Necronomicon, Obsession, The Official Splatter Movie Guide, Oriental Cinema, Outré, The Overlook Film Encyclopedia of Horror, Painful Excursions, Photon, Psychotronic, The Psychotronic Encyclopedia of Film, The Psychotronic Video Guide, Reflections of a Teenage Gorehound, Samhain, Scarlet Street, Scary Monsters, Schlock-O-Rama, Scream Queens Illustrated, The Seal of Dracula, Sex-Murder-Art, The Shape of Rage, Shivers, Shock Value, Shock X-Press, Sickoid, Slaughter House, The Sleaze Merchants, Sleazoid Express, Spaghetti Splatter Holocaust, Splatter Movies, The Splatter Times, Starburst, Terror on Tape, Toxic Horror, Trash Compactor, Trashfiend, The Trashfiend's Guide to Collecting Videotapes, Trashola,

Trauma, The Underground Film Bulletin, Uncut, Ungawa, Variety Movie Guide, Video Junkie Magazine, Video Movie Guide, Video Watchdog, The Video Watchdog Book, Videooze, Videosonic Arts, and World of Fandom.

Special thanks go out to: Lorren Bell, Devon Bertsch, Jackie Currie, Charles Dawson, Laurie Dawson, Duane Eilf, Robin Harris, F. Paul Russell, Larry Schemel, Jon Shapiro, Melany Shapiro, Gerald Stine, Judy Stine, Tim Towns, Michael von Sacher-Masoch, T. Andrew Wahl, and anyone else who offered their assistance in editing or collecting information for this book, or who offered support while it was in production, or who—overcome by a sadistic streak that would make the Marquis himself flinch—said, "But you *have* to watch this film ... it has gore in it."

Contents

Preface

As of 2003, the phenomenon known as the splatter film will be forty years old, a rather short existence when one considers the venerable age of cinema itself. Although pornography is considered the black sheep of this medium, its half-brother the splatter film is only more acceptable by default. Similarly maligned by the public consensus, both of these genres are said to appeal only to the "prurient" interest of filmgoers (pornography's yin to the splatter film's yang; sex and violence, the cornerstones of American entertainment). It is easy to see why people are quick to judge such films, as their aims are often simple: to evoke one of two base emotions, to shock or to titillate. Detractors feel justified in their claims that these films amount to little more than crass exploitation; even diehard fans can't easily ignore the shoddy production values and lack of artistry that are prevalent in adult films and splatter fare. It is not that they *can't* aspire to something more—such directors as George Romero, David Cronenberg and Jorg Büttgereit have shown this time and time again—but many simply choose not to explore the possibilities.

Since the splatter film was branded at birth, it is not surprising that it has had only a modicum of success in shedding its bad reputation. (Even the horror film itself is often snubbed by many cineastes, despite its ability to cover "serious" issues just as successfully as "serious" movies.) By fans and film historians alike, the concept of the splatter film is marked by the Herschell Gordon Lewis "opus" *Blood Feast* (1963), the first film to shamelessly wallow in gratuitous violence to a nauseating extreme. This misbegotten child came into the world kicking and screaming, an inevitability that few people wished to recognize.

The remainder of the sixties was the equivalent of the first few years of a child's life. It was heard, its cries an irritating reminder of its existence, yet it was rarely seen. It wasn't until the 1970s—its "terrible twos," as it were—that it took its first real steps. Like a young child who has discovered mobility, the splatter film began testing its boundaries, pushing the envelope

1

"UNRELENTING EXCITEMENT!
A TRULY ORIGINAL HAUNTED HOUSE
THRILLER!" —Tobe Hooper, Director of
POLTERGEIST

"ONE OF THE MOST
FRIGHTENING
HORROR FILMS
I HAVE EVER
SEEN."
—Kim Henkel,
Author of
THE TEXAS
CHAINSAW
MASSACRE

7 DOORS OF DEATH

TERRY LEVENE presents an AQUARIUS ASSOCIATES 1 release of an AQUARIUS PRODUCTIONS presentation
Starring KATHERINE MacCOLL • DAVID WARBECK • SARAH KELLER • TONY SAINT JOHN and VERONICA LAZAR
Director of Photography GLENN KIMBELL • MUSIC by MITCH and IRA YUSPEH
Executive Producer RON HARVEY • Screenplay ROY CORCHORAN • Editor JIM MARKOVIC • Directed by LOUIS FULLER
Produced by TERRY LEVENE • Distributed by AQUARIUS RELEASING, INC. • Prints by TECHNICOLOR®
COPYRIGHT AQUARIUS ASSOCIATES 1—ALL RIGHTS RESERVED

DOLBY STEREO   IN SELECTED THEATRES

R RESTRICTED
UNDER 17 REQUIRES ACCOMPANYING
PARENT OR ADULT GUARDIAN

American ad mat for *L'Alidila* (1981).

at every given opportunity. This narcissistic decade made up its formative years, and was most crucial in its growth and development as an art form. The only people around to put their foot down were its adoptive guardians, both reluctant about parenthood. The MPAA and its ratings board played the part of mother for the thankless child, and its father was public concern, a misguided husband who had influence over his wife's decisions, but was just as prone to turn a blind eye, hoping the little beast would simply go away.

But to the chagrin of many, it didn't disappear into the night. The 1980s marked its childhood, a time of reckless abandon that was most notably restricted—not by the censors, but by its own immaturity. Its imagination stifled, it often preferred to play the same games over and over again instead of looking elsewhere for intellectual stimulation. Unfortunately, the brand of shame it wore with pride had left an indelible mark on its psyche as well as its flesh.

There were two factors that most contributed to how we define the splatter films from the 1980s, both

of which came about during the end of the previous decade.

The first was the advances in technology as it pertained to special effects, especially as it applied to prosthetics make-up and animatronics. Prior to this, there were very few special effects artists who had made names for themselves; the legendary Dick Smith was one of the only artisans to garner any real respect for his craft. The 1970s became a stomping ground for aspiring effects artists inspired by his efforts and fueled by such magazines as *Famous Monsters of Filmland*. These determined individuals—Rick Baker, Rob Bottin, Tom Savini and Stan Winston among them—helped take special effects as it applied to the splatter film to levels heretofore unexplored. No longer

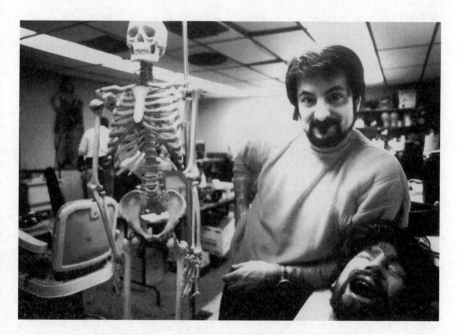

Special effects artist Tom Savini in his studio (1985).

would movies be relegated to displaying only the aftereffects of a particularly violent confrontation, facilitated with poorly crafted latex limbs, red paint and animal viscera. Now the act itself could be shown with more aplomb, facilitated by complex prosthetics and remote controlled mechanical apparatuses.

Unfortunately, it was the second factor that held the splatter film back, a factor that kept it from exploring its potential. This tumorous growth was given the name of the slasher movie, and it is this label that has become synonymous with the splatter film.

The late 1970s saw a revival of the psycho killer film, originally precipitated by Alfred Hitchcock's *Psycho* in 1960. The sixties displayed an interest in similarly staged psychological shockers, as they promised a level of suspense that monster films were no longer able to generate among filmgoers, due to their caricature horrors. The trademarks of the psycho killer film were exploited in the seventies as well, by low-budget American fare and Italian *giallo* thrillers alike, as it proved a convenient way to take advantage of the weakened restrictions in film. It wasn't until John Carpenter's *Halloween* (1978) and Sean S. Cunningham's *Friday the 13th* (1980) that this subgenre truly came into its own. In light of the intense popularity of these two films, hack filmmakers began churning out a slew of copycats that lifted the stalk 'n' slash formula and stripped it down to its barest essentials. Using little more than a holiday as an oh-so-clever backdrop, these painfully conven-

tional slice 'n' dicers spotlighted rutting teens being dismembered and eviscerated by a masked killer over the course of ninety minutes. Many of these filmmakers held a complete disregard for conventions such as characterization, relying instead on tired archetypes; the "imaginative" deaths always held center stage, titillation used to spice up the otherwise uneventful gaps between the perfunctory bloodshed.

Occasionally, there were exceptions, but this was the rule more often than not. And since the slasher film and the splatter film were inseparable, the genre found itself facing yet another hurdle.

As could be expected, the best films from this genre are those that don't rely entirely on "gore for gore's sake." (Not that this can't hold its own as entertainment; very few of the

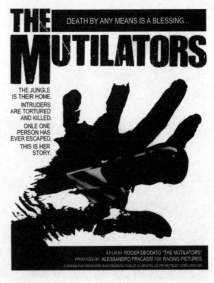

Alternate ad mat for *Inferno in Diretta* (1985).

splatter movies by cult filmmakers Herschell Gordon Lewis and Lucio Fulci can be considered anything more than violent exploitation, but their respective followings clearly attest to their popularity.) Some of the most noteworthy splatter films are both artistically crafted *and* thought provoking, and hold their own against mainstream outings because they surpass genre expectations. These efforts are splatter films because the depiction of graphic violence is an integral part of the story and a reflection of the undeniably dark themes these artists wish to share. Granted, films like *Day of the Dead* (1985), *Henry— Portrait of a Serial Killer* (1986) and *Nekromantik* (1987) could have been made without such "gratuity," but then they probably wouldn't have had the impact they do were they stripped of the gore.

As a teen growing up in the 1980s (a desolate time compared to my childhood in the 1970s), I was there to witness firsthand the continued growth of the splatter film, for better or for worse (usually the latter). So impressed by the tension of *Halloween* and the realistic effects of *Friday the 13th*, I wasted no time in renting every slasher film littering the shelves of our local video outlet. Much to my dismay, only some of these knock-offs boasted reasonably impressive effects work, and fewer still could be considered suspenseful.

Since a young age I had been fascinated by the art of special effects, so I continued to look elsewhere for films that might sate my interest in

Director George Romero in a publicity still for *Day of the Dead* (1985).

such illusory commitment. As I mentioned in the preface to *The Gorehound's Guide to Splatter Films of the 1960s & 1970s*, *Dawn of the Dead* had left a considerable impression on me. Unfortunately, most zombie films made in the wake of Romero's sequel were unsatisfying, although they *did* fare better than slasher movies as whole. I probably would have given up on them as well if it weren't for the third film in that series, *Day of the Dead*, which I happened to catch at a local theater that everyone in town referred to as "The Stickyfoot."

Along with a group of loyal friends who had a similar reverence for *Dawn of the Dead*, I decided to make this an affair to remember. One could only imagine the looks on the faces of the other theater patrons as a group of seven teenage boys in full zombie make-up and silk-screened *Day of the Dead* t-shirts (both facilitated by myself for this occasion) stumbled into the lobby, trying our damnedest not to sully the place with fake blood. Although we undoubtedly made a scene, we were otherwise respectful, giving the theater owner no good reason to kick our sorry asses back into the street. As much as we built up the release of this film, it is surprising that none of us were disappointed, as little could live up to our expectations. But it did.

(It was at this selfsame theater that one of these aforementioned friends and I caught a small independent feature called *The Evil Dead*. Neither of us liked it. We would have walked out of the theater in disgust if we hadn't decided to get our money's worth and heckle the screen relentlessly. We were both surprised when we discovered years later that this director actually *did* have some talent. Although I've enjoyed much of Sam Raimi's work since, I still am unimpressed by his directorial debut, even though it was an admirable effort in light of the nonexistent budget.)

Most of my exposure, though, was through video, not theatrical means. Confined to being a video junkie at a fairly young age, I rented and purchased these films indiscriminately, hoping to discover the next Dario Argento or Stuart Gordon. To somehow justify this compulsion, I began producing a hand-stapled, photocopied fanzine called *Sickoid*. After a few issues, the format improved, and to commemorate this I changed the name to *Reflections of a Teenage Gorehound*. With my graduation from high school, I folded the magazine—intent on pursuing more "serious" endeavors—but started it up again a few years later as *Painful Excursions*. By the close of the 1980s, I had successfully chronicled (in a rather primitive manner) the growth of the genre during this decade, as seen through the eyes of a young fan. (With *GICK! The Journal of Horror, Splatter & Exploitation Films* and its latest incarnation, *Trashfiend*, I continued to write about the splatter film phenomenon, although these later publications focused more on pre–1980s fare.)

I originally began compiling the material for this book and its predecessor in 1989, having already seen most of what that decade had to offer in the way of genre films. Although still a fan at the time, I was not so young as to be entirely subjective. Thirteen years later, I am more able to put into perspective these cinematic contributions—however poorly conceived—although its not an altogether easy task when one considers the power of nostalgia. (It never ceases to amaze me that some of the films I did or didn't find entertaining at fourteen I now hold in a completely different regard more than two decades later.)

Hopefully, this book will do one of two things: offer the younger horror enthusiasts an enjoyable and informative look at the films of a decade in which they were too young to appreciate, or offer the older fans a nostalgic guidebook to the much-maligned films of their youth. Of course, it can be a valuable reference book for hardcore cineastes as well, but I assume most of them will keep it on a shelf just out of reach of prying eyes.

How to Use This Book

With *The Gorehound's Guide to Splatter Films of the 1980s*, I have attempted to compile an exhaustive filmography of splatter films from that decade that fall within the definition of a splatter film, detailed in the Preface. Since this book includes not just American productions, but splatter films the world over, it cannot hope to be complete due to the fact that many of these movies have never been released on video outside of their respective countries. Also, anyone who actually *succeeded* in watching every one of these suckers ever produced would no doubt be traumatized for life. Spending the rest of my years drinking my meals through a straw is not what I would call a life, so I will settle with this book being *nearly* complete.

All of the films included in this book are arranged alphabetically and are accompanied by information that the film student or casual reader might find important, insightful or interesting. Inclusions are broken down thus:

Original title of film (Year of Production)

Production company [Country of origin]

DIR: Director(s)
PRO: Producer(s)
SCR: Screenwriter(s) [Availability of source material and/or movie novelization with author and/or publisher]
DOP: Director(s) of Photography
EXP: Executive Producer(s)
SFX: Special Effects
MFX: Make-Up Effects
VFX: Visual Effects
MUS: Music Composer(s) [Availability of soundtrack and record label]
STR: Cast [Listed in alphabetical order.]
AKA: Alternate titles
Approximate running time; B&W and/or color [I have also listed if a film was released in 3-D, or if it was shot on videocassette, as many independent features are.]
DVD: Availability on DVD [Video label; printed running time of print; widescreen letterboxing

9

(LBX); and the language of print and subtitles, if not in English.] *Note: When a running time of a particular videocassette is erroneously cited on the box or label, the actual running time of the print rounded to the nearest minute is noted in parenthesis immediately following the listed time.*

VHS: Availability on videocassette [Same general information as DVD.]

Note: Please see information below for specifications of DVD and VHS formats, as well as a key to video labels.

ADL: A selected adline used to promote the film for either its theatrical or video release.

Of utmost importance are my highly biased, often unrelenting reviews of the film which immediately follow the technical information. As always, I do my darnedest to point out any and all redeeming qualities of each and every film (not an easy chore, I assure you), even if it is bona fide horse pucky.

For the more sensitive gorehounds, I have also included a " 🐂 🐂 🐂 " warning if a particular film contains scenes of animal cruelty or slaughterhouse footage. (I use these two terms to loosely differentiate whether the scenes are before or after-the-fact.) This information is geared specifically towards those individuals who wish to avoid or simply be prepared for such footage, and is not meant to blacklist such films. If you don't care, ignore it. (As you'll see, I hold a number of

these films in high regards despite these scenes ... but that won't stop me from bitching about it insistently.)

On a similar note, I've included a " 🔪 🔪 🔪 " warning if the film contains actual surgery or autopsy footage. Although I do not find such scenes morally offensive, I do find them quite repugnant and I do like *some* forewarning as to what to expect ... even though my finger never strays far from the fast-forward button.

Although I avoided listing the original MPAA ratings for the films (it's safe to assume that most were released with an R rating), I have marked those movies that contain hardcore sex footage with the classic XXX rating. (Of course, this rating doesn't actually exist and has never been recognized by the MPAA. For those who are unaware, this was originally a ploy by adult filmmakers to convince their audience that *their* films were "harder" than the usual adult fare, thus deserving three Xs as opposed to a meager one.) This is simply to warn people who do not wish to see penetration shots outside of the violent, metaphorical variety that can be found in most slasher pics.

Since I have included numerous foreign, non–English titles, certain guidelines need to be clarified so as to avoid any confusion that might arise due to language barriers.

First, non–English titles are arranged alphabetically by the first word other than articles (i.e. as in English, where we ignore "a", "an" or "the"). Lest you feel the need to drag out your trusty old foreign dictionaries, I've included a list of common articles for French, German, Italian, Portuguese, Spanish and Japanese below:

A	Der	El	Il	Le	O	Une
As	Die	Gli	L'	Les	Un	Uno
Das	Ein	I	La	Lo	Una	Za

Second, standard transliterations of non–Romanized (i.e. Asian) titles are listed when a Romanized version of the title is unavailable. (Obviously, it would be unfeasible for me to reproduce these titles using the actual Asian ideograms. And how I would go about alphabetizing them is beyond me.) Transliterated Asian titles are listed alphabetically, and are followed by translations whenever available.

A Quick Note About DVD and Video Formats

With so many different formats of videos and DVDs currently in use around the globe, it is easy to get confused about what is and what isn't compatible. Below I have included a breakdown of the most commonly used formats for both mediums, and in which countries they are the standard.

DVD (Region 1) is specific to the United States and Canada.
DVD (Region 2) is specific to Western Europe, the Middle East, Japan, South Africa and Greenland.
DVD (Region 3) is specific to Taiwan, Korea, the Philippines, Indonesia and Hong Kong.

DVD (Region 4) is specific to Mexico, South and Central America, Australia, New Zealand, the Pacific Islands and the Caribbean.
DVD (Region 5) is specific to C.I.S., Eastern Europe, India, most of Africa, North Korea and Mongolia.
DVD (Region 6) is specific to China.

VHS (NTSC) is specific to the United States, Canada, Japan, South America and the Philippines.
VHS (PAL) is specific to Europe, Hong Kong, Australia and most African and Asian countries.
VHS (SECAM) is specific to France, the USSR and some African countries.

To differentiate these when listing video availability, I list the former as DVD1 through DVD6, and the latter as VHS1 through VHS3. (Most American consumers simply need to know that their machines will probably only play DVD1 or VHS1.)

Key to Countries of Origin

In order to conserve space, I have used abbreviations for the countries of origin. A list of abbreviations is given below alphabetically.

Au = Australia
Be = Belgium
Br = Brazil
Ca = Canada
Cz = Czechoslovakia
Fr = France

HK = Hong Kong
Hu = Hungary
In = Indonesia
It = Italy
Ja = Japan
Li = Liechtenstein
Ma = Malaysia
Mx = Mexico
Ne = Netherlands
NZ = New Zealand
Ph = Philippines
Po = Portugal
PR = Puerto Rico
Sw = Sweden
Sz = Switzerland
Th = Thailand
UK = United Kingdom
US = United States
WG = West Germany

Key to Video Labels

In order to conserve space, I have used acronyms for the names of video labels when listing information pertaining to specific releases. A list of acronyms is given below alphabetically.

ABA = Abacus Entertainment
ABE = Anchor Bay Entertainment
ACT = Action Vidéo
AFD = Arrow Film Distribution
AHE = Academy Home Entertainment
AIP = AIP Home Video, Inc.
ALL = All Seasons Entertainment
ALP = Alpha Video
AME = American Home Entertainment
API = Applause Productions, Inc.
APX = A-Pix Entertainment
ARR = Arrow Video

AVI = Avid Entertainment
AVO = AVO Film Home Video
BDV = Black Diamond Home Video
BMV = Burning Moon Home Video
BWV = Brent Walker Video
CAM = Camp Video
CAN = Cannon Video
CAR = Caribbean ABC Video
CAS = Castle Home Video
CBL = CBL Video
CBS = CBS/Fox Video
CCC = Cinema City Company, Ltd.
CCL = Cinema Club
CEI = Complete Entertainment, Inc.
CGV = Cinema Group Home Video
CHA = Charter Entertainment
CHE = Celebrity Home Entertainment
CIN = CineReal
CLV = City Lights Home Video
CNC = Concorde Video
CND = Condor Video
CNG = Congress Video
CNH = CineHollywood
COF = Constan Films
COL = Columbia Video
COM = Commercial Factors
CON = Continental Video
CTS = Columbia/TriStar Home Video
CUL = Cult Video
DAP = Dead-Alive Productions
DAY = Day Connection
DIA = Diamond Entertainment
DIG = Digital Entertainment, Ltd.
DIR = Direct Video
DIV = Digital Versatile
DMP = Donna Michele Productions
DUR = DuraVision
ECE = EC Entertainment
ECF = European Creative Films
EDE = Edde Entertainment
EIV = Entertainment in Video

ELT = Elite Entertainment
EMB = Embassy Home Entertainment
EMI = Thorn EMI Video
FFV = 4 Front Video
FHV = Forum Home Video
FLV = Fox Lorber Home Video
FME = Full Moon Entertainment
FOV = Fox Hills Video
FOX = Fox Video
FTV = Film Threat Video
GEM = Gemstone Entertainment
GHV = Goodtimes Home Video
GRI = Grindhouse Releasing
HBO = HBO Video
HCG = Home Cinema Group
HFE = Hollywood Family Entertainment
HQV = HQV
IHV = International Home Video
III = III Star Video
ILV = Interlight Video
IMG = Image Entertainment
IMP = Imperial Entertainment Corporation
INT = Interglobal Video
IVE = International Video Entertainment
IVP = International Video Presentations
JAP = Japan Home Video Company, Ltd.
JEF = JEF Films International
KET = Ketchum Video
KEY = Key Video
KLV = Karl-Lorimar Home Video
KVP = Key Video Productions
LDV = LD Video
LET = Lettuce Entertain You, Inc.
LIG = Lightning Video
LIV = Live Home Video
LUM = Lumina Film
MAG = Magnum Entertainment

MAR = Marathon Video
MCA = MCA Home Video
MEC = Medusa Communications, Ltd.
MED = Medusa Video
MET = Metrodome Distribution
MHE = Media Home Entertainment
MIA = MIA Video Entertainment
MID = Midnight Video
MNM = Midnite Movies
MOG = Mogul Communications
MON = Monterey Home Video
MOV = Movie Time
MPA = Video MPA
MRQ = Marquis Video
MTX = MNTEX Entertainment
MUA = MGM/UA Home Video
MWG = Movies with Guts
MYR = Myrsine Home Video
NAV = Navarre Video
NCV = New Concorde Home Video
NEL = Nelson Entertainment
NEW = New Line Home Video
NOU = Nouveau Entertainment, Ltd.
NSV = New Star Video
NWV = New World Video
OCS = Ocean Shores Video
ODY = Odyssey Video
OFF = Off Hollywood Video
ORI = Orion Home Video
PAN = Panarecord
PAR = Paragon Video Productions
PCM = Professional Cine Media
PEE = Peerless Films
PHV = Paramount Home Video
PIO = Pioneer Video
PLN = Planet Distribution
PLV = Planet Video
PMD = Platinum Media Distributors
POL = Polygram Video

PRE = Premiere Entertainment
PRI =Prism Entertainment
PRO = Pro-Active Entertainment
QUA = Queasy Art
RAE = Rae Don Entertainment
    Group
RAI = Rainbow Audio & Video, Inc.
RAV = Raven Releasing
RCA = RCA/Columbia House
    Home Video
RCV = René Château Video
RED = Redemption Video
REP = Replay Video
RHI = Rhino Home Video
RPV = Republic Pictures Home
    Video
RSG = RSG Video
SCR = Screen Edge
SGE = Southgate Entertainment
SHV = Starmaker Home Video
SIM = Simitar Video
SKO = Skorpion Home Video
SLE = Slaughterhouse Entertain-
    ment
SNR = Synergy
SON = Sony Video
SOV = Sovereign Multimedia, Ltd.
SPI = Saturn Productions, Inc.
SPO = SPO Video
STS = Sterling Silver
SUN = Sunset Video
SVS = SVS, Inc.
SWV = Something Weird Video
SYN = Synapse Films
TAI = Tai Seng Video Marketing
TAP = Tapeworm Video
TAR = Tartan Video
TCF = 20th Century Fox Home
    Entertainment
TDK = TDK Super Video
TEL = Televideo & Music
TEM = Tempe Video
THR = Thriller Video

TJV = Tokuma Japan Video
TOP = Top Video
TRO = Troma Team Video
TVC = Trend Video Concepts
TWE = TransWorld Entertainment
UCV = Urban Classics Video
UHV = United Home Video
UNI = Universal Home Video
USA = USA Home Video
VCI = VCI Home Video
VCP = Video City Productions
VDA = VidAmerica
VDS = VDS Video
VDY = Video Dynamic
VEA = Videatrics
VEN = Ventura Distribution
VES = Vestron Video
VFP = Video for Pleasure
VFP = Videofilm Promotions
VGM = Video Gems
VIC = Video Communications
VID = Vidmark Entertainment
VII = VCII
VIM = Videomedia
VIP = Vipco
VIR = VirginVision
VIS = Vista Video
VIV = Virgin Video
VSM = Video Search of Miami
VSV = Very Strange Video
VTC = VTC
VTR = Video Treasures
VVV = Volledige Versie Video
WAR = Warner Brothers Home
    Video
WIZ = Wizard Video
WOR = World Video
WOV = World of Video 2000

DVD and Video Sources

    The appendix includes an extensive listing of legitimate video companies and distributors that may aid you in tracking down specific titles included in this book.

Index

This index includes not only every film and person appearing in the main section of the book, but also pseudonyms and alternate titles.

Notes About Changes

Those readers who have read my previous book, *The Gorehound's Guide to Splatter Films of the 1960s and 1970s*, may have noticed some changes in this follow-up volume, all of which I feel are improvements on the original format.

First, in a feeble effort to come out of the Dark Ages, I have expanded the list of available video formats to include DVD, which has since become a valuable source for previously out of print films. I have also made efforts to include not only NTSC videocassettes and Region 1 DVDs (both of which are the standards in the United States), but also formats commonly used in other countries for overseas readers.

Second, due to the larger girth of this second volume, I have adapted numerous acronyms in order to conserve space. Keys for all of these abbreviations are given in this section.

Third, I have abandoned the previous "hardgore" rating, as the lines blur considerably when trying to judge the amount of bloodshed in splatter films from the 1980s. Furthermore, this—as with any rating that tries to measure either quantity

or quality of a film—becomes superfluous when the reviewer already describes the film in some detail.

It is for a similar reason that I refuse to apply a five-star rating system, as many reviewers do. Not only can this be deceptive—being subjective, it doesn't indicate *why* the reviewer thinks it is or isn't a worthwhile film—I believe it a pointless endeavor to rate all movies using such a system, as some films simply cannot be judged on the same merits as others. Trashy productions like *Blood Freak* [1971] are worth their weight in gold, and are a heck of a lot more enjoyable than most mainstream films, but giving it a justly deserved five stars when it is far from competently produced would only confuse readers as to what constitutes a "good" movie. Better for the reader if the reviewer instead takes the time to state *why* it is worth watching, and avoid this type of shorthand altogether.

Fourth, in my list of video sources, I am now excluding any bootleg outfits that sell tapes "from one collector to another." I feel that even mentioning these individuals somehow condones and even legitimizes such practices, so I will no longer do so. My suggestion is that, if a film isn't currently available on video or DVD, either wait until it *is* released by a legitimate outfit, or write to any of the companies who specialize in obscure films in order to let them know there is a demand for a particular title. This way, you—the consumer—have a better chance of getting a quality product, and the people involved in the original production of the film actually get paid for their blood, sweat and tears.

Most of the other changes are small and may even go by undetected by the casual reader. (For example, for my animal cruelty warning I've replaced the three dogs with three cats. Why? Because I like cats better than dogs, and thus find the new warning more aesthetically pleasing.)

The Films

The Aberdeen Experiment *see* **Scared to Death**

Der Abgrund der Lebenden Toten *see* **L'Abîme des Morts-Vivants**

L'Abîme des Morts-Vivants [The Abyss of the Living Dead] (1981)

Eurociné [Fr/Sp]

DIR: Jesús Franco Manera; PRO: Daniel Lesœur; SCR: Marius Lesœur; DOP: Max Monteillet; SFX: Richard Green; MUS: Daniel J. White

STR: Caroline Audret, Manuel Gélin, France Jordan, Henri Lambert, Myriam Landson, Jeff Montgomery, Eric Saint-Just and Eric Villard

AKA: *Der Abgrund der Lebenden Toten* [The Abyss of the Living Dead]; *Bloodsucking Nazi Zombies*; *Grave of the Living Dead*; *Oase der Zombies* [Oasis of the Zombies]; *Oasis of the Zombies*; *Le Trésor des Morts Vivants* [The Treasure of the Living Dead]

Approximately 85m; Color

DVD1: *Oasis of the Zombies* [IMG; 85m; LBX]; VHS1: *Oasis of the Zombies* [GEM; 82m]; *Oasis of the Zombies* [IMG; 85m; LBX]; *Oasis of the Zombies* [WIZ; 90(85)m]

ADL: *The Ultimate Confrontation with the Flesh-Eating Living Dead!*

There's this oasis somewhere in the African desert, you see, and, well, some zombie refugees from World War II, and a cache of looted nazi gold. And there's lots of zooms. Lots and lots of those, yes indeed (it *is* a Jesse Franco flick, after all), but not much else.

Franco has helmed some adequately made, even—dare I say it—

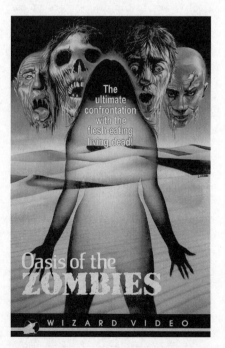

Video box art for *L'Abîme des Morts-Vivants* (1981), Wizard Video.

17

engaging films, but far too many of the entries in his voluminous catalog are neither. *L'Abime des Morts-Vivants* is no exception. This is a slipshod Euro-quickie, made on a budget that wouldn't buy a used car in Tijuana, with no attention paid to artistry. Continuity is nonexistent. Characters are shallow and uninteresting. And the biggest crime of all, the zombies are barely a notch above those found in Umberto Lenzi's *Incubo sulla Città Contaminata* (1980), not because the effects work here is any better (the "zombie head on a stick" will attest to that), but only because it is a tad more imaginative. (At least Franco's crew tried to cover up the seams by gluing live worms to the poor actors' faces, if that means anything.) The gore amounts to little more than smeared blood, although there is one obligatory gut-munching scene depicting desperate actors chewing on butcher shop leftovers draped over someone's midriff.

Lucky for us, Franco made *two* versions of this film. (Geez ... wouldn't *one* have sufficed?) The other version—which utilizes Spanish actors for most of the leading roles—was released as *La Tumba de los Muertos Vivientes*.

The Abomination (1988)

Donna Michele Productions [US]
DIR: Bret McCormick; PRO: Matt Devlin and Bret McCormick; SCR: Bret McCormick; DOP: Richard Strait; SFX: Dark FX, Ltd.; MUS: Kim Davis, Richard Davis and John Hudek
STR: Gaye Bottoms, Victoria Chaney, Van Connery, Scott Davis, Jude Johnson, Brad McCormick, Suzie Meyer, Bubba Moore, Rex Morton and Blue Thompson
Approximately 90m; Color
VHS1: *The Abomination* [DMP; 90m]

A young man's mother, obsessed with a televangelist who she thinks can cure her of cancer, "lays hands" on her TV set and promptly vomits up her malignant tumor. Now homeless, the offending growth takes foot and climbs down her son's gullet while he's sawing logs. A few days later he gets sick, throws it back up, and sticks it under his bed frame like a wad of bubblegum. The young man then goes on a killing spree, shoving the resulting corpses under his bed as well. Tummy now full, the creature begins reproducing, and their human slave proceeds to make mincemeat out of the small town's populace in order to keep the little beasties fed.

The Abomination is undeniably heavy on the gore, but the filmmakers didn't have enough sense to spread on the blood just a little thicker, as too many latex seams become evident when pig gut isn't used to facilitate the effects. Someone involved with this production must have been proud of the results, though, because the first five minutes are packed with blood-drenched footage that are the "highlights" still to come, shown via flashbacks. (Definitely a stupid move on the filmmakers' part; anyone with an ounce of brains—Yours Truly excluded—will turn this sucker off once they realize that these *are* the film's highlights.)

Although *The Abomination* is—for the most part—on par with *Return of the Aliens—The Deadly Spawn* (the over-the-top no-budget grue, cheesy synth score and 16mm grain can be held partially responsible for the comparison), the toothy monsters in this flick aren't nearly as convincing or ingratiating. (One almost wonders if they may be leftover props from the sexploitation flick *Please Don't Eat My Mother* [1972], a softcore remake of a certain Roger Corman movie featuring a man-eating plant. Yes, they're *that* bad.) Also, the aforementioned padding is quite irksome, as some of the scenes are recycled two, even three times before the opening credits even roll. At least Ed Wood had the decency to spread it out a little over the course of his films.

The Little Shop of Horrors (1960) meets David Cronenberg's *The Parasite Murders* (1976), minus the sum of their budgets.

Absurd see **Rosso Sangue**

Aenigma [Enigma] (1987)

A.M. Trading International [It], Sutjeska Film [Yu]

DIR: Lucio Fulci; PRO: Boro Banjack and Ettore Spagnolo; SCR: Lucio Fulci and Giorgio Mariuzzo; DOP: Luis Ciccarese; EXP: Walter Bigari; SFX: Production Film 82 S.N.C.; MUS: Carlo Maria Cordio

STR: Riccardo Acerbi, Lijljana Blagojević, Rade Colović, Sophie d'Aulan, Dragan Ejelogrlić, Lucio Fulci, Zoran Lesić, Zorica Lesić, Jared Martin, Lara Naszinski, Jennifer Naud, Ulli Reinthaler, Franciska Spahić, Kathi Wise, Dusica Zegarać and Mijljana Zirojević

AKA: *Di las Garras del Diablo* [In the Grip of the Devil]

Approximately 89m; Color

DVD1: *Aenigma* [IMG; 89m; LBX]; VHS1:*Aenigma* [IMG; 89m; LBX]

Saint Mary's College, Boston. Kathy, the cleaning lady's daughter, is an awkward girl harassed relentlessly by her peers. Following a particularly vicious prank, she winds up in the hospital, comatose. Shortly thereafter, a new girl shows up ("For me, a successful year means making out with as many gorgeous boys as possible") and things start getting a little weird

around campus. (An aerobics instructor is killed by his own mirror image, a student is suffocated by snails, you know—the usual hazing antics.)

Technically, this is one of Fulci's more competent productions; unfortunately, the weak, derivative material can't support the film no matter how nice it looks. The direction is surprisingly adept, and the photography quite stylish, but the dialogue gets painfully stilted at times, and the plot developments are highly unlikely. (The script proves to be engaging if only because the screenwriters are able to weave several concurrent storylines without losing the viewer.) For the most part, Fulci once again mimics his peers; *Aenigma* bears a striking resemblance to Dario Argento's *Phenomenon*, but here the director doesn't have the skill to successfully pull off such a contrived script.

The gore is not as over-the-top as what can be found in most of Fulci's horror fare (of course, very little could ever hope of topping *Zombi 2* [1979] in sheer gratuity), but it still boasts some juicy moments. These sequences—gory decaps and some cannibalism thrown in for good measure—are either dreams or hallucinations, so one wonders if they were mere afterthoughts, inserted simply to placate Fulci's legion of diehard fans.

Carrie meets *Patrick*, by way of the Big Boot.

Aerobicide see **Killer Workout**

After Death see **Oltre la Morte**

Agguato sul Fondo [Ambush from the Deep] (1984)

Filmes International [Fr], Les Filmes

du Griffon [Fr], National Cinematografica [It], Nuova Dania Cinematographica [It]

DIR: Lamberto Bava; PRO: Mino Loy; SCR: Gianfranco Clerici, Dardano Sacchetti and Frank Walker; DOP: John McFerrand; MFX: Ovidio Taito; SFX: Germano Natali; MUS: Antony Barrymore

STR: William Berger, Paul Branco, John Garko, Dagmar Lassander, Valentine Monnier, Lawrence Morgant, Iris Peynado, Michael Sopkiw and Cinthia Stewart

AKA: *Devil Fish; Devilfish; Devouring Waves; Shark—Rosso del l'Oceano* [Shark—Blood in the Ocean]

Approximately 96m; Color

VHS1: *Devilfish* [VID; 92(96)m]

ADL: *Sink Your Teeth into Pure Terror.*

Riding the crest of *Jaws* (1975) and *Tentacles* (1976)—one of the many films Spielberg's hit inspired—this early Lamberto Bava effort features a prehistoric fish that not only is an ancestor of the modern day shark, but also sports tentacles. Even worse, it can asexually reproduce, so it's up to the heroes to take it down before it repopulates the oceans.

Tired shocks and bad science make up this mostly dreary, uninspired monster flick. There is an abundance of chewed bodies, and even some fairly nifty monster effects, but it never really amounts to anything more than a mindless creature feature riddled with uninteresting characters and stock shark footage.

Lamberto Bava, son of *giallo* pioneer Mario, finally made his mark a few years later with the *Démoni* series, which again emphasized (to a mind-numbing degree) grue over substance. Sink or swim, they say, although the answer seems pretty obvious to me.

L'Aldilá *[The Beyond] (1981)*

Fulvia Film S.r.L. [It]

DIR: Lucio Fulci; PRO: Fabrizio de

Spanish ad mat for *L'Aldilá* (1981).

Angelis; SCR: Lucio Fulci, Giorgio Mariuzzo, and Dardano Sacchetti; DOP: Sergio Salvati; SFX: Germano Natali; MFX: Gianetto de Rossi; MUS: Fabio Frizzi [Soundtrack from Beat Records and Eibon Records]

STR: Pier Luigi Conti, Laura de Marchi, Giovanni de Nava, Cinzia Demonreale, Anthony Flees, Lucio Fulci, Veronica Lazar, Katriona MacColl, Maria Pia Marsala, Michele Mirabella, Antoine Saint John, Gianpaolo Saccarola and David Warbeck

AKA: *L'Au-Dela* [The Beyond]; *Die Geisterstadt der Zombies* [The Ghost Town of Zombies]; *The Hereafter; Hotel der Verdoemden* [Hotel of the Damned]; *El Mas Alla* [The Beyond]; *As Sete Portas do Inferno* [The Seven Gates of Hell]; *The Seven Doors of Death; Seven Doors to Death; Las Siete Puertas del Infierno* [The Seven Gates of Hell]; *Über dem Jenseits* [The Beyond]; *Ein Zombie Hing am Glockenseil* [A Zombie Hangs from the Bell Rope]

Approximately 91m; Color

DVD1: *The Beyond* [ABE; 91m; LBX];

VHS1: *The Beyond* [ABE; 91m; LBX]; *The Seven Doors of Death* [THR; 86m]; *Seven Doors to Death* [LDV; 85m]; VHS2: *The Beyond* [VIM; RTU]; *The Beyond* [VIP; 83m]

ADL: *Don't Go in Unless You're Ready to Die.*

A renovated hotel in New Orleans conveniently houses one of the seven doorways to Hell ... much to the chagrin of the new owner. The strange goings-on eventually force the entrepreneur to delve into the history of the failed establishment, and she isn't particularly happy with what she finds out.

In his unofficial sequel to the infamous *Paura nella Città dei Morti Viventi*, Lucio Fulci (1927–1996) continues to do what he does best—unapologetic splatter films with little or no pretensions outside of shocking jaded audience members with outbursts of high-voltage gore. This time, though, he decided to sprinkle a little spice on the still-steaming viscera by introducing to the formula violence and supernatural gobbledygook an almost coherent storyline. (Granted, the story gets so bold as to interfere with the carnage, but we can't have it all.) Also present are some stylistic trappings that actually lend themselves to the inherent gothicism; unfortunately, the more effective scenes have been shamelessly pilfered from his peers. (Most blatant is a scene that mirrors the death of the blind pianist in Dario Argento's *Suspiria* (1977), a film many consider the pinnacle of spaghetti splatter.)

For those individuals who tire easily from heavy or prolonged doses of old-fashioned horror, be relieved to know that Fulci couldn't go too long a stretch without employing his trademark butchery; by midway through the second reel things kick back into high gear as victim after victim is gobbled up by hungry corpses with predictably sour attitudes. The best of both worlds? It may have been, if the effects work wasn't, on the whole, quite shoddy.

Only five gates to go, Lucio! (Okay ... so maybe we shouldn't be holding our breaths.)

Alien—Die Saat des Grauens Kehrt Züruck *see* **Alien 2 sulla Terra**

Alien II *see* **Contaminazione**

Alien 2 *see* **Alien 2 sulla Terra**

Alien 2—Llega a la Tierra *see* **Alien 2 sulla Terra**

Alien 2 sulla Terra [Alien 2 on Earth] (1980)

Production company unknown [It]

DIR: Ciro Ippolito; PRO: Ciro Ippolito; SCR: Ciro Ippolito; DOP: Silvio Fraschetti; EXP: Ciro Ippolito; SFX: Donald Patterly; MFX: Lamberto Marini; MUS: The Oliver Onions

STR: Benny Aldrich, Robert Barrese, Mark Bodin, Claudio Falanga, Vincent Falanga, Belinda Mayne, Don Parkinson, Judy Perrin and Michele Soavi

AKA: *Alien 2*; *Alien 2—Llega a la Tierra* [Alien 2—Arrival on Earth]; *Alien—Die Saat des Grauens Kehrt Züruck*— The Seeds of Horror Return]; *Alien Terror*; *Le Monstre Ataque* [The Monster Attacks]; *Strangers*

Approximately 80m; Color

VHS2: *Alien 2* [KVP; 80m; In English w/Greek subtitles]; *Alien Terror* [VTC; 102(80)m]

A returning space capsule splashes down in the Pacific Ocean, bringing with it yet another gift of alien eggs. (Geez ... where do they find them all?) A telepathic cave explorer (groan) is having nightmares about monsters; meanwhile, people are having their faces ripped off by the unseen parasites. (One little girl does-n't seem too particularly perturbed by her own bloody disfigurement, crying as if she had stubbed her toe or some-thing equally superficial.) One of the eggs is inadvertently carried along on a spelunking expedition by the afore-mentioned telepath and her cave-hopping buddies, and hatches none too soon to make short work of the uninteresting characters.

If you thought *Contaminazione* (1980) was bad, then avoid this un-eventful clunker at all costs. This life-less horror flick spends the first half of the film putting the viewer to sleep (Woohoo! More stock footage!), then the second futilely trying to make amends with cheesy amorphous crit-ters and second-rate gore effects. (Buckets of red paint are dumped over the victims' faces, but to no avail.) Just as debilitating is the cop-out ending, and the fact that the beastie-to-end-all-beasties that pursues the lone survivor is never actually shown. If it weren't for the really cool "mon-ster-vision," we'd never even know he was there.

The natural cave formations used as a backdrop are completely wasted; had they graced a more able horror film, the effect would have been stun-ning. Even the Goblin-esque sound-track does nothing to improve the ex-perience. (Unless, of course, one already has a penchant for crappy Italian monster flicks.)

Not my idea of eighty minutes well spent.

Alien Contamination *see* **Contaminazione**

Alien Predator (1985)

Continental Motion Pictures Inc. [Sp/US]

DIR: Deran Serafian; PRO: Carlos Aured Alonso and Deran Serafian; SCR: Deran Serafian; DOP: Tote Trenas; EXP: Eduard Sarlui and Helen Sarlui; SFX: John Balandin; MFX: Margaret Bessara, James Cummins, Mark Shostrom and Bill Sturgeon; MUS: Thomas Chase and Steve Rucker

STR: Christina Augustin, Yousaf Bokhari, J.O. Bosso, Dennis Christopher, Pablo Garcia, Martin Hewitt, Lynn-Holly Johnson, Yolanda Palomo, Luis Prendes, Carlos Ramirez and Christina San Juan

AKA: *Alien Predators*; *Cosmos Mortal* [Mortal Cosmos]; *The Falling*; *Mutant 2*

Approximately 90m; Color

VHS1: *Alien Predator* [TWE; 92 (90)m]; *Alien Predators* [VTR; 92(90)m]

ADL: *There Is No Place to Hide...*

Apparently, in May of '73, NASA launched the Skylab Space Station into orbit around Earth. Objective? To perform a series of highly classi-fied experiments that could not take place on good old *terra firma*. Five years later, Skylab's orbit decays and it crash lands back on earth ... with a little surprise on board. Although kept in check for a few years, the alien parasite being harbored by the gov-ernment escapes, making life hell for three teens on a European vacation. (I don't think it could have been any worse had Chevy Chase and the Gris-wold clan been present for the pro-ceedings.)

Not a great film by anyone's stan-dards, but enjoyable nonetheless. *Alien Predator* is competently di-rected, and boasts characters that prove at least somewhat sympathetic, in spite of the silly mistakes the scriptwriters force them to make. Some effective gore punctuates the tense proceedings that unabashedly borrows (okay, *steals*) key scenes and ideas from the granddaddy of xeno-phobia itself, *Alien* (1979), but the awkward scripting and some unre-strained silliness keep it from being anything but a B-movie.

Furthermore, the second half of *Alien Predator* veers off from its main inspiration and begins treading simi-lar ground as that of Lamberto Bava's *Démoni* (made the same year), and even has the same inexcusable ending that appears to be inserted purely for the shock value, despite the breech in the film's already tenuous logic.

An engaging distraction at best.

Alien Predators *see* **Alien Predator**

Alien Terror *see* **Alien 2 sulla Terra**

Aliens (1986)

Brandywine Productions [UK/US]
DIR: James Cameron; PRO: Gale Anne Hurd; SCR: James Cameron; DOP: Adrian Biddle; EXP: Gordon Carroll, David Giler and Walter Hill; SFX: Stan Winston; VFX: The L.A. Effects Group Inc.; MUS: James Horner
STR: Bill Armstrong, Jay Benedict, Michael Biehn, Barbara Coles, Valerie Col-gan, Holly de Jong, Blain Fairman, Al Matthews, Paul Maxwell, Mac McDonald, Alibe Parsons, Bill Paxton, Alan Polonsky, Paul Reiser, Mark Rolston, Ricco Ross, Cynthia Scott, Trevor Steedman, Tip Tip-ping, Carl Toop and Sigourney Weaver
Approximately 154m; Color
DVD1: *Aliens* [FOX; 154m; LBX];
VHS1: *Aliens* [FOX; 154m; LBX] *Aliens* [TCF; 138m; LBX]
ADL: *This Time It's War.*

After being in suspended anima-tion for fifty-seven years, Ripley is re-vived by the government. The au-thorities don't seem to believe her story about the rock on which the Nostromo had landed, until they find their communication severed with the colonists terra-forming the selfsame asteroid. She is asked to accompany a crack marine corps to the site, only to find the colony crawling with bugs. Really big, really pissy bugs.

This dazzling gung-ho sequel to Ridley Scott's *Alien* (1979) takes a more comic-book approach than its moody predecessor. It is easy to see why it was such a hit, as it succeeds on so many levels, appealing to horror, science fiction, and action/adventure fans alike. *Aliens* may be little more than an adrenalized take on the alien monster films of the fifties (with some elements from Akira Kurosawa's *The Seven Samurai* [1954] thrown in for good measure), but it does it excep-tionally well.

Aliens also boasts some of Stan Winston's best effects work to date. (With films like this to his credit, it's hard to believe he started out on such no-budget pics as *Dr. Black and Mr. Hyde* and *Zoltan—Hound of Dracula*, 1976 and 1977 respectively). Present are many of its predecessor's bloody trademarks, including an obligatory chest-bursting scene, just in case any-one forgot this was a sequel.

The cast is top notch, led by Sigourney Weaver reviving her en-during character of Ripley from the first film. Also on hand is Lance (*Mil-lennium*) Henriksen as a sympathetic android, Bill (*Near Dark*) Paxton as a nutty soldier, and Paul (*Mad About You*) Reiser as a conniving business executive.

Alligator (1980)

Alligator Inc. [US]
DIR: Lewis Teague; PRO: Brandon Chase; SCR: John Sayles; DOP: Joseph Mangine; EXP: Robert S. Bremson; SFX:

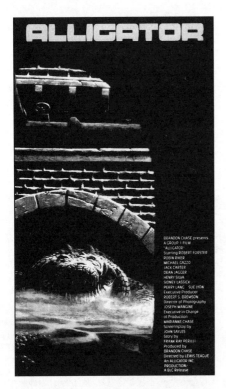

Video box art for *Alligator* (1980), Lightning Video.

Richard O. Helmer; MFX: Robert Short; MUS: Craig Hundley

STR: Jim Alquist, Royce D. Applegate, James Arone, Danny Baseda, Jim Boeke, Simmy Bow, Bart Braverman, Jom Brockett, Ed Brodow, Leslie Brown, Kendall Carly Browne, Bella Bruck, Jack Carter, Barry Chase, Jo Jo d'Amore, Jeradio de Cordovier, Vincent de Stefano, Robert Doyle, Corky Ford, Robert Forster, Michael Gazzo, John F. Goff, Harold Greene, Elizabeth Halsey, Stan Haze, James Ingersoll, Dean Jagger, Patti Jerome, Anita Keith, Tom Kindle, Perry Lang, Sydney Lassick, Frederick Long, Philip Luther, Sue Lyon, Larry Margo, Michael Mazurki, Micol, Peter Miller, Michael Misita, Gloria Morrison, Margaret Muse, Buckley Norris, Richard Partlow, Charles B. Penland, Pat Petersen, Margie Platt, Dick Richards, Robin Riker, Henry Silva, Angel Tompkins, Tink Williams, John Lisbon Wood and Nike Zachmanoglou

Approximately 92m; Color
DVD2: *Alligator* [DIG; 87m]; VHS1: *Alligator* [LIG; 92m]; VHS2: *Alligator* [DIG; 87m]

Although this monster flick relies on an urban legend to lay the groundwork (Remember the one about alligators being flushed down the toilet and thriving in the sewers?), award-winning screenwriter John Sayles makes up for this by tackling a number of social issues even as unfortunate stand-ins are being ripped to shreds by an oversized saurian. (The anti-vivisection angle and potshots at American consumerism are the most recurring subjects; although a bit heavy-handed at times, they make for some of the film's more disturbing—as well as amusing—moments.)

The gore never strays far from severed limbs littering the sets, but the alligator effects—the most convincing I've seen in this caliber of film—make up for the repetitive grue. (Even though you know it's little more than an average-size specimen running rampant amid miniaturized sets, it's still easy to be impressed by the pre–CGI effects work.) The rest of the production values are consistently average—even dangerously mediocre at times—with only an obligatory twist ending to mar the indelible proceedings.

For the most part, *Alligator* is a predictable, albeit enjoyable, little romp that is easily worth the modest price of admission. (Hey ... any film that actually shows young children being chewed up by large toothy reptiles couldn't be all bad, now could it?)

Alone in the Dark (1982)

New Line Cinema [US]
DIR: Jack Sholder; PRO: Robert
Shaye; SCR: Jack Sholder; DOP: Joseph
Mangine; EXP: Benni Korzen; MFX: Tom
Brumberger, Don Lumpkin and Tom Sa-
vini; MUS: Renato Serio
STR: Norman Beim, Ken Burns,
Phillip Clark, Frederick Coffin, Ralph Cor-
rado, Jr., Steve Daskawisz, Laura Esterman,
Deborah Hedwall, Dorothy Dorian James,
Brent Jennings, Mallory Jones, Annie Ko-
rzen, Martin Landau, Carol Levy, Michael
Medieros, Jack Palance, Robert Pastner,
E.D. Phillips, Larry Pine, Donald Pleas-
ence, Paula Raflo, Keith Reddin, Earl
Michael Reid, Jana Schneider, Dwight
Schultz, Lin Shaye, The Sic F*cks, Lee Tay-
lor-Allan, Erland van Lidth, Elizabeth
Ward, Gordon Watkins and John Weissman
Approximately 92m; Color
VHS1: *Alone in the Dark* [CTS; 92m];
Alone in the Dark [NEW; 92m]
ADL: *When the Lights Go Out the Ter-
ror Begins.*

Four dangerous psychotics escape from a high security mental institution and hole up in their new
psychiatrist's house, much to the chagrin of his family. And, well, that's the
story in a nutshell.

Although *Alone in the Dark* isn't
exactly routine slasher fare, the script
still proves too predictable to make
for an engrossing thriller. There are
some good if not characteristic performances from several top-notch B-
actors, among them Martin (*Space:
1999*) Landau, the late Donald (*Halloween*) Pleasence, Dwight (*A-Team*)
Schultz, and He Whose Name is
Plastered All Over the Reissued
Video Release After His Success with
City Slickers (easily the most ham-
fisted of the lot; sorry Jack). Landau,
Pleasence, and Palance have never
been loonier; granted, it isn't much of
a stretch for Pleasence, and even less

for Palance, whose melodramatic approach rivals that of William Shatner.

The gore is pretty standard, but
the one thing that makes the film
fairly hard to stomach at times are the
stereotyped punk rockers used to il-
lustrate the decline of social mores.
(John Waters' scene with L7 in *Serial
Mom* [1994] offers a similarly orchestrated stab; but whereas Waters' humorous approach is tongue-in-cheek
satire, *Alone in the Dark* proffers a narrow-minded attack on a musically
oriented subculture beyond the filmmakers' understanding. Boo, hiss.)
Interesting, but far from required
viewing.

L'Altro Inferno [The Other Hell] (1980)

Cinemec Produzione [It/Sp]
DIR: Bruno Mattei; PRO: Arcangelo
Picchi; SCR: Claudio Fragasso; DOP:
Giuseppe Bernardini; MFX: Giuseppe Fer-
ranti; MUS: Goblin
STR: Andrea Aureli, Francesca Car-
meno, Carlo de Mejo, Susan Forget, Franco
Garofalo, Paola Montenero, Daniela Samu-
eli and Franca Stoppi
AKA: *Guardian of Hell*; *The Presence*;
Terror en el Convento [Terror in the Con-
vent]
Approximately 89m; Color ❉ ❉ ❉
VHS1: *The Other Hell* [LET; 90(88)m];
The Other Hell [LIV; 88m]; *The Other Hell*
[VES; 88m]; VHS2: *Terror en el Convento*
[RED; 89m]
ADL: *Say Your Prayers.*

This pleasant little film opens
with a nosy nun discovering a hidden
laboratory within the convent, and
not only does it contain insurmount-
able mounds of skulls, but one of her
sisters dead on a slab, naked save for
her habit. (They just *had* to leave the
habit on, didn't they?) And just when

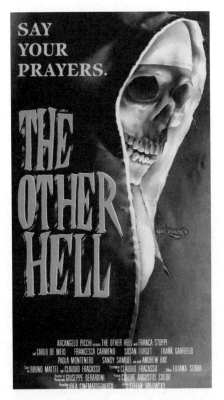

SAY
YOUR
PRAYERS.

THE OTHER HELL

ARCANGELO PICCHI presents THE OTHER HELL with FRANCA STOPPI
with CARLO DE MEJO   FRANCESCA CARMENO   SUSAN FORGET   FRANK GARFEELD
PAOLA MONTENERO   SANDY SAMUEL and ANDREW RAY
Story BRUNO MATTEI   Music CLAUDIO FRACASSO   Screenplay CLAUDIO FRACASSO   Editor LILIANA SERRA
Photography GIUSEPPE BERARDINI   in COLORE AUGUSTUS COLOR
Produced by IDEA CINEMATOGRAFICA   A film by STEFAN OBLOWSKY

Video box art for *L'Altro Inferno* (1980),
Vestron Video.

you think, "it doesn't get much better
than this," another of her order enters
stage right and cuts out the dead girl's
uterus, all the while raving maniacally
about "the Devil's tool." ("The first
thing to do when embalming a simple nun is to cleanse her evil, starting
... there! That's the place! The evil
starts there ... between her legs. The
genitals are the door to *evil.*") She
takes a breather from her post-
mortem surgery to introduce her uninvited guest to the preserved remains
of the Mother Superior, then stab her
to death. All of this in the first five
minutes, accompanied by the sounds
of Italy's premiere rock-horror com-

posers, Goblin. Unfortunately—much
like Argento's *Suspiria* (1977), another
film with which the aforementioned
band was involved—*L'Altro Inferno*
never surpasses the opening sequence,
and actually becomes sluggish once
the filmmakers try to make sense out
of the proceedings.

    L'Altro Inferno also dishes up
stigmata, buckets of maggots, zombies, some *giallo*-like trappings, and a
few wonderfully surreal contrivances.
(In the best Bava tradition, the attic
in the convent is not only filled with
cobwebs but also child-sized man-
nequins dangling by nooses. In all
likelihood, the set designer simply became bored one day during a shoot
and announced, "Hey ... I know what
would look cool in here!" but it's still
effective.) The ending is painfully
hokey, and is accommodated by some
very amateurish burn make-up, but
these detract little from the fact that
L'Altro Inferno is a pleasant reminder
as to just *why* Italian trash horror has
such a cult following.

Amazon Savage Adventure *see*
Inferno in Diretta

Amazonia—La Jungle Blanche *see*
Inferno in Diretta

American Nightmare (1981)

    Mano Films Ltd. [US]
    DIR: Don McBrearty; PRO: Ray
Sager; SCR: John Sheppard; DOP: Daniel
Hainey; EXP: Anthony Kramreither and
Paul Lynch; MUS: Paul Zaza
    STR: Latty Aubrey, Paul Bradley,
Mike Copernan, Neil Dainard, Lawrence
Day, Marty Doyce, Page Fletcher, Tom
Harvey, Michael Ironside, Peter Lavender,
Don MacQuarrie, Nancy Oliver, Alexandra
Paul, Lora Staley, Claudia Udy, Bunty Webb
and Lenore Zann

Video box art for *American Nightmare*
(1981), Media Home Entertainment.

Approximately 85m; Color
VHS1: *American Nightmare* [INT;
90(85)m]; *American Nightmare* [MHE;
85m]

This seedy murder mystery involving prostitution, incest, and
blackmail has been coyly disguised as
a slasher film, which it qualifies as, if
only for the abundance of slit throats.
Despite the sleazy goings-on, it does
boast a passably interesting script and
a few believable performances ... but
not much else. (To give it some credit,
American Nightmare does make several attempts to deconstruct sexist
connotations common to such films,
but these are put into uncomfortable

perspective by the seemingly endless,
obligatory T&A shots—usually incorporated as strip joint footage—that
make up a good third of the film's
running time.)
    The story? Oh, that. Granted, it's
not expendable, but if the aforementioned topics don't interest you, the
plot devices linking these unpleasant
subjects surely won't sway anyone.
    With its dated feel, *American
Nightmare* will undoubtedly interest
fans of '70s sleaze more than fans of
'80s horror and splatter, so if you're
looking for more "modern" slasher
fare, look elsewhere. (And, yes the
producer is the same actor who contributed to several H.G. Lewis films,
most notable as Montag the Magician
in the 1970 atrocity *The Wizard of
Gore*.)

American Nightmare (1984)

2000 A.D. Productions [US]
    DIR: Buddy Giovinazzo; PRO: Buddy
Giovinazzo; SCR: Buddy Giovinazzo;
DOP: Stella Varveris; EXP: Michael Herz
and Lloyd Kaufman; SFX: Ralph Cordero
II; MFX: Ralph Cordero II, Jeff Mathes,
Brian Powell and Ed Varuolo; MUS: Ricky
Giovinazzo
    STR: Martin Blank, Ginny Cattano,
Jim Cooney, Mary Cristadoro, Tom Desan-
tis, Tom Devito, Colette Geraci, Bobby
Giovinazzo, Carmine Giovinazzo, Ricky
Giovinazzo, Claire Harnedy, Doo Kim, Lori
Labar, Yan Lai, Asaph Livni, Joe Loach,
Don Loftin, Leo Lunney, Mitch Maglio,
Jeff Mathes, Jimmy May, Barry McBride,
Dean Mercil, Bob Mireau, Howie Murphy,
Nick Nasta, Ed Pepitone, Vincent Petrizzo,
Ray Pinero, Janet Ramage, Arthur Saunders,
Veronica Stork, Melissa Tait, Stacey Tait,
Brendan Tesoriero, Michael Tierno, Leif
Vetland and Nancy Zawada
    AKA: *Combat Shock*
    Approximately 99m; Color
    DVD1: *Combat Shock* [TRO; 99m];
VHS1: *Combat Shock* [PRI; 92(85)m]; *Com-
bat Shock* [TRO; 99m]

ADL: *Fighting, Killing, Maiming, Agent Orange and Torture Cages Were the Easy Part!*

American Nightmare isn't by any means a bad movie once it gets started; until then, the viewer is forced to wade through needlessly drawn out scenic footage that highlights our "hero" wandering aimlessly, looking for Viet Cong in what are probably the wilds of Upstate New York. (Okay, so they couldn't afford location shooting, but they *could* afford to trim some of the exhaustive expository footage.) Somehow, the shell-shocked vet lives to see the mid-'80s, surrounded by unconvincing junkies begging for smack and bums just begging to get rolled. (These scenes are almost as tiring as the opening travelogue; some streamlining would do this film wonders, even if the end product was only an hour or so in length.)

The meat of the film is the pathetic life of our aforementioned browbeaten veteran, and it is here where the director should have focused more. Unable to pull himself out of debt, he finds himself laden with a family he can't support, in particular a mutant child who is apparently the outcome of his exposure to Agent Orange during the war. Needless to say, depression gets the best of him and he eventually snaps. (*Eraserhead* meets *Rambo*? Sounds as good a comparison as any.)

Gore is fairly sparse—albeit effective—and there are a few stray moments of offbeat humor. (During an interview at an unemployment office, the interviewer stops to announce to the unemployable vet, "Life is hot, Franky, and because it is hot, I am compelled to remove my jacket." Come again?)

On an up note, *American Nightmare* is thoroughly depressing stuff, and boasts one of the most nihilistic endings that have ever graced a genre film. Few films manage to capture the disparity that poverty offers, and this is where Giovinazzo is most successful. With a bigger budget—and a more, shall we say, conservative editor at the reigns—I think it's safe to say that he could have produced some impressive stuff if given half a chance.

An American Werewolf in London (1981)

Universal Pictures [UK/US]
DIR: John Landis; PRO: George Folsey, Jr.; SCR: John Landis; DOP: Robert Paynter; SFX: Effects Associates Inc.; MFX: Rick Baker; MUS: Elmer Bernstein and Various Artists [Soundtrack from Polygram Records]
STR: Jenny Agutter, John Altman, Bob Babenia, Sean Baker, Joe Belcher, Claudine Bowyer, Elizabeth Bradley, Michele Brisigotti, Sidney Bromley, Geoffrey Burridge, Michael Carter, Brenda Cavendish, Gypsy Dave Cooper, Johanna Crayden, Anne-Marie Davies, Rufus Deakin, Linzi Drew, Griffin Dunne, Peter Ellis, Colin Fernandes, Mark Fisher, Alan Ford, Dennis Fraser, Brian Glover, Christine Hargreaves, George Hilsdon, Keith Hodiak, Paula Jacobs, Lila Kaye, Paul Kember, Will Leighton, Gerry Lewis, Rik Mayall, Don McKillop, Lucienne Morgan, Albert Moses, David Naughton, John Owens, Frank Oz, Cynthia Powell, Roger Rowland, Paddy Ryan, John Salthouse, David Schofield, Christopher Scoular, Ken Sicklen, Frank Singuineau, Susan Spencer, Denise Stephens, Gordon Sterne, Mary Tempest, Lesley Ward and John Woodvine
Approximately 97m; Color
DVD1: *An American Werewolf in London* [UNI; 97m; LBX]; VHS1: *An American Werewolf in London* [MCA; 97m]; *An American Werewolf in London* [UNI; 97m; LBX];

An American Werewolf in London [VES; 97m]

An American tourist (David Naughton, the "Dr. Pepper guy" who sang and danced his way through a slew of embarrassing television commercials) is bitten by a werewolf while walking the moors one night with his college buddy. His friend, killed in the attack, comes back to haunt him (decomposition taking its toll between each successive visit), urging him to kill himself. The unknowingly afflicted young man shrugs off the odd encounters, distracted by a bad case of puppy love for his nurse, played by Jenny (*Logan's Run*) Agutter. When he's not bumping uglies with his caretaker (nice bedside manner, that), he spends his nights wreaking havoc and eating the very proper natives.

Despite the graphic gore and bloodletting, this was a surprisingly big hit for director John (National Lampoon's *Animal House*) Landis, which received widespread attention for the groundbreaking effects that reinvented the rules applied to werewolf films. (These merits should be shared with its peer, *The Howling*, which came out the same year and boasted some equally impressive effects work. Ironically, *The Howling*'s effects artist, Rob Bottin, originally studied under Landis' hired hand, Rick Baker.) The film's success can also be attributed to its effective mix of humor and shocks; this combustible mixture usually results in really bad movies whose wit is as sophomoric as the bloodshed is gratuitous, but director/screenwriter Landis keeps the film from becoming a parody of itself.

Das Amulett des Bösen *see* **L'Occhio del Male**

And When She Was Bad *see* **There Was a Little Girl**

Angel Heart (1987)

Carolco [US]
DIR: Alan Parker; PRO: Elliott Kastner and Alan Marshall; SCR: Alan Parker [Based on the novel *Falling Angel* by William Hjortsberg]; DOP: Michael Seresin; EXP: Andrew G. Vajna; SFX: J.C. Brotherhood; MUS: Trevor Jones [Soundtrack from Polygram Records]
STR: Lisa Bonet, Robert de Niro, Stocker Fontelieu, Michael Higgins, Eliott Keener, Brownie McGhee, Charlotte Rampling, Mickey Rourke and Elizabeth Whitcraft
Approximately 113m; Color
DVD1: *Angel Heart* [LIV; 113m]; VHS1: *Angel Heart* [IVE; 113m]; VHS2: *Angel Heart* [FFV; 109m]
ADL: *Harry Angel Is Searching for the Truth ... Pray He Doesn't Find It.*

A private detective (Mickey Rourke) is hired to find a singer who "escaped" from a mental institution ten years previous. The client—played to the hilt by de Niro—is a mysterious "Louis Cyphre." (A slap on the wrist to anyone who doesn't figure out this thinly veiled pseudonym by the time I've finished this sentence.) Part detective film, part supernatural offering, the movie's involvement with voodoo-oriented black magic is downplayed with a decidedly stringent avoidance of pyrotechnics and the like, making the hokum much easier to swallow than what is usually dished up in similar fare (i.e. *The Believers* and *The Serpent and the Rainbow*, 1987 and 1988 respectively).

Angel Heart is well paced, stylish, and occasionally unsettling. Unfortunately, this horrific stab at film noir is not nearly as unpredictable as the screenwriters would like you to think. Without treading over territory already strip-mined by exploitation filmmakers, Alan Parker provides us with a wonderfully pretentious splatter film for people who might not be too swift on the uptake, but have grown tired of Jason and Freddy's antics. The excellent performances by some name actors also garners it some additional respectability and merit, which says a lot considering that this is not the usual "safe" Hollywood fodder diluted by what is considered acceptable in mainstream films.

Some controversy surrounded Bonet's decision to star as Harry Angel's love interest: Rumor has it that some TV execs didn't approve of her involvement with said film and her mutual contract with *The Cosby Show*. (Rumor also has it that, surprisingly, Bill supported her decision.) I guess they didn't like the idea of a highly rated, family-oriented television show star flaunting it all in incestuous, gore-drenched sex scenes—the selfsame footage that was forcibly removed from the film so it could receive a more "accessible" R-rating. Go figure. (Get the uncut version if you wish to see what all the hype was about.)

Angoscia *see* **Anguista**

Anguish *see* **Anguista**

Angustia [Anguish] (1986)

Luna Films [Sp], Samba PC [Sp]
DIR: Juan Jose Bigas Luna; PRO: Pepon Coromina; SCR: Michael Berlin and Juan Jose Bigas Luna; DOP: Josep M. Civit;

EXP: George Ayoub and Andres Coromina; SFX: Paco Teres; MUS: Jim Pagan
STR: Nat Baker, Josephine Borchaca, Michael Chandler, Jose M. Chucarro, Jordi Estivill, John Garcia, Merche Gascon, Vicente Gil, Gustavo Gili, Victor Guillen, Michael Heat, Angela Jove, Edward Ledden, Michael Lerner, Robert Long, Isabel Garcia Lorca, Patricia Manget, Alberto Merelles, Miguel Montport, Javier Moya, Antonella Murgia, Clara Pastor, Talia Paul, Diane Pinkley, George Pinkley, Benito Pocino, Janet Porter, Francesca Rabella, Antonio Regueiro, Joaquin Ribas, Juame Rios, Evelyn Rosenka, Zelda Rubenstein and Pedro Vidal
AKA: *Angoscia* [Anguish]; *Anguish*; *Blind Terror*
Approximately 89m; Color ♠♠♠
DVD1: *Anguish* [ABE; 89m; LBX];
VHS1: *Anguish* [ABE; 89m; LBX]; *Anguish* [KEY; 85m]
ADL: *The Eyes of the City Are Mine.*

I'm going to purposely avoid giving a synopsis of this film as it would give away too many details that might hinder the element of surprise; as it is, I'm going to have a difficult time keeping my mouth shut. (The box does warn, however, that it contains "scenes of powerful hypnosis, shocking crimes and unrelenting terror." They had *me* hooked.)

Anguista is a modestly ambitious horror film that somehow transcends the genre and the gimmicks employed. Borrowing elements from such diverse filmmakers as William Castle, Dario Argento, and Luis Buñuel, Juan Jose Bigas Luna (abridged to Bigas Luna on English prints) manages to create a striking little ode to horror movies without being overtly sentimental or condescending.

For once, the gimmicks employed in the film (in particular the overused film-within-a-film device) are not only used to great effect but are an integral part of the production itself. The secondary production, *The Mommy* (starring Lerner and Rubinstein in probably the best performances of their careers), pays homage to "Hypno-Vision" and other Castle-like contrivances. (Granted, I'm too young to have experienced the draw of films like *The House on Haunted Hill* [1958] in the theater, but it doesn't mean I can't appreciate the ingenuity behind them.)

Throw in buckets of snails and real eye surgery footage, and you have a really twisted, perception-skewering slasher film that has been undeservedly overlooked.

Anthropofago *see* **Anthropophagus**

Anthropofago—The Savage Island *see* **Anthropophagus**

Anthropophage *see* **Anthropophagus**

Anthropophagus [Man-Eater] (1980)

Filmirage [It], PCM International [It] DIR: Aristide Massaccesi; PRO: Oscar Santaniello; SCR: Aristide Massaccesi and Luigi Montefiore; DOP: Aristide Massaccesi; MFX: Pietro Tenoglio; MUS: Marcello Giombini

STR: Simone Baker, Mark Bodin, Margaret Donnelly, Tisa Farrow, Zora Kerova, Robert Larsen, Mark Logan, Luigi Montefiori, Rubina Rey, Vanessa Steiger and Saverio Vallone

AKA: *Anthropofago* [Man-Eater]; *Anthropofago—The Savage Island*; *L'Anthropophage* [The Man-Eater]; *Anthropophagous* [Maneater]; *Anthropophagus the Beast*; *Anthropophalus* [Man-Eater]; *Gomia, Terror en el Mar Egeo* [Gomia, Terror in the Aegean Sea]; *The Grim Reaper*; *Man Beast*; *Der Maneater* [The Man-Eater]; *Der Menschenfresser* [The Man-Eater]

Approximately 88m; Color
DVD1: *The Grim Reaper* [DIV; 88m]; VHS1: *Anthropofago* [VIS; 88m; in English w/Portuguese subtitles]; *Anthropofago—The Savage Island* [MID; 88m]; *Anthropophagus the Beast* [VFP; 88m]; *Anthropophalus* [MPA; 95(88)m; in French]; *The Grim Reaper* [MHE; 81m]; *The Grim Reaper* [MON; 87m]
ADL: *It's Not Fear That Will Tear You Apart. It's Him!*

A group of island-hopping teens find themselves stranded on a rock where tagalong Tisa Farrow (Mia's real life sister) plays nanny for a blind girl. Things wouldn't be so bad if most of the islanders hadn't been gobbled up by a lunatic (played by screenwriter Montefiori) who acquired a taste for *long pig* while lost at sea with his wife and child.

This little excursion does for cannibalism what the same director's *Buio Omega* (1979) did for necrophilia, and is almost as unpleasant an outing. (I mean that in a *good* way, of course.) Most of the gore is relegated to the last thirty minutes of the film, which most prints have trimmed to varying degrees. Of note is an oft-removed and somewhat distasteful scene that has our antagonist chewing on a hastily removed fetus, for which the make-up artists used a skinned rabbit to facilitate the effect. Forgoing any subtleties, Massaccesi also has our resident man-eater ravenously attack his very own intestines after he is critically wounded with a well-placed pickaxe.

A host of dry rot–ridden corpses, and a testosterone-laden score mixed by an apparently deafened sound editor also contribute to the film's overzealous appeal. (If it were a Goblin-inspired soundtrack, and not a

ANTHROPOPHALUS

Video box art for an alternate release of *Anthropophagus* (1980), Videofilm Promotions.

Moog-driven score, *à la Dr. Butcher, M.D.*, most viewers would have inevitably complained of ruptured eardrums.) Production values are passable, but they seem somewhat primitive when compared to Massaccesi's aforementioned corpse-screwing opus filmed the previous year. (Technically, his follow-up, *Rosso Sangue* [*aka Anthropophagus II*; 1981]— a sequel in name only—is superior to its predecessor, but far less engaging.)

Although the cinematography is credited to Enrico Biribicchi, this film was actually shot by the director.

Enjoyable Euro-trash that will surely whet the appetites of most gorehounds.

Anthropophagus II *see* Rosso Sangue

Anthropophagus the Beast *see* Anthropophagus

El Anticristo II *see* The Unholy

Apocalipsis Canibal *see* Inferno dei Morti-Viventi

Apocalisse Domani [Apocalypse Tomorrow] (1982)

New Fida Organisation [It], José Frade PC [Sp]

DIR: Antonio Margheriti; PRO: Maurizio Amati and Sandro Amati; SCR: Antonio Margheriti and José Martinez Molla; DOP: Fernando Arribas; EXP: José Frade; SFX: Bob Shelley; MFX: Gianetto de Rossi; MUS: Alessandro Blonksteiner

STR: Jere Beery, Linzia de Carolis, Laura Dean, Doug Dillingham, John Geroson, William H. Gribble, Cindy Hamilton, May Heatherly, Tony King, George Nikas, Vic Perkins, Giovanni Lombardo Radice, Joan Riordan, Benjamin Rogers, Don Ruffin, Ronnie Sanders, John Saxon, Lonnie Smith, Elizabeth Turner, Ralph Pruitt Vaughn, Wallace Wilkinson and Ray Williams

AKA: *Asphalt-Kannibalen* [Cannibals in the Streets]; *Cannibal Apocalypse; Cannibals in the City; Invasion of the Flesh Hunters; Jäger der Apokalypse* [Apocalypse Hunter]; *Savage Apocalypse; Savage Slaughterers; The Slaughterers; Virus*

Approximately 98m; Color ⚄ ⚄ ⚄

DVD1: *Cannibal Apocalypse* [IMG; 96m; LBX]; VHS1: *Invasion of the Flesh Hunters* [VES; 90m]; VHS2: *Cannibal Apocalypse* [REP; 90m]

ADL: *There are some things worse than death!*

Despite the fact that director Margheriti has been one of Italy's most prolific genre filmmakers since the early '60s, his work continuously stands out from that of other exploitation filmmakers. This is not so much due to a recognizable style or

POWs in Vietnam...starved in captivity... released with a taste for human flesh.

Alternate ad mat for *Apocalisse Domani* (1982).

above-average production values (both of which contribute to his better films), but to his ability to take then-current trends and tired formulas and rework them into something reasonably engaging. *Apocalisse Domani* is a perfect case in point. Here he manages to avoid many of the clichés that are inherent to whatever subgenre he exploits. For example, the rampant cannibalism in *Apocalisse Domani* is neither the work of the hungry dead nor Stone Age savages, but of Vietnam vets and their affected kin who have acquired a rare disease. Maybe it doesn't make much sense, but once the viewer has accepted this strange condition, the film manages to breathe a little life into an extremely stale subgenre. (One character attributes the anthropophagia to

"some kind of biologic mutation due to a psychic alteration." Huh?)

John Saxon, a talented but chronic B-actor, stars as one of the aforementioned vets who leads a small group of contagion-ridden victims pursued by authorities. (The film's otherwise obvious intention to make a statement on the plight of Vietnam vets is surprisingly underscored, the subtlety making it all the more effective.) It is interesting to note that, although repelled by their actions, the audience is easily lulled into sympathizing with the cannibalistic-prone fugitives, despite the actions they take in order to survive.

Undoubtedly, there are many elements lifted from its obvious inspiration, *Dawn of the Dead* (1978), but even with these, Margheriti pulls a few left hooks. There are four protagonists (three men—one black—and one woman), but *they* are the flesh eaters themselves. At one point, one of them (Deodato regular Giovanni Lombardo Radice in what is easily his buggiest role ever) is pursued through a mall by bikers. Saxon's wife is a newscaster, and their precarious marriage riddled with complications. Furthermore, the incubation of the virus period is extremely inconsistent (as it was in Romero's film), able to yield results anywhere from a few hours to a few years, depending on what the script calls for.

Decent performances and some legitimate shocks help to smooth out the occasionally rocky production values. Unfortunately for us, the only print available in the US is almost completely bereft of the really nasty bloodshed. (A scene with Euro-fave Radice and an overworked bone saw never made it to these shores, and neither did one with him suffering from a rather large hole in his chest, courtesy of a cop's double-barrel shotgun.) Ironically, gratuitous bloodshed was not something director Margheriti was fond of depicting, which is surprising since much of his '70s fare is actually quite violent. Regardless, *Apocalisse Domani* easily rates as one of his most enjoyable outings, in spite of these excesses.

Aquarius *see* **Deliria**

Aquarius—Theater des Todes *see* **Deliria**

Aquella Casa al Lado del Cementerio *see* **Quella Villa Accanto al Cimitero**

Arabella l'Angelo Nero [Arabella the Black Angel] (1987)

Arpa International [It]
DIR: Stelvio Massi; PRO: Paolo di Tosto and Armando Novelli; SCR: R. Filippucci; DOP: Stelvio Massi; MUS: Serfran
STR: Francesco Casale, Tinì Cansino, Renato d'Amore, David d'Ingeo, Giosè Davì, Vinicio Dimanti, Ida Galli, Carlo Mucari, Rena Niehaus, Evelyn Stewart and Valentina Visconti
AKA: *Black Angel*
Approximately 87m; Color
VHS1: *Arabella l'Angelo Nero* [SKO; 90(87)m; In Italian]
ADL: *An Erotic Thriller Where the Vice Is Not Sin.*

A man with a camera follows Arabella—a sexually frustrated housewife—to the Inferno Regency, a castle that caters to sado-masochists. Police raid the establishment, and one of the officers has his way with the desperate woman, with the rape being captured on film by her faceless fol-

lower. She goes home to her verbally abusive husband, a writer by trade who was crippled on their wedding day. (Once again, this proves the adage that fellatio and moving vehicles do not mix.) The cop—her purse in his possession—comes to her house the following day for a repeat performance, and is bludgeoned to death with a mallet after her hubby catches him going down on her. They bury the body in the backyard, but, much to their chagrin, the photographer notices the cop's disappearance and does a little math.

Aside from acres of bare flesh and softcore sex, this slick and sleazy giallo thriller dwells on the death of many a horny man dispatched with a rather nasty looking pair of scissors. Although the identity of the killer is fairly obvious early on, there are enough twists to accommodate the sordid goings-on. Adding to the fun is a catfight, some bloody emasculations, a disturbing dream sequence, and a flaming queen in leather playing accordion on the lawn of the castle who tells Arabella, "I can tell you sport mammary glands." Good dubbing, that.

Director Massi (here hiding under his oft-employed pseudonym of "Max Steel") helmed a slew of spaghetti westerns in the 1960s, and also directed such "notable" exploitation films as *Perché Quelle Strane Gocce di Sangue sul Corpo di Jennifer?* (1972) and *Mondo Cane 3* (1986).

Arabella the Black Angel *see* **Arabella l'Angelo Nero**

El Asesino de Rosemary *see* **The Prowler**

Asesino del Futuro *see* Futurekill

Asphalt-Kannibalen *see* Apocalisse Domani

Astaron—Brut des Schreckens *see* Contaminazione

El Ataque de los Zombies Atomicos *see* Incubo sulla Città Contaminata

L'Au-Dela *see* L'Aldilá

Aullido *see* The Howling

Ausgeburt der Hölle *see* Rosso Sangue

L'Avion de l'Apocalypse *see* Incubo sulla Città Contaminata

Baby Blood (1989)

Exo 7 Productions [Fr], Partner's Productions [Fr]
DIR: Alain Robak; PRO: Joelle Malberg, Irene Sohm and Ariel Zeitoun; SCR: Serge Cukier and Alain Robak; DOP: Bernard Dechet; EXP: Joelle Malberg and Irene Sohm; MFX: Benoît Lestang; MUS: Carlos Acciari and Simon Boswell
STR: Jacques Audiard, Eric Averlant, Philippe Belin, Caroline Blanvillain, Sophie Blanvillain, Arsene Burgonde, Pierre Cadeac, Alain Chabat, Éric Dangremont, Alain Doyen, Kodjo Eboucle, Emmanuelle Escourrou, François Frapier, Jean-François Gallotte, Pierre Garnier, Dan Garzon, Jonathan Garzon, Roselyne Geslot, Christian Guerinel, Thierry Guerinel, Jerzy Kowynia, Piotr Kukla, Jean-Yves Lafesse, Chimbot le Chien, Thierry le Portier, Marc Linbe, Christine Malberg, Marine Malberg, Barbara Michotek, Claude Najeau, Joanna Orzechowska, Jean-Pierre Piardon, Yann Piquer, Jocelyn Pirio, Roger Placenta, Alain Robak, Jean-Claude Romer, Christophe Rossignon, Remy Roubakha, Anne Singer, Christian Sinniger, Jean-Marc Toussaint, Dominique Treillou, Caroline Vie, Roger Zacconi and Zoe

AKA: *The Evil Within*
Approximately 85m; Color
VHS1: *The Evil Within* [APX; 88(85)m]; VHS2: *Baby Blood* [HCG; 88(85)m; French w/English subtitles]
ADL: *It's Time to Feed the Baby.*

A zoo in Central Africa acquires a new leopard; unbeknownst to everyone involved, the feline harbors an alien-like, primordial parasite. The critter eventually tears its way out and "impregnates" a busty, gap-toothed lion tamer. Soon after, she begins hearing a voice in her head—the monster's, of course—which whines about being fed. Much like Audrey from Roger Corman's *The Little Shop of Horrors* (1960), not only is it petulant, but human blood seems to be the only thing it can keep down. (Before long, the killing becomes perfunctory for the surrogate mother; at one point she even makes her unborn guest say "please" before she finishes off the victim.)

Although *Baby Blood* is worth seeing because it's one of the goriest flicks to ever come out of France (a country not revered for its horror or splatter fare), it's also a fairly endearing effort. Unfortunately, what could have been a film of serious merits is hindered by innumerable factors. Some of the photography is innovative, but much of the camerawork is sloppy to the point of amateurish. The script offers some engaging, thought-provoking concepts, yet seems to avoid tackling the obvious, like "Why doesn't anyone notice the fact that the young woman in question is always drenched in blood?" Even worse for English-speaking viewers, those responsible for redubbing the film found it necessary to make the monster sound like a whiny asthmatic. (Think "What if Erkle from *Family Matters* had replaced James Earl Jones as the voice of Darth Vader?")

Still, the brutal violence and subtle humor makes *Baby Blood* a memorable film, and it is because of these qualities it has gained something of a cult reputation (despite being butchered for its American release under the completely generic title of *The Evil Within*). All in all, it's quite touching. Really.

Two parts Zulawski's *Possession* (1981) plus one part Henenlotter's *Brain Damage* (1988).

Backwoods *see* **Geek!**

Backwoods Massacre *see* **Midnight**

Bad Taste (1987)

WingNut Films [NZ]
DIR: Peter Jackson; PRO: Peter Jackson; SCR: Ken Hammon, Tony Hiles and Peter Jackson; DOP: Peter Jackson; SFX: Peter Jackson; MFX: Peter Jackson; MUS: Michelle Scullion

STR: Peter Jackson, Dean Lawrie, Mike Minett, Pete O'Herne, Terry Potter, Craig Smith, Peter Vere-Jones and Doug Wren

Approximately 90m; Color
DVD1: *Bad Taste* [ABE; 90m; LBX]; VHS1: *Bad Taste* [ABE; 90m]; *Bad Taste* [MAG; 90m]; VHS2: *Bad Taste* [FFV; 87m]

Ugly BEMs with a taste for human flesh post a base on Earth so they can collect enough of this universal "delicacy" to start an intergalactic fast food joint specializing in *long pig*. A New Zealand special-forces group, AIDS (Alien Investigation and Defense Service), is sent to quash their nefarious plans, and a literal bloodbath ensues.

Video box art for *Bad Taste* (1987), Magnum Entertainment.

This, Jackson's impressive debut feature, is a disgusting, albeit riotously funny, splatter flick that owes as much to films like *Dawn of the Dead* (1978) as it does to *Monty Python and the Holy Grail* (1975). As with films such as *Basket Case* (1982), the low-budget restraints actually add to its odd charm. Some of the special effects may not be great, but in a humorous context such as this, they're quite satisfactory.

Jackson followed *Bad Taste* with a string of enjoyable over-the-top splatter flicks, including *Meet the Feebles* (1990) and *Dead Alive* (1991). For those unaware, yes, these films were directed by the selfsame chap from down under who brought us the critically acclaimed *Heavenly Creatures* (1994) and Tolkein's epic *Lord of the Rings* (2002) trilogy. Geez ... who would've thunk it?

Barbarian Goddess *see* **Mondo Cannibale** (1980)

Basket Case (1982)

Shapiro-Glickenhaus Entertainment [US]

DIR: Frank Henenlotter; PRO: Edgar Ievins; SCR: Frank Henenlotter; DOP: Bruce Torbet; EXP: Arnie Bruck and Tom Kaye; MFX: John Caglione, Jr., and Kevin Haney; MUS: Gus Russo

STR: Chris Babson, Ilze Balodis, Beverly Bonner, Diana Browne, Joe Clarke, Billy Freeman, Sean McGabe, Ruth Neuman, Lloyd Pace, Richard Pierce, Tom Robinson, Kerry Ruff, Terri Susan Smith, Dorothy Strongin, Kevin Vanhentenryck and Robert Vogel

Approximately 91m; Color

DVD1: *Basket Case* [IMG; 91m]; VHS1: *Basket Case* [MHE; 89m]; *Basket Case* [SWV; 91m]; *Basket Case* [VTR; 89m]; VHS2: *Basket Case* [TAR; 85m]

ADL: *The Tenant in Room 7 Is Very Small, Very Twisted and Very Mad.*

A young man carrying a wicker basket rents a room in a seedy hotel in downtown New York. Something in the basket is carrying a chip on its shoulder nearly as large as itself, and is forced to rely on his "big" brother to make amends for being wronged by a cadre of unethical medical practitioners.

Few modern horror films achieve or deserve the cult status bestowed upon them by opportunistic ad men and second-rate film reviewers. *Basket*

Video box art for *Basket Case* (1982), Media Home Entertainment.

Case is one such film, having garnered its reputation without ever having seen a decent release. The innovation and verve this movie displays surpasses its innumerable shortcomings, all products of a film that qualified as destitute before the cameras even started rolling. The fact that most of the "actors" had probably never stepped foot in front of a camera prior to this only adds to the movie's squalid charm; their talents may be slim, but their presence is priceless. (Of mild interest is the screen debut of Scott Valentine from *Family Ties—*

if you use your frame advance, you may be able to pick him out of the crowd—and an uncredited appearance by porn star Jerry Butler as a bar patron.)

And not to forget the other half of "cheap and nasty," *Basket Case* boasts numerous gore-drenched murders, all rendered in a way that is more representative of 1970s fare. It is of little surprise that the film offers an onscreen dedication to the Godfather of Gore himself, Herschell Gordon Lewis.

So far, there's been two sequels of proportionally higher budgets by the same filmmaker, but neither has managed to capture the audacious charm of the original. Whereas the humor in the later outings is much more pronounced and intentional, the tongue-in-cheek approach of *Basket Case* works unnervingly well with the horrifically surreal aspects. Even the trite revenge motif is used with great results here, but loses its power in the future installments.

Apparently calling it quits as a filmmaker about ten years ago, Frank Henenlotter is currently helping to peddle the "Sexy Shockers from the Vault" line for Something Weird Video. From his reviews for these films, one can't mistake the love he has for trash cinema, and it shows in his first effort more than any other.

Battalion 2 *see* **The Return of the Living Dead—Part II**

The Beast Within (1981)

United Artists [US]
DIR: Philippe Mora; PRO: Harvey Bernhard and Gabriel Katzka; SCR: Tom Holland [Based on the novel *The Beast Within* by Edward Levy]; DOP: Jack L.

Richards; EXP: Jack B. Bernstein; MFX: Thomas R. Burman; SFX: Fred J. Cramer and Garry J. Elmendorf; MUS: Les Baxter STR: R.G. Armstrong, Luke Askew, Bibi Besch, Paul Clemens, Ronny Cox, Don Gordon, J. Boyce Holleman, Natalie Nolan Howard, John Dennis Johnston, L.Q. Jones, Malcolm McMillan, Fred D. Meyer, Kitty Moffat, Logan Ramsay, Ron Soble and Meshach Taylor

Approximately 98m; Color
DVD1: *The Beast Within* [MUA; 98m; LBX]; VHS1: *The Beast Within* [MUA; 98m]

While on her honeymoon, a newlywed wife is raped by a hairy beast (no ... *not* her husband). Seventeen years later, their seemingly normal, average son starts to suffer from an "occult malignancy" which doctors claim is simply a pituitary gland going full-tilt boogie. Realizing it has something to do with the illegitimate boy's *real* father, the couple goes back to the town where the incident occurred, but they have a heck of a time getting any answers out of the hick residents.

Although *The Beast Within* is a quaint little tale of cicadas and cannibalism, it sadly suffers from innumerable shortcomings, including way below-average acting and a make-it-up-as-you-go-along script with little explanation for the resident beastie (a feeble looking monster than can best be described as Spielberg's ET on steroids). Gore is plentiful, but it comes across as rather laughable thanks to some overused bladder effects. (Remember *Spasms* [1983] anyone?) If anything good can be said of this, *The Beast Within* proves—once and for all—that metamorphosis in the 1980s was far messier—and apparently more painful—than it was with the screen monsters of yesteryear.

"There's something terrible happening in there," one character responds dryly as the teen begins to mutate in the next room. Methinks they may have been referring to the make-up appliances reserved for the hapless actor.

Luckily, the film does cut to the quick early on, and it manages to throw in enough playful references to keep the diehard horror fan's attention fixed. (A mortician named "Dexter Ward" didn't get past me, nor was it lost on other Lovecraftophiles, I'm sure.)

Similar in tone to (and just as sleazy as) *The Incubus* (1981) and *Amityville II—The Possession* (1982), *The Beast Within* is silly, maybe, but good for a few cheap thrills.

Beasts *see* **Flesh and the Bloody Terror**

The Beasts' Carnival *see* **El Carnaval de las Bestias**

Beautiful Screamers *see* **Silent Madness**

The Being (1981)

Bad Dreams Inc. [US]
DIR: Jackie Kong; PRO: William Osco; SCR: Jackie Kong; DOP: Robert Ebinger; MFX: Mark Bussan and Thom Shouse; SFX: Mark Bussan and John Eggett; MUS: Don Preston
STR: Larry Babcock, Tracy Barry, Ellen Blake, Ruth Buzzi, Dave Clark, Rexx Coltrane, Johnny Commander, Patrick Cunningham, Johnny Dark, John Elliott, José Ferrer, Kinky Friedman, Cury Germann, Brad Ginther, Marianne Gordon, Eric Helland, Mary Hold, Jefferson Jewell, Martin Landau, Murray Langston, Dorothy Malone, Richard Marcus, Jerry Marin, Roland Onffrey, Nancy Osco, Roxanne Cybelle Osco, Kent Perkins, Bill Rawlinson, Jay Sherlock, Chief Sherwin, James Simmerman, Roger Smith and Brian Swain
AKA: *Freak*; *The Pottsville Horror*
Approximately 92m; Color
VHS1: *The Being* [HBO; 92m]; *The Being* [MHE; 92m]

This is more typical early '80s Midwestern monster fare, with the prerequisite sex and gore (although the lighting is too poor to see much of either). Production values are pretty standard as well, with the exception of some piecemeal editing and continuity that makes the ride bumpier than it should have been.

This time around, the monster is a cyclopean meatloaf that seems to suffer the same debilitation as that of the hydrocephalic critters from *Inva-*

Video box art for *The Being* (1981), Media Home Entertainment.

sion of the Saucer Men (1957). Martin (*Space: 1999*) Landau and comedian Ruth Buzzi (as an anti-smut activist) lend their names to the cast, and both appear in a goofy dream sequence that should have been left on the cutting room floor. There's a scene involving a cat almost entirely lifted from *Alien* (1979), and the frequently overused "Is it really over?"–style ending does nothing but underscore the movie's lack of originality.

Director Jackie Kong went on to do the equally derivative but (debatably) more enjoyable *Blood Diner* six years later.

La Bestia y la Espada Mágica
[The Beast and the Magic Sword] (1983)

Acónito Films [Sp], Amachi Films [Ja]
DIR: Jacinto Molina Alvarez; PRO: Augusto Boué; SCR: Jacinto Molina Alvarez; DOP: Julio Burgos; EXP: Julia Salinero and Masurao Takeda; SFX: Juan Ramón Molina
STR: Jacinto Molina Alvarez, Sigheru Amachi, Junko Asahina, Charly Bravo, Violeta Cela, José Luis Chinchilla, Irene Daina, Antonio Durán, Beatriz Escudero, Yoko Fuji, Elena Garret, Mitsuaki Hori, Yoshiro Kitamachi, Makiko Kitashiro, Jiro Miyaguchi, Sara Mora, Seijun Okabe, Conrado San Martín, Soburo Sauri, José Vivó, Gérard Tichy Wondzinski and Takenori Yamase
AKA: *The Werewolf and the Magic Sword*
Approximately 109m; Color

The year is 938 A.D., and Waldemar Daninsky is called in to fight a duel with a rumored vampire. In return for his services, Waldemar demands the king's youngest daughter's hand in marriage. The king agrees, and the bad guy is quickly quashed. Unfortunately, his dead nemesis had

friends in low places, namely a witch and her dwarf assistant who sports a ping-pong ball eye. She curses Waldemar and his lineage before being brought down herself, and soon he's off in search of a cure for his rather nasty malady. He makes his way to Kyoto, and before you can say "sushi to go, please," our barrel-chested lycanthrope is chewing his way through hordes of pony-tailed samurai and their quickly defrocked women.

Although fans of the "El Hombre Lobo" films should be delighted with this entry, they'll probably be equally ticked off by the director's choice to rewrite and revamp his character's origin yet again. (C'mon, … pick an origin and stick with it, why don't you? Geez.) Also, the gore and sleaze quotient is low when compared to previous efforts, yet the make-up itself has hardly changed a hair since it was first conceived fifteen years earlier. (Yes, he still looks like a giant, drooling Ewok. Emphasis on the drooling.) Overall, the production values are much higher, making it seem as if this film was a last ditch attempt to make his movies more accessible to the masses.

What makes this film stand out from its predecessors, though, is Naschy's attempt to combine the popular excesses of Spanish trash horror with that of Japanese cinema. (Samurai zombies are one thing, but the koto they relentlessly abuse on the soundtrack has got to go.) Why this film didn't get better distribution I'll never know. (Imagine the possibilities had it broken him into the mainstream! *El Hombre Yojimbo! Lone Werewolf and Cub!* Please, someone stop me…)

At the very least, it's a hell of a lot better than Hammer's attempt to cross genres ten years earlier with *The Legend of the Seven Golden Vampires* (1973).

The Beyond *see* **L'Aldilá**

Beyond Dream's Door (1988)

Beyond Dream's Door Co. [US]
DIR: Jay Woelfel; PRO: Dyrk Ashton; SCR: Jay Woelfel; DOP: Scott Spears; SFX: Scott Simonson; MUS: Jay Woelfel

STR: Nick Baldasare, John Dunleavy, Catherine Enke, Rick Kesler, Susan Pinsky, Lucas Simpson, Norm Singer, Darby Vasbinder, Daniel White, Marge Whitney and others.

Approximately 86m; Color [Partially shot on video]
VHS1: *Beyond Dream's Door* [VDA; 86m]
ADL: *It Takes Its Victims and Hides Them in Your Nightmares!*

Just what we need ... another shoddy *A Nightmare on Elm Street* clone focusing on kids suffering from bad dreams, precipitated by a supernatural entity who apparently has nothing better to do with his time. (They—the filmmakers, I assume—claim it was inspired by a D.H. White poem, but I don't think the late wordsmith would be pleased with the affiliation.) The acting is sub-par, and most of the gore is lousy; a few of the better, more visceral effects manage to make it to the level of simply bad. (They even managed to screw up what could be considered the only truly inspired scene, one involving a cow-skulled revenant. At least we have to give them credit for being consistent.) And, to make it a truly painful excursion, some of this mess was shot on video. (They did have the sense to film-look some of it, al-though it makes little difference when one is watching the movie with his or her finger glued to the fast-forward button on the remote.)

Hey, *Deep Red*, *Horrorfan* and *Slaughterhouse* supposedly gave it good ratings. Is it any wonder why *these* magazines aren't still around?

Beyond the Door III (1989)

CFS Avala Film [Yu], Trihoof Investments B.V. [US]
DIR: Jeff Kwitny; PRO: Ovidio Gabriele Assonitis; SCR: Sheila Goldberg; DOP: Adolfo Bartoli; EXP: Ovidio Gabriele Assonitis; SFX: Angelo Mattei; MUS: Carlo Maria Cordio

STR: Tanya Alexander, Dusko Bulajic, Sarah Conway Ciminera, William Geiger, Savina Gersak, Bogdan Jakus, Mary Kohnert, Miroljub Leso, Andrej Maricic, Milutin Micovic, Predrag Milenkovic, Mario Novelli, Igor Pervic, Olga Poznatov, Reneé Rancourt, Ramiz Sakic, Jeremy Sanchez, Ljiljana Sljapic, Bo Svenson, Ratko Tankosic, Dusan Tasic, Alex Vitale, Ron Williams, Susan Zelouf and Victoria Zinny

AKA: *Death Train*
Approximately 93m; Color
VHS1: *Beyond the Door III* [RCA; 94(93)m]
ADL: *Some Doors Are Best Left Closed.*

A group of students take a trip to Europe in order to view firsthand an ancient Balkan rite. Unbeknownst to them, one of the girls in their midst is destined to be wed to Satan during this ceremony, and her peers are to be chalked up as convenient sacrifices.

A sequel in name only, this meandering supernatural shocker is ultimately a forgettable and silly excursion, despite an unconventional structure. *Beyond the Door III* is further hindered by bad actors (save for Bo Svenson, who shows he has some range by playing a Serbo-Croatian professor), and what has to be some of the most unconvincing miniatures to ever grace a horror film of this caliber. Worst of all, the script is marred by some of the most outrageous hokum to be found in a supernatural thriller, including a contrived plot device involving a possessed train. (A scene that has it derail and pursue some unwary victims across the countryside is too laughable to be scary.) The cinematography is more than adequate (thanks to Full Moon regular Bartoli), however, and there is some nasty gore thrown in for good measure.

Some doors are best left closed; yes indeed.

Bio Hazard *see* **Biohazard**

Biohazard (1985)

Viking Films International [US]
DIR: Fred Olen Ray; PRO: Fred Olen Ray; SCR: Fred Olen Ray; DOP: Paul Elliott and John McCoy; EXP: T.L. Lankford and Art Schwaitzer; MFX: Kenneth J. Hall and Jon McCallum; VFX: Bret Mixon; MUS: Drew Neumann and Eric Rasmussen
STR: Brad Arrington, Michael Bober, Mika Bonavia, Carroll Borland, Loren Crabtree, William Fair, Richard Hench, Donald G. Jackson, Robert King, Ray Lawrence, Frank McDonald, Brett Miller, Arthur Payton, David Pearson, Angelique Pettyjohn, George Randall, Aldo Ray, Christopher Ray, Fred Olen Ray, Charles Roth and Robin Shurtz
AKA: *Bio Hazard*
Approximately 89m; Color
VHS1: *Bio Hazard* [CON; 84(89)m]; *Bio Hazard* [MTX; 90(84)m]
ADL: *It Feeds on Human Flesh!*

First and foremost, ignore the video box synopsis. (Haven't you learned anything by now?) Not only is it erroneous, it has a tendency to make a mountain out of a molehill when it *does* stray close to the truth. *Biohaz-*

Video box art for *Bio Hazard* (1985), Continental Video.

ard is nothing more than yet another dumb alien-on-the-loose flick, taking as many cues from the influential *Alien* (1979) as it does from the slew of B sci-fi flicks that reigned during the era of McCarthyism. (To give credit where it's due, there are some interesting concepts which form the basis of this film; the same material, though, was handled much better in *Shadowzone* (1989), which relies less on the aforementioned staples.)

Yes, as with most of Ray's earlier flicks, the acting kind of sucks (although the script probably deserves as much blame as the delivery), and the monster effects are of the bargain-basement variety. (Here, especially, is where the movie resembles '50s space garbage more than Ridley Scott's breakthrough film.) Also, the throw-away twist ending comes much too soon ... or not soon enough, depending on just how engaging you find the movie. On the upside, there are a few effective corpses and some legitimate laughs. (An old woman's "Speed Kills" speech should garner more than a few chuckles from desperate viewers.) And, well, upside, downside, take your pick, silicone-enhanced Angelique Pettyjohn—ex-porn actress and *Star Trek* guest star—does bare all, but that revelation is about as surprising as the stupid ending.

Bad but far more engaging than Ray's later exploitation efforts.

The Bite (1989)

Towa Productions [Ja], Viva Entertainment [US]

DIR: Frederico Prosperi; PRO: Ovidio Gabriele Assonitis; SCR: Frederico Prosperi and Susan Zelouf; DOP: Roberto d'Ettorre Piazzoli; EXP: Ovidio Gabriele Assonitis, Franco Prosperi and Kenichi Tominaga; SFX: Screaming Mad George; MUS: Carlo Maria Cordio

STR: Deke Anderson, Shiro Appleby, Ana Maria Auther, Sommer Betsworth, Suzanne Celeste, Terrence Evans, Al Fann, Jamie Farr, Jose Garcia, Savina Gersak, Barbara Glover, Sydney Lassick, Bruce Marchiano, Marianne Mellerleile, David Ode, J. Eddie Peck, Jill Schoelen, Sandra Sexton, Bo Svenson, Shawn Tierney, Tanker Trucker and Tiny Welles

AKA: *Curse II—The Bite*
Approximately 98m; Color
VHS1: *Curse II—The Bite* [MUA; 98m]; *Curse II—The Bite* [TWE; 97(98)m]
ADL: *The First Bite Is the Deepest!*

A couple on their way to Albuquerque take a shortcut and wind up in a small Arizona town conveniently situated near a nuclear base. The young man is bitten by a snake, and his hand turns into one itself. With a ten-foot forked tongue. Really. Would I cook up something *this* stupid?

As if *The Curse* (1987) wasn't bad enough, some dipshit producers had to follow it up with a crappier-than-thou unrelated sequel. The ridiculous premise is backed up by a ridiculous pseudo-scientific explanation. Highlights include laughable gore, Screaming Mad George's most embarrassing effects work to date, and some of the phoniest Swedish accents this side of the Chef from *The Muppet Show*. Unfortunately, this movie does boast Jamie Farr, in one of his biggest roles outside of *M*A*S*H*, as the town doctor; I'm betting he rued the day that the Emmy award-winning show was cancelled.

Bad news, despite what other critics may have claimed.

Bits and Pieces (1985)

Celluloid Conspiracy Inc. [US]

DIR: Leland Thomas; PRO: Richard Bansbach, Michael Koby and Leland Thomas; SCR: Michael Koby and Leland Thomas; DOP: Richard Bansbach; EXP: Michael Koby; MFX: John Naulin; MUS: Don Chilcott and Rene Kakebeen

STR: Richard Bansbach, Elaine Bartolone, Sandy Brooke, Brian Burt, Thomas L. Callaway, Tally Chanel, Bob Cole, M. Kam Cooney, Nidia Cota, Ralph Duran, Larry Gries, Andrea Jungert, Lloyd Jay Keiser, Michael Koby, Sheila Lussier, Michael Mandeville, Don Molins, Catherine Newburn, Carla Y. Reynolds, Mike Rick, David St. Amant, Kathy St. Amant, Suzanna Smith, Chris Solari, Andrew Solis, Elena Thomas, Leland Thomas, Devon Ward, Jeanine Ward, Maria Waschak, Dino Zaffina and S.E. Zygmont

Approximately 86m; Color
VHS1: *Bits and Pieces* [TWE; 86m]

A woman leaving a male strip joint is abducted by a tie-wearing weirdo whose deceased mom talks to him through a mannequin. Unfortunately for the woman, she's the seventh in a string of serial killings perpetrated by the buggy momma's boy. He dresses his kidnapped victims in the dead woman's clothes, but it's all for naught as it's little more than a failed attempt at reenacting Joe Spinnel's shtick from *Maniac* (1980). *Bits and Pieces* plays by the book, and does so with such little heart that you can't help but be bored stiff by the tired slicing 'n' dicing. (Although there's a fair amount of blood splashing the scenery, there's hardly an entrance wound in sight, if that's what you're looking for.)

Best left forgotten.

Der Biß der Schlangfrau *see*
The Lair of the White Worm

Black Angel *see* **Arabella l'Angelo Nero**

Black Magic with Buddha *see*
Nao Mo

Black Magic with Butchery *see*
Nao Mo

A Blade in the Dark *see* **La Casa con la Scala nel Buio**

The Blob (1988)

TriStar Pictures [US]
DIR: Chuck Russell; PRO: Jack H. Harris and Elliott Kastner; SCR: Frank Darabont and Chuck Russell [movie novelization by David Bischoff, from Dell Books]; DOP: Mark Irwin; EXP: Andre Blay; MFX: Tony Gardner; SFX: Lyle Conway; VFX: Dream Quest Images; MUS: Michael Hoenig
STR: Kristen Aldrich, James Arnett, Rick Avery, Robert Axelrod, Opelene Bartley, Billy Beck, Beau Billingslea, Don Brunner, Candy Clark, Del Close, Frank Colli-

son, Noble Craig, Richard Crenna, Jr., Peter Crombie, Jeffrey de Munn, Kevin Dillon, Erica Eleniak, Douglas Emerson, Judith Flanagan, Charlene Fox, Ricky Paull Goldin, Portia Griffin, Michael Kenworthy, Art la Fleur, Clayton Landey, Donovan Leitch, Jennifer Lincoln, Pons Maar, Jacquelyn Masche, Wade Mayor, Paul McCrane, Julie McCullough, Bill Moseley, Jack Nance, Jamison Newlander, Moss Porter, Jack Rader, Joe Seneca, Margaret Smith, Shawnee Smith, Sharon Spelman, Charlie Spradling, Teddy Vincent and David Weininger
Approximately 92m; Color
DVD1: *The Blob* [CTS; 92m; LBX];
VHS1: *The Blob* [RCA; 92m]

As per the original, a small isolated town is terrorized by a giant corrosive booger from outer space. This Hollywood updating attempts to up the ante, though, with high tech effects and a paranoid twist involving germ warfare and a government conspiracy. Everyone involved, though, simply goes through the motions, making the viewer wonder, "Why bother in the first place?"

The Blob's biggest downfall is its predictability: Every joke, every shock, every plot device, every gosh darn line of dialogue is seen coming ten minutes before the hammer falls. This has nothing to do with the fact that it's a remake, and everything to do with the fact that the filmmakers were so afraid that the viewer might miss something. Sure, it's fun to see the title critter swallow up half a town—women and children withstanding—but it would've been much more enjoyable were there *some* suspense. It *is* a monster flick, after all.

Most of the cheap thrills involve the big-budget effects, even though some of them are pretty tacky. The twist ending—involving comic book writer Del Close playing a buggy priest—works well, but (thankfully) they didn't take the opportunity given them and make a sequel.

Stick to the original, and maybe Hollywood will eventually remember *why* it's usually pointless to remake something deemed a classic.

Die Blond Göttin *see* **Mondo Canibale** (1980)

Blood Butchers *see* **The Blood Eaters**

Blood Cult (1985)

United Entertainment Pictures [US]
DIR: Christopher Lewis; PRO: Linda Lewis; SCR: Stuart Rosenthal; DOP: Paul MacFarlane; EXP: Bill F. Blair; MFX: Robert Brewer and David Powell; MUS: Bob Slane

STR: Julie Andelman, Christi Beavers, Robbie Cobb, Paul Cowdin, Mary Dickens, Bob Duffield, Charles Ellis, Bryan Gilbreath, Fred Graves, Josef Hardt, Joy Jordan, Bennie Lee McGowan, Allison O. Meilia, David Brent Stice, Catherine L. Tolin, James Vance, Carolyn Wallace, Dot Wishman, David Woods and Charlie Yip

Approximately 89m; Color [Shot on video]

DVD1: *Blood Cult* [VCI; 89m]; VHS1: *Blood Cult* [UHV; 89m]

A pact of devil worshippers doing their best Alice Cooper impersonations (there's more runny eyeliner here than in the flood which swept Jimmy Bakker's trial, for crying out loud) spend their off-hours worshipping the god "Caninus." And—as could be surmised from the video box synopsis—the viewer is offered a slew of screaming, scantily clad coeds (imagine that—in a slasher film, of all places) begging a masked assailant to spare their lives. In the "best" H.G. Lewis tradition, our killer uses his meat cleaver to make mincemeat out of the victims, gleefully ignoring their pleas. Of course, it's the means to an end for the cult, which ends up being comprised of just about everyone in town, save for the geriatric hero. And the dead girls.

It's not as inept as most shot-on-video productions go, and it would probably be passable no-budget sludge on film, but the medium of video only emphasizes its shortcomings. Of which there are many: Poor production values, a tired and threadbare script, actors who couldn't act their way out of a wet paper bag, you know—the usual.

To give credit where it's due, the director did improve upon his craft with *The Ripper*, another shot-on-video gorefest, and *Revenge*, the sequel to *Blood Cult*; but neither of these are worth owning either.

Blood Cult 2 *see* **Revenge**

Blood Delirium *see* **Delirio di Sangue**

Blood Diner (1987)

Lightning Pictures [US], PMS Filmworks Inc. [US]
DIR: Jackie Kong; PRO: Jimmy Maslon; SCR: Michael Sonye; DOP: Jürg Walther; EXP: Lawrence Kasanoff and Ellen Steloff; SFX: Bruce Zahlava; MUS: Don Preston

STR: Alisa Alvarez, Bob Avacado, Barbara Babbins, Cynthia Baker, Michael Barton, Effie Bilbrey, Bonnie Bradigan, Rick Burks, Jane Cantillion, Cynthia Cantrell, Cathy Cooper, Alan Corona, Carl Crow, Roxanne Cybelle, Rogert Dauer, David Dressel, Drew Godderis, Lisa Guggenheim, Laurie Guzda, Karen Hazelwood, Sean Holton, Aron Illa, LaNette la France, Dino Lee, Bob Loya, The Luv Johnsons, Deanne McCain, Max Morris, Tanya Papanicolas,

John Randall, Sir Rodenheaver, Deseree Rose, Gary Scherzer, John Barton Shields and Eva Swidereka
Approximately 88m; Color
VHS1: *Blood Diner* [VES; 88m]

You know its tongue is firmly in its cheek when the movie begins with a disclaimer establishing that "All of the mutilations, bodily dismemberments and cannibal rituals were performed by seasoned professionals ... please do not attempt any of these stunts at home." (This may or may not predate a similar disclaimer that accompanies *Hollywood Chainsaw Hookers* [1987], which also captures much of the—ugh—flavor of said film as well.)

Blood Diner is essentially a loose (and unofficial) sequel to *Blood Feast* (1963), and it is obvious that the director has a soft spot in her heart for H.G. Lewis' preeminent gore film. (Jackie Kong was also responsible for *The Being*, so her devotion to the genre has been duly noted.) In *Blood Diner*, the nephews of the deceased Fuad Ramses (called something else here, but which I forgot to jot down) pick up where he left off, under the inept supervision of their uncle's cognizant, albeit displaced, brain. Yes, it's even worse than it sounds.

Although slicker than most "gore-omedies" of the time, it's the same old tired jokes that'll make any veteran splatterpunk wince in embarrassment. *Blood Diner* dishes up a *few* amusing skits, but just enough to save it from the same slop bucket that claimed such "luminary" outings as *Bloodsuckers from Outer Space* (1984). I know, I know ... they can't all be *Bad Taste* or *Re-Animator*, but it would be nice if they tried a *little* harder.

The Blood Eaters (1980)

CM Productions [US]
DIR: Charles McCrann; PRO: Charles McCrann; SCR: Charles McCrann; DOP: David Sperling; SFX: Craig Harris; MUS: Ted Shapiro
STR: Alyssa Allyn, John Amplas, Charles Austin, Judy Brown, Gerald Cullen, Philip Garfinkel, Dennis Graber, Kevin Hanlon, Bob Hanson, Craig Harris, James Hart, Paul Haskin, Dennis Helfend, Pat Kellis, Ronald Kienhuis, John Kuhi, Bob Larson, Debbie Link, James McGonigal, Roger Miles, Hariet Miller, Debra O'Leary, Kim Roff, Claude Scales, Beverly Shapiro and William Shetterly
AKA: *Blood Butchers*; *Forest of Fear*; *Toxic Zombies*
Approximately 88m; Color
VHS1: *Toxic Zombies* [QUA; 85(88)m]; *Toxic Zombies* [VEA; 85(88)m]
ADL: *They Thought They Were Just Killing Some Weeds. Instead, They Grew a Whole New Kind of Crop!*

A small band of marijuana farmers hiding in the mountains kill two federal marshals. The authorities— still unsure of their exact location— retaliate by spraying the hills with Dromax, an experimental herbicide that has some rather nasty side effects. (Namely, it turns those exposed into—Surprise!—flesh-eating ghouls.)

This fairly obscure zombie gut-muncher exhibits all the charm of a '70s homegrown effort: Cut-rate performances, low-tech gore effects, and an oft-grating Moog synthesizer score predominate. If you prefer your films to be adequately made, then you might want to look elsewhere; if you can handle some grit in your gore sandwich, then you should have no problem keeping down this early *Dawn of the Dead* rip-off. Granted, it borrows more from earlier films, like Jorgé Grau Sola's *Non Si Deve Pro-*

Video box art for *The Blood Eaters*
(1980), Queasy Art.

fanare il Sonno dei Morte (1974) and
John Hayes' *Garden of the Dead*
(1972), but Romero's sequel was surely
the impetus for *Toxic Zombies* getting
made. Romero fans will probably
want to check it out, if only for the
presence of John (*Martin*) Amplas.

For zombie film completists or
fans of low-rent splatter only.

Blood Frenzy (1987)

Hollywood Family Entertainment [US]
DIR: Hal Freeman; PRO: Hal Free-
man; SCR: Ted Newsom; DOP: Richard
Pepin; MFX: John Goodwin; MUS: Digital
Arts
STR: Claire Cassano, John Clark,
J'Aime Cohen, Hank Garrett, Eddie Laufer,
Lisa Loring, Wendy MacDonald, Tony
Montero, Chuck Rhae, Lisa Savage, Monica
Silveria and Carl Tignino
Approximately 90m; Color
VHS1: *Blood Frenzy* [HFE; 90m]

More tepid slasher fare, this one
takes place in the desert, *à la The Hills
Have Eyes* (1977). The numerous
graphic (albeit unconvincing) slit
throats in no way makes up for the
gratuitous character exposition we're
forced to accept in the place of, well,
a plot. (After sitting through two-
thirds of the running time listening
to the intended victims whine and
bitch and moan and generally act
neurotic, I was more than a little eager
to see the killer get it in gear and save
me—the unfortunate viewer—from
having to sit through another twenty
or thirty minutes of the same. Much
to my chagrin, though, the overacting, courtesy of my alleged savior, was
even more excruciating than that
which preceded it.)

Forgettable, unnecessary, and …
hold on a minute, let me grab my thesaurus…

Blood Massacre (1987)

Applause Productions Inc. [US]
DIR: Don Dohler; PRO: Dan Buehl,
Don Dohler and Barry Gold; SCR: Dan
Buehl, Don Dohler and Barry Gold; DOP:
Christopher Chrysler and Jeffrey Herberger;
EXP: Howard N. Esbin; MFX: John Cosen-
tino and Larry Schlechter; MUS: Jon Chris-
topher and Dan Linck
STR: Theresa Crain, Lisa Defuso,
James di Angelo, Anne Frith, Barry Gold,
Ted Hakim, Thomas Humes, Lucille Jolle,
David Kodeck, Don Leifert, Howard Le-
vine, Robin London, Mary McFaul, Herb
Otter, Jr., Karl Otter, Mary Ann Pence,
Lucie Poirier, Richard Ruxton, Grace Stahl,
George Stover, Twilight Titan, Gerard
Vanik and Paul Wilson
Approximately 90m; Color
VHS1: *Blood Massacre* [III; 90m]

A group of criminals (with names like Rizzo and Pauly, go figure) kill a woman while holding up a video store. (One perceptive witness advises the cops with a straight face, "You better catch this guy ... he's gonna hurt somebody!") In the second best *Last House on the Left* (1972) tradition, they head for the country, holing up in an isolated farmhouse—against the owners' wishes, of course. The victimized family gets revenge—here's the punchline—by eating them. (Uh-oh ... now I'm having *Los Ojos Azules de la Muneca Rota* [1973] flashbacks.)

More grade–Z genre fare from Don Dohler; unfortunately, this lacks the charm of his earlier, usually sci-fi oriented outings. (He should've stuck to aliens instead of trying his hand at slasher flicks.) The editing is lousy, and degenerates into abysmal during what constitutes the film's action sequences. There's gore galore, but it's particularly shoddy and relegated to the last third of the film. (Even if one finds these effects palatable, the viewer is sure to lose any admiration he or she may have when subjected to the papier-mâché prosthetics employed during the ridiculous finale.) Also of note is the sheer amount of nonsensically placed dialogue; methinks this may have been a ploy, as the viewer may be too distracted by their own "Huh?"s to realize just how bad the rest of the film is.

I wasn't surprised to discover that this, alas, was Mr. Dohler's last film. (Maybe we should let him take a crack at the 20th Century Fox *Alien* franchise instead of pursuing these other avenues. I'm game, how about you?)

Blood Salvage (1988)

High Five Productions [US], Paragon Arts International [US]

DIR: Tucker Johnston; PRO: Martin J. Fischer and Ken C. Sanders; SCR: Tucker Johnston and Ken C. Sanders; DOP: Michael Karp; EXP: Evander Holyfield and Ken C. Sanders; MFX: Bill Johnson

STR: Dan Albright, Bridget Bennett, Lori Birdson, Tommy Chappelle, Byron Cherry, Ed Corbin, Margaret Crosby, Rubin Devore, Lou Duva, Bridgette Fennell, Betsy Gilmer, Andy Greenway, Krista Harris, Christian Hessler, Keith Holder, Evander Holyfield, Frank Kube, Tracy Lester, Anne McGarity, Christine Morris, Danny Nelson, Chanda Palmer, Gil Roper, Clarissa Sanders, Ken Sanders, Sr., Kelly Saul, John Saxon, P.J. Shinall, Lonnie Smith, Michele Smith, Ralph Pruitt Vaughn, Suzanne Ventulett, Ray Walston, Christine Wennersten, Laura Whyte, Mike Witfield and Robert Wynn

AKA: *Mad Jake*

Approximately 98m; Color

VHS1: *Blood Salvage* [MAG; 98m]

ADL: *If Jake Can't Fix It, It's Been Dead Too Long.*

A family with a handicapped daughter falls into the clutches of some psycho rednecks that—much to the victims' chagrin—become obsessed with the wheelchair-bound girl. Outside of this, most everything else—from the opening sequence to an onscreen rendition of "Bringing in the Sheaves"—was patently stolen from Hooper's *The Texas Chainsaw Massacre Part 2* (1986). (It won't be difficult for viewers to spot the stand-ins for the cook, the hitchhiker, and Leatherface, I assure you.) It only deviates from that film's formula in that our white trash killers fix cars instead of making chili, and that instead of practicing anthropophagia, they run a similarly cannibalistic operation— black market organ harvesting. Of course the donors are a bit reluctant to part with their wares, but this is the only thing that makes the proceedings even remotely interesting.

Blood Salvage does have good production values, but the inadequate acting brings the whole kit and caboodle down a few notches. Saxon—the only veteran in the bunch outside of Ray (*My Favorite Martian*) Walston—even screws up, unable to keep his fake southern accent for more than a few lines at a time. Worst of all, the obligatory rednecks chew up the scenery, acting like a bunch of psychotic retards. (Not that they're particularly bad at it, as far as psychotic retards go, but the shtick gets real old, real fast.) Also, the black humor and schlock-ridden contrivances more often than not fail, if only because of the derivative script. Trust me—you've seen it all before, folks. And better.

Blood Sisters (1987)

Reeltime Distribution Corp. [US]
DIR: Roberta Findlay; PRO: Walter E. Sear; SCR: Roberta Findlay; DOP: Roberta Findlay; MUS: Michael Litovsky and Walter E. Sear
STR: Lynnea Benson, Thomas Biscione, Amy Brentano, Ruth Collins, Derek Conte, Brigette Cossu, Jesse d'Angelo, Mikhail Druhan, Dan Erickson, John Fasano, Patricia Finneran, Gretchen Kingsley, Pam la Testa, Marla MacHart, Robert P. Masci, Shannon McMahon, Elisabeth Rose, Cjerste Thor, Michael Tilton, Seraphine Warrington and Brian Charlton Wrye
Approximately 86m; Color
VHS1: *Blood Sisters* [SON; 86m]
ADL: *Their Hazing Was a Night to Dismember.*

College hazing forces a group of teens to spend the night in an abandoned whorehouse, haunted by the ghosts of the prostitutes killed in a massacre that occurred there thirteen years earlier. If that isn't enough, someone very much alive is stalking the desperate participants and dispatching them by whatever means necessary.

Not nearly as interesting as Roberta Findlay's '60s work (made with late husband/co-conspirator Michael Findlay), this film will put the audience to sleep long before it manages to snag their attention. *Blood Sisters* amounts to little more than conventional slasher fare, with some haunted house hokum thrown in to keep the viewer from realizing this until it's too late. True to most of Findlay's output, there's more skin than bloodshed. (Still fresh from an extended stint as an XXX filmmaker, she utilizes many of the same conventions picked up from working in the adult film industry. I guess some habits are hard to shake.) True to the work of many women filmmakers, the characterization in *Blood Sisters* is generally a notch above that in the output of their testosterone-ridden peers, but this is lost amidst the film's shortcomings: Inept continuity, an aimless storyline, etc. And worst of all—particularly noticeable, it being a Findlay film—it's boring and unimaginative. (At least her earlier movies never suffered this fate, no matter how abysmal they were. I guess sometimes it just doesn't pay to improve.)

Blood Song (1982)

Allstate Film Company [US], Mountain High Enterprises [US]
DIR: Alan J. Levi; PRO: Frank Avianca and Lenny Montana; SCR: Frank Avianca, James Fargo and Lenny Montana; DOP: Steve Posey; EXP: Stefan B. Sofro and Len Turner; SFX: Rick Hatcher; MUS: Monty Turner and Rob Walsh

STR: David Arndt, Frankie Avalon, Antoinette Bower, Norman Brecke, Dane Clark, Roydon Clark, William Kirby Cullen, Candace Dickey, Roger Diedrich, Jenifer Eskat, Erick Fisher, Jeffery Isham, Victor Izay, Richard Jaeckel, Dennis P. Karroll, Jim Kimball, Kit Lewis, Carla McKizzick, Lenny Montana, Noelle North, Don Perry, Beverly Salicko, Christopher Scarano, Elliott Silverstein, Joseph Stanfill and Donna Wilkes

AKA: *Dream Slayer; Melodia Siniestra* [Sinister Melody]

Approximately 90m; Color

VHS1: *Blood Song* [ABA; 90m]; *Blood Song* [VIC; 90m]; *Dream Slayer* [HQV; 90m]

Much like in *The Eyes of Laura Mars* (1978), a crippled girl "sees" a series of brutal killings and eventually crosses paths with the killer himself. (Geez, her of *all* people should have seen that plot development coming.) The expected chase ensues, with everyone eventually catching up to a very unsatisfying finale.

As derivative as the script may be, *Blood Song* is surprisingly palatable; this, I feel, is due mostly to the sympathetic *and* believable characters portrayed herein—with the exception of the killer himself. The melodrama that predominates the film early on will presumably bore most gorehounds, though, who will fast-forward to the bloody—albeit predictable—action. (The gore is slim, but a few effectively brutal scenes might make it worth your wait.) An annoying synth score and a tacky "out-of-the-eye" optical effect are the only real blemishes on what are otherwise average production values.

What's most surprising about *Blood Song* is the presence of Avalon as a psychopath, whose impetus to murder was having seen his father chew on the wrong end of a gun when he was a wee lad. He relives the experience by tooting on a wooden pipe his dad made him prior to each killing. (After hearing him play, I can see why his father painted the walls with his own gray matter. Were some music lessons too much to ask for?) For those of you who don't recognize the name, Frankie Avalon starred in a slew of beach films back in the 1960s; ask your parents, they'll remember. If only Annette could see him now.

Blood Splash *see* **Nightmare**

Blood Tracks (1985)

Smart Egg Pictures [Sw/US]

DIR: Mats Helge; PRO: Tom Sjoberg; SCR: Mats Helge and Anna Wolf; DOP: Hans von Dittmer; EXP: Georg Zeçeviç; SFX: Mats Helge and Dick Ljunggren; MFX: Dick Ljunggren; MUS: Dag Unenge and Easy Action

STR: Ingemar Anderson, Lars-Gunnar Anderson, Per-Olof Borhult, Fatima Bruzelius, Robin Bruzelius, Easy Action, Tommy Ellgren, Michael Fitzpatrick, Derek Ford, Jeff Harding, Lotte Heise, Mats Helge, Helena Jacks, Naomi Kaneda, Frances Kelly, Jonathan Kosakow, Karina Lee, Anders Linberg, Sonja Llind, Chris Lynn, Kee Marcello, Peter Merrill, Frederick Offren, Joakim Osterllind, Brad Powell, Harriet Robinson, Tina Shaw, Filippa Silverstope, Alex Tyrone, Freddie van Gerber, Torsten Wahllind, Jesper Westerlund and Zin Zan

Approximately 82m; Color

VHS1: *Blood Tracks* [VIS; 82m]

ADL: *Terror on the Slopes!*

Somehow I'd gotten suckered into sitting through this unmitigated dross *twice*; apparently, I didn't remember just how bad it was the first time through and felt the need to unconsciously punish myself so I wouldn't make the same mistake in the future.

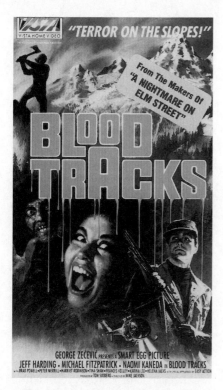

Video box art for *Blood Tracks* (1985), Vista Home Video.

(Unfortunately, I ain't that savvy; a couple of more films of this caliber and I'll be eating my dinner through a straw.)

Despite an almost interesting intro and some nice location shooting, *Blood Tracks* scrapes the proverbial bottom. A group of ultra-obnoxious glam-metal rockers get picked off by some of *The Hills Have Eyes'* distant kin, to absolutely no one's chagrin. If the screenwriters wanted to garner any sympathy for the victims, where did they get the ludicrous idea that making them whiny rock stars would do the trick? The filmmakers also made the mistake of inserting some unbearable MTV-style videos

in the mix, and a really grating glam-metal soundtrack. Does anyone take these rock 'n' roll horror flicks seriously? And where do filmmakers get the impression that this subgenre is marketable? Why am I asking you? Too many questions, too many ... damn. I dropped my straw.

There is also some nasty gore—all of it after the fact—but in no way does it compensate for having to sit through more than five minutes of this turkey. For reasons that should be self evident, director Mats Helge employed the pseudonym "Mike Jackson" for this flick. If you had any sense, you'd keep your distance as well.

Bloodmoon (1989)

Village Roadshow Pictures [Au]
DIR: Alec Mills; PRO: Stanley O'-Toole; SCR: Robert Brennan; DOP: John Stokes; EXP: Graham Burke and Gregory Coote; SFX: Lance Cornell and April Harvie; MUS: Brian May
STR: Michael Adams, Christine Amor, Sean Anderson, Narelle Arcidiacono, Stephen Bergin, Christophe Broadway, Warwick Brown, David Clendinning, Sue-yan Cox, Craige Cronin, Michelle Doake, Jane Dormaier, Les Evans, Lisa Hamilton, Jonathan Hardy, Hazel Howson, Shawn Kristofer, Sue Lawson, Leon Lissek, Kesha Loy, Damien Lutz, Suzie MacKenzie, Karen Miers, Anya Molina, Brian Moll, Jo Munro, Gregory Pamment, Tess Pike, Justin Ratcliffe, Kate Riley, Samantha Rittson, Matthew Smith, Helen Strube, Helen Thomson, Ray Turner, Chris Uhlmann, Elizabeth Williams and Ian Williams
Approximately 101m; Color
VHS1: *Bloodmoon* [LIV; 104(101)m]
ADL: *The Last Full Moon You'll Ever See.*

A psychopathic killer—with a penchant for strangling his victims with barbed wire, snipping off their fingers, and plucking out their eyes— is stalking the grounds of a girls' school. Otherwise, it's business as usual, with the film focusing on the drama of teen life in Cooper's Bay.

This Aussie slasher flick trades in the usually cardboard teen fodder for character exposition, but becomes bogged down in the process. Furthermore, the whodunit aspects are all but discarded, as the killer's identity is revealed halfway through the film. Without this mystery, the murders seem even more out of place. So, once all is said and done, *Bloodmoon* amounts to little more than a *Beverly Hills 90210* episode with some teen flesh and grisly murders thrown in for good measure.

Bloodsuckers from Outer Space (1984)

One-of-Those Productions [US]
DIR: Glen Coburn; PRO: Rick Garlington; SCR: Glen Coburn; DOP: Chad D. Smith; EXP: Carl Boyd Latham; MFX: J.P. Joyce and Tim McDowell; SFX: Tim McDowell; MUS: Rick Garlington and Various Artists [Soundtrack from One-of-Those Music]
STR: Robert Bradeen, John Brigham, Derel Chick, Charles Coburn, Glen Coburn, Franny Coppenbarger, Christine Crow, David Cunningham, Joyce Dixon, John Duvall, Laura Ellis, Dan Gallion, Rick Garlington, Wayne Greene, Jack Hammack, Chris Heldman, Billie Keller, Paul la Rocque, John Latham, Dennis Letts, Thom Meyers, Kris Nicolau-Sharpley, Julie P. Oliver-Touchstone, Pat Paulsen, Roy Russell, Charlie Seybert, Darrell Shelton, Jim Stafford, Richard Wainscott, Samantha Walker, John Webb and Jack Wilkinson
Approximately 79m; Color
VHS1: *Bloodsuckers from Outer Space* [KLV; 79m]

I didn't have to wait for the opening credits to start rolling to know I was in trouble. It was painfully obvious from the video cover that this was going to be a major turd, and a waste of the sixty-some-odd cents I had plunked down to rent it. (If you must know, a local video store was having a "six movies for four bucks" special, and I decided to rent stuff I wouldn't have otherwise watched, if only to complete the book you now hold. As for the other five I rented, I don't remember what they were, but I do know that *Bloodsuckers from Outer Space* was the stinkiest of the lot. Geez, the things I do for you guys.)

Anywho, I think this is supposed to be a comedy; I couldn't tell that from the half of the film I *did* sit through. (The fast-forward button on my remote—yeah, the only button with the paint worn off of it—dutifully took care of the rest.) The production values (sans the bargain-basement effects) are passable, considering the obviously threadbare budget, but in no way does that make up for the tired shtick. In retrospect, I wish it had been shot on video so there wasn't *anything* going for it, like so many homegrown efforts. At least then I could have just surfed my way to the end credits without feeling an ounce of guilt.

Granted, there is one amusing scene (an offscreen sexcapade that almost demolishes a house), and a crack about a rubber ducky solicited a chuckle or two as well, but in no way does this film change my opinion about "gore-omedies" and their pathetic, jaundice-ridden ilk. Peter Jackson's efforts are an exception, as is the occasional aberration—*Re-Animator* and *Cannibal! The Musical* come to mind—but, unfortunately, "splatstick" usually sees the light of day when desperate filmmakers realize, "Gee, this movie really bites ... how about we just play it for laughs instead?"

I wonder if I complain, you think they'd reimburse my sixty-some-odd cents? If I tied them to a chair and force them to sit through *Bloodsuckers from Outer Space*, without the benefit of fast-forward capabilities, I'm sure they'd be more than happy to compensate me.

Bloodsucking Nazi Zombies *see* **L'Abîme des Morts-Vivants**

Bloody Bird *see* **Deliria**

The Bloody Dead (1987)

Independent-International Motion Pictures Corp. [US/WG]
DIR: Samuel M. Sherman and Alfred Vohrer; PRO: Horst Wendlandt; SCR: Herbert Reinecker [Based on the novel *Die Blau Hand* by Edgar Wallace]; DOP: Ernst W. Kalinke; MFX: Edward French; MUS: Martin Böttcher

STR: Albert Bessler, Otto Czarski, Thomas Danneberg, Gudrun Genest, Richard Haller, Fred Haltiner, Karin Kenklies, Klaus Kinski, Diana Körner, Helga Lander, Carl Lange, Harald Leipnitz, Hermann Lenschau, Ilse Pagé, Peter Parten, Harry Riebauer, Siegfried Schürenberg, Heinz Spitzner and Ilse Steppat
Approximately 80m; Color
VHS1: *The Bloody Dead* [VSV; 80m]
ADL: *Discover the Knife-Hand That Slashed Throats ... Before Freddy Was Born!*

A twin escapes from an asylum and gladly takes the place of his twin brother, who is conveniently missing. Meanwhile, some psycho wielding a medieval gauntlet (complete with retractable blades, of course) is making bacon of the locals. And then ... sound a little familiar? It should, if you're at all familiar with the Edgar Wallace-inspired *krimi* films of the 1960s, or Kinski's outings of the same time period. From the video box alone I was able to deduce this to be a retitling of *Die Blau Hand* (The Blue Hand; 1968), released here as *The Creature with the Blue Hand*. (The lame adline was the first clue.) But— Surprise!—I was only partly right.

Apparently, Independent-International secured the rights to this film sometime in the '80s, and filmed additional gore scenes for an intended 1987 re-release. (Independent-International—home to exploitation moguls Al Adamson and Samuel M. Sherman—was infamous for their patchwork creations. Pick any Sherman or Adamson epic, and you'll have a prime example of what one can accomplish with scraps of unused footage and previously released productions, as well as a new, sordid moniker to hide the fact that you've already paid money to see it once. Wonders to behold, they are.)

The new footage—all of seven minutes worth—involves a cannibalistic inmate at the aforementioned institution, and boasts some pretty intense gore effects, especially as far as Independent-International's other films are concerned. Although many sources are vague, at least one claims that this additional footage was lensed by Sherman himself, and was done because it would have been too costly to replace the "gore" footage that was excised from the original US print.

Except for the three inserts, it's pretty much the same damn film (even retaining the dubbing from its initial US release). But this may not necessarily be a good thing. Salvaged from the original movie (unfortunately) is the overbearing score that— thirty years later—is unintentionally comical, particularly when the killer is unmasked and his nefarious plot exposed.

Despite my nostalgic fondness for the original film (before it was mussed up by Independent-International), this version's still a keeper.

Bloody Moon see **Die Säge des Todes**

Bloody Pom Poms see **Cheerleader Camp**

Boarding House see **Boardinghouse**

Boardinghouse (1982)

Blustarr Films Inc. [US]
DIR: Johnn Wintergate; PRO: Peter Baahlu; SCR: Jonema; DOP: Jan Lucas and Obee Ray; SFX: Johnn Wintergate; MFX: Johnn Wintergate
STR: Hawk Adley, Brian Bruderlin, Michael Burke, Jon Buxer, Tim Campbell, John Chase, Christopher Conlan, Chris Cristin, Alexandra Day, Dean Disico, Elizabeth Hall, Victoria Herron, Kalassu Kay, Belma Kora, Michele Krieger, Mary McKinley, Tom Mones, Carla Nansel, Tracy O'Brian, Mark Prines, Joel McGinnis Riordan, Elliot van Koghbe, Jim Vincioni, Allen R. Warren, Cindy Williamson, A'Ryen Winter and Rosane Woods
AKA: *Boarding House*; *Housegeist*
Approximately 95m; Color [Shot on video]
VHS1: *Boarding House* [PAR; 95m]
ADL: *...Where the Rent Won't Kill You, but Something Else Will!*

An asthmatic killer with telekinetic powers escapes from a sanitarium and moves into a boarding house that caters primarily to topless women. Lots of bloody hokum results. (Geez,

is there anyone who *can't* move things with the power of their mind in this flick?)

As far as I know, I think this was the first shot-on-video splatter flick, and how it managed to inspire others to make the same mistake, I'll never know. (Maybe the resulting flood of videocam productions can be attributed to a deluded "Hey ... I can do better than that!" psychology.) Awful handheld videography tempered with unnecessary zooms and cheesy video effects, help to distract the viewer from the overacting (when it's adept enough to be labeled as such). There's a lot of third-rate gore to be had, but it doesn't compensate for, well, *anything*.

Godawful lousy, thank you.

Body Count see **Camping del Terrore**

The Boogens (1981)

Zaft International Pictures Inc. [US]
DIR: James L. Conway; PRO: Charles E. Sellier, Jr.; SCR: Bob Hunt and David O'Malley [Based on the novel *The Boogens* by Charles E. Sellier, Jr., and Robert Weverka]; DOP: Paul Hipp; SFX: Kenneth Horn, Doug Kramer, William Munns and Jon Reeves; MUS: Bob Summers
STR: Rebecca Balding, John Crawford, Med Flory, Jeff Harlan, Jon Lormer, Anne-Marie Martin, Fred McCarren, Marcia Reider, Peg Stewart and Scott Wilkinson
AKA: *Engendros Macabros* [Macabre Embryos]
Approximately 95m; Color
VHS1: *The Boogens* [RPV; 95m]
ADL: *There Is No Escape!*

After a string of "accidents" in 1912, a silver mine is closed down, but is re-opened almost seventy years later. Some strategically placed dyna-

American lobby card for *The Boogens* (1981).

mite opens up an underground lake strewn with the bones of unlucky miners reported MIA. Unbeknownst to two couples, the house they're staying in was built directly over the self-same network of tunnels that is also home to some rather toothy-looking critters with a hankering for human flesh.

The Boogens makes for engaging monster fare, thanks to some passable character development and adept direction. The film even boasts some tense moments, with some effective scenes of people being dragged into the creatures' lair while remaining off screen. Even the plot holes and contrivances are easy to overlook (except maybe why on earth the mines feed into everyone's basements), but, alas, the beasts themselves—the key to all good monster flicks—are pretty

damned silly looking when they finally get around to exposing their rubbery hides. A rather disappointing lot, especially considering the build-up.

The gore is sparse, but reasonably brutal, with all of the killings being executed by tentacles tipped with razor-sharp spurs. We are also treated to a fair amount of Boogens-cam, and one of the most enjoyable dog actors to ever endure the demands of a horror movie. (Even people like myself, who despise poodles, will get a kick out of this pooch's screen presence.)

Brought to us by the people responsible for such "documentaries" as *Beyond and Back* (1978) and *In Search of Historic Jesus* (1980), *The Boogens* is just as fanciful an outing but—suffice it to say—a heck of a lot more interesting.

Boogeyman 2 *see* Boogeyman II

Boogeyman II (1982)

New West Films [US]
DIR: Bruce Starr; PRO: Ulli Lommel;
SCR: David Herschel, Ulli Lommel and
Suzanna Love; DOP: Philippe Carr-Forster
and David Sperling; EXP: Jochen Breiten-
stein and David du Bay; SFX: CMI Ltd. and
Craig Harris; MUS: Tim Krog
STR: Rhonda Aldrich, Raymond Boy-
den, John Carradine, David d'Arner, Ashley
du Bay, Gillian Gordon, Howard Grant,
Shannah Hall, Ron James, Mina Kolb, Ulli
Lommel, Nicholas Love, Suzanna Love,
Rock MacKenzie, Felicite Morgan, Rafael
Nazario, Jane Pratt, Bill Rayburn, Bob
Rosenfarb, Natasha Schiano, Leslie Smith,
David Swim, Llewelyn Thomas, Sholto von
Douglas, Sarah Jean Watkins, Ann Wilkin-
son, Jay Wright and Cindy Zeising

Video box art for *Boogeyman II* (1982),
VCII.

AKA: *Revenge of the Boogeyman*
Approximately 79m; Color
VHS1: *Boogeyman 2*; *Boogeyman II*
[GEM; 79m]; *Boogeyman II* [VCII; 79m]
ADL: *You Didn't Listen to Mama the
First Time ... Now He's Back Again!*

If you suffer from a severe case of
déjà vu while watching this sequel,
don't fret. Not only is it a retread of
the original, but it recycles a tremen-
dous amount of footage from *The
Boogeyman* (1977) as well.

Although all of the bloodshed in
the first half of this film is culled from
its predecessor, you'll quickly find
yourself wishing they had stolen *more*
once the filmmakers kick in with their
own contributions. Not content with
using the old standbys (butcher
knives, meat cleavers, axes, chainsaws,
etc.), *Boogeyman II* shows some originality and uses, shall we say, more
unconventional tools of vengeance. An
electric toothbrush. Shaving cream.
An exhaust pipe. Oh, and let's not
forget the horsehead BBQ tongs. Yes
... horsehead BBQ tongs. Needless to
say, whatever atmosphere its predecessor *did* manage to convey is long-
since gone in this patchwork atrocity,
and no amount of recycling is going
to bring it back for a second round.

The Borrower (1989)

Vision Pictures Inc. [US]
DIR: John McNaughton; PRO: Steven
A. Jones and R.P. Sekon; SCR: Richard Fire
and Mason Nage; DOP: Julio Macat and
Robert C. New; EXP: William H. Coleman;
SFX: Steve Galich; MFX: Kevin Yagher
Productions; MUS: Ken Hale, Steven A.
Jones and Robert McNaughton
STR: Tom Allard, Tony Amendola,
Madchen Amick, Tracy Arnold, B.J. Barie,
Geri Betzler, Rae Dawn Chong, Tami Clat-
terbuck, Stuart Cornfeld, Steve de Clark,
Robert Dryer, Antonio Fargas, Cindy Folk-

erson, Neil Giuntoli, Don Gordon, Pam Gordon, Will Gotay, Rif Hutton, Daniel Inskip, Heath Jobet, Steve Landi, Jack Lightsy, Christopher MacLean, Lorrie Marlow, John Martinuzzi, Bentley Mitchum, Pamela Norris, Larry Pennell, Will Robinson, Mark Rosenblatt, Sam Scarber, Darryl Shelly, Chad Taylor, Tom Towles, Richard Wharton, Rob Williams, Tonya Lee Williams and Gregory Wolf
Approximately 97m; Color
VHS1: *The Borrower* [CAN; 97m]
ADL: *Don't Lend Him Anything You Can't Afford to Lose!*

An alien killer comes to Earth aided by the ability to assume a human guise. On the downside, his head has a nasty habit of exploding, so he's constantly on the lookout for noggins which he can "borrow" from Los Angeles' populace. Tommy Chong's daughter Rae Dawn plays a cop investigating the series of mysterious decaps. (Seems to me she's been in an awful lot of genre films as of the late '80s. Since she can actually *act*, you won't hear me putting up a fight.)

The Borrower is—what I assume to be, anyway—a schlocky, tongue-in-cheek homage to all those gory alien-on-the-loose flicks of the past few decades. And if it's *not* a pastiche of such B-grade horrors, it's a sad departure for the genius behind *Henry—Portrait of a Serial Killer* (1987). As can be rightfully ascertained, gore is plentiful, although the effects leave something to be desired.

Hey, at least Antonio "Huggy Bear" Fargas is on hand for the fun.

Il Bosco *see* **Notte nel Bosco**

Brain Damage (1988)

Palisades Entertainment [US]
DIR: Frank Henenlotter; PRO: Edgar Ievins; SCR: Frank Henenlotter; DOP:

Video box art for *Brain Damage* (1988), Paramount Home Video.

Bruce Torbet; EXP: Andre Blay and Al Eicher; MFX: Gabriel Bartalos; MUS: Clutch Reiser and Gus Russo
STR: Theo Barnes, Michael Bishop, Beverly Bonner, Vicki Darnell, Angel Figueroa, Joe Gonzales, Don Henenlotter, Rick Herbst, Jennifer Lowry, Gordon MacDonald, Kenneth Packard, Artemes Pizarro, John Reichert, Bradlee Rhodes, Ari Roussimoff, Michael Rubenstein, Lucille Saint-Peter, Kevin Vanhentenryck, Slam Wedgehouse and Zacherle
Approximately 89m; Color
DVD7: *Brain Damage* [IMG; 86m; LBX]; VHS1: *Brain Damage* [PHV; 89m]; *Brain Damage* [RAV; 90(86)m]

A young man stumbles across Aylmer, a dopey-eyed, crooning parasite that gets his hosts hooked on a powerful and addictive hallucinogenic that his body provides. In turn, his hosts are forced to procure for him the only foodstuff that he can apparently stomach ... and it isn't McDonald's.

This is a wonderful follow-up to *Basket Case* (1982), Henenlotter's first feature film. Although distinct, both movie share several commonalties, namely theme and formulaic approach. (A young man is coerced into playing host to a parasitic entity, and is forced to kill to sate the creature's lust for blood.)

Although production values are a step up, and the humor more pronounced, Henenlotter doesn't hold back on the grue. (One scene, though—involving fellatio and brain-eating, the details of which I won't go into here—was originally trimmed by censors because of the coupling of sex and violence. As if anyone would, or *could*, get any ideas from something as *outré* as this. Morons.) Also true to form, Hennenlotter wastes no time giving unhoned actors awkward dialogue to recite while acting neurotic throughout. (Speaking of which, even *Basket Case wunderkin* Kevin Vanhentenrych makes a cameo appearance, playing—who else?—some freak carrying around a wicker basket. I laughed, anyway.)

Unfortunately, the make-up effects are substandard, but Henenlotter has the sense to throw in buckets of the red stuff from off screen whenever things start to get a bit dry, helping to cover the shortcomings of the prosthetics. Aylmer, our parasitic co-star, is particularly unconvincing, but in this case—no pun intended—the cartoonish approach actually works, especially when one takes the

tongue-in-cheek script into consideration. And, yes, he does look a bit phallic. (Hmmm ... do I sense someone making a statement about male sexuality?)

It may not be as "good" as *Basket Case*, but it's the next best thing.

Breeders (1986)

Taryn Productions Inc. [US]
DIR: Tim Kincaid; PRO: Cynthia de Paula; SCR: Tim Kincaid; DOP: Arthur D. Marks; EXP: Charles Band; SFX: Matt Vogel; MFX: Edward French; MUS: Don Great and Tom Milano
STR: Leeanne Baker, Brian Barnes, Amy Brentano, Mae Cerar, Norris Culf, Doug Devos, Derek Dupont, Teresa Farley, Owen Flynn, Edward French, Dan Geffen, Rose Geffen, Raheim Grier, Adriane Lee, Mark Legan, Lance Lewman, Matt Mitler, Natalie O'Connell, Kent Perkins, Frances Raines, Pat Rizzolino, Roxie, Louis Spudeas and Michael Zezima
Approximately 76m; Color
DVD1: *Breeders* [MUA; 93m; LBX]; VHS1: *Breeders* [MUA; 93m]; *Breeders* [WIZ; 90(76)m]
ADL: *These Aliens Don't Want to Phone Home...*

Alien spores infect select humans so that they can sniff out and rape women walking the streets of New York City—in particular, virgins. (Apparently, *everyone* of the female persuasion in New York is a virgin; even more unlikely are the actresses they—the filmmakers—hired to play the roles of these "unsullied" women.) The survivors are impregnated so as to perpetuate the alien species; the horny boogers have set up a nest in the sewers for the knocked-up hosts, who spend their days bathing in slime and feeling up one another.

Breeders is exploitation in the purest sense. Unfortunately, it lacks the allure that similar films held a

Video box art for *Breeders* (1986), Wizard Video.

beasties decide to tear their way out of the unsuspecting hosts. And, yes, the effects are about as impressive as could be expected. Which, well, isn't.

A serious consideration only for those who find the idea of nude aerobics appealing.

decade earlier. Although not inept, the film is particularly wooden. The script relies entirely on convenience; everything hinges on the actresses admitting that their maidenheads are intact and—Presto!—a slimy critter pops out of the woodwork to deflower them. Titillation takes precedence, with nearly every scene accommodating needless T&A. (Are the extended scenes of nude aerobics *really* necessary?) Granted, there's not an ounce of silicone in sight, but this is little consolation. Furthermore, most of the actors who grace the screen exhibit the emotional range of doorstops, and the continuity, well, isn't.

The gore consists mostly of spurting blood and overused bladder effects employed whenever our bloated

Bride of Re-Animator (1989)

50th Street Films [US]
DIR: Brian Yuzna; PRO: Brian Yuzna; SCR: Rick Fry and Woody Keith; DOP: Rick Fichter; EXP: Hidetaka Konno, Keith Walley and Paul White; MFX: Screaming Mad George and KNB EFX Group, Inc.; VFX: David Allen Productions, Magical Media Industries Inc. and Doublin EFX; MUS: Richard Band

STR: Bruce Abbott, David Bynum, Jeffrey Combs, Irene Forrest, Friday, David Gale, Claude Earl Jones, Kathleen Kinmont, Johnny Legend, Mary Sheldon, Mel Stewart, Michael Strasser, Marge Turner and Fabiano Udenio

AKA: *Re-Animator 2*
Approximately 97m; Color
DVD7: *Bride of Re-Animator* [PIO; 99(97)m; LBX]; DVD2: *Re-Animator 2* [MEC; 93m]; VHS1: *Bride of Re-Animator* [LIV; 99(97)m]
ADL: *Date. Mate. Re-Animate.*

Herbert West and his sidekick Dan are back to wreak more havoc, but West isn't the only one with a faltering foothold on reality this time out. (Don't ask how he managed to survive being crushed to death by a giant, animated intestine, or what happened to his partner's girlfriend in the interim. I guess some things are best left to the viewer's imagination.) The somewhat derivative script— echoing, as the name implies, *The Bride of Frankenstein* (1935)—is little more than a convenient scenario for our unorthodox medical students to continue in their experiments involving the re-animation of dead tissue. It

Date.
Mate.
Re-animate.

H.P. LOVECRAFT'S

BRIDE OF
RE-ANIMATOR

LIVE
HOME VIDEO

Video box art for *Bride of Re-Animator* (1989), Live Home Video.

seems West, though, has succeeded in taking his theories one step further and actually creating new life from the juxtapositioning of re-animated parts.

This is one of those exceptions when it comes to the unwritten law of the sequel. Not only does this film rival its predecessor, it actually exceeds it in scope, particularly in reference to the special effects. (Even the most hardcore *Re-Animator* fans have to admit that its gratuitous gore was downright shoddy overall.) Although the sequel's make-up is still weak in areas (due, if anything, to its sometimes comic-book approach), there

are some amazingly gruesome gore effects that will satisfy even the more jaded splatterpunks.

Jeffrey Combs is back, reprising the role that gave him instant genre recognition, as is Bruce Abbott and David Gale. (What, no "giving head" scene?) Taking Stuart Gordon's lead, accomplice Brian Yuzna—making his directorial debut—succeeds in picking up where his ex-partner left off. (Yuzna went on to direct a slew of palatable sequels for various low-rent franchises, although as far as *they* were concerned, it wasn't much of a challenge to outdo their predecessors.) The tongue-in-cheek splatstick comedy is still prevalent, thanks to some silly monsters and West's sardonic one-liners, complimenting the gratuity. Lovecraft may not be too pleased with the affiliation, but fans that like their humor wet shouldn't be disappointed by this entry.

The Broken Mirror *see* **Non Avere Paura della Zia Marta**

Brutal Sorcery *see* **Du Gu**

The Burning (1980)

Miramax Pictures [US]
DIR: Tony Maylam; PRO: Harvey Weinstein; SCR: Peter Lawrence and Bob Weinstein [Based on the novel *The Burning* by Graham Masterton]; DOP: Harvey Harrison; EXP: Michael Cohl, Andre Djaoui and Jean Ubaud; MFX: Tom Savini; MUS: Rick Wakeman
STR: Jason Alexander, Leah Ayres, Brian Backer, Shelley Bruce, Sarah Chodoff, Lou David, Jeff de Hart, Bonnie Deroski, Ned Eisenberg, Carrick Glenn, Carolyn Houlihan, Holly Hunter, Larry Joshua, Kevin Kendall, Bruce Kluger, Keith Mandell, Brian Matthews, Jerry McGee, J.R. McKechnie, Mansoor Najee-Ullah, George Parry, Willie Reale, John Roach, Reid Ron-

dell, Ame Segull, Fisher Stevens, K.C. Townsend, John Tripp and James van Verth
AKA: *Carnage*
Approximately 91m; Color
VHS1: *The Burning* [HBO; 90m]; *The Burning* [MUA; 91m]; *The Burning* [EMI; 90m]
ADL: *The Most Frightening of All Maniac Films!*

This shameless retread of *Friday the 13th* has its moments, but has been deservedly forgotten amidst the glut of slasher flicks that followed in *that* film's wake. *The Burning*'s only real point of interest is the participation of effects wizard Tom Savini; he has even been quoted as saying he chose to do this film instead of *Friday the 13th—Part 2* because he thought the

The most frightening of all maniac films!

"Uncanny . . . grisly and convincing . . . a truly grotesque monster."   —THE MIAMI HERALD

THORN EMI VIDEO

Video box art for *The Burning* (1980), Thorn EMI Video.

script was more promising. In retrospect, he must feel pretty gosh darn silly, considering that—for all intents and purposes—it's the same damn film.

Even more ironic is the fact that about a minute's worth of the gore was cut prior to its theatrical release (an uncut version has only recently surfaced on video), leaving little of Savini's assumed magic intact. Why the producers—not the ratings board, in this case—decided to do this is beyond me; you'd think they would have realized that a slasher film without the obligatory bloodshed would not go over well with its intended audience. *Especially* when teens wanted to see how someone was going to top *Friday the 13th* in pure gratuity.

For what it's worth, this uncredited adaptation of a Masterton novel is a notch above *Friday the 13th—Part 2*, but splitting hairs is not my favored method for gauging quality.

Caligula—La Storia Mai Raccontata [Caligula— The Untold Story] (1981)

Metaka Corporation S.A. [It]
DIR: Aristide Massaccesi; SCR: Aristide Massaccesi and Lugi Montefiori; DOP: Aristide Massaccesi; EXP: Alexander Sussman; SFX: Roy Nottingham; MUS: Carlo Maria Cordio
STR: John Alin, Charles Borromel, Sasha d'Arc, Larry Dolgin, Oliver Finch, Alex Freyberger, Laura Gemser, David Cain Haughton, Ulla Luna, Michele Soavi, Gabriele Tinti and Fabiola Toledo
AKA: *Caligula II—The Forbidden Story*; *Emperor Caligula—The Garden of Taboo*; *The Emperor Caligula—The Untold Story*; *L'Imperatore Caligula [The Emperor Caligula]*
Approximately 116m; Color XXX
VHS1: *The Emperor Caligula—The Untold Story* [TWE; 100m]; VHS2: *Caligula II—The Forbidden Story* [MOV; 111(116)m];

English w/Dutch subtitles]; DVD1: *Caligula—The Untold Story* [PRO; 92m]
ADL: *He Crossed a Line Most People Never Dare to Make.*

This treatment of the infamous Roman leader's escapades revolves around *Emanuelle*'s Gemser and her plan to assassinate the titular tyrant after he casually rapes a member of her then-burgeoning cult of Christianity; the girl kills herself during the assault, and her boyfriend—the only other witness—is slain. Gemser the good little virgin deflowers herself with a sculpted black dildo in church, then joins the emperor's harem. After a few quick lessons, she is indoctrinated into her new life via the demands of a Roman orgy. Of course, the gluttonous proceedings are bloodied by a gladiatorial skirmish, staged for the benefit of the audience. (Once the carnage is cleared, it's back to the sins of the flesh; a live horse is brought out and, well, it's Tijuana revisited.) Then things get *really* messy.

Although not as slick as *Gore Vidal's Caligula* (1980), the lack of gloss actually benefits this film, putting the subject matter in a very suitable light. Whereas Guccione's opus is pretentious and almost glorifying in its presentation, Massaccesi's knock-off comes across more as gritty documentation. (How historically accurate either film is, I won't dare to venture a guess, since I think we can assume that the screenwriters took a great deal of artistic license.)

The gore is gratuitous, with an early tongue-sawing sequence particularly repellent. (Oh, and let's not forget the poor chap who gets impaled with a spear in a manner that makes suppositories look positively quaint.)

And, like *Gore Vidal's Caligula*, the uncut version contains hardcore sex footage to make it an even sleazier affair ... as if it needed any help. Unfortunately, this uncut edition of *Caligula—La Storia Mai Raccontata* has yet to be made available domestically.

Caligula—The Untold Story *see* **Caligula—La Storia Mai Raccontata**

Caligula II—The Forbidden Story *see* **Caligula—La Storia Mai Raccontata**

Cameron's Closet (1987)

Smart Egg Pictures [US]
DIR: Armand Mastroianni; PRO: Luigi Cingolani; SCR: Gary Brandner [Based on the novel *Cameron's Closet* by Gary Brandner]; DOP: Russell Carpenter; EXP: Georg Zeçeviç; MFX: Rose Librizzi, Alex Rambaldi and Carlo Rambaldi; SFX: Greg Landerer; VFX: Ermanno Biamonte; MUS: Harry Manfredini
STR: Bond Bradigan, Doc D. Charbonneau, Dort Donald Clark, Scott Curtis, David Estruardo, Mel Harris, Gary Hudson, Tab Hunter, Kim Lankford, Skip E. Lowe, Chuck McCann, Leigh McCloskey, Kerry Nakagawa, Raymond Patterson, Frank Pesce, Cotter Smith, Wilson Smith and Paul W. Zeçeviç
Approximately 87m; Color
VHS1: *Cameron's Closet* [SVS; 87m]
ADL: *A New Place to Look for Terror.*

Tab Hunter is the high-strung father of a boy with telekinetic powers; going by his attitude, he must have seen *Carrie* one too many times. Unfortunately, he didn't heed de Palma's warning and, well, his screen time is cut short (much like the actor's career). The tike is sent to live with his mother and her bitchy boyfriend, and soon she realizes *why* she never tried to get custody of her only son. As it turns out, the boy's not directly responsible for all of the mayhem that ensues; instead, the blame is rightfully placed on the head of some Mayan devil god who has decided that "it's time to come out of the closet." So to speak.

This, a typical Mastroianni production, offers very human characters (unlike the usual Hollywood archetypes) but is hindered by silly psychotechnics and a tacky rubber monster. The hokey proceedings lack the subtlety and logic necessary to coerce the viewer into suspending his or her disbelief for an hour and a half. And, for us splatterpunks, we are offered a handful of gory deaths realized with sub-par effects. Doesn't this man ever hire anyone with any artistic ability? Or is he just able to make even good effects look bad? Since Mastroianni's strength is with people, methinks he should find a new genre to exploit and stay away from effects-laden horror films altogether.

Camper see **Paura nel Buio**

Campfire Tales see **The Legend Lives**

Camping del Terrore [Camp of Terror] (1986)

Racing Pictures S.r.L. [It/US]
DIR: Ruggero Deodato; PRO: Alessandro Fracassi; SCR: Alessandro Capone, Luca d'Alisera, Sheila Goldberg and Dardano Sacchetti; DOP: Emilio Loffredo; SFX: Roberto Pace; MUS: Joel Goldsmith and Claudio Simonetti
STR: Nancy Brilli, Mimsy Farmer, Nicola Farron, Valentina Forte, Clelia Fradella, Stefano Galantucci, Lorenzo Grabau, David Hess, Sven Kruger, Andrew J. Lederer, Stefano Madia, Luisa Maneri, Charles Napier, Bruce Penhall, Elena Pompei, Ivan Rassimov, John Steiner, Cynthia Thompson and Fabio Vox
AKA: *Body Count*; *Camping della Morte* [Camp of the Dead Women]; *The Eleventh Commandment*
Approximately 83m; Color
VHS2: *Body Count* [IHV; 90(83)m; English w/Dutch subtitles]

Someone in a cheesy Halloween mask is hacking up obnoxious teens on a campground that was supposedly built on an Indian burial ground. Of course, we—the viewers—don't buy the hokey pretenses and know it's somebody with something more akin to personal vengeance on their mind.

It is difficult to believe that Ruggero Deodato, the filmmaker who brought us such unrelenting genre films as *Cannibal Holocaust* (1979) and *La Casa Sperduta nel Parco* (1981), helmed this painfully generic slasher film. Stilted dialogue, gratuitous '80s dancing, and a stupid shock ending make it particularly hard to endure. (Ex-Goblin member Simonetti supplied the score, but even his contribution seems uninspired.)

Deodato, why hast thou forsaken us?

Camping della Morte see **Camping del Terrore**

Campsite Massacre see **The Final Terror**

Campus Killings see **Splatter University**

Canibal Feroz see **Cannibal Ferox**

Cannibal Apocalypse see **Apocalisse Domani**

Cannibal Campout (1988)

Donna Michele Productions [US]
DIR: Tom Fisher and Jon McBride;
PRO: Tom Fisher and Jon McBride; SCR:
John Rayl; DOP: Tom Fisher; EXP: Jon
McBride; SFX: Joseph Salhab; MUS:
Christopher A. Granger

STR: Ray Angelic, Amy Chludzinski,
John Farrell, Christopher A. Granger, Car-
rie Lindell, Richard Marcus, Jon McBride,
Gene Robbins, Joseph Salhab and Nanoy
Sciarra

Approximately 88m; Color [Shot on
video]

VHS1: *Cannibal Campout* [DMP;
88m]

"What you are about to see is
based upon true accounts and conjec-
ture and is a delineation of actual
events which transpired at an inde-
terminable time to persons of less
than genuinely equivocal authentic-
ity." Either someone is trying to be
funny, or they abuse their thesaurus
more than I do.

Okay, everybody, it's time for a
math test. Four teens on campout +
two friends planning a practical joke
+ three redneck cannibals = what,
folks? If you guessed pretty much
anything except "a good movie,"
you're absolutely right. Even the few
attempts at humor don't save face for
this lousy shot-on-video production.

Co-conspirator Jon McBride
also perpetrated the goreless *Wood-
chipper Massacre* (1987), but at least
that effort had some charm, despite
its homegrown ineptitude. This one
makes up for lost time by piling on
the grue, but it seems no amount of
stage blood can hide the rubber and
chicken giblets used to create the
effects.

And you thought math was hard.

Cannibal Ferox [Ferocious Cannibals] (1981)

Dania Film [It], Medusa Distribuzione
[It], National Cinematografica [It]
DIR: Umberto Lenzi; PRO: Antonio
Crescenzi; SCR: Umberto Lenzi; DOP:
Giovanni Bergamini; EXP: Antonio Cre-
scenzi; MFX: Gino de Rossi; MUS: Roberto
Donati and Maria Fiamma Maglione

STR: Janos Bartha, Giovanni Berga-
mini, Richard Bolla, Lorraine de Selle, Meg
Fleming, Zora Kerova, Walter Lucchini,
Danilo Mattei, Riccardo Petrazzi, Perry
Pirkanen, Giovanni Lombardo Radice, El
Indio Rincon and Venantino Venantini

AKA: *Canibal Feroz* [Ferocious Can-
nibals]; *De Kannibalen Vallen Aan!*; *Let Them
Die Slowly*; *Make Them Die Slowly*; *Mondo
Cannibale* [Cannibal World]; *Die Rache der
Kannibalen* [The Revenge of the Cannibals];
Woman from Deep River

Approximately 93m; Color ⚔ ⚔ ⚔
DVD1: *Cannibal Ferox* [IMG; 93m;
LBX]; VHS1: *Cannibal Ferox* [GRI; 93m];
Cannibal Ferox [MWG; 93m; LBX]; *Make
Them Die Slowly* [THR; 92m]; VHS2: *Can-
nibal Ferox* [REP; 89(93)m]; *Cannibal Ferox*
[VIP; 86m]; *Canibal Feroz* [COF; 86m];
Make Them Die Slowly [MYR; 93m]

"This motion picture is one of the
most violent films ever made. There
are 24 scenes of barbaric torture and
sadistic cruelty graphically shown. If
the representation of disgusting and
repulsive material upsets you, please
do not view this film." The tagline got
my interest ... unfortunately.

A woman anthropologist and her
two friends are off tramping about in
the Amazon, trying to prove her the-
sis that "cannibalism as an organized
practice of human society does not
exist, and historically has never existed." They run into a small-time
drug pusher and his wounded friend
who claim to have been accosted by
cannibals, and the whole lot of tourists quickly find themselves being
hunted down by the voracious natives.

Sadly, this is one of the closest things to a "good" film Lenzi has ever perpetrated, but even though it's better than, say, *Incubo sulla Città Contaminata* (1980), it's nothing to shout about. Granted, close-ups of a native chewing on the remains of a still-twitching grub worm does help to set the tone of the film, but I think it's safe to say that a filmmaker with any *real* talent could have avoided such a shot altogether and still create atmosphere. For the most part, *Cannibal Ferox* is not only typical in execution of the much-maligned Italian cannibal epics, but probably stands as the definitive entry.

Although our heroine claims that cannibalism never existed on a societal level, that it is a myth perpetrated throughout our history by so-called "civilized man" to justify acts of cultural genocide on third-world countries, the filmmakers contest this, if only to take advantage of the viewers' xenophobia. Having exploited the natives and our fears of the primitive mind, any social statements that this film attempts to make fall on deaf ears as they—the filmmakers—have proven themselves guilty of the selfsame prejudices displayed by the people they condemn. Of course, the same can be said for this particular genre altogether, and no amount of fast talk will fool the more conscientious viewers for even a second.

And while we're on the subject of exploitation, it's not worth wading through the sickening displays of animal cruelty (staged or simply "documented") for the few interesting gore scenes. A graphic castration is the *crème de la crème*, although a female variation on *A Man Called Horse*-style hanging does clock in at a close second.

If, having never seen any Green Hell films, you have found your interest piqued by these reviews, check out Ruggero Deodato's *Cannibal Holocaust* (1979) instead for what is probably the only *truly* worthwhile film of the lot, even though it falls prey to many of the same faltering ethics. If that outing doesn't turn you away, feel free to work your way down from there.

Cannibal Hookers (1987)

Hollywood International Pictures [US]
DIR: Donald Farmer; PRO: Donald Farmer and Gary J. Levinson; SCR: Donald Farmer; DOP: Tony Fabian, Richard Kashanski and Glenn Kral; SFX: Bill Barschdorf and Brian Sipe; MUS: Das Yahoos and Jana Silver
STR: Mark Arnold, Sheila Best, Matt Borlenghi, Bonnie Bradigan, Eric Caiden, Dusty Carlson, Tommy Carrano, Diana Cruz, Rod Dailey, Kristie Etzold, Michelle Fox, Marya Gant, Katina Garner, Drew Godderis, Wayne Hyde, Annette Kellogg, Dena Kellogg, Gary J. Levinson, Michael Liberty, Richard Liberty, Ron McGonigle, Nancy Milholland, Annette Munro, Sky Nicholas, Cheryl Rusa, Donald Trimborn and Amy Waddell
Approximately 65m; Color [Shot on video]
VHS1: *Cannibal Hookers* [MAG; 90(65)m]

And you thought Fred Olen Ray's *Hollywood Chainsaw Hookers* (1988) sucked.

Needless to say, the title succinctly sums up the proceedings: A bunch of skanky strippers-turned-actresses stumble through the sets, chewing on latex prosthetics when not doing the same to the scenery, flaunting their sometimes silicone-enhanced wares for all to see.

This film could very well be the quintessential shot-on-video horror flick, productions that rarely elevate themselves above the same amateurish mix of blood and boobs that predominate this medium-inspired subgenre. Director Farmer—most notable as the publisher of *The Splatter Times*, one of the most influential and groundbreaking magazines devoted to splatter films—has averaged a little more than one film a year since he made the move to filmmaking in 1986, and not all of these are horror films. He is also an ordained minister.

Cannibal Hookers was later released as Volume Three in the "I Will Dance on Your Grave" series offered by Magnum Video. (A couple of the other entries were perpetrated by Farmer as well, so be warned.)

Includes film clips from Tony Malanowski's *Curse of the Screaming Dead* (1976). (Zombies, of course! You can't have a shot on video production without zombies showing up *somewhere*.)

Cannibal Virus *see* **Inferno dei Morti-Vivent**

I Cannibali *see* **Mondo Cannibale** (1980)

Cannibals *see* **Mondo Cannibale** (1980)

Cannibals in the City *see* **Apocalisse Domani**

Cannibals in the Streets *see* **Apocalisse Domani**

Carnage (1981) *see* **The Burning**

Carnage (1983)

Jaylo International Films Inc. [US]
DIR: Andy Milligan; PRO: Lew Mishkin; SCR: Andy Milligan; DOP: Andy Milligan
STR: Albert Alfano, Chris Baker, Michael Chiodo, William Cooner, Leslie den Dooven, Rosemary Egan, Lon Freeman, Jogn Garritt, Chris Georges, Bill Grant, Victor Logan, David Marks, Judith Mayes, Ché Moody, Ellen Orchid, Susan Ortiz, Jack Poggi, Lola Ross, Ray Trail, Deeann Veeder and Joseph Vitagliano
Approximately 92m; Color
VHS1: *Carnage* [MHE; 91(92)m]
ADL: *See Home Appliances Slice and Dice ... People!*

A desperate couple consummates their marriage by painting the walls with their brains. (Awww ... how romantic.) Three years later, another couple purchases the suicide house, only to have their home appliances pick up bad attitudes. Of course, the ghosts—unhappy at the prospect that somebody's marriage is going over better than theirs did—are responsible for all of the booga booga table tapping; when that doesn't do the trick, they take out their ire on the cleaning lady until she takes a straight razor to her own throat. It's downhill from there for the newlyweds, with the bloodthirsty ghosts no longer willing to eke out a living as mere poltergeists.

Carnage is, ultimately, little more than a slow-moving, cheesy spook show with a bucket full of gore smearing the stale routine. There is no suspense, as the haunted house shtick is played by the book, every last prop in sight being dragged around the place with fishing line. (Who ever said this stuff doesn't show up on film needs to double-check their eyeglass prescription.) When the grue does kick in, we are instantly reminded that this *is* an Andy Milligan flick, and that the effects in his production rarely rise above that of bottom-of-the-barrel. (Taking even his earliest gore efforts into account, *Carnage* contains the worst evisceration ever perpetrated for the sake of celluloid; is that spaghetti they used for the entrails, or am I just imagining things?)

The remainder of the production values are heads and tails above Milligan's previous films, yet still primitive enough to capture that wonderful '70s feel despite the '80s production stamp.

For Andy Milligan fans only. (Is there a support group for such lost souls? If anyone out there has their number, I need it.)

El Carnaval de las Bestias [The Carnival of the Beasts] (1980)

Dálmata Films S.A. [Sp], Hori Kikaku Seisaku [Ja]

DIR: Jacinto Molina Alvarez; SCR: Jacinto Molina Alvarez; DOP: Alejandro Ulloa; EXP: Jacinto Molina Alvarez and Hideo Sasai; MUS: CAM

STR: Silvia Aguilar, Jacinto Molina Alvarez, Ramón Centenero, Luis Ciges, Rafael Conesa, Roxana di Pre, Tito García, Azucena Hernández, Rafael Hernández, Paloma Hurtado, Alexia Loreto, Kogi Moritugu, Lautaro Murúa, Eiko Nagashima, Ricardo Palacios, Manuel Pereiro, Pepe Ruiz and Julia Salinero

AKA: *The Beasts' Carnival*; Human Beasts; *The Pig*

Approximately 90m; Color ❦❦❦
VHS1: *Human Beasts* [ALL; 90m]

Everybody's favorite Spanish horror star heads the cast as a mercenary who is hired by a Japanese "firm" to secure some diamonds for them, and knocks up the boss' sister in the process. After a little double-crossing,

he hightails it to Spain and—after a bloody skirmish with his ex-employers—is nursed back to health by a doctor and his three daughters. The family seems normal enough at first—one daughter even giving the killer a new lease on life—but things take a turn for the worst.

The crime elements which the film tries so hard to establish becomes secondary to the more horrific circumstances that befall our beloved anti-hero. In other words, don't be fooled by the video box synopsis that makes this out to be little more than an action/adventure flick; the presence of Paul Naschy (*né* Jacinto Molina Alvarez) should be enough to tip you off that this film is not exactly your standard potboiler. There is plenty of gore, the highlight being an attack by man-eating pigs, and—just so you know they aren't playing by the rules—the ghost of the doctor's deceased wife shows up to make matters more interesting.

El Carnival de las Bestias does boast some outstanding production values (at least when placed side by side with Naschy's earlier horror films), but the abundance of T&A and the inclusion of man-eating pigs are subtle reminders that Spanish trash is just that, regardless of how much money one pours into it. (It's a shame Japanese investors couldn't have kept this up for a few more years; it would've been nice to see what else Naschy could've accomplished with some decent financial backing.)

Not surprising, Paul Naschy makes a very convincing Napoleon Bonaparte. (And, no, that comment wasn't out of left field.)

La Casa 2 *see* **Evil Dead II**

La Casa 3—Ghosthouse [The House 3—Ghost House] (1987)

Filmirage [It/US]
DIR: Umberto Lenzi; PRO: Donatella Donati and Aristide Massaccesi; SCR: Cinthia McGavin; DOP: Franco delli Colli; EXP: Robert Gould, Dan Maklansky and Roland Park; MUS: Simon Boswell and Piero Montanari

STR: Robert Champagne, William J. Devany, Kristen Fougerousse, Ron Houck, Martin Jay, Hernest McKimnoro, Willy M. Moon, Ralph Morse, Susan Muller, Donald O'Brien, Greg Scott, Mary Sellers, Kate Silver, Alain Smith and Lara Wendel

AKA: *La Casa de los Muertos* [The House of the Dead]; *Ghosthouse*
Approximately 91m; Color
VHS1: *Ghosthouse* [IMP; 91m]

A little girl is reprimanded for knifing the family pet; while she's being consoled by an oversized stuffed clown, her parents are butchered. Twenty years later, a couple is drawn to the house after receiving a desperate plea for help over their ham radio. Suffice it to say, their presence kick starts all of the necessary hokum.

Initially interesting, *La Casa 3—Ghost House* fails to live up to its potential, instead relying on second-rate *Amityville Horror*-style theatrics. The acting is similarly lacking, as are the special effects. (When jars explode from the pressure, the pyrotechnics artists don't bother concealing the flashes made by the charges.)

The film is gorier than what one would expect: People are dispatched by (in no particular order) an axe, a butcher knife, hedge clippers, a claw hammer, a fan blade, a guillotine, and lots and lots of glass. We're talking Fulci city here, folks, so if you don't care how or why the carnage piles up, then this should be as good as gold to you.

And what's with the backmasked children's song? It sounds like someone's saying "Hey, Bob ... are you there? Are you there? Are you there?" but I'm not certain. (Apparently, some of the music was lifted from Boswell's score for *Deliria* [1987], but I don't recall *this* being it.)

La Casa al Fondo del Parco *see* **Quella Villa in Fondo al Parco**

La Casa con la Scala nel Buio [The House of the Dark Staircase] (1981)

National Cinematografica [It], Nuova Dania Cinematografica [It]
DIR: Lamberto Bava; SCR: Elisa Livia Briganti and Dardano Sacchetti; DOP: Gianlorenzo Battaglia; SFX: Giovanni Corridori; MUS: Guido de Angelis and Maurizio de Angelis

STR: Valeria Cavalli, Giovanni Frezza, Stanko Molnar, Lara Naszinski, Andrea Occhipinti, Anny Papa, Michele Soavi and Fabiola Toleda

AKA: *A Blade in the Dark*; *La Maison de la Terreur* [The House of Terror]
Approximately 104m; Color
DVD1: *A Blade in the Dark* [ABE; 104m; LBX]; VHS1: *A Blade in the Dark* [ABE; 104m; LBX]; *A Blade in the Dark* [LIG; 96m]

A musician is hired to work on the score for a horror film, and retreats to an isolated villa to compose it. Unfortunately for him, his tranquility is threatened, first by some strange goings-on that allude to a supernatural presence, then by a string of seemingly unrelated murders. Neither the hero nor the viewer, though, is given enough clues as to *why* the killer is stalking him and/or his premises.

This, Lamberto Bava's second stint as a full-fledged director, is a fairly engrossing *giallo* thriller, al-

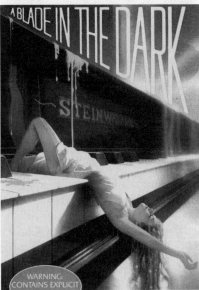

Top: Japanese one-sheet for *La Casa con la Scala nel Buio* (1981). *Bottom:* Video box art for *La Casa con la Scala nel Buio* (1981), Lightning Video.

though it probably owes more to his peer Dario Argento than his iconoclastic father Mario. This is most evident in the stylistic nuances that, intriguing as they may be, make little sense within the context of the film. The threadbare motive and brutal displays of violence are also a dead giveaway as to the source of his inspiration.

With the kid from Fulci's *Quella Villa Accanto al Cimitero* (House by the Cemetery, 1981), bee-stung lips and all, and another Argento protégé, Michele Soavi, director of the acclaimed *Dellamorte, Dellamore* (Of Death, of Love, 1993). (Soavi also functioned as assistant director.) Both play small but crucial parts and—spoiler forthcoming—both appear in drag.

Easily one of Bava's more effective films, although fans that prefer the campy excesses of *Demoni* (Demons, 1985) will be quick to disagree.

A Casa de Cemitério *see* **Quella Villa Accanto al Cimitero**

La Casa de los Muertos *see* **La Casa 3—Ghosthouse**

Catacombs (1988)

Eden Ltd. [US], Empire Pictures [US]
DIR: David Schmoeller; PRO: Hope Perello; SCR: Giovanni di Marco and R. Barker Price; DOP: Sergio Salvati; EXP: Charles Band; MFX: Thomas Floutz; SFX: Renato Agostini; MUS: Pino Donaggio
STR: Ian Abercrombie, Omero Bartolini, Feodor Chaliapin, Roberto di Cicco, Antonio Dispensieri, Vernon Dobtcheff, Giordano Falzoni, Franco Fazi, G. Ferretti, Benedetto Fortino, Francesco Fusari, Mapi Galán, Julian Jenkins, Alfredo Manotti, Etore Martino, Adriana Grampa Michel,

Nicola Morelli, Sarco Nale, Michael Pasby, Brett Porter, Lino Prevato, Nicole Ricci, Ted Rusoff, Laura Schaeffer, E. Leslie Thomas, Timothy van Patton, Felix Weiner and Jeremy West
AKA: *Curse IV—The Ultimate Sacrifice*
Approximately 84m; Color
VHS1: *Curse IV—The Ultimate Sacrifice* [CTS; 84m]
ADL: *The Curse Never Rests...*

The Abbey of San Pietro en Valle, 1506. An exorcism doesn't pan out, so the monks decide to wall up the still living man suffering from a bad case of the "devil made me do it"s. Almost five-hundred years later, an American teacher visits the abbey to investigate the catacombs beneath the venerable monastery ("the last significant monument to Christian antiquity"). Of course, the aforementioned wall is breached, and we have a hokey horror flick on our hands in no time flat.

Okay, so *Catacombs* is the prototypical Full Moon film: A nicely photographed, adeptly directed horror flick that boasts likable characters and above-average effects. (There are some interesting things achieved here, though, with the simplest means, especially film reversal.) Furthermore, there are some nice comedic touches, many of which are supplied by the sometimes eccentric, but very human monks that make up most of the cast. Unfortunately, the final confrontation is not only quite cheesy, but also rather anticlimactic. (The fact that it essentially reiterates well-worn themes from *The Exorcist* [1973] doesn't help matters, either.) All in all, *Catacombs* is a rather enjoyable low-key horror film, despite the fact that it never amounts to much in the end.

Filmed in 1988, this movie was shelved until 1993 due to Empire Picture's bankruptcy.

Cellar Dweller (1987)

Dove Corporation Ltd. [It/US]
DIR: John Carl Buechler; PRO: Bob Wynn; SCR: Kit du Bois; DOP: Sergio Salvatti; EXP: Charles Band; MFX: John Carl Buechler and Mechanical & Makeup Imageries; MUS: Carl Dante
STR: Pamela Bellwood, Jeffrey Combs, Yvonne de Carlo, Michael S. Deak, Vince Edwards, Floyd Levine, Debrah Mullowney, Brian Robbins and Cheryl-Ann Wilson
Approximately 77m; Color
VHS1: *Cellar Dweller* [MUA; 77m]; *Cellar Dweller* [NWV; 80(77)m]; *Cellar Dweller* [RSG; 80(77)m]

1955. A comic book artist who draws his inspiration from an ancient tome on demonology accidentally brings to life one of his creations. Thirty-some years later the house where the dead artist lived is now an art institute, run by Yvonne (*The Munsters*) de Carlo. A young burgeoning artist arrives who wants to revive the dead artist's comic which initially inspired her to pick the vocation, and she finds herself not only having to deal with the selfsame monster that killed her hero, but—worst of all—she finds herself trapped in a house with a bunch of pretentious buffoons who call themselves "artists."

I'm going to gloss over the specifics on this pre–Full Moon shocker; it sucks eggs, and that's all you need to know. What I want to mention is the scriptwriter's ineptitude when it came to researching facts for this podunk monster flick: Specifically, the world of the comic artist. I guess they didn't think an actual comic artist would ever watch their lousy little film, giving them room for whatever artistic license they saw fit to use.

Having worked in the business for at least six years (and being fairly knowledgeable in the field *before* I took it up as a short-lived vocation), I've got an itchy trigger finger and a pocket full of rounds.

First and foremost, comic book artists are not "cartoonists"; both are entirely different fields, and one is invariably offended when referred to as the other. The dead artist's style in the film is patented '70s, not '50s (let alone the fact that it contained liberal uses of nudity, unheard of in mainstream comics and not seen until the underground comics revolution that didn't start until the tail end of the '60s). Furthermore, the art was actually done by Frank Brunner, an artist who made his name in—you guessed it—the '70s. (I guess they thought comic book art is interchangeable regardless of the time period, even though it's just as distinct as fashions, styles of cars, etc.) They also make comic illustrating out to be quite an easy task (you know, those lazy artists); whereas most artists do an average of one to two pages a day, this inexperienced hack whips out one in two minutes … complete with washes and zip tone!

Oh, and there's other things that will insult the intelligence of not only artists, but of anyone with an ounce of sense, like the 6 oz. container of white-out that holds at least two quarts of the stuff. (You couldn't buy that at J.K. Gill, believe you me.) Or the fact that paper not only *burns* when it comes into contact with fire, but that it is much more combustible than people.

The movie? Shallow characterization predominates, and the title monster barely passes muster. There is a fair amount of gratuity, but only a decap is at all noteworthy.

Truly, truly embarrassing.

Cementerio del Terror [Cemetery of Terror] (1985)

Dynamic Films Inc. & Producciones Torrente S.A. [Mx]

DIR: Rubén Galindo, Jr.; PRO: Raúl Galindo; SCR: Rubén Galindo, Jr.; DOP: Luis Medina and Rosalio Solano; EXP: Rodolfo Galindo; MFX: Ken Diaz; SFX: Raul Falomir; MUS: Chucho Zarzosa

STR: Francisco Adel, Edna Bolkan, Erika Buenfil, Eduardo Capetillo, René Cardona III, Jacqueline Castro, Alfonso Cervera, Isaac Chavira, Mauricio Chico, Marta Galindo, Santiago Galindo, Andrés García, Jr., Gabriela Garcia, Lorenza Garcia, Virginia Garcia, Luis Godinez, Pablo Godinez, José Gómez, Alfred Ibanez, Cervando Manzetti, Raúl Meraz, Mineko Mori, Leonardo Noriega, José Gómez Parcero, Maria Rebeca, Bety Robles, César Adrian Sanchez, Ricardo Serrano, Hugo Stiglitz, Adrian Vargas, César Velasco, Usi Velasco, Leo Villnueva and Lili Zoto

Approximately 91m; Color

VHS1: *Cementerio del Terror* [CIN; 91m; Spanish]

Some kids steal the body of a seemingly inhuman killer from the morgue in order to perform some hokey rituals in the graveyard at night (*à la Children Shouldn't Play with Dead Things*). They are quickly rained out, abandoning their fun and games and hightailing it to an old house. Of course, they didn't stick around long enough to see their success, but before long the graveyard's patronage has followed them to their intended make-out spot, including the resuscitated killer sporting very strong, very sharp fingernails.

Even if you can't understand a lick of Spanish, this is a fun little

Mexican lobby card for *Cementerio del Terror* (1985).

zombie romp for people who can't get enough of ye olde gut-munchers. Being typical for the genre, the gore quotient (slapdash as it may be) is fairly high, and only a few hairs short of the undiluted carnage for which Fulci became renowned. (Had it not all been relegated to the second half of the film, it could have conceivably given Lucio himself a run for his money.) Due to primitive resources, the filmmakers have succeeded in capturing a '70s feel, enhancing the film's stillborn charm. Even the obligatory haunted house shenanigans seem uncomfortably at home.

Fulci's *Quella Villa Accanto al Cimitero* meets Raimi's *The Evil Dead*, minus the obligatory eye gouging and Bruce Campbell.

El Cementerio Maldito *see* **Pet Semetary**

A Cena col Vampiro [Dinner with a Vampire] (1988)

Dania Film [It]
DIR: Lamberto Bava; SCR: Lamberto Bava and Dardano Sacchetti; DOP: Gianfranco Transunto; EXP: Massimo Manasse and Marco Grillo Spina; MFX: Rosaro Prestopino; SFX: Paolo Ricci; VFX: Sergio Stivaletti; MUS: Simon Boswell and Mario Tagliaferri

STR: Daniele Aldrovandi, George Hilton, Valeria Milillo, Roberto Pedicini, Patrizia Pellegrino, Riccardo Rossi, Isabel Russinova, Stefano Sabelli, Yvonne Sciò, Igor Zalewski and Letizia Ziaco

Approximately 90m, Color

A film crew breaks into a hidden crypt, discovering a sealed sarcophagus. One of the crewmembers accidentally cuts himself and—in the best Hammer tradition—inadvertently awakens a hungry vampire, in this case Count Urich. Years later, having since settled into a modern lifestyle, the Count holds "auditions" for a proposed horror film. The winners (in this case, two lousy singers, a lousy actor, and a lousy comedian) are invited to his castle for the weekend. They are greeted by a manservant who bears an uncanny resemblance to Marty Feldman from *Young Frankenstein* (1974), and sounds like Monty Python's patented Mr. Gumby. It turns out that the Count is tired of immortality and wants his guests to end his life. The trick is, they need to figure out the one way in which he can be killed. Unfortunately for them, a crucial clue was mistakenly withheld by the harebrained hunchback.

Bava must've been in a funky mood when he concocted this one. At times a straightforward horror film (with such gory highlights as hearts being ripped out and the obligatory meltdown), *A Cena col Vampiro* tends to lean towards the comedic, whether it be tongue-in-cheek or slapstick. (From the pastiches of old black and white horror films offered in the film's latter half, it is probably safe to assume that—despite any modern conventions—*A Cena col Vampiro* is also an homage to the creature flicks of yesteryear.) Unfortunately, its schizoid tendencies make it an awkward viewing experience, and the humor is often downright insipid. (The finale is sure to draw a grimace from even the more hare-brained viewers.) For every inspired moment, there's five minutes of bad Transylvanian accents or contrived hokum. The film is almost saved by its lavish cinematography and impressive sets, but these are ultimately superficial, at best.

Occasionally amusing and sometimes impressive, *A Cena col Vampiro* never lives up to its potential.

The Chainsaw Devil *see* **Mil Gritos en la Noche**

Cheerleader Camp (1988)

Bloody Pom Pom Productions Inc. [US]

DIR: John Quinn; PRO: Jeff Prettyman and John Quinn; SCR: David Lee Fein and R.L. O'Keefe; DOP: Bryan England; SFX: Tom Surprenant; MUS: Joel Hamilton and Murielle Hodler-Hamilton

STR: Vickie Benson, Dave Delgado, Lucinda Dickey, Rebecca Ferratti, George Flower, Leif Garrett, Lorie Griffin, Tom Habeeb, William Johnson, Mike Knox, Kathryn Litton, Travis McKenna, Krista Pflanzer, Craig Piligian, Chris Prettyman, Jeff Prettyman, John Quinn, Frank Reinfield, Betsy Russell and Teri Weigel

AKA: *Bloody Pom Poms*

Approximately 88m; Color

VHS1: *Cheerleader Camp* [PRI; 89(88)m]

ADL: *Competition Was Murder at Cheerleader Camp*

Maybe I got ahold of a bad batch of popcorn while watching this by-the-book stalk 'n' slash, but I inexplicably found it almost, uhm ... engaging. Even more incredible, I swear some of the performances are even, uhm ... convincing. This doesn't make it a good film by any means, and maybe not even worth the ninety minutes I spent wading through it, but any slasher flick that manages to transcend the low standards inherent to it *in any way* deserves some credit. (Even if it is a pat on the head before you throw the bastard out the door.)

Would I watch it again or actually purchase a copy? Well, uhm ... probably not, unless I got into the same batch of tainted kernels again. (Okay, I admit it. For two bucks, I'll buy damn near anything, food poisoning withstanding.)

For those who care at all, *Cheerleader Camp* also features a fairly early appearance of porn star Teri Weigel (one of the "big-uns" girls from *Married with Children*), and she, well, "exposes" the fact that this was made before she was disfigured by silicone implants.

La Chiesa [The Church] (1989)

ADC S.r.L. [It], Cecchi Gori Group [It], Reteitalia [It], Tiger Cinematografica [It]

DIR: Michele Soavi; PRO: Dario Argento; SCR: Dario Argento, Lambert Bava, Franco Ferrini, Dardano Sacchetti and Michele Soavi [Based on the short story "The Treasure of Abbot Thomas" by M.R. James]; DOP: Renato Tafuri; SFX: Renato Agostini, A. & G. Corridori and Sergio Stivaletti; MUS: Simon Boswell, Keith Emerson, Philip Glass, Goblin and Fabio Pignatelli [Soundtrack from Cinevox Records]

STR: Tomas Arana, Asia Argento, Roberto Caruso, Feodor Chaliapin, Roberto Corbiletto, Barbara Cupisti, Olivia Cupisti, Gianfranco de Grassi, Alina de Simone, Claire Hardwick, Lars Jorgensen, John Karlsen, Katherine Bell Marjorie, Riccardo Minervini, Daria Nicolodi, Enrico Osterman, Micaela Pignatelli, Patrizia Punzo, Hugh Quarshie, Giovanni Lombardo Radice, John Richardson, Matteo Rocchietta, Michele Soavi and Antonella Vitale
Approximately 102m; Color
DVD: *The Church* [ABE; 102m; LBX];
VHS1: *The Church* [SGE; 110(102)m]
ADL: *In This Unholy Sanctuary You Haven't Got a Prayer...*

One of Europe's first cathedrals is placed on the site of a massacre perpetrated by a group of Teutonic Knights during the time of the crusades. Modern day, the seal placed on the grave that makes up the church's foundation is broken, and, well, all hell breaks loose, quite literally.

Originally proposed as an entry in Lamberto Bava's *Démoni* series, *La Chiesa* bears little resemblance to those films (although Soavi's picture is actually much more deserving of such a moniker). Although still early in the director's career, and riddled with its fair share of faults, *La Chiesa* is a stunning genre film that displays much of the selfsame verve that marks more successful Italian horror fare. Granted, much of this can be attributed to Argento's guiding hand—evident in much of the film—but Soavi has since proven that he is a capable artist independent of his mentor. The photography is lavish, the staging exhilarating, and the plot devices used to distance it from Bava's aforementioned films interesting enough on their own accord. A soundtrack by Argento cohorts Goblin and Keith Emerson doesn't hurt, either.

The film's biggest hindrance is the script's inability to keep any kind of a reign on the supernatural elements. When kept to a minimum here, they are effective and actually quite spooky, but when allowed free reign, the film degenerates into a string of spook show "boos" that detract from the oppressive atmosphere. (One of these sequences was "borrowed" almost directly from a well-known painting by fantasy artist Boris Vallejo.)

With the screen debut of Argento's daughter, Asia; an appearance from that director's ex-wife Daria Nicolodi (as a grade school teacher); Giovanni Lombardo Radice as a priest (a nice change of face for him, I'm sure); and director Soavi in an uncredited screen appearance as a policeman.

Oh, I almost forgot; you splatterpunks shouldn't be too disappointed either. It's almost worth a look for what has to be the nastiest "death by jackhammer" scene I've seen to date. (*And* it's a suicide, no less.)

Christmas Evil (1980)

Edward R. Pressman Productions [US]
DIR: Lewis Jackson; PRO: Pete Kameron and Burt Kleiner; SCR: Lewis Jackson; DOP: Ricardo Aronovich; EXP: Jerold Rubenstein; SFX: Tom Brumberger; MUS: Don Christensen, Joel Harris, and Julia Heyward
STR: Sheila Anderson, Robert Ari, Horace Bailey, Ray Barry, Arthur Bressler, John Brockman, Chris Browning, Philip Casnoff, Mark Chamberlin, Nancy Clark, Jeffrey de Munn, Jim Desmond, Francine Dumont, Pamela Enz, Danny Federid, Andy Fenwick, Peter Friedman, Sam Gray, Lance Halcomb, Brian Hartigan, Owen Hollander, Tyrone Holmes, Lloyd David Host, David Hughes, Dianne Hull, Joe Jamrog,

IST CAME "HALLOWEEN" ...
THEN "FRIDAY 13TH" ...
and NOW
THIS CHRISTMAS
YOU BETTER BELIEVE IN SANTA... OR HE'LL SLAY YOU.

Christmas Evil
...the night he dropped in.
Written and Directed By LEWIS JACKSON
IN COLOR

American one-sheet for *Christmas Evil* (1980), Edward R. Pressman Productions.

Joan Jonas, Burt Kleiner, Michael Klinger, Bobby Lesser, Brandon Maggart, Mark Margolis, Ellen McElduff, Scott McKay, Will McMillan, Peter Neuman, Brian Neville, Jennifer Novtney, Patricia Richardson, Elizabeth Ridge, William Robertson, Gus Salud, Lisa Sloan and Colleen Zenk
    AKA: *Terror in Toyland; You Better Watch Out*
    Approximately 92m; Color
    DVD1: *Christmas Evil* [TRO; 92m]; VHS1: *Christmas Evil* [PRE; 92m]; *Christmas Evil* [SPI; 92m]
    ADL: *You Better Believe in Santa ... or He'll Slay You.*

"As a boy, he saw Mommy making love to Santa Claus. As an adult, he is a crazed killer who has kept a list of all the girls who have been good, and all the girls who have been bad. It's Christmas time, and all the bad girls are in trouble. A man dressed as Santa Claus is stalking the streets, brutally murdering innocent girls. Who's to say if the kindly old gent, whose knee your daughter sits upon, is a maniacal murderer?"

No, he doesn't kill innocent girls as the video box insists, but instead vents his ire on fellow employees and the like who bully him and generally make his life miserable. (Not that this is a morally sound case for murder, but it does make our resident anti-hero more sympathetic.) As for the "I saw Mommy kissing Santa Claus" (or, in this case, "I saw Mommy kissing Santa Claus' you-know-what") reasoning behind our psychopath's impairment, it is far from credible, but with this film's tongue-in-cheek approach, I doubt any other explanation would seem as sound.

Technically, the film is adequate at worst, and boasts some effective editing. Throw in a *Frankenstein*-inspired scene of the "villagers" chasing our pathetic St. Nick through the streets with torches, and a finale that was copped by Spielberg for a Christmas episode of *Amazing Stories* some years later, and you have the strangest darn Yuletide slasher flick to probably ever see the light of day. (I'm thinking *this* should have spawned a franchise instead of the notorious 1984 film *Silent Night, Deadly Night*, don't you?)

C.H.U.D. (1984)

New World Pictures [US]
DIR: Douglas Cheek; PRO: Andrew Bonime; SCR: Parnell Hall; DOP: Peter Stein; EXP: Larry Abrams; MFX: John Caglione, Jr., and Edward French; MUS: David A. Hughes
STR: Frank Adu, Raymond Baker, Graham Beckel, John Bedford-Lloyd, Beverly Bentley, Ivar Brogger, Sandford Clark, Brenda Currin, Christopher Curry, James Dudley, Carey Eidel, Frankie R. Faison, Shana Lee Farrell, Hallie Foote, Peter Michael Goetz, John Goodman, Kim Guest, Justin Hall, Parnell Hall, Cordis Heard, John Heard, Eddie Jones, Lou Leccese, Ruth Maleczech, George Martin, Laurie Matios, Sam McMurray, Mark Mikulski, Kelly Nichols, Michael O'Hare, Gene O'Neill, Jon Polito, Vic Polizos, J.C. Quinn, John Ramsey, William Joseph Raymond, Patricia Richardson, Rocco Siclari, Daniel Stern, Jay Thomas and Robert Toupin
AKA: *Chud—Infierno Bajo la Ciudad* [Chud—Hell Under the City]
Approximately 88m; Color
DVD1: *C.H.U.D.* [ABE; 88m; LBX]; VHS1: *C.H.U.D.* [ABE; 88m]; *C.H.U.D.* [MHE; 88m]; *C.H.U.D.* [VTR; 87m]
ADL: *They're Not Staying Down There Any Longer.*

An epidemic of missing persons—including that of a police Captain's wife—is somehow linked to an EPA probe going on below the city streets. As it turns out, something—or a whole lot of somethings—with a hankering for human flesh are thriving in the sewers. (C.H.U.D., among other things, is an acronym for "Cannibalistic Humanoid Underground Dwellers," the term cannibalistic used

erroneously, since these creatures are, technically, no longer human, and they don't dine on one another.)

Although the portrayal of homeless people seems unconvincing, the characterization is above par. (Keep an eye out for John Goodman in an early role as a cop.) The monsters, though, fare even worse than the vagrants; besides the fact they look so damn rubbery, someone in production had the bright idea of making their eyes glow. (The monsters were designed by—irony noted—underground comic artist Tim Boxell, responsible for illustrating *Image of the Beast* and *Amputee Love*, as well as some twisted contributions to *Bizarre Sex*. Due to his contributions in the field, I hate to pin the blame on him for the glowing eyes.)

In the way of gore, there are a few excessive moments, but most of these are more effective in the stills I remember clipping out of *Fangoria* magazine in my high school years. (Hey, I couldn't just leave my peechees bare, now could I?)

More environmentally corrupt horrors from a genre that can never get enough of them. Evident, it seems, from this film's nearly worthless sequel.

C.H.U.D. II *see* **C.H.U.D. II—Bud the Chud**

C.H.U.D. II—Bud the Chud (1989)

Lightning Pictures [US]
DIR: David Irving; PRO: Jonathan D. Krane; SCR: Ed Naha; DOP: Arnie Sirlin; EXP: Lawrence Kasanoff and Richard Keatings; MFX: Make-Up & Effects Laboratories Inc.; MUS: Nicholas Pike
STR: Peter Beckman, Sarah Berry,

Gregg Binkley, Frank Birney, Eric Boles, Bill Calvert, Larry Cedar, James F. Dean, Jo Ann Dearing, Tony Edwards, Robert Englund, Jonathan Farwell, Norman Fell, Tricia Leigh Fisher, Geoffrey Forward, Winifred Freedman, Gerrit Graham, Jami Lynn Grenham, Rich Hall, Bianca Jagger, Sandra Kerns, Zachariah Sage Kerns, Mark S. Lane, Larry Linville, June Lockhart, Marvin J. McIntyre, Alissa Marie Mello, Richard Moore, Kelly O'Brien, Judd Omen, Mary Margaret Patts, Andy Pelish, Gregory Phelan, Priscilla Pointer, Jack Riley, Brian Robbins, Suzanne Schmitt, Warren Selko, Ritch Shyoner, Andy Steinlen, Robert Symonds and Robert Vaughn.

AKA: *C.H.U.D. II*
Approximately 84m; Color
DVD2: *C.H.U.D. II—Bud the Chud* [CTS; 84m]; VHS1: *C.H.U.D. II* [VES; 84m]; VHS2: *C.H.U.D. II—Bud the Chud* [CCL; 84m]

What was it that I said about nearly worthless sequels? This one's about a disease-ridden cannibal that likes to mug for the camera before taking a bite out of his unwary victims. Needless to say, those bitten end up sporting the same greasepaint and going after the same game.

Despite a few funny scenes (just don't ask me what they were), this condescending gore-omedy appears to be aimed at adolescent splatterpunks who buy *Fangoria* magazine only for the pictures and comical captions. To add insult to injury, *C.H.U.D. II*'s connection with its predecessor is *extremely* tenuous; apparently, someone sought to cash in on the success of *C.H.U.D.*, however one may define it.)

With scads of forgotten television actors and bit-players, including Robert (*The Man from U.N.C.L.E.*) Vaughn as a psychotic army general, and even an uncredited cameo by Robert "Freddy Krueger" Englund.

If you must chastise yourself, at least wait until this sucker shows up on cable.

Chud—Infierno Bajo la Ciudad *see* **C.H.U.D. II—Bud the Chud**

The Church *see* **La Chiesa**

La Cité de la Peur *see* **Icubo sulla Città Contaminata**

City of Blood (1987)

New World Pictures [SA]
DIR: Darrel Roodt; PRO: Anant Singh; SCR: Mary-Ann Lindenstadt and Darrel Roodt; DOP: Paul Witte; MUS: Lloyd Ross
STR: John Carson, Susan Coetzer, Charles Comyn, Norman Coombes, Gys de Villiers, Liz Dick, Ken Gampu, Morrison Gampu, Bentley Keomonde, Megan Kruskal, Abigail Kubeka, Greg Latter, Dudu Michize, Nicky Rebelo, Robin Singh, Muriel Smith, Sheena Stannard, Joe Stewardson, Sean Taylor, Lynne White, James Whyle and Ian Yule
Approximately 96m; Color
VHS1: *City of Blood* [MAG; 96m]
ADL: *Pray You Can Escape.*

Someone is dispatching prostitutes in an African city with a spiked club, in a manner that harkens back to primitive rituals and spirit warriors. A coroner tries to solve the case, knowing that the string of murders is apt to fuel already precarious racial relations.

City of Blood is a tense thriller that deals with—on the surface, anyway—a possibly supernatural serial killer; the guts of the film, though, focus on the racial tension prevalent in Africa in the mid–1980s. Although there is some gore to be had, splatterpunks looking solely for slasher-oriented fare are sure to be bored by the political trappings and social under-pinnings of the film. Those approaching *City of Blood* with an open mind shouldn't be disappointed, even pleasantly surprised by this intelligently made horror film.

Production values are pretty good, taking into consideration what the filmmakers did and didn't have at their disposal, and the conditions in which the film was probably made. *City of Blood*'s only real weakness is the sometimes inspired but more-often-than-not-confusing editing that proves distracting.

Exceptional for its approach and its ability to confront the viewer and their preconceived notions of third world racism, *City of Blood* is an excellent example of what can be done within the ill-defined limits of the genre. (Don't expect an enjoyable respite, though; the experience can be summed up by the downbeat ending that is pretty heavy even by *my* morbid standards.)

City of the Living Dead *see* **Paura nella Città dei Morti Viventi**

City of the Walking Dead *see* **Incubo sulla Città Contaminata**

Colegialas Violadas *see* **Die Säge des Todes**

La Colina del Terror—Encuentro con la Diablo *see* **The Hills Have Eyes Part II**

Combat Shock *see* **American Nightmare** (1984)

Contaminazione [Contamination] (1980)

Alex Cinematografica S.r.l. [It], Barthonia Film [WG], Lisa Film [WG]
DIR: Luigi Cozzi; PRO: Claudio Mancini; SCR: Luigi Cozzi and Erich Tomek; DOP: Giuseppe Pinori; SFX: Giovanni Corridori, Giorgio Ferrari and Claudio Mazzoli; MUS: Goblin
STR: Pier Luigi Conti, Carlo de Mejo, Gisela Hahn, Louise Marleau, Marino Masé, Ian McCulloch, Carlo Monni and Siegfried Rauch
AKA: *Alien II*; *Alien Contamination*; *Astaron—Brut des Schreckens* [Astaron—Brood of Terror]; *Toxic Spawn*; *Het Zaad van Mars* [The Seed from Mars]
Approximately 88m; Color
VHS1: *Alien Contamination* [PAR; 90(84)m]; *Toxic Spawn* [LET; 90(88)m]; VHS2: *Contamination* [ECF; 88m]
ADL: *You Can Feel Them in Your Blood...*

A boat full of alien eggs is discovered in a New York harbor; since these eggs carry spores that infect humans and cause them to explode, authorities are a little concerned. The cargo is traced back to South America, and it is discovered that the eggs are being dispersed by one of two astronauts who survived a mission to Mars ("the Cyclops Star," everyone is eager to point out, despite the fact that Mars is a *planet* and doesn't even boast *one* eye). Unfortunately for the rotten apple, the other survivor is Fulci splatfest veteran Ian McCulloch (*Zombi 2, Paura nella Città dei Morti Viventi*, etc.), who is determined *not* to let his ex-partner give the entire human race a rather nasty case of heartburn.

Alien Contamination immediately kicks into high gear with some particularly meaty gore scenes, but sputters out shortly thereafter, unable to regain any real momentum. The filmmakers were smart enough *not* to show the boss monster until the very end of the movie, as most viewers will be sawing some ZZZs before reaching the finale. (Far from the biomechanical bug that dominates the film that inspired this low-rent knock-off, the creature herein resembles one of Corman's *papier-mâché* beasties from the 1950s more than it does H.R. Giger's unparalleled nightmare.)

Production values are typical of Italo-horror at the time, and the soundtrack is an uneventful affair by trend-setting prog-rock band Goblin, with the better parts of the score sounding like outtakes from their work on Romero's *Dawn of the Dead*. (Furthermore, the soundtrack for

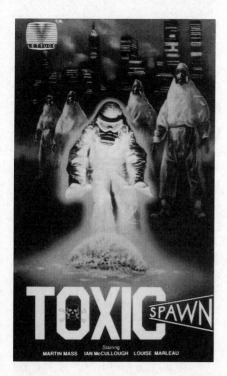

Video box art for *Contaminazione* (1980), Lettuce Entertain You Inc.

Alien Contamination is pockmarked by some particularly obnoxious sound effects, one of the culprits being what is most likely a barking seal looped ad infinitum.)

If all you care about are slo-mo chest-bursting scenes, then look no further, as it doesn't get any splashier than this. If, however, you want suspense, or an intelligent script, or a top-notch cast and crew, or ... well, you get my drift. (This film ended up on Elvira's TV show quite a few years back now, minus the gore, of course; having seen this truncated version, I realized early on what the film's *only* redeeming features were.) If you like this, check out the similarly slipshod *Alien 2 sulla Terra*, perpetrated the same year.

Cosmos Mortale *see* **Alien Predator**

The Craving *see* **El Retorno del Hombre Lobo**

Crawlspace (1986)

Empire Pictures [It/US]
DIR: David Schmoeller; PRO: Roberto Bessi; SCR: David Schmoeller; DOP: Sergio Salvati; EXP: Charles Band; MFX: John Carl Buechler and Mechanical & Make-Up Imageries Inc.; MUS: Pino Donaggio
STR: David Abbott, Talia Balsam, Sally Brown, Carol Ann Francis, Jack Hiller, Klaus Kinski, Take McClure, Kenneth Robert Shippy and Barbara Whinnery
AKA: *Fou à Tuer* [Killing Mad]
Approximately 80m; Color
VHS1: *Crawlspace* [LIG; 80m]

Klaus Kinski plays the owner of an apartment building who was once a doctor in Buenos Aires. It seems he learned his specialized skills from his father, a high-ranking Nazi medical officer in World War II. Now Kinski,

Video box art for *Crawlspace* (1986), Lightning Video.

all grown up, spends his days peeping on women from an elaborate ventilation duct, and building insidious devices to use on those who get a little too close to learning his many well-guarded secrets.

Despite the many slasher film contrivances, *Crawlspace* actually manages to evoke some chills, in part due to Kinski's performance, and in part to some well-staged tension. (A reoccurring scene of Kinski playing Russian roulette is, surprisingly, quite intense, even if it was done better in *The Deer Hunter*.) Had the film avoided many of the pitfalls common to exploitation films, it may have achieved something akin to Agustin Villaronga's *Tras el Cristal* (In a Glass Cage, 1986); instead, it settles for being a predictable but fairly effective thriller graced with a handful of disturbing images.

Production values are about on par with Charles Band's later Full Moon productions, (although the outstanding score by Pino Donaggio outshines anything Charles' brother Richard ever conceived). It's a shame that Band now spends all of his time and energies with his various franchises of pint-sized horrors (*Puppet Master, Demonic Toys, Dollman*, etc.), especially since he once saw fit to produce above-average contributions to the genre such as this.

Crazy Fat Ethel II *see* **Criminally Insane 2**

Creature *see* **Titan Find**

Créature *see* **Titan Find**

Creepers *see* **Phenomena**

Creepozoids (1987)

Titan Productions Inc. [US]
DIR: David de Coteau; PRO: David de Coteau and John Schouweiler; SCR: David de Coteau and Burford Hauser; DOP: Thomas L. Callaway; EXP: Charles Band and Linnea Quigley; MFX: Peter Carsillo and Thomas Floutz; SFX: Thomas L. Callaway; MUS: Guy Moon

STR: Ken Abraham, Michael Aranda, Richard Hawkins, Kim McKamy, Linnea Quigley and Joi Wilson

Approximately 72m; Color
VHS1: *Creepozoids* [CLV; 72m]; *Creepozoids* [UCV; 72m]; VHS2: *Creepozoids* [MET; 69m]

ADL: *Your Flesh Will Creep Right Off Your Bones.*

"1998—Six years after the super-powers have engaged in a devastating nuclear exchange. Earth is now a blackened husk of a planet. Tiny clusters of survivors eke out a miserable existence in the ruins of the cities, and bands of deserters roam the barren wastelands ... hiding from mutant nomads and seeking shelter from the deadly acid rains."

Anywho, one such band discovers an "abandoned" bunker, and a convenient place for Ms. Quigley to jump into a shower. Of course, they're not alone, and the already small group is pared down to the bare minimum by genetically engineered boogers.

Despite the fact that this is probably the best de Coteau flick I've seen to date, recommending it would be like suggesting one contract gonorrhea instead of congenital herpes. The monsters are about all you can expect from a no-budget *Alien* rip-off. (The infamous dinner sequence from said film is "borrowed" almost verbatim, except that the infectee gets ugly and dies after taking a bite of food. Amino acid overload, of course. Another suffers a similar fate, oozing Quaker State Pennzoil from every orifice.) As bad as the title critters are, though, they have nothing on the giant rat and baby monster that also plague the dimwitted heroes. (The cast tries *really* hard to convince us that they're scared by the aforementioned rodent, but even *real* actors would have difficulty pulling that off.)

Linnea Quigley fans should be warned that if they do decide to sit through it for her obligatory nude scenes, they should at least have the decency to turn the sound off. (Did someone say "stilted dialogue"?) The gore is poorly executed, so the rest of us have little or no reason to check it out.

If you want more rubber for your buck, then you've come to the right place.

Creeps *see* **Night of the Creeps**

Creepshow (1981)

Laurel Group [US]
DIR: George A. Romero; PRO: Richard P. Rubenstein; SCR: Stephen King; DOP: Michael Gornick; EXP: Salah M. Hassanein; MFX: Tom Savini; SFX: Cletus Anderson; VFX: David Stipes; MUS: John Harrison

STR: Chuck Aber, John Amplas, Cletus Anderson, Tom Atkins, Adrienne Barbeau, Ted Danson, David Early, Darryl Ferrucci, Christine Forrest, Robert Harper, Ed Harris, Hal Holbrook, Kate Karlowitz, Don Keefer, Joe King, Stephen King, Viveca Lindfors, Jon Lormer, E.G. Marshall, Pater Messer, Nann Mogg, Leslie Nielsen, Carrie Nye, Bingo O'Malley, Elizabeth Regan, Gaylen Ross, Iva Jean Saraceni, Tom Savini, Martin Schiff, Warner Shook, Charles van Eman and Fritz Weaver

Approximately 120m; Color
VHS1: *Creepshow* [WAR; 120m]; VHS2: *Creepshow* [ALP; 120m]
ADL: *The Most Fun You'll Ever Have Being Scared!*

This anthology is a loving tribute to the EC comics of the '50s, in particular their horror titles which quite often pushed the envelope of good taste. Unfortunately, Romero decided to go a little overboard on the gimmicky comic-style matte work and word balloons (courtesy of Jack Kamen); although innovative, it is ultimately distracting and depreciates any chills the film may have achieved. (At times, the film seems to be aimed primarily at young teens, both in its approach and its "gore-lite" status.

Had producers made a couple of trims to avoid the R rating, *Creepshow* may have proven to be more successful.) The first segment, "Father's Day," is the type of supernatural revenge fare with which EC has become synonymous. The second, "The Lonely Death of Jordy Verrill," has screenwriter King hamming it up as in inbred farmer who, apparently, has never seen *The Blob* (1958). (After seeing this, it's no wonder he's usually consigned to cameos in films and not given the lead.) "Something to Tide You Over," the third segment, has Gaylen (*Dawn of the Dead*) Ross and Ted (*Cheers*) Danson as an adulterous couple, and Leslie (*The Naked Gun*) Nielsen as her possessive husband. Although another stab at the "vengeance beyond the grave" formula, this one proves to pack a little more punch, thanks to some fairly disturbing ideas. The fourth, "The Crate," deals with an English professor (Hal Holbrook) who—after a series of "accidents"—concocts a plan to conveniently dispose of obnoxious wife Barbeau. This segment does boast some suspense, as well as the bulk of the gore *Creepshow* manages to scrape up. The last segment, "They're Creeping Up on You," is a lame killer cockroach story that should have been stuffed somewhere in the middle of the selections, if not discarded altogether. There is also a cute little wraparound sequence starring King's son as a boy not altogether happy about Dad tossing his cherished horror comics in the trash (playing to our sympathies, I see).

Fun, but extremely disappointing considering some of the people involved.

Creepshow 2 (1987)

Laurel Group [US]
DIR: Michael Gornick; PRO: David Ball; SCR: George A. Romero; DOP: Richard Hart and Tom Hurwitz; EXP: Richard P. Rubenstein; MFX: Howard Berger and Edward French; MUS: John Harrison, Les Reed and Rick Wakeman
STR: David Beecroft, Daniel Beer, Cheré Bryson, Lois Chiles, Phillip Dore, Jeremy Green, Page Hannah, Don Harvey, David Holbrook, Domenick John, Daniel Tucker Kamin, George Kennedy, Stephen King, Dorothy Lamour, Holt McCallany, Kaltey Napoleon, Maltby Napoleon, Richard Parks, Frank S. Salsedo, Paul Satterfield, Tom Savini, Joe Silver, Dean Smith, Shirley Sonderegger, Tyrone Tonto and Tom Wright
AKA: *Macabras Historias de Horror* [Macabre Stories of Horror]
Approximately 96m; Color
DVD1: *Creepshow 2* [ABE; 96m; LBX]; DVD2: *Creepshow 2* [CCL; 85m]; VHS1: *Creepshow 2* [ABE; 96m]; *Creepshow 2* [SHV; 89m]; VHS2: *Creepshow 2* [CCL; 85m]

Yes, it's yet another anthology of grisly EC-inspired horror stories, but this offering doesn't have as much charm as its predecessor. Although the stories here are more in tune with the type once offered by EC comics (which folded under censorial pressure in 1955), the problem lies therein. Where *Creepshow* came across as an homage to titles like *Tales from the Crypt* (which obviously influenced both Romero and King as children), the scripts in *Creepshow 2* are even more derivative, thus little more than carbon copies of their inspiration. Even worse, the direction by cinematographer Michael Gornick seems flat, making one doubt his sincerity towards the material.

The first segment, "Ole' Chief Woodinhead," is a predictable revenge piece involving a dimestore Indian. The second, "The Raft," is an aquatic variation of *The Blob*; despite its derivative nature, it manages to create some mild tension. And, last but not least, "The Hitchhiker" does an admirable job of delivering the goods, piling shocks atop the grue. It's fairly predictable as well, but comes closest to capturing the spirit of EC.

Includes an animated wraparound sequence, and effects artist Tom Savini as *Creepshow 2*'s host, "The Creep."

Criminally Insane 2 (1987)

Irmi Films [US]
DIR: Steve Millard; PRO: Frances Millard; SCR: Steve Millard; DOP: Karil Ostman
STR: Priscilla Alden, Robert Copple, Charles Egan, Lisa Farros, Michael Flood, Jane Lambert, Sonny Larocca, C.L. Lefleur, Gina Martine, Cliff McDonald and Sandra Shotwell
AKA: *Crazy Fat Ethel II*
Approximately 59m; Color [Shot on video]
VHS1: *Crazy Fat Ethel II* [VTR; 60(59)m]
ADL: *Never Come Between Ethel and a Well-Stocked Refrigerator!!*

"Thirteen years ago, Ethel was judged 'criminally insane.' Now the mental ward is overcrowded, and the budget has been cut, so Ethel is back on the street!!"

Well, kinda sorta. Everyone's favorite overweight cannibalistic-prone psychopath is back, and she still has an appetite for destruction. Sent to live in a halfway house, she's back to her old tricks again ... mostly eating, of course. Still, Ethel manages to knock off a few of the other patients in between bites. (One of them thinks he's a spider. Yes, a spider.)

It's doubtful that *Crazy Fat Ethel*

II would have captured some of *Criminally Insane*'s whacko charm had it been committed to celluloid instead of videotape. (Even grainy Super 8 stock wouldn't have saved this sucker, believe you me.) And after seeing the new footage, I'm not at all surprised they recycled about half of the first film, working it into *Crazy Fat Ethel II* as flashbacks. Yes, half. There's no way in hell there's more than thirty minutes of new footage here ... but you're not going to hear me raising a stink. What isn't flashback material is unbearably tedious and droll; the lack of a soundtrack to cover up the static hiss of the cheap videocam makes it even more belaboring to sit through. (Not that Millard was a great filmmaker to begin with, but it's amazing how much he forgot about the rudimentary aspects of filmmaking in the interim.)

Crazy Fat Ethel II is an inept patchwork creation unworthy of any association with its predecessor.

Crocodile (1981)

Cobra Media [Th]
DIR: Sompote Sands; PRO: Robert Chan and Dick Randall; SFX: Stephane Goulet
STR: Nat Puvanai, Tany Tim, Kirk Warren and Angela Wells
Approximately 95m; Color 🐊🐊🐊
VHS1: *Crocodile* [EMI; 95m]
ADL: *From the Slimy Depths of the Ocean ... Nature Explodes with Savage Fury!*

It's *Jaws* meets *Godzilla* in this Asian chomp-a-thon that purports to make an environmental statement, but shows its true colors with the type of geek-oriented exploitation which—although fairly common in most Asian films—is usually taken to such extreme degrees in the Italian canni-

Curse 84

bal epics of the 1970s. Watching a real crocodile ravage a toy boat is pretty fun, to be sure, but witnessing one of its kin being eviscerated while still alive certainly isn't my idea of entertainment.

Aside from its questionable ethics, *Crocodile* is a slow moving and poorly made production that has little to offer to anyone except the desperate trash fiend, and even they will have to wonder, "Was it all worth it?"

Regardless of your tastes, *Crocodile* does not come recommended.

Curse (1987) *see* **The Devil in Snake**

The Curse (1987)
TransWorld Entertainment [It/US]
DIR: David Keith; PRO: Ovidio Gabriele Assonitis; SCR: David Chaskin [Based on the short story "The Colour Out of Space" by Howard Phillips Lovecraft]; DOP: Robert D. Forges; EXP: Moshe Diamant; SFX: Ron Petruccione; VFX: Kevin Erham; MUS: Franco Micalizzi
STR: Claude Akins, Steve Carlisle, David Chaskin, Malcolm Danare, Steve Davis, Kathleen Jordon Gregory, Cooper Huckabee, David Keith, Hope North, John Schneider, Amy Wheaton and Wil Wheaton
AKA: *The Farm; La Maldición* [The Curse]
Approximately 92m; Color
VHS1: *The Curse* [ABE; 92m]; *The Curse* [MHE; 92(87)m]; *The Curse* [VTR; 92(87)m]
ADL: *It Takes Your Body. And Your Mind. Then It Takes You Straight to Hell...*

What a waste òf celluloid this turned out to be. I'm surprised producer Assonitis, who is responsible for his own fair share of dreck (*Chi Sei?* [1974], aka *Beyond the Door*, coming readily to mind), didn't use his "Oliver Hellman" pseudonym on this turkey. The few nice touches introduced to

this updating of a popular H.P. Lovecraft piece are completely wasted; *The Curse* is not only predictable and derivative of other popular horror films, it is so poorly made that it begs the question of why it wasn't shelved following the first screening. (The lack of an ending and an unexplained prelude would lead one to believe that the producers ran out of money before filming was completed anyway; the finances definitely weren't squandered on special effects, that's for certain.)

Italian gore-meister Lucio Fulci functioned on *The Curse* as associate producer and optical effects coordinator (under the oh-so-inconspicuous pseudonym of "Louis Fulci").

If you're dead set on seeing a film adaptation of the piece, go back and watch Daniel Haller's *Die, Monster, Die!* (1965) instead; it may not be as faithful, but I'll take an aging Karloff over a dimwitted eighties production any day of the week.

Curse II—The Bite *see* **The Bite**

Curse IV—The Ultimate Sacrifice *see* **Catacombs**

Curse of the Blue Lights (1988)
Tamarack Corp. [US]
DIR: John Henry Johnson; PRO: John Henry Johnson; SCR: John Henry Johnson; DOP: John Henry Johnson; EXP: William A. Johnson; MFX: Wizard Effects Group; MUS: Randall Crissman
STR: James Asbury, Marty Bechina, Chuck de Broder, Deborah Devencenty, Kent E. Fritzell, Becky Golladay, Willard Hall, Bettina Julias, Patrick Keller, Clayton A. McCaw, Brent Ritter, George Schanze, Mark Thalhamer, Tom Villagrama and Don Warren
Approximately 96m; Color

VHS1: *Curse of the Blue Lights* [MAG; 96m]

ADL: *...and the Dead Shall Inherit the Earth.*

I'm not even going to bother to give you the run-down. This puppy's so bad you'd swear it was nothing more than a kid's film with some obligatory gore thrown in for good measure. The highlights (as they are) include really shoddy make-up effects (someone should notify the authorities about the flagrant waste of latex), actors who have difficulty reciting even the simplest of lines (and those that do manage to accomplish this little feat take the opportunity to ham it up), and one of the most uneventful sword fights that has ever graced the silver screen (even watching it on fast forward, the viewer may be inspired to curl up for a nap).

I'm not finished yet. *Curse of the Blue Lights* is not only one of the worst zombies films I've ever seen (suddenly, *Redneck Zombies* doesn't seem so bad), it is without a doubt one of the most painful experiences I've ever had short of having my wisdom teeth removed without anesthesia. (Where's the Novocain when you *really* need it?) And, no, it does *not* qualify as "so bad it's good." The dividing line between watchable and unwatchable garbage may be thin and ill-defined (as well as completely subjective), but even the more desperate trash fiends like myself won't find anything redeemable about this sad production. ("...and the dead shall inherit the video market" *should* have been the tagline.)

C'mon ... you *know* the movie's bad when I'm forced to rely so heavily on parenthetical expressions.

Cut and Run *see* **Inferno in Diretta**

La Dagyde les Sexandroïdes (1987)

Les Productions Vidéo Self [Fr]
DIR: Michel Ricaud; PRO: Alain Braud and Marina Weingarten; SCR: Michel Ricaud; DOP: Philippe Polliopoulos; SFX: Daniel Dubois
Approximately 57m; Color [Shot on video]

Okay, this pointless anthology is an inexcusable load of horse pucky, plain and simple, but it deserves some mention if only because it's so gosh darn weird.

The first segment—the only one that actually works as a narrative—has a prostitute being brutalized by a man with a voodoo doll fashioned from a Barbie. While in the bathroom of a bar, she has her clothes ripped off (by someone off screen who isn't supposed to be there), then bleeds from every orifice as the man sticks pins in the doll's eyes and crotch. Reasonably unpleasant.

The second has a woman shoot a "monster" in a dungeon. After he walks off wounded, she does a striptease and plays with fire. The dolt in bad make-up comes back and kisses her, whereupon she coughs up a rubber spider. He then tortures her, piercing her nipples (for real), piercing her tongue (faked), and piercing her breasts (again, for real). She then cuts herself with a straight razor. (Real? Faked? You be the judge.) He responds to this act of self-mutilation by cutting out her eye and eating it. (This is obviously faked, but it's still pretty gosh darn gross.) After ripping out her innards, the two all but walk off into the sunset. No ... I'm not making any of this up.

The third has a widow visiting her husband's funeral. He comes to as a vampire (the cheesy plastic teeth are a sure giveaway), foams at the mouth, tears her clothes off, bites her, then climbs back in the coffin for a snooze. Having collapsed, she leaps up, wearing white greasepaint and sporting her own pair of Halloween fangs, and starts dancing to Tina Turner music. Fifteen minutes and half an album later, she climbs into the coffin with her undead hubby and places a "Do Not Disturb" sign on their makeshift love nest. Again, I'm not making any of this up.

Unfortunately, I probably make this film sound much better than it actually is, so if you are compelled to scout this sucker out, don't come crying to me when you find yourself wasting twenty bucks on a lousy bootleg you'll end up dubbing over.

Dark Eyes of the Zombie *see* **Uccelli Assassini**

Dawn of the Mummy (1981)

Harmony Gold Ltd. [Eg/It/US]

DIR: Franco Agrama; PRO: Franco Agrama; SCR: Franco Agrama, Ronald Dobrin and Daria Price; DOP: Sergio Rubini; EXP: Lewis Horwitz; MFX: Luigi Batistelli, Tony di Dio, Jr., and Farid Abdoul; MUS: Shuki Y. Levy [Soundtrack from Saban Records]

STR: Ali Azab, Diane Beatty, Ellene Faison, Ali Gohar, Ibrahim Khan, Brenda King, Ahmed Laban, Joan Levy, Laila Nasr, George Peck, Ahmed Ratib, Baher Saied, John Salvo and Barry Sattels

AKA: *El Despertar de la Momia* [The Awakening of the Mummy]; *Die Rache der Mumie* [The Revenge of the Mummy]

Approximately 92m; Color

VHS1: *Dawn of the Mummy* [EMI; 93(92)m]

A cruel pharaoh is laid to rest, and—as law dictates—all of his servants are buried alive in his final resting place. The tomb is discovered three thousand years later; while an "entrepreneur" is looking for the pharaoh's fabled treasure, a camera crew from a ritzy New York magazine uses the crypt for a photo shoot. Making King Tut's

Video box art for *Dawn of the Mummy* (1981), Thorn EMI Video.

curse look like an idle threat, the dead pharaoh Saphirama exacts his vengeance in person, with a little help from his servants. Not content with simply ripping the faces off of those who desecrated their tomb, the bloodthirsty mummies make their way to the nearest city, eviscerating anyone who happens to cross their dusty path. (I know being out of circulation for three thousand years would make one hungry, but these guys' appetites just won't quit.)

Despite the titular similarity to Romero's *Dawn of the Dead*, *Dawn of the Mummy* actual owes everything to Amando de Ossorio's *El Ataque de los Muerte Sin Ojos* (1973) and Lucio Fulci's *Zombi 2* (1980). Gore is plentiful (with a preference for pig offal over latex viscera), but the make-up is kind of shabby, the mummies looking no better than most Italian ghouls. (The lead mummy, though, does pass muster; obviously, more time was spent on him than his less than convincing minions.) Oddly enough, the sexploitation value is virtually nonexistent, with nary a nipple in sight. (No sex? In an Italian film? What were they thinking?) The production values, though, are fairly typical of Italian fare, marred only by some overzealous actors and numerous continuity problems. (How in the hell did the pharaoh's servants end up buried in the sand dunes when they were entombed with him? Screenwriters—especially in exploitation films—are prone to making some boneheaded mistakes, but oversights like this are unforgivable.)

A fun little zombie stomper with all of the gory fixings.

Day of the Dead (1985)

Laurel Group [US]
DIR: George A. Romero; PRO: Richard P. Rubenstein; SCR: George A. Romero; DOP: Michael Gornick; EXP: Salah M. Hassanein; MFX: Tom Savini; SFX: Steve Kirshoff and Mark Mann; VFX: Jim Danforth; MUS: John Harrison
STR: Terry Alexander, John Amplas, Lori Cardille, Jarlath Conroy, Antonie di Leo, Phillip G. Kelliams, G. Howard Klar, Richard Liberty, Ralph Marrero, Gregory Nicotera, Joe Pilato, Howard Sherman, Taso N. Stavrakis and others.
AKA: *El Dia de los Muertos* [The Day of the Dead]
Approximately 102m; Color
DVD0: *Day of the Dead* [ABE; 102m; LBX]; DVD2: *Day of the Dead* [AFD; 101m]; VHS1: *Day of the Dead* [ABE; 102m]; *Day of the Dead* [MHE; 100m]; VHS2: *Day of the Dead* [FFV; 101m]
ADL: *The Darkest Day of Horror the World Has Ever Known!*

A paramilitary group consisting of soldiers and scientists have, under orders, holed themselves up in an abandoned missile silo in an effort to find a cure for the zombie infestation that has wiped out much of the population. With cabin fever taking its toll, the two halves find themselves constantly at odds. The soldiers want nothing more than to destroy their stock of "experimental subjects," zombies captured above and penned nearby for their convenience. The scientists resist pressure from their adversaries, even though there is no cure in sight. All the while, the undead they seek to dispose of are taking their first baby steps towards acquiring knowledge.

Despite having his proposed budget cut back just prior to shooting, Romero went ahead and salvaged his script, still managing to come up with a brilliant film that more than does justice to its predecessors (*Night of the Living Dead* and *Dawn of the Dead*, 1968 and 1978, respectively). The characters are all too human, their desperation all too real. Much bleaker than the previous film, *Day of the Dead* uses humor sparingly; although a few moments are intended to tickle the viewer's funny bone, most are used to add extra depth to the characters and make them that much more sympathetic. To compliment the tense proceedings are effects that mark this as the pinnacle of Tom Savini's career as a make-up artist. The gore-strewn finale even eclipses *Dawn of the Dead*'s infamous bloodbath, and is far more convincing than that film's groundbreaking effects work. (Few films have succeeded in offering both quantity and quality, as one is usually sacrificed for the other.)

By far, one of the top ten splatter films ever made, and not a bad little movie altogether.

With director George Romero and *Splatter Times* publisher Donald Farmer making cameos as zombies.

La Dèa Cannibale *see* **Mondo Cannibale** (1980)

Dead Heat (1987)

New World Entertainment Ltd. [US]
DIR: Mark Goldblatt; PRO: David Helpern and Michael Meltzer; SCR: Terry Black; DOP: Robert D. Yeoman; MFX: Steve Johnson; SFX: Patrick Read Johnson; VFX: Ernest D. Farino; MUS: Ernest Troost
STR: Monty Ash, Steven R. Bannister, Shane Black, Clarence Brown, Cate Caplin, Monty Cox, Lindsay Frost, Chip Heller, Lew Hopson, H. Ray Huff, Steve Itkin, Stephen Jacques, Peter Kent, Claire Kirkconnell, Monica Lewis, Keye Luke, Pons Maar, Darren McGavin, Dick Miller, Ben Mittleman, Tom Nolan, Peggy O'Brien, Yvonne Peattie, Robert Picardo, Joe Piscopo, Vincent Price, Martha Quinn, Ivan E. Roth, Mike Saad, Dawan Scott, Mel Stewart, Toru Tanaka, Ron Taylor, Beth Toussaint, Pamela Vansant and Treat Williams
Approximately 86m; Color
VHS1: *Dead Heat* [NWV; 86m]
ADL: *You Can't Keep a Good Cop Dead.*

Dead Heat is a cop-buddy film with a twist: One of them dies and spends the rest of the film helping his partner track down the man responsible for creating an army of zombies … himself included. Unfortunately, they have a bit of a time limit; he has less than ten hours before he "dissolves into an organic stew."

Although the movie sacrifices coherency for laughs, this is one of the better "gore-omedies" to have been released, thanks to the cast and better-than-usual backing from New World Pictures. Joe Piscopo is quick with the one-liners, and there are a few scenes that—God forbid!—are actually funny. One of the better moments has our motley duo attacked by a revived side of beef in a butcher shop. Of course, everything therein gets the *Re-Animator* treatment, sparking the comment, "Zombie duck heads. What a concept." With that said, not everything is as witty as the screenwriters probably thought it was. (Detective "Roger Mortis?" It is puns such as this that make me wince more than any "violence to the eye" scene from a Lucio Fulci film.)

Outside of the gaping plot holes and glaring continuity problems, *Dead Heat* also suffers from some bad CGI, then in its infancy. But with Vincent Price and Darren (*Kolchak— The Night Stalker*) McGavin on hand for the fun, the film is far from being a complete waste.

The Dead Next Door (1988)

Amsco Studios [US]
DIR: J.R. Bookwalter; PRO: J.R. Bookwalter and Jolie Jackunas; SCR: J.R. Bookwalter; DOP: Michael Tolochko, Jr.; EXP: Samuel M. Raimi; MFX: J.R. Bookwalter, Ron Contenza, Mike Davy, Bill Morrison, Sean Rodgers and Michael Todd; MUS: J.R. Bookwalter and Various Artists
STR: J.R. Bookwalter, Bruce Campbell, Lester Clark, Emilio Cornachione, Floyd Ewing, Jr., Peter Ferry, Barbara Gay, Roger Graham, Michael Grossi, Kelly Helmick, Jolie Jackunas, Jon Killough, Robert Kokai, Maria Markovic, Bill Morrison, Jennifer Mullen, Matt Patrick, Bogdan Pecic, Jerry Porter, Jeffrey Scaduto, Scott Spiegel, Michael Todd, Michael Tolochko, Jr., Joe Wedlake, Jeff Welch and others.
AKA: *Mondo Zombie* [Zombie World]
Approximately 82m; Color
VHS1: *The Dead Next Door* [TAP; 85(82)m]; *The Dead Next Door* [TEM; 84(82)m]
ADL: *The Neighborhood's Gone to Hell.*

Akron, Ohio, is suddenly overrun by the living dead. Five years later in Virginia, "Zombie Squads" are on patrol searching for human survivors. With the help of a scientist, one group discovers the source of the virus, but they find themselves at odds with a "Reverend Jones" and his fanatical cultists who have found convenient ways to exploit their dead-but-not-down-for-the-count brethren.

The Dead Next Door is a mindless zombie gutmuncher that tries to pick up where *Dawn of the Dead* (1978) and *Day of the Dead* (1985) left off. Although there's nary an original bone in its desiccated body, this film stands as an almost endearing homage to Romero's aforementioned classics.

The fact that the filmmakers are horror fans is self-evident; damn near every character is named after luminary genre figures: Savini, Romero, King, Raimi, Carpenter, et al.

Unlike most knock-offs, *The Dead Next Door* actually succeeds with some of its humor; a scene with zombie rights activists carrying protest signs that read "Let the dead walk" actually shows some wit, something rare in such films. Samuel (*The Evil Dead*) Raimi (who functioned on *The Dead Next Door* as an uncredited executive producer) makes a cameo, and the voice of his leading man Bruce Campbell makes a guest appearance as well. Fans of homegrown horror might also recognize a few of the other names, people who went on to be "successful" shot-on-video filmmakers. (I guess success is defined by having sold more than a dozen copies of one's film on video.)

Despite all of its inherent limitations, J.R. Bookwalter's directorial debut is actually somewhat enjoyable, and an ambitious effort considering the budget (or lack thereof). Now if only the rest of his films showed half the verve that this sucker does.

Dead Pit (1989)

Cornerstone Productions Company [US]
DIR: Brett Leonard; PRO: Gimel Everett; SCR: Gimel Everett and Brett Leonard; DOP: Marty Collins; EXP: Jack A. Sunseri; SFX: Ed Martinez; MUS: Dan Wyman
STR: Michael Alu, Joan Bechtel, Lizzie Byrd, Tim Craighead, Sheila dé Maris, Skyy Diaz, Frederick Dodge, Rorey Edelman, Mara Everett, Randy Fontana, Damon Foster, Randy Foster, Steffen Gregory Foster, Stephen Fritch, Geha Getz, Danny Gochnauer, Marcia Gray, Jeff Gru-

bic, Nettie Heffner, Stanford Isaac, Michael Jacobs, Kaldonia, Bill Kemper, Robert Kvenild, Cheryl Lawson, Heather Lloyd, Scott Malpass, Brett Murmann, Dale Pearson, Lynette Rogers, Gary Ruble, Jason Slate, Jeremy Slate, Luana Speelman, Willy Strasser, Steve Strom, Jack A. Sunseri, Irwin Swan, Irene Teagardin and Jay Wikner
AKA: *La Fossa del Terror* [The Pit of Terror]
Approximately 95m; Color
DVD2: *Dead Pit* [MNM; 97(95)m]; VHS1: *Dead Pit* [IMP; 95m]

With a strong pre-credits sequence setting the stage, *Dead Pit* repeatedly catches the viewer off guard by offering a non-formulaic approach, and throws in some lavish photography for good measure. The script offers the viewer a few other nice surprises along the way (although one of the "shocking" revelations is a blatant gimmee that demands a response of "no shit.") Everything seems to be moving along nicely, at least—that is—for the initial two-thirds of the film. At this point, the *please* turns out to be all *tease* when it deteriorates into yet another unnecessary zombie flick.

Granted, our antagonist (the resurrected doctor) looks pretty stupid with his painted eyebrows and glowing eyes, but he does manage to deliver a few good Freddy-style one-liners. When told early on, "you're a doctor ... you're supposed to be *saving* lives!" he calmly responds, "I've done life ... now I'm doing death." (Unfortunately, some of these quips were copped from classier, or more innovative, genre outings; *Hellraiser* and *The Howling* come immediately to mind.)

The gore is abundant, with quality ranging from good to disturbingly effective (save for the climactic melt-

down, fairly crude when compared to the preceding bloodshed).

Dead Pit is worth a look-see, even though it is ultimately disappointing.

Deadbeat at Dawn (1988)

Asmodeus Productions Inc. [US]
DIR: Jim van Bebber; PRO: Michael King; SCR: Jim van Bebber; DOP: Michael King; MFX: Jim van Bebber; MUS: Ned Folkerth and Mike Pierry
STR: Steve Bognar, John Bradley, Steve Brown, Tom Burns, Dave Calabro, Michael T. Capone, Andy Carrol, Rob Craeger, Sue Ann Crule, Calisto Cruz, Mary Jo Dawes, Ned Folkerth, Marcelo Games, Maureen Gentner, Mark Gillespie, John Gnann, Sid Gnann, Charlie Goetz, Stu Grasberg, Paul Harper, Tom Harris, Lill Hendler, Debbie Hichadel, Mike Hile, Phil Hile, Pal Hughes, Barbara Kerr, Michael King, Steve King, Barry Landy, Loretta Landy, Carol Lee, Rich Leiser, James McCullars, Joe Monahan, Mark Monell, Chris Moore, Megan Murphy, Leslie Orr, Jeff Osbourne, Dave Parker, Andrew Pearson, Nate Pennington, Marc Pitman, Joel Pohlman, Pete Puchin, Bob Radford, Julia Reichert, Rick Saintnov, Jim Sayer, Doug Sharp, Anita Stenger, Bill Stover, Dan Trihschuh, Randy Valentine, Jim van Bebber, Ric Walker, Dave White and Rob Zinser
Approximately 85m; Color
DVD1: *Deadbeat at Dawn* [IMG; 85m]; VHS1: *Deadbeat at Dawn* [KET; 80m]
ADL: *He Quit the Gangs. They Killed His Girl. He Became ... Deadbeat at Dawn!*

Goose (van Bebber) is a gang member who is pressured by his occult-dabbling girlfriend to go straight. While he makes a half-assed attempt to do so, she is brutally murdered by members of a rival gang. This precipitates the expected vendetta, although our antihero is so coked up and drunk that he can barely stand. (Had this not been made years before, I would say this was a half-baked take on *The Crow* [1994], minus the supernatural overtones.)

Deadbeat at Dawn finds itself mostly unhindered by the restraints of an almost nonexistent budget. With some inspired editing and photography, this film surpasses its peers by the sheer power of innovation and dedication. The lack of professional actors also does little to deter it, and in some cases actually adds to the gritty realism. Surprisingly, there's a fair amount of martial arts on display; none of it's great—hell, some of it may not even be that good—but at least it's handled realistically and in a down-to-earth fashion. Last but not least is the gore, typically brutal and equally realistic, as per usual for no-budget *wunderkind* van Bebber.

I may be making this film out to be more than it actually is, but van Bebber never ceases to amaze me with what he can create from virtually nothing. (Aspiring filmmakers should take some cues from this guy; don't wait around for something to happen, make it happen, and do the best with what you have at your disposal.)

Deadly Eyes (1982)

J.G. Arnold and Associates Ltd. [US], Northshore Investments Ltd. [US]
DIR: Robert Clouse; PRO: Paul Kahnert and Jeffrey Schechtman; SCR: Charles Eglee [Based on the novel *The Rats* by James Herbert]; DOP: René Verzier; EXP: J. Gordon Arnold; MFX: Makeup Effects Labs; SFX: Malivoire Productions Inc.; MUS: Anthony Guefen
STR: Sara Botsford, Wendy Bushell, David Cardoza, Scatman Crothers, Dora Dainton, Lesleh Donaldson, James B. Douglas, Roger Dunn, Michael Fawkes, Steven Fearnley, Kevin Foxx, Sam Gordon, Sandy Grant, Sam Groom, Til Hanson, John Stephen Hill, Michael Hogan, Lorraine Housego, Suzanne Housego, David Hughes, Jaime Hyland, Charles Jolliffe, Joseph Kelly, Lisa Langlois, Cec Linder, Bruce O.R. Marshall, Paul McCallum, Mike McManus, George Merner, Brian Morrison, Bridget O'Sullivan, Guy Sanvido, Kevin Sheard, Jack van Evera, Jacquie van Wart, Lee-Max Walton, Bunty Webb, Jon Wise, Tod Woodcroft and Mary Anne Ziewkiewicz
AKA: *Night Eyes*; *Las Ratas Asesinas* [The Killer Rats]
Approximately 87m; Color
VHS1: *Deadly Eyes* [WAR; 87]

C'mon, guys … rats went out in the '70s. How can anybody even think of topping Andy Milligan's patchwork opus *The Rats Are Coming! The Werewolves Are Here!* (1972)?

Seriously, though, *Deadly Eyes* is an adequately made horror flick that will appeal to fans of the socially conscious monsteramas that were proliferate during the previous decade. Sure, the script is riddled with enough conveniences to obliterate any suspense. And sure there's a surprising amount of sloppy hand-held camerawork for a film of this caliber. But, hey, the first person to be gobbled up by the big-boned vermin is a baby, so *Deadly Eyes* automatically gets four stars in my book.

There are buckets of gore to be had, to be sure, but the highlights of the film are the rats themselves (or yet another spur in the film's side, depending on how serious you take your critter flicks). Taking its cue from *The Killer Shrews* (1959), the oversized rodents are no more than small dogs in drag. Of course, this really *special* effect gives the film that edge, that touch of realism so desperately lacking in modern horror fare. (Okay, let's see now … dachshunds, or 20 lb. latex-covered animatronics. It *is* more cost efficient just to clean up after the dolled up pooches, so dogs it is! Yes, I'm being facetious.) The group shots of the "rats" aren't bad considering, but the close-ups leave much to be desired. (For the scenes where you actually see them taking bites out of their victims, the puppies are replaced by what looks like toothy hand puppets; suffice it to say, these are slightly less than convincing.)

Well, anyway, there's lots of fun to be had for everyone. (Except maybe actor Scatman Crothers, who doesn't seem to fare well in horror films. I guess monsters just take a shine to him.)

Deadly Manor (1989)

Castor Films S.A. [Sp/UK]
DIR: José Ramón Larraz; PRO: Brian Smedley-Aston and Angel Somolinos; SCR: José Ramón Larraz; DOP: Tote Trenas; EXP: Enrique Bellot, Alexander W. Kogan, Jr., and Barry Tucker; MFX: Boaz Stein; SFX: George Giordano and Peter Kunz; MUS: Cengiz Yaltkaya
STR: Jennifer Delora, Claudia Franjul, Liz Hitchler, Mark Irish, Jerry Kernion, Kathleen Patane, Greg Rhodes, William Russell, Greg Scott and Clark Tufts
AKA: *Savage Lust*
Approximately 86m; Color
VHS1: *Savage Lust* [AIP; 90(86)m]
ADL: *She Has a Lust for Life—Pray It's Not Yours!*

A group of vacationers pick up a mighty suspicious hitchhiker and wind up staying the night in a seemingly abandoned house. Nearby on the front yard, a wrecked car serves as a shrine for a car crash victim, and the house is wallpapered with the self-same dead girl's photo. They find a closet full of human scalps while checking out the joint, but are still reluctant to leave, leaving a good hour

for them to be knocked off by the killer lurking nearby.

Sadly, Larraz' films have gotten progressively worse over the years, although even the worst of them have *something* to offer the desperate horror fan. There are some inspired touches (an ominous cracked wall, a scrapbook of unorthodox crime scene photos, etc.), but these are easily overlooked amidst the conventional horror film trappings. There are a few surprises (the hero doesn't fare as well as one would think) and the gore is passable, but the characters are shallow and the make-up effects are bad, so one can't win for losing.

Deadly Spawn *see* **Return of the Aliens—The Deadly Spawn**

Deadtime Stories (1987)

Scary Stuff Productions Inc. [US]
DIR: Jeffrey S. Delman; PRO: William Paul; SCR: Jeffrey S. Delman, Edward Kiernan and Charles F. Shelton; DOP: Daniel B. Canton; EXP: William J. Links; MFX: Edward French; SFX: Bryant Tauser; MUS: Taj
STR: John Bachelder, Heather L. Baley, Michael Berlinger, Ron Bush, Lisa Cain, Oded Carmi, Careline Carrigan, Phyllis Craig, Brian de Persia, Catheryn de Prume, Ivan de Prume, Jeffrey S. Delman, Beth Felty, Kathy Fleg, Kevin Hannon, Leigh Kilton, Melissa Leo, Fran lo Pate, Michael Mars, Pat McCord, Michael Mesmer, Matt Mitler, Jim Nocell, Nicole Picard, Harvey Pierce, Anne Redfern, Casper Roos, Timothy Rule, Lesley Sank, Robert Seldon, Rondell Sheridan, Bryant Tauser, Thea, Robert Trimboli, Scott Valentine, Suzanna Vaucher and Leif Wennerstrom
AKA: *Freaky Fairy Tales*
Approximately 83m; Color
VHS1: *Deadtime Stories* [CGV; 83m]
ADL: *Nobody Lives Happily Ever After.*

This anthology—a splatterpunk take on children's fairy tales—is, well, pretty forgettable, despite it being a commendable attempt to "update" said stories.

The first segment, borrowing liberally from several different sources, stars Scott (*Family Ties*) Valentine and boasts little more than passable effects and a cute ending. The second is a predictable pastiche of "Little Red Riding Hood," with some gratuitous sex and a werewolf; it fares a little better than the first segment, but is still far from noteworthy. The third (and best) is a contrived updating of "Goldilocks and the Three Bears," engaging if *only* because of its outlandishness. The jokes are rather insipid, and it would have been in the screenwriters' best interests to drop the telekinesis angle altogether, but it is somehow charming nonetheless. Gore is sprinkled liberally throughout the production, but I dare say none of it is worth writing home about.

Wait to catch it on late-night cable.

Death Dorm (1981)

Jeff Obrow Productions [US]
DIR: Stephen Carpenter and Jeffrey Obrow; PRO: Jeffrey Obrow; SCR: Stephen Carpenter, Stacey Gaichino, and Jeffrey Obrow; DOP: Stephen Carpenter; MFX: Matthew Mungle; MUS: Chris Young
STR: Kay Beth, Jimmy Betz, Chandre, Thomas Christian, Richard Cowgill, Bill Criswell, Dennis Ely, Pamela Holland, Jake Jones, Laurie Lapinski, Chris Morrill, Robert Richardson, Woody Roll, Stephen Sachs, Chris Schroeder, David Snow and Daphne Zuniga
AKA: *The Dorm That Dripped Blood*; *Pranks*
Approximately 84m; Color
VHS1: *The Dorm That Dripped Blood* [MHE; 84m]
ADL: *When the Party Was Over ... the Killing Began!*

As can be ascertained from the various titles, another gaggle of expendable teenagers get themselves butchered for no other reason than to placate really bored splatterpunks. (Is it asking too much to expect *some* kind of story to accompany the grue?) As slasher creed insists, a different weapon is employed for each and every killing: knife, drill, baseball bat with ten-penny nails hammered through it—whatever's handy, I guess. Still, the killings are rote, lifeless; the special effects are as much to blame as the direction. (Most of the other production values are similarly lackluster as well.) And don't expect any suspense or tension; this is as predictable as it gets.

Unlike some of its peers—*Hell Night* (1981), *Sleepaway Camp* (1983), etc.—this one has not aged well.

Death Row Diner (1988)

Camp Motion Pictures [US]
DIR: B. Dennis Wood; PRO: Salvatore Richichi; SCR: James Golff, Salvatore Richichi and Dennis Wood; SFX: Greg Blocker; MUS: Brad Allen and Peter Prince
STR: Michael Antin, Michelle Bauer, Jodi Berkoff, Jon Blatt, Richard Bloom, John Content, Donna Dandini, David James Golff, James Grizzle, Papa Raphael Gueavaba, Brooke Healey, Alex K., Lob Keem, Dana Lis Mason, Mark Mayers, Dennis Mooney, Rick Preston, Jay Richardson, Salvatore Richichi, Frank Sarcinello, Sr., Frank Sarcinello, Jr., Tom Schell, Chuck Trutnik, Howard Ward, Jr., and Dennis Wood
Approximately 90m; Color [Shot on video]
VHS1: *Death Row Diner* [CAM; 90m]

The Big House, 1948. Otis Wilcox is a man sent to the chair for a crime he didn't commit, and—even worse—he's sent to his death without a last meal. As he's pumped full of volts, he screams, "I'm hungry," just before issuing his last gasp. Forty years later, the prison—now deserted—becomes the setting for a low-budget monster flick. Right on cue, the ghost of the aforementioned prisoner returns (with the help of cheap digital videocam effects) to exact revenge while filling his empty gut.

Oh ... did I mention this is also a comedy? (At least I *think* that was the filmmakers' intentions.)

To be blunt, films this bad should be illegal. (About midway through this dreck I decided to let the tape run its course while I worked on three days worth of dirty dishes. The only thing I regretted was not letting them pile up a few more days so as to eat up the rest of the ninety minutes.) The humor—or what passes as such—relies on mock pulp-style narration, sophomoric TV spoofs, an obnoxious *Crocodile Dundee* stand-in who says "mate" far too often and sports a swastika tattoo, and the worst Elvis impersonator this side of the King of Rock himself (credited only as a "soundalike," which is *still* pushing things a wee bit). The gore effects are not only bad, but unnecessarily gratuitous, even as far as "gore-omedies" are concerned. (I'm sorry, but even *I* feel it's not in a filmmaker's best interest to waste a few gallons of blood on a simple strangulation.)

Thankfully, the director gave up any aspirations of being a filmmaker and became an editor for sexploitation films soon after this movie saw the light of day.

And by the way, it only got *worse* after I returned from doing the dishes. (Hmmm ... I think the grout in my bathroom is calling me.)

Death Screams (1981)

A&A Productions Inc. [US]
DIR: David Nelson; PRO: Ernest Bouskos and Charles Ison; SCR: Paul C. Elliott; DOP: Darrell Cathcart; EXP: Ernest Bouskos and Charles Ison; SFX: Barbara Galloway and Worth Keeter; MUS: Dee Barton
STR: Sharon Alley, Monica Boston, Jimmy Bouskas, Mike Brown, Jennifer Chase, Josh Gamble, William T. Hicks, Bill Ison, Debbie Ison, Jody Kay, Susan Kiger, John Kohler, David Lenthall, Mary Fran Lyman, Hans Manship, Barbara McClarty, Bob Melton, Penny Miller, Gail Minton, R.C. Nanney, Gene Pool, Kurt Rector, Andrea Savio, Larry Sprinkle, Helene Tryon and Martin Tucker
AKA: *House of Death; Night Screams*
Approximately 89m; Color
VHS1: *House of Death* [VGM; 90(89)m]; *House of Death* [VIR; 89m]
ADL: *He Wants Their Bodies ... in Pieces.*

A couple making out on their motorbike near an old railroad are strangled, their bodies dumped into the river. (The corpses spend the entirety of the film thereafter floating downstream—improbable, but amusing nonetheless.) The killer is just warming up, although he takes his sweet time in picking up where he left off. (The second murder is almost an hour into the film; I guess he just lost track of the running time.) Eventually, a handful of twenty-something high schoolers make the mistake of partying in the woods, having stumbled into a graveyard before they realize something is terribly amiss. By then, our machete-wielding psycho is scrambling to make short work of the lot of them before the end credits roll.

Despite the generic synopsis, *House of Death* is redeemable in that it offers more in the way of character development than most slasher flicks,

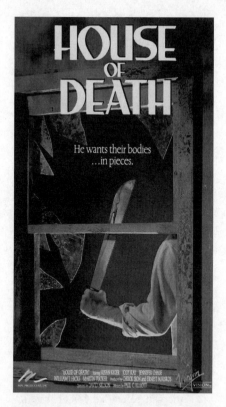

Video box art for *Death Screams* **(1981), VirginVision.**

with some convincing performers and believable small-town blather to back it up. There is also some intentional humor that—God rest our souls—works! (Although some may find it more disturbing than amusing, the best scene involves the aforementioned floaters, nude and bloody, still caught on some rocks in the riverbed as the end credits role over the top of them. Now *that's* funny.)

Unfortunately, shortcomings are also many. First is the lack of blood in the first hour; once it does kick in, though, the heads start piling up like cordwood. Second is the overabundance of carnival stock footage. (Rid-

dle me this: How come whenever a carny comes to town, someone *has* to make a horror film around it?) Others are minor points, like seeing a train sneak up on a woman. Or the fact that, despite the video release title, none of the killings are committed in a house until the last ten-or-so minutes.

Directed by the real life son of Ozzie and Harriet, and brother of singer Ricky Nelson. (And they thought he wouldn't amount to much. He showed *them*.)

Death Train *see* **Beyond the Door III**

Death Warmed Up (1984)

The Tucker Production Company Ltd. [NZ]

DIR: David Blyth; PRO: Murray Newey; SCR: David Blyth and Michael Heath; DOP: Jame Bartle; MFX: Bryony Hurden and Rosalind McCorquodale; SFX: Kevin Chisnall; MUS: Mark Nicholas

STR: Gary Day, Norman Fairley, Tina Grenville, Jonathan Hardy, Ken Harris, Karam Hau, Michael Hurst, Bruno Lawrence, Nat Lees, David Letch, Judy McIntosh, Eva Radich, Norelle Scott, Geoff Snell, Margaret Umbers, William Upjohn, Ian Watkin and David Weatherly

AKA: *La Maldición de los Zombies* [The Curse of the Zombies]

Approximately 83m; Color

DVD2: *Death Warmed Up* [AFD; 78m]; VHS1: *Death Warmed Up* [VES; 83m]

A prominent neurosurgeon has left a prestigious position in order to work on his own, somewhat unethical experiments in private. Seven years later, he is the head of Trans Cranial Applications, a "psychiatric hospital" that specializes in creating zombies. One of his original patients has since been rehabilitated and wants revenge, so it's off to the island institute with three of his closest friends, most of whom think they are simply on vacation.

This zombie flick from somewhere down under is one of those rare attempts where the filmmakers make a serious effort to break the mold established with *Night of the Living Dead*, yet retain the elements that make such films so popular. *Death Warmed Up* is an engaging, off-kilter horror film that bears more than a few similarities to Peter Jackson's early efforts. (Although extreme at times, the gore is nowhere near as copious as it is in Jackson's priceless splatterfests. Splatterpunks might get a little antsy, as it does take a while for the bodies to start stacking up like cordwood, but there are some grueling scenes of brain surgery to help tide one over until then.) Although humor is prevalent, it's much darker than that found in such films as *Bad Taste*, but with all of the oddball characters and headbursting, you can't help but make comparisons.

Director Blyth went on to make another paranoid medical thriller, the anemic *Red-Blooded American Girl* (1990); he probably would have been better off just making a sequel to *Death Warmed Up*, as it looks like that was his intention with this film's ironic, albeit lame, ending.

Mike Boom makes a cameo.

La Déese Blonde *see* **Mondo Cannibale** (1980)

La Déese Cannibale *see* **Mondo Cannibale** (1980)

Deliria *[Delirium] (1987)*

Filmirage [It]
DIR: Michele Soavi; PRO: Aristide Massaccesi and Donatella Donati; SCR: Luigi Montefiorel; DOP: Renato Tafuri; SFX: Robert Gould, Dan Maklansky, Roland Park, and Alan Sloane; MUS: Guido Anelli, Simon Boswell and Stefano Mainetti

STR: Richard Berkeley, David Cain Haughton, Barbara Cupisti, Domenico Fiore, Robert Gligorov, Sheila Goldberg, Dan Gordon, Claude Jurman, Mickey Knox, Clain Parker, Mark Parkinson, Loredana Parrella, Martin Philips, Helen Porter, Dominique Portier, Giovanni Lombardo Radice, Rackel Roskoff, James E.R. Sampson, Simone Sardon, Albert Schultz, Sandy Schultz, Ulrike Schwerk, Mary Sellers, Frank Seneca, Jo Anne Smith, Michele Soavi and Piero Vida

AKA: *Aquarius*; *Aquarius—Theater des Todes* [Aquarius—Theater of Death]; *Bloody Bird*; *Delirio* [Delirium]; *Sound Stage Massacre*; *Stage Fright*

Approximately 92m; Color
DVD1: *Stage Fright* [ABE; 92m; LBX]; VHS1: *Stage Fright* [IMP; 95(90)m]; VHS2: *Stage Fright* [RED; 87m]

A crash rehearsal for an *avant-garde* musical, "The Night Owl," is plagued by a psychopathic killer who has escaped from a nearby sanitarium. The director aims to capitalize on the wardrobe mistress getting axed, and forges on, unaware that the murderer isn't going to settle for a body count of one.

Whereas the first half of *Deliria* is fairly typical, lacking anything even remotely resembling innovation, Argento protégé Michele Soavi manages to save the remainder of the film with his flair for style and pacing (much like his patriarch). Other similarities—a pounding rock score, unrelenting brutality, and a theater production as a backdrop for the killings—also beg comparison. Unfortunately, when *Deliria* does work, it comes across as

Video box art for *Deliria* (1987), Imperial Entertainment.

little more than a mimeograph of Argento's influential films. (Soavi fared much better in his later works; although they still bear Argento's influence, they are more representative of Soavi's own vision.)

Much like Argento's work, it also seems that inspiration is in short supply until the carnage begins. Although not nearly as "balletic" as his mentor's, the violence here is equally brutal. For splatterpunks, here's the score: A knifing, a pickaxe to the mouth, another gored by a very long drill, a chainsaw, an axe decap, and a particularly gruesome scene of a woman being torn in two. Suffice it to say, the proceedings were only about a bucket of pig gut short of it qualifying for the Fulci stamp of approval.

On hand are such luminary Italian screen stars as John Morghen (né Giovanni Lombardo Radice) as a flaming homosexual, and the director himself as a cop who thinks he looks like James Dean.

Consider it a worthwhile update of Peter Walker's *Asylum of the Insane* (1973).

Delirio *see* **Deliria**

Delirio di Sangue [Delirium of Blood] (1988)

Cine Decima [It]
DIR: Sergio Bergonzelli; SCR: Sergio Bergonzelli; DOP: Raffaele Mertes; SFX: Delio Catini, Corridori and Raffaele Mertes; MUS: Nello Ciangherotti
STR: Brigitte Christensen, John Phillip Law, Olivia Link and Gordon Mitchell
AKA: *Blood Delirium*
Approximately 87m; Color
VHS2: *Blood Delirium* [TEL; 89(87)m; Greek subtitles]

A woman who likes to set the table in the nude is accosted by a rather obnoxious poltergeist that claims to be her twin spirit. We then see this "twin" in her deathbed, ranting about two candles becoming one. Upon her demise, her husband, Vincent van Gogh (yes … van Gogh) creates a kinky reconstruction of his wife, it's failure somehow inspiring him to make a wise career move and destroy all of his paintings. He eventually hooks up with the aforementioned woman who—of course—is the spitting image of his dead lover. Suddenly, he thinks he's that painter from H.G. Lewis' *Color Me Blood Red* (1965), and all hell breaks loose, although it's not nearly as exciting as one would imagine Hell being.

Alas, this contrived, convoluted,

and rather silly horror film can't even afford to cash in on its own geek value. The film's only real highlight is a rather amusing scene where the artist's manservant confesses his love to his mistress' corpse, then proceeds to feel her up and mount her ... while the bereaved husband is playing the organ not twenty feet away. And you thought love triangles were passé. There is no gore until the film reaches the halfway mark, whereupon *Delirio di Sangue* tries to liven up the meandering proceedings with some brutal dismemberments. It doesn't help much, of course, but for those having already sat through half the film, it's something of a respite from the tedium.

The book *Spaghetti Nightmares* refers to *Delirio di Sangre* as "an abortive piece of cinema," and I am inclined to agree.

Un Delitto Poco Comune [A Common Little Crime] (1987)

Globe Films [It], Tandem Cinematografica [It], Reteitalia [It]

DIR: Ruggero Deodato; PRO: Pietro Innocenzi; SCR: Gigliola Battaglini, Gianfranco Clerici and Vincenzo Mannino; DOP: Giorgio di Battista; SFX: Fabrizio Sforza; MUS: Pino Donaggio

STR: Caterina Boratto, Daniele Brado, Lewis E. Ciannelli, Renato Cortesi, Ruggero Deodato, Edwige Fenech, Mapi Galán, Daniela Merlo, Donald Pleasence, Antonella Ponziani, Giovanni Lombardo Radice, Fabio Sartor, Carola Stagnaro, Benito Stefanelli, Al Yamanouchi and Michael York

AKA: *Off-Balance*; *Phantom of Death*; *Squilibrio* [Imbalance]; *La Tueur de la Pleine Lune* [The Terror of the Full Moon]

Approximately 95m; Color

VHS1: *Phantom of Death* [VID; 95(91)m]

ADL: *How Do You Catch the Uncatchable?*

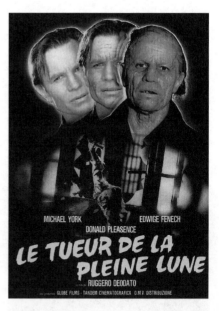

Alternate ad mat for *Un Delitto Poco Comune* (1987).

A pianist with ninja flashbacks (*Logan's Run*'s Michael York) is stricken with a disease similar to Progeria (premature aging) and goes on a killing spree. (Although it is kept a secret early on in the film, they quickly disclose the killer's identity, probably aware that the ad campaign would give it away anyway. Which it did.) First it's his unfaithful wife, then it's on to the bearer of bad news concerning his failing health, and so on; never at a shortage for "deserving" victims, he even offs a man who comments on his thinning hair. Being a bit defensive is understandable, but—needless to say—this guy is a little too gosh darn touchy about his condition.

Un Delitto Poco Comune isn't nearly as silly as it sounds, but it is still a far cry from the films that garnered Deodato acclaim (or notoriety, depending on your point of view). Although adeptly made, sadly unaccounted for is the disturbing intensity that punctuated such infamous genre films as *Cannibal Holocaust* (1979) and *La Casa Sperduta nel Parco* (1980). Premise aside, this effort is little more than a plodding suspense film, despite the participation of an excellent cast. The gore is relegated, it seems, to necks spurting copious amounts of blood, so splatterpunks won't find a whole lot of variety herein.

Although Deodato has yet to recapture the charm of his earlier films, he has made such admirable attempts as *The Washing Machine* (1992). (Still, I don't think he'll ever be able to make amends for such mid–'80s actioners as *I Barbari* [1987]; I don't know about you, but it'll take another *Cannibal Holocaust* if I'm ever to forgive him *that* trespass.)

Delizie Erotiche [Erotic Delights] (1980)

Kristal Film [It]
DIR: Aristide Massaccesi and Bruno Mattei; SCR: Luigi Montefiori; DOP: Aristide Massaccesi; MUS: Nico Fidenco
STR: Manlio Certosino, Dirce Funari, Annj Goren, Luigi Montefiori and Lucia Ramirez
AKA: *Porno Holocaust*
Approximately 97m; Color XXX

There's not much of a story here, folks, except for the fact that a group of people show up at an island, only to be accosted by a "monster" (a well-endowed black guy in a Robinson Crusoe get-up sporting awful make-up prosthetics). When the tourists aren't doing the nasty amongst themselves, the women are being raped by the brute and his gargantuan member. That is, save for one girl whom he abducts, but for whom he picks flowers instead. (She doesn't seem too terribly upset over her predicament, despite the bodies piling up around her.)

Most of the film follows the conventions of low-rent pornography; everything is cued so as to allow one sex scene to be followed by another, with the only breaks being when the participants decide to change positions. Once the monster shows up mid-way through, the sex scenes are interspersed with no-budget gore, if only to make sure the viewer hasn't fallen asleep to the rather uneventful screwing, I would assume. One man has his head crushed in with a large rock (ground hamburger is promptly affixed to his face and drenched in fake blood), a friend suffers a similar fate after kissing a log, and another has his chest torn open since there's nothing else lying around with which to brain him.

If you can stomach this dreck, check out Massaccesi's similarly inclined *Le Notti Erotiche de Morti Viventi* (1979).

Demented (1980)

Four Features Partner Ltd. [US], I.W.D.C. [US]
DIR: Arthur Jeffreys; PRO: Arthur Jeffreys and Michael Smith; SCR: Alex Rebar; DOP: Jim Tynes; EXP: Alex Rebar and Rick Whitfield; MFX: Dale Brady and Robert Burman; MUS: Richard Tufo [Soundtrack from MSP Records]
STR: Deborah Alter, Jay Belinkoff, Stephen Blood, Bryan Charles, Kathryn Clayton, Mark del Castille, Sallee Elyse, John Green, Mark Justin, J. Kelly, Bill Martin, Edward Talbot Matthews, Robert Mendel, Bosco Palazzolo, Douglas Price and Herbert Stretcher

Video box art for *Demented* (1980), Media Home Entertainment.

Approximately 88m; Color
VHS1: *Demented* [MHE; 92(88)m]
ADL: *Revenge is Sweet ... and Deadly*

A woman is gang raped by four men on her ranch, their identities concealed beneath stockings. Traumatized, she ends up staying at a sanitarium for a short jaunt, and is released probably too soon for her own good. Before long, hallucinations become commonplace; to make things worse, some local kids decide to torment her while her hubby's away porking some money-hungry floozy. (At least these new predators decided to spring for Halloween masks instead of pantyhose.) No one believes her, of course, chalking her claims up to the aforementioned hallucinations. So—as the back of the video box promises—she "castrates and murders her intruders by shotgun and meat cleavers, ignoring their pleas for mercy."

No, there's no subtlety here, folks. *Demented* is exactly what it sounds like: A seedy exploitation flick cashing in on the popularity of *Day of the Woman* (1977), aka *I Spit on Your Grave*. The only reason I included this rape/revenge flick was because it actually has some nasty gore, and what are some of the best meat cleaver killings I've seen in quite some time. Of course, you have to wade through over an hour's worth of grimy melodrama and very unpleasant sexploitation, but I guess that's the price for those who are running out of '70s genre films in which to wallow.

One of the actors, going by the name of "Bruce Gilchrist," is famed porn actor Harry Reems (*né* Herbert Stretcher). In fact, *Demented* has the look and feel of some of the better late '70s porn, so I wouldn't be surprised to find out that the filmmakers actually got their start in the skin trade. And to think that some people might actually look at this as a step *up*.

Screenwriter Alex Rebar starred in *The Incredible Melting Man* (1977) and has been involved with numerous other exploitation flicks as well.

Demon Queen (1986)

Camera 1 Productions [US]
DIR: Donald Farmer; PRO: Donald Farmer and David Reed; SCR: Donald Farmer; DOP: David Reed; MFX: Rick Gonzales; SFX: Carole Reed; MUS: Jan Haflin
STR: David Blood, Cliff Dance, Mary

Fanaro, Ric Foster, Mark Holman, Debbie Leigh, Michele Poncier, Lauren St. Michael, Dennis Stewart, Robert Tidwell, Patti Valliere and Annett van Grinsveu
Approximately 54m; Color [Shot on video]
VHS1: *Demon Queen* [MOG; 54m]

A man picks up a girl for a one-nighter; apparently, she's not impressed by his sexual performance, as she promptly plucks out his heart with her bare hands. Something of a story begins to unfold, but—being particularly unimpressed by the performances of everyone involved—I promptly fast-forwarded to the gore, as this is the *only* reason this film was made. (In retrospect, I should've kept my scan button engaged; the effects aren't nearly as impressive as the pics on the back of the video box made them out to be.) Somewhere along the line, a zombie epidemic ensues. Oh, boy.

Demon Queen is mostly on a par with 1980s shot-on-video porn, complete with a cheesy synth score and an abundance of T & A that borders on the tedious. (The only part of the film worth pausing at involved the interior of a video store and their shelves stocked with display box horror films.) Even at the conservative running time—at least six minutes of which were credits—this was a hard one to sit through. Good thing it wasn't any longer, if only because I might've had to replace the batteries in my remote before the film ran its course.

Following this debut, director Farmer went on to do a slew of other no-budget features, but—from what I've seen insofar—he should have stuck with publishing instead. (His

sadly short-lived *The Splatter Times* was an inspiration to many a young splatterpunk, myself included.) His heart is in the right place, and he obviously loves what he's doing, but I just damn well hope he got a knack for this filmmaking thing after these early efforts. (Maybe if someone gave him a 16mm camera and some film stock...)

Démoni [Demons] (1985)

DAC Film [It]
DIR: Lamberto Bava; PRO: Dario Argento; SCR: Dario Argento, Lamberto Bava, Franco Ferrini and Dardano Sacchetti; DOP: Gianlorenzo Battaglia; MFX: Rosario Prestopino and Sergio Stivaletti; SFX: Corridori & Company; MUS: Claudio Simonetti and Various Artists
STR: Fiore Argento, Guido Baldi, Urbano Barberini, Lamberto Bava, Stelio Candelli, Bettina Ciampolini, Paola Cozzo, Giuseppe Mauro Cruciano, Sally Day, Nicoletta Elmi, Geretta Giancarlo, Natasha Hovey, Jasmine Maimone, Eliana Miglio, Marcello Modugno, Peter Pitsch, Bobby Rhodes, Lino Salemme, Enrica Maria Scrivano, Alex Serra, Michele Soavi, Claudio Spadaro, Nicole Tessier, Fabiola Toledo and Karl Zinny
AKA: *Demonios* [Demons]
Approximately 88m; Color
DVD0: *Demons* [ABE; 88m; LBX]; DVD2: *Demons* [PMD; 88m; LBX]; VHS1: *Demons* [ABE; 88m; LBX]; *Demons* [NWV; 89(88)m]; *Demons* [RSG; 89(88)m]
ADL: *They Will Make Cemeteries Their Cathedrals and the Cities Will Be Your Tombs.*

A man in a mask (Soavi) hands out free tickets to the premiere showing of a cheesy horror film about bored teens discovering the tomb of Nostradamus. In the theater, a prostitute cuts herself on a prop demon mask and—while everyone is distracted by the low-rent horror flick—turns into a rat-toothed glowing-eyed monster with a voracious appetite.

Despite the supernatural impetus, the proceedings adhere to precedents set by zombie films in the last thirty years as the desperate theatergoers try to find a way out of the theater without being bitten and/or clawed by "infected" individuals.

This nonsensical shocker has gained something of a following from splatterpunks who were bored with American fare in the mid–'80s. It does offer some mindless fun, to be sure, but there are too many continuity problems, tacky monster effects, and bad dialogue for it to be taken seriously or to be enjoyed unconditionally. Obviously intended for a mass market, *Démoni* is far too patronizing, even packing the soundtrack full of obnoxious pop and glam metal tunes that would only appeal to indiscriminate high schoolers of the time. (Even ex–Goblin member Simonetti's theme song is enough to make one want to take advantage of the mute button on one's remote.) As a fan of spaghetti cinema, the only real appreciation I have for this film is that it helped a generation of *Fangoria* readers to search out other Italian genre efforts, thus potentially exposing them to the many exceptional films and filmmakers that the Big Boot had and has to offer (including the likes of Michele Soavi, who functioned here as an assistant director).

Although it's Lamberto Bava's most famous film, *Démoni* is far from his best. (After this, one almost forgets he showed promise early on with *Macabro* and *La Casa con la Scala nel Buio*, 1980 and 1983 respectively.)

Démoni 2—L'Incubo Ritorna [Demons 2—The Nightmare Returns] (1987)

DAC Film [It]
DIR: Lamberto Bava; PRO: Dario Argento; SCR: Dario Argento, Lamberto Bava, Franco Ferrini and Dardano Sacchetti; DOP: Gianlorenzo Battaglia; EXP: Ferdinando Caputo; MFX: Rosario Prestopino; SFX: Corridori & Company; MUS: Simon Boswell and Various Artists

STR: Asia Argento, Anita Bartolucci, Bruno Bilotta, Furio Bilotta, Nancy Brilli, Virginia Bryant, Antonio Cantafora, Dario Casalini, Robert Chilcott, Luca de Nardo, Lorenzo Flaherty, Yvonne Fraschetti, Angela Frondaroli, Andrea Garinei, Karen Gennaro, Lorenzo Gioielli, Annalie Harrison, Eliana Miglio, David Knight, Marina Loi, Caroline Christina Lund, Davide Marotta, Michele Mirabella, Stefano Molinari, Luisa Passega, Pascal Persiano, Giovanna Pini, Fabio Poggiali, Bobby Rhodes, Kim Rhone, Silvia Rosa, Lino Salemme, Maria Chiara Sasso, Andrea Spera, Coralina Cataldi Tassoni, Monica Umena, Pasquale Valente and Marco Vivio

AKA: *Demons 2*; *Demons 2—The Nightmare Continues*; *La Profecia Satanica* [The Satanic Prophecy]
Approximately 91m; Color
DVD0: *Demons 2* [ABE; 91m; LBX]; DVD2: *Demons 2* [PMD; 95(91)m; LBX]; VHS1: *Demons 2* [IMP; 88m]

A group of teens sneak into what's left of Italy (the Big Boot, Spaghetti Central, pick yer euphemism) after it has been overrun by the rat-fanged pissers from *Démoni*. Jumping a barbed-wire barricade, they find a claw in the muck, unaware of the problems that may result. Of course, even if the viewer is privy to the fact that this scenario is only a movie within a movie doesn't make an iota of difference, as, being a sequel to *Démoni*, these toothy muckabouts are able to—Boo!—cross the threshold from film to "make-believe," here leaping out of a TV screen and generally making nuisances of themselves in an apartment complex.

The son of illustrious filmmaker Mario Bava, Lamberto was just making a name for himself as a capable filmmaker when he started churning out the entries in his popular, but rather tactless, *Démoni* series. (Since Argento had a hand in these, you almost wonder if he were somehow threatened by Bava's burgeoning film career, thus taking it upon himself to make sure his protégé would never rise above the level of a hack filmmaker. Food for thought.) Even if one doesn't get their hopes up—and why would they?—this sequel is still a disappointing mess. Although it seems to owe something to Cronenberg's *The Parasite Murders* (1976), *Démoni 2* is more reminiscent of the abysmal *The Video Dead* (1987). Why anyone would want to do a take off of *that* film is beyond me.

The rather bloody effects—the only reason to even bother with a film like this in the first place—is much worse than those which took center stage in its overrated predecessor. (Lay off the bladder effects, all right guys? You can tell they're prophylactics under latex, so you're not fooling anybody.) Topping off the lame gore are some bad stop-motion, an infected dog equipped with a set of rat-teeth and glowing eyes, and a chest-bursting scene which proffers a *Gremlins*-like prodigy.

Hey, wasn't that *Bill & Ted's* Alex Winter playing the demon that gets the ball rolling? Hmmm ... must've been my imagination.

Demonios *see* **Démoni**

Demons *see* **Démoni**

Demons 2 *see* **Démoni 2—L'Incubo Ritorna**

Demons 2—The Nightmare Continues *see* **Démoni 2—L'Incubo Ritorna**

The Demons of Ludlow (1983)

Ram Productions Inc. [US], Titan International Ltd. [US]

DIR: Bill Rebane; PRO: Bill Rebane; SCR: William Arthur; DOP: Bill Rebane; EXP: Barbara J. Rebane; MFX: Denise Bednar and Alan Rebane; SFX: Vern Hyde; MUS: Ric Coken and Steven Kuether

STR: Michael Accardo, Angailica, Don Arthur, Richard Ausman, Paul Bernard, Genevieve Brown, James E. Chamberlain III, Stephanie Cushna, C. Dave Davis, Robert Dawson, William Dexter, Debra Dulman, Jose Granados, Deanne Hass, Richard W. Lange, Carol Perry, James R. Robinson, Patricia J. Statz, Paul von Hausen and Mary Walden

Approximately 92m; Color

VHS1: *The Demons of Ludlow* [TWE; 83(92)m]

In the midst of celebrating its bicentennial, the small isolated town of Ludlow receives a "Harmonium" from the estate of Ethan Ludlow III, the founder's now deceased descendent. It seems that Ethan Senior, though, was banished from Ludlow—one of America's earliest settlements—for witchcraft, and even had his hands lopped off by his peers so he couldn't play his glorified harpsichord. Before too long, the townsfolk begin dropping like flies—that is, when they're not too wrapped up in their own petty little lives.

This film brings up innumerable questions. First, when does 185 years make a bicentennial? Second, how is it that, in films, pianists and organists can make the music sound like something besides what they're obviously playing? Third, why would a ghost be inclined to rip the clothes off of its female victims before killing them? C'mon ... inquiring minds want to know.

Yes, *The Demons of Ludlow* does get pretty nasty for a Bill Rebane film, with a handful of gory eviscerations and blood-drenched decapitations, but this in no way makes up for the fact that it lacks much of the engaging charm of his earlier outings. (For those unfamiliar with his work, Rebane has—with such efforts as *Rana, the Legend of Shadow Lake* [1975] and *The Capture of Bigfoot* [1979] under his belt—tried to single-handedly make Wisconsin the Hollywood of the Midwest. Despite his penchant for engaging characters and enjoyably silly monsters, he didn't succeed.) Unfortunately, being a no-budget spook show effort, Rebane tries to squeeze in as much hokum as the script would allow; sorry, but props being levitated by "invisible" wires, or being shaken by someone just off screen just isn't scary anymore. *Especially* when the execution is so poor.

Though reminiscent of *The Fog* (1979), *The Demons of Ludlow* lacks John Carpenter's once magical flair. (Where's George "Buck" Flower when you need him?) If it's any consolation, the film looks like it was made in the 1970s, despite the fact it was lensed in 1983.

Los Depredores de la Noche *see* **Les Prédateurs de la Nuit**

Descanse en Piezas [Rest in Pieces] (1987)

Calepas International Inc. [UK/Sp] DIR: José Ramón Larraz; PRO: José Frade; SCR: Santiago Moncada; DOP: John Tharp and Manuel Rojas; SFX: Arthur Brilliant; MUS: Greg Debelles
STR: Scott Thompson Baker, Fernando Bilbao, Robert Case, Tony Isbert, Carole James, Daniel Katz, Dorothy Malone, David Rose, Antonio Ross, Jeffrey Segal, Patty Shepard, Jack Taylor and Lorin Jean Vail
Approximately 88m; Color
VHS1: *Rest in Pieces* [IVE; 90(88)m]

A young woman inherits her aunt's six million dollar estate after her curious death; the old nutter not only committed suicide, but videotaped the proceedings as well. Her niece moves into the newly acquired home with her hubby, and the house wastes no time in boning up on its Amityville 101 skills: Clothes rearrange themselves, automobiles start up on their own, a piano teaches itself to play one note over and over and over, etc. Even worse, their oddball neighbors turn out to be dead acquaintances of the deceased aunt, all having offed themselves in the selfsame asylum in which she was a resident. (Worst of all, they don't seem to take kindly to chamber music, if their brutal treatment of a quartet is any indication; maybe they're just particular.)

Except for some conventional ghostly goings-on, *Descanse en Piezas* is a fairly unpredictable effort from the man responsible for the wonderfully sleazy yet atmospheric *Vampyres, Daughters of Dracula* (1974). Unfortunately, it has none of the charm of Larraz' earlier genre outings. Adeptly made and reasonably engaging, the film suffers from a dependency on tired hokum, a lead actress who has all the subtlety of Sweeny Todd in a Supercuts, and a confusing, unsatisfying shock ending. There is also the matter of seemingly relevant mysteries that lead nowhere, in particular an abandoned house to which no one can find the keys ("Who occupies the vacant house across the street?" our heroine asks with a straight face), and an all-but-forgotten basement room filled with rotting greens. Gore is sparse, enough to tease the average splatterpunk but not substantial enough to whet their appetites.

A barely passable shocker from a man whose career still warrants further examination.

El Descuartizador *see*
Leatherface—Texas Chainsaw Massacre III

El Descuartizador de New York *see*
Lo Squartatore di New York

El Desierto de los Zombies *see* **La Tumba de los Muertos Vivientes**

El Despertar de la Momia *see* **Dawn of the Mummy**

The Devil (1981)

Production company unknown [HK]
DIR: Jen Chieh Chang; PRO: Mao Hung Chi and C.H. Wong; SCR: Luk Pak Sang; DOP: Li Shih Chieh; MUS: Wang Mao Shan
STR: Hung Lieh Chen, Mei Hua Chen, Shao Tung Chow, Wei Hung Ho, Yang Chi Lin, Wen Bin Liu, Yin Shang Liu, Bin Lo, Ti Ou, Ming Tien, Pao Yu Wang and Shen Yuan
Approximately 90m; Color 𝄪𝄪𝄪
VHS1: *The Devil* [VCP; 90m]
ADL: *Crawling Horror from the Depths of Hell!*

This is still one of the nastier Asian gore films I've been lucky enough to stumble across; the opening five minutes are guaranteed to have the milquetoasts running for any available exits. Punctuating the typical classified-style "ghost seeks revenge" storyline is an array of dimestore pyrotechnics, inept make-up effects, and—last but not least—a whole gaggle of desperate actors willing to swallow and throw up on cue buckets of verminous fauna: centipedes, snakes, earthworms, snakes, snails, maggots, snakes, millipedes, and, well ... more snakes. Unfortunately, the viewer is occasionally distracted from the nauseating tomfoolery by the inept dubbing, a token "cute" kid, and scattered scenes of animal cruelty (in addition to any abuse arising from the vomit-related scenarios described above).

The Devil is a relatively accessible introduction to the wacky world of Asia's more extreme brand of geekhorror cinema. It may be typical for Eastern spook show fare, but at least it's much more imaginative than its Western counterparts.

Not for all tastes (pun most certainly intended).

The Devil in Snake (1987)

Production company unknown [In]
DIR: Yeung Kong; PRO: Angle Jo
STR: Susan Brandy, Chang Hoi, Lai Hon, Maria Jo, Li Sua Kwon, Isabel Lopez, Hoi San and Elisa Ye
AKA: *Curse*
Approximately 86m; Color
VHS1: *Curse* [OCS; 86m; Chinese w/English subtitles]

A young woman tries to leave her abusive, wheelchair-bound hubby, but her true love is killed on the day they are set to take flight. Overcome with grief, she kills herself, but is reincarnated so as to track down her similarly resuscitated lover. Eventually, she follows him to the Philippines, but finds herself forced to seek an evil sorcerer's aid in order to make him hers. And just when this supernatural love story has nearly lulled the viewer to sleep, the film switches gears and, well, gets really funky. In the sorcerer's domain we see women being herded into cages by dwarves with whips while people in skeleton costumes dance. Those seeking his help are raped by the devil-worshipping magician, their virginity taken in trade for his love potions. Promises are broken, curses are thrown, and before long *The Devil in Snake* is wallowing in the grade–Z excesses of its Indonesian contemporaries.

Unfortunately, the only gore intact in the American print (most scenes are obviously clipped of any bloodshed) is that which depicts our sorcerer getting his just desserts in the end, splitting down the middle, every orifice spewing gobs of blood-soaked vermin: Worms, insects, mice, and— of course—snakes. Lots and lots of snakes. (Although there is no blatant animal cruelty, it is apparent that some of them probably didn't fare very well considering the circumstances.) Left reasonably intact, though, is the T&A and numerous softcore sex scenes. (Being an import, most of the pubic shots have been fogged, obscuring the incriminating follicles.) Throw in some martial arts and shrimping, and you have another fairly strange genre effort from South Asia.

Unfortunately, despite there being lots of snakes, drooling dwarves, foot fetishism, and the Asian custom of barfing up live insects and various other small animals, *The Devil in Snake* is a pretty tepid viewing experience (*especially* with all of the cuts made to the American release). So, unless films like this are your bag, *The Devil in Snake* should remain at the bottom of your list.

Devil Story *see* **Il Était une Fois … le Diable**

Di las Garras del Diablo *see* **Aenigma**

El Dia de los Muertos *see* **Day of the Dead**

Dial Help *see* **Inferno in Diretta**

Dinner with a Vampire *see* **A Cena col Vampiro**

Diyu Wu Men (1980)

Seasonal Film Corporation [HK]
DIR: Hark Tsui; PRO: Cheung Kuen and See-Yuen Ng; SCR: Wai-Cheuk Szeto; DOP: Hung Chuen Lau
STR: Hung Gao, Kwok-Choi Han, Siu-Keung Tsui, Kam-Seng Wong, and David Wu
AKA: *Hell Has No Gates*; *Kung Fu Kannibalen* [Kung Fu Cannibals]; *No Door to Hell*; *We Are Going to Eat You*
Approximately 90m; Color 🌂 🌂 🌂

An isolated community apparently suffers from a protein-deficient diet, as they have the unpleasant habit of eating any and all visitors to the island. They get more than what they bargained for, though, when a government official (Agent 999), hot on the trail of a renowned criminal (Rolex), shows up uninvited, inadvertently throwing a wrench into their anthropophagic machinery.

Diyu Wu Men is a wacky Asian take on the Italian cannibal epics of the '70s, exhibiting not just some extreme gore, but also Hong Kong's penchant for comedic action. Most of the chop-socky stunt work will be too stagy for modern-day filmgoers raised on the likes of Jackie Chan and Sammo Hung, although some of the choreography here is very similar to those stars' humor-inclined execution.

With a soundtrack comprised of flagrant lifts (in particular, Goblin's main theme from *Suspiria*), and some of the ugliest people *ever* to appear in a film.

Loads of fun for those with an adventurous streak.

DNA Formula Letale [DNA Lethal Formula] (1987)

Filmirage [It]
DIR: Luigi Montefiore; PRO: Donatella Donati; SCR: Luigi Montefiore; DOP: Gianlorenzo Battaglia; MFX: Maurizio Trani; SFX: Maurizio Trani; MUS: Pahamian
STR: Jason Arnold, Catherine Baranov, Stephen Brown, Harry Cason, Anna Colonna, Wally Doyle, Laura Gemser, Gene le Brock, Wayne Potrafka, Serina Steinberg, Allison Stokes, Tom Story, David Wicker and Tim Wright
AKA: *Metamorphosis*; *Regenerator*
Approximately 96m; Color
VHS1: *Metamorphosis* [IMP; 93m]

DNA Formula Letale holds promise early on, despite being entirely derivative of Cronenberg's *The Fly*. Unfortunately, once the interesting premise has been established, it quickly degenerates into an '80s take on tacky '50s style B-horror films. Stiff acting, an obnoxious soundtrack, crappy make-up effects, and a not-as-menacing-as-they'd-like-you-to-think-it-is *papier-mâché* monster

make the viewing experience that much more wretched. (But, hey, it's got a groovy video box that lights up and makes spooky sounds, so it *has* to be good, right?)

Although filmed in the states, this Italian quickie was perpetrated by Aristide Massaccesi cohort Luigi Montefiore, star of *Anthropophagus* and *Rosso Sangue*. And, yes, he should've stuck to acting.

Dr. Butcher, M.D. (1980)

Aquarius [It/US]
DIR: Roy Frumkes and Marino Girolami; PRO: Terry Levene; SCR: Fabrizio de Angelis and Marino Girolami; DOP: Roy Frumkes and Fausto Zuccoli; EXP: Ron Harvey; SFX: Fabrizio de Angelis, Rosario Prestopino and Maurizio Trani; MUS: Nico Fidenco and Walter E. Sear
STR: Sherry Buchanan, Dakkar, Alexandra delli Colli, Linda Fumis, Víctor Israel, Ian McCulloch, Donald O'Brien, Peter O'Neal, Walter Patriarca and Roberto Resra
Approximately 81m; Color
VHS1: *Dr. Butcher, M.D.* [PAR; 81m]; *Dr. Butcher, M.D.* [THR; 81m]
ADL: *He Is a Depraved, Sadistic Rapist; a Bloodthirsty Killer … and He Makes House Calls.*

Someone is breaking into a New York hospital and borrowing organs and various body parts from cadavers used in medical studies. When it turns out to be a medical student with a hankering for *long pig*, a reporter, a nurse (who also just *happens* to have a degree in anthropology … how convenient), and a doctor follow their only lead (a tattoo) to Kito, an island in the Archipelago. Not only are the native inhabitants there vicious cannibals, but a doctor on the selfsame island is conducting rather unethical experiments using humans as guinea pigs, the results being mindless, lum-

Video box art for *Dr. Butcher, M.D.*
(1980), Thriller Video.

bering zombies with a bad case of the uglies.

This unrepentant gorefest makes up for its lack of originality by being overwhelmingly contrived … in an endearing sort of way. There's lots of nauseating fun with eviscerations, eye gougings, and dismemberments on the part of the cannibals, not to mention the tongue-snipping, scalp-peeling, brain-stealing exploits of the resident physician. (To date, this film boasts the most impressive use of an outboard motor ever shown in a film. Needless to say, the poor sap's face it comes into contact with doesn't fare too well.) With all of the gore, it's easy to look past the low-rent production values and conveniences offered by a sometimes lazy script. Like so many Italian cannibal epics,

it even reiterates themes concerning modern man and the archetypical savage. Here this theme isn't used to justify the onscreen butchery and general abuse of live animals that usually punctuate Green Hell efforts, as such real-life atrocities are avoided altogether.

Dr. Butcher, M.D. is actually Marino Girolami's *La Regina dei Cannibali* (1979), re-edited by American distributors to include additional footage from *Tales to Rip Your Heart Out,* an incompleted film by Roy Frumkes. (So, if you couldn't figure out why there were scenes of zombies stumbling out of a graveyard at the film's onset, now you know.)

Zombi 2 (1979) meets *Cannibal Ferox* (1981) by way of the Filipino "Blood Island" films.

Dr. Yuen and Wisely *see* **The Seventh Curse**

Document of the Dead *(1989)*

Roy Frumkes Productions [US], The School of Visual Arts [US]
DIR: Roy Frumkes; PRO: Roy Frumkes; SCR: Roy Frumkes; DOP: Reeves Lehman; EXP: Len Anthony and Studio Entertainment; MUS: Rick Ulfik
STR: John Amplas, Steve Bissette, Christine Forrest, Roy Frumkes, Michael Gornick, Nicole Potter, George A. Romero, Richard P. Rubenstein, Tom Savini, Susan Tyrrell and Gahan Wilson
Approximately 84m; B&W and Color
DVD1: *Document of the Dead* [SYN; 84m]; VHS1: *Document of the Dead* [OFF; 76m]; *Document of the Dead* [SYN; 84m]

The core of this documentary is a behind-the-scenes look at the making of George Romero's' classic gutmuncher *Dawn of the Dead* (1978), lensed by Frumkes while working towards a degree at the School of Visual

Arts. It was eventually finished in 1989 while Frumkes was on the set of another Romero/Argento collaboration, *Two Evil Eyes*. (A lengthy piece details a particularly problematic special effect applied in Romero's half of the anthology.) The package is rounded out with a slew of short interviews with cast and crew, as well as footage from other Romero productions (*Night of the Living Dead*, *Martin*, and *Monkeyshines—An Experiment in Fear*), plus some footage from the European cut of *Dawn of the Dead* (released thereabouts as *Zombie*), most of which was included in Anchor Bay Entertainment's remastered Director's Cut of the same film.

Document of the Dead seems to be a rather comprehensive look at the man who started the whole zombie trend ... until one realizes that not one mention is made of *Day of the Dead* (1985), the third film in the infamous trilogy. (Some stills are shown during the final credits, but this is little more than an afterthought.) Why they overlooked this film is beyond me (the notion of it being simply an oversight is unthinkable). In addition to this glaring exclusion, the film is also occasionally bogged down by pretentious pontification from narrators who aren't nearly as familiar with Romero's work as they'd like you to believe.

Required viewing for both splatterpunks and aspiring filmmakers.

De Doder van New York *see* **Lo Squartatore di New York**

Don't Go in the Woods (1981)
James Bryan Films [US]
DIR: James Bryan; PRO: Roberto

Gomez and Suzette Gomez; SCR: Garth Eliassen; DOP: Henry Zinman; MUS: H. Kingsley Thurber

STR: Dale Angell, Mary Gail Artz, David Barth, Carolyn Braza, Angie Brown, Leon Brown, Jr., Linda Brown, Brad Carter, Ken Carter, McCormick Dalten, Tom Drury, Garth Eliassen, Cecilia Fannon, Susan Farrs, Ruth Grose, Jaren Harbrecht, Bonnie Harris, James P. Hayden, Eric Jenkins, Randy Kleffer, Gerry Klein, Amy Martell, Jack McClelland, Frank Clitus Muller, Matt Muller, Matt Noone, Alma Ramos, Larry Roupe, Tom Ruff, Ann St. Michael, Valetta Saunders, Bill Stockdale, Laura Trefts, Ebin Whiting, Jon Williams, Jeff Wood and Henry Zinman

AKA: *Don't Go in the Woods ... Alone*
Approximately 91m; Color
VHS1: *Don't Go in the Woods* [VES; 88(91)m]
ADL: *Everyone Has Nightmares About the Ugliest Way to Die!* (Me? Mine is choking to death on my own vomit while watching a film of this caliber. I wouldn't want *that* in my obituary.)

My God! Something in the woods is killing people! Why? Because A: It makes for cheap location shooting; B: You city slickers let exploitation filmmakers cash in on your deep-seated paranoia of trees; and C: One doesn't have to hire a screenwriter for these plotless exercises. Furthermore, if one doesn't want to spring for monster effects, they can simply make the killer a deranged mountain man or similarly inbred redneck.

Below par on all counts. (Inept actors and a cheesy synth score are the exception, as these manage to plumb even greater depths.)

Does a bear shit in the woods? Sure it does, but we needn't step in it.

Don't Go in the Woods ... Alone *see* **Don't Go in the Woods**

Don't Open 'Til Christmas see
Don't Open Till Christmas

Don't Open Till Christmas (1984)

Spectacular International Films [UK]
DIR: Alan Birkinshaw and Edmund Purdom; PRO: Steve Minasian and Dick Randall; SCR: Derek Ford and Alan Birkinshaw; DOP: Alan Pudney; MFX: Pino Ferranti; SFX: Coast to Coast Ltd.; MUS: Des Dolan

STR: Pat Astley, John Aston, Kelly Baker, Adrian Black, Wilfred Corlett, Wendy Danvers, Des Dolan, Nicholas Donnelly, Ashley Dransfield, Maria Eldridge, Derek Ford, Ken Halliwell, Lawrence Harrington, Derek Hunt, Mark Jones, Ricky Kennedy, Alan Lake, Kevin Lloyd, Ray Marioni, Belinda Mayne, Paula Meadows, Caroline Munro, George Pierce, Edmund Purdom, Max Roman, Gerry Sundquist and Sid Wragg

AKA: *Don't Open 'Til Christmas*; *Fröhliche Weihnachten* [Merry Christmas]; *Non Aprite Prima di Natale* [Don't Open Until Christmas]

Approximately 86m; Color

VHS1: *Don't Open Till Christmas* [VES; 86m]; VHS2: *Don't Open Till Christmas* [VES; 80(86)m]

ADL: "*...t'was the Night Before Christmas, and All Through the House Not a Creature Was Stirring ... They Were All Dead!*"

Don't Open Till Christmas is drab British tripe about a masked killer doing away with every Old Saint Nick that crosses his or her path. (One nude model in a fur-lined red coat is spared, if only because the scriptwriters couldn't figure out a more convenient way to give the inept police some much needed leads.)

Granted, this is yet another heaping plate full of uninspired dreck, but for once, a country besides the good old US of A is responsible. Although murders are plentiful, the killings are rote and the gore just as lame. (Stab wounds spurting H.G. Lewis–style red paint seems to be a favorite of the effects people.) There is a castration scene, but it is probably the most pathetic emasculation ever to be committed to celluloid. *Don't Open Till Christmas* also boasts the most unconvincing flashback explanation employed by a slasher film, and some priceless dialogue. (A storefront Santa walks into a bar and is confronted with the lascivious query, "So, Santa, did you bring me any presents?" to which he replies, "I'm not the real one." Guess he's never heard of role-playing.)

Don't open until Christmas? Hell, why bother taking it out of the box at all.

Doom Asylum (1983)

Seidbourd World Enterprises [US]
DIR: Richard Friedman; PRO: Steve Menkin; SCR: Rick Marx; DOP: Larry Revene; EXP: Alexander W. Kogan, Jr., and Barry Tucker; MFX: Vincent J. Guastini; SFX: Vincent J. Guastini; MUS: Dave Erlanger and Jonathan Stuart

STR: Dawn Alvan, Ruth Collins, Kristin Davis, Farin, Paul Giorgi, William Hay, Harvey Keith, Steve Menkin, Patty Mullen, Kenny L. Price, Michael Rogen and Harrison White

Approximately 78m; Color

VHS1: *Doom Asylum* [AHE; 77(78)m]

ADL: *It'll Send Shivers Up Your Funnybone!*

A car crash victim isn't quite dead when he ends up on the slab, but—aside from having his face peeled off by an impatient coroner—he's not faring too poorly. Ten years later, his daughter and a group of friends decide to party at an abandoned asylum, and, well, you can put two and two together, I'm sure.

Yes, *Doom Asylum* is another desperate cry to "Save the Celluloid," as it doesn't warrant the film that was used to make it. Like most horror comedies, this movie is neither scary nor funny, and will probably only find a following among thirteen-year-old *Fangoria* readers who are too busy seeking tits and gore to realize that efforts like this are sophomoric drivel. The jokes are stale, and the special effects are mostly awful. But hey, any movie that touts its star as a Penthouse Pet of the Year has got to be good, hasn't it? (Yeah, those models sure can act, can't they? Heck, they don't even *need* acting lessons. Born thespians, one and all.)

I would never have guessed that the director made this in the midst of a television career that spans such series as *Tales from the Darkside* and *Lois & Clark*.

Doomed to Die *see* **Mangiati Vivi**

The Dorm That Dripped Blood *see* **Death Dorm**

Dream Slayer *see* **Blood Song**

Dreamaniac (1986)

Taryn Productions Inc. [US]
DIR: David de Coteau; PRO: David de Coteau; SCR: Helen Robinson; DOP: Howard Wexler; MFX: Linda Nottestad and Tom Schwartz; MUS: Don Great and Tom Milano
STR: Thomas Bern, Brent Black, Cynthia Crass, Lisa Emery, Brad Laughlin, Kim McKamy, Bob Pelham, Lauren Peterson, Matthew Phelps, Sylvia Summers, Michael Warren and Linda Watts
Approximately 80m; Color
VHS1: *Dreamaniac* [WIZ; 80m]
ADL: *You Don't Have to Go to Elm Street to Have a Nightmare.*

This early straight-to-video shocker is more of the usual from de Coteau: A house full of stupid, hormonally-charged teens are routinely killed in however grisly a fashion the effects persons can muster. Granted, there is a little more sex and violence than what is usually called for in such pics, but this isn't always a plus. (The gore is nasty, but isn't sawing off someone's head with a *drill* going a little overboard? And it isn't even done well, for crying out loud.) There are also several attempts at humor, but these are poorly aimed efforts to cover up the other shortcomings of the film. (Okay, so the scene where a girl throws up on her boyfriend and her ex is amusing, as is the just-for-laughs ending, but neither make the proceedings worth wading through.)

"Wake up and die!" the adline screams. Personally, I suggest you stay asleep so you don't have to suffer through this dreck in the first place.

Du Gu (1986)

Production company unknown [HK/Th]
DIR: Ling Pan
STR: Lily Chan, Hoi-Shan Kwan and Hon Chi Lai
Approximately 86m; Color ⚔ ⚔ ⚔
VHS1: *Brutal Sorcery* [OCS; 86m; Chinese w/ English subtitles]

A taxi driver is told by a fortuneteller that his life will take a turn for the worse, and at the very least he can expect a crippling illness. His fate, though, is even worse than he expected, as he suddenly becomes a magnet for ghosts, each wanting him to give them rides in his cab. Among them are the spirits of two lovers killed by a "black magic death curse" and buried apart from each other in different graveyards. His job? To dig up the corpses and ship them back to their home country where they can join one another in the afterlife.

Although it sounds like fairly typical Asian spook show fare, those familiar with such films won't be too terribly surprised to find out that it is also steeped in gratuity. (The best scene involves an actor's stomach bursting open, spewing offal and mealy worms.) The viewer can also expect abundant T&A, cheesy animated ghosts, flashbacks within flashbacks, and a possessed man who does a song and dance number—"You Can't Escape from Love." Those wacky Asians.

Director Pan also helmed *Xiong Zhou* (1986), aka *Blood Sorcery*, the same year. Actor Kwan appeared in numerous Jackie Chan films, in particular the entries in his *Project A* series.

Edge of Hell *see* **Rock 'n' Roll Nightmare**

Edge of the Axe *see* **Filo del Hacha**

The Eleventh Commandment *see* **Camping del Terrore**

The Emerald Jungle *see* **Mangiati Vivi**

Emperor Caligula—The Garden of Taboo *see* **Clagula—La Storia Mai Raccontata**

Emperor Caligula—The Untold Story *see* **Clagula—La Storia Mai Raccontata**

Engendros Macabros *see* **The Boogens**

Epitaph (1987)

City Lights Home Video [US]
DIR: Joseph Merhi; PRO: Joseph Merhi and Richard Pepin; SCR: Joseph Merhi; DOP: Richard Pepin; EXP: Ronald L. Gilchrist; VFX: Jim Crouch, Constance J. Damron, Aaron Sims and Judy Yonemoto; MUS: John Gonzalez
STR: Paula Jamison, Liz Kane, Flint Keller, Mike Mendoza, R.W. Munchkin, Delores Nascar, Natasha Pavlova, Ed Reynolds, Linda Tucker Smith and Jim Williams
Approximately 90m; Color
VHS1: *Epitaph* [CLV; 90m]

A family moves into an old house that was once a church. Shortly after their arrival, while everyone else is away from the house, the mother comes onto a young painter. When he not so subtly resists her advances ("I've had all I can take with you and all the horny old bags I meet on this stinkin' job"), the rebuked wife does a permanent number on him with a butcher knife. Apparently, this is not an isolated occurrence, as her husband, although frustrated with his wife's appalling habit, seems to have gotten pretty damn good at digging graves. Somehow, the painter survives the attack (amazing, considering that each time she struck him it was up to the hilt) *and* being buried alive, so he decides to exact revenge with a pick-axe. And here we are, only a third of the way into the film.

Passably engaging but far from being a great film, *Epitaph* is not completely formulaic, and—for better or worse—the slashing often takes a backseat to the abundant melodramatics. The gore is standard, although there is a fairly nasty torture scene involving a rat. (The poor rodent isn't the one being tortured, but it was probably traumatized more than the other actor involved.)

Director Merhi went on to do a number of made-for-cable erotic thrillers—films that usually fail on both counts—as well as a slew of B action flicks.

Il Était une Fois ... le Diable [Once Upon a Time ... the Devil] (1986)

Albatros Films [Fr], Condor Films [Fr]
DIR: Bernard Launois; SCR: Bernard Launois; DOP: Guy Maria; MFX: Plastic Studio; SFX: André Trielli; MUS: Paul Piot and Michel Roy
STR: Catherine Day, Nicole Desailly, Christian Paumelle, Marcel Portier, Véronique Renaud and Pascal Simon
AKA: *Devil Story*
Approximately 72m; Color

A pig-faced psychopath kills a couple of campers and tosses their corpses down a well. Another man makes the mistake of asking the self-same "le Monstre" for directions to the nearest gas station, and suffers a similar fate. And just when the viewer is about ready to write the film off as a silly monster-cum-slasher flick, it switches gears and begins to focus on a man and his disturbed wife who take up in a creaky seaside hotel. Even the whole look and feel of the film changes from cut-rate exploitation to passable Euro-gothic fare; one almost wonders if it's two entirely different unfinished films pasted together. Everyone forgets about "le Monstre"—at least for a while, anyway—as everything now begins to revolve around a ghost ship and a re-animated Egyptian mummy. (How does everything tie in together? Don't ask

me. Heck, I doubt if even the scriptwriter knows.)

Obviously, the gore is one of the reasons, if not *the* reason, this flick was propagated to begin with. The viewer is greeted with lots of loving close-ups of spurting blood, as well as a particularly nasty—albeit ridiculously staged—evisceration. Unfortunately, when actors aren't being dispatched, we are offered nothing more exciting than a very agitated horse (who—to everyone's chagrin—receives more screen time than any of its human counterparts).

Despite the charming contrivances, *Il Etait une Fois ... le Diable* is just one more reason why French cinema rarely ventures or strays into splatter territory. (You'd think being only a stone's throw from Italy they would have *some* clue.) One may actually be surprised to find out that this was the director's last film, not his first, in a string of obscure offerings. I was.

L'Eventreur de New York *see* **Lo Squartatore di New York**

Evil Clutch *see* **Notte nel Bosco**

The Evil Dead (1982)

Renaissance Pictures Ltd. [US]
DIR: Samuel M. Raimi; PRO: Robert G. Tapert; SCR: Samuel M. Raimi; DOP: Tim Philo; EXP: Bruce Campbell, Samuel M. Raimi and Robert G. Tapert; MFX: Tom Sullivan; VFX: Bart Pierce; MUS: Joe lo Duca [Soundtrack from Varèse Sarabande]
STR: Betsy Baker, John Cameron, Bruce Campbell, Barbara Carey, Gwen Cochanski, Hal Delrich, Bob Dorian, Phil Gillis, Dorothy Guttridge, David Horton, Debie Jarczewski, Joanne Kruse, Don Long, Ivan Raimi, Samuel M. Raimi, Theodore Raimi, Kurt Rauf, Ellen Sandweiss, Stu Smith, Scott Spiegel, Mary Beth Tapert,

Robert G. Tapert, Wendall Thomas, Bill Vincent and Sarah York
Approximately 85m; Color
DVD0: *The Evil Dead* [ABE; 85m; LBX]; VHS1: *The Evil Dead* [ABE; 85m]; *The Evil Dead* [CNG; 89(85)m]; *The Evil Dead* [EMI; 85m]

Five young people purchase a cottage retreat once rented by an anthropologist who discovered the infamous "Book of the Dead" in the Sumerian ruins of Kandar. They make the mistake of playing back a pre-recorded incantation, and—Presto!—instant Kandarian demon summoning. With the only access—a bridge—put out of commission by supernatural forces, they find themselves with their hands full.

"The most ferociously original horror film . . ."
— Stephen King, Author of THE SHINING and THE DEAD ZONE

Video box art for *The Evil Dead* (1982), Thorn EMI Video.

Granted, *The Evil Dead* deserves recognition for what Raimi and crew did on a minuscule budget, but—outside of some stray inspired moments (courtesy of Raimi's staging and Bruce Campbell's performance)—this film is an overrated shocker that suffers from abysmal effects work, sub-par acting, and a complete lack of continuity. (Campbell wouldn't have the opportunity to show his comedic range until the "sequel" made five years later.) Of course, every splatterpunk and his grandmother will be quick to hail this film as a "cult classic," a title it deserves simply because of its reputation and not because of its contribution to the genre, so I'll just cut this short so as not to accrue *too* much hate mail.

Me? I saw it in the theater upon its initial theatrical showing and heckled it all the way through. And I had no problem getting most of the audience to join along. (I had to get my money's worth *somehow*.)

Evil Dead II (1987)

Renaissance Pictures Ltd. [US]
DIR: Samuel M. Raimi; PRO: Robert G. Tapert; SCR: Samuel M. Raimi and Scott Spiegel; DOP: Peter Deming and Eugene D. Shlugleit; EXP: Alex de Benedetti and Irvin Shapiro; MFX: Mark Shostrom; SFX: Vern Hyde; VFX: Doug Beswick Productions Inc. and Rick Catizone Anivision; MUS: Joseph lo Duca
STR: Josh Becker, Sarah Berry, Denise Bixler, Bruce Campbell, Mitch Cantor, Richard Domeier, Jenny Griffith, Lou Hancock, Dan Hicks, Thomas Kidd, John Peaks, Samuel M. Raimi, Theodore Raimi, William Preston Robertson, Roc Sandstorm, Scott Spiegel and Kassie Wesley
AKA: *La Casa 2* [The House 2]; *Evil Dead 2—Dead by Dawn*
Approximately 85m; Color
DVD0: *Evil Dead 2—Dead by Dawn*

[ABE; 85m; LBX]; DVD1: *Evil Dead II*
[ABE; 95(85)m; LBX]; VHS1: *Evil Dead II*
[VTR; 95(85)m; LBX]; *Evil Dead 2—Dead
by Dawn* [ABE; 84(85)m]; *Evil Dead 2—
Dead by Dawn* [VES; 84m]
    ADL: *2 Terrifying. 2 Frightening. 2
Much!*

    Picking up where the previous
film left off (kind of, but not really),
Evil Dead II reiterates its predecessor's action after discarding all of the
extraneous characters, then brings in
another handful of victims to be
mauled, possessed, and generally harassed by those wacky Kandarian
demons. (The sequel, though, begins
to make ties with H.P. Lovecraft's
Cthulhu mythos, the renaming of the
book "the Necronomicon" being the
most significant change.)
    Here the tone is decidedly more
playful than the first. Campbell is
given the opportunity to ham it up
considerably, and thus steals the show.
(I couldn't see his star power from the
first film, but here he proves himself
able to give Jim Carey a run for his
money in the slapstick department.)
Raimi's inventive photography, staging, and editing valiantly vies for
screen time with the adept lead actor,
though, displaying the talent he was
purported to have in the first film but
which rarely materialized. (It is no
surprise that, whereas *Evil Dead* guaranteed them a following, *Evil Dead
II* was the breakthrough film for both
Raimi and Campbell that helped to
get their foot in the door at Hollywood.)
    Evil Dead II is much improved
over the original in every other way as
well. It is undeniably slicker (granted,
this takes the edge off the shocks at
times), and the effects aren't nearly as

shoddy, despite the fact they're still
too rubbery to be effective. Unfortunately, the third film—*Army of Darkness*—went even further in this direction, sacrificing any shocks and
gratuitous bloodshed for laughs. (Bad
move; it wasn't funny.)

Evil Dead 2—Dead by Dawn *see*
    Evil Dead II

Evil Dead Trap *see* **Shiryo No Wana**

Evil Laugh (1986)

    Wildfire Productions [US]
    DIR: Dominick Brascia, Jr.; PRO:
Steven Baio and Dominick Brascia, Jr.;
SCR: Steven Baio and Dominick Brascia,
Jr.; DOP: Stephen Sealy; EXP: Arthur
Schweitzer and Krishna Shah; MFX: David
Cohen; MUS: David Shapiro
    STR: Steven Baio, Dominick Brascia,
Jr., Jody Gibson, Susan Grant, Tony Griffin,
Gary Hays, Kim McKamy, Donna Nevada,
Myles O'Brien, Karyn O'Bryan, Jerold
Pearson, Hal Shafer, Tom Shell, Johnny
Venocur and Howard Weiss
    Approximately 87m; Color
    VHS1: *Evil Laugh* [CHE; 90(87)m]
    ADL: *Martin's Back ... and He'll Scare
You—to Death!*

    Evil Laugh is effortless tripe
about a bunch of medical students
partying at a friend's newly acquired
home who are taken out one by one by
a killer with an "evil" Pee Wee Herman laugh. (The "Stay Away" spray-
painted all over the house doesn't
seem to be a deterrent, it seems, although the viewers shouldn't take this
warning so lightly.) There is nothing,
I repeat, *nothing* worthwhile or even
remotely memorable about this waste
of celluloid. Everything about *Evil
Laugh*, from the technical to the creative ends, is sub-par at best. Maybe,
somewhere within, there's a kernel of

inspiration or ingenuity, but if there is, I couldn't find it. The whole of the film is overwhelmed by the fact that the filmmakers made no effort to do anything new or different, nor did they make any attempts to do it at least as well as everyone else.

Director Brascia functioned primarily as an actor in B films.

Evil Spawn (1987)

American-Independent Productions [US], Camp Motion Pictures [US]
DIR: Kenneth J. Hall; PRO: Anthony Brewster; SCR: Kenneth J. Hall; DOP: Christopher Condon; MFX: Thomas Floutz and Cleve Hall; SFX: Dan Bordona, Ralph Miller III and Christopher Ray; MUS: Paul Natzke
STR: Forrest J Ackerman, Mark Anthony, Bobbie Bresee, John Carradine, Michael S. Deak, Leslie Eve, Jerry Fox, Pamela Gilbert, Drew Godderis, Chris Kobin, Gary J. Levinson, Sue Mashaw, Roger McCoin, Donna Shock and John Terrence
Approximately 90m; Color
VHS1: *Evil Spawn* [CAM; 90m]
ADL: *Tonight ... She Will Love Again—and Kill Again!*

Bobbie (*Mausoleum*) Bresee is an actress (so to speak) who turns down a role in the excretory *She-Devil* so as to make herself available for the much classier *Savage Goddess*. (Say, that does sound like a step up.) Because of her fading beauty, she loses that as well, and is approached by a doctor who wants her to take part in some rather questionable rejuvenation experiments. Being a no-budget, sleazy horror film, the results go from bad to worse ... as does everything else about this film.

The script is actually a notch above what you might expect from such a film, if only because it is al-most an exact remake of Roger Corman's *The Wasp Woman* (1959), and almost as ludicrous as its predecessor. The directing, on the other hand, is fairly abysmal, as is the acting, as are the make-up effects, as is the ... let's see, what have I forgotten? A pathetically invalid Carradine (in what has to be one of his last roles, if not his last) doesn't make things any brighter, and the same could be said for the unnecessary and completely obligatory shock ending. To be blunt, the whole thing should have been shot on video, if only so an hour and a half of celluloid would have been saved.

"Sounds like something out of a bad science fiction film," one actor remarks. Bingo! Emphasis on the "bad."

Creating some unnecessary confusion for many viewers and film historians, *Evil Spawn* was re-edited with new footage by Fred Olen Ray and Ted Newsom a few years later and released as *The Alien Within*.

The Evil Within see **Baby Blood**

Evilspeak (1982)

Coronet Film Corporation [US], Leisure Investment Co. [US]
DIR: Eric Weston; PRO: Sylvio Tabet and Eric Weston; SCR: Joseph Garofalo and Eric Weston; DOP: Irv Goodnoff; EXP: Sylvio Tabet; MFX: Make-Up Effects Lab; SFX: John Carter and Harry Woolman; MUS: Roger Kellaway
STR: Kristine Alskeg, R.G. Armstrong, Sam Baldoni, Jane Bartelme, Hamilton Camp, Sue Casey, Joseph Cortese, De Forest Covan, Deborah Dawes, Dick Drake, Kenny Ferrugiaro, Louie Gravance, Jim Greenleaf, Lynn Hancock, Alan Harris, Thomas Hillard, Clint Howard, Victor Husberger, Jr., Claude Earl Jones, Katherine Kelly Lang, Loren Lester, Bennett Liss, Kathy McCullen, Richard Moll, Lenny Montana, Haywood Nelson, Leonard

O'John, Nadine Reimers, Don Stark, Robert Taylor and Charles Tyner
AKA: *Mensajero de Satanás* [Messenger of Satan]
Approximately 92m; Color
DVD2: *Evilspeak* [DIG; 90m]; VHS1: *Evilspeak* [TCF; 92m]; VHS2: *Evilspeak* [DIG; 90m]

Ron's estranged brother Clint (*Gentle Ben*) Howard gets to actually *star* in a film for a change, instead of being relegated to a small supporting role. (He may not have a lot of range at his disposal, but he's always interesting to watch.) Anywho, Clint headlines the film as a geek (imagine that!) at a military academy who eventually takes revenge on his abusive peers with the help of his PC and the spirit of a devil worshipping, excommunicated monk whose church formed the physical foundation of the aforementioned boys' school. (The defrocked monk is played by the always-intimidating Richard Moll, who tended to play heavies before landing the role of Bull Shannon in *Night Court*.)

Most of the deaths are fairy gruesome, with some over-the-top gore punctuating the wacky finale. (So when did pigs become Satan's pet of choice? Were the screenwriters actually aware of the role this animal played in the bible's earliest depictions of an exorcism, or were they just a handy way to mete out some of the executions?) Some of the supernatural pyrotechnics come across as tacky, and the capabilities of computers are, shall we say, exaggerated. (Hey, I remember what a PC was capable of twenty years ago, and it wasn't much.) Otherwise, the film is enjoyable although not outstanding, both in re-

spect to production values and overall content.

Revenge of the Nerds (1984) by way of old Scratch himself.

The Eye of the Evil Dead *see* **L'Occhio del Male**

Eyes of a Stranger (1981)

Warner Brothers [US]
DIR: Ken Wiederhorn; PRO: Ronald Zerra; SCR: Mark Jackson; DOP: Mini Rojas; MFX: Tom Savini; MUS: Richard Einhorn
STR: Richard Allen, José Bahamande, Steven Belgard, Toni Crabtree, Madeline Curtis, Michael de Silva, George de Vries, John di Santi, Peter du Pré, Tony Federico, Dan Fitzgerald, Rhonda Flynn, Joe Friedman, Herb Goldstein, Robert Goodman, Luke Halpin, Timothy Hawkins, Sarah Hutcheson, Amy Krug, Alan Lee, Jennifer Jason Leigh, Gwen Lewis, Jillian Lindig, Kitty Lunn, Melvin Pape, Ted Richert, Stella Rivera, Bob Small, Kathy Suergiu, Lauren Tewes, Tabbetha Tracey, Pat Warren and Sonia Zomina
AKA: *Los Ojos de un Extraño* [The Eyes of a Stranger]
Approximately 85m; Color
VHS1: *Eyes of a Stranger* [WAR; 88(85)m]

Eyes of a Stranger is generic early '80s slasher fare about a rapist-slash-murderer that doesn't hesitate to wallow in the clichés: A female newscaster being stalked by an obsessive killer, a blind girl trapped in her apartment by the same, etc. To further the lack of innovation, most of the murders involve nasty throat slashings, perpetrated by effects artist Savini who undoubtedly got bored with his contributions. The only highlight of *Eyes of a Stranger* is that it shows some clips from one of Wiederhorn's earlier efforts, *Shock Waves* (1976), by far the best underwater mutant zombie Nazi film ever. (And that's not an accolade to be taken lightly.)

With Jennifer Jason Leigh in one of her earliest roles.

Faceless *see* **Les Prédateurs de la Nuit**

Fall Break *see* **The Mutilator** (1983)

The Falling *see* **Alien Predator**

Fanatic *see* **The Last Horror Film**

Fanatical Extreme *see* **The Last Horror Film**

The Farm *see* **The Curse** (1987)

Fear *see* **L'Ossessione Che Uccide**

Feurtanz der Zombies *see* **Inferno**

Une Fille pour les Cannibales *see* **Mondo Cannibale** (1980)

Filles Traquées *see* **La Nuit des Traquées**

Filo del Hacha [Edge of the Axe] (1987)

Calepas International Inc. [Sp/US]
DIR: José Ramón Larraz; PRO: José Frade; SCR: Joaquín Amichatis, Javier Elorrieta and José Frade; DOP: Tote Trenas; EXP: Lara Polop; MFX: Colin Arthur; SFX: Colin Arthur; MUS: Javier Elorrieta
STR: Joy Blackburn, Barton Faulks, May Heatherly, Fred Holliday, Christina Marie Lane, Elmer Modlin, Alicia Moro, Page Moseley, Conrado San Martín, Patty Shepard and Jack Taylor
Approximately 91m; Color
VHS1: *Edge of the Axe* [FHV; 91m]

A woman is killed in a car wash by an axe-wielding maniac. Before the community has recovered from this grisly crime, one couple finds a pig's head in their bed, and an exterminator and his computer whiz buddy discover a corpse stashed away in the basement of a bar. From there, the story dives into a fair amount of mildly interesting but seemingly unrelated subplots. By film's end, though, *Filo del Hacho* has degenerated into a fairly generic slasher flick, having traded the mystery elements for the more standard stalk 'n' slash routine. (Even the killer is scared to break the mold, hiding behind a featureless white mask *à la* Jason Vorhees and Michael Myers.)

Despite its insistence on playing it safe in the latter half of the film, *Filo del Hacho* still manages to be an engaging psycho-on-the-loose flick. Although the director himself has been quoted as saying that this is his most disappointing film, it is a hell of a lot better than the dreck it sought to emulate. Production values are probably the best Larraz has ever had to work with, although this makes little difference, as he has been able to accomplish some commendable work on the lowest of budgets. Numerable red herrings, and the presence of Jack Taylor (performing some spooky organ music), gives it an extra edge as well.

Competent slasher fare from the man who brought us *The House That Vanished* (1973) and *Vampyres, Daughters of Dracula* (1974).

The Final Terror (1981)

Watershed Co. [US]
DIR: Andrew Davis; PRO: Joe Roth; SCR: Jon George, Neil Hicks and Ronald Shusett; DOP: Andreas da Videscu; EXP:

Samuel Z. Arkoff; MFX: Ken Myers; MUS: Susan Justin
STR: Akosua Busia, Lori Lee Butler, John Friedrich, Daryl Hannah, Ernest Harden, Jr., Cindy Harrell, Richard Jacobs, Tony Maccario, Mark Metcalf, Joe Pantoliano, Donna Pinder, Irene Sanders, Lewis Smith, Rachel Ward, Jim Youngs and Adrian Zmed
AKA: *Bump in the Night*; *Campsite Massacre*; *The Forest Primeval*
Approximately 84m; Color
VHS1: *The Final Terror* [VES; 90(84)m]
ADL: *Without Knowing They Have Awakened an Unknown Force—Can Anyone Survive?*

A youth work detail goes on what they assumed would be an innocuous camping trip, but are besieged by a killer who we are led to believe is a crazed mother and/or her illegitimate son. In the tried and true tradition of *Friday the 13th*, unsympathetic teens are brutally murdered, in the woods, usually while bumping uglies. At one point, *The Final Terror* goes off on a *Deliverance* kick, but this—and whatever other deviations the screenwriters make in the script—isn't enough to salvage the stale proceedings. (Worse yet, the gore is quite restrained when compared to the aforementioned inspiration, so anyone looking for an effects-laden slaughterfest will undoubtedly be disappointed.)
Forgettable.

555 (1988)

King Video Productions [US]
DIR: Wally Koz; PRO: Wally Koz; SCR: Roy M. Koz; DOP: Lamar Bloodworth; EXP: Wally Koz; MFX: Jeffrey Lyle Segal; MUS: Frankie Rodriguez
STR: Ricardo Alvarez, Mara-Lynn Bastian, Christine Cabana, Jeff Dieter, Charles Fuller, Bob Grabill, Skip Grisham, Scott Hermes, Greg Kerouac, Roy M. Koz, Wally Koz, Temple Mead, Pat Mongoven, Greg Neilson, Richard Orchard, Anita Reformado, Frankie Rodriguez, Doreen Semese, B.K. Smith, David Trelford and Anne Walker
Approximately 90m; Color [Shot on video]
VHS1: *555* [SLE; 90m]

A couple is butchered while making their own oil spill on a secluded beach. An old army colonel witnesses the murder, and claims the killer was a hippie, complete with love beads, bellbottoms and other stereotypical paraphernalia. A couple in a van doing the Blitzkrieg Bop is next in line, and by this time a police sergeant is acting awfully suspicious. The pathetic Manson wannabe (Polyester? Charles would never wear polyester!) spends almost every waking minute sharpening his knives, preparing for the murders that he perpetrates every five years.

Being a shot on video production, no one will—or should—have high expectations for this number. Production values are low, with the gore being the focal point of the film (go figure). The story amounts to little more than three cops on stake outs or interrogating their only witness, and—even though much of the acting is better than what one might expect—none of the main players have the chops to carry the weak premise.

The effects are splashy, but more often than not unconvincing. (The wounds don't spray much blood, but the prop knives sure do.) Although the first two killings are mostly off screen, the murders get progressively gorier, serving up severed fingers, decaps, and an evisceration. The scriptwriter also tries to up the ante by throwing in a nasty scene involving necrophilia, but *Nekromantik* this isn't.

Flesh and the Beast *see* **There Was a Little Girl**

Flesh and the Bloody Terror (1988)

Production company unknown [HK]
DIR: Teddy Robin Kwan and Yu Kong Yun; PRO: Wallace Cheung; SCR: Fong Ling Ching and Lee Ten; DOP: Bob Thompson
STR: Juk-Si Cheng and Fong Ling Ching
AKA: *Beasts*
Approximately 72m; Color XXX

Five young people on a camping excursion are accosted by a band of thieves. One girl is brutally and graphically raped, and her brother is killed trying to pursue the perpetrators. None too happy, their father goes after the gang members, knocking them off in bloody and sometimes inventive ways.

Flesh and the Bloody Terror is a typical rape/revenge potboiler that borrows elements from *Last House on the Left* (1972) and its progeny. Production values, though, are not much better than what can be found in most chop socky fare. But don't worry about having to sit through an hour and a half of obnoxious dubbing, because the sound editors decided to drown out most of the dialogue with '80s pop music pilfered from these shores. What's surprising is that one of the directors behind *Flesh and the Blood Terror* is Yu Kong Yun (*aka* Dennis Yu), the man behind *Xiong Bang* (1981), an enjoyable and fairly well written supernatural flick.

The reason for the hardcore rating is the aforementioned rape scene that—although it depicts no intercourse—does show some explicit finger penetration, as well as one of the rapist's very erect penises. (The editing during and after this particular scene is unusually jumpy, leading me to believe that there may have been even *more* footage, probably hardcore as well, but I have nothing to substantiate this.)

I don't know about you, but this is definitely not *my* idea of entertainment.

Flesh Eater (1989)

H&G Films Ltd. [US]
DIR: S. William Hinzman; PRO: S. William Hinzman; SCR: S. William Hinzman and Bill Randolph; DOP: Simon Manses; EXP: David Gordon; MFX: Gerald Gergely; MUS: Erica Portnoy
STR: Charis Kirkpatrick Acuff, David Ashby, Lutz Bacher, Rik Billock, Allan T. Bross, Chris Bross, Eileen E. Carper, Dean A. Custozzo, Matthew C. Danilko, Kristy Dettore, Adena Dodds, Karen L. Gergely, Michael Gornick, Heidi Hinzman, Mark Hinzman, S. William Hinzman, Bill Ingalls, Dave Kelly, Jim Kelly, Barry Kessler, Kevin Kindlin, Scott Knechtel, William Andrew Laczko, Tom Madden, Theresa Marie, Bonnie Mastandrea, Denise Morrone, John Mowod, Dan Perko, David Phelps, Paula Recchio, Kathleen Marie Rupnik, James J. Rutan, Andrew Sands, Steven B. Sands, Lisa Smith, Carl W. Sodergren, David A. Sodergren, Jackie Sodergren, Susan Marie Spier, Mark Strycula, Vincent Suryinski, Taryn Thomas, Michelle Vensko, Leslie Ann Wick and Steve Yount
AKA: *Zombie Nosh*; *Revenge of the Living Zombies*
Approximately 85m; Color
VHS1: *Revenge of the Living Zombies* [MAG; 85m]; VHS2: *Zombie Nosh* [VIP; 86(85)n]

A stump puller discovers a sealed tomb, guarded by a pentagram-carved stone and the inscription "This evil which will take flesh and blood from thee and turn all ye unto evil." (Truly scary, that.) Of course, he opens it up and—Surprise!—it's Bill Hinzman, wearing the same skivvies he sported as the lead zombie in George A. Romero's *Night of the Living Dead* (1968). Soon thereafter, a carload of stupid twenty-something teens wander into the fray, just waiting to be gobbled up by low-rent actors in white grease paint. The survivors are forced to find refuge in an abandoned farmhouse, of all things, but the supernatural contagion eventually makes it way to more densely populated areas, leaving them nowhere to turn.

There's nothing that *isn't* lame about this backyard take on the film in which Hinzman had taken part twenty-one years prior. The zombies grunt and growl with the worst of them, although they prefer to do most of their bloodstained handiwork off screen. (A gut-muncher without the prerequisite over-the-top gore will surely disappoint those viewers who usually search out this fare.) There's also an obligatory shower scene, funny in that during a skirmish immediately thereafter, the girl's robe refuses to budge, exposing nothing; in what has to be a joke, Bill Hinzman makes a point of tearing the stubborn clothing off of the young woman once he manages to kill her. Aside from this, the only high points are a cheesy animation title sequence, and a scene in which a little girl dressed as an angel for Halloween gets bitten by a trick-or-treating Hinzman. (I laughed, anyway.)

A Bill Hinzman vanity production.

The Fly (1986)

Brooksfilms [US]
DIR: David Cronenberg; PRO: Stuart Cornfeld; SCR: David Cronenberg and Charles Edward Pogue; DOP: Mark Irwin; MFX: Chris Walas; SFX: Louis Craig and Ted Ross; VFX: Hoyt H. Yeatman; MUS: Howard Shore [Soundtrack from Varèse Sarabande]
STR: Joy Boushel, Leslie Carlson, George Chuvalo, Michael Copeman, David Cronenberg, Geena Davis, John Getz, Jeff Goldblum, Shawn Hewitt and Carol Lazare
Approximately 96m; Color
DVD1: *The Fly* [TCF; 96m; LBX]; VHS1: *The Fly* [CBS; 96m]

Matthew Brundle (Jeff Goldblum) is an eccentric scientist who discovers a means of teleportation; unfortunately for him, he's having some difficulty getting his invention to recognize the difference between flesh and inanimate objects. A writer for a science magazine (Geena Davis) takes a liking to the man while doing an exclusive on him, much to the chagrin of her boss-cum-ex-boyfriend. Eventually, the scientist irons the wrinkles out of his discovery, but runs into an unexpected snag after he decides to use himself as a guinea pig.

Probably David Cronenberg's most mainstream effort, this is an inventive, profound, and even quite—God forbid—*moving* take on the classic 1958 horror film of the same name. Wonderful performances, thought-provoking script, effective shocks ... the film's only weakness comes from the sad-looking title creature. (It not only doesn't live up to the promise of the remainder of the effects, it's actually quite detrimental when it comes to the viewer's suspension of disbelief. Chris Walas tried to make up for this with his sequel, with some success.) There are some "gross out" effects (for which reviewers like Leonard Maltin berated *The Fly*), but they are all perfectly acceptable within the context of the movie.

It may be a "sell-out" film, but at least Cronenberg proved he could even do *this* well.

The Fly II (1989)

Brooksfilms [US]
DIR: Chris Walas; PRO: Steven-Charles Jaffe; SCR: Frank Darabont, Mick Garris, Jim Wheat and Ken Wheat; DOP: Robin Vidgeon; EXP: Stuart Cornfeld; MFX: Dennis Pawlik and Joanne Smith; SFX: Chris Walas, Inc.; VFX: Available Light Ltd.; MUS: Christopher Young [Soundtrack from Varèse Sarabande]
STR: Pat Bernel, Gary Chalk, Harley Cross, John Getz, Jeff Goldblum, Saffron Henderson, Ann Marie Lee, Matthew Moore, Andrew Rhodes, Lee Richardson, Rob Roy, Eric Stoltz, William Taylor, Frank C. Turner, Jerry Wasserman and Daphne Zuniga
Approximately 105m; Color
DVD1: *The Fly II* [TCF; 96m; LBX;]; VHS1: *The Fly II* [CBS; 105m]; VHS2: *The Fly II* [TCF; 100m]

Picking up about, oh, nine months after the first film, *The Fly II* has the dream birth sequence from *The Fly* become a reality. (They have a stand-in for Geena Davis, though. Guess she thought she was above horror films by this point in time, or demanded too much money to return for all of three minutes.) Despite being removed from a chrysalis-looking egg, the child seems quite normal ... until the doctors realize the boy is growing at an accelerated speed, about four times the average. He becomes the pride and joy of Bartok Industries, and seems reasonably content with the situation (even picking up his father's experiments where he

left off) until he discovers their ulterior motives.

Although this film tries *really* hard not to be, it rarely amounts to anything more than a Hollywood sequel that has lost sight of its predecessor's intent. Still, it's a lot of fun, and even the shallow melodrama is painfully endearing. The only area where it may actually surpass the original's is in the effects department. Granted, Eric Stoltz' transformation make-up is below par, but the monster—as stiff as it may be—is a hell of a lot more menacing than the one in *The Fly*, as it doesn't look quite so much like a dime-store novelty. The sequel is also considerably gorier, although all of this is relegated to the end. (A nasty elevator "accident," and a nauseating meltdown highlight the bloodier proceedings.) Of course, the focus on effects probably has something to do with the fact that *The Fly II* is the directorial debut of Chris Walas, a veteran effects artist who contributed his talents to the first film.

Follia Omicida *see* **L'Ossessione Che Uccide**

Food of the Gods—Part 2 *see* **Gnaw—Food of the Gods II**

Forbidden World (1982)

New World Pictures [US]
DIR: Allan Holzman; PRO: Roger Corman; SCR: Tim Curnen; DOP: Timothy Suhrstedt; MFX: John Carl Buechler and Don Oliviera; SFX: Steve Neill, Dennis Skotak and Robert Skotak; VFX: Deborah Gaydos
STR: Michael Bowen, June Chadwick, Linden Chiles, Dawn Dunlap, Fox Harris, Raymond Oliver, Don Oliviera, Scott Paulin and Jesse Vint

AKA: *Mutant*
Approximately 82m; Color
VHS1: *Forbidden World* [EMB; 77m]

This is, simply put, one of the *grosser Alien*-inspired knock-offs. (To give credit where credit's due, though, it's more of a throwback to '50s B-science fiction horror than its predecessor.) Apparently taking its cue from the word-of-mouth popularity of said film's infamous chest-bursting scene, *Forbidden World* runs with the concept and sees just how far it can go with the gross-out effects. The creature itself is—at best—fair to middling, but all of the effects work is drenched in so much stage blood that it can't help but make the grades.

Production peaks include some pretty impressive post–*Star Wars* outer space effects, and exhaustive bouts of machine gun editing. On the downside, the passable actors are given a script that would put a strain on seasoned professionals, and the grating '50s influenced score only drives in the point that *Forbidden World* is nothing but a contrived updating of the selfsame pictures. There is also a surprising abundance of gratuitous nudity, which—although adding to the overall sleaze quotient—seems awfully out of place.

If you like alien critter flicks, and you're willing to put your brain on hold for a while, check it out.

The Forest (1981)

Wide World of Entertainment [US]
DIR: Donald M. Jones; PRO: Donald M. Jones; SCR: Evan Jones; DOP: Stuart Asbjornsen; EXP: Frank Evans; MUS: Richard Hieronymus and Alan Oldfield
STR: Marilyn Anderson, John Batis, Steve Michael Brody, Becki Burke, J.L. Clark, Tony Gee, Donald M. Jones, Jeanette Kelly, Stafford Morgan, Corky Pigeon, Dean Russell, Elaine Warner and Ann Wilkinson
AKA: *Terror in the Forest*
Approximately 85; Color
VHS1: *The Forest* [PRI; 90(85)m]; *The Forest* [SHV; 90(85)m]
ADL: *If You Come to the Woods, You Might Be the Meal*

While *The Forest* is thoroughly contrived, and it deluges the viewer with inane dialogue, you may be a tad disappointed to find out that these are the film's finer points. (That and the fact it has the look and feel of a 1970s live-action Disney flick.) *The Forest* is painfully conventional slasher fare about dumb kids in the woods being killed by an unseen killer (as if I needed to hum a few bars). Even if this sucker shows up on late-night TV, I suggest you change the channel

Video box art for *The Forest* (1981), Prism Entertainment.

unless you're suffering from a severe bout of insomnia.

The most surprising revelation in this ineffectual shocker was discovering that it was helmed by the same man responsible for such exploitation "classics" as *Schoolgirls in Chains* (1973) and *The Love Butcher* (1975). Geez, what happened to the guy?

Forest of Fear *see* **The Blood Eaters**

Forever Evil (1987)

B&S Productions [US]
DIR: Roger Evans; PRO: Jill Clark; SCR: Freeman Williams; DOP: Horacio Fernandez; EXP: Bill F. Blair and Betty S. Scott; MFX: J.C. Matalon and Nightmares International; VFX: Roger Evans; MUS: Rod Slane
STR: Marcy Bannor, David James Campbell, Karen Chatfield, Jon Cox, James Ebdon, Kayve Glasse, Richard Hamner, Tracey Huffman, Howard Jacobsen, Diane Johnson, Kent Johnson, Jeffrey Lane, Susan Lunt, Polly MacIntyre, Red Mitchell, Dana Ryder, Charles Trotter, Barbara Williams, Freeman Williams, Natalie Williams and Richard Zamecki
Approximately 110m; Color
VHS1: *Forever Evil* [UHV; 107(110)m]
ADL: *It Is Evil Beyond Time and Imagination ... Forever Watching ... Waiting ... Killing!*

A group of friends on a weekend outing find themselves picked off by an unseen entity with glowing eyes and its zombie servant. A lone survivor teams up with a woman who went through a similar ordeal, and they find themselves entrenched in a netherworldly conspiracy being carried out by the cult of Yog Kothag.

Although it starts out as an ineffectual *Evil Dead* knock-off (there's even a manhandling tree thrown in for good measure), *Forever Evil* quickly switches gears, owing more to H.P.

Lovecraft's timeless pulp horrors than Raimi's no-budget shocker. Non-formulaic, with an above-average script, the film is dragged down by the abundance of booga booga shocks, tacky visual effects, and a zombie which is nothing more than someone sporting a $19.95 Halloween mask. There are some passable gore effects, the highlight being an evisceration that initiates the carnage; unfortunately, the effects used during a number of dream sequences relating to the selfsame act are pretty damn poor.

Not great, nor even very good, but just interesting enough to keep the viewer from finding something *constructive* to do.

Formation of a Ghost *see* **Shiryo No Wana**

La Fossa del Terror *see* **Dead Pit**

Fou à Tuer *see* **Crawlspace**

Frayeurs *see* **Paura nella Città dei Morti Viventi**

Freak *see* **The Being**

Freaky Fairy Tales *see* **Deadtime Stories**

Friday the 13th (1980)

Georgetown Productions Inc. [US]
DIR: Sean S. Cunningham; PRO: Sean S. Cunningham; SCR: Victor Miller; DOP: Barry Abrams; EXP: Alvin Geiler; MFX: Tom Savini; MUS: Harry Manfredini
STR: Willie Adams, Kevin Bacon, Laurie Bartram, Peter Brouwer, Ronn Carroll, Harry Crosby, Rex Everhart, Sally Anne Golden, Walt Gorney, Debra S. Hayes, Adrienne King, Dorothy Kobs, Ari Lehman, Ron Millkie, Robbi Morgan, Mark

Nelson, Betsy Palmer, Ken L. Parker, Mary Rocco and Jeannine Taylor
AKA: *Vendredi 13* [Friday the 13th]; *Viernes 13* [Friday the 13th]; *Vrijdag de 13de* [Friday the 13th]
Approximately 95m; Color ✬✬✬
DVD1: *Friday the 13th* [PHV; 95m; LBX]; VHS1: *Friday the 13th* [PHV; 93(95)m]; VHS2: *Friday the 13th* [WAR; 83m]

Since I've got eight more of these suckers to watch and review, I'm avoiding anything extraneous or superfluous, so here's your synopsis. Camp Crystal Lake, 1958, closed after two counselors are killed while screwing around. Twenty-two years later, camp reopened. More counselors. More deaths.

This is the sucker that helped kick off the slasher genre, as well as establish the formula and each and every plot device employed by such films. Of course, similar blame can be laid at *Halloween*'s feet, although Carpenter's film predated *Friday the 13th*, and didn't dwell on gratuity like its younger sibling. And without the gratuity, most slasher films have nothing else to offer, so...

In the over twenty years since *Friday the 13th* was released, it has spawned nine sequels, has inspired countless knock-offs, and has made Jason Vorhees a household name, making him second only to Freddy Krueger as the American bogeyman of choice in the 1980s. (What's funny is that Jason Vorhees was not the killer in the film that precipitated the franchise, and failed to show his ugly puss in the fifth installment as well.)

Sure, it's mindless stalk 'n' slash fare no matter how you look at it, but it's still more watchable than 99 percent of the dreck that followed in its

wake. Furthermore, Tom Savini's special effects still hold up fairly well, if only because—again—most everything done since has been sub-par.

Lest I forget to mention it, *Friday the 13th* marks the screen debut of Kevin Bacon. (Not that many of you probably care, but it's a bit of obligatory trivia that I can't forget to include lest *Leonard Maltin's Movie Guide* be one up on me. God forbid.) Next...

Friday the 13th—Part 2 (1981)

Georgetown Productions Inc. [US]
DIR: Steve Miner; PRO: Steve Miner and Dennis Murphy; SCR: Ron Kurz; DOP: Peter Stein; EXP: Lisa Barsamian and Tom Gruenberg; MFX: Carl Fullerton; SFX: Steve Kirshoff; MUS: Harry Manfredini
STR: Kirsten Baker, David Brand, Stu Charno, China Chen, Steve Daskawisz, John Furey, Warrington Gillette, Walt Gorney, Adrienne King, Marta Kober, Carolyn Lauden, Jack Marks, Tom McBride, Betsy Palmer, Jaime Perry, Bill Randolph, Tom Shea, Amy Steel, Lauren-Marie Taylor, Russell Todd, Jall Voight and Jerry Wallace
Approximately 86m; Color
DVD1: *Friday the 13th—Part 2* [PHV; 86m; LBX]; VHS1: *Friday the 13th—Part 2* [PHV; 86m]; VHS2: *Friday the 13th—Part 2* [PHV; 83m]

Taking its cue from the shock ending of *Friday the 13th*, Mrs. Vorhees' mongolitic son Jason is alive and well and living near Camp Crystal Lake, the site of the previous film's bloodbath. This sequel opens with the young woman who cut his dear old mum down in her prime finding the lady's desiccated head in her Frigidaire, and she's dispatched before the opening credits roll. (Of course, this is padded with about five minutes worth of footage from the first film, in case by chance the viewer missed the only worthwhile entry in the series.)

His mother seemingly avenged, it's back to his old stomping ground, with yet another group of teens ready to become lunchmeat at the hands of the most threadbare franchise to date.

Yes, if you've seen one *Friday the 13th* flick, you've pretty much seen them all, but after watching each film back to back (The horror! The horror of it all!), I'm surprised by the fact that the producers managed to make each and every entry worse than the last. The only real difference between this film and its predecessor is that there was some mystery as to the killer's identity in the first flick; here it's a given, making the slaughtering quite rote. (Of course, the gore isn't nearly as impressive either, as Savini didn't grace this film with his talents.) The edict of "sex = death" remains the linchpin of the series; although one can see why that was true when Mrs. Vorhees was exacting revenge here it is exposed as a cheap ploy to not only up the skin quotient, but to exploit the viewers' basest fears. Why bother building suspense the old fashioned way (i.e. hard work and innovation) when you can simply create a false sense of vulnerability? (This is one of the reasons why many a filmmaker insists on the obligatory shower scene … aside from the gratuity, of course.) Next…

Friday the 13th—Part III (1982)

Jason Productions Inc. [US]
DIR: Steve Miner; PRO: Frank Mancuso, Jr.; SCR: Martin Kitrosser and Carol Watson; DOP: Gerald Feil; EXP: Lisa Barsamian; MFX: Make-Up Effects Labs; SFX: Martin Becker; MUS: Harry Manfredini and Michael Zager
STR: Terry Ballard, Richard Brooker, Gloria Charles, Steve Daskawisz, John Furey, Annie Gaybis, Rachel Howard, David Katims, Dana Kimmell, Paul Kratka, Cheri Maugans, Terence McCorry, Charles Messenger, Steve Miner, Kevin O'Brien, Betsy Palmer, Catherine Parks, Jeffrey Rogers, Nick Savage, Tracie Savage, Gianni Standaart, Amy Steel, Steve Susskind, Perla Walter, David Wiley and Larry Zerner
AKA: *Friday the 13th 3-D*
Approximately 96m; Color [3-D]
DVD1: *Friday the 13th—Part III* [WAR; 96m; LBX]; VHS1: *Friday the 13th—Part III* [PHV; 96m]; VHS1: *Friday the 13th—Part III* [PHV; 91m]

By now the scriptwriters had honed their formula to a razor's edge, leaving nothing even remotely resembling a storyline. When *Friday the 13th—Part III* isn't playing by the book, it's exploiting the cheap shocks that completely hinge on the 3-D effects that accompanied the film's theatrical release. (And, no, they aren't far removed from those found in SCTV's *Dr. Tongue's House of 3-D*, if anyone in the audience remembers *that* spoof of 3-D films.) Besides this pathetic ploy, the only thing that differentiates *Part III* from the previous entry is a grating updating of the theme music that works a drum machine into the mix. So, if you must watch it, go ahead and mute it. No, I mean the whole film. Don't worry … you won't miss a thing.

I will give it credit, though, for what has to be the worst effects sequence to ever grace a *Friday the 13th* film (now *that's* a feat)—namely, Jason squeezing a victim's head until the unfortunate's eye pops out at the cameras, the wire it is attached to being more than a little obvious. Next…

Friday the 13th 3-D *see* **Friday the 13th—Part III**

Friday the 13th Part 4 *see* **Friday the 13th—The Final Chapter**

Friday the 13th—The Final Chapter (1984)

Friday Four Inc. [US]
DIR: Joseph Zito; PRO: Frank Mancuso, Jr.; SCR: Barney Cohen; DOP: João Fernandes; EXP: Lisa Barsamian and Robert M. Barsamian; MFX: Tom Savini; SFX: Reel EFX Inc.; MUS: Harry Manfredini
    STR: E. Erich Anderson, Judie Aronson, Kirsten Baker, Peter Barton, Kimberly Beck, Richard Brooker, Peter Brouwer, Ronn Carroll, Steve Daskawisz, Tom Everett, Rex Everhart, Corey Feldman, Joan Freeman, Lisa Freeman, John Furey, Thad Geer, Crispin Glover, Walt Gorney, Wayne Grace, Alan Hayes, Bonnie Hellman, Frankie Hill, Barbara Howard, Dana Kimmell, Adrienne King, William Kirby, Marta Kober, Paul Lukather, Bruce Mahler, Jack Marks, Tom McBride, Lawrence Monoson, Arnie Moore, Camilla More, Carey More, Betsy Palmer, Robert Perault, Jaime Perry, Antony Ponzini, Jeffrey Rogers, Gene Ross, Nick Savage, Abigail Shelton, Amy Steel, Lauren-Marie Taylor, Russell Todd, John Walsh, Ted White and Robyn Woods
AKA: *Friday the 13th Part 4*
Approximately 90m; Color
DVD1: *Friday the 13th—The Final Chapter* [WAR; 90m; LBX]; VHS1: *Friday the 13th—The Final Chapter* [PHV; 90m]; VHS2: *Friday the 13th—The Final Chapter* [PHV; 88m]

This one's *almost* got a story, but don't take that as a recommendation. Jason's corpse is (prematurely) taken to a morgue, and is resuscitated by the heavy breathing of two horny staff members nearby. Making his way back to Camp Crystal Lake, a trail of bodies in his wake, he meets his match in a young horror film geek (Corey Feldman) and his sister. And again, in case you missed the first three installments, footage of those films are dutifully included as well.

Having secured a target audience, this one attempts to placate the hardcore horror fans by not only giving innumerable nods to the genre (conveniently accommodated by our young hero's hobby), but by buying back the talents of Tom Savini. (Knowing the artist's dislike for the first film, you know it *had* to have been the money.) Aside from this, it's the same old equation. The only real point of interest is what has to be either some clever humor on the part of the screenwriter, or a knack for redundancy. During the last reel, everyone—and I mean *everyone*—is either thrown or they throw themselves out of a window. (Geez, even the family pooch does a slo-mo defenestration. Argento, eat your heart out.) Next...

Friday the 13th V—A New Beginning (1985)

Paramount Pictures [US]
DIR: Daniel Steinmann; PRO: Timothy Silver; SCR: David Cohen, Martin Kitrosser, and Daniel Steinmann; DOP: Stephen L. Posey; EXP: Frank Mancuso, Jr.; MFX: Martin Becker; SFX: Reel EFX Inc.; MUS: Harry Manfredini
    STR: Anthony Barrile, Suzanne Bateman, Dominick Brascia, Jr., Todd Bryant, Curtis Conaway, Juliette Cummins, Bob de Simone, John Robert Dixon, Corey Feldman, Jeré Fields, Tiffany Helm, Melanie Kinnaman, Richard Lineback, Carol Locatell, Ric Mancini, Ed Matthews, Tom Morga, Miguel A. Núñez, Jr., Corey Parker, Jerry Pavlon, Shavar Ross, Marco St. John, John Shepherd, Ron Sloan, Caskey Swaim, Mark Venturini, Debi Sue Voorhees, Vernon Washington, Chuck Wells, Ted White, Dick Wieand, Rebecca Wood and Richard Young
Approximately 92m; Color
DVD1: *Friday the 13th V—A New Beginning* [PHV; 92m; LBX]; VHS1: *Friday the 13th V—A New Beginning* [PHV; 92m]; VHS2: *Friday the 13th V—A New Beginning* [PHV; 87m]

A young man (the horror film geek from *Friday the 13th—The Final Chapter*) is institutionalized, and within only hours of his arrival—surprise!—a killing spree ensues. Of course, the viewer is made to think that our buggy hero and his violent temper are responsible, but that would be too obvious. (Now we know why these films stay away from anything remotely resembling a story; their pathetic displays of logic aren't equipped to deal with anything more complicated than "Jason kills.")

A New Beginning can only tout itself as such because of the lack of Jason's presence. Our readily disposable victims include a wide variety of tired stereotypes. There's Vinny and his greaser buddy, both looking like rejects from a Sha Na Na revival; Junior and his ma, a couple of inbred rednecks who—apparently—are the comedy relief; and the remainder of the characters can just as easily be pigeonholed by their color or upbringing. And not to disappoint the fans, the politics are the same: You have sex ... you die. You think about having sex ... you die. (You'd think the religious right would just *love* these pictures for the messages they impart.)

The film is not nearly as graphic as previous entries, so splatterpunks will probably find *A New Beginning* pretty disappointing. Of course, if the selfsame fans had half a brain, they wouldn't get their hopes up, regardless of the gore quotient.

I only have one question. What in Sam Hill is a hockey mask doing in that hospital room dresser? Next...

Friday the 13th Part VI—Jason Lives *see* **Jason Lives—Friday the 13th Part VI**

Friday the 13th Part VII—The New Blood (1987)

Friday Four Inc. [US]
DIR: John Carl Buechler; PRO: Iain Patterson; SCR: Manuel Fidello and Daryl Haney; DOP: Paul Elliott; MFX: Magical Media Industries Inc.; MUS: Harry Manfredini and Fred Mollin
STR: Diane Almeida, Jennifer Banko, Diana Barrows, Kimberly Beck, Jeff Bennett, Kevin Blair, Susan Blu, William Butler, Larry Cox, Darcy DeMoss, Corey Feldman, Tony Goldwyn, C.J. Graham, Staci Greason, Kane Hodder, Elizabeth Kaitan, Debora Kessler, Terry Kiser, Heidi Kozak, Lar Park Lincoln, Thom Mathews, Nancy McLoughlin, Michael Nomad, John Otrin, Delano Palughi, Jon Renfield, Michael Schroeder, Susan Jennifer Sullivan, Lauren-Marie Taylor, Craig Thomas and Ted White
Approximately 88m; Color
VHS1: *Friday the 13th Part VII—The New Blood* [PHV; 88m]; VHS2: *Friday the 13th Part VII—The New Blood* [PHV; 84m]

Like bad leftovers, Jason just keeps coming back. As if the series wasn't already inundated with enough senseless hokum, the screenwriters for this sucker decided to throw *Carrie* into the mix. Furthermore, this—like just about every other film in the godforsaken series—is padded out with clips from previous entries. Do they *really* think the viewers are that ignorant or ... oh, never mind.

Of note, Harry Manfredini does seem more inspired this time around, flexing his chops a bit with the series' trademarked score, but except for this and the supernatural subplot, it's more of the same old, same old. (Gosh darn, imagine that.)

The violence in this entry is actually quite restrained (on the insis-

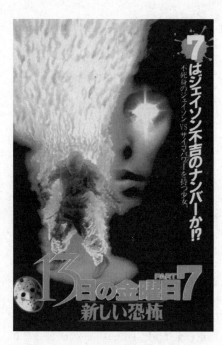

Japanese ad mat for *Friday the 13th Part VII—The New Blood* (1987).

tence of Buechler, who didn't want this to be another effects-laden slaughterfest), but—being a *Friday the 13th* film—I couldn't refuse its inclusion in this book even if my only justification for reviewing it was "for posterity." (Of course, if I could have found a way to avoid the whole lot of them, I *would* have. Biased? You bet your sweet ass I'm biased! Most people who have sat through the entire series did so because—egads—they *wanted* to.) Next...

Friday the 13th Part VIII— Jason Takes Manhattan (1989)

Horror Inc. [US]
DIR: Rob Hedden; PRO: Randolph Cheveldave; SCR: Rob Hedden; DOP: Bryan England; MFX: Jamie Brown; SFX:

Reel EFX Inc.; VFX: Effects Associates Inc.; MUS: Fred Mollin
STR: Ace, Roger Barnes, Michael Benyaer, Barbara Bingham, Vinny Capone, Martin Cummins, Gordon Currie, Jensen Daggett, Alex Diakun, Vincent Craig Dupree, Peggy Hedden, Fred Henderson, Saffron Henderson, Kane Hodder, Kelly Hu, David Longworth, Sharlene Martin, Timothy Burr Mirkovich, Warren Munson, Tiffany Paulsen, Amber Pawlick, Scott Reeves, Peter Mark Richman, Sam Sarkar and Todd Shaffer
Approximately 96m; Color
VHS1: *Friday the 13th Part VIII—Jason Takes Manhattan* [PHV; 96m]

Hey! Guess what? That shit for brains killing machine in a hockey mask is back! Having dispatched everyone within spitting distance of Camp Crystal Lake, Jason boards a cruise ship and makes his way to New York to boost the waning body count. In fear of being redundant, I'll save recounting the rest of the film for you. (Did I mention the rockers? How about the fact that Jason can apparently teleport now? Kill me now. Please ... just kill me now.)

Except for the change in scenery, nothing has changed. There is nothing impressive about this film, the eighth entry in what has to be the most insufferable series in horror cinema. *Jason Takes Manhattan* is the granddaddy of pointless exercises, its sole existence hinging on the old proverb "a fool and his money are soon parted." Lucky for us, many of these fools—the addle-minded splatterpunks who have supported the series throughout—weren't going to fall for it this time around, as profits forced producers to reassess their plans of making *Friday the 13th* an annual event. (Many were lured back in four years later, though, by the promise that *Jason Goes to Hell—The Final Friday* would be the last film. What makes *The Final Friday* any different than *The Final Chapter*? Absolutely nothing. Yet another Jason outing wormed its way into the theaters last year, if only to emphasize the point.) C'mon, enough is enough, people ... bury what's dead.

Fröhliche Weihnachten *see* **Don't Open Till Christmas**

From a Whisper to a Scream (1986)

Whisper-Scream Limited Partnership [US]

DIR: Jeff Burr; PRO: William Burr and Darin Scott; SCR: Jeff Burr, C. Courtney Joyner, and Darin Scott; DOP: Craig Greene; EXP: Bubba Truckadaro; MFX: Rob Burman; MUS: Jim Manzie

STR: Sergio Aguire, Nicos Argentiogorgis, Paul Barberi, Ashli Bare, Jahary Bennett, Martine Beswick, Ron Brooks, Tommy Burcher, Barney Burman, Miriam Byrd-Nethery, Harry Caesar, Rosalind Cash, Christopher Cobb, C.J. Cox, Rick Cox, George Davies, Whit Davies, Leon Edwards, David Ford, Clu Gulager, Bob Hannah, Mark Hannah, Katherine Kaden, Terry Kiser, Terry Knox, Didi Lanier, Megan McFarland, Cameron Mitchell, Justin Nowell, Tommy Nowell, Gordon Paddison, Vincent Price, Angelo Rossitto, Frank Shaheen, Nancy Shaheen, David Styncromb, Lawrence Tierney, Susan Tyrrell, Chastity Waters, Tim Wingard, Gene Witham and Tony Wright

AKA: *The Offspring*
Approximately 99m; Color
VHS1: *The Offspring* [IVE; 99m]

This cleverly disguised anthology utilizes a wraparound sequence starring Vincent Price as the uncle of a woman (Martine Beswick) sent to the chair for murder. He tells of the family's tainted bloodline, his examples being the four segments that comprise the film. The first involves a

man who has some grisly wet dreams about a co-worker; one thing leads to another and, well, you know. The second has a wounded criminal on the lam being saved by an old witch doctor (two hundred years old, to be precise). The crook is intent on discovering the man's secret of eternal life, and ends up doing his own interpretation of "Johnny Got His Gun." The third involves the owner of a carnival who holds power over its sideshow residents. A glass eater tries to escape his clutches, but he finds himself suffering from a delayed case of indigestion. The fourth is, for the sake of argument, little more than a Civil War–era *Children of the Corn* (1984).

From a Whisper to a Scream is, surprisingly, consistently interesting, trying and usually succeeding in offering original concepts, even though most take an EC-style approach. Although the gore starts out fairly mild, it gets nastier as the film progresses; unfortunately, some of the effects are too shoddy to be effective. The film's only other weakness is the really atrocious post-synch dubbing, something you would not expect from a movie of this caliber.

Of particular interest, though, is the sheer number of B-names involved. (Geez, it's almost stifling.) Even if you don't recognize the names, you're sure to recognize faces from innumerable other horror films.

From Beyond (1986)

Taryn Productions Inc. [It/US]

DIR: Stuart Gordon; PRO: Brian Yuzna; SCR: Dennis Paoli [Based on the short story "From Beyond" by Howard Phillips Lovecraft]; DOP: Mac Ahlberg; EXP: Charles Band; MFX: John Naulin and Mark Shostrom; SFX: John Carl Buechler

and Mark Shostrom; VFX: Anthony Dou-
blin; MUS: Richard Band [Soundtrack from
Enigma Records]
    STR: Regina Bleesz, Karen Christen-
feld, Jeffrey Combs, Barbara Crampton, Ken
Foree, John Leamer, Bruce McGuire, Andy
Miller, Carolyn Purdy-Gordon, Del Russel,
Ted Sorel, Bunny Summers and Dale Wyatt
    Approximately 85m; Color
    VHS1: *From Beyond* [VES; 85m]
    ADL: *Humans Are Such Easy Prey.*

An experiment to stimulate the
pineal gland by Dr. Edward Pretorius
(Sorel) goes awry; the police discover
the remains of his headless corpse,
and are forced to lock away his buggy
assistant Crawford (Combs). A young
psychologist with unorthodox views
(Crampton) decides to recreate the
experiment in order to get to the bottom of Crawford's apparent psychosis.
Come to find out, the "resonator" not
only awakens the supposedly dormant
pineal, it also causes an inter-dimen-
sional breach.

    In light of the success of *Re-An-
imator* (1985), the team of Gordon,
Yuzna and Band returned with several of their leads in tow to do another updating of a piece by cult pulp
writer H.P. Lovecraft. (Suffice it to
say, much artistic license is taken with
the source material, the most notable
being the "sexing up" of the writer's
habitually sexless work.) Although
not as much fun as its predecessor,
From Beyond actually benefits from its
darker, more serious tone. Not to say
that the film doesn't have its moments
of humor; it's hard to imagine a movie
starring Jeffrey "Herbert West"
Combs that didn't have some comedic
touches. (A scene where a crazed
Combs compares Pretorius getting his
head bitten off to that of a ginger-
bread man is priceless.)

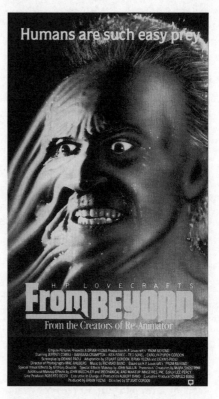

Video box art for *From Beyond* (1986),
Vestron Video.

    The special effects are a tad bet-
ter than what was found in *Re-Animator*, but they still leave much to be
desired. (The stop-motion animation
is particularly bad.) Some of the visuals are very reminiscent of John
Carpenter's *The Thing*, and there's a
fairly cool beastie that could be a relative to the sand worm from *Dune*
(1984).

    With Ken (*Dawn of the Dead*)
Foree as a wisecracking cop who has
a thing for dumplings.

Die Fürsten der Dunkelheit *see*
   Prince of Darkness

Futurekill (1984)

Magic Shadows [US]
DIR: Ronald W. Moore; PRO: John
H. Best and Gregg Unterberger; SCR:
Ronald W. Moore; DOP: Jon Lewis; EXP:
Don Barker; MFX: Robert A. Burns and
Kathleen Hagan; MUS: Robert Renfrow
STR: Joe Abner, Byron Blandford,
Cap Brooks, Marilyn Burns, Kate Caden-
head, Deborah Damm, Doug Davis, Paul
Deaton, Cathy Durkin, Barton Faulks,
Gabriele Folse, Charles Gruber, Elizabeth
Henshaw, Bill Johnson, Craig Kanne, Karin
Kay, Nick McFarran, David Moerbe, Edwin
Neal, Wade Reese, Rob Rowley, Rebecca
Scoggin, Jeffry Scott, Geren Smith, Jessie
Sublett and Alice Villarreal
AKA: *Asesino del Futuro* [Future
Killer]; *Night of the Alien*; *Splatter*
Approximately 83m; Color
VHS1: *Futurekill* [VES; 83m]
ADL: *In the Future—the Mutants Rule!*

Even though it could never
amount to anything more than a
scaled-down version of John Carpenter's *Escape from New York* (1981), *Futurekill* is still predictable drivel fueled by unrepentant stereotypes and
routine stalk 'n' slash proceedings.
Production values are substandard,
with abysmal continuity to help distract the viewer from its other failings. (Most of their monies were
probably expended when they hired
Swiss painter H.R. Giger to do the
art for the one-sheet, and even that is
pretty uninspired.)

A really sad return to the silver
screen for Edwin Neal and Marilyn
Burns, the hitchhiker and sole survivor from *The Texas Chain Saw Massacre*, respectively.

Galaxy of Terror (1981)

New World Pictures [US]
DIR: Bruce D. Clark; PRO: Roger
Corman; SCR: Bruce D. Clark; DOP:
Jacques Haitkin; MFX: Thom Shouse; VFX:

Tom Campbell and Brian Chin; MUS:
Barry Schrader
STR: Edward Albert, Bernard Behr-
ens, Jack Blessing, Robert Englund, Sid
Haig, Zalman King, Erin Moran, Taaffe
O'Connell, Mary Ellen O'Neill, Ray Wal-
ston and Grace Zabriskie
AKA: *Mindwarp—An Infinity of Ter-
ror*; *Planet of Horrors*; *Planeta del Terror*
[Planet of Terror]; *Quest*
Approximately 85m; Color
VHS1: *Galaxy of Terror* [EMB; 85m]
ADL: *Hell Has Just Been Relocated.*

Riding the coattails of *Alien* and
the resulting slew of sci-fi/horror
crossbreeds, *Galaxy of Terror* differs in
that it doesn't rely upon a single BEM
for ninety minutes of mayhem, and
instead draws its inspiration from
such films as *Forbidden Planet* (1956).
After a healthy introduction that
mimics the opening scenes of Ridley's
trend-setting film (a crew of space-
farers land on a desolate planet and
stumble across artifacts of a long-
since-dead civilization), most similarities end.

Using the transubstantiated fears
of the crew as a trip-hammer to numerable exotic, violent (and often
ludicrous) deaths, the film spends
whatever time remaining trying to
shamefacedly cover up the obviously
contrived proceedings with forced
characterization and pseudo-mystical
philosophizing.

The cast—composed almost entirely of small screen has-beens and
B-film veterans—make an admirable
go of the situation. (Of special note
are Erin [*Happy Days*] Moran, Robert
Englund in a pre–Freddy Krueger appearance, and exploitation favorite
Sid Haig.) Generally, the effects are
passable, but the film does benefit
greatly from some nicely composed

alien backdrops, which are extremely impressive considering the low budget. The filmmakers also succeed in building some atmosphere, but some of the scenes—one of a woman being raped by an overgrown mealworm springs immediately to mind—are unintentionally laughable and remind us that, yes, *Galaxy of Terror* never amounts to much more than a cheesy B-film.

The Gates of Hell *see* **Paura nella Città dei Morti Viventi**

Geek! (1986)

Overlook Films Ltd. [US]
DIR: Dean Crow; PRO: Maureen Sweeney; SCR: Charles Joseph; DOP: Jon Gerard; SFX: Phil Yeary; MUS: Skeet Bushor
STR: Brad Armacost, Leslie Denise, Dick Kreusser, Gary Lott, Christina Noonan, Jack O'Hara and Diane Sommerfield
AKA: *Backwoods*
Approximately 89m; Color ⁎⁎⁎
VHS1: *Backwoods* [CGV; 89m]
ADL: *Deep in the Backwoods the Darkness Can Kill!*

"It's a trip of terror when two campers cross paths with a reclusive mountain man named Eben. In the days that follow, the couple is slowly drawn into Eben's dark and troubled world—a world of memories and a secret too hideous to reveal. Intrigued by the mystery, Jamie and Karen wander through the woods, gradually coming to realize that someone, slowly and relentlessly is stalking them."

Geek! is a fairly nondescript exploitation effort that boasts some convincing performances but little else. The antagonist of the original title is—I can safely say without giving too much away—an inbred boy who, sure

enough, bears more than a little resemblance to the all–American sideshow freak that spawned the endearing and enduring slang term. The boy's father, a rather convincing hillbilly redneck, tells the unfortunate couple: "He's not a man. He's not a boy. He don't even pass for a critter." (That's because he bites the heads off livestock, you old fart.)

Backwoods is passably engaging, considering the simple-minded story and sparse cast, and it boasts just enough gore to pique a splatterpunk's interest, but it's nothing to hoop and holler about.

Die Geisterstadt der Zombies *see* **L'Aldilá**

Ghosthouse *see* **La Casa 3— Ghosthouse**

Gnaw—Food of the Gods II (1988)

Rose & Ruby [Ca]
DIR: Damian Lee; PRO: Damian Lee and David Mitchell; SCR: Richard Bennett and E. Kim Brewster; DOP: Curtis Petersen; EXP: Andras Hamori and Robert Misiorowski; MFX: David B. Miller; VFX: Ted Rae; MUS: Dennis Haines and Steve Parsons [Soundtrack from Filmtrax Records]
STR: Real Andrews, Jackie Burroughs, Deborah Cass, Eduardo Castillo, Michael Copeman, Paul Coufos, Kimberly Dickson, Colin Fox, Kate Healey, Ian Higgins, Stuart Hughes, Christina James, Alex Jefferies, Howard Jerome, Robert Kennedy, David Koyle, Geoffrey Link, David Lyle, Michael Malcolm, Sean Mitchell, Frank Moore, David B. Nichols, Arm Offe, Frank Pelegrino, Maxine Rennes, Lisa Schrage, Catherine Swing, Katherine Walkiewkz and Mike Werb
AKA: *After Food of the Gods*; *Food of the Gods—Part 2*
Approximately 86m; Color

VHS1: *Food of the Gods—Part 2* [IVE; 90(86)m]
ADL: *It's Their Party … You Can Die If You Want To.*

Young Bobby suffers from a growth deficiency … until he's given an experimental growth hormone. "Something went wrong," as he's now about ten feet tall (and still growing) and suffers from a severe case of potty mouth. (Remember the giant rubber hand from *Attack of the 50 Foot Woman*? It looks like someone salvaged it from another studio's prop department.) A botanist (yes, a *botanist*) is brought in to iron out the wrinkles; a group of animal activists muss about his lab, freeing a pack of infected rodents into the streets.

Besides being a fairly abysmal production, the scriptwriters clumsily exploit the public fears of both technology and animal activism. (The narrow-minded views of science rival that of old B-science fiction films, and the cardboard cutout anti-vivisectionists don't fare well either.) On the upside, we get a rat killer who thinks he's Clint Eastwood (the exterminator with no name?), synchronized rat swimming, gurney-cam, a great wet dream sequence that involves more than just a growing erection, and scads of half-eaten corpses.

If *Deadly Eyes* didn't sate your desire to see people torn to ribbons by hordes of oversized rodents, this half-baked horror flick should do the trick.

Gomia, Terror en el Mar Egeo *see* **Anthropophagus**

Goremet—Zombie Chef from Hell (1986)

Swanfilms [US]
DIR: Don Swan; PRO: Don Swan; SCR: Jeff Baughn, William Highsmith, and Don Swan; DOP: Don Swan; EXP: Loy Dellinger, William Highsmith, and Jon Lamphere; SFX: Warren Graham; MUS: Steve Cunningham, Dan Smith, and Don Swan
STR: Charles Barger III, Jeff Baughn, C.W. Casey, Cindy Castanio, Chuck Clubb, Loy Dellinger, Theo Depuay, Bob Highsmith, Johnny Howie, Kelley Kunicki, Alan Marx, Joy Merchant, Woody Mitchell, Michel O'Neill, Rocky Oliviero, Jeff Pillars, John Rodgers, Billy Scott, Dan Sinski, Tina Webster, Bob Whitman and Arnold William
Approximately 90m; Color

This 8mm no-budget H.G. Lewis–inspired trash is actually a commendable effort by an unrepentant fan of the genre, even though this outing appears to be a warm-up to a career that never got off the ground. (Maybe it's for the best, I don't know.) *Goremet—Zombie Chef from Hell* suffers from the usual detriments: slapdash editing, awful synth score, and annoying video effects. The gore, though (as primitive as it is), is laid on pretty gosh darn thick. (A scene involving a "headless water fountain" would have been right at home in Joel Reed's *The Incredible Torture Show* [1976], aka *Bloodsucking Freaks*.)

Story? Think Jackie Kong's *Blood Diner* with a supernatural twist. (Okay, so the living brain wasn't exactly grounded in reality, but when I say supernatural I mean as in … oh, why bother.)

Not an enriching experience by anyone's standards, but worthy of some kind of mention. (Had it been shot on video, I probably wouldn't have been nearly as forgiving.)

The Graduation *see* The Prowler

Grave of the Living Dead *see* L'Abîme des Morts-Vivants

The Grim Reaper *see* Anthropophagus

The Grim Reaper II *see* Rosso Sangue

Grito de Panico *see* Scared to Death

El Grito Silencioso *see* The Silent Scream

Großengriff der Zombies *see* Incubo sulla Città Contamina

Guardian of Hell *see* L'Altro Inferno

Halloween II (1981)

Dino de Laurentiis Corp. [US]
DIR: John Carpenter and Rick Rosenthal; PRO: John Carpenter and Debra Hill; SCR: John Carpenter and Debra Hill [Film novelization by Jack Martin, from Zebra Books]; DOP: Dean Cundey; EXP: Joseph Wolf and Irwin Yablans; SFX: Frank Munoz; MUS: John Carpenter and Alan Howarth [Soundtrack from Varèse Sarabande]
STR: Ana Alicia, Brian Andrews, Lucille Benson, Catherine Bergstrom, Anne Bruner, Robin Coleman, Howard Culver, Jamie Lee Curtis, Charles Cyphers, Nichole Drucker, Cliff Emmich, Leigh French, Gloria Gifford, Lance Guest, Adam Gunn, Roger Hampton, Alan Haufrect, Dennis Holahan, Jeffrey Kramer, Nancy Kyes, Pamela McMyler, Ty Mitchell, Tony Moran, Tawny Moyer, Donald Pleasence, Jonathan Prince, Ford Rainey, Kyle Richards, Leo Rossi, Pamela Susan Shoop, Ken Smolki, Nancy Stephens, Jack Verbois, Hunter von Leer, Bill Warlock, Richard Warlock and John Zenda
AKA: *Halloween II—Das Grauen Kehrt Zurück* [Halloween II—The Gray Returns]

Approximately 92m; Color
DVD1: *Halloween II* [GHV; 93(92)m; LBX]; *Halloween II* [UNI; 93(92)m; LBX]; DVD2: *Halloween II* [CAS; 87m]; VHS1: *Halloween II* [GHV; 93(92)m; LBX]; *Halloween II* [MCA; 92m]; *Halloween II* [UNI; 93(92)m]
ADL: *The Nightmare Isn't Over!*

Picking up right where the last film left off (one of the few sequels in film history ever to do so), Michael Myers is alive and well and still persistent about offing Jamie Lee Curtis, and anybody else who gets in his way. (The screenwriters even offer a fairly convincing reason as to *why* he's got his sights set on the poor teen.) Also reprising his role as Dr. Loomis is Donald Pleasence, apparently the only person who knows that Michael is "pure evil," and not just some nut in a William Shatner mask (which was altered this time around to avoid any messy legal problems—like it could have *hurt* Bill's career).

Although this sequel seemed pretty damn cool when I was, oh, about twelve, it's not nearly as impressive twenty-some years later. (Great, the first R-rated film I saw in a theater, and it had to be this sucker.) There are innumerable attempts to try and capture the tension of *Halloween*, but they are all in vain. Instead, *Halloween II* has more in common with the fungus inadvertently spawned by *Halloween* than its predecessor. (The filmmakers even replaced Carpenter's unnerving piano score with a "souped up" synth remix. Egads.) Outside of the premise that forms the crux of the film, nothing herein is plausible in any way. Everything is contrived solely for shock effect, with all logic thrown to the wayside. There is enough gore to help it qualify it as the splatter film *Halloween* wasn't ... but it wasn't worth the sacrifice.

Apparently, Carpenter wasn't happy about the way Rosenthal was handling it either, and stepped in to direct some of it himself. It didn't help.

Halloween II—Das Grauen Kehrt Zurück *see* **Halloween II**

Halloween III— Season of the Witch (1982)

De Laurentiis Entertainment Group [US]

DIR: Tommy Lee Wallace; PRO: John Carpenter and Debra Hill; SCR: John Carpenter and Debra Hill; DOP: Dean Cundey; EXP: Joseph Wolf and Irwin Yablans; MFX: Thomas R. Burman; SFX: Jon G. Belyeu; MUS: John Carpenter and Alan Howarth STR: Tom Atkins, Jadeen Barbor, Al Berry, Martin Cassidy, Loyd Catlett, Michael Currie, Paddi Edwards, Michael W. Green, Jeffrey D. Henry, Nancy Kyes, John McBride, Norman Merrill, Joshua Miller, Stacey Nelkin, Maidie Norman, Dan O'Herlihy, Patrick Pankurst, Bradley Schachter, Essex Smith, Garn Stephens, Ralph Strait, Jon Terry, Michelle Walker, Tommy Lee Wallace, Richard Warlock and Wendy Wessberg

AKA: *Halloween III—Die Nacht der Entscheidung* [Halloween III—The Night of the Decision]; *Halloween III—El Imperio de las Brujas* [Halloween III—The Empire of the Witches]

Approximately 96m; Color

DVD0: *Halloween III—Season of the Witch* [GHV; 98m; LBX]; DVD2: *Halloween III—Season of the Witch* [MIA; 92m]; VHS1: *Halloween III—Season of the Witch* [GHV; 96m]; *Halloween III—Season of the Witch* [MCA; 98(96)m]; *Halloween III—Season of the Witch* [UNI; 96m]; VHS2: *Halloween III—Season of the Witch* [MIA; 92m]

ADL: *The Night No One Comes Home.*

A man clutching a Halloween mask is accosted by some well-dressed

Video box art for *Halloween III—Season of the Witch* (1982), MCA Home Video.

men, but escapes and is hospitalized. Dr. Challis (Tom Atkins) is drawn into a conspiracy after the old man has his head turned into a bowling ball by one of his pursuers, who immediately immolates himself thereafter. It seems a Halloween mask company, Silver Shamrock Novelties, might have something to do with the inexplicable events that offer nods to *The Stepford Wives* (1975) and Asian horror films.

Much to the chagrin of many viewers, this installment in the series not only makes no mention of Michael Myers, but also has absolutely nothing to do with the other entries. Opinions differ, though. John

Carpenter wanted to avoid remaking the same film again, and made the wise choice of turning the franchise into something else. His idea was to produce a new, unrelated horror film every year for a Halloween release, their only ties being the holiday itself. Unfortunately, no one bought it, and the series was dropped until producers—seeing how profitable *Friday the 13th* and its sequels were—brought it back from the dead six years later.

Despite the absence of Michael, this entry is more of a Carpenter film than any other sequel. Even though he didn't helm this one, it bears his mark on everything, from the staging and camerawork that evokes all of his previous efforts, to the effectively droning score that is reminiscent of his and Alan Howarth's work on *The Thing*. *Halloween III* is even successful in creating some of the selfsame tension the first film generated, in spite of the illogical contrivances and precarious hokum. We'll even excuse Carpenter patting himself on the back when a clip of *Halloween* is shown on television and advertised as "the Immortal Classic."

Of course, after all is said and done, if there's any one thing the viewer will remember, it's the nerve-wracking Silver Shamrock jingle, sung to the tune of "London Bridge Is Falling Down" and played ad infinitum (or would that be "ad nauseum?").

Halloween III—Die Nacht der Entscheidung *see* **Halloween III—Season of the Witch**

Halloween III—El Imperio de las Brujas *see* **Halloween III—Season of the Witch**

Halloween 4—The Return of Michael Myers (1988)

Trancas International [US]
DIR: Dwight H. Little; PRO: Paul Freeman; SCR: Alan B. McElroy; DOP: Peter Lyons Collister; EXP: Moustapha Akkad; MFX: Magical Media Industries Inc.; SFX: Larry Fioritto; MUS: Alan Howarth [Soundtrack from Varèse Sarabande]
STR: Karen Alston, Nancy Borgenicht, Jordan Bradley, Robert Conder, Richy Cumba, Stephanie Dees, Walt Logan Field, Carmen Filpi, Michael Flynn, Don Glover, Ellie Gottwald, Danielle Harris, Ron Harrison, Eric Hart, David Jensen, Sasha Jenson, Richard Jewkes, Rand Kennedy, Kathleen Kinmont, Harlow Marks, M.I. McDonnell, Raymond O'Connor, Jeff Olson, Michael Pataki, Donald Pleasence, Danny Ray, Leslie L. Rohland, Gene Ross, Beverly Booth Rowland, Michael Ruud, Don Ré Sampson, Tami Sanders, Beau Starr, Richard Stay, George Sullivan and George P. Wilbur
Approximately 88m; Color
DVD1: *Halloween 4—The Return of Michael Myers* [ABE; 90(88)m]; DVD2: *Halloween 4—The Return of Michael Myers* [DIG; 84m]; VHS1: *Halloween 4—The Return of Michael Myers* [ABE; 90(88)m]; *Halloween 4—The Return of Michael Myers* [CBS; 88m]

Pleasence is once again stalking our favorite shoe-in for William Shatner, and is given ample opportunity to recite the same damn monologue he's been reciting for three films now. ("He is *evil* ... pure *evil*.") Michael is on his way back to Haddonfield, but he's not looking for just anyone of which to make short work; he has a purpose. (And apparently it's not just to rake in the profits of one of horror's longest-running franchises, although this seems more palpable than that given by the screenwriters.)

To give credit where it's due, there is some attempt to stay true to

Carpenter's original vision. Regardless, *Halloween 4* is just what you would expect: a redundant sequel that offers nothing new to the formula inadvertently established in the decade prior. Besides the expected reiteration, *Halloween 4* suffers from some hefty drawbacks. Most distracting is that the viewers' suspension of disbelief is taxed beyond belief. How did Michael and Dr. Loomis survive the gas explosion that punctuated *Halloween 2*? What happened to Jaime Lee Curtis' character, and why is Michael content with going after her lineage? And for moving at a snail's pace, Michael sure gets around, doesn't he? (Me, I imagine him running like the dickens whenever anyone's back is turned, trying to make up for lost time. Of course, seeing him out of breath might not be good for his image.) Without the logic that was applied to the first film—as tenuous as it may have been—anything remotely resembling suspense is gone, replaced by—at best—a few cheap shocks. Also of note is the insincere ending that tries to bring the series full circle, and would have been a pathetic attempt even if the franchise had ended with this installment.

Gore is minimal, almost nonexistent (much like in the first), but for reasons of both posterity and consistency, I have included it here as well.

Halloween 5—The Revenge of Michael Myers (1989)

Trancas International [US]
DIR: Dominique Othenin-Girard; PRO: Ramsey Thomas; SCR: Shem Bitterman, Michael Jacobs and Dominique Othenin-Girard; DOP: Robert Draper; EXP: Moustapha Akkad; MFX: KNB EFX Group; SFX: Greg Landerer; MUS: Alan Howarth [Soundtrack from Varèse Sarabande]
STR: Karen Alston, Steve Anderson, Jay Bernard, Betty Carvel, Jonathan Chapin, Frank Como, Stanton Davis, Troy Evans, John Gilbert, Tamara Glynn, Ellie Gottwald, Danielle Harris, Tom Jacobsen, Frank Kanig, Wendy Kaplan, Jeffrey Landman, Russ McGinn, Angela Montoya, Jack North, Jon Richard Platten, Donald Pleasence, Fenton Quinn, Max Robinson, Harper Roisman, Don Ré Sampson, Donald L. Shanks, Beau Starr, David Ursin, Matthew Walker and Patrick White
Approximately 98m; Color
DVD1: *Halloween 5—The Revenge of Michael Myers* [ABE; 98m; LBX]; DVD2: *Halloween 5—The Revenge of Michael Myers* [DIG; 97m]; VHS1: *Halloween 5—The Revenge of Michael Myers* [ABE; 98m; LBX]; *Halloween 5—The Revenge of Michael Myers* [CBS; 96m]
ADL:*Michael Lives ... and This Time They're Ready!*

This far into the series, *Halloween 5* has absolutely nothing going for it. All traces of Carpenter and his influence are long gone. Half of the cast from *Halloween 4* is on hand to add some continuity, but most of them are dispatched early on, and the few remaining can do little to save this sinking ship. (Even the token kid, fairly innocuous in the previous entry, begins to wear on one's nerves this time out.) There are some major discrepancies between the two films, which the screenwriters try to iron out by rewriting the facts bridging the two. (Did they honestly think that no one would recognize the changes, and that they would fall for the shoddy manipulation? Just because Raimi somehow got away with it in the *Evil Dead* films doesn't mean that they have the right to change their minds between productions.)

Even worse, *Halloween 5* adheres

to every slasher convention in the book. The addition of gore this time around only emphasizes the similarities between this installment and the *Friday the 13th* series, as does the open ending that avoids anything remotely resembling a conclusion. To make matters worse, the screenwriters saw fit to introduce a "mystery" character whose purpose is never revealed, obviously a cheap lure to keep viewers from passing over the inevitable sequel. Those viewers actually suckered in by this ploy were probably none to happy to find that the follow-up threw this subplot away altogether.

Halloween Party *see* **Night of the Demons** (1987)

Happy Birthday to Me (1980)

The Birthday Film Company Inc. [Ca] DIR: J. Lee Thompson; PRO: John Dunning and André Link; SCR: Timothy Bond, Peter Jobin and John C.W. Saxton; DOP: Miklos Lente; MFX: The Burman Studio; MUS: Bo Harwood and Lance Rubin
STR: Sharon Acker, Melissa Sue Anderson, Damir Andrei, Jack Blum, Tracy Bregman, Griffith Brewer, Matt Craven, Lawrence Dane, Louis del Grande, Gina Dick, Lesleh Donaldson, David Eisner, Glenn Ford, Terry Haig, Frances Hyland, Alan Katz, Nick Kilbertus, Michel Rene Labelle, Lisa Langlois, Ron Lea, Walter Massey, Steven Mayoff, Stephanie Miller, Earl Pennington, Maurice Podbrey, Richard Bebiere, Karen Stephen, Jérôme Tiberghien, Vlasta Vrana, Murray Westgate and Lenore Zann
Approximately 110m; Color
VHS1: *Happy Birthday to Me* [RCA; 108(110)m]
ADL: *Six of the Most Bizarre Murders You Will Ever See.*

A young girl (*Little House on the Prairie*'s Melissa Sue Anderson) suffers from apparent blackouts following an accident where her mother is killed and she is forced to undergo experimental brain surgery. As her birthday approaches, her rich friends begin dropping like flies.

Despite a good cast, some interesting twists, and above-average production values, *Happy Birthday to Me* is flat and rarely engaging splatter fare. (It may be better than 90 percent of the slasher dreck made in the last twenty years, but that *still* isn't saying a heck of a lot.) The murders are quite gruesome, but not extremely gory, boasting a few ingenious murders which have since become mainstays in stalk 'n' slash cinema. (This, of course, includes the stock party scene, complete with corpses and party hats.)

As a horror film, it barely passes muster; as an almost-two-hour-long drama, it doesn't fare much better.

Hardcover *see* **I, Madman**

The Haunting of Hamilton High *see* **Hello Mary Lou—Prom Night II**

Das Haus an der Friedhofsmauer *see* **Quella Villa Accanto al Cimitero**

Headhunter (1988)

Gibraltar Releasing Organization Inc. [US]
DIR: Francis Schaeffer; PRO: Jay Davidson; SCR: Len Spinell; DOP: Hans Kühle; EXP: Joel Levine; MFX: Elaine Alexander and Kevin Brennan; MUS: Julian Laxion
STR: Isaac Albert, John Barrett, June Chadwick, Wayne Crawford, John Fatooh, Steve Kanaly, Helena Kriel, Ted le Platt, Kay Lenz, Anna Molefe, Gordon Mulholland, Jim Neill, Frank Notaro, Al Roberts, Barrie Saint Clair, Robert Lai Thom and Sam Williams
Approximately 91m; Color
VHS1: *Headhunter* [AHE; 92(91)m]
ADL: *Black Magic. Pure Terror.*

A Nigerian tribe pisses off one of their devil gods, so he goes after the members, following the last of them to Miami and exacting revenge in a predictably bloody fashion. The police are stumped (pun certainly intended) by a series of murders where witch doctors and the aforementioned refugees are found with their noggins lopped off; two officers finally glean the above information from some of the survivors, and go about trying to crack the case without any support from their skeptical superiors.

This laid back horror film is actually quite successful as a drama; thanks to some wonderful performances and an engaging script, it is easy to identify with the characters involved. As a horror film, though, *Headhunter* is sorely lacking, as the director is much more adept with the low-key proceedings than the tacky, obligatory shocks that occasionally punctuate the film. (Had the filmmakers at least done away with the poorly executed decaps and gauche sparkler effects, it would have been easier to take it a little more seriously.) There are some tense moments, but these rarely involve the title boogeyman, and instead hinge on the somber atmosphere that permeates the remainder of the film.

With clips from Robert Clarke's *The Hideous Sun Demon* (1959). Sadly, the make-up effects from *that* film are far superior to what can be found herein.

Heartstopper (1988)

Thinker Productions Inc. [US]
DIR: John A. Russo; PRO: Charles A. Gelini; SCR: John A. Russo; DOP: John Rice; EXP: Robert A. Donell and Charles A.

Gelini; MFX: Tom Savini; VFX: Rick Catizone; MUS: Paul McCullough
STR: Bob Abbott, Chuck Aber, Jonathan Adams, Maria Barney, Deanna Bennett, Greg Besnak, Carla Bianco, Christopher Bill, Bill Danzel III, June de Phillips, William Duncan, Degan Everhart, Steve Figore, Pam Fischer, Greg Funk, Lou Grippo, John Hall, Sylvia Hatchin, Kevin Kindlin, Tommy la Fitte, Tammy Mader, Wolfgang McClosey, Susan McGregor-Laine, Sheila McKenna, Bud Mellot, Ana Munoz, Bingo O'Malley, Michael J. Pollard, Ken Reid, Richard Rifenstein, Frank Salerno, Peggy Sanders, Lia Savini, Tom Savini, Tom Schaller, Jim Sharp, Glen Shorter, Paul Stockhausen, Dianne Ulan, John C. Wanamaker, Jaiyson White and Moon Unit Zappa
Approximately 97m; Color
VHS1: *Heartstopper* [TEM; 96(97)m]

Pittsburgh, 1776: Dr. Benjamin Latham is hanged for trumped up charges of witchcraft. Over two hundred years later a little girl dies under mysterious circumstances, the work of a vampire—the aforementioned scapegoat. But it seems he's not alone, as a copycat killer is making the rounds, screwing the corpses to boot. A pretty nice guy for being a bloodsucker, Dr. Latham is disgusted by the killer's work and decides to track him down on his own time.

Even if the components are all fairly traditional, *Heartstopper* offers a fairly unconventional storyline. (Unfortunately, it tries offering some pseudo-scientific explanations for vampirism that come out sounding more outlandish than the hokum we've come to accept.) There is also some stilted dialogue, obtrusive voice-overs, a pandering metal soundtrack, and some tacky stop-motion animation, but it's still fairly engaging nonetheless.

Of course, with Tom Savini as

the resident effects artist, there is some graphic and unsettling effects work, even though it seems a little rote by his standards. (This is also one of the few times he's been given a starring role in a film; although adequate, one can see why he was—at least up until that point in time—relegated to supporting roles.)

Hell Night (1981)

BLT Productions Inc. [US]
DIR: Thomas de Simone; PRO: Bruce Cohn Curtis and Irwin Yablans; SCR: Randolph Feldman; DOP: Mac Ahlberg; EXP: Chuck Russell and Joseph Wolf; MFX: Kenneth Horn and Tom Schwartz; SFX: Court Wizard Productions; MUS: Dan Wyman
STR: Peter Barton, Linda Blair, Kevin Brophy, Cary Fox, Ronald Gans, Suki Goodwin, Gloria Heilman, Jenny Neumann, Hal Ralston, Jimmy Sturtevant and Vincent van Patten
AKA: *Noche Infenal* [Hell Night]
Approximately 101m; Color
DVD0: *Hell Night* [ABE; 102(101)m; LBX]; VHS1: *Hell Night* [ABE; 102(101)m] *Hell Night* [MHE; 100(101)m]; VHS2: *Hell Night* [ODY; 101m; LBX]
ADL: *Pray for Day*

Everyone's favorite head turner, Linda Blair, is a new pledge whose initiation involves spending the night in Garth Manor, a seemingly abandoned murder house. Turns out—surprise!—the mutant progeny of the last owner still reside there, and, no, they don't take too kindly to college coeds dropping in unannounced.

Hell Night is one of those early '80s stalk 'n' slash quickies that—although universally despised at the time, despite the fact they made money—is actually quite endearing in retrospect. (Of course, this may be in light of the dreck which continued to be churned out years thereafter.) Sure,

Video box art for *Hell Night* (1981), Media Home Entertainment.

everything's cued far in advance, and, sure, we know who the only survivor is before the initial credits finish rolling, and, sure, the gore is nothing we haven't seen before. And, sure, it doesn't have an original bone in its misbegotten little body, but there are some nice sets, and, okay ... so it has some nice sets. And cool one-sheet art.

Wait a minute; isn't there something missing? Nudity. *Hell Night* has *no* nudity. Really, how many slasher flicks involving teens doing illicit things by the light of the moon can you think of that have no skin? (No, *before* the MPAA got ahold of them? Yeah, thought so.) This wouldn't seem quite so strange if it hadn't been helmed by de Simone, an ex-porn filmmaker who used to direct under the name "Lancer Brooks." Maybe he adamantly avoided any nudity in this effort because he wanted to put his smutty past behind him. I say "adamantly" because anyone having sex in the film is fully clothed. Odd … really odd.

Mike Boom makes a cameo.

Hell of the Living Dead *see* **Inferno dei Morti-Viventi**

Hellbound—Hellraiser II (1988)

Film Futures [US]
DIR: Tony Randel; PRO: Christopher Figg; SCR: Peter Atkins; DOP: Robin Vidgeon; EXP: Clive Barker and Christopher Webster; MFX: Image Animation; SFX: Bob Keen; MUS: Christopher Young [Soundtrack from Crescendo Records]
STR: Simon Bamford, Imogen Boorman, Doug Bradley, Sean Chapman, Catherine Chevalier, Edwin Craig, Kenneth Cranham, Clare Higgins, William Hope, Deborah Joel, Ashley Laurence, Bradley Lavelle, Angus MacInnes, Oliver Parker, Oliver Smith, James Tillitt, Ron Travis, Nicholas Vince and Barbie Wilde
Approximately 98m; Color
DVD1: *Hellbound—Hellraiser II* [ABE; 99(98)m; LBX]; *Hellbound—Hellraiser II* [NWV; 93m]; DVD2: *Hellbound—Hellraiser II* [CCL; 89m; LBX]; VHS1: *Hellbound—Hellraiser II* [ABE; 107(98)m; LBX]; *Hellbound—Hellraiser II* [NWV; 93m]; *Hellbound—Hellraiser II* [SHV; 96m; R-Rated version]; *Hellbound—Hellraiser II* [SHV; 98m; Unrated edition]
ADL: *Time to Play*

Picking up where the original production left off, *Hellbound* offers (besides a slew of flashback sequences recycling footage from *Hellraiser*) a new—albeit temporary—addition to Barker's pantheon of hell-spawned sado-masochistic monks. (As con-

trived as the new member of the order may seem, he's downright charming when compared to what passed as cenobites in *Hellraiser III—Hell on Earth*.) Ashley Laurence is back, ready to be victimized once again, as is her stepmother (Clare Higgins), suffering from the selfsame skin condition that befell her lover—Ashley's uncle—in the first film. And—of course—so is Doug Bradley as Pinhead, the lead cenobite that has become the poster boy for the series.

The first half of the film manages to capture the same low-key dread that made *Hellraiser* a worthwhile horror film (thanks to Clive Barker's dark vision). Unfortunately, *Hellbound* becomes too ambitious for its own good, eventually sacrificing the gothic grandeur for comic book–style action. The film also suffers from some awkward dialogue that even the seasoned talents have difficulty pulling off, and an effects-laden "twist" ending that would have been better left on the cutting room floor. Still, despite its faults, it gives no indication as to just how far the franchise would fall in years to come. (Refer to *Hellraiser III—Hell on Earth* [1992] as to just how bad it would get. Or, better yet, avoid that film altogether.)

Not a bad sequel, considering the accomplishments of its predecessor, even though it falls short during the final reel.

Hello Mary Lou—Prom Night II (1987)

Simcon Limited in Trust [Ca]
DIR: Bruce Pittman; PRO: Peter Simpson; SCR: Ron Oliver; DOP: John Herzog and Brenton Spencer; EXP: Peter Haley and Peter Simpson; MFX: Nancy Howe; MUS: Paul Zaza

STR: Steve Atkinson, Lorretta Bailey, Michael Evans, John Ferguson, Marek Forysinski, Vincent Gale, Beth Gondek, Glen Gretsky, Kirk Greyson, Terri Hawkes, Deryck Hazel, Beverley Hendry, Michael Ironside, Howard Kruschke, Robert Lewis, Justin Louis, Wendy Lyon, Judy Mahbey, Paul McGaffey, Richard Monette, Larry A. Mussor, Joan Olsen, David Robertson, Dennis Robinson, Lisa Schrage, Brock Simpson, Jay Smith and Wendell Smith
AKA: *The Haunting of Hamilton High* Approximately 97m; Color
VHS1: *Hello Mary Lou—Prom Night II* [ABE; 97m]; *Hello Mary Lou—Prom Night II* [VIR; 97m]

Mary Lou Maloney is a good little Catholic slut who is caught bumping uglies with someone other than her date at the school prom. He retaliates with a vengeful prank, accidentally immolating her as she is about to be crowned prom queen. Thirty years later, a troubled teen accidentally invokes the spirit of the late tease who feels it is high time she gets the honor she rightfully deserved.

This unrelated sequel refuses to stray far from the usual possession/hokey-vengeance-from-beyond-the-grave subgenres. (And just so you can easily pin a date on it, the screenwriters also opted to include some hallucinatory Freddy-style happenings offered by way of cheesy dream sequences.) Some of the hokum works when kept low-key (in particular a devilish rocking horse that accosts our heroine), but the inevitable overkill imminently destroys any atmosphere.

Performances are sometimes a notch above the rest, thanks in part to the presence of Michael Ironside. (Having been typecast as the villain, here he plays the school principle, so he's not *too* far removed from his usual roles.) Gore is minimal, with most of

the *Carrie*-inspired mayhem ensuing during the finale. *Hello Mary Lou— Prom Night II* does depict the most flagrant abuse of hairspray, so viewers with good fashion sense and weak stomachs may want to keep their distance. (If teasing one's hair were made a crime, this actress would be given the chair.)

Ray Sager (Montag the Magician from H.G. Lewis' *The Wizard of Gore*) was a co-producer.

Hellraiser (1987)

New World Entertainment Ltd. [UK/US]
DIR: Clive Barker; PRO: Christopher Figg; SCR: Clive Barker [Based on the novella *The Hellbound Heart* by Clive Barker]; DOP: Robin Vidgeon; EXP: Mark Armstrong, David Saunders, and Christopher Webster; MFX: Bob Keen; MUS: Christopher Young
STR: Antony Allen, Dave Atkins, Frank Baker, Simon Bamford, Gay Baynes, Sharon Bower, Doug Bradley, Niall Buggy, Michael Cassidy, Sean Chapman, Leon Davis, Clare Higgins, Robert Hines, Grace Kirby, Ashley Laurence, Kenneth Nelson, Raul Newney, Oliver Parker, Andrew Robinson, Pamela Sholto, Oliver Smith and Nicholas Vince
AKA: *Puerta al Inferno* [Door to Hell] Approximately 93m; Color
DVD1: *Hellraiser* [ABE; 93m; LBX]; DVD2: *Hellraiser* [CCL; 90m; LBX]; VHS1: *Hellraiser* [ABE; 105(93)m]; *Hellraiser* [ABE; 118(93)m; LBX]; *Hellraiser* [NWV; 94(93)m]; VHS2: *Hellraiser* [CCL; 90m]
ADL: *He'll Tear Your Soul Apart.*

A pleasure seeker obtains a Lament Configuration, a puzzle box that—when solved—opens up a doorway to a dimension overseen by the Cenobites, a race of sado-masochistic demons. The man's brother and his family move into the selfsame house where he was abducted by the creatures, and accidentally brings him—well, *most* of him, anyway—back to Earth. Before he can completely reform himself (with the help of his brother's adulterous wife), the Cenobites realize their victim has given them the slip.

This is Clive Barker's directorial debut (as far as feature-length films are concerned), and is a stylish and imaginative splatter film whereupon he proves himself just as adept behind the camera as he is behind the keyboard. Based on one of his own short stories, *Hellraiser* is an excellent representation of the man's oeuvre, a film that exhibits both his penchant for dark fantasy and for extreme violence. His vision is brought to fruition by an excellent cast and some highly impressive effects. (Although bearing the mark of technical advances made in the last decade, the effects work also has a "juicy" quality that has hardly been seen since the '70s.) One of the monsters is pretty gosh darn cheesy, as is the silly ending, but it's still a remarkable independent horror film nonetheless.

Needless to say, this movie helped catapult Barker from underground icon to mainstream acceptance. Unfortunately for this film, the popularity of *Hellraiser*—or, more specifically, the popularity of the lead Cenobite quaintly referred to as "Pinhead"—demanded that it become a franchise. Although the sequel, *Hellbound—Hellraiser II*, is an admirable effort, the series went downhill immediately thereafter. (The term "scraping bottom" comes immediately to mind.)

Henry—Portrait of a Serial Killer (1986)

Fourth World Productions Inc. [US]
DIR: John McNaughton; PRO: Lisa Dedmond, Steven A. Jones and John McNaughton; SCR: Richard Fire and John McNaughton; DOP: Charlie Lieberman; EXP: Malik B. Ali and Waleed B. Ali; MFX: Jeffrey Lyle Segal; SFX: Lee Ditkowski; MUS: Ken Hale, Steven A. Jones and Robert McNaughton
STR: Waleed B. Ali, Tracy Arnold, Ray Atherton, Augie, Anne Bartoletti, Frank Coranado, Mary Demas, Donna Dunlap, Kristin Finger, Pamela Fox, Brian Graham, Cheri Jones, Ted Kaden, David Katz, Tom McKearn, Lily Monkus, Kurt Naebig, Monica Anna O'Malley, Anita Ores, Megan Ores, Sean Ores, Benjamin Passman, Rick Paul, Bruce Quist, Michael Rooker, John Scafidi, Flo Spink, Denise Sullivan, Erzsabet Sziky, Lisa Temple, Tom Towles, Peter van Wagner and Eric Young
Approximately 82m; Color
VHS1: *Henry—Portrait of a Serial Killer* [MPI; 90(82)m]
ADL: *He's Not Freddy, He's Not Jason ... He's Real*

Based loosely on the real life exploits of serial killer Henry Lee Lucas and cohort Otis Toole, this film focuses on the relationship between the killers and Otis' sister Becky, who moves in with the two while she attempts to sort out a failed marriage. Meanwhile, Henry lures his drug pushing pervo friend into his world of murder, showing his new accomplice the ropes, as it were. In a new city with no friends, Becky finds herself attracted to her brother's reserved roommate, mistaking his gentleman-like instincts for love.

A disturbing and thought-provoking film, *Henry—Portrait of a Serial Killer* is a bleak character study of an individual for whom violent murder is an everyday part of life, and for whom this is the only thing that offers

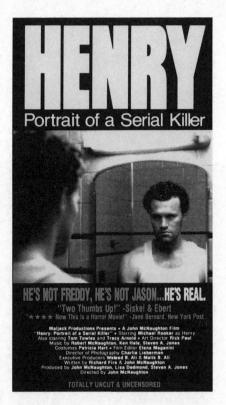

Video box art for *Henry—Portrait of a Serial Killer* (1986), MPI Home Video.

him any sort of comfort. His abusive childhood is touched upon, not to justify his compulsions but to offer some insight as to how real monsters are made.

Rooker is perfect as the title character, instilling a cold aloofness into the role that only occasionally allows for a protracted moment of seething rage. (When Rooker says, "My mama was a whore," one can't help but shudder.) Tom Towles is also unnervingly convincing as his sleazier-than-thou protégé Otis, who—despite an initial reluctance—seems to go through with the killings not out of necessity, like Henry, but for the sheer perverted pleasure it offers him. In both cases, neither performance falls prey to the Hollywood stereotype of a manic, wisecracking psycho that has become a staple in the genre.

Cinematically, the film is more than competent, considering the low budget, although an abundance of TV-style fades are ultimately distracting. There is some gore, relegated mostly to after-the-fact still-lifes of the carnage left in Henry's wake. (An effectively disturbing touch has the victims' pleas for help accompanying the aftermath.) One of the more unnerving scenes has the two videotaping their massacre of a suburban family, which Otis later watches obsessively, trying to vicariously relive the moment.

Due to its disturbing tone, the MPAA refused to award *Henry—Portrait of a Serial Killer* an R-rating, even though it was less graphic, and far less gratuitous, than many horror films being released at the time. It was finally released (in both unrated and R-rated editions) several years later, despite the fact it had received much fanfare from both fans and critics alike (if only because it showed that the genre was capable of producing something other than *Friday the 13th* clones).

The Hereafter (1981) *see* **L'Aldila**

The Hereafter (1983)
Dolan-Melsack [NZ]
DIR: Michael Melsack; PRO: Des Dolan; SCR: Michael Melsack; DOP: David Daynes; SFX: Roger Venton; MUS: Philip Love and Terry Mills
STR: Lindsey Allen, Al Greer, Yvette Gunter, Marina Lee, Steven Longhurst, Michael Lynch, Peter Neal, Catherine Row-

lands, David Slater, Neil Wilkinson, Harry Willowski and Wendy Young
Approximately 84m; Color
VHS1: *The Hereafter* [MOG; 84m]

A young man constantly harangued by his invalid father is finally freed of his obligations, thanks to a fatal accident. The old man's will specifies that his son must live on the estate if he is to see any of the vast inheritance. A shuttered room figures into the equation, once belonging to a great uncle who killed himself after his lover was drowned by his discerning family members. Oh, yeah ... there's a curse on the bloodline, due to the suicide.

Some table-tapping nonsense ensues, but wait! It's all a ploy to drive the young man away from his inheritance (a scenario much abused by low-rent shockers), but now that this plot device is out of the way—not even half of the film's running time having seen the light of day—it's time for *The Hereafter* to switch gears and get on with some real business.

The Hereafter is better than one would have expected, a fairly ambitious effort considering the budget. (Try your best to ignore the shitty make-up effects which grace the video box; there *is* a reason why it looks so bad, just so you know.) Production values are on par with most of the independent New Zealand flicks that make it to these shores (*Bad Taste*, *Body Melt*, etc.).

Unfortunately, *The Hereafter* isn't as outrageous as those films, and isn't nearly as interesting either. (The same can be said for the gore as well, which doesn't kick in until the last third of the film.)

Hide and Go Shriek (1987)

New Star Entertainment Inc. [US]
DIR: Skip Schoolnik; PRO: Dimitri Villard; SCR: Michael Kelly; DOP: Eugene D. Shlugleit; EXP: Robby Wald; SFX: Screaming Mad George; MUS: John Ross
STR: Donna Baltron, Ronald Colby, Brittain Frye, Scott Fults, Bunky Jones, Sean Kanan, Michael Kelly, Scott Kubay, Jeff Levine, Larry Lyons, Ria Pavia, James Serrano, Annette Sinclair, Donald Mark Spencer, George Thomas, Robin Turk and Joe White
Approximately 94m; Color
VHS1: *Hide and Go Shriek* [NSV; 94m]

Eight horny teens (at least some of them *look* like teens, for a change) decide to spend the night in a large furniture store owned by one of the boy's father. Of course—unbeknownst to them—a psychopathic killer is locked in with them; apparently, these young adults hadn't seen their share of slasher flicks, as they are oblivious to all but their hormones. (God ... haven't I written this all down somewhere before?)

Hide and Go Shriek is only notable for a few small detours. First, it goes entirely against the grain by having the story's two virgins be the first to be dispatched by the perfunctory killer. Second, the ending actually came as some surprise. (Not the "shock" ending crudely tacked on the end, of course, but the revelation previous to that.)

And, well, that's about it. The rest is strictly by the book, folks. (Gore is equally typical, although a little restrained, save for a fairly successful decap.)

If you come across this sucker in the video store, I suggest you just do what the title suggests.

The Hills Have Eyes Part II (1984)

Hills Two Corp. [US]
DIR: Wes Craven; PRO: Barry Cahn and Peter Locke; SCR: Wes Craven; DOP: David Lewis; EXP: Adrienne Fancy; SFX: Richard Brownfield; MUS: Harry Manfredini

STR: Michael Berryman, Kevin Blair, John Bloom, Janus Blythe, Edith Fellows, Peter Frechette, Lance Gordon, Kane Hodder, Robert Houston, Penny Johnson, Susan Lanier, John Laughlin, Brenda Marinoff, Arden Roger Meyer, David Nichols, Willard Pugh, Colleen Riley, Martin Speer, Tamara Stafford, Virginia Vincent and James Whitworth

AKA: *La Colina del Terror—Encuentro con el Diablo* [Terror in the Hills—Encounter with the Devil]

Approximately 86m; Color
VHS1: *The Hills Have Eyes Part II* [HBO; 86m]; *The Hills Have Eyes Part II* [EMI; 86m]

ADL: *So You Think You're Lucky to Be Alive...*

Video box art for *The Hills Have Eyes Part II* (1984), Thorn EMI Home Video.

A busload of motocross enthusiasts break down in the desert, accompanied by a now-civilized Ruby (one of the cannibals from this film's predecessor) and Beast, the German shepherd that was responsible for knocking off most of her clan. Of course, the uninteresting and very disposable twenty-somethings take shelter in a not-so-abandoned mining camp, which just so happens to be the current residence of Jupiter's heretofore-unmentioned big brother, the Reaper, and his nephew Pluto.

By this time in his quickly waning career, Wes Craven had a handful of well-crafted shockers under his belt (*The Last House on the Left*, *The Hills Have Eyes*, *Deadly Blessing*, and *A Nightmare on Elm Street*), as well as some made-for-TV films (*A Stranger in Our House*, *Chiller*, *Invitation to*

Hell) and one true embarrassment (*Swamp Thing*). Still, *The Hills Have Eyes Part II* can be considered the point of no return for the director, as he has never fully recovered from what has to be the worst choice he ever made as a filmmaker.

The Hills Have Eyes Part II is a painful reiteration of a film that is considered one of the pinnacles of '70s independent horror. Aside from a complete lack of originality, the contrived script forfeits logic for cheap shocks; not only is it an embarrassment of a sequel, it falls short of the many half-baked knock-offs inspired by the success of its predecessor. The running time (and threadbare script) is padded with recycled footage from *The Hills Have Eyes*, presented as flashbacks by the returning characters. (Even the dog has a flashback, for crying out loud. I've heard of desperate plot devices, but *this* is ridiculous.)

Reprising their roles from the first film is Janus Blythe as a very old looking Ruby, and Michael Berryman as Pluto. Bobby shows up just long enough in the opening sequences to look angst-ridden and remind the viewer of what happened seven years earlier.

The gore is standard slasher-level carnage, and—being thus—lacks even the slightest visceral impact. Besides being weak stalk 'n' slash fare, *The Hills Have Eyes Part II* shares two other similarities with the *Friday the 13th* series: The participation of composer Harry Manfredini (whose lame score is even tacked onto the poorly re-edited, recycled footage), and the presence of stuntman Kane (Jason Vorhees) Hodder. The only other real point of interest is Al Adamson regular John Bloom trying to fill Papa Jupe's shoes. (Hey, even taking into account that Bloom's claim to fame is starring in such brain-damaged epics *Dracula Vs. Frankenstein* and *Brain of Blood*, this is a step down.)

"The following film is based on fact." Methinks the only fact that underlies this film is that everyone sells out for the right price. Truly wretched, this.

Hollow Gate—Das Tor des Todes
see **Hollowgate**

Hollowgate (1988)

City Lights Home Video [US]
DIR: Ray Dizazzo; PRO: Joseph Merhi and Richard Pepin; SCR: Ray Dizazzo; DOP: Voya Mikulic; EXP: Ronald L. Gilchrist; MFX: Judy Yonemoto; SFX: Don Power; MUS: John Gonzales
STR: Katrina Alexy, Dana Balicki, Bartholomew Bottoms, Ted Buck, George Cole, Vanessa Commerson, Jeff Culver, Denise Dougherty, Richard Dry, Robert Gallo, Charlie Ganis, Gabe Goldschmidt, Jamie Hack, Mario Hernandez, Patricia Jacques, Lisa la Rosa, Jody Lange, Craig Lechman, Richard London, Jerry Marble, J.J. Miller, Carly Pepin, Genevieve Pepin, Addison Randall, Pat Shalsant, Michelle Smith, Kelly Struyck, Nicole Struyck, Scott Tenen, Stephanie Tenen, Beth Toomy, Eric Wilson, Biff Yeager and Jennifer Zdenek
AKA: *Hollow Gate—Das Tor des Todes* [Hollow Gate—The Gate of Death]
Approximately 84m; Color
VHS1: *Hollowgate* [CLV; 84m]

Two couples partying over state lines get suckered into making a delivery to a mansion for a costume rental shop. The house is owned by an old woman and her grandson, who—by the way—is a tad nutters; by the time they arrive, they find that the outpatient had finally gotten the nerve to plant a pair of shears in granny's eye socket. He then goes after the teens, sporting different costumes for each murder and killing the kids accordingly. (And it all dates back to a traumatic bobbing for apples incident. No, I'm *not* making this up.)

Although not completely formulaic (at least in structure), *Hollowgate* is nonetheless a tiring experience for the viewer, exhibiting all of the signs of typical Merhi drudgery. (For what it's worth, he might as well have directed it instead of acting simply as producer.) Not as inept as it could have been, the film still offers nothing that could be commended, either in thought or execution. For stalk 'n' slash enthusiasts only.

Hollywood Chainsaw Hookers (1987)

American-Independent Productions [US], Savage Cinema [US]
DIR: Fred Olen Ray; PRO: Fred Olen Ray; SCR: T.L. Lankford and Fred Olen Ray; DOP: Scott Ressler; EXP: James Golff, Nick Marino and Salvatore Richichi; MFX: Sally Kay; MUS: Michael Perilstein
STR: Esther Alise, Michelle Bauer, Tricia Burns, Jerry Fox, Gunnar Hansen, Jeffrey Hill, Gerry Jenkins, Gary J. Levinson, Dennis McNuey, Jerry Miller, Charles O'Hair, Sandy Palm, Linnea Quigley, Jay Richardson, Michael Sonye, Steve Welles, Dawn Wildsmith, Jimmy Williams and Susie Wilson
AKA: Hollywood Hookers
Approximately 90m; Color
DVD1: Hollywood Chainsaw Hookers [VEN; 105(90)m; LBX]; DVD2: Hollywood Chainsaw Hookers [MNM; 75m; LBX]; VHS1: Hollywood Chainsaw Hookers [VEN; 90m]; VHS2: Hollywood Chainsaw Hookers [MNM; 75m]
ADL: They Charge an Arm and a Leg!

"The chainsaws used in this Motion Picture are *real* and *dangerous*! They are handled here by seasoned professionals. The makers of this Motion Picture advise strongly against anyone attempting to perform these stunts at home. Especially if you are naked and about to engage in strenuous sex. My conscience is clear. Fred Olen Ray." Unfortunately, the rest of the film never gets any better than this onscreen warning or the original adline (clever, that).
Hollywood Chainsaw Hookers is a sophomoric, campy gore flick tailored for splatterpunks who think Leather-

face and shower scenes are "rad." There are, as the title implies, buckets of the red stuff, usually thrown from off screen onto scantily clad models (I hesitate to use the term "actresses") that can barely wield a chainsaw, let alone a bad pun.
The "seasoned" veterans here are Gunnar Hansen and Linnea Quigley. Sad, really, in that their most notable contributions to cinema are, respectively, squealing like a pig while wearing a human skin mask and performing a striptease on a tombstone in the rain. (I wonder if they had anything to do with the announced sequel, *Student Chainsaw Nurses*, never getting made, as both of them deserve better.)
For better or for worse, this is the film that seemed to set the course for director Ray: Low budget films with passable production values that rely almost entirely on the exploitive use of sex and violence. In fact, comparisons to Roger Corman (producing marketable films quickly on budgets that just barely squeak by) would not be out of line. People like myself, though, have a difficult time swallowing intentional camp, as it inevitably fails to capture the magic that the so-bad-they're-good films from yesteryear evoke, and this is why modern filmmakers will never succeed where those like Corman tried so hard not to.
Mildly amusing, at best.

Hollywood Hookers *see* **Hollywood Chainsaw Hookers**

Hollywood's New Blood (1989)

Jamestown Productions [US]
DIR: James Shyman; PRO: Ron Fos-

ter; SCR: James Shyman; DOP: Robert Birchall; EXP: Meredith Jo Mischen and James Shyman; MFX: Kelly Ford; MUS: Emilio Kauderer and Jamos Studios

STR: Kent Abrams, Martie Allyne, Joe Balogh, Lynn Dee, Ken Denny, Allen Francis, Bobby Johnston, Francine Lapensee, Donna Lynn, Lynne Pirtle, George Spellman and Al Valletta

Approximately 77m; Color

VHS1: *Hollywood's New Blood* [RAE, Inc.; 90(77)m]

ADL: *Where Acting Dead Can Be Fatal.*

An acting class decides to hold a seminar at an old house just outside of Hollywood which, of course, has a checkered past. During the '50s and '60s the place was used as a set for horror films; on what was to be its last day, some stagehands got sloppy and blew up the wrong house, killing eight. Rumors have it that the three Clouster brothers are intent on revenge, and have been seen hanging out around the place at night. Say ... sounds awfully convenient, don't you think?

Yes, *Hollywood's New Blood* is yet another unnecessary contribution to stalk 'n' slash cinema. Still another group of inept young actors (and I ain't talking *characters* here) are methodically dispatched without the slightest itch of suspense on the part of desperate filmmakers looking to break into the business, but unwilling to actually make a film that is little more than an open sore on the backside of horror cinema.

The gore is mostly after the fact, and relegated to ready-made slashings, save for a slightly more ambitious injury to the eye, and—what may be the only inspired moment in the entire film—a death by skull. The carnage is the work of three unconvincing hobos, faces smeared with greasepaint and oatmeal. The already lifeless proceedings are padded with extensive scenes of the mist-filled woods (if you want atmosphere, you've got to do better than that), and what I think is supposed to be a music video. (The film is capped off by an extended ten-minute remix of the theme song—already painful in its shorter, edited form—accompanied by scenes from the movie. Talk about insult to injury.)

Holocausto de los Zombies *see* **La Regina dei Cannibali**

El Hombre Rata *see* **La Casa al Fondo del Parco**

Home Sweet Home *see* **Lurkers**

Honeymoon Horror (1982)

Omega Cinema Productions Company Ltd. [US]

DIR: Harry Preston; PRO: Nick Calpeno; SCR: Deanne Kelly; DOP: David Preston; EXP: Norman Brown, Ken Chock, and Michael Wyckoff; MFX: Shane Johnson; SFX: Bryan Owen; MUS: Ron di Lulio

STR: Fari Addington, Cheryl Black, James Cassey, Jade Cherie, William Clarke, Michael Crabtree, Margi Curry, Jane Fradue, Paul Franski, Kathy Johnson, Jillian Kaye, Leslie McKinley, Jerry Meagher, Jan Norton, William F. Pecchi, Megan Ready, Philip Thompson, Bob Wagner, Mary Lou Whitman and Michael Wyckoff

Approximately 90; Color

VHS1: *Honeymoon Horror* [SON; 90m]

ADL: *'Til Death Do Us Part.*

A man is presumably killed following the discovery of his wife's infidelity, but—surprise!—he pops up years later when his wife and her hubby-to-be decide to open an island resort for newlyweds. Of course, the ex-husband being spiteful as well as a bit deranged, his adulterous wife isn't the only one to suffer his wrath. Not everyone is quickly dispatched, though, as the time between murders seems unbearably long, with little else to offer during the interim. (There's a fair amount of bed hopping, but only one brief flash of nudity, so anyone expecting the obligatory flesh to tide them over during these lulls will be sorely disappointed.)

Although the copyright date insists this was a 1982 production, one would swear this was made in the mid-'70s. All of that decade's earmarked style is present, including shoddy production values; even the gore has that cheap, primitive look that relies more on editing than prosthetics to garner the results. That said, the only viewers who would receive *any* gratification from *Honeymoon Horror* would be those fans that never managed to drag their sorry butts out of the '70s. (Yes, myself included.) Everyone else will be relieved when the honeymoon is over.

Horrible *see* **Rosso Sangue**

Horror House *see* **The Horror Show**

Horror Planet *see* **Inseminoid**

Horror Queen *see* **Notte nel Bosco**

The Horror Show (1989)

United Artists [US]
DIR: David Blyth and Jim Isaac; PRO: Sean S. Cunningham; SCR: Leslie Bohem and Allyn Warner; DOP: Mac Ahlberg; MFX: KNB EFX Group; VFX: Available Light Ltd.; MUS: Harry Manfredini
STR: Terry Alexander, Lewis Arquette, Armand Asselin, Robert V. Barron, Thom Bray, Matt Clark, Bobby Collins, Meshell Dillon, Aron Eisenberg, Greg Finley, Lance Henriksen, Stephen A. Henry, Brion James, Zane Levitt, Larry McCormick, Jack McGee, Alvy Moore, Oliver Muirhead, David Oliver, Dedee Pfeiffer, John Sistrunk, Rita Taggart, Lawrence Tierney and Greg Kean Williams
AKA: *Horror House*; *House 3*; *House III—The Horror Show*
Approximately 94m; Color
DVD2: *House III* [DIG; 95(94)m]; VHS1: *The Horror Show* [MUA; 95(94)m]
ADL: *They Tried to Electrocute "Meat Cleaver" Max. It Didn't Work.*

Serial killer Max Jenke (Brion James) is given the chair, but his evil is transformed into an electrical current so he can come back and make life hell for a cop and his family. Due to the killer's intangible form and penchant for bad puns, *The Horror Show* inevitably wanders into Freddy territory; by film's end, it shamelessly treads the path swathed by the numerous *A Nightmare on Elm Street* sequels, as well as their countless clones.

The Horror Show is only really notable for some of the performances therein (excepting, of course, an obnoxious token kid who you really, *really* want to become a statistic before the end credits roll). Lance Henriksen is, well ... Lance Henriksen, so you can't go wrong there. Celluloid bad guy Brion James passes muster as the killer, admirable in that he manages to pull it off despite the weak script.

There is some brutal gore, but the focus is on the same flashy pyrotechnics that tend to punctuate modern supernatural fare. (With all this money, though, you'd think they could've refrained from using the by-now familiar cat sound effect from the *Walt Disney's Chilling, Thrilling*

Sounds of the Haunted House Halloween record. Not that I actually expect them to pull a cat's tail for realism, but c'mon...)

The *Horror Show* was originally intended as an entry in the *House* series, but was ultimately marketed as an unrelated film because producers decided it was a little too intense to follow the other, more comedic efforts. Also of interest, Isaacs replaced David (*Death Warmed Up*) Blyth as director a week into filming, for reasons currently unknown. (And why Allyn Warner insisted on the catchall pseudonym of "Alan Smithee" for his credit, I don't know, but it probably has something to do with the above switch.)

Hospital Massacre (1981)

The Cannon Film Group Inc. [US]
DIR: Boaz Davidson; PRO: Yoram Globus and Menahem Golan; SCR: Marc Behm; DOP: Nicholas von Sternberg; EXP: Geoffrey Rose; SFX: Joe Quinlivan; MUS: Arlen Ober
STR: Gay Austin, Judy Baldwin, Marian Beeler, Barbi Benton, Lanny Duncan, Bill Errigo, Michael Frost, John Greene, Don Grenough, Beverly Hart, Elizabeth Hoy, Billy Jacoby, Ann Charlotte Lindgren, Chip Lucia, Thomas McClure, Jonathan Moore, Gloria Jean Morrison, Michael Romano, Tammy Simpson, Karyn Smith, Jilly Stathis, Den Surles, Jon van Ness, John Warner Williams and Elly Wold
AKA: *Ward 13*; *X-Ray*
Approximately 89m; Color
VHS1: *Hospital Massacre* [MUA; 89m]

It's easy enough to do, so forget the story. *Hospital Massacre* is standard early '80s slasher fare that inevitably suffers from the usual shortcomings. On top of that, attempts at suspense are too forced to be effective (and when given the opportunity, they screw it up by telegraphing

everything far in advance), and every last man is implicated as the masked killer in order to distract the viewer from the obvious.

So what's left is the gore, most of which consists of brutal stabbings. (One scene, though, involves a bone saw, and actually deserved more screen time than it received.) The film's only other "highlight" is a humorous and truly inspired scene involving three immobile patients in body casts being affronted by *Playboy* Playmate of the Year Barbi Benton screaming (as shrill as humanly possible), "Can somebody help me?"

Of course, if you have a soft spot (or is that a *hard* spot?) for Ms. Benton, her innumerable nude scenes will probably be the only impetus you'll need to rent this sucker.

Hot Love (1985)

JB Films [WG]
DIR: Jörg Buttgereit; PRO: Jörg Buttgereit; SCR: Jörg Buttgereit; DOP: Jörg Buttgereit; SFX: Jörg Buttgereit and Daktari Lorenz; MUS: Daktari Lorenz and John Boy Walton
STR: Jörg Buttgereit, Norbet Hähnel, Marion Koob-Liebing, Patricia Leipold, Daktari Lorenz, Franz Rodenkirchen and Simone Schulz
Approximately 40m; Color
VHS1: *Corpse Fucking Art* [FTV; 40m]

Hot Love is an extremely primitive featurette from the director of the infamous *Nekromantik* series. A young man sporting devil locks and sideburns (a poor attempt at covering up his receding hairline) falls madly in love, only to later find that his one and only is two-timing him (the other man being played by the director, proving here that he should stay *behind* the camera). He begins stalking her, and, after violently raping his true love, he promptly kills himself. Nine months later she gives birth, in what has to be the most ludicrous—albeit disgusting—birth scenes ever put to 8mm film. The illegitimate child (played with utmost conviction by a make-up laden baby doll) eventually mutates into a corpse-like incarnation of its real father, killing both the mother and her boyfriend. The end.

There is some outrageous (albeit poorly executed) gore, but the film displays little of the style that would later punctuate Buttgereit's full-length features. There is an exemplary piano score from the unmistakable team of Lorenz and Walton, but, sadly, this is the only real highlight of the film and sounds miserably out of place.

Hot Love is available as a bonus on Film Threat's video release of *Corpse Fucking Art*. (Thank God, because I would hate to actually have to *pay* for a copy.) Pretty awful, but I guess everyone has to start *somewhere*. For Buttgereit completists only.

Hotel der Verdoemden   *see*   **L'Adilá**

House 3   *see*   **The Horror Show**

House III—The Horror Show   *see*   **The Horror Show**

The House by the Cemetery   *see*   **Quella Villa Accanto al Cimitero**

House of Death   *see*   **Death Screams**

House of Evil   *see*   **The House on Sorority Row**

The House on Sorority Row (1982)

VAE Productions [US]
DIR: Mark Rosman; PRO: John G. Clark and Mark Rosman; SCR: Mark Rosman; DOP: Timothy Suhrstedt; EXP: W. Thomas McMahon and John Ponchock; MFX: Rob E. Holland and Make-Up Effects Lab; MUS: Richard H. Band, 4 Out of 5 Doctors and Joel Goldsmith
STR: Tom Bothwell, Karl B. Bromwell, Patti Chambers, Arthur Crockett, Hilary Crowson, Kathryn Davidov, Eileen Davidson, Ellen Dorsher, Jodi Draigie, Ed Heath, Lois Kelso Hunt, Nanna Ingvarsson, Harley Kozak, Michael Kuhn, Christopher Lawrence, Peter McClung, Kathryn McNeil, Robin Meloy, Ruth Moss, Ken Myers, Celeste Poirier, Van Santvoord, Jean Schertler, Michael Serio, Charles Sero, Larry Singer, Brian T. Small, Eric Smith, Alan Treadwell, Ruth Walsh and Janis Zido
AKA: *House of Evil; Seven Sisters*
Approximately 91m; B&W and Color
DVD1: *The House on Sorority Row* [ELT; 92m; LBX]; VHS1: *House of Evil* [DUR; 90(91)m]; *The House on Sorority Row* [VES; 90(91)m]

Six sorority sisters decide to stay behind a few days once school's closed to party, and their housemother is none too pleased. After the bitter old woman slashes one of their waterbeds, they decide to stage a vicious practical joke that results in a fatal accident. The predictable stalk 'n' slash immediately ensues.

The House on Sorority Row has competent production values, but this in no way compensates for the rote proceedings (been there, done that), the lack of gratuitous sex and violence (it *is* a slasher film, after all), the presence of 4 Out of 5 Doctors (an obnoxious '80s rock band), and a shitty finale. What, did the editor misplace the last five minutes of the film? Or did they decide to purposefully rile up the viewer by not revealing who the killer was after all of the build-up? We *know* it is supposed to be the old woman's supposedly deceased son—that was made obvious from square one—but everything implies that the killer is someone we've seen during the proceedings. And, no, I didn't miss something while fast-forwarding through the uneventful parts; I actually sat through the whole godforsaken mess (not out of choice, mind you; my girlfriend at the time wanted to see it because it starred Eileen Davidson, who later went on to become a fairly respectable soap actress).

The House Outside the Cemetery
see **Quella Villa Accanto al Cimitero**

Housegeist *see* **Boardinghouse**

The Howling (1980)
Avco Embassy Pictures Corp. [US]
DIR: Joe Dante; PRO: Jack Conrad and Michael Finnell; SCR: John Sayles and Terence H. Winkless [Based on the novel *The Howling* by Gary Brandner]; DOP: John Hora; EXP: Daniel H. Blatt and Steven A. Lane; MFX: Rob Bottin; SFX: Roger George; VFX: David Allen; MUS: Pino Donaggio [Soundtrack from Varèse Sarabande]
STR: Forrest J Ackerman, Belinda Balaski, Herb Braha, Joe Bratcher, Elisabeth Brooks, Robert A. Burns, John Carradine, Roger Corman, Dennis Dugan, Sarina C. Grant, Margie Impert, Patrick Macnee, Chico Martinez, Kevin McCarthy, Jim McKrell, Don McLeod, Dick Miller, James Murtaugh, Steve Nevil, Daniel Núñez, Michael O'Dwyer, Robert Picardo, Slim Pickens, Ivan Saric, John Sayles, Bill Sorrells, Christopher Stone, Meshach Taylor, Kenneth Tobey, Dee Wallace, Bill Warren, Noble Willingham and Wendell Wright
AKA: *Aullido* [Howl]; *Das Tier* [The Beast]
Approximately 91m; Color
DVD1: *The Howling* [MUA; 91m;

LBX]; VHS1: *The Howling* [EMB; 90(91)m]; *The Howling* [MUA; 91m]; VHS2: *The Howling* [FFV; 87m]

Newscaster Karen White sets herself up as bait to catch Eddie, an obsessive fan who also has the unusual distinction of being one of New York's most brutal serial killers. After a close call, authorities nail him, but she is left traumatized by the whole ordeal. Under doctor's orders, she takes a most overdue vacation with her hubby to a coastal wood-side retreat. She soon finds out that—through no coincidence—the retreat was also Eddie's home before he moved on to the Big Apple.

"ABSOLUTELY UNIQUE...scenes that win audience gasps, deservedly." —People Magazine
"ONE OF THE BEST WEREWOLF MOVIES EVER MADE. The special effects are brilliant beyond all description." —Los Angeles Magazine

Video box art for *The Howling* (1980), Embassy Home Video.

Although overshadowed by the success of *An American Werewolf in London* (released the same year), *The Howling* is in no way inferior. (Ironically, the effects work here—some of the best of its type to date—was created by Rob Bottin, a protégé of Rick Baker, the artist who supplied the work for that *other* werewolf film.) Thankfully, the groundbreaking effects are complimented by adept direction, good performances, inspired editing, and some impressive art direction (thanks to Robert A. Burns, the man responsible for giving *The Texas Chain Saw Massacre* its rustic charm).

Best of all, the script was written by John Sayles, one of the more prestigious names to come out of Corman's school of exploitation filmmaking. *The Howling* is probably the most intelligently written film about lycanthropy in the history of horror cinema. Sayles also takes the opportunity to make his trademarked stabs at whatever societal concerns had worked their way under his skin: pop psychology, the media, you name it. (The friction between "new age" lycanthropy and more traditional werewolfism could even be taken as an analogy for the generation gap, the orthodoxy, what have you.) On top of it all, *The Howling* displays a fair amount of wit.

Although the lead performers deserve their share of credit, some of the supporting players deserve a special mention as well. (John Carradine and Dick Miller have small roles, and Roger Corman—among others—makes a cameo appearance, but they don't count.) A better or more physically convincing actor couldn't have

been picked for the role of Eddie, one of the most chilling monsters in horror cinema; the actors playing his family may not have his charisma, but they are graced with similarly lupine characteristics that help them convince the viewer of their heritage without make-up. Thanks in part to their contributions, *The Howling* is actually quite scary at times, with the initial sting being one of the more harrowing sequences of its type. Of course, the seedy atmosphere adds to the tension and helps to establish the psychosexual origins of the werewolf myth.

The film is not perfect, faltering when the amount of effects becomes overwhelming; the fiery finale is accompanied by some tacky transformations (which look worse when compared to Eddie's more impressive coming-out earlier on) and some awkward stop-motion photography that was—thankfully—kept to a minimum in the final edit.

The Howling's biggest fault, though, was that it spawned (so far) six sequels of varying degrees of inferiority. (If you *must* check any of them out, settle for the fifth and sixth films in the series, and leave well enough alone.)

The Howling II *see* **Howling II— Your Sister Is a Werewolf**

Howling II—Your Sister Is a Werewolf (1984)

Granite Productions [Cz/US] DIR: Philippe Mora; PRO: Steven A. Lane; SCR: Gary Brandner and Robert Sarno [Based on the novel *Howling II* by Gary Brandner]; DOP: Geoffrey Stephenson; EXP: Grahame Jennings; MFX: Jack Bricker and Cosmetikinetics Inc.; MUS:

Stephen Parsons [Soundtrack from Film Trax Records]

STR: Jitka Asterova, Steven Bronowski, John Brown, Reb Brown, James M. Crawford, Sybil Danning, Simon Etchell, Patrick Field, Shirley Hanson, Marsha A. Hunt, Valerie Kaplanova, Ed Kleynen, Anna Maria Kolarova, Jan Kraus, Jiri Krytinar, Ladis Law, Christopher Lee, Hana Ludvikova, Miriam Lugerova, Ferdinand Mayne, Annie McEnroe, Jimmy Nail, Ivo Nierderle, Judd Omen, Stephen Parsons, Chris Pye, Ludmila Safarova, Jared Seide, Petr Skarke, Igor Smrzik, Miro Sustr and Steve Young

AKA: *Howling II—Your Sister Is a Werewolf; Stirba the Werewolf Bitch*

Approximately 87m; Color

VHS1: *Howling II* [POL; 91(87)m]; *Howling II* [EMI; 91(87)m]; *Howling II* [HBO; 91(87)m]

ADL: *Torture, Death and Destruction Reign Supreme in the Castle of Werewolves.*

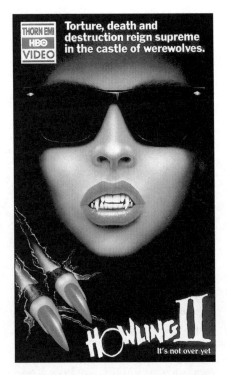

Video box art for *Howling II—Your Sister Is a Werewolf* (1984), Thorn EMI/ HBO Video.

The brother of *The Howling*'s female protagonist is approached during her funeral by an occult investigator (Christopher Lee) who tells him that, not only was his sister a werewolf, but that the birthday of the Mother of All Werewolves is fast approaching, whereupon all lycanthropes must reveal their true faces. (Hers, it seems, is that of buxom Sybil Danning, in a role that must have been a blight to even *her* career.) They track the she-wolf down to "the Dark Country" (Transylvania, of course) and waste no time in decimating her cult of loyal followers.

Now for the bad news. *Howling II* is not only an inferior sequel (surprise!), it's a pretty miserable film altogether. The acting is abysmal. The special effects and, heck, *most* of the action is underexposed (which is probably for the best). The location shooting is completely wasted, even though it's Czechoslovakia and not

Romania as they claim. Tacky optical effects abound. (Gee ... Danning can make her cape glow. Whoopee.)

But wait ... there's more. The script plays around with standard werewolf folklore, with no explanation as to the changes. (Some werewolves can only be killed with titanium and not silver? Why, you ask? Beats me. I'm only reviewing this load of dog dookie.) Female werewolves are forced to gallivant around in black leather underwear, for no other reason than because it looks exotic. Throw in a club full of stereotyped punkers, the tackiest werewolf sexcapades ever filmed, and—to add insult to injury to *The Howling*—a restaging of the finale from its predecessor. (Sure, Dee Wallace doesn't look like a rabid poodle this time out—a second-rate Paul Naschy, maybe, but not a rabid poodle.) I won't even mention the Sybil Danning bodice-ripping scene that is recycled, oh, no less than ten times during the closing credits. (Which—lucky us—is also accompanied by the "punk" band Babel and their less-than-rousing Howling theme song.) Please just kill me now.

What's truly scary, though, is that the series managed to fall even further with...

Howling III (1987)

Bancannia Pictures [Au]
DIR: Philippe Mora; PRO: Philippe Mora and Charles Waterstreet; SCR: Philippe Mora [Based on the novel *The Howling III* by Gary Brandner]; DOP: Louis Irving; EXP: Steven A. Lane, Robert Pringle and Edward Simons; MFX: Bob McCarron; SFX: Steve Courtney; MUS: Allan Zavod [Soundtrack from Film Trax Records]

STR: Aminatta Joy Abraham, Mary Acres, Brian Adams, Imogen Annesley, Peter Armstrong, Max Aspin, Peter Baird, Bob Barrett, Andreas Bayonas, Leigh Biolos, Dasha Blahova, Burnham Burnham, David Cahill, Ric Carter, Bill Collins, Ralph Cotterill, Lionel Curtin, Alan Dargin, Tony Deary, Roger Eagle, Jon Ewing, Max Fairchild, Rodney Francis, Mary Haire, Maia Horniak, Barry Humphries, Paul Lennon, Penny Linden, Glenda Linscott, Alec Maksimovich, Bob McCarron, Gary McGuire, Barry Otto, Christopher Pate, Michael Pate, Jerome Patillo, Alan Penny, Wayne Pleace, Steve Rackman, Lee Rice, Patrick Rowe, Megan Shapcott, Danielle Sharp, Steve Shaw, Robert Simper, Gerry Skilton, Carole Skinner, Max Skipper, Frank Thring, Sam Toomey, Pieter van der Stolk, Jenny Vuletic, Fred Welsh, Deby Wightman and William Yang

AKA: *Howling III—The Marsupials*
Approximately 98m; Color
VHS1: *Howling III* [VIS; 94(98)m];

DVD1: *Howling III—The Marsupials* [ELT; 98m; LBX]

A young lycanthrope high tails it from a marsupial werewolf clan in the outback (the town of "Flow"—how witty) and hooks up with an assistant director working on the film *Shapeshifter—Part 8*. She becomes pregnant, and an accident reveals her birthright to the authorities, so it's up to her significant other and a couple of sympathetic friends to get her to safety.

What could have been the most innovative, thought-provoking entry in this indefatigable series is instead reduced to being the most inconsistent, slapdash, and hokey film of the

Video box art for *Howling III* (1987), Vista Home Video.

bunch. The effects are the quintessential of bad, which is funny considering that those shown in a mock horror film ("It Came from Uranus") aren't much worse than what is passed off as "the real McCoy." (The forced perspective doesn't help.) Furthermore, the editing and continuity are sloppy, and the actors either amateurish or downright inept. With the haphazard filmmaking portrayed here, it is difficult to see what were once some intriguing concepts underlying the action.

Oh, and there's not much gore to speak of, but I felt inclined to include this film in order to prepare you for...

Howling III—The Marsupials *see* **Howling III**

Howling IV—The Original Nightmare (1988)

Allied Vision [US]
DIR: John Hough; PRO: Harry Alan Towers; SCR: Freddie Rowe and Clive Turner; DOP: Godfrey Godar; EXP: Steven A. Lane, Avi Lerner, Robert Pringle and Edward Simons; MFX: Steve Johnson's S.F.X. Inc.; MUS: David George
STR: Norman Anstev, Dale Cutts, Megan Davies, Lamya Derval, Ralph Draper, Kate Edwards, Bill Foertsch, Dennis Folbigge, Beryl Gresan, Antony Hamilton, Anthony James, Hugh Jobling, Maxine John, Megan Kruskal, Greg Latter, Tulio Moneta, Susanne Severeid, Dennis Smith, Diana Tilldon-Davis, Clive Turner, Peter Ware, Michael T. Weiss and Romy Windsor
AKA: *Howling IV*
Approximately 94m; Color
VHS1: *Howling IV—The Original Nightmare* [AVI; 94m]; *Howling IV—The Original Nightmare* [IVE; 94m]

A writer suffering from a nervous breakdown retreats to a country cottage for a much-overdue vacation with her husband. The rural town of Drago—gosh darn it all to hell—is populated by werewolves. (Starting to sound awfully familiar, isn't it?) Savvy to the locals' despicable plans, a nun's ghost tries to warn the young woman, but it's too little, too late.

Talk about going through the motions. This completely generic werewolf flick does little more than rehash the film responsible for instigating this long-running series, and when it does offer something "new," it's been pilfered from other, less successful horror films. (I've been told this is closer to Brandner's original novel than the first film, but I no longer have the stomach to find out for myself.) Even worse, the acting is stiff, and the direction stale. There is some gore, but it is a long time coming, and not worth the wait. The only thing that could even remotely be considered a highlight are the transformation effects—at least those early on—as they are inevitably accompanied by some rather messy meltdowns (think *Street Trash*, but low on Technicolor). So unless you're hard up for crappy werewolf films, I suggest you sit this one out. Granted, it may be more competent than *The Howling III*, but it's a far more embarrassing outing than...

Howling V—The Rebirth (1989)

Lane Pringle Productions [Hu/US]
DIR: Neal Sundström; PRO: Clive Turner; SCR: Freddie Rowe and Clive Turner; DOP: Arledge Armenaki; EXP: Gary Barber, Steven A. Lane, Robert Pringle and Edward Simons; MFX: Max Effects; MUS: The Factory
STR: Victoria Catlin, Ben Cole, Philip Davis, Stephanie Faulkner, József Madaras,

Jill Pearson, Elizabeth Shé, William Shockley, Mark Sivertsen, Mary Stavin, Benata Szatler, Nigel Triffitt and Clive Turner
Approximately 99m; Color
VHS1: *Howling V—The Rebirth* [AVI; 99m]; *Howling V—The Rebirth* [IVE; 99m]

Budapest, 1489: One of the most powerful families in Europe is slaughtered by one of their own in an effort to sever a tainted bloodline. Unfortunately, a child survives. Exactly five hundred years later (what a coincidence!), a group of tourists attend the grand re-opening of the castle where the massacre occurred, and—don't let it out that I told you—one of the guests is the direct descendant of the aforementioned survivor.

Some of the individuals responsible for the previous installment saw fit to try and redeem themselves with this one. Although *Howling V* is not a remarkable film by anyone's standards, it is a competent werewolf flick that tries to break the mold (or rather go back to its roots) by adding gothic settings and instilling a certain amount of mystery into the proceedings. Granted, it is not very successful as a straight whodunit, but it's an admirable attempt regardless.

The script is palatable, with some above average performances to help smooth over its weaker moments. Some tension is actually achieved, kudos going to both the director and the authentic location shooting. Gore is restricted to a slew of torn throats— most of which are after the fact—and a humorous decap. But, hey, at least the werewolf looks halfway decent this time out; I didn't think I'd ever recover from the phony abominations that were proliferate in *The Howling III.*

A passable werewolf flick that positively shines when compared to the other sequels.

Het Huis bij het Kerkhof *see* **Quella Villa Accanto al Cimitero**

Hullujenhuone *see* **There Was a Little Girl**

Human Beasts *see* **El Carnaval de las Bestias**

Humanoids from the Deep (1980)

New World Pictures [US]
DIR: Jimmy T. Murakami and Barbara Peters; PRO: Martin B. Cohen and Roger Corman; SCR: Frederick James; DOP: Daniel Lacambre; MFX: Rob Bottin; SFX: Roger George; MUS: James Horner
STR: Frank Arnold, Amy Barret, Rob Bottin, Breck Costin, Shawn Erler, Denise Galik, Lisa Glaser, Hoke Howell, Lyle Isom, Meegan King, Jonathan Lehan, Don Maxwell, Doug McClure, Bruce Monette, Vic Morrow, Anthony Penya, Linda Shayne, David Strassman, Lynn Theel, Greg Travis, Ann Turkel, Cindy Weintraub, Henry T. Williams and Jo Williams
AKA: *Monster*; *Les Monstres de la Mer* [The Monsters of the Sea]
Approximately 82m; Color
DVD0: *Humanoids from the Deep* [NCV; 80(82)m]; VHS1: *Humanoids from the Deep* [NCV; 80(82)m]; *Humanoids from the Deep* [WAR; 82m]
ADL: *Sea Beasts on the Prowl—for Human Mates.*

A small fishing community is besieged by a horde of mutated prehistoric fish with an insatiable appetite for human flesh ... whether it be for food, or for reproductive purposes.

Now that *that's* out of the way, let's get to the finer points of this film, the pinnacle of the fish monster subgenre. *Creature from the Black Lagoon?* Sure, it's an all right horror film, but

Humanoids from the Deep showed everything that its granddaddy only hinted at. I'm sure the gill man *wanted* to bump uglies with Julie Adams, but he was too much of a milquetoast to follow through with it. Also, with three films to his credit, not *once* did he ever knock off a little kid, yet the humanoids mange to lay waste to half a city's underage population in the last fifteen minutes of the film. Now *that's* dedication.

Humanoids from the Deep was made back in the days when Corman was still pumping out good exploitation films. Purportedly, he did not feel that Peters' ecological monster movie had enough bite for modern filmgoers, so the King of the Bs had additional scenes of gratuity filmed to help liven things up a bit, i.e. boobs and blood. Lots of boobs and blood. The mix of sincere introspection at racial tensions and ecological concerns with, well, lots of boobs and blood makes for an odd mélange, to say the least. (Did I mention the cheesy *Alien*-style chest-bursting scene tacked onto the end? Uhm, just pretend I didn't.)

Aside from the buckets of chum, the monsters—if anything—are the prime reason to check it out. Especially the critters with the *reeealy* long arms. (Kudos go to Rob Bottin for creating what have to be the coolest looking fish monsters ever to grace the silver screen. Especially the ones with the *reeealy* long arms.)

Humanoids from the Deep did for fish monster movies what *The Howling* did for werewolf flicks.

Humongous (1981)

Humongous Productions Ltd. [Ca]
DIR: Paul Lynch; PRO: Anthony Kramreither; SCR: William Gray; DOP: Brian R.R. Hebb; EXP: Michael M. Stevenson; MFX: Brenda Kirk; SFX: Martin Malvoire; MUS: John Mills Cockell
STR: Janit Baldwin, Joy Boushel, Lane Coleman, Page Fletcher, Shay Garner, Janet Julian, John McFadyen, Garry Robbins, Mary Sullivan, David Wallace and John Wildman
Approximately 92m; Color
VHS1: *Humongous* [EMB; 93(92)m]
ADL: *It's Loose ... It's Angry ... and It's Getting Hungry!*

A woman is raped during a party, the unborn's father killed immediately thereafter by a pack of trained guard dogs. She spends the remainder of her life locked up on her family's privately owned island, outsiders avoiding the

Video box art for *Humongous* (1981), Embassy Home Entertainment.

place in fear of the madwoman and the property which has since become overrun with wild dogs. Thirty-six years after the accident, a handful of twenty-somethings are forced to take refuge on the small island after their boat goes down. Of course, if you haven't figured it out by now, the dogs are the least of their problems.

From the director of *Prom Night* (made the previous year) comes another *Friday the 13th* knock-off, although this one bears more of a resemblance to *Hell Night* than anything. (Even the shameless exploitation of congenital birth defects—this one being acromegaly, the selfsame affliction from which '30s character actor Rondo Hatton suffered—is present and accounted for.) And like the other films it emulates, the proceedings are painfully predictable; only the location shooting and some effective editing keep the film from being completely mundane. Even the gore is typical of the subgenre (albeit a little restrained).

Ray (*The Wizard of Gore*) Sager functioned as assistant director.

Hunter's Blood (1986)

Hunter's Blood Ltd. Partnership [US] DIR: Robert C. Hughes; PRO: Myrl A. Schreibman; SCR: Emmett Alston [Based on the novel *Hunter's Blood* by Jere Cunningham]; DOP: Tom de November; EXP: Judith F. Schuman; MFX: Make-Up Effects Laboratories Inc.; MUS: John d'Andrea

STR: Samuel Bottoms, Charles Cyphers, Connie Danese, Lee de Broux, Kim Delaney, David de Shay, Dennis Dorantes, Billy Drago, Gene Glazer, Bruce Glover, Clu Gulager, Mickey Jones, Ron la Pere, Allen Lerner, Daniel McFeeley, Burr Middleton, Billy Million, Michael Muscat, Mayf Nutter, Bryan Rasmussen, Jerry Ratay, Beverly E. Schwartz, Nan J. Seitz, Ken Swofford, Billy Bob Thornton, Joey Travolta, Joe Verroca and Ray Young
Approximately 101m; Color
VHS1: *Hunter's Blood* [EMB; 102(101)m]
ADL: *Out There, No One Hears You Scream*

Five hunters go off into the mountains for some rest and relaxation. First they get into a brawl at the Amionite Velvet Lounge ("No Bare Feet, No Bare Chests, No Coloreds"), and whilst trying to skedaddle, they are forced off the trail. Some game wardens warn them about "two-legged bloodsuckers" and "hunters coming up missing," and before too long our macho antagonists discover the culprits are a clan of phony butt-raping hicks.

Suffice it to say, *Hunter's Blood* offers tired *Deliverance*-style hijinks, hindered by a lack of sympathetic characters; the hunters are all assholes, and the rednecks are, well, rednecks. What makes this film at all notable is a couple of things. First, the film includes a very early appearance of Billy Bob (*Slingblade*) Thornton, but the number of readers who actually care about this trivia makes this factoid, well, trivial. The second, though, is the gore. Not only is *Hunter's Blood* exceptionally graphic for this type of fare, the effects are surprisingly well executed. A graphic skinning, a decap, and what has to be probably the best shotgunned head ever committed to film are the highlights amidst various other scenes of bloodshed. It's just sad that such inspired carnage is relegated to a fairly uninteresting backdrop.

But, hey, it's better than Hughes' *Memorial Valley Massacre*, made two years later. Not that he had far to drop, but *still...*

I, Madman (1988)

TransWorld Entertainment [US]
DIR: Tibor Takács; PRO: Rafael Eisenman; SCR: David Chaskin; DOP: Bryan England; EXP: Paul Mason and Helen Sarlui; MFX: Randall William Cook; SFX: Frank Ceglia; VFX: Randall William Cook; MUS: Michael Hoenig
    STR: Tom Badal, Mary Baldwin, Kevin Best, Randall William Cook, Bob Frank, Mary Pat Gleason, James Quincey Hendrick, Stephanie Hodge, Michelle Jordan, Christopher Kriesa, Roger la Page, Marty Levy, David P. Lewis, Vincent Lucchesi, Steven Memel, Rafael Nazario, Clayton Rohner, Stan Roth, Murray Rubin, Vance Valensia, Bruce Wagner, Nelson Welch, Jenny Wright and Jeff Yesko
    AKA: *Hardcover*
    Approximately 90m; Color
    VHS1: *I, Madman* [ABE; 90m]; *I, Madman* [MHE; 90m]

An aspiring actress finds herself immersed in the works of pulp writer Malcolm Brand, whose grisly books *Much of Madness, More of Sin* and *I, Madman* are curiously labeled as nonfiction. ("Makes Stephen King read like Mother Goose," one character remarks.) Eric Kessler, the antagonist of the novels—who has sliced off all of his features in order to impress the woman he loves—has somehow found a way to breach the line between fantasy and reality, and goes on a killing spree in order to replace his disfigured countenance, just as it is described in the books.
    Even though *I, Madman* bears numerous similarities to other supernatural-oriented serial killer flicks, this atypical take on the slasher genre is a reasonably impressive effort from the director of *The Gate* (1987). Kessler proves to be a fairly spooky

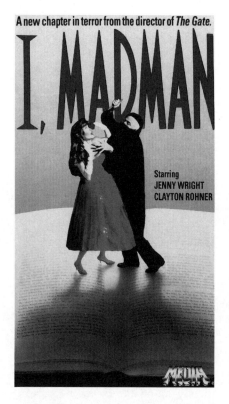

A new chapter in terror from the director of *The Gate.*

Starring
JENNY WRIGHT
CLAYTON ROHNER

Video box art for *I, Madman* (1988), Media Home Entertainment.

and original villain, owing as much to the weird pulps of yesteryear as to modern fare. (He does bear a striking resemblance to Robert Englund's titular portrayal of the *Phantom of the Opera*, but that film—also worthwhile—was made a year later.) For once, the obligatory grue is accompanied by some adequately suspenseful moments, thanks primarily to an intelligent and not altogether predictable script. (Although I do have a problem with the unlikely antiquarian bookstore clerk who would never in a million years be employed by such an establishment, even out of nepotism.)
    The inspired touches and adept

blurring between fantasy and reality are complimented by solid production values, not the least of which is some wonderful stop-motion animation of a hybrid jackal-man by Cook, who also contributed his talents to Takács' aforementioned debut and its sequel. Not many artists can touch Ray Harryhausen's superlative work, but Cook is one of the few to come close.

Im Schatten des Kilimandscharo *see* **In the Shadow of Kilimanjaro**

The Imp (1981) *see* **Xiong Bang**

The Imp (1987)

Titan Productions [US]
DIR: David de Coteau; PRO: David de Coteau and John Schouweiler; SCR: Sergei Hasenecz; DOP: Stephen Ashley Blake; EXP: Charles Band; MFX: Craig Caton; MUS: Guy Moon
STR: Carla Baron, Michelle Bauer, George Flower, Hal Havins, Andras Jones, Kathi Obrecht, Linnea Quigley, Michael Sonye, Brinke Stevens, Robin Stille and John Stuart Wildman
AKA: *Sorority Babes in the Slimeball Bowl-O-Rama*
Approximately 79m; Color
DVD0: *Sorority Babes in the Slimeball Bowl-O-Rama* [FME; 77(79)m]; VHS1: *Sorority Babes in the Slimeball Bowl-O-Rama* [UCV; 80(79)m]
ADL: *In a Bowling Alley from Hell, There's Only One Way to Score...*

A handful of coeds break into a bowling alley in order to pass a sorority initiation rite, and inadvertently release a jive talking, Muppet-like imp from a pilfered trophy. The wishes they receive for their deed go sour, and before long everyone is turned into rejects from *The Evil Dead.* How's that for threadbare *and* ridiculously contrived?

Here's a real turd that tried to pass itself off as a "cult classic." Little more than a vehicle for the three reigning queens of 1980's B-films (Stevens, Quigley, and Bauer under the pseudonym of McClellan), *The Imp* appeals to the lowest common denominator, mixing gratuitous T&A with sophomoric humor and some wretched gore effects. (Any surprise it's a de Coteau film?) The movie's only redeeming feature is the presence of genre walk-through George "Buck" Flower, who presumably was so embarrassed by his part in the film that he used the pseudonym of "C.D. le Fleur."

Unless you want to spend twenty minutes ogling Michelle Bauer's tits, I suggest you pass.

L'Imperatore Caligula *see* **Caligula—La Storia Mai Raccontata**

In the Shadow of Kilimanjaro (1986)

Intermedia Productions [SA/UK]
DIR: Raju Patel; PRO: Guatam Das and Jeffrey M. Sneller; SCR: T. Michael Harry and Jeffrey M. Sneller; DOP: Jesus Elizondo; EXP: Sharad Patel; SXP: Bachu Patel; VFX: Malcolm Bubb, Paul Gilby and Robert Roach; MUS: Arlon Ober
STR: Don Blakely, Jim Boeke, Timothy Bottoms, Michele Care, Patty Foley, Patrick Gorman, Calvin Jung, Irene Miracle, John Rhys-Davies, Leonard Trolley, Ka Vundla and Mark Watters
AKA: *Im Schatten des Kilimandscharo* [In the Shadow of Kilimanjaro]
Approximately 96m; Color ⚔ ⚔ ⚔
VHS1: *In the Shadow of Kilimanjaro* [USA; 94(96)m]
ADL: *Violent Death Was the Easy Way Out!*

In the Shadow of Kilimanjaro claims to be "based on a real story";

although I don't doubt there is a kernel of truth to the proceedings, I think it's safe to assume that the scriptwriters took some artistic license. Apparently, a severe drought caused the animals indigenous to the area to go a little buggy, in particular an enormous pack of baboons. Like many of the fictional "nature's revenge" films of the '70s, *In the Shadow of Kilimanjaro* follows a handful of individuals first discovering the problem, then spending the remainder of the movie trying to keep their asses intact.

Compared to other films in the aforementioned subgenre, this is one of the better, more convincing entries. (I'm sure that having it be based—no matter how tenuous—on actual events gives it some weight.) Production values are good, and it is intelligently written, save for a particularly unconvincing finale. There is some extremely intense gore (a rarity for this kind of film), the success due in part to the exemplary special effects (except, that is, for a couple of really, *really* fake baboons used for extreme close-ups during the attacks; it couldn't have been any worse had someone shoved one of those wind-up monkeys with cymbals in front of the camera lens).

The only perturbing fact was that, although the producers "wish to make it known that not a single animal was mistreated during the making of *In the Shadows of Kilimanjaro*," they chose to utilize stock footage of real monkeys being shot out of trees early on in the film.

Apparently not wanting to make a career out of more extreme cinema, director Patel went on to produce a string of children's features.

Inconsciente *see* **L'Ossessione Che Uccide**

Incubo sulla Città Contaminata [Nightmare in the Contaminated City] (1980)

Dialchi Film [It], Lotus Internacional Film [Sp]

DIR: Umberto Lenzi; PRO: Diego Alchimede and Luis Méndez; SCR: Antonio Cesare Corti, Luis María Delgado and Piero Regnoli; DOP: Hans Burman; MFX: Franco di Girolami and Giuseppe Ferranti; MUS: Stelvio Cipriani

STR: Achille Belletti, Ugo Bologna, Charles Borromel, Pierangelo Civera, Frank Clement, Stefania d'Amario, Alejandro de Enciso, Ottaviano dell'Acqua, Eduardo Fajardo, Tony Felleghi, Mel Ferrer, Meg Fleming, Sara Franchetti, Umberto Lenzi, Antonio Mayans, Maria Rosario Omaggio, Benito Pacifico, Francisco Rabal, Giovanni Lombardo Radice, Silvano Scandariato, Carmen Martínez Sierra, Hugo Stiglitz, Laura Trotter, Sonia Viviani, José Yepes and Manolo Zarzo

AKA: *El Ataque de los Zombies Atomicos* [The Attack of the Atomic Zombies]; *L'Avion de l'Apocalypse* [The Airplane of the Apocalypse]; *La Cité de la Peur* [The City of the Fear]; *City of the Walking Dead*; *Großengriff der Zombies* [Grip of the Zombies]; *La Invasión de los Zombies Atómicos* [The Invasion of the Atomic Zombies]; *Nightmare City*; *Zombies Atomicos* [Atomic Zombies]

Approximately 92m; Color

VHS1: *City of the Walking Dead* [AME; 92m]; *City of the Walking Dead* [CON; 90(92)m]; *Nightmare City* [TDK; 92m; w/Japanese subtitles]

ADL: *Just When You Thought the Dead Were Buried...*

An unscheduled plane lands at an airport carrying a buttload of well-armed and pissed-off zombie soldiers. (Atomic radiation is responsible. Natch.) Before one can pontificate "Geez ... didn't Romero already do this? And better?" a plague of bloodlust and bad make-up is spreading across the countryside like wildfire.

Just when you thought the dead were buried
CITY OF THE WALKING DEAD
Starring Mel Ferrer
Directed by Umberto Lenzi
Rated R
In Current Theatrical Release

Video box art for *Incubo sull Città Contaminata* (1980), Continental Video.

This film, released here under the homogenized title of *City of the Walking Dead*, is bad even by Lenzi's already low standards. A derivative script, haphazard continuity, and low-grade special effects are only part of the all around poor production values. (The more etiquette-minded zombies have the decency to wipe their mouths after draining a hapless victim of blood, but this usually results in them smearing the stage make-up in the process.) The photography and acting are passable, but that's it for quality.

There is gore aplenty, but—as I've mentioned—the execution is abysmal. Highlights include a dancer getting her breast sliced off by one of the hungry dead, and innumerable shotgunned craniums, but there is no flesh-eating *per se*. (Apparently, the effects budget couldn't spring for butcher shop leftovers.)

Even throughout all of the ensuing mayhem, the hero and his wife somehow manage to spend a little quality time philosophizing about the zombie scourge. The "it was only a dream ... or was it?" premonition-style ending is taken to an unbearable extreme, and looks to be a poor attempt to pad out the short running time with recycled footage. And let's not forget the gratuitous jazzercize numbers. Egads.

Simply put, *Incubo sulla Città Contaminata* is probably the worst professionally-made, post-*Night of the Living Dead* zombie flick to date. Even some of the shot-on-video efforts manage to outdo this imported clunker.

Inferno (1980)

Produzioni Intersound [It]

DIR: Dario Argento; PRO: Claudio Argento; SCR: Dario Argento and Daria Nicolodi; DOP: Romano Albani; EXP: Salvatore Argento and William Garroni; MFX: Mario Bava; SFX: Germano Natali; MUS: Keith Emerson [Soundtrack from Cinevox Records]

STR: Feodor Chaliapin, Jr., James Fleetwood, Eleonora Giorgi, Ryan Hilliard, Gabriele Lavia, Veronica Lazar, Rodolfo Lodi, Luigi Lodoli, Leopoldo Mastelloni, Leigh McCloskey, Fulvio Mingozzi, Irene Miracle, Daria Nicolodi, Paolo Paoloni, Ania Pieroni, Sacha Pitoëff, Rosario Rigutini, Michele Soavi and Alida Valli

AKA: *Feuertanz der Zombies* [Firedance of the Zombies]; *Infierno* [Inferno]

Approximately 106m; Color

DVD0: *Inferno* [ABE; 106m; LBX]; VHS1: *Inferno* [ABE; 106m; LBX]; *Inferno* [KEY; 107(106)m]; VHS2: *Inferno* [TCF; 101m; LBX]

This, an indirect sequel to Argento's own *Suspiria* (1977), and the second in the proposed "Three Mothers" trilogy, revolves around Mater Tenebrarum ("the Mother of Darkness") who resides in New York. A woman finds a book about the Three Mothers in a hole-in-the-wall bookstore and discovers that she herself lives in one of the houses built for the infamous witches by the alchemist Varelli. She "disappears" soon thereafter, so her brother drops his studies in Italy and comes to the rescue, only to find himself wrapped up in the mysteries surrounding both his sibling's disappearance and the building in which she lived.

Visually, this is by far one of Argento's most accomplished films, combining Hitchcock-like staging, Bava-like lighting and photography, and Peckinpah-like choreography for the violence; yet, as a whole, it is undeniably Argento. It also rates as both his most striking and poetic work to date. It does not suffer from a threadbare script, as did *Suspiria*, but—on the same note—it can be quite confusing, to the point where repeated viewings may be required for the viewer to unravel everything themselves, and there are far too many coincidences to be taken lightly. While it takes great pains to separate itself from its predecessor without forfeiting that film's pervasive themes, *Inferno* makes a lazy choice of reiterating *Suspiria*'s fiery finale.

Sadly, this was Mario Bava's last film; although he is only credited as a make-up artist, it is rumored that he actually directed a handful of scenes. His son, Lamberto, was assistant director.

Inferno dei Morti-Viventi [Hell of the Living Dead] (1981)

Beatric Film [It], Films Dara [Sp]
DIR: Bruno Mattei; PRO: Sergio Cortona; SCR: José María Cunillés and Claudio Fragasso; DOP: John Cabrera; EXP: Sergio Cortona; MFX: Giuseppe Ferranti; MUS: Goblin

STR: Pep Ballenster, Joaquín Blanco, Bruno Boni, Patrizia Costa, Cesare di Vito, Josep Lluís Fonoll, Piero Fumelli, Franco Giraldi, Víctor Israel, Selan Karay, Esther Mesina, Margit Evelyn Newton, Robert O'Neil, Sergio Pislar, Gaby Renom and Bernard Seray

AKA: *Apocalipsis Canibal* [Cannibal Apocalypse]; *Cannibal Virus*; *Hell of the Living Dead*; *Night of the Zombies*; *Virus*; *Zombie Creeping Flesh*; *Zombie Inferno*; *Zombie of the Savanna*

Video box art for *Inferno dei Morti-Viventi* (1981), Vestron Video.

Approximately 100m; Color ⍟ ⍟ ⍟
DVD1: *Hell of the Living Dead* [ABE;
103(100)m; LBX]; VHS1: *Night of the Zombies* [VES; 101(100)m]
ADL: *They Eat the Living!*

A leak at a nuclear plant creates a zombie rat that kills a worker, turning him into—go figure—a ravenous ghoul. The expected plague ensues, with black-faced zombies stumbling after walking sacks of pig gut. A group of swat team members decide to take a little trip to the jungle, coming across a busload of tourists that have been attacked by natives infected with the virus. The survivors make their way back to civilization, only to find that the city is even worse off than the countryside.

This shameless retread of George Romero's 1978 splatter-fest *Dawn of the Dead* (and, to some degree, Lucio Fulci's *Zombi 2*, made the following year) seems undeterred by its lack of originality, forging forward with the sort of gratuity on which all post–*Night of the Living Dead* zombie films are wholly dependent. Its source of inspiration is only made more obvious in that, save for the opening theme, most of the soundtrack by Goblin was swiped from *Dawn of the Dead* and *Contaminazione*.

The production's sorest point, though, is not its derivative nature, but the fact that almost twenty minutes of stock travelogue footage was used to pad out the film ... with very little of it matching. (Most of these scenes were cannibalized—no pun intended—from raw footage used in the Japanese produced *mondo* flick *Guinea Ama* [1974], a film which purported to depict modern day cannibals in Papua New Guinea. Not wanting to let any of it go to waste, director Mattei used some of the unused footage in his 1980 shockumentary *Sesso Perverso, Mondo Violenta* as well.)

Suffice it to say, *Inferno dei Morti-Viventi* is for diehard splatterpunks and zombie film completists only.

Inferno in Diretta *[Live from Hell]* (1985)

Racing Pictures S.r.L. [It/US]
DIR: Ruggero Deodato; PRO: Alessandro Fracassi; SCR: Cesare Frugoni and Dardano Sacchetti; DOP: Alberto Spagnoli; MFX: Alberto Blasi and Maurizio Trani; SFX: Penta Studio, S.r.L.; MUS: Claudio Simonetti
STR: Willie Aames, Luca Barbareschi, Michael Berryman, Karen Black, Lisa Blount, Richard Bright, Penny Brown, Carlos de Carvalho, Ottaviano dell'Acqua, Ruggero Deodato, Edward Farrelly, Valentina Forte, Roffredo Gaetani, Eriq Lasalle, Richard Lynch, Barbara Magnolfi, Leonard Mann, John Steiner and Gabriele Tinti
AKA: *Amazon Savage Adventure*; *Amazonia—La Jungle Blanche* [Amazonia—The White Jungle]; *Cut and Run*; *Dial Help*; *Infierno en el Amazonas* [Hell in the Amazon]; *The Mutilators*
Approximately 90m; Color
DVD1: *Cut and Run* [ABE; 90m; LBX]; VHS1: *Cut and Run* [NWV; 87m]; VHS2: *Amazonia—La Jungle Blanche* [VDS; 87m]; *Cut and Run* [MEC; 84m]; *Inferno in Diretta* [PAN; 86(90)m]
ADL: *Death by Any Means Is a Blessing...*

Although *Inferno in Diretta* is more of a straightforward action/adventure flick than anything else, there's just too much going for it to *not* to recommend it. First, it's helmed by Ruggero Deodato, the selfsame filmmaker responsible for such disturbing genre films as *Cannibal Holocaust* (1979) and *La Casa Sperduta nel Parco* [The House on the Edge of the Park] (1980). Second, it has Michael

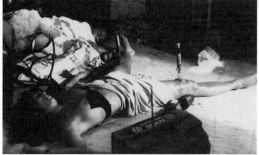

Top: Mexican lobby card for *Inferno in Diretta* (1985). *Left:* Promotional still for *Inferno in Diretta* (1985).

Berryman (which doesn't seem to be much of a consolation when one finds out he plays opposite Willie Aames— yes, *that* Willie Aames from *Eight Is Enough* and *Charles in Charge*—whose ineptitude in dramatic roles is sorely understated). And third, the score is by ex–Goblin member Claudio Simonetti, and—even though it does get a little *too* exuberant at times—is as good as anything the aforementioned band ever produced for Ar-

gento. (Okay, so maybe it isn't as memorable as their score for *Profondo Rosso* [Deep Red] (1975), but you have to give him credit for producing work even remotely comparable to their '70s output.) There are other reasons, but—outside of the high-voltage gore—most of them are overshadowed by the above highlights.

Inferno in Diretta is quite similar to *Cannibal Holocaust* in its approach, although here the media (represented by investigative reporters tracking down drug dealers instead of filmmakers documenting third-world cannibalism) is shown in a less cynical, more empathetic light (if only because it would have been a great undertaking to make them nastier than the opportunistic monsters in *Cannibal Holocaust*). Unfortunately for American audiences, almost all references to cannibals (and the resulting gore) have been replaced with stale footage of, well, Willie Aames. Damn the MPAA.

Under the pre-production title of *Marimba*, this film was originally slated to be directed by Wes Craven, and to star Tim McIntire, Dirk (*Battlestar Galactica*) Benedict and Christopher Mitchum.

Worth a look if any of the above reasons are deemed sufficient.

Infierno *see* **Inferno**

The Initiation (1982)

Initiation Association Ltd. [US]
DIR: Larry Stewart; PRO: Scott Winant; SCR: Charles Pratt, Jr.; DOP: George Tirl; EXP: Jock Gaynor and Bruce Lansbury; SFX: Jack Bennet; MUS: Gabriel Black and Lance Ong
STR: Christi Michelle Allen, Christopher Bradley, Jerry L. Clark, Dan Dickerson, Robert Dowdell, Mary Davis Duncan, Cheryl Foster, Lance Funston, Clu Gulager, Patti Heider, Ronald M. Hubner, Joy Jones, Marilyn Kagan, Kathy Lee Kennedy, Paula Knowles, Peter Malof, Rusty Meyers, Vera Miles, Traci Odom, Diane Page, Frances Peterson, James Read, Trey Stroud, Jennifer Suttles, Melissa Toomin, Hunter Tylo, Andrea Vaccarello and Daphne Zuniga
Approximately 97m; Color
VHS1: *The Initiation* [EMI; 97m]
ADL: *They Pledge Themselves to Be Young, Stay Young … and Die Young.*

A little girl catches her mother bumping uglies with someone who is not her daddy. She promptly takes a kitchen knife to the man, but daddy walks in before she can finish the job. During the scuffle, her father (conveniently) gets booze spilled on him, then (even more conveniently) brushes up against the open fireplace. The scene cuts to pledge night many years later, with a sorority house full of—gasp!—half naked college girls. Their initiation involves breaking into a department store owned by the father of one of the girls and stealing the security guard's uniform. The next day someone escapes from a sanitarium. Is it the girl's disfigured father? Or is it someone else who witnessed the accident?

Despite its intentions, *The Initiation* doesn't exploit the expected con-

Video box art for *The Initiation* (1982), Thorn EMI Video.

ventions as much as similar films have in the past (*Hell Night, Pledge Night,* etc.), and is made a little more bearable by the addition of some tongue-in-cheek humor. Unfortunately, the last thirty minutes degenerates into typical slasher fare. (Let's see: Death by machete? Check. Axe? Check. Hand rake? Check. Knife? Some things are always a given. Bow and arrow? Check. Harpoon gun? Check.) Of course, the presentation of the opening sequence as either a dream or a memory is an attempt to distract the viewer from the killer's identity, but otherwise, it's a fairly predictable excursion.

DIR: Norman J. Warren; PRO: Richard Gordon and David Speechley; SCR: Gloria Maley and Nick Maley; DOP: John Metcalfe; EXP: Peter M. Schlesinger; MFX: Make-Up Effects Ltd.; SFX: Camera Effects and Oxford Scientific Films; MUS: John Scott

STR: Jennifer Ashley, David Baxt, Stephanie Beacham, Robin Clarke, Judy Geeson, Steven Grives, Barry Houghton, Dominic Jephcott, Rosalind Lloyd, Kevin O'Shea, Robert Pugh, John Segal, Victoria Tennant, Trevor Thomas and Heather Wright

AKA: *Horror Planet*; *Inseminoid—Un Tempo nel Futuro* [Inseminoid—A Time in the Future]; *Inseminoide—Inseminacion Extraterrestre* [Inseminoid—Extraterrestrial Insemination]

Approximately 93m; Color

DVD0: *Inseminoid* [ELT; 93m; LBX];

Inseminoid (1981)
Jupiter Film Productions Ltd. [UK]

American one-sheet for *Inseminoid* (1981).

Video box art for *Inseminoid* (1981), Embassy Home Entertainment.

VHS1: *Horror Planet* [EMB; 93(92)m]; *Inseminoid* [ABE; 93m; LBX]; VHS2: *Inseminoid* [BWV; 93m]; *Insemonoid* [SOV; 89m] ADL: *A Far from Human Birth*

An interstellar archeological expedition stumbles across a network of caves that houses the skeletal remains of an extinct race. The only survivor of an accidental explosion is found clutching a handful of crystals; he goes crazy, attacking his crewmates, and is eventually brought down. To make matters worse, star Judy Geeson is accosted by one of the aliens—very much alive, to everyone's chagrin—and is impregnated. She goes bonkers as well, and begins cannibalizing the corpses of those crewmembers she fells.

There are some interesting deviations from the post-*Alien* formula, but—ultimately—*Inseminoid* is an inferior clone of the same. Everything onscreen reflects the low budget: Special effects, sets, and the sub-par acting. (The token beasties—crucial to such films—are silly looking at best.) There is an abundance of blood and gore, but much of this was excised for its Stateside release.

Let's just say that Ridley Scott has nothing to fear from this film.

Inseminoid—Un Tempo nel Futuro *see* **Inseminoid**

Inseminoide—Inseminacion Extraterrestre *see* **Inseminoid**

La Invasión de los Zombies Atómicos *see* **Incubo sulla Città Contaminata**

Invasion of the Flesh Hunters *see* **Apocalisse Domani**

Island of Blood *see* **Whodunit**

Jäger der Apokalypse *see* **Apocalisse Domani**

Jason Lives—Friday the 13th Part VI (1986)

Terror Productions Inc. [US]
DIR: Tom McLoughlin; PRO: Don Behrns; SCR: Tom McLoughlin; DOP: Jon Kranhouse; MFX: Chris Swift and Brian Wade; SFX: Martin Becker and Reel EFX Inc.; MUS: Alice Cooper and Harry Manfredini

STR: Alan Blumenfeld, Jennifer Cooke, Darcy DeMoss, Temi Epstein, Matthew Faison, Tom Fridley, Tony Goldwyn, C.J. Graham, Vincent Guastaferro, Renee Jones, David Kagen, Cynthia Kania, Bob Larkin, Sheri Levinsky, Thom Mathews, Nancy McLoughlin, Wallace Merck, Michael Nomad, Kerry Noonan, Justin Nowell, Tommy Nowell, Taras O'Har, Ron Palillo, Roger Rose, Whitney Rydbeck, Ann Ryerson, Michael Swan and Courtney Vickery

AKA: *Friday the 13th, Part VI—Jason Lives*; *Martes 13—Part VI Jason Vive* [Tuesday the 13th—Part IV Jason Lives]

Approximately 87m; Color
DVD1: *Friday the 13th, Part VI—Jason Lives* [PHV; 87m; LBX]; VHS1: *Jason Lives—Friday the 13th Part VI* [PHV; 87m]; VHS2: *Friday the 13th, Part VI—Jason Lives* [PHV; 87m]

Jason's maggot-ridden corpse is resuscitated by a well-placed makeshift lightning rod and a well-timed bolt of lightning. The two responsible are Ron (*Welcome Back, Kotter*) Palillo (in what has to be the low point of his career) and who I assume to be the lead from *A New Beginning*. On hand for fodder is the usual gaggle of horny campers, as well as a horde of paintball-packing weekend warriors.

Jason Lives is not only *another* worthless entry in one of the longest running (and redundant) series in the history of cinema, it is by far the most generic of the lot, with a complete disregard for logic and common sense that is unprecedented even in *this* series.

By this time, Jason had become the antithesis of literate horror, representing everything shallow and trite about an already precarious genre. The paint-by-numbers slaughter this film offers will only appeal to those individuals looking for the most rudimentary of catharsis; even children raised on *Goosebumps* will see it for what it is, and pass it up for the more mature offerings with which their school library can supply them. Its wit and cinematic savvy can be summarized by the following exchange: "We better turn around." "Why?" "Because I've seen enough horror movies to know any weirdo wearing a mask is never friendly." And so the script decrees. Next…

De Kannibalen Vallen Aan! *see* **Cannibal Ferox**

Killer Crocodile (1989)

Fulvia Film S.r.L. [It]
DIR: Fabrizio de Angelis; PRO: Fabrizio de Angelis; SCR: Fabrizio de Angelis and Dardano Sacchetti; DOP: Sergio d'Offizi; MFX: Gianetto de Rossi; SFX: Roberto Ricci; MUS: Riz Ortolani
STR: Marte Amilgar, Dionisio Castro, Anthony Crenna, Franklin Dominguez, Ann Douglas, Nic Gavin, Ennio Girolami, Julian Hampton, John Harper, Van Johnson, Gray Jordan, Sherrie Rose and William Wohrman
Approximately 88m; Color

A group investigating a radioactive waste dump on a South American island run into yet another toxic-spawned critter, in this case a twenty-foot bloodthirsty croc with a hankering for eco-freaks. That said, there's actually a story behind all of this, and since there's no mystery as to *what's* responsible for all of the killing, I'll leave the rest for the viewer to discover.

Having seen just about every killer animal film ever made, I actually found *Killer Crocodile* to be much better than expected, if only because of some good performances and an engaging storyline. (The *only* thing that seems reiterative is the recycled *Jaws* theme.) The best news, though, concerns our toothy nemesis, as he is actually one of the grooviest-looking beasties to come along for quite some time, and his grisly demise is one of the splashiest as well. The gore is also pretty brutal, blood and meat tossed about whenever our resident monster manages to latch onto an unsuspecting swimmer. Of course, there's no blood when a Cabbage Patch doll gets eaten, but watching that is no less enjoyable.

Worth checking out if it ever makes it this far upstream.

Killer Workout (1986)

Maverick Films Ltd. [US], The Winters Group [US]
DIR: David A. Prior; PRO: Peter Yuval; SCR: David A. Prior; DOP: Peter Bonilla; EXP: David Winters and Marc Winters; SFX: United Film Works; MUS: Todd Hayen
STR: Michael Beck, Richard Bravo, David James Campbell, Dianne Copeland, Veronica Davis, Andrea Drever, Lori E. Forsberg, Kris Hagerty, Joel Hoffman, Sheila Howard, Krysia Javid, Lorain Joyner, Monica Karlson, Marcia Karr, Elizabeth Keeme, Irene Korman, Kima Lindquist, Denise Martell, Fritz Matthews, Carol

Maxwell, Lynn Meighan, Kathi Miller, Laurel Mock, Elke Muller, Deborah Norris, Ted Prior, Larry Reynolds, John Robb, Kellyann Sebatasso, Pat Statham, Eddie Swilling, Teresa Truesdale, Richard Turner, Teresa van der Woude, Charles Venniro and Sharon Young
AKA: *Aerobicide*
Approximately 89m; Color
VHS1: *Killer Workout* [AHE; 89m]; VHS2: *Aerobicide* [SOV; 82m]

A girl goes on a vengeful killing spree after being disfigured in a freak tanning booth accident. Armed with nothing but an oversized safety pin, she hacks her way through an aerobics class, then ... sounds like a comedy, right? I'm not laughing. Especially after paying a buck to rent this sucker just so I could get the credits. Anywho, as if the murders weren't tedious enough, each one is followed by a meticulously well-rehearsed aerobics drill. One right after another. It just doesn't end. Seriously ... *it just doesn't end!*

All of the B's are present: Bare breasts, blood, big hair, bad music, bad scripting, bad acting, etc. Out of all the slasher films I've been forced to sit through (again, it never ends), this one has got to be the most painful excursion of the lot.

If you're the kind of pathetic geek who whacks off to your sister's aerobicize videos, then you're in luck. Otherwise, keep your distance.

Killing Birds *see* **Uccelli Assassini**

The Killing of Satan (1983)

Cinex Films Inc. [Ph]
DIR: Efren C. Piñon; PRO: Pio C. Lee; SCR: Jose Mari Avellana; DOP: Ricardo Herrera; EXP: Conrado Puzon; MFX: Cecine Baun; SFX: Jun Marvella; VFX: ELG Arts & Ads; MUS: Ernani Cuenco
STR: Cecille Castillo, Charlie Davao, Paquito Diaz, George Estregan, Elizabeth Oropesa, Ramon Revilla and Erlyn Umali
Approximately 93m; Color
VHS1: *The Killing of Satan* [PAR; 95(93)m]
ADL: *What Powers Should a Man Possess to Challenge the Prince of Darkness?*

A small village is besieged by a magician in red tights and a cape ("the Prince of Magic") and his just as colorful henchman. Their savior comes in the form of Lando, an ex-con who was sent to prison for killing the antagonist's brother. After they kidnap Lando's daughter and beat the snot out of his wife, the reluctant hero journeys to the bad guy's island lair and finds himself confronted by more than just a podunk Dr. Strange knock-off.

This one's a hoot and a half, people. Everyone in the film displays magical prowess: The bad guys all shoot power rays from their fingertips (their adversaries prefer to use their elbows, it seems), or engage in really intense staring contests, and when that doesn't work, they simply slug it out. All of the hokum is outrageously conceived, added onto the film after the fact by someone with great patience and a box of colored markers. The mad magician is aided by "cobra men" and—of course—old Scratch himself (complete with horns, a pitchfork, and a tail—natch). There's even a rotting mummy with a ping-pong-ball eye, which subtly graces the back of the video box as well.

Even though one would swear that this film was intended for a very young audience, *The Killing of Satan* is not without its gratuitous sex and violence. T&A is the order of the day in the magician's lair; his harem of

WHAT POWER
SHOULD A MAN
POSSESS TO
CHALLENGE
THE PRINCE OF
DARKNESS?

THE KILLING OF

SATAN

starring
RAMON REVILLA
ELIZABETH OROPESA
GEORGE ESTREGAN
CHARLIE DAVAO
produced by PIO C. LEE · directed by EFREN C. PIÑON

PARAGON
VIDEO PRODUCTIONS

Video box art for *The Killing of Satan* (1983), Paragon Video Productions.

(extremely) young looking abductees are kept in a large cage, doing little more than standing for the entirety of the film, displaying their wares to anyone who cares. The gore is sparse, but surprisingly intense. (There is one ripped face prosthetic that is passable, but the highlight is a man getting crushed by a possessed boulder. This scene is not only outrageously gory, but also hilariously funny, and could easily be inserted into a theatrical Monty Python skit without anyone being the wiser.)

And if it wasn't bad enough, the inept dubbing should garner a few extra laughs. (When one character proclaims, "Uncle Miguel is dead," someone immediately asks, "You mean uncle Miguel is dead?" Geez,

where is there room for misinterpretation in that sentence?) Trash fiends rejoice!

Killing Spree (1987)

Twisted Illusions Inc. [US]
DIR: Tim Ritter; PRO: Al Nicolosi; SCR: Tim Ritter; DOP: Mark Pederson; EXP: Vincent Miranda; MFX: Joel Harlow and Mark Pederson; MUS: Perry Monroe
STR: Alan Brown, Bruno, B. Casey Campfield, Greg Campfield, Raymond Carbone, Christina de Tequesta, Tracy Drolet, Asbestos Felt, Norm Kahl, Courtney Lercara, Richard Lustic, Paul Merkel, Jr., Vincent Miranda, Bobby Newman, Al Nicolosi, Norman, Darlene Nowocien, Bruce Paquette, Cloe Pavel, Alice Penner, Mel Pitler, Jimmy Riblitt, Tim Ritter, Johnny Rough, Rachel Rutz, Kieran Turner, Dwayne Willis and Joel D. Wynkoop
Approximately 88m; Color
VHS1: *Killing Spree* [MAG; 88m]

An overworked airplane mechanic goes on, well, a killing spree after he comes to the conclusion that his wife of six months is cheating on him with his best friend, the electrician, the TV repairman, and, well, just about every other guy who strays in front of the camera.

Everything about this production is inept. Realizing its inadequacies, *Killing Spree* tries to cover up its own stink with what amounts to really desperate attempts at humor. (A weird dream sequence with the killer's adulterous wife sporting a pair of lips that make Mick Jagger's look petite is one of the highlights, sad to say.) Furthermore, you can see the crucial twist coming a mile away, whereas the shock ending isn't nearly as predictable, if only because no seasoned screenwriter would ever attempt such a ridiculous feat. And, worst of all, as the gore escalates, the special make-up effects get progressively worse.

In light of the film's innumerable shortcomings, who even *needs* to mention the obnoxious synth score?

Kung Fu Kannibalen *see* **Diyu Wu Men**

El Laberinto de las Arañas *see* **Il Nido del Ragno**

The Lair of the White Worm (1988)

Vestron Pictures [UK]
DIR: Ken Russell; PRO: Ken Russell; SCR: Ken Russell [Based on the novel *The Lair of the White Worm* by Bram Stoker]; DOP: Dick Bush; EXP: Dan Ireland and William J. Quigley; MFX: Image Animation; SFX: Alan Whibley; VFX: Tony Lawrence; MUS: Stanislas Syrewicz
STR: Paul Brooke, Peter Capaldi, Imogen Claire, Miranda Coe, Sammi Davis, Amanda Donohoe, Linzi Drew, Paul Easom, Christopher Gable, Hugh Grant, James Hicks, Stratford Johns, Caron Anne Kelly, David Kiernan, Matthew King, Gina McKee, Ross Murray, Andy Norman, Fiona O'Conner, Catherine Oxenberg, Lloyd Peters, Chris Pitt, Caroline Pope, Jackie Russell, Elisha Scott, Tina Shaw and Bob Smith
AKA: *Der Biß der Schlangfrau* [The Bite of the Bolting Woman]
Approximately 93m; Color
DVD0: *The Lair of the White Worm* [PIO; 93m; LBX]; VHS1: *The Lair of the White Worm* [VES; 93m]

A young man discovers the fossils of a "white worm," an extinct prehistoric creature that was worshipped by early man ... or so he thinks. The skeletal remains are stolen, instigating a series of bizarre murders across the quaint Irish countryside.

Although quite lighthearted when compared to Russell's other genre offerings (*The Devils*, *Altered States*, etc.), *The Lair of the White Worm* still

showcases some of the director's penchant for disturbing, often surreal imagery, much of which saves the film from tumbling headlong into horror film pastiche. The "Nudge, nudge. Wink, wink. Know what I mean?" humor is charming at times, but is often laid on so thick that the more suspenseful scenes don't pack nearly the wallop they should. Regardless, there are some wonderful performances that shine through the one-liners and thick Irish brogues.

The gore is sparse, but gratuitous when shown; most of the bloodshed is commandeered by a series of "flashbacks" that suffer greatly from having been patched together using very primitive CGI. (This is particularly distracting in that the film tries unbearably hard to give everything an antiquated feel.)

Enjoyable, although a little disappointing considering the filmmaker and the source material.

The Last Horror Film (1982)

Sphere Productions Ltd. [US]
DIR: David Winters; PRO: Judd Hamilton and David Winters; SCR: Judd Hamilton, Tom Klassen, and David Winters; DOP: Tom de Nove; MFX: Peter McKenzie; SFX: John Humphreys, Michael Jones, and Jean Scott; MUS: Jesse Frederick and Jeff Koz
STR: George Altschul, John Austin, Dennis Beasnard, Stanley Susanne Benton, Corina Burkli, Melissa Carr, Malgosia Casey, Sean Casey, June Chadwick, John Claude, Peter Darcy, Holly de Jong, Tom de Nove, Ronald Dessautels, Valerie Devereaux, Judy Duckett, Mai Britt Finseth, Devin Goldenberg, Lavana Hakim, Chip Hamilton, John Hamilton, Judd Hamilton, Tammy Hamilton, Marty Heckleman, Joanne Hicks, Sharon Hughes, Mark Hutchinson, Glenn Jacobson, David Jones, Noreen Kantala, John Kelly, Marika

Laususer, Robin Leach, Jenny Lipman, Katia Malmio, Henri Marchal, Richard Masner, Tony McCann, Caroline Munro, Marty Ollstein, Simone Overman, Robert Paget, Jane Rawlins, Patty Salier, Joe Spinell, Mary Spinell, Don Talley, Valerie, George Valismis, Luke Walter, Jane Wellman, Mary Jose Welsch, William Whittington, David Winters and J'Len Winters
    AKA: *Fanatic*; *Fanatical Extreme*
    Approximately 86m; Color
    DVD0: *Fanatic* [TRO; 86m]; VHS1: *Fanatic* [TRO; 86m]; *The Last Horror Film* [MHE; 87(86)m]

Obviously inspired by the questionable success of William Lustig's *Maniac* (1981), *The Last Horror Film* reunites the stars from said film for more stalk 'n' slash action. This film, though, follows obsessed taxi driver Vinny Durand (Spinell), who goes to Cannes in order to convince B-actress Jana Bates (Caroline Munro) to be in his (nonexistent) horror film. Upon his arrival, someone starts knocking off anyone who seemingly stands in the way of her appearing in the delusional protagonist's magnum opus. Although *The Last Horror Film* tries valiantly to blur the dividing lines between reality and cinematic fantasy, it boils down to nothing more than opportunistic slasher dreck that tries to make the most out of its backdrops. (One of the only high points is a scene during the film festival when we see booths of distribution and production companies pandering their wares, including one plastered with posters from Jean Rollin efforts, and a glimpse of a man who resembles the selfsame director.) Of course, it's not a complete waste of time, as it's always fun to see Spinell bug-eyed and, well, just plain buggy; but *Maniac* this isn't. (The lame splatter effects will attest to this.)

A truncated version of this film showed up in the horror anthology *Thriller Zone* (1995) as a segment entitled "Fanatical Extremes."

The Last Slumber Party (1988)

B&S Productions [US]
    DIR: Stephen Tyler; PRO: Jill Clark; SCR: Stephen Tyler; DOP: Georges Cardona; EXP: Bill F. Blair and Betty S. Scott; MFX: Richard Landwehr and John Woodruff; MUS: John Brennan, Danilo Bridgens and Firstryke
    STR: Paul Amend, Barbara Claiborne, Claire Cooney, Danny David, Lance Descourez, Darcy Devine, Jan Jensen, Nancy Meyer, Mary Louise Michel, Rick Polizzi, Jim Taylor, Stephen Tyler, David Whitley and Joann Whitley
    Approximately 71m; Color
    VHS1: *The Last Slumber Party* [UHV; 80(71)m]
    ADL: ...*Where the Girls Are Dying for a Good Time.*

A paranoid schizophrenic doctor waiting in line for a pre-frontal lobotomy escapes from the hospital and makes life a living heck for three graduates holding a slumber party. Gee ... *there's* a story.

I get the distinct impression that some kid spent his college tuition money to make this picture, and I bet his parents were none too pleased. *The Last Slumber Party* is just what we needed ... a half-baked rehash of *Slumber Party Massacre* that exhibits every cliché, every lame shock and plot device (yes, there *is* a shower scene) that has become the staples of the modern slasher film. As if that wasn't enough, it even boasts an obnoxious '80s metal soundtrack that will surely put some wear and tear on your mute button. (How could we ever thank Firstryke for their contribution, aside from a letter bomb?)

Yet another poster child for the "Save the Celluloid" foundation.

Latidos de Pánico [Panicked Heartbeats] (1983)

Aconito Films [Sp]
DIR: Jacinto Molina Álvarez; PRO: Jacinto Molina Álvarez; SCR: Jacinto Molina Álvarez; DOP: Julio Burgos; EXP: Augusto Boué; MUS: Moncho Alpuente and Servando Carballar
STR: Jacinto Molina Álvarez, Charly Bravo, Pedro de las Heras, Lola Gaos, Carol Kirkham, Silvio Miró, Paquita Ondiviela, José Sacristan, Salvador Sáinz, Julia Salinero, José Vivó and Manuel Zanzo
Approximately 92m; Color

Latidos de Panico opens with a quaint little scene of a nude woman running through the woods, pursued by a knight on horseback, the infamous caballero Alaric de Mannac who could—apparently—give the Knights Templar a run for their money in sheer depravity. No sooner has he revealed himself to be Paul Naschy (*né* Jacinto Molina Alvarez), then he begins to tenderize her with a morningstar. (Ouch.) Four hundred years later, we cut to the knight's descendant, who is caring for his wife who suffers from a serious heart condition. Thinking it would do her some good, he takes his ailing spouse to his ancestral family home and, well, I'm sure you can see where this is heading.

Even though it depends on many of the staples of Spanish horror cinema, this—one of Naschy's later efforts—is an extremely admirable effort. The production values on display here are as good as any of Naschy's films have ever seen, as is the script, which boasts enough double-crossing and twists and turns to com-pliment any Italian crime thriller. The gore may be sparse, but it is brutal (to say the least) and worth the wait in most cases.

Definitely recommended for Paul Naschy fans and Spanish horror aficionados.

Leatherface—Texas Chainsaw Massacre III (1989)

New Line Cinema [US]
DIR: Jeff Burr; PRO: Robert Engelman; SCR: David J. Schow; DOP: James L. Carter; MFX: KNB EFX Group Inc.; MUS: Jim Manzie and Patrick Regan [Soundtrack from Enigma Records]
STR: Jennifer Banko, Ron Brooks, William Butler, Miriam Byrd-Nethery, David Cloud, Beth de Patie, Tom Everett, Ken Foree, Kate Hodge, Toni Hudson, R.A. Mihailoff, Viggo Mortensen, Joe Unger, Dwayne Whitaker, Michael Shamus Wiles and Caroline Williams
AKA: *El Descuartizador* [The Chopper]; *Leatherface—The Texas Chainsaw Massacre III*
Approximately 82m; Color
VHS1: *Leatherface—The Texas Chainsaw Massacre III* [NEW; 85(82)m; LBX]; *Leatherface—The Texas Chainsaw Massacre III* [RCA; 82m]
ADL: *He Puts the Teeth in Terror*

This film hinges on the premise that the events in *The Texas Chainsaw Massacre II* simply never happened, *and* that Leatherface was the only member of the Sawyer family to survive and elude authorities, *and* that he's been busy the last fifteen years, laying low and raising a family of his own. (Even as head of the clan, he's never been able to shake his "whipping boy" status.) Anywho, a brother and sister driving across country inadvertently comes a knocking, unfamiliar with this family's peculiar brand of country hospitality. Ken (*Dawn of the Dead*) Foree plays a survivalist who gets caught in the crossfire ("My name's Benny ... I'm the sorry ass bastard you almost hit"), and is the *only* saving grace in this sorry ass film.

This is simply a failed attempt to franchise Texas' resident saw freak-slash-cannibal. Although it may have been a vaguely interesting sequel had it not disregarded the Chainsaw mythos, any film trying to follow-up *The Texas Chain Saw Massacre* will inevitably fail. Presumably, Hooper realized this when he cooked up his sequel, taking an entirely different approach so that when it failed to live up to expectations, it would still be an entertaining film. *Leatherface*, though, shamelessly cops entire scenes from the original, and—although I'm sure they would claim it was done in homage—it reeks of stale reiteration.

Oh, and by the way: It looks like much of the gore was probably left on the cutting room floor, so if you're looking for over-the-top carnage, you may want to look elsewhere.

Maybe the adline should've read: "He puts the teeth in *this film bites.*" That would have made a *little* more sense, anyway.

Leatherface—The Texas Chainsaw Massacre III *see* **Leatherface—Texas Chainsaw Massacre III**

The Legend Lives (1981)

The Legend Lives Company [US]
DIR: Joe Giannone; PRO: Gary Sales; SCR: Joe Giannone; DOP: James Momel; EXP: Sam Marion; MFX: Rich Alonzo and Johanne Hansen; SFX: William Depaolo, Rob E. Holland, John Luckavic and Matt Vogel; MUS: Stephen Horelick and Gary Sales
STR: Harriet Bass, Jan Claire, Stephen

Clark, Paul Ehlers, Tony Fish, Carl Fredericks, Deidre Higgins, Seth Jones, Vicki Kenneally, Lori Mathes, Shelley Mathes, Alexander Murphy, Jr., Jane Pappidas, Gaylen Ross, Trais Sawyer, Jimmy Steele, Michael Sullivan and Tom Veilleux
AKA: *Campfire Tales*; *Madman*; *Madman Marz*
Approximately 88m; Color
DVD1: *Madman* [ABE; 88m; LBX]; VHS1: *Madman* [ABE; 88m; LBX]; *Madman* [EMI; 89(88)m]
ADL: *They Thought They Were Alone.*

"It all started during a campfire at North Sea Cottages, a special retreat for gifted children..." A campfire tale relates the story of a farmer who went buggy and chopped up his family with an axe. He was lynched and mutilated by the none-too-happy townsfolk, but his body—and those of his family—were gone by morning. Supposedly, saying his name aloud will bring him 'round, so some wise ass who's never seen a horror film gets the bright idea to ... well, you know.

Although grounded in urban legend, this slasher flick shamelessly reiterates the proceedings from *Friday the 13th* to such an extent that it might as well have been one of that film's many sequels. Production values are similarly lackluster, although *The Legend Lives* doesn't boast the effects artistry of Tom Savini's caliber to make it noteworthy. The film's only high point is the presence of *Dawn of the Dead*'s Gaylen Ross (under the pseudonym of Alexis Dubin) as the camp counselor-cum-heroine, although even she doesn't live to see the end credits. If you're not a diehard *Dawn of the Dead* fan, then this isn't much of a selling point, but it's all that it's got.

Forgettable.

Lentávát Tappajat *see* Piranha Part
Two—The Spawning

Let Them Die Slowly *see* Cannibal
Ferox

Leviatán *see* Los Perros de la
Muerte

The Living Dead Girl *see* La Morte
Vivante

Lucker the Necrophagous (1986)

Desert Productions [Be]
DIR: Johan Vandewoestijne; PRO:
Filip Beys, André Coppens and Johan Van-
dewoestijne; SCR: John Kupferschmidt and
Johan Vandewoestijne; EXP: Johan Vande-
woestijne; MFX: Filip Beys; SFX: Filip Beys;
MUS: Geert Beernaert and Peter Bonne
STR: Heidi Calewaert, Tony Castillo,
Marie Paule Claes, Eddy Cosaert, Veerle
Dendooven, John Edwards, Francis Impe,
Let Jodts, Nico Karadjiam, Joachim Kes-
teloot, Freek Neirynck, Werner Onré, Mar-
tine Scherre, Frans Schwepens, Frank van
Laecke, Carry van Middel, Nick van Suyt
and Helga Vandevelde
AKA: *Necrophagous*
Approximately 84m; Color

John Lucker is a simple killer
with simple needs. Having just escaped from a sanitarium (where he
was incarcerated for murdering eight
young women), he decides to make up
for lost time by going on a little binge,
erstwhile "cleaning his pipes." It
seems his "simple" needs involve rape
and murder, but not quite in that
order. (Those ass-backwards necro-
philes ... God bless 'em.) He's also a
cannibal, to which the title eludes, but
that's secondary. (The terms "necro-
phile" or "anthropophagous" would
have shed more light on his predilections, though, as a large percentage of
the population perform necrophagia,
sometimes three times in a day.)

Yes, this flick can get pretty repulsive, predating *Nekromantik* by a
year in its graphic depiction of "that
unspeakable sex act." Unfortunately,
this film is simply brash, with little or
no style to compliment the disturbing
goings-on. (The only stylistic touch
easily recalled is the use of the "rocking chair-cam"; the cinematographer
must've seen *The Headless Eyes* the
night before filming.) Although in-
disputably gory, most of the blood
spilled is the gallons spit up by the
victims, who have a penchant for
doing so regardless of how they die.

Well, there's not much else to re-
port, as not much really happens between the scenes of carnage. No real
character development. No dialogue.
No exposition. Nothing. Lots and lots
of nothing. Even watching a time-
compressed, seventy-one minute version proved to be a tedious experience.

If you must see it, borrow it from
someone suckered into buying a bootleg of it; you'll be happy that you did-
n't shell out your own hard-earned
cash for it. (Hey, that's what I did.)

Lune de Sang *see* Die Säge des
Todes

Lurkers (1987)

Reeltime Distributing Corp. [US]
DIR: Roberta Findlay; PRO: Walter
E. Sear; SCR: Ed Kelleher and Harriette
Vidal; DOP: Roberta Findlay; MFX: Ed-
ward French; MUS: Walter E. Sear
STR: Jodi Armstrong, C.C. Banks,
Eva Baumann, Tom Billett, Wayne Bur-
cham, Tara Lyn Catanzaro, Carissa Chan-
ning, Ruth Collins, Ric Frank, Florence
Galperin, Shana Sear Gaskill, Anne Grind-
lay, Nancy Groff, Danielle Leonard, Roy
McArtur, Christine Moore, Dana Nardelli,
Gil Newsom, Lynne Nonnenmacher, Peter

Oliver-Norman, Debbie Rochon, Deanna Rossi, Janeen Rossi, Lauren Ruane, Timothy Rule, Walter E. Sear, Dayne Shapiro, Elka Shapiro, Jeanette Smith, Bonnie Sterner, Gregory Sullivan, Marina Taylor, William Titus, Moira Tobey, Steve Villalobos, Jeffrey Wallach and Gary Warner

AKA: *Home Sweet Home*
Approximately 95m; Color
VHS1: *Lurkers* [MHE; 95m]
ADL: *Cathy's Childhood Nightmares Are Back ... and This Time They're Going to Get Her.*

As a child, Cathy was plagued by an abusive mother, sadistic peers, and a bunch of stupid looking ghosts; as an adult, she doesn't fare much better. She meets a photographer and things are going reasonably well until the nightmares kick in. Her brother— now a priest—tells her to keep her distance. (I guess that's what she gets for inviting him to her wedding.) From there, *Lurkers* becomes *The Sentinel* (1977) by way of *Carnival of Souls* (1962), minus the verve of either of those films.

This cheesy supernatural flick is a fairly innocuous outing, plodding and gore-lite (save for a particularly repulsive scene involving a sledgehammer and some poor sap's head). And, even though Findlay hasn't improved much in her (by this time) twenty-odd years in the business, it's difficult *not* to find some charm in her grade Z productions. (I mean, how many people—besides Andy Milligan—were still making '70s films this far into the '80s, hmmm?) Of course, Roberta Findlay's later horror output doesn't hit the same nerves as the films she worked on with her late hubby (*Shriek of the Mutilated*, *Slaughter*, and—my personal favorite—*A Thousand Pleasures* come immediately

to mind), but she should still be commended for her no-budget innovation. (Regardless, those awful synth horns have got to go.)

Probably best reserved for Findlay aficionados.

Macabras Historias de Horror *see* **Creepshow**

Mad Jake *see* **Blood Salvage**

Madhouse *see* **There Was a Little Girl**

Madman *see* **The Legend Lives**

Madman Marz *see* **The Legend Lives**

La Maison de la Terreur *see* **La Casa con la Scala nel Buio**

La Maison Près du Cimetière *see* **Quella Villa Accanto al Cimitero**

The Majorettes (1987)
Major Films [US]
DIR: S. William Hinzman; PRO: John A. Russo; SCR: John A. Russo [Based on the novel *The Majorettes* by John Russo]; DOP: Paul McCollough; EXP: J.C. Ross; MFX: Gerald Gergely; SFX: Gerald Gergely; MUS: Paul McCollough

STR: Teresa Almendarez, Kristan Blake, Joe Blakely, Jacqueline Bowman, Earl Brandstetter, George Brennan, Allen Bross, Angel Canalungo, Gina Cotton, Daryl Darak, Joy Deco, Tom E. Desrocher, Angela Eckerd, Terrie Godfrey, Dave Gordon, Carl Hetrick, Bonnie Hinzman, Heidi Hinzman, S. William Hinzman, Denise Huot, Mark V. Jevicky, Harold K. Keller, Kevin Kindlin, Edna Kleitz, Frank Krauss, Mary Jo Limpert, Kristen Lintner, Robert Lintner, Tom Madden, Dana Maiello, Melissa Marko, Colin Martin, Amy Mathesiuf, William R. Mott, Christine Mura, Eileen Mura, Jennifer Mura, Jackie Nicoll, Joe Pas-

sarillo, Tammy Petruska, Elaine Restad, Lynn Restad, Abby Roach, Wilbur Roncone, Jay Ross, John A. Russo, Sueanne Seamens, Andrea Spence, Russ Streiner, M. Therian, Roland Tournat and Mike Wilson
AKA: *One by One*
Approximately 93m; Color
VHS1: *The Majorettes* [VES; 93m]
ADL: *Sis, Boom, Blood. You're Dead.*

A photographer who has a penchant for hanging out in the ventilation shaft of the girls' locker room at school (hey, how convenient for the ogle-minded viewer) may be a crazed killer making short work of young women in a small town. Meanwhile, a caretaker scheming to kill off an old woman in order to filch her inheritance decides to take advantage of the killings. Having initiated these two tenuously related storylines, *The Majorettes* quickly resumes its place as a predictable entry in the stalk 'n' slash sweepstakes. There are some plot twists about an hour into the film, but it's too little, too late. (The same can be said for the forced religious symbolism; it may have worked in Russo's earlier—and far superior—offering, *Midnight* [1980], but here it is simply extraneous.)

The highlights of the film (of course) are the abundance of slit throats and the gratuitous T&A, the cornerstones of slasher cinema. Less noteworthy are the cheesy synth score, an obnoxious Jerry Lewis–type punk, and stilted dialogue that one would swear was swiped from a bad soap opera. Last but not least is the most *convenient* finale I've seen to date, where an entire gang of motorcycle punks is *conveniently* dispatched, and everything caught in the crossfire *conveniently* blows up. Gee, what are the odds of that? (It just goes

to show that it takes a writer of the highest order to come up with such clever twists.)

Pretty sad, really. You expect this kind of dreck from newbies, but finding out that *The Majorettes* involves three of the people who had a hand in *Night of the Living Dead* is pretty disturbing, I assure you.

Make Them Die Slowly *see* **Cannibal Ferox**

La Maldición *see* **The Curse**

La Maldición de los Zombies *see* **Death Warmed Up**

Il Malocchio *see* **L'Occhio del Male**

Man Beast *see* **Anthropophagus**

Mangeurs d'Hommes *see* **Mondo Cannibale** (1980)

Mangiati Vivi [Eaten Alive] (1980)

Dania Film [It], Medusa Distribuzione [It], National Cinematografica [It]
DIR: Umberto Lenzi; PRO: Mino Loy and Luciano Martino; SCR: Umberto Lenzi; DOP: Frederico Zanni; SFX: Paolo Ricci; MUS: Carlo Maria Cordio and Maria Fiamma Maglione
STR: Janet Agren, Alfred Joseph Berry, Francesco Fantasia, Mel Ferrer, Meg Fleming, Gianfranco Goduti, Gerald Grant, Robert Kerman, Me Me Lai, Carl Longhi, Ivan Rassimov, Michele Schmiegelm, Paola Senatore and Robert Spafford
AKA: *Doomed to Die*; *The Emerald Jungle*; *Mangiati Vivi dai Cannibali* [Eaten Alive by the Cannibals]
Approximately 92m; Color 🎞🎞🎞
DVD2: *Eaten Alive* [VIP; 81m]; VHS1: *The Emerald Jungle* [CON; 92m]; *Mangiati Vivi* [ECE; 89m]; VHS2: *Eaten Alive* [VIP; 81m]

A cult leader named Jonas governs a "purification village" in an isolated stretch of South American jungle. (It is made even more unreachable considering their next-door neighbors are a fierce tribe of cannibals with particularly atrocious table manners.) With the help of a hero-for-hire, a girl tracks down her missing sister to the commune, where she has been taken under Jonas' wing. Of course, the protagonists find themselves between a rock and a hard place trying to escape from the Green Hell into which they've stumbled.

This contrived cannibal flick tries really hard to broaden the inherently limited range of the Green Hell subgenre by introducing an equally exploitive storyline that shamelessly basks in the steaming remains of the Jim Jones massacre. (Let's see: A religious cult leader named "Jonas," a South American commune, poisoned Kool-aid, mass execution … yep, everything's accounted for.) Otherwise, it's typical for this subgenre, although it might be even more unwatchable than most Green Hell efforts in that it wallows in animal evisceration for damn near half the film's running time. If the sight of a monkey being eaten alive by a hungry croc doesn't make your stomach churn, that of his reptilian cousin being skinned alive by natives should do the trick. On hand to add to the geek-show proceedings are some (real) ritualistic piercings and a (faked) *Make Them Die Slowly*–style emasculation. And, of course, racism and sexism abounds. Gee … imagine that.

Recommended only for those with no sense of ethics or aesthetics.

Mangiati Vivi dai Cannibali *see* Mangiati Vivi

Manhattan Baby *see* L'Occhio del Male

Maniac (1980)

Maniac Productions Inc. [US]
DIR: William Lustig; PRO: Andrew Garroni and William Lustig; SCR: C.A. Rosenberg and Joe Spinell; DOP: Robert Lindsay; EXP: Judd Hamilton and Joe Spinell; MFX: Tom Savini; SFX: Tom Savini; MUS: Jay Chattaway [Soundtrack from South East Records and Varèse Sarabande]
STR: Jimmy Aurichio, Nelia Bacmeister, Joan Baldwin, James Brewster, Candace Clements, Tracie Evans, Terry Gagnon, Carol Henry, Kim Hudson, Louis Jawitz, Randy Jurgensen, Gail Lawrence, William Lustig, Hyla Marrow, Sharon Mitchell, Rita Montone, Caroline Munro, Jeni Paz, Frank Pesce, Kelly Piper, Tom Savini, Billy Spagnuolo, Denise Spagnuolo, Joe Spinell, Linda Lee Walter and Janelle Winston
AKA: *Maniaco* [Maniac]
Approximately 85m; Color
VHS1: *Maniac* [ABE; 85m; LBX]; *Maniac* [MHE; 88(80)m]; *Maniaco* [TOP; 88(80)m; Portuguese subtitles]
ADL: *I Warned You Not to Go Out Tonight…*

This is it, what many people consider the lowest depths ever plumbed by the slasher film; an irredeemable splatterfest that panders to only the most sadistic misfits. There is hardly a "respectable" film reviewer that hasn't spoken out against this movie, a film whose testament is a sad statement about a society so utterly desensitized to violence, jaded by the ever-increasing brutality portrayed on the silver screen. That's what *they* say, anyway.

Maniac is not an art film by any means, nor is it a great film, but it is in invaluable tool in putting into per-

DIGITALLY REMASTERED COLLECTOR'S EDITION

JOE   CAROLINE
SPINELL   MUNRO

I WARNED YOU
NOT TO GO OUT
TONIGHT

MANIAC

"Maniac" Starring Joe Spinell • Caroline Munro
Associate Producer John Packard • Special Make-Up Effects by Tom Savini
Music by Jay Chattaway • Screenplay by C.A. Rosenberg and Joe Spinell
Executive Producers Joe Spinell and Judd Hamilton
Produced by Andrew Garroni and William Lustig
Directed by William Lustig

Video box art for *Maniac* (1980), Anchor Bay Entertainment.

spective how our society perceives violence. Unlike most slasher films—in particular the indefatigable *Friday the 13th* series—*Maniac* does not glorify the violence, approaching it as something "fun." It is a gritty, disturbing and sordid affair that follows the exploits of a very deranged individual, the viewer's pity turning to revulsion every time he takes a victim. Many of the selfsame individuals who can be heard hooting and hollering every time Jason Vorhees makes an addition to his ever-increasing body count will probably be repulsed by the actions of Joe Spinell's much more convincing portrayal of a serial killer.

(Whereas Jason is the ultimate anti-hero, an indestructible killing machine whose motivation is beyond everyone save for maybe the scriptwriter, Spinell's tortured monster is pathetic and rarely worthy of anything more than contempt.) Granted, *Friday the 13th* may be cathartic for the aforementioned jaded society, but which response seems healthier?

Not to say that *Maniac* doesn't exploit the popular tenets of sex and violence; it does, but the proceedings never come across as aggrandizing. The bloodshed is brutal, complimented by some of Tom Savini's most impressive work; the scalpings that are the killer's trademark are the most unnerving effects of its type ever committed to the screen. The sex is fairly reflective of its 42nd Street origins, and is even more convincing in that many of the actresses involved were fairly big names in the adult film industry. (Some, like Sharon Mitchell, were synonymous with '70s porn, as was Abigail Clayton, appearing here under her real name of Gail Lawrence.) Although director Lustig was probably just trying to cash in on a trend that came to typify '80s horror, *Maniac* is ultimately something more than most of the slasher films which preceded, and inevitably followed, it.

Just ignore Leonard Maltin, why don't you?

Maniac Cop (1988)

Shapiro-Glickenhaus Entertainment [US]

DIR: William Lustig; PRO: Larry Cohen; SCR: Larry Cohen; DOP: Vincent J. Rabe; EXP: James Glickenhaus; MFX: More Than Skin Deep; SFX: Hollywood Special Effects; MUS: Jay Chattaway

STR: Lee Arnone, Tom Atkins, Wina

Aversen, Nick Barbaro, Lou Bonacki, Barry Brenner, Bruce Campbell, Victoria Catlin, James Dixon, Nay K. Dorse, Corey Eubanks, George Flower, Jill Gatsby, Rocky Giordano, John F. Goff, William J. Gorman, Jon Greene, Teddy M. Haggarty, Danny Hicks, Erik Holland, Dennis Junt, Marcia Karr, Judy Kerr, Jake la Motta, Laurene Landon, Judy Levitt, Jason Lustig, William Lustig, Vic Manni, Sheree North, Tito Nunez, Daniel Ortiz, Louis Pastore, Frank Pesce, Bernie Pock, Ed Polgardy, Samuel M. Raimi, Carla Y. Reynolds, Jef Richard, Richard Roundtree, William Smith, Adele Sparks, Tom Taylor, Ingrid van Dorn, Bill Waldron, Luke Walter, Alma Washington, Patrick Wright, Nicholas Yee and Robert Z'Dar

Approximately 92m; Color

DVD1: *Maniac Cop* [ELT; 92m; LBX]; DVD2: *Maniac Cop* [SNR; 81m]; VHS1: *Maniac Cop* [ABE; 85m; LBX]; *Maniac Cop* [TWE; 92m]; VHS2: *Maniac Cop* [SNR; 81m]

ADL: *You Have the Right to Remain Silent ... Forever!*

A cop is set up and sent to the state pen, where he is killed by convicts he had put away himself. He comes back as a vengeance-minded zombie, intent on taking down those responsible for the injustice in the bloodiest fashion he can muster as judge, jury and executioner.

Maniac Cop is an utter disappointment considering the names involved. The film shows none of the intensity that punctuated *Maniac* (1980), Lustig's most infamous effort. Even worse, *Maniac Cop* was penned by Larry Cohen, a filmmaker whose works usually excel despite the limitations of their exploitation film backgrounds. (C'mon, guys, we know you *both* can do better than this.)

Trying to soften the blow, I would assume, is the presence of several genre personalities, including filmmaker Sam (*The Evil Dead*)

Raimi and his leading man, Bruce Campbell (in what has to be the most restrained role of his career).

The gore is pretty blasé, and the make-up on Z'Dar as the titular killing machine is downright shoddy. (He fared just as bad in the 1987 film *Grotesque.*)

I have to sit through two more of these damnable things? Geez, someone up there hates me.

Maniaco *see* **Maniac**

El Mas Alla *see* **L'Aldilá**

Masacre en la Fiesta *see* **Slumber Party Massacre**

Masacre en Texas 2 *see* **The Texas Chainsaw Massacre 2**

Mausoleo *see* **Mausoleum**

Mausoleum (1982)

Western International Pictures [US]

DIR: Michael Dugan; PRO: Robert Barich and Robert Madero; SCR: Robert Barich and Robert Madero; DOP: Robert Barich; EXP: Michael Franzese and Jerry Zimmerman; MFX: John Carl Buechler and Maurice Stein; SFX: Roger George; MUS: Jamie Mendoza-Nava

STR: Blake Barich, Joyce Barich, John Brannigan, Bobbie Bresee, Norman Burton, Ron Cannon, Gene Edwards, Julie Garfinkel, Marjoe Gortner, Richard Guarino, Laura Hippe, Joel Krame, Joe Lipsher, Mildred Lipsher, Chu Chu Malave, Sheri Mann, Di Ann Monaco, Julie Christy Murray, La Wanda Page, Jay Saunders, Maurice Sherbanee, Bill Vail, Eileen Zimmerman, Lori Zimmerman and Michael Zimmerman

AKA: *Mausoleo* [Mausoleum]

Approximately 97m; Color

VHS1: *Mausoleum* [EMB; 96(97)m]; *Mausoleum* [NEL; 96(97)m]

ADL: *Centuries of Evil Have Just Awakened ... and No One Is Safe.*

Apparently, the firstborn females in the Nomed family (yes ... most of the viewers will have picked up on the backmasking—groan) are possessed by demons. The only living family member to qualify for this honor is Bobbie Bresee, who's not doing too bad until she seduces the gardener, then kills him with a hand rake. More soon follows. Somehow (don't ask me, I was having trouble paying attention to the film) all of these strange events revolve around a mausoleum. We have a title!

Let's see what we got here ... slamming doors, levitations, glowing green eyes, an overworked smoke machine, and biting demon breasts. Yes ... biting demon breasts. (It's even sillier than it sounds.) On the production end, there are some crappy visual effects, some passably extreme gore, and some awful, awful, *awful* makeup effects. Everything else is, for lack of a better word, pretty dreary.

Somehow, this film guaranteed Ms. Bresee a place in the unofficial B-queen Hall of Fame. Why, I really don't know, as she's not that good of an actress (if her performance here is any indication), and she only did one other genre film as far as I know, the even more lamentable *Evil Spawn* (1987).

To be avoided, unless you have a yen to see Bresee's breasts, with or without teeth.

Meet the Feebles (1989)

WingNut Films [NZ]
DIR: Peter Jackson; PRO: Jim Booth and Peter Jackson; SCR: Peter Jackson, Danny Mulheron, Stephen Sinclair and Frances Walsh; DOP: Murray Milne; SFX: Steve Ingram; MUS: Peter Dasent
STR: Eleanor Ajtken, Donna Aker-sten, Terri Anderton, Sean Ashton-Peach, Carl Buckley, Stuart Devenie, Sarah Glensor, Mark Hadlow, Ross Jolly, Danny Mulheron, George Port, Brian Sergent, Peter Vere-Jones, Ian Williamson, Doug Wren, Justine Wright and Mark Wright
Approximately 105m; Color
VHS1: *Meet the Feebles* [DAP; 105m]; *Meet the Feebles* [JEF; 92m]; VHS2: *Meet the Feebles* [AFD; 93m]; DVD1: *Meet the Feebles* [COM; 92m]; DVD2: *Meet the Feebles* [AFD; 93m]
ADL: *Hell Hath No Fury Like a Hippo with a Machine Gun.*

"The producers wish to advertise that no puppets were ever killed or maimed during the production of this film."

In the interest of warning puppet rights activists, I wish to point out that this onscreen claim is an outright lie. Not only were a godforsaken number of puppets killed and maimed during the production of *Meet the Feebles*, they were flagrantly abused and exploited in every other conceivable fashion as well. Needless to say, the puppet lovers among you would be horrified by the fate that befell the entire cast of said film. If Mr. Jackson's heinous crimes against our stuffed brethren is ever brought to the public's attention, we can only hope and pray that the authorities will not sanction such malicious acts, and make an example out of him by sending him to bed without dinner, or—public support be willing—ground him for an entire week.

Rumor has it that *Meet the Feebles* was originally denied release in this country because Muppets creator Jim Henson was, shall we say, a little perturbed by not only the similarities between his progeny and Jackson's irreverent creations, but that the Feebles represented the darker side of the human idiom. Not content with crooning shallow tunes and parlaying homogenized quips, the Feebles lie, cheat, steal, drink, smoke, shoot heroin, cheat on their spouses, spread venereal diseases, and—occasionally—go on gore-drenched killing sprees. They are racists, misogynists, panty sniffers, coprophagiacs, blackmailers, sodomists, drug dealers, and—I was saving the worst for last— pretentious artists. But goddamn if they aren't funny. (There's an essay somewhere in here, believe you me.)

As of this writing, Jackson just finished shooting his epic, a trilogy of films adapting J.R.R. Tolkien's influential fantasy series *Lord of the Rings*. How someone can make the jump from such films as *Bad Taste* and *Meet the Feebles* to one of the most expensive productions to ever come out of Hollywood probably has a lot of cineastes doing a double take.

Melodia Siniestra *see* **Blood Song**

Memorial Day *see* **Memorial Day Massacre**

Memorial Valley Massacre (1988)

Motion Picture Corp. of America [US], Vertex Motion Pictures [US]
DIR: Robert C. Hughes; PRO: Brad Kzevoy and Steven Stabler; SCR: Robert C. Hughes and George Francis Skrow; DOP: James Mathers; EXP: Peter Fornstam and Bjorn Friberg; MFX: Peter Geyer; MUS: Jed Feuer
STR: Jay Byron, John Caso, Eddie D., Charles Douglass, Marc Ezralow, Dan S. Fambeau, Susan Frailey, Livington Holmes, Linda Honeyman, Michael Inglese, Julie Jachim, Jimmy Justice, Chris Keene, Bradford E. Kelly, John Kerry, Lesa Lee, Leon Martel, Mark Mears, Cameron Mitchell, Bob Moore, Erin O'Leary, David S. Perry,

Zig Roberts, B.B. Selco, William Smith, Michael Spenard, Christina Sullivan and Dusty Woods
AKA: *Memorial Day*
Approximately 92m; Color
VHS1: *Memorial Valley Massacre* [ORI; 93(92)m]
ADL: *Just When You Thought It Was Safe to Go Back in the Tent...*

A recently opened, but still unfinished, recreational park in *Memorial Valley Massacre* just so happens to be the stomping ground of a feral man bent on killing the guests. Whoopee. *Memorial Valley Massacre* hinges on a *silly* premise, accompanied by an even *sillier* stock caveman. (Remember TV's Saturday morning show *Bigfoot and Wild Boy* from the *Krofft Super Show*? I had lost most recollection of this grade school guilty pleasure until this film reluctantly made its way into my deck.) The film tries really hard to be politically correct, which is a pretty *silly* thing for a slasher film to do. There is gore. A fair amount of it, really, but all of it is poorly executed.

Uhm ... *silly* seems to be the only word that comes to my mind.

Mesanjero de Satanás *see* **Evilspeak**

Menschenfresser, Der *see* **Anthropophagus**

Metamorphosis *see* **DNA Formula Letale**

Midnight (1980)

Congregation Company [US], Independent-International Pictures Corp. [US]
DIR: John A. Russo; PRO: Donald M. Redinger; SCR: John A. Russo [Based on the novel *Midnight* by John A. Russo]; DOP: Paul McCullough; EXP: Daniel Q. Kennis and Samuel M. Sherman; MFX:

Tom Savini; SFX: Greg Besnak, Raymond Laine, and John A. Russo; MUS: Paul Mc-Collough and One Man's Family

STR: John Amplas, Greg Besnak, John Blaho, Amy Brinton, LaChele Carl, Daniel Costello, Kenneth Croyle, Connie Gori, Billy Green, Jim Grippo, Lou Grippo, Doris Hackney, John Hall, Charles Jackson, Bob Johnson, Ann Kambes, Don Kamerer, David Marchick, Armand Martin, David McCullough, Bud Mellot, Doug Mertz, Tom Milas, Maura Minteer, Jackie Nicoll, Prank Pryzbylski, Eugene Ratkiewicz, Chris Riblett, John Rice, Jack Ruffing, Raymond Russo, Glenn Shannon, Debra Smith, Lawrence Tierney, Melanie Verliin, Robin Walsh, Lucian White and Ellie Wyler

AKA: *Backwoods Massacre*

Approximately 94m; Color

VHS1: *Midnight* [VID; 88(94)m]

ADL: *Madness Begins When the Clock Strikes Twelve.*

A young woman runs away from home, trying to free herself from her alcoholic, sexually abusive stepfather. She is picked up by two guys in a van, and the three—on the run from the police after a grand display of shop-lifting—stumble across four devil-worshipping siblings bent on obtaining human sacrifices.

Midnight is an adeptly made low budget horror film, despite the simple arithmetic involved. (*Midnight* = *The Texas Chain Saw Massacre*–Texas + Pittsburgh – scary redneck cannibals + cardboard redneck Satanists.) With the story based on one of his novels, director/screenwriter John Russo (who also co-authored *Night of the Living Dead*) tries to interject charac-ter development and religious alle-gory into the otherwise stale pro-ceedings; unfortunately, it seems forced, especially in respect to the for-mer. (Even the otherwise capable cast—which includes *Martin*'s John Amplas and *Reservoir Dog*'s Lawrence

Tierney—has difficulty with the stilted and often contrived dialogue.) To the film's credit, though, it does manage to keep the viewer's interest throughout.

There is a fair amount of gore, although one wonders if anything is missing, as several publicity stills for *Midnight* depict either alternate scenes specifically staged for these still shots, or footage that didn't make it into the final cut. Regardless, the bloodshed is typical of Savini's work for the time: brutal and sometimes quite convincing. Much of it does look better in the stills, though.

The only other problem many

Video box art for *Midnight* (1980), Vid-mark Entertainment.

viewers may have with *Midnight* is the grating '70s bar rock theme song that endlessly intones, "You're on your own, you're all alone, you can't go home." I swear I'll frigging scream if I'm ever confronted by this tune again. (Of course, I'd own the soundtrack if there was one, but that's beside the point.)

Miedo en la Ciudad de los Muertos Vivientes *see* **Paura nella Città dei Morti Viventi**

Mil Gritos Tiene la Noche [A Thousand Cries in the Night] (1981)

Almena Film Production [Sp], Fort Films [PR]

DIR: Juan Piquer Simón; PRO: Stephen Miniasian and Dick Randall; SCR: Aristide Massaccesi and Juan Piquer Simón;

YOU DON'T HAVE TO GO TO TEXAS FOR A CHAINSAW MASSACRE

This film contains scenes of explicit violence and may be offensive

Alternate ad mat for *Mil Gritos Tiene la Noche* (1981).

DOP: Juan Mariné; EXP: Edward L. Montoro; SFX: Basilio Cortijo; MUS: Librado Pastor

STR: Carmen Aguado, Pilar Alcón, Paco Alvez, Carlos H. Aztarán, Franco Braña, Nicholas A. Burd, Cristina Cottrelli, Mario de Barros, Alejandro de Enciso, Hilda Fuchs, Silvia Gambino, Christopher George, Lynda Day George, May Heatherly, Alejandro Hernández, Víctor Iregua, Emilio Linder, Isabel Luque, Leticia Marfil, Roxana Nieto, Edmund Purdom, Ian Sera, Paul L. Smith, Jack Taylor and Gérard Tichy Wondzinski

AKA: *The Chainsaw Devil; Pezadas* [Pieces]; *Pieces*

Approximately 89m; Color

VHS1: *Pieces* [VES; 89m]; VHS3: *Pieces* [CBS; 87m]

ADL: *You Don't Have to Go to Texas for a Chainsaw Massacre!*

Someone with a chainsaw and a love for jigsaw puzzles is making short work of young schoolgirls, pilfering select pieces he needs to make his own dream girl. It's up to the authorities to discover the psychopath's identity before the word "coed" is dropped from their school policy.

Although predictable in every sense of the word, this gory sleazefest makes up for its shortcomings with its over-the-top approach. Bearing as many similarities to Italy's *giallo* thrillers as it does to post–*Halloween* slasher flicks, *Mil Gritos en la Noche* exploits both genres without adding anything new to either. Opening with a preposterous basis for the killer's obsession with making a flesh and bone jigsaw puzzle, the film continues to sacrifice all credibility and coherency to the gods of sex and violence. Even worse, what little realism the film managed to hold onto throughout the dire proceedings is traded in for a ridiculous shock ending, a joke so staggering that one is inclined to think that the filmmakers weren't exactly taking any of this business seriously.

Mil Gritos en la Noche is undeniably splashy; sets are inevitably spattered with the red stuff as body parts fly. This film is the quintessential gorefest, bereft of anything in the way of style, intelligence, and good taste. If your needs are simple, and you lack the discriminating taste of your peers, then help yourself. (Of course, masochists like myself will suffer any indignity just to see Jack Taylor do his thing.)

Maybe you don't have to go to Texas for a chainsaw massacre, but you sure the hell don't have to go nearly as far as Spain for a bad movie.

Mindwarp—An Infinity of Terror *see* **Galaxy of Terror**

Mondo Cannibale [Cannibal World] (1980)

Eurociné [Fr]
DIR: Jesús Franco Manera; PRO: Franco Prosperi; SCR: Jesús Franco Manera and A.L. Mariaux; DOP: Luis Colombo; SFX: Michael Nizza; MUS: Roberto Pregadio
STR: Ramón Ardid, Pier Luigi Conti, Monique Delaunay, Jérome Foulon, Anouchka Lesœur, Jesús Franco Manera, Olivier Mathot, Antonio Mayans, Shirley Night, Lina Romay, Anne Marie Rosier and Sabrina Siani
AKA: *Barbarian Goddess*; *Die Blonde Göttin* [The Blonde Goddess]; *I Cannibali* [The Cannibals]; *Cannibals*; *La Dèa Cannibale* [The Cannibal Goddess]; *La Déese Blonde* [The Blonde Goddess]; *La Déese Cannibale* [The Cannibal Goddess]; *Une Fille pour les Cannibales* [A Young Girl for the Cannibals]; *Mangeurs d'Hommes* [Man-Eaters]; *Mondo Cannibale 3 Teil—Die Blonde Göttin* [Cannibal World Part 3—The Blonde Goddess]; *Sexo Caníbal* [Sex Cannibal]; *White Cannibal Queen*

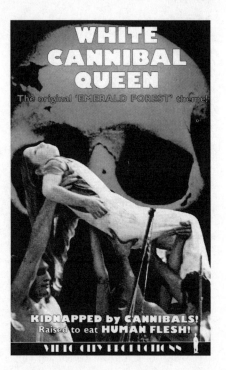

Video box art for *Mondo Cannibale* (1980), Video City Productions.

Approximately 90m; Color
VHS1: *Cannibals* [DAY; 87m]; *Mondo Cannibale* [ACT; 86m]; *White Cannibal Queen* [VCP; 90m]; VHS2: *Cannibals* [CNH; 87m]
ADL: *Kidnapped by Cannibals! Raised to Eat Human Flesh!*

While on a scientific expedition, a family is attacked by cannibals. The mother is promptly gobbled up, whereas the father escapes with one less appendage to his name. The young daughter is presumed dead, but Daddy hasn't given up. Several years after the incident, he packs his bags and heads back to South America to discover that—not only is she still alive—she has been raised by the natives as a "White Goddess" (apparently the only "English" they know outside of some "oom papa mau mau" lyrics).

Despite some nasty gore, this is probably the worst cannibal epic to ever make it to these shores. It's no surprise when one discovers that it was perpetrated *not* by some Italian hackmeister, but *the* Spanish hackmeister Jesús Franco Manera. He may produce some engaging works when fiddling around with his own obsessions and fetishes, but his works-for-hire tend to be—how can I put this delicately?—the most unwatchable pieces of excrement ever to hit the silver screen. The terms "crude" and "hackneyed" don't even begin to describe some of these films. Although *Mondo Cannibale* isn't as taxing as some of his even less-inspired works, it is still a really, *really* bad movie.

The production values are simply abysmal, with complete and utter disregard for realism and continuity. The "natives" are obviously well groomed Spaniards (some with mustaches and sideburns, no less!) painted up like excommunicated members of KISS. Another dead giveaway that it wasn't filmed on location is the terrain; methinks that palm trees and manicured lawns probably aren't indigenous to the area affectionately known as "Green Hell."

Although most cannibal films are inherently racist, this one is mired in it, from the embarrassing native-speak (oogly oogly to you too) to the racist fantasies that form the crux of the "White Goddess" plot device. Sure, the film may not exploit real natives, but it sure sets them back a few centuries.

But wait, there's more. As I mentioned earlier on, gore is dished out liberally, but the carnage is photographed in extreme close-up, with the camera often out of focus. Obviously, this was to save on the spendy effects that usually punctuate these films. No need to make it look good; just get a tight shot of someone chewing on raw meat wrapped around someone's limb, douse it with red paint, blur the image or run it in slomo, and—bingo!—SPFX Are Us.

As a testament to their frugality, Eurociné let Julio Pérez Tabernero pilfer this film for recycled footage, which he used in the equally unwatchable *Terror Caníbal* the same year. Furthermore, American prints cite Franco Prosperi as the director of *Mondo Cannibale*; although a hack in his own right, I don't think that even *he* has made anything as bad as this.

Mondo Cannibale (1981) *see* **Cannibal Ferox**

Mondo Cannibale 3 Tiel—Die Blonde Göttin *see* **Mondo Cannibale** (1980)

Mondo Zombie *see* **The Dead Next Door**

Monster (1980) *see* **Humanoids from the Deep**

Monster Dog *see* **Los Perros de la Muerte**

Monster Hunter *see* **Rosso Sangue**

Le Monstre Ataque *see* **Alien 2 sulla Terra**

Les Monstres de la Mar *see* **Humanoids from the Deep**

Moon Stalker (1989)

Cinema & Theatre Seating Ltd. [US] DIR: Michael O'Rourke PRO: Sally Smith; SCR: Michael O'Rourke; DOP: Michael Goi; EXP: Eldon Nygaard; SFX: Ken Balles; MUS: Douglas Pipes
STR: Ernie Abernathy, Mark Archuletta, Joe Balogh, Joseph Christopher, Ron K. Collie, Larry Coven, Jil Foor, Blake Gibbons, Tom Hamil, Ken Hanes, Susan Hannah, Tracy Hutton, Sioux-Z Jessup, Neil Kinsella, Greg Mardon, John Marzilli, Ann McFadden, Kelly Mullis, Pamela Ross, Myron Sayan, Carl Soloman, Joleen Tropp, Ingrid Vold, Alex Wexler and Sam Williams
AKA: *Camper Stamper*
Approximately 92m; Color
VHS1: *Moon Stalker* [CEI; 92m]
ADL: *There's a Bad Moon Rising ... and It Just Got Worse.*

Good news: *Moon Stalker* was, despite soured expectations, *not* shot on video. Bad news: Well, the bad news is that it was made at all. There's a killer with squeaky galoshes, that much I do remember. And—a death knell to most modern day slasher films—most of the killings are off screen. The score is a *little* better than most, showing some slight nods to John Carpenter. And, well, having sat dumbly (emphasis on "dumb") through too many damnable slasher flicks in a row, I think I may have suffered a permanent memory lapse. Go figure.

If I ever get the nerve to sit through this sucker again, I'll let you know just how bad it was. It *was* bad, of that I'm sure.

La Morte Vivante [The Living Dead Girl] (1982)

Les Films ABC [Fr], Films Aleriaz [Fr], Films du Yaka [Fr]
DIR: Jean Rollin; PRO: Sam Selsky; SCR: Jacques Ralf and Jean Rollin; DOP: Max Monteillet; SFX: Benoît Lestang; MUS: Philippe d'Aram
STR: Carina Barone, Patricia Besnard-Rousseau, Françoise Blanchard, Jean-Pierre Bouyxou, Veronique Carpentier, Jean Cherlian, Jean Herel, Delphine Laporte, Fanny Magieri, Jacques Marbeuf, Mike Marshall, Sandrine Morel, Lise Overman, Alain Petit, Marina Pierro, Veronique Pinson, Jean Rollin, Laurence Royer, Sam Selsky and Dominique Treillou
Approximately 91m; Color
DVD0: *The Living Dead Girl* [IMG; 91m]; DVD2: *The Living Dead Girl* [PLN; 83m; LBX; French and English w/English subs]; VHS1: *La Morte Vivante* [VSM; 86m; LBX; French and English w/English subtitles]; VHS2: *The Living Dead Girl* [RED; 91m; French w/English subs; LBX]

Three guys make the dire mistake of dumping toxic waste in the catacombs near an old chateau, as a leakage resuscitates the body of a young woman who had died only days before. She awakens with an insatiable appetite for blood (natch), ripping out the throats of the uninvited guests. She makes her way home—the aforementioned chateau—and spends her days pining over the absence of her childhood friend. Meanwhile, an American photographer and his petulant actress girlfriend—having seen the dead girl roaming about—enter the picture, wanting her to pose for them. Eventually, the dead girl's aforementioned friend returns, having been sent notice of her demise. It isn't long before she's acquiring victims for her friend, and even offering her own blood in order to keep her alive.

Despite the over the top gore, this is by far one of Rollin's most haunting pieces of work. It is no surprise that it is essentially a variation on themes offered in Sheridan le Fanu's gothic classic *Carmilla*, as that book touches on many of the selfsame staples crucial to the director's earlier works: vampires, crumbling castles, suppressed lesbianism, and the like. Despite the gratuity, though, *La Morte Vivante* is much less exploitive than his earlier work, reaching a level of poetry as it examines the relationship between the dead girl and her friend. Gone are the days of garishly staged sex scenes, fuzzed out guitar scores, and rubber bats; at this point in his career, Rollin opted for a more subtle approach.

That is, except for the gore. Had the special effects been passable, they would not have been so detrimental, so distracting from the film's finer points; even the gallons of blood splashed across the sets can't hide the latex seams. Rarely would I suggest such a thing, but this film would be improved *immensely* by excising much of the gore, leaving only the after-the-fact carnage, as it cheapens the remainder of the proceedings.

Also of interest in *La Morte Vivante* is the captivating beauty of actress Marina Pierro; no stranger to French genre films, she also starred in Walerian Borowczyk's exemplary *Dr. Jekyll et les Femmes* (1981).

An often-breathtaking piece of work from one of the few artists working in the genre.

Mother's Day (1980)

Mother's Day Company [US]
DIR: Charles Kaufman; PRO: Charles Kaufman and Michael Kravitz; SCR: Charles Kaufman and Warren D. Leight; DOP: Joseph Mangine; EXP: Alexander Beck; MFX: Josie Caruso and Rob E. Holland; SFX: Josie Caruso and Rob E. Holland; MUS: Phil Gallo and Clem Vicari
STR: Marshall Auerbach, Ed Battle, Robert Carnegie, John Castellano, Louis Cogie, Robert Collins, Marsella Davidson, Silas Davis, John Fanelli, Suzie Fried, Leilani Gerrè, Joel Greenberg, Nancy Henderickson, Katya, Stanley Kaufmen, Timmy Leight, Kevin Lowe, Scott Lucas, Deborah Luce, Lawrence Mayer, Holden McGuire, Billy Ray McQuade, Vince Piccalo, Tiana Pierce, John Radom, Sheldon Reide, Doreen Richardson, Rose Ross, Karl Sandys, Sture Sjostedt, Bill Smith, Steve Sturm and Gwen van Highland
AKA: *Muttertag* [Mother's Day]
Approximately 90m; Color
DVD1: *Mother's Day* [TRO; 90m]; VHS1: *Mother's Day* [MHE; 98(90)m]; *Mother's Day* [TRO; 90m]; VHS2: *Mother's Day* [CUL; 94(90)m; Dutch subtitles]
ADL: *I'm So Proud of My Boys—They Never Forget Their Mama.*

Video box art for *Mother's Day* (1980), Media Home Entertainment.

Three college roommates get together for their annual mystery retreat, ending up on a camping trip in the middle of Nowhere, New Jersey. Unexpectedly, they are abducted, beaten and brutally raped by two backwoods perverts and their just as buggy mother. (They play out shallow, sadistic psychodramas put on not only for their sick pleasures but for their mother's amusement as well.) One of the girls dies; her friends have a chance to escape, but return to exact vengeance on their tormentors.

Mother's Day is not quite the simplistic sado-fare that the above synopsis might imply. This often-disturbing film spends much of its ninety minutes making pointed stabs at consumerism, pop psychology, TV culture, parental expectations, and even the gratuitous excesses of the '70s. (The movie even pokes fun at the slasher genre, but these jibes probably would've been looked upon as tired plot devices—cheesy shock ending included—were it not for the other satirical jabs.) Accompanying the societal ribbings (at least on the part of the protagonists) is sufficient character development, a rarity in slasher films. Unfortunately, with the exception of maybe "Ike," the killers are cartoonish and completely unconvincing, leavening much of the film's disturbing nature.

The violence is quite brutal at times, but relegates itself to early and later on in the film, with a few nasty gore scenes thrown in for good measure. One of the most grueling scenes, though, involves a severe case of rope burn that is sure to make even the more jaded viewers flinch.

Surprisingly, this was co-produced by Lloyd Kaufman (Charles' brother) and Michael Herz, the founders of Troma. (Surprising in that *Mother's Day* is actually a decent production, which is more than can be said for most of *their* films. If it wasn't for nepotism, Troma would be shy at least one passable flick.)

Mountain Top Motel *see* **Mountaintop Motel Massacre**

Mountaintop Motel Massacre (1983)

Jim McCullough Productions [US]
DIR: Jim McCullough, Sr.; PRO: Jim McCullough, Sr.; SCR: Jim McCullough, Jr.; DOP: Joseph Wilcots; MFX: Drew Edward Hunter; MUS: Ron di Lulio

STR: Rhonda Atwood, Linda Blackenship, James Bradford, Greg Brazzel, Major Brock, Anna Chappell, Angela Christine, Amy Hill, Marian Jones, Jill King, Foster Litton, Virginia Loridans, Will Mitchell and Bill Thurman

AKA: *Mountain Top Motel*
Approximately 95m; Color
DVD1: *Mountaintop Motel Massacre* [ABE; 95m; LBX]; VHS1: *Mountaintop Motel Massacre* [NWV; 95m]; *Mountaintop Motel Massacre* [ABE; 95m; LBX]
ADL: *Please Do Not Disturb Evelyn. She Already Is.*

Evelyn Chambers is released from a mental hospital after a three-year stay. Apparently, the Bible-thumping missus went a little buggy after catching her daughter "conjurin' spirits" in the root cellar, and almost took the girl's head off with a sickle. Conveniently enough, she now runs a mountain retreat, a business that keeps her supplied with a modest but stable influx of victims for whenever she gets the urge to relive old times. (For someone with an obvious dislike of animals, she sure uses a lot of them

Muerte

Although *Mountaintop Motel Massacre* has a nice, cozy low-budget feel to it, it relies too much on formula; the tepid stalk 'n' slash conventions are sure to garner disapproval from fans who are even the least bit discriminating with their horror films. There are some gory sickle slashings, but even these murders are similarly uninspired.

Great adline, though.

La Muerte del Chacal [The Death of the Jackal] (1984)

Casablanca Producciones S.A. [Mx]
DIR: Pedro Galindo III; PRO: Eduardo Galindo and Santiago Galindo; SCR: Gilberto de Anda; DOP: Miguel Arana; EXP: Eduardo Galindo; SFX: Jorge Farfan; MUS: Nacho Mendez
STR: Victor Alaniz, Fernando Almada, Mario Almada, Fernando Benavidez, Ruben Benavidez, Jorge Busto, Larry Casanova, Aurora Chavira, Olivia Collins, Nina Kovars, Cristina Molina, Nilo Ortiz, Lizzeta Romo and Severiano Suarez
Approximately 91m; Color
VID: *La Muerte del Chacal* [CND; 91m; Spanish]

A black-gloved, sword cane-wielding psychopath and his two bloodthirsty Dobermans haunt an old shipyard, but he quickly moves his business to a strip of seedy grind houses once the desperate teenagers take the hint that making out on the abandoned ships he likes to frequent is *not* a good idea. Since it becomes obvious early on who the killer is, the screenwriters decide to unmask him halfway through the film, and even have him captured shortly thereafter by the archetypical mustachioed Hispanic cop. With only an hour of the film's running time under his belt, the killer takes the opportunity to escape and resume his spree, and even squeezes in enough time to exact revenge on his captor.

La Muerte del Chacal is not quite complex enough to pass as a giallo thriller, and is therefore relegated to the dung heap that is home to the generic slasher flick. Unlike its peers, though, most of the gore never amounts to much more than him running people through with the aforementioned sword (although a number of the victims do end up hanging from meat hooks in a scene that is easily one of the more striking images in the film). The production values are okay, and there are some nice sets, but everything comes across as rather stale.

At least it's proof that Mexico *is* capable of churning out something besides wrestling superhero pics and boring potboilers. (Just kidding ... sort of.)

Murder by Mail *see* **Schizoid**

Murder Weapon (1989)

Gerardfilm Ltd. [US]
DIR: David de Coteau; PRO: Fred Kennamer and Linnea Quigley; SCR: Ross A. Perron; DOP: Michael Seaman; EXP: David de Coteau; MFX: David Barton; MUS: Del Casher
STR: Michelle Bauer, Rodger Burt, Damon Charles, Allen First, Michael Jacobs, Jr., Michael Jacobs, Sr., Victoria Nesbitt, Linnea Quigley, Karen Russell, Richard J. Sebastian, Brinke Stevens, Stephen Steward, Allen Tombello and Lyle Waggoner
Approximately 90m; Color
VHS1: *Murder Weapon* [CGV; 90m]
ADL: *Sex Isn't Their Only Weapon...*

Geez ... will de Coteau ever make an interesting film, or will he continue to spend his career filming ninety minute slots of gratuitous sex, gratuitous violence, and shallow character development (usually in that order of importance)? But then again, when you have such B-queens as Linnea Quigley, Michelle Bauer and Brinke Stevens at your disposal, who needs a story? Just pander to sexually repressed horror fans, and you're sure to have a successful straight-to-video B-film on your hands.

I'll admit, *Murder Weapon* does boast an impressive scene involving a sledgehammer to the cranium, but it just wasn't worth it. Is it time for my mush?

Mutant (1982) *see* **Forbidden World**

Mutant 2 *see* **Alien Predator**

Mutant Hunt (1987)

Taryn Productions Inc. [US]
DIR: Tim Kincaid; PRO: Cynthia de Paula; SCR: Tim Kincaid; DOP: Thomas Murphy; EXP: Charles Band; MFX: Edward French; MUS: Tom Milano
STR: Nancy Arons, Leeanne Baker, Manuel Cordero, Ralph Crawford, Michael Cummings, Damian, Doug Devos, Mary Fahey, Owen Flynn, Rick Gianasi, Eluah Goodman, William Higgs, Ron Hill, Michael Iozzino, Asia Kio, Adriane Lee, Mark Legan, Eliza Little, Ed Mallia, Chris McNamee, Max Mollison, Hector Morales, Henry Oliver, Bill Peterson, Ron Reynaldi, Pedro Rosa, Christina Sisinni, Manuel Siverio, Stormy Spill, Lenny Tobi, Warren Ulaner, Marc Umle, Taunie Vernon, Joel von Orsteiner and Leon Woods
Approximately 90m; Color
VHS1: *Mutant Hunt* [LIG; 90m]
ADL: *New York: The 21st Century, It's Open Season on Cyborgs.*

"Too gory for the silver screen," the video box exclaims ... but *we* know better, don't we. We know *ex-*

actly why this sucker went straight to video, and it isn't because the MPAA decreed it unsuitable for a theatrical release (common sense, maybe, but not the MPAA). Having already questioned this dubious claim, we won't be too surprised to find out that *Mutant Hunt* is not nearly as gory as they'd like us—the consumers—to believe. First rule to keep in mind when watching exploitation films: No matter what the movie poster or video box claims, assume that the opposite is probably true.

Anywho, it's nice to see that not much has changed in the next century. Sure, we have androids running around using laser technology and the like, but everyone's still wearing Fruit of the Looms and driving the same old beat-up convertibles. Hey, it doesn't look like fashion has changed much either, so unless they're in the midst of an '80s revival, I think it's safe to assume that the budget didn't allow for costuming. (There are a few stray examples of gaudy, new-wavish future wear that are a staple of futuristic adventure films, but—thankfully—only a few.)

The acting is abysmal, and the effects horrendous. And, of course, all of the androids are simply cut-rate terminators, but this is to be expected from any films dealing with bio-mechanics—especially low budget films—made in the wake of Cameron's groundbreaking sci-fi actioner. Oh, and the choreography for the fight scenes are not only laughable, but pretty bad even for this level of film-making. (Everyone, and I mean *everyone* in *Mutant Hunt* thinks they're a frigging kick boxer; even a walk-on victim taking out his trash at four in the morning exhibits a few sad moves. Is it safe to assume that Jean-Claude van Damme was also a hot Hollywood commodity at the time?) I know *I've* got better things to do with my time.

The Mutilator (1983)

OK Productions [US]
DIR: Buddy Cooper and John S. Douglass; PRO: Buddy Cooper; SCR: Buddy Cooper; DOP: Peter Schnall; MFX: Mark Shostrom and Anthony Showe; SFX: Michael Minard; MUS: Michael Minard
STR: Michelle Bach, David Bell, John Bode, Darryl Case, Jan Case, Kay Case, Wendy Case, Jack Chatham, Dee Clodfelter, Phil Collins, A.B. Cooper, Hallock Cooper, Pamela Weddle Cooper, Trace Cooper, Steve Davis, Jenny Grice, Greta Groves, Jimmy Guthrie, Bill Hitchcock, Pat Jordon, Morey Lampley, Dail Lowery, Ruth Martinez, Miriam Mason, Andrea McLean, Matt Mitler, Ben Moore, Tom Outlaw, Jennifer Price, Frances Raines, Connie Rogers, Chris Sarosy, David Sledge, George Sutton, Bruce Taylor and Fred Tillery
AKA: *Fall Break*
Approximately 86m; Color
DVD2: *The Mutilator* [VIP; 85m]; VHS1: *The Mutilator* [VES; 86m]
ADL: *By Sword. By Pick. By Axe. Bye Bye.*

A young boy accidentally shoots his mother while cleaning his father's guns. (That's a birthday present daddy won't be forgetting for quite some time, methinks.) Years later, the traumatized little Samaritan is all grown up, and takes a group of friends to his father's seaside condo for some rest and relaxation. And if the title didn't clue you in, someone has it in for the unsuspecting teens, and you've got *one* guess who's holding a grudge.

Okay, so we've got a weak premise, stilted dialogue, almost inept performers, and a low body count; with the exception of the latter, this could be a description of just about every other slasher flick. The gore is a little heavier than what is expected of its ilk (hence the R and unrated editions), and it isn't half bad, but it really isn't worth waiting around for. Just say "Bye Bye" as the adline insists.

Muttertag *see* **Mother's Day**

My Bloody Valentine (1981)

Canadian Film Development Corp. [Ca], Famous Players [Ca], Secret Film Co. [Ca]
DIR: George Mihalka; PRO: John Dunning, André Link and Stephen Miller; SCR: John Beaird; DOP: Rodney Gibbons; MFX: Tom Burman, Ken Diar and Thomas R. Hoerber; MUS: Paul Zaza
STR: Neil Afleck, Jeff Banks, Peter Cowper, Cynthia Dale, Gina Dick, Don Francks, Jeff Fulton, Lori Hallier, Patricia Hamilton, Pat Hemingway, Alf Humphreys, Paul Kelman, Keith Knight, Tom Kovacs, Sand Leim, Carl Marotte, John McDonald, Marguerite McNeil, Jim Murchison, Larry Reynolds, Rob Stein, Helen Udy, Jack van Evera, Pat Walsh, Terry Waterland, Fred Watters and Graham Whitehead
Approximately 92m; Color
VHS1: *My Bloody Valentine* [PHV; 91m]
ADL: *There's More Than One Way to Lose Your Heart...*

Valentine's Day, 1960: Five miners are trapped in a mine after an explosion, but only one survives, thanks to the option of cannibalism. (Shades of the obscure 1974 horror flick *The Severed Arm?*) After spending a year in a mental institution, the miner returns to his hometown to kill those responsible for the oversight, and promises to continue the spree unless they put a kibosh on the town's annual Valentine's Day dance. Needless to say, they reluctantly agree to the terms

... until twenty years later, that is, when the incident has been nearly forgotten. Unfortunately for them, the killer is still around, and intends to keep his promise, taking Valentine's Day motifs to a bloody extreme.

This is a competent but utterly predictable slasher flick from the early '80s that, surprisingly, is somewhat endearing in retrospect. (Admittedly, I harbor some nostalgia for *My Bloody Valentine*, but I think I can say objectively that it is pretty gosh darn good when compared to its peers. And, yes, it's almost interchangeable with *The Prowler* (1980), but I have some sick liking for that film as well.) There are some great sets to accommodate the stalk 'n' slash, and some particularly vicious killings ... at least there was in the original version.

Apparently, the MPAA started to crack down on graphic violence when this film was released, so the producers of *My Bloody Valentine* were forced to make numerous heavy-handed cuts in order to receive an R-rating. (Its only stateside video release is the same butchered print that was released theatrically.) Unbeknownst to many, an uncut version of this film made its way onto cable television in the early eighties, so only the lucky few who recorded it off of Showtime have in their possession an unadulterated print. (It looks like I'm not alone in wanting to see it receive a more respectable release, as the uncut version of *My Bloody Valentine* is one of the most requested films of its ilk. No, I'm not making that up.)

Nailgun Massacre (1985)

Futuristic Films [US]
DIR: Bill Leslie and Terry Lofton; PRO: Terry Lofton; SCR: Terry Lofton; DOP: Bill Leslie; EXP: Linda Bass and L. Lofton; SFX: Terry Lofton; MUS: Whitey Thomas

STR: Mike Bendall, Diana Bober, Aaron Carrol, Aaron Chadwick, Mike Coady, Michael Cullins, Amy Deitrich, Thomas Freylac, Staci Gordon, Randy Hayes, Joann Hazelbarth, Frances Heard, John Holden, Charles Ladeate, Monica Lawless, Sabrina Lawless, Beau Leland, Terry Lofton, Kim Mathis, Michelle Meyer, Tom Meyers, Kit Michell, Jerry Nelson, Rocky Patterson, Roger Payne, John Price, Ron Queen, Pamela Rene, John Rudder, Rob Slyker, Martin Smith, Connie Speer, Taleesa van Tassel, Billy Wedlow, Mark Woodcock and Shelly York

Approximately 84m; Color
VHS1: *Nail Gun Massacre* [MAG; 90(84)m]
ADL: *It's Cheaper Than a Chainsaw!*

A group of small town hard-hats rape a young woman, and before anyone can say "I Spit on Your Grave," a masked killer brandishing a nail gun begins, uhm, nailing the culprits, as well as any other construction workers who happen to pass through town looking for work. Eventually, the killer is forced to broaden his/her horizons, taking his/her ire out on just about anyone who wanders in sight of the opportunistic script. (Spoiler: The filmmakers try desperately to disguise the killer's sex, but unfortunately a motorcycle helmet and a voice synthesizer just don't quite do the trick. They even go so far as to use—obviously—female stunt doubles, despite the fact that the killer is supposed to be the raped girl's father!)

This exercise in low-rent filmmaking is a typically lame slasher flick, loaded with abundant nudity (mostly silicone enhanced) and embarrassing puns. (You've heard all the one-liners before, although probably delivered with more grace and eloquence than they are here.)

Nail Gun Massacre is inexcusable sexist tripe that will only appeal to indiscriminate splatterpunks.

Nao Mo *[Sorcerer]* (1983)

Production company unknown [HK]
DIR: Lo Lieh; PRO: Gracy Wong; SCR: Chiu Chi Kin; DOP: Wong Wing Lung; EXP: Wong Lit Tat
STR: Elane Kim, Chau Koo, Kuan Tai Chen, Lo Lieh, Chau Sing and On-On Yu
AKA: *Black Magic with Buddha*
Approximately 91m; Color

Papua New Guinea. Two men discover a mummy hidden deep within a cave. As per the ritual, they stab its heart, its head splits open, and they bag its brain. The younger of the two sneaks it through customs (via the old "now you see it, now you don't" mummy brain in a box trick) and finds himself with a squishy variation on the genie in a bottle. Unfortunately, he doesn't follow his friend's advice to destroy it with holy water after making his wish; pretty soon, neighbor animals begin showing up on his doorstep, dead, their gray matter consumed by—you guessed it!—the mummy brain. It soon runs out of pets, so the man and his family find themselves falling prey to the *Fiend without a Face* reject and a number of its friends. Then things start getting *really* funky.

Although this Asian shocker has a high cheese factor (say what?), *Nao Mo* gets an "A" for effort. This helping of chop socky splatter is bland in execution, but the "brain devil" makes the whole mess much more palatable than it probably should be. Gore is

sparse but nasty, and the soundtrack is filched almost entirely from *Alien* and *Phantasm*. (Apparently, Goldsmith is quite popular in Hong Kong, as evidence by so many of the films that have "borrowed" his scores, including this one.)

Outré, even by Asian standards.

Near Dark (1987)

The Near Dark Joint Venture [US]
DIR: Kathryn Bigelow; PRO: Steven-Charles Jaffe; SCR: Kathryn Bigelow and Eric Red; DOP: Adam Greenberg; EXP: Edward S. Feldman and Charles R. Meeker; MFX: Gordon Smith; VFX: Fantasy II Film Effects Inc.; MUS: Tangerine Dream [Soundtrack from Varèse Sarabande]
STR: Billy Beck, Roger Aaron Brown, Kenny Call, Ed Corbett, Bill Cross, Gary Wayne Cunningham, Troy Evans, Leo Geter, Jenette Goldstein, S.A. Griffin, Gordon Haight, Lance Henriksen, Neith Hunter, Jan King, Danny Kopel, Paul Michael Lane, William T. Lane, Marcie Leeds, James le Gros, Gary Littlejohn, Joshua Miller, Eddie Mulder, Adrian Pasdar, Bill Paxton, Tony Pierce, Don Pugsley, Theresa Randle, Bob Terhune, Tim Thomerson, Thomas Wagner, Robert Winley and Jenny Wright
Approximately 94m; Color
VHS1: *Near Dark* [HBO; 94m]
ADL: *At Dawn They Hide. At Dusk They Wake. At Night They Search for Blood. Pray for Daylight.*

While a young cowpoke hooks up with a nubile bloodsucker, and things aren't so bad until he meets her friends: A gang of roving vampires with bad attitudes and poor grooming habits. He is reluctantly initiated into their ranks, all the while his family searches for him, combing the state and harassing the authorities.

Before going on to helm some fairly spendy Hollywood productions, Kathryn Bigelow directed this interesting and passably entertaining vampire flick. (One interesting aspect about *Near Dark* is that not once during the entirety of the film does anyone utter the dreaded "V" word. There's not even any mention of the pesky bloodsuckers by name on the back of the original video box.) The screenwriters make some attempts to ground the vampire myth in reality; unfortunately, artistic license is usually employed for reasons of convenience and not just to make the supernatural motif more plausible.

The best reason to check out *Near Dark* (besides some rather grisly and disturbing effects work) is the cast. Lance (*Pumpkinhead*) Henriksen is sinister as ever, playing the leader of the vagabond parasites. As the boy's concerned father, Tim (*Trancers*) Thomerson proves he is capable of more than just throwing around one-liners for the audience's amusement. And—last but not least—cocky Bill (*Aliens*) Paxton (in the role of the most sadistic, wisecracking member of the bloodthirsty gang) gives it his all, creating a villain who is as charming as he is scary. It's worth a peek, anyway.

Necrophagous *see* **Lucker the Necrophagous**

Nekromantik (1987)

JB Films [WG]
DIR: Jörg Buttgereit; PRO: Manfred O. Jelinski; SCR: Jörg Buttgereit and Franz Rodenkirchen; DOP: Uwe Bohrer; SFX: Jörg Buttgereit, Daktari Lorenz and Franz Rodenkirchen; MUS: Hermann Kopp, Daktari Lorenz and John Boy Walton
STR: Christiane Baumgarten, Henri Boeck, Splat Brose, Michael Büschke, Jörg Buttgereit, Hapunkt Fix, Elke Fuchs, Fritz Fuchs, Daniela Geburtig, Volker Hauptvogel, Wilfried Hoog, Manfred O. Jelinski, Susa Kohlstedt, Hagen Koob-Liebing, Marion Koob-Liebing, Heinz Langner, Lasko, Patricia Leipold, Daktari Lorenz, Harald Lundt, Beatrice Manowski, Mutfak Reisse, Manfred Repnow, Franz Rodenkirchen, Margit Im Schlaa, Colloseo Schulzendorf, Clemens Schwender, Simone Spörl, Holger Suhr, Heike Surban, Heini Walton and Harald Weis
Approximately 74m; Color ⚔ ⚔ ⚔
VHS1: *Nekromantik* [FTV; 74m; German w/English subtitles]
ADL: *Death Is Just the Beginning.*

"Warning: Some of this film may be seen as grossly offensive and should not be shown to minors!!!" There's an understatement if I've ever heard one. Even if they hadn't seen this world renowned "video nasty" (an impossi-

Video box art for *Nekromantik* (1987), Film Threat Video.

bility until Film Threat Video gave it a legitimate release a few years back), gorehounds everywhere were aware of its existence, a film that was cited as the last word in cinematic necrophilia. Little is left to the viewer's imagination as a street sweeper collects goodies from the sites of various auto accidents or the like to be used in his and his girlfriend's slightly screwed up sex life. Both, it seems, are obsessed with dead things, be it parts, the whole enchilada, what have you. When the breadwinner brings home the putrefying corpse of a murder victim, things start getting a bit intense. His biggest nightmare comes true, though, when he becomes the third wheel, and she runs off with her new love in tow. Having lost his job as well, he is forced to take desperate measures in picking up where he had left off.

Buttgereit's amazing directorial skill, even burgeoning here, manages to shine through what could conservatively be referred to as a limited budget. *Nekromantik* is decidedly stark, almost nihilistic, intensified by convincing performances, a beautiful, evocative score, and some of the nastiest effects work ever conceived. Unfortunately, Buttgereit's decision to use actual footage of a rabbit being graphically butchered almost brings the film down to the level of the *mondo*-oriented cannibal epics of yesteryear. If you can stomach such scenes, though, or don't mind using your fast-forward button, than *Nekromantik* is recommended, both to gorehounds who think they have seen it all, and to those interested in truly transgressive cinema.

Neon Maniacs (1986)

Cimarron Productions [US], Kelly Park Associates [US]
DIR: Joseph Mangine; PRO: Christopher Arnold and Steven D. Mackler; SCR: Mark Patrick Carducci; DOP: Joseph Mangine and Oliver Wood; EXP: H. Frank Dominguez and Bernard E. Goldberg; MFX: Makeup Effects Labs; MUS: Nendall Schmidt [Soundtrack from Easy Street Records]
STR: Mark Allen, Allan Aperlo, Matthew Asner, James Atcheson, Amber Austin, Zac Baldwin, Frank Baleno, Gene Bicknell, Alfred Boyer, Victor Elliot Brandt, Barry Buchanan, Daniel Burrell, Chuck Cohen, Clarke Coleman, Jerome L. Dennae, Andrew Divoff, Trish Doolan, Jessie Lawrence Ferguson, Dick Frattali, Scott Guetzkow, Joel Steven Hammond, Alan Hayes, Katherine Heard, Chuck Hemingway, Anthony Henderson, Kathy Hooker, Marta Kober, John la Fayette, Elizabeth Lauren, Shawn Lieber, Donna Locke, Douglas Markel, Solly Marx, Doyle McCurley, Scott McKenna, Susan Mierisch, Shari Moskau, David Muir, Cooper Neal, Tom Noble, P.R. Paul, Teri Ralston, Bo Sabato, Leilani Sarelle, Chuck Secor, Joseph Shirley, James H. Smith, T.J. Snell, Cynthia Sprink, Michael Todd, Mark Twogood, Jeff Tyler, Mario Valdez, Betty Vaughan, Robert E. Veilliux, Michael Walter, Lydia Weiss and David Wellington
Approximately 90m; Color
VHS1: *Neon Maniacs* [LIG; 90m]
ADL: *Night Falls. So Do Their Victims.*

"When the world is ruled by violence, and the soul of mankind fades, the children's path shall be darkened by the shadows of the Neon Maniacs." Yeah, whatever ... just shut your pie hole so we can get through this with as little pain as possible.

A fisherman finds an animal skull and touched up photos of the title monsters, apparently letting them loose on whatever hapless twentysomething teenagers get in their way. It seems that the only thing standing between them and world domination is a horror fan-slash-aspiring film-maker. (Sure, she looks kind of cute in a Nostromo cap, but her idea of what makes a good horror flick is pretty sad, sloughing off any empathy we might have shown for the character.) The "Neon Maniacs" are little more than mutant renditions of the Village People (doctor, lawyer, Indian chief ... yes indeed, all present and accounted for) sporting cheesy prosthetics that melt when they come in contact with water. The gore doesn't suffer the same indignities as the make-up, but it's still pretty trite.

Directed by the cinematographer of *Mother's Day*.

Not to be mistaken for a good film.

New Year's Evil (1980)

Cannon Films Inc. [US]
DIR: Emmett Alston; PRO: Yoram Globus and Menahem Golan; SCR: Leonard Neubauer; DOP: Edward Thomas; EXP: Billy Fine; MUS: W. Michael Lewis, Lauren Rinder, and Various Artists [Soundtrack from Cannon Records]
STR: John Alderman, Celena Allen, Jim Amormino, Jennie Anderson, Lyle Baker, Bill Blair, Richard Brown, Jerry Chambers, Ryan Collier, Teri Copley, Grant Cramer, Anita Crane, Tim Cutt, Christine Davis, Mark Defrain, Alicia Dhanifu, Michael Frost, Barry Gibberman, Randy Gould, Jon Greene, Don Grenough, Jay Happstein, Ricky Israel, Edward Jackson, Bob Jarvis, Richard E. Kalk, Roz Kelly, Mark Korngute, Clarisse Kotkin, Doug le Mille, Larry Lindsey, John London, Cynthia MacArthur, Jodie Mann, Mike Mihalich, Jed Mills, Karen Mills, Louisa Moritz, Kip Niven, Taaffe O'Connell, Rozanne Orbis, Lyle Pearcy, Mark L. Rosen, Wendysue Rosloff, Justin Rubin, Linda Terito, Julie Kaye Towery, Adrienne Upton, Chris Wallace, Michelle Waxman and Jerry Zanitsch
Approximately 88m; Color
VHS1: *New Year's Evil* [CAN; 88m]

To be perfectly honest, I saw this film when it was first released on video, and I have been dreading having to go back and watch it again almost two decades later. I can also say, with complete and utter sincerity, that it *still* blows.

Graced with inept actors and an addle-minded screenplay, *New Year's Evil* tries to hide the fact it's an exploitive load of horse-pucky by deluging the viewer with half-baked social commentary that amounts to nothing more than narrow minded stabs at the punk subculture. (Uh oh, Yours Truly on the warpath *again*.) Accompanying their conservative stance is what amounts to their perception of how punk bands look and sound; the soundtrack and live bands consists of little more than nerve-wracking metal-rock that is the exact antithesis of "new wave" music (a term which had already outlived its usefulness by this point in time). Obviously, no one did their homework (they were probably too spooked by the image to actually *go* to a concert), but even taking that into consideration, they disregard common sense. (Why they assumed stage divers leap into empty pits and not the audience is beyond me; even the stoned imbeciles they portray would know better than *that*.) But I digress.

New Year's Evil—besides being a punk's worse nightmare—is completely worthless as a slasher film, as it is quite tame by standards set by similar films of the time. Furthermore, *New Year's Evil* lacks anything even remotely resembling suspense, style, or intensity, relying entirely on the aforementioned spectacle to keep the viewer's already strained interest.

Mexican lobby card for *Il Nido del Ragno* (1988).

New York Ripper *see* Lo Squartatore
di New York

Il Nido del Ragno [The Nest of
the Spider] (1988)

Reteitalia Splendida Films [It]
DIR: Gianfranco Giagni; PRO: To-
nino Cervi; SCR: Riccardo Arragno, Tonino
Cervi, Cesare Frugoni and Gianfranco
Manfredi; DOP: Nino Celeste; SFX: Sergio
Stivaletti; MUS: Franco Piersanti
STR: Stéphane Audran, William
Berger, Bill Bolender, Arnaldo dell'Acqua,
Bob Holton, Attilla Löte, John Morrison,
Claudia Muzi, Massimiliano Pavone, Paola
Rinaldi, Valeriano Santinelli, László Sipos,
Maghareta von Krauss and Roland Wy-
benga
AKA: *El Laberinto de las Arañas* [The
Labyrinth of the Spider]; *The Spider Laby-
rinth*
Approximately 83m; Color
VHS2: *The Spider Labyrinth* [CBL;
86(83)m]

A professor of Oriental lan-
guages gets stuck going to Budapest
to reestablish contact with another
scholar on a sabbatical. On the day of
his arrival, the old man is found dead,
hanging by a rope and covered with
cobwebs. The professor is none too
pleased, as he has a serious aversion to
spiders (thanks to an oh-so-traumatic
childhood experience), but stays on
nonetheless to conduct an investigation into the strange and untimely
death.

Although the gore doesn't start
kicking in for a good forty minutes,
this is an engaging and beautifully
staged horror film. Several of the scenarios are very Argento-esque, and
the presence of Mario Bava's spirit
can be sensed as well, in regards to
both the elaborate lighting and the
roving camerawork. In other words,

Il Nido del Ragno is a spaghetti horror fan's dream ... at least for the first couple of reels.

Much like *Maschera di Cera*—but not nearly as serious a case—the film holds unlimited promise early on, then sacrifices everything for cheap thrills as it nears its crescendo. Although the unveiling of the monster's lair is pretty encouraging, the make-up effects are stagy and ineffectual; a monstrous offspring that doesn't show its rubbery hide until the end is particularly bad, and at best comes off as a dime-store copy of *The Thing*. And the shoddy stop-motion animation makes matters even worse.

If you can look past the pathetic effects and the disappointing finale, than it might be worth your while.

Night Beast (1982)

Amazing Film Productions [US]
DIR: Don Dohler; PRO: Don Dohler; SCR: Don Dohler; DOP: Richard Geiwitz; EXP: Amazing Film Productions; MFX: James Chai and Larry Schlechter; SFX: Kent Burton; VFX: John R. Ellis; MUS: Jeffrey Abrams and Robert J. Walsh
STR: Glenn Barnes, Chris Burke, Greg Dohler, Kim Dohler, David Donoho, Dick Dyszel, Dane Ellis, Rick Ernest, Anne Frith, Richard Geiwitz, Fred Gibmeyer, Tom Griffith, Christopher Gummer, Eleanor Herman, Karin Kardian, Don Leifert, Dennis McGeehan, Don Michaels, Monica Neff, Richard Nelson, David Parson, Larry Reichman, Bump Roberts, Richard Ruxton, Steve Sandkuhler, Jerry Schuerholz, George Stover, Hank Stuhmer, Dick Svehla, Gary Svehla, Chris White, Bill Wieman, Rose Wolfe and Jaime Zemarel
AKA: *Nightbeast*
Approximately 82m; Color
VHS1: *Nightbeast* [PAR; 82m]; VHS2: *Nightbeast* [TRO; 81m]

For some inexplicable reason, I have a fondness for Dohler's low-tech horror/sci-fi films. (Methinks it might have something to do with the coverage of his first film, *The Alien Factor* (1977), in an issue of *Famous Monsters of Filmland* I bought off the newsstand when I was but a wee lad of ten. One of said film's goofy aliens graced the gaudy pink cover as well.) With a faithful troupe of backyard actors and an aspiring special effects crew, he made a handful of films that bear his signature, as well as another unmistakable mark: that of movies made by fans, for fans.

Night Beast is another one of his homegrown efforts that does a commendable job with obviously limited resources, although this film does sport more finesse than his earlier productions. Unfortunately, it hasn't aged as well as the others, having been made amidst the glut of '80s alien-on-the-loose fare. In their wake, this is a fairly predictable entry in the annals of post–*Alien* films, offering little more than the selfsame staples and plot devices. Regardless, *Night Beast* still has a certain *je-ne-sais-quoi* that keeps me from lumping it in with the rest.

And, yes, there is gore; more than what one usually expects to see in a Dohler film. (He made the complete jump into splatter territory with his 1988 effort *Blood Massacre*, a disappointing film, even though he managed to—once again—squeeze aliens into the storyline.) Although not as toothy, the title critter does give *The Alien's Deadly Spawn* a run for its money. Not an easy task, I assure you.

Primarily for Don Dohler fans. (Namely, me. And *Midnight Marquee* magazine, the publishers of which having weaseled their way into the cast.)

Night Breed (1989)

Morgan Creek Productions Inc. [UK/US]

DIR: Clive Barker; PRO: Gabriella Martinelli; SCR: Clive Barker [Based on the novel *Cabal* by Clive Barker]; DOP: Robin Vidgeon; EXP: James G. Robinson and Joe Roth; MFX: Image Animation; VFX: Image Animation, VCE, Inc. and Westbury Design & Optical; MUS: Danny Elfman

STR: John Agar, Valda Aliks, Simon Bamford, Tony Bluto, Anne Bobby, Richard Bowman, Doug Bradley, Catherine Chevalier, David Cronenberg, Scott Gilmore, Charles Haid, Alan Harris, Bernard Henry, Lindsay Holiday, Stephen Hoye, Tom Hunsinger, Carolyn Jones, Daniel Kash, Vincent Keene, Bradley Lavelle, Eric Loren, Peter Marinker, Ted Maynard, Christine McCorkindale, Mac McDonald, Kenneth Nelson, Oliver Parker, Hugh Quarshie, Kim Robertson, Nina Robertson, Hugh Ross, George Roth, McNally Segal, Bob Sessions, Craig Sheffer, Kathy Sinclair, Malcolm Smith, Richard van Spall, Nicholas Vince, Mitch Webb, Debora Weston and David Young

Approximately 101m; Color

DVD1: *Night Breed* [WAR; 101m; LBX]; VHS1: *Night Breed* [MHE; 102 (101)m]; *Night Breed* [WAR; 101m]

ADL: *Come Meet the Dead of Night.*

Boon, a troubled young man suffering from bad dreams, is fingered as a serial killer by his psychiatrist. Before being nabbed by the cops, he discovers the location of what he presumes to be the imaginary city of Midian, and goes to find sanctuary in the fabled refuge for "lost tribes" (i.e. monsters). Before gaining admittance, he is shot and killed by police, but not before being bitten by one of its testier residents.

As Clive Barker's writing wandered from outright horror into the realms of dark fantasy, so did his films. Eschewing the sado-gothic trappings of *Hellraiser* for Freudian-fueled modern primitivism, Barker creates a world where the monsters—despite all of their failings—are the protagonists. Although the theme of "there are no greater monsters than man" has been overused in a slew of more caustic horror offerings, the director/writer takes it to a comic book extreme here. Because of this, *Night Breed* does get a little campy at times, but it is through a more lighthearted approach that Barker aids the viewer in associating with his monstrous heroes.

Barker's stylish direction is a given, and it is accompanied by excellent production values, including what has to be Elfman's most intense, most inspired score to date. The sets are breathtaking at times, at least in reference to Midian (the underground city itself, not the stagy graveyard above).

Performances are good as well, with kudos going to filmmaker David Cronenberg, cast here as the psychiatrist-cum-serial killer. (Considering Cronenberg's demeanor and his background, one would swear that this role was tailor made for him.) Doug (*Hellraiser*) Bradley is also on hand, unrecognizable in the innocuous role of the breed's soothsayer.

There is some intense gore … or was some, I should say. Although still a bloody offering, much of the film's "gratuity" was cut just prior to its theatrical release, probably in order to obtain an R rating. Also a disappointment is the make-up; although some of the effects work is excellent, much of it is cheap looking, thus ineffectual. (This can be excused, considering the sheer quantity of special effects this film demanded—*Night Breed* probably showcases more monsters in a single production than any other film before or since—but it remains a shortcoming nonetheless.)

Night Eyes see **Deadly Eyes**

Night Life (1989)

Creative Movie Marketing [US]
DIR: David Acomba; PRO: Charles Lippincott; SCR: Keith Critchlow; DOP: Roger Tonry; MFX: Craig Reardon; SFX: Edward French; MUS: Roger Bourland

STR: Matthew Asner, John Astin, Alan Blumenfeld, Richard Butler, Erik Cord, Kenneth Ian Davis, John de Bello, Warwick Deeping, Darcy deMoss, Lisa Fuller, Anthony Geary, Scott Grimes, Arlene Harris, Patricia P. Hurley, G.E. Miller, Buckley Norris, Mark Pellegrino, Cheryl Pollak, Philip Proctor, Spiro Razatos, Mike Reynolds, Ross Vachon, Ed White, Charles Woods and Biff Yeager

Approximately 92m; Color
VHS1: *Night Life* [RCA; 92m]
ADL: *There's Good Reason to Be Afraid of the Dark.*

A smart-ass geek working at a mortuary harasses and is harassed by a group of jocks and their Barbie-doll girlfriends. He and his cute grease monkey pal aren't safe from their tormenting, though, even when Death steps in, it seems.

Night Life is a well-paced zombie flick that boasts some fairly intelligent scriptwriting (vas ist das?) and even (mein Gott!) some suspense. The zombie antics don't kick in until about midway through, which is actually good because the build-up surpasses the predictable shenanigans of the living dead. Unfortunately, everything that this film initially has going for it starts to fade as it careens towards its sad climax. (Sure, the shock ending is kind of cute, but by this point the viewer will be eager to stuff the film into the video rewinder.)

Another of the film's strengths is star John (*The Addams Family*) Astin; going against typecasting, here he plays a real prick of a mortician, quashing his previously established image as a lovable eccentric. There is some gore, although it seems that the effects artists were saving up their reserve of fake blood for Astin's particularly messy—albeit poetic—demise. (There's no "I'm feeling much better now" here, that's for sure.) Unfortunately, the special effects leave something to be desired, and seem almost as uninspired as the latter half of the film.

Night of the Alien see **Futurekill**

Night of the Creeps (1986)

TriStar Pictures Inc. [US]
DIR: Fred Dekker; PRO: Charles Gordon; SCR: Fred Dekker; DOP: Robert C. New; EXP: William Finnegan; MFX: David B. Miller; VFX: Ted Rae and David Stipes; MUS: Barry de Vorzon and Stan Ridgway

STR: Elizabeth Alda, Tom Atkins, Howard Berger, Katherine Britton, Todd Bryant, Alice Cadogan, Beal Carrotes, Elizabeth Cox, Richard de Haven, Chris Dekker, Tex Donaldson, Earl Ellis, Emily Fiola, Daniel Frishman, Joseph S. Griffo, June Harris, Ken Heron, Dave Alan Johnson, Jay Arlen Jones, Allan J. Kayser, Robert Kerman, Robert Kino, Robert Kurtzman, Jack Lightsy, Jason Lively, Steve Marshall, Brian McGregor, David B. Miller, Dick Miller, Russell Moss, David Oliver, David Paymer, Vic Polizos, Ted Rae, Ivan E. Roth, Leslie Ryan, Richard Sassin, Craig Schaeffer, Dawn Schroeder, Evelyne Smith, Suzanne Snyder, Bruce Solomon, Arick Stillwagon, Wally Taylor, Kevin Thompson, Jim Townsend, Jay Wakeman, Keith Werle, Jill Whitlow and John J. York

AKA: *Creeps*
Approximately 89m; Color
VHS1: *Night of the Creeps* [HBO; 89m]
ADL: *The Good News Is Your Date Is Here. The Bad News Is … He's Dead.*

A crew of baby-butt extraterrestrials eject a canister into space, and it just so happens to land in what appears to be Patty Duke's hometown. From there it becomes a pastiche of *The Blob*, except that the interstellar booger has been replaced with a *Night of the Living Dead*–style virus. Following that film's cue, it eventually settles into *Return of the Living Dead* meets *They Came from Within*. If you're thinking that *Night of the Creeps* is nothing more than a simple-minded homage to all of our favorite horror films, you're right, except that—unlike most films that attempt to pay tribute to such trend setting movies—this one actually elicits a few laughs, and is even quite charming when all is said and done.

Although production values are passable, only the content is consequential. *Night of the Creeps* has a little bit of everything: some surprisingly heavy-handed gore; clips from Ed Wood's *Plan 9 from Outer Space* (1959); a zombie cat; ex–Go Go's member Jane Wiedlin on the soundtrack; characters named Romero, Carpenter, and Hooper; and Dick Miller asking Tom Atkins "if it's Halloween or something."

Director Dekker tried to pull of another homage with *The Monster Squad*, made a year later, but failed on most counts *that* time out.

Night of the Demons (1987)

Halloween Partners Ltd. [US], Meridian Pictures [US]

DIR: Kevin S. Tenney; PRO: Joe Augustyn; SCR: Joe Augustyn; DOP: David Lewis; EXP: Walter Josten; MFX: Steve Johnson; MUS: Dennis Michael Tenney

STR: Alvin Alexis, Harold Ayer, Allison Barron, Marie Denn, Karen Ericson, Lance Fenton, William Gallo, Hal Havins, Clark Jarrett, Donnie Jeffcoat, Jr., Amelia Kinkade, Cathy Podewell, Linnea Quigley, James W. Quinn, Philip Tanzini and Jill Terashita

AKA: *Halloween Party; La Noche de los Demonios* [The Night of the Demons]

Approximately 90m; Color

DVD2: *Night of the Demons* [MNM; 86m]; VHS1: *Night of the Demons* [RPV; 90m]

ADL: *Angela Is Having a Party, Jason and Freddy Are Too Scared to Come ... But You'll Have a Hell of a Time.*

A group of stupid teens (aren't they all?) go to the abandoned Hall House for a Halloween party. (Not only was the place once a funeral parlor, it was the site of a mass slaughter perpetrated by the resident mortician-cum-necrophile on his own family.) They inadvertently let loose a demon biding his time in the crematorium furnace, which promptly possesses all the females of the group, who then go about making short work of their partners.

In the vein of *Démoni* and *The Evil Dead*, *Night of the Demons* is a mindless shocker that tries to update stock haunted house horrors without straying too far from the conventions. Unlike the aforementioned entries, though, *Night of the Demons* lacks the verve that made those films at least watchable. (Sorry, but the scene with Linnea Quigley shoving a tube of lipstick into her nipple does not qualify this as a recommendable film, no matter what the other critics say.) Production values are homogenized, save for the across-the-board bad acting. Lame gore predominates. *Night of the Demons* does boast a campy but cool animated intro, but after that it's fast forward territory.

Personally, I would suggest you

skip the series altogether and save yourself the rental fees.

Night of the Zombies *see* **Inferno dei Morti-Viventi**

Night Ripper! (1986)

Video Features [US]
DIR: Jeff Hatchcock; PRO: Jeff Hathcock and John Tomlinson; SCR: Jeff Hathcock; DOP: Joe Dinh; MFX: Paul Herndon; MUS: Bill Parsley
STR: April Anne, Phil de Carlo, Nick de Santis, Simon de Soto, James Hansen, Courtney Lercara, Danielle Louis, Valerie Maddox, Jim Mann, Jillian Marone, Rebecca Nitkin, Claire Paradis, Lee Richards, Lawrence Scott, Suzanne Tegman, Brad Thoennes, Larry Thomas, Tami Tirgrath, Robyn Truxal and Drew Walker
Approximately 89m; Color [Shot on video]
VHS1: *Night Ripper!* [IVP; 88(89)m]
ADL: *Get Ready for a Night-Stalking, Blood-Gushing Nightmare!*

Video box art for *Night Ripper!* (1986), International Video Presentations.

Granted, *Night Ripper!* may be more adept than most shot on video fare (due to the fact that the director had previous experience in film), but most of you probably know that this doesn't mean squat since—chances are—they inevitably suck and are rarely comparable to even the worst celluloid production.

As could be expected from the title, the film's main impetus is the display of extremely graphic effects. Although not shabby (and, again, better than most shot on video fare), it's nothing to write home about. Some of the actors are, well, actually actors, instead of just friends and family of the crew. And there is enough of a story to keep one from hitting the snooze button on the alarm. Just barely. Regardless of the film's ability to just scrape by at above average (again, for shot on video fare, not *real*

cinema), it has nothing new to offer an already overworked genre. Simply put, no inspiration, all reiteration.

Night Ripper! does offer the viewer some irritations, though. First, everyone in the film is a frigging photographer. *Everyone.* (A minor offense, to be sure, but it just goes to show how lazy some scriptwriters get, their stories entirely dependent on convenience.) Second—and hardest to overlook—is the fact that the killer is a militant lesbian, and her sexual proclivities are the impetus to the murders. (Some similarly perturbing politics show up in the director's earlier—and surprisingly sleazier—outing, *Victims!* But, hey, at least that one wasn't shot on video.)

For homegrown enthusiasts only.

Night Train to Terror (1985)

Visto International Inc. [US]
DIR: John Carr, Phillip Marshak, Tom McGowan, Jay Schlossenberg-Cohen and Greg C. Tallas; PRO: Edmund J. Bodine, Jr., Darryl A. Marshak and Jay Schlossenberg-Cohen; SCR: Philip Yordan; DOP: Frank Byers, Art Fitzsimmons, Bruce Makoe, Susan Maljan and Byron Wardlaw; EXP: Stanford Hale, William F. Messerli, Carl Newell and William Stroup; MFX: Martin L. Dorf; SFX: Martin L. Dorf; VFX: William R. Stromberg & Associates; MUS: Steven Arthur Yeaman and Casey Young

STR: Rick Arbuckle, Rick Barnes, Lori Bell, Arthur M. Braham, Robert Bristol, Richard Bulik, William Charles, Marlie Clark, Faith Clift, Norma Clift, Micki Anne Corbin, Peter Creadick, Juan Luis Curiel, Barbara de Vandre, Lou Edwards, Anne Fairchild, Jini Flynn, Georgia Geerling, Maurice Grandemaison, Donna Grillo, Meredith Haze, Eva Hesse, Meredith Kennedy, John Phillip Law, Marc Lawrence, Stacy Lyons, Linda Maderas, Carla Marlenee, Elizabeth Martin, Cameron Mitchell, Richard Moll, Melanie Montilla, Chantel Morogeus, Angela Nicoletti, Charles Parker, Sharon Ratcliff, Mark Ridley, Robyn Russel, Dina Lee Russo, Richard Sanford, T.J. Savage, Jamie Scoggin, J. Martin Sellers, Joe Sheron, Klint Stevenson, Evan A. Stoliar, Amy Sussman, Christie Wagner, Earl Washington, Lisa Watkins, Gabriel Whitehouse, Barbara Wyler, Byron Yordan and Philip Yordan, Jr.

AKA: *Shiver*

Approximately 93m; Color

DVD0: *Night Train to Terror* [SIM; 93m]; VHS1: *Night Train to Terror* [PRI; 98(93)m]; *Night Train to Terror* [VTR; 93m]

ADL: *A Rock Band Gives Their Final Performance on a Hell Bound Trip into the Outer Reaches of Horror!*

I bet you're wondering "Why so many credits?" Even for an anthology, a hell of a lot of people were involved on the production end of it. Well, I'm going to let you in on something...

With an unfinished film under their belts, some filmmakers came up with a grand way of getting it released as is. Having been involved with two other films released in the late '70s, they obtained the rights to these obscure outings, trimmed them down to, oh, about thirty minutes each (ouch! that's what I call a close shave) and—bingo!—instant anthology. All they needed to do then was film a wraparound sequence that tenuously linked the three segments. Well, no time to actually write much of a script, but they knew this band a friend of theirs was in, so they could just film them performing a few numbers to pad it out. All they needed was a name and an adline to tie it all together, and straight to video it went. Oh, Al Adamson would be proud.

The first segment is the unfinished film proffered here as "The Case of Harry Billing." Damn good thing it was never finished because—despite lots of gratuity—this piece about people being abducted and their body parts being sold to medical school is plodding even at half an hour. As unnerving as it is, seeing Richard (*Night Court*) Moll playing a sadistic rapist is the highlight. The second, "The Case of Gretta Connors," is actually what is left of the quirky 1970s melodrama *Death Wish Club*. Stripped of its humor, it becomes completely worthless. The third, "The Case of Claire Hansen," is the remnants of *The Nightmare Never Ends* (1980), an obscure splatter film that doesn't fare much better. The wraparound consists of God and Satan quibbling over souls on a train, all the while some really obnoxious rock band panders to brain dead MTV fans next door.

You've been warned.

Nightbeast *see* **Night Beast**

Nightbreed *see* **Night Breed**

The Nightkillers *see* **Silent Madness**

Nightmare (1981)

Goldmine Productions Inc. [US]
DIR: Romano Scavolini; PRO: John
L. Watkins; SCR: Romano Scavolini; DOP:
Gianni Fiore Coltellacci; EXP: David Jones;
MFX: Edward French; SFX: Les Larrain
and William R. Milling; MUS: Jack Eric
Williams
STR: Tara Alexander, Randy Arieux,
Raymond Baker, Tommy Bouvier, Craig
Cain, Carl Clifford, C.J. Cooke, Mik Crib-
ben, Mark Davis, Kathleen Ferguson, Dan-
ielle Galiana, Lonnie Griffis, Christina
Keefe, William S. Kirksey, George Kruger,
Candy Marchese, Geoffrey Marchese, David
Massar, William R. Milling, Mary Lee
Parise, Kim Patterson, Tammy Patterson,
William Paul, Scott Praetorius, Danny
Ronan, Frank Rothery, Sharon Smith, Baird
Stafford, Michel Sweney, Robert Tenvooren,
Ken Thomas, Scott Trotter, Danny Watkins
and Susan Webb
AKA: *Blood Splash*; *Nightmares in a
Damaged Brain*; *Schizo*
Approximately 89m; Color
VHS1: *Nightmare* [CON; 89m];
VHS2: *Nightmare* [VFP; 99(89)m]; *Night-
mares in a Damaged Brain* [WOV; 93(89)m]
ADL: *The Dream You Can't Escape
Alive!*

An outpatient suffering from
"schizophrenia, mild amnesia, and
homicidal dream fixation seizures"
makes a trip from Florida (against his
doctor's orders) to New York and begins stalking a single mother and her
children. Turns out, the man caught
his parents playing S&M games when
he was a child, and beheaded his
mother with an axe. (Don't worry ...
although they make some attempt to
be vague, it's obvious early on who
was responsible for the murder.)
This low budget, sometimes tir-

ing splatterfest boasts little more than
some above-average performances
and—when given the opportunity—
gratuity. (The term "reveling" comes
to mind, even though it is curiously
conservative with the nudity and gore
at times.) The script offers the viewer
few, if any, surprises, and even makes
a half-baked attempt to copy Bava's *Il
Rosso Segno della Follias* (1971) by having the killer trying to piece together
his lost memories. (Each murder is
accompanied by a flashback which
gets him that much closer to revealing the identity of his mother's killer,
obviously himself.)
A marginally interesting early
stalk 'n' slash gorefest at best, *Nightmare's* claim to fame is the controversy
surrounding the participation of a
certain special effects artist. Credited
as "Special Effects Director," artist
Tom Savini purportedly claimed that
he did nothing more than offer some
over-the-phone assistance to the production of this film, and threatened
them with a lawsuit if they didn't remove his name from movie posters
and video box covers. Although most
of the special effects were actually created by Les Larrain, William Milling
and Edward French, there is ample
evidence that Tom Savini *was* on the
set of the film and acted to a much
greater degree than he supposedly
claims. (One damning photo can be
found in the book *Spaghetti Nightmares* by Gaetano Mistretta and Luca
M. Palmerini, and depicts Mr. Savini
himself showing a young star how to
swing a rather nasty-looking axe.)
How much of this is true, and how
much is rumor is anyone's guess.
Now if only the movie were as
interesting as this side note.

Nightmare 2—Die Rache see
A Nightmare on Elm Street
Part 2—Freddy's Revenge

Nightmare Beach see La Spiaggia
del Terrore

Nightmare City see Incubo sulla
Città Contaminata

Nightmare Island see The Slayer

A Nightmare on Elm Street (1984)

Media Home Entertainment [US], New Line Cinema [US], Smart Egg Pictures [US]

DIR: Wes Craven; PRO: Robert Shaye; SCR: Wes Craven; DOP: Jacques Haitkin; EXP: Stanley Dudelson and Joseph Wolf; MFX: David B. Miller; MUS: Charles Bernstein [Soundtrack from Varèse Sarabande]

STR: Jason Adams, David Andrews, Ronee Blakley, Ed Call, Nick Corri, Johnny Depp, Robert Englund, Charles Fleischer, Paul Grenier, Shawshawnee Hall, Don Hannah, Leslie Hoffman, Heather Langenkamp, Jeff Levine, Sandy Lipton, Mimi Meyer-Craven, Carol Pritikin, Brian Reise, John Saxon, Lin Shaye, Jack Shea, Joe Unger, Joseph Whipp, Donna Woodrum and Amanda Wyss

AKA: *Pesadilla en la Calle del Infierno* [Nightmare on the Street of Hell]

Approximately 92m; Color

DVD1: *A Nightmare on Elm Street* [NEW; 92m; LBX]; VHS1: *A Nightmare on Elm Street* [MHE; 92m]; *A Nightmare on Elm Street* [NEW; 92m; LBX]; VHS2: *A Nightmare on Elm Street* [EIV; 88m]

ADL: *If Nancy Doesn't Wake Up Screaming ... She Won't Wake Up at All!*

A young girl is having nightmares about being harassed by a child molesting serial killer that plagued her neighborhood years before, and who was lynched by concerned parents. Somehow, his spirit has survived, entering the dreams of his in-tended victims, while possessing the ability to make their deaths a reality.

Anyone reading this will undoubtedly be familiar with the series or—at the very least—its sadistic wisecracking antagonist, Freddy Krueger. Somehow, he has become a prominent part of Americana, surpassed only by the instant recognition of Mickey Mouse, Superman, and Dracula. By the end of the 1980s, he had become America's superlative bogeyman, the embodiment of children's greatest fears. In the process, an interesting psychological phenomenon took place; Freddy Krueger became not only a hot commodity, but also a virtual anti-hero in the eyes of the general public.

The film? *A Nightmare on Elm Street* is a somewhat effective (albeit overrated) shocker that proved to be the beginning of the end for director Craven. Although a passable horror film, it's not nearly as visceral as such early efforts as *Last House on the Left* and *The Hills Have Eyes*. Everything is sacrificed for simple shocks; the script is forced, the dialogue awkward, and the movie refuses to adhere to even its own skewered sense of logic. Essentially, *A Nightmare on Elm Street* is silly hokum that boasts little in the way of decent effects, a necessity in a film that relies on the viewers' suspension of disbelief. Character actor Robert Englund is definitely the high point of the picture, but neither the actor nor the character can carry this for more than one film without becoming a self-parodying caricature.

Enjoyable, but definitely not worth its weight in sequels.

A Nightmare on Elm Street 2—
Freddy's Revenge *see* A
Nightmare on Elm Street
Part 2—Freddy's Revenge

Nightmare on Elm Street Part 2—Freddy's Revenge (1985)

Heron Communications Inc. [US], New Line Cinema [US], Smart Egg Pictures [US]

DIR: Jack Sholder; PRO: Robert Shaye; SCR: David Chaskin; DOP: Jacques Haitkin; EXP: Stephen Diener and Stanley Dudelson; MFX: Mark Shostrom and Kevin Yagher; VFX: Paul Boyington; MUS: Christopher Young [Soundtrack from Varèse Sarabande]

STR: Allison Barron, Marshall Bell, Edward Blackoff, Donna Bruce, Robert Chaskin, Christie Clark, Steve Eastin, Robert Englund, Melinda O. Fee, Clu Gulager, Jonathan Hart, Hope Lange, Kimberly Lynn, Thom McFadden, Kim Myers, Mark Patton, Kerry Remsen, Robert Rusler, Steven Smith, Hart Sprager, Sydney Walsh, Lyman Ward, Joann Willette and Brian Wimmer

AKA: *Nightmare 2—Die Rache* [Nightmare 2—The Revenge]; *A Nightmare on Elm Street 2—Freddy's Revenge*; *Pesadilla en Elm Street 2—La Venganza de Freddy* [Nightmare on Elm Street 2—The Revenge of Freddy]

Approximately 87m; Color

DVD1: *A Nightmare on Elm Street 2—Freddy's Revenge* [NEW; 87m; LBX]; VHS1: *A Nightmare on Elm Street 2—Freddy's Revenge* [MHE; 87m]; *A Nightmare on Elm Street 2—Freddy's Revenge* [NEW; 87m]

A bunch of adults trying to pass themselves off as high school students are besieged by everyone's favorite child molester-cum-Hollywood horror icon. This time, the new kid on the block moves into the selfsame house where all of the action from *A Nightmare on Elm Street* took place. (Go figure.) Apparently, Freddy is looking for a host so as to achieve transubstantiation (pretty big word to

use in reference to one of these flicks) and leave the realm of dreams behind.

Reiterating its predecessor, *Freddy's Revenge* should have been a vain attempt to perpetuate a franchise; unfortunately, it worked. The dream sequences are tedious, and the film is virtually goreless until the "big" finale (which is capped off with a predictable bullshit ending). Some of the more laughable scenes—like an exploding bird, or a leather-wearing, sado-masochistic gym teacher tied up with jump ropes and whipped with wet towels—are almost amusing, but they aren't worth the price of admission. (Pass on this sucker if only to avoid an uninvited *Risky Business*-style musical number. God, those exhibitions turn my stomach.)

I'm not going to bother elaborating any further because this is one of those cases where, if you haven't already seen it, you probably don't intend to.

A Nightmare on Elm Street Part III
see A Nightmare on Elm Street
3—The Dream Warriors

A Nightmare on Elm Street 3— Dream Warriors (1987)

Heron Communications Inc. [US], New Line Cinema [US], Smart Egg Pictures [US]

DIR: Chuck Russell; PRO: Robert Shaye; SCR: Wes Craven, Frank Darabont, Chuck Russell and Bruce Wagner; DOP: Roy H. Wagner; EXP: Wes Craven and Stephen Diener; MFX: Greg Cannom, Mark Shostrom, and Kevin Yagher; VFX: Doug Beswick Productions Inc. and Dream Quest Images; MUS: Angelo Badalamenti

STR: Stacey Alden, Patricia Arquette, Mary Brown, Brooke Bundy, Dick Cavett, Kristen Clayton, Melanie Doctors, Donna Durham, Rodney Eastman, Robert Englund, Larry Fishburne, Zsa Zsa Gabor,

Bradley Gregg, Ira Heiden, Paul Kent, Clayton Landey, Heather Langenkamp, Nan Martin, Sally Piper, Priscilla Pointer, Michael Rougas, Jennifer Rubin, Ken Sagoes, John Saxon, Jack Shea, Rozlyn Sorrell, Penelope Sudrow and Craig Wasson

AKA: *A Nightmare on Elm Street Part III*; *Pesadilla en Elm Street 3—Dream Warriors* [Nightmare on Elm Street 3—Dream Warriors]

Approximately 96m; Color

DVD1: *A Nightmare on Elm Street 3—The Dream Warriors* [NEW; 96m; LBX]; VHS1: *A Nightmare on Elm Street 3—The Dream Warriors* [MHE; 96m]; *A Nightmare on Elm Street 3—The Dream Warriors* [NEW; 96m]

ADL: *If You Think You'll Get Out Alive, You Must Be Dreaming...*

This time out, we've got a whole gaggle of insomniacs doing battle with the prince of nightmares. Unfortunately, there isn't one person in the sorry lot with which one can empathize, as they are all pathetic, whiny, and/or shallow introverts who really don't deserve to live, let alone be given the screen time they receive. (And this is saying a great deal coming from a pathetic, whiny, and—more often than not—shallow introvert. Won't Hollywood *ever* get us right?) It's really no wonder Freddy reached anti-hero status, considering the cannon fodder the scriptwriters offer to him.

Despite a few (very few) inspired moments, *The Dream Warriors* is more of the same, although this is the first film to truly capitalize on its pandering franchise status. (Taken to even greater extremes with the next two films, I might add.)

The film opens with Edgar Allan Poe's classic quote "Sleep. Those little slices of death. How I loathe them." It's a good thing he never lived to see a Freddy film, otherwise he would have found something much less profound to abhor.

A Nightmare on Elm Street 4— The Dream Master (1988)

Heron Communications Inc. [US], New Line Cinema [US], Smart Egg Pictures [US]

DIR: Renny Harlin; PRO: Robert Shaye and Rachel Talalay; SCR: Brian Helgeland and Scott Pierce; DOP: Steven Fierberg; EXP: Stephen Diener and Sara Risher; MFX: R. Christopher Biggs, Steve Johnson, Magical Media Industries Inc., Screaming Mad George and Kevin Yagher; VFX: Dream Quest Images; MUS: Craig Safan [Soundtrack from Chrysalis Records and Varèse Sarabande]

STR: John Beckman, Kisha Brackel, Brooke Bundy, Wanda Bursey, Hope Marie Carlton, Kristen Clayton, Duane Davis, Rodney Eastman, Robert Englund, Richard Garrison, Danny Hassel, Jake, Andras Jones, Tuesday Knight, Jeff Levine, Joanna Lipari, Joie Magidow, Jacquelyn Masche, Nicholas Mele, Judy Montana, Toy Newkirk, Pat O'Neal, Linnea Quigley, Cheryl Richardson, Ken Sagoes, Robert Shaye, Brooke Theiss, Lisa Wilcox and Mickey Yablans

Approximately 99m; Color

DVD1: *A Nightmare on Elm Street 4—The Dream Master* [NEW; 99m; LBX]; VHS1: *A Nightmare on Elm Street 4—The Dream Master* [MHE; 99m]; *A Nightmare on Elm Street 4—The Dream Master* [NEW; 99m]

ADL: *Terror Beyond Your Wildest Dreams.*

Freddy's up to his old tricks again ... emphasis on "old." In fact, "venerable" or even "tired" would probably be more apropos.

It is no surprise that this Slumberland outing was perpetrated by Renny Harlin, director of the Hollywood mega-hit *Die Hard* (1988) and its sequels. The gloss is laid on thick, further diluting any shocks. Everything herein adheres to strict, ho-

213 [Nine]

mogenized Hollywood standards; even the effects by Screaming Mad George—the most conceptually interesting of the lot—are fairly unimpressive.

Only two more to go...

A Nightmare on Elm Street 5—The Dream Child see A Nightmare on Elm Street—The Dream Child

A Nightmare on Elm Street— The Dream Child (1989)

Heron Communications Inc. [US], New Line Cinema [US], Smart Egg Pictures [US]

DIR: Stephen Hopkins; PRO: Rupert Harvey and Robert Shaye; SCR: Leslie Bohem; DOP: Peter Levy; EXP: Sara Risher and Jon Turtle; MFX: David Miller Studios and KNB EFX Group Inc.; VFX: Alan Munro; MUS: Jay Ferguson [Soundtrack from Jive Records and Varèse Sarabande]

STR: Erika Anderson, Ron Armstrong, Valorie Armstrong, Michael Ashton, Beatrice Boepple, Matt Borlenghi, Noble Craig, E.R. Davies, Burr de Benning, Beth de Patie, Will Egan, Stacy Elliott, Robert Englund, Clarence Felder, Wally George, Steven Grives, Danny Hassel, Whitby Hertford, Jennifer Honneus, Jake Jacobs, Anne Lamaje, Gerry Loew, Kara Marie, Don Maxwell, Roxanne Mayweather, Nicholas Mele, Kelly Jo Minter, John R. Murray, Ted Nugent, Marne Patterson, Cameron Perry, Rudy Sarno, Joe Seely, Mark Siegler, Eric Singer, Mike Smith, Pat Sturges, Cesar Anthony Torres, Peter Trencher and Lisa Wilcox

AKA: A Nightmare on Elm Street 5— The Dream Child

Approximately 91m; Color

DVD1: A Nightmare on Elm Street 5— The Dream Child [NEW; 90(91)m; LBX]; VHS1: A Nightmare on Elm Street 5—The Dream Child [MHE; 91m]; A Nightmare on Elm Street 5—The Dream Child [NEW; 90(91)m]

ADL: It's a Boy!

Yes, the entire storyline hinges on the fact that Freddy is now a daddy. Beyond that, it's the same old shenanigans on Elm Street.

Not only is this installment less coherent than previous films, it's even more technically incompetent despite the fact that it was helmed by Stephen (Predator 2) Hopkins. Unless you're a diehard (i.e. brain dead) fan of the series and/or antagonist, stay away as it offers nothing outside of the usual cheesy effects and bad puns. (It's no wonder the fan base for these films get younger and younger; despite the gratuity, it doesn't seem that far a cry from The Mighty Morphin' Power Rangers. Geez.)

Nightmare Vacation see Sleepaway Camp

Nightmare Vacation II see Sleepaway Camp 2—Unhappy Campers

Nightmare Vacation III see Camp 3—Teenage Wasteland

Nightmares in a Damaged Brain see Nightmare

976-EVIL (1988)

Horrorscope Inc. [US]

DIR: Robert Englund; PRO: Lisa M. Hansen; SCR: Brian Helgeland and Rhet Topham; DOP: Paul Elliott; EXP: Paul Hertzberg; MFX: Kevin Yagher; SFX: Kevin McCarthy and Sandra McCarthy; MUS: Thomas Chase and Steve Rucker

STR: Don Bajema, Darren Burrows, J.J. Cohen, Greg Collins, Wendy Cooke, Ed Corbett, Lezlie Deane, Sandy Dennis, Stephen Geoffreys, Bert Hinchman, Gunther Jenson, J.J. Johnston, Joanna Keyes, Jim Landis, Thom McFadden, Christopher Metas, Jim Metzler, Pat O'Bryan, Demetre Phillips, Robert Picardo, Quigley, Roxanne Rogers, Maria Rubell, Mindy Seeger, Jon Slade, Cynthia Szigeti, Jim Thiebaud, Larry Turk and Paul Willson

Approximately 104m; Color
DVD2: *976-EVIL* [DIG; 90m];
VHS1: *976-EVIL* [RCA; 105(104)m]

Hoax, a nebbish whipping boy blessed with a domineering, religiously overzealous mother, turns to a "horrorscope" line that eventually turns him into a vengeful demon. His rebel without a clue cousin, Spike, is by now used to saving his ass, but this is more than even he can handle (especially when his kickdog cousin is smitten by his new trashy girlfriend). A reporter for a religious *Weekly World News*–style tabloid gets involved, as does the boy's principal.

This is the directorial debut of Robert "Freddy Krueger" Englund, and—so far—the only film to his credit as a filmmaker. (Just because he is a good character actor doesn't mean he can make a good film. Far from it.) *976-EVIL* is a hopelessly derivative script riddled with stale Hollywood archetypes; Stephen Geoffreys (Evil Ed from *Fright Night*) manages to add some pathos to the role of Hoax, but only because he's always so damn good as the nebbish whipping boy. Production values are average, and the gore doesn't really kick in until the last reel.

Although it is better than many of the *Carrie* rip-offs, someone with some money took that to mean more than it does. A sequel followed.

La Noche de los Demonios *see* **Night of the Demons**

La Noche del Hombre Lobo *see* **El Retorno del Hombre Lobo**

Non Aprire Prima di Natale *see* **Don't Open Till Christmas**

Non Avere Paura della Zia Marta [Do Not Fear Aunt Marta] (1989)

Alpha D.C. Production [It]
DIR: Mario Bianchi; PRO: Antonio Lucidi and Luigi Nannerini; SCR: Mario Bianchi; DOP: Silvano Tessicini; EXP: Augusto Carminito; MUS: Gianni Esposito
STR: Lucy Arland, Jessica Moore, Sacha Orwin, Norren Parker, Maurice Poli, Adriana Russo and Gabriele Tinti
AKA: *The Broken Mirror, The Murder Secret*
Approximately 88m; Color
VHS1: *The Murder Secret* [VDY; 88m; LBX; Japanese subs]

A man and his family are off to the country to visit his aunt Martha, who—following a brief stay in an institution—has been living in South America for the last thirty years. They arrive, and are told that she is due back in a few days. The caretaker shows them around, giving them free reign of the place ... save for the "boarded up" entrance to the basement where they are obviously not welcome. While waiting around for their kooky relative to show up, the guests spend their time sullying the sheets, falling for the caretaker's lame excuses, and—not soon enough—getting knocked off by an unseen assailant.

"Supervised" by the man who brought us such tasteful excursions as *Zombi 2* (1979) and *Paura nella Città dei Morti Viventi*, *Non Avere Paura della Zia Marta* is a simple-minded, predictable gore flick that reeks more of Fulci's formula gorefests than many of Fulci's own films made around this time. Production values are average, but bad acting abounds. The murders are graphic, though the execution (excuse the bad pun) is lousy. (Most of the killings involve decapitation; although one may—with a stretch of the imagination—accept having one's head lopped off by a chainsaw, the death involving an oak chest is a little more difficult to swallow.) Highlights include a trademarked Fulci maggot-ridden corpse, a very crude *Psycho*-esque shower scene, and, spoiler one, a very non–Hollywood style script that sees fit *not* to spare the children from the violent fates that befall their parents. But then, spoiler two, there's the typical cheat "it was only a dream" ending, which is guaranteed to elicit more than a few groans of disapproval.

Sorry, folks, but there's not much here that I can recommend.

Nothing Underneath *see* **Sotto il Vestito Niente**

Notte nel Bosco [Night in the Woods] (1988)

Fomar Film [It]
DIR: Andreas Marfori; PRO: Agnese Fontana; SCR: Andreas Marfori; DOP: Marco Isoli; MFX: Bruno Biagi, Elisa Calcinari, Paolo Forti and Donatella Mondani; MUS: Adriano Maria Vitali
STR: Elena Cantarone, Luciano Crovato, Stefano Molinari, Diego Ribon and Coralina Cataldi Tassoni
AKA: *Il Bosco* [The Woods]; *Evil Clutch*; *Horror Queen*
Approximately 85m; Color
VHS1: *Evil Clutch* [RHI; 85m]; VHS2: *Evil Clutch* [TRO; 80m]
ADL: *Her Kiss May Be Heaven, But Her Touch Is Hell!*

A couple pick up a woman who—unbeknownst to them—has a spider-like appendage that slides out of her crotch and rips out the innards of any unsuspecting men she succeeds in seducing. Shortly thereafter, they meet up with a horror writer who wears aviation goggles and—due to a tumor—is forced to talk through a voice synthesizer. He sets them down and tells them a story—with his listeners as the main characters—about a woman who comes back from the grave after her lover stabs her to death on a beach. (This pointless exercise manages to waste a good ten minutes, as well as increasing the gore quotient.) From there it's on to bad movie Hell.

This low-renter is undoubtedly gory, but no amount of gore is worth this abuse. The special effects are abysmal; ping-pong balls cut in half and placed over someone's eyes is one of the more *effective* examples. The rest of the production values are not nearly as inept, but are unimpressive nonetheless.

It's amazing that with so many *good* Italian films awaiting release in the states, *this* one gets the honors.

La Nuit des Traquées [The Night of the Hunted] (1980)

Impex Films [Fr]
DIR: Jean Rollin; SCR: Jean Rollin; DOP: Jean-Claude Couty; EXP: Lionel Wallmann; SFX: Évelyne Belkodja; MUS: Gary Sandeur
STR: Grégoire Cherlian, Jean Cherlian, Véronique Délaissé, Christiane Farina, Vincent Gardère, Jacques Gatteau, Catherine Greiner, Jean Hérel, Dominique Journet, Rachel Mhas, Bernard Papineau, Natalie Perrey, Dominique Saint-Cyr, Cyril Val and Brigitte van Meerhaegue
AKA: *Filles Traquées* [Hunted Girls]; *Night of the Cruel Sacrifice*; *The Night of the Hunted*
Approximately 88m; Color
DVD0: *The Night of the Hunted* [RED; 88m; LBX]; VHS2: *La Nuit des Traquées* [SUN; 88m; In French]

Okay, bear with me here; an English language version of the film was unavailable domestically when I penned this review, so I might not have as good a grasp on the proceedings as I'd like.

On a rainy night, a man almost runs over a frantic woman; she has lost her memory; he picks her up and takes her back to his place. Trying to piece her life together, they eventually work out that she's a patient at some kind of institution. She ends up back there just in time for one of the attendants to go on a killing spree. It looks like the director may be involved in some ethically questionable experiments, but what they are were beyond me.

Taking a break from his trademarked vampire epics, director Rollin not only changed his focus but the setting as well, which may account for the film's ineffectual visuals. The rotting châteaux and decrepit graveyards have been replaced with the sort of sterilized sets more at home in David Cronenberg's science-gone-awry features. Without the gothic atmosphere that usually inspires Rollin to great heights, *La Nuit des Traquées* is little more than a string of graphic murders and softcore sex romps.

Rollin's direction isn't completely wasted, though, as some of his nuances still shine through. (The inherent paranoia harkens back to his film *La Vampire Nue* [1969], with certain parts of *La Nuit des Traquées* coming across as a nod to this early effort.) The gore, typical of Rollin's output at the time, isn't great, although it is a notch above that which marred *La Morte Vivante*, if only because the camera doesn't dwell on the carnage

here nearly as much as it did in that film.) And as usual, Brigette Lahaie (née van Meerhaegue) has an undeniably powerful screen presence, due not only to her exquisite beauty, but to her ability to do something so many other adult film actresses are incapable of doing: acting.

Worth seeing, but wait for an English language release so you have *some* idea of what's going on. (With any luck, Redemption will have released it domestically by the time this book sees print.)

Oase der Zombies *see* **L'Abime des Morts-Vivants**

Oasis of the Zombies *see* **L'Abime des Morts-Vivants**

L'Occhio del Male [The Eye of Evil] (1982)
Fulvia Film [It]
DIR: Lucio Fulci; PRO: Fabrizio de Angelis; SCR: Elisa Livia Briganti and Dardano Sacchetti; DOP: Guglielmo Mancori; MFX: Maurizio Trani; VFX: Studio 4; MUS: Fabio Frizzi [Soundtrack from Beat Records and Graveside Entertainment]
STR: Vincenzo Bellanich, Brigitta Boccoli, Andrea Bosic, Cosimo Cinieri, Christopher Connelly, Carlo de Mejo, Cinzia de Ponti, Giovanni Frezza, Lucio Fulci, Laura Lenzi, Mario Moretti, Tonino Pulci and Martha Taylor
AKA: *Das Amulett des Bösen* [The Amulet of the Evil One]; *The Eye of the Evil Dead*; *Il Malocchio* [The Evil Eye]; *Manhattan Baby*; *The Possessed*
Approximately 91m; Color ×× ×× ××
DVD1: *Manhattan Baby* [ABE; 91m; LBX]; VHS1: *Manhattan Baby* [ABE; 91m; LBX]; *Manhattan Baby* [BDV; 90(89)m]; *Manhattan Baby* [LIG; 90(89)m]
ADL: *Terror Is Born!*

While on an archeological expedition with her family in Egypt, a

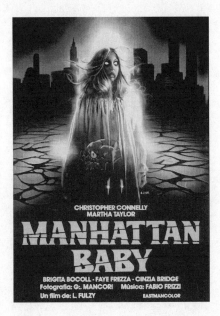

CHRISTOPHER CONNELLY
MARTHA TAYLOR

MANHATTAN BABY

BRIGITA BOCOLL · FAYE FREZZA · CINZIA BRIDGE
Fotografia: G. MANCORI　Música: FABIO FRIZZI
Un film de: L. FULZY　　　　　　　EASTMANCOLOR

French ad mat for *L'Occhio del Male* (1982).

young girl stumbles across a talisman, while her father makes the mistake of disturbing a consecrated temple of evil. He is blinded and sent back to New York, whereupon a series of spooky goings-on ensue.

Having just finished a string of offal-drenched films that garnered him instant notoriety, Lucio Fulci decided to take a more "subtle" approach with this hokey outing. Unfortunately, it doesn't generate the atmosphere that *L'Aldila* or *Quella Villa Accanto al Cimitero* did, nor does it have nearly the gratuity needed to distract the viewer from this sad fact. (There is some gore to compliment the cheesy proceedings, but there isn't the prerequisite pig gut to cover up the rubber seams.) Production values are equally chintzy; the photography is terribly underexposed, and is made worse by Fulci's penchant for close-ups (mostly eyes, just waiting to get jabbed by something, one thinks). Considering when this film was made, *L'Occhio del Male* is painfully unimpressive.

The Awakening (1980) by way of the Big Boot.

Off-Balance *see* **Un Delitto Poco Commune**

The Offspring *see* **From a Whisper to a Scream**

Los Ojos de un Extraño *see* **Eyes of a Stranger**

Oltre la Morte [Beyond Death] (1988)

Flora Film [It/Ph]
DIR: Claudio Fragasso; SCR: Rossella Drudi; DOP: Luis Ciccarese; MFX: Franco di Girolami; SFX: Rodolfo Terrente; VFX: Francesco Paolocci and Gaetano Paolocci; MUS: Al Festa [Soundtrack from Variety Film]
STR: Candice Daly, Jim Gaines, Adrianne Joseph, Jim Moss, Nick Nicholson, Chuck Peyton, Massimo Vanni and Don Wilson
AKA: *After Death*; *Zombie 4—After Death*
Approximately 88m; Color
VHS1: *After Death* [SPO; 88m; Japanese subtitles]

Scientists hole up on a remote tropical island rife with voodoo, investigating the properties of local herbs in order to find ways "to conquer death." The chief's daughter dies of Leukemia, and the natives blame their uninvited guests. Before you know it, the unconvincing eggheads are overtaken by an army of drooling demons intent on revenge, with only a young girl surviving the massacre. Twenty years later, a boat load of vacationers (one of whom is the aforementioned survivor, all grown up) chance upon the island, as does a group of mercenaries for hire and three more scientists. Needless to say, the odds are stacked against the lot of them.

Although unofficially cited as an entry in Lucio Fulci's *Zombi* series, *After Death* might as well have been the third installment in the same director's "Gates of Hell" series, initiated by *Paura nella Città dei Morti Viventi* (1980) and followed by *L'Aldilá* (1981), as *After Death* focuses on the mythical third gate bridging Earth and the underworld. It could just as well be another entry in Lamberto Bava's *Demoni* series, with which this film also has been mistakenly associated.

Furthermore, *Oltre la Morte* stands as little more than a carbon copy of George Romero's *Dawn of the Dead* (1978). This becomes evident once the heroes' ranks are stripped down to three men and one woman, two of the men "fighters" and one of them black. Following this equation, it's easy to figure out who will be the next to die.

Production values are average, with some nice tropical sets adding an exotic air to the proceedings. Unfortunately, the "demons" are little more than Romero-style zombies in black jumpsuits and bad make-up, with the goings on facilitated by distracting optical effects and an obnoxious rock score. There is some extreme gore, but—in light of all of the film's influences—this is a given. At least some of the effects are "slimier" than what one might expect.

Almost engaging as mindless mayhem, but ultimately forgettable.

One by One *see* **The Majorettes**

Opera (1988)

A.D.C. Production [It], Cecchi Gori Group [It], Tiger Cinematografica [It]
DIR: Dario Argento; PRO: Dario Argento; SCR: Dario Argento and Franco Ferrini; DOP: Ronnie Taylor; EXP: Ferdinando Caputo; MFX: Antonio Corridori, Giovanni Corridori and Germano Natali; SFX: Renato Agostini; MUS: Various Artists [Soundtrack from Cinevox Records]
STR: Urbano Barberini, Francesca Cassola, Ian Charleson, Barbara Cupisti, Maurizio Garrone, Cristina Giachino, Gyorivany Gyorgy, Bjorn Hammer, Antonino Iuorio, Cristina Marsillach, William McNamara, Daria Nicolodi, Elizabeth Norberg-Schulz, Michele Pertusi, Peter Pitsch, Michele Soavi, Sebastiano Somma, Carola Stagnaro, Coralina Cataldi Tassoni and Antonella Vitale
AKA: *Terror at the Opera*
Approximately 107m; Color
DVD1: *Opera* [ABE; 107m; LBX];
VHS1: *Opera* [ABE; 107m; LBX]; *Terror at the Opera* [EDE; 107m]; *Terror at the Opera* [SGE; 107m]

The diva of an *avant garde* updating of *Macbeth* (natch) is hospitalized after an accident. Soon thereafter, her replacement finds herself stalked by a madman who enjoys tying her up and making her watch as he brutally kills her friends and acquaintances. The needles he tapes beneath her eyelids guarantees she doesn't miss a thing.

Although a loose retelling of Gaston Leroux' *The Phantom of the Opera*, this—Argento's last substantial offering—is a *giallo* thriller in every sense of the word. Although the story is too transparent to be effective (unless, of course, it was *supposed* to be obvious to throw the viewer off track), the film is carried entirely by the intense visuals and innovative staging.

makes for some truly disturbing scenes. The movie's only weak point is the soundtrack; although the heavy metal selections often make a nice counterpart to the classical score, it ultimately cheapens the overall effect, coming across as something to placate the younger audience members. Recommended.

Video box art for *Opera* (1988), Southgate Entertainment.

Going just by the cinematography, this appears to be his most inspired film since the underrated *Inferno*; the bird's eye POV shots, and the almost microscopic view of a single bullet traversing the distance of a peephole in slow motion, are but two of the more groundbreaking shots this film offers.

The remaining production values are slick enough to please more "discriminating" filmgoers, but not so much that they dilute the director's intensity (which seems to be the case in subsequent efforts). The gore is as nasty as anything in Argento's previous films, and, coupled with the coerced voyeurism mentioned above,

The Oracle (1985)

Laurel Films Inc. [US]
DIR: Roberta Findlay; PRO: Walter E. Sear; SCR: R. Allen Leider; DOP: Roberta Findlay; MFX: Jean Carballo; SFX: Horrorefx; MUS: Michael Litovsky and Walter E. Sear
STR: Lou Bacotti, Lou Batholomew, Alexandra Blade, Juan Calderon, Rebecca Collins, G. Gordon Cronce, Chris Maria de Koron, Victoria Dryden, John Dwight, Tory Estern, John Ford, Stacey Graves, Rafael Guadalupe, Mari Kasiner, Pam la Testa, Joan Leonard, Dan Lutzky, Ethel Mark, Christopher Marzulli, Ted Mejia, John Munn, Roger Neil, Einar O. Peterson, Caroline Capers Powers, Lee-Allen Richardson, Lowell Richardson, Jr., Felix Rivera, Irma St. Paule, James Styles, Dog Thomas and Joe White
Approximately 94m; Color
VHS1: *The Oracle* [USA; 94m]
ADL: *Jennifer Has Seen the Future*

An old woman kicks it, leaving behind a house full of magical paraphernalia. The proprietor gives a planchette (a glamorized Ouija board) to a new renter, who in turn gives it to her hubby for a Christmas gift, and a tacky séance ensues. With the protagonists unable to get rid of the thing, it eventually coughs up a booger that attaches itself to a man's leg, causing him to hallucinate and stab himself to death. Meanwhile, a sexually maladjusted ox (an overweight woman trying to pass herself off as a man) is doing short work of the local pros. And, yes, it all ties together in the end. (Somehow, the screenwriter manages to weave two distinct story-lines together—one dependent on slasher proceedings, the other on hokum—but by the second half it proves itself to be little more than a retread of the 1978 film *The Eyes of Laura Mars*.)

This is, by far, one of Findlay's more professional efforts, and one of her more interesting films since her pre-porn work of the early '70s. (There is some sex—natch—but it's sparse and quite tame, considering.) There is an extremely graphic murder ten minutes into the film, and al-though the rest of the gore never reaches this level (save maybe for a grisly meltdown), it's all wonderfully gratuitous. Oh, but let's not forget the silly floating head monster, and the overacting on the part of just about every actor involved.

Mostly for fans of Findlay's low-rent horrors.

Orgias Sangrienta *see* **Die Säge des Todes**

L'Ossessione Che Uccide [The Obsession That Kills] (1980)

Dionysio Cinematografica S.r.L. [It], Nouvelle Cinevog [Fr]

DIR: Riccardo Freda; PRO: Enzo Boetani, Giuseppe Collura and Simon Mizrahi; SCR: Antonio Cesare Corti, Riccardo Freda and Fabio Piccioni; DOP: Cristiano Pogany; MUS: Franco Mannino

STR: Martine Brochard, Silvia Dionisio, Henri Garcin, Laura Gemser, Fabrizio Moroni, Stefano Patrizi, John Richardson and Anita Strindberg

AKA: *Fear; Follia Omicida* [Homicidal Madness]; *Inconsciente* [Unconscious]; *Paura* [Fear]; *Satan's Altar; The Wailing*

Approximately 92m; Color

VHS1: *Fear* [WIZ; 90(89)m]
ADL: *The Ultimate Journey into Terror...*

After trying to kill an actress on the set of his new film, an actor de-cides to take some time off and visit his mother in the countryside, ac-companied by his co-workers and his girlfriend. Apparently, mommy is not too fond of her son's lover, and a lit-tle too fond of her son (who also just happens to bear an uncanny resem-blance to his dead father whom he ap-parently knifed when he was but a child). Before long, someone's trying to knock off the uninvited guests in many a grisly fashion.

Although it has its moments, this is a far cry from Freda's groundbreak-ing ode to necrophilia, *L'Orribile Segreto de Dr. Hichcock* [The Horrible Secret of Dr. Hichcock; 1962]. *L'Ossessione Che Uccide* is not an incompe-tent effort (although the viewer is as-saulted by the whir of the camera in far too many scenes), and is even in-spired at times, but it is far too ex-ploitive to qualify as effective horror. Furthermore, the hackneyed gore ef-fects cheapen the film's overall impact.

The story refuses to settle on any one keynote. Instead, the viewer is dished up Satan worshippers, psychic phenomenon, incest, and some big spoonfuls of *giallo*-inspired mayhem. (The hokum is quite unnecessary, and at best distracts the viewer from the more important issues.) Because of the numerous plot devices, there are some interesting twists, but—lo and behold—you will be correct in your assumptions that, yes, the butler did it after all.

The film does close with some powerful imagery (religious symbol-

Video box art for *L'Ossessione Che Uccide* (1980), Wizard Video.

ism, go figure), thankfully avoiding the cheap shock endings which usually castrate otherwise effective horror films.

With Laura Gemser from the infamous Black Emanuelle films.

The Other Hell *see* **L'Altro Inferno**

Parasite (1982)

Embassy Pictures [US]
DIR: Charles Band; PRO: Charles Band; SCR: Alan Adler, Frank Levering and Michael Shoob; DOP: Mac Ahlberg; EXP: Irwin Yablans; MFX: Allan A. Apone, Lance Anderson, James Kagel and Stan Winston; SFX: Doug White; MUS: Richard Band
STR: Luca Bercovici, Vivian Blaine, James Cavan, Cherie Currie, James Davidson, Al Fann, Robert Glaudini, Natalie May, Joel Miller, Demi Moore, Freddie Moore, Joanelle Romero, Cheryl Smith and Scott Thomson
AKA: *Parasito* [Parasite]

Approximately 85m; Color [3-D]
DVD0: *Parasite* [FME; 85m]; VHS1: *Parasite* [FME; 85m]; *Parasite* [WIZ; 85m]
ADL: *The Futuristic Monster Movie*

This low-budget sci-fi/horror offering takes most of its cues from *Alien*, focusing on the selfsame fears of xenophobia and parasitism. But— as could be expected—*Parasite* is nothing more than a string of cheap shocks, perpetrated by a young Charles Band (who would go on to create Full Moon Studios, among other, less successful production companies). Being a futuristic film, *Parasite* is considerably hindered by its "conservative" budget; had the filmmakers chosen to stick with a modern day setting, the viewers' suspension of disbelief wouldn't be tested so greatly, and would have made for a more effective film.

A particularly wooden performance is offered by lead Robert Glaudini, and the remainder of the cast is passable at best. (Of interest, though, is the debut of a then-unknown Demi Moore, and a bit part by Cherie Currie from the Runaways, a '70s all-female rock group that featured Joan Jett and Lita Ford before they went "solo.")

The film does have its share of gore on display (some of which was created by a still virtually unknown Stan Winston), but none of it is worth noting. Furthermore, most of the shocks were geared specifically for the film's 3-D theatrical release, and are completely lost upon seeing it on video.

Parasito *see* **Parasite**

Party des Schreckens *see* **There Was a Little Girl**

Patrick Is Still Alive *see* **Patrick Vive Ancora**

Patrick Lebt! *see* **Patrick Vive Ancora**

Patrick Vive Ancora [Patrick Still Lives] (1980)

Stefano Film [It]
DIR: Mario Landi; PRO: Gabriele Crisanti; SCR: Piero Regnoli; DOP: Franco Villa; SFX: Vincenzo Napoli and Rosario Prestopino; MUS: Berto Pisano
STR: John Benedy, Gianni Dei, Maria Angel Giordan, Paolo Giusti, Sacha Pitoëff, Carmen Russo, Franco Silva and Anna Veneziano
AKA: *Patrick Is Still Alive*; *Patrick Lebt!* [Patrick Lives!]
Approximately 89m; Color

Not so much a sequel as a really tepid remake of *Patrick* (1978), this lame supernatural horror film is noteworthy only because of its gratuitous nature. T&A is prevalent, although the cinematographer—much like Jesse Franco—has difficulty tearing away from the actresses' pubic regions. When the gore finally kicks in almost an hour into the film, the viewer may wish they had dispensed with the murders altogether, as the cameraman still doesn't have to stray far. The most infamous scene involves a woman getting skewered by a rotisserie. The fact that it is shown—as explicit as such a scene could be—entering her vagina and exiting out through her mouth is what makes it extremely repugnant. Director Landi had already attempted a similarly staged murder in his just as deplorable slasher flick *Giallo a Venezia* one year earlier.

Not worthy of anything *but* the notoriety it received.

Paura *see* **L'Ossessione Che Uccide**

La Paura *see* **Paura nella Città dei Morti Viventi**

Paura nel Buio [Fear in the Dark] (1989)

Filmirage [It]
DIR: Umberto Lenzi; PRO: Aristide Massaccesi; SCR: Umberto Lenzi and Olga Pehar; DOP: Jerry Phillips; MUS: Piero Montanari
STR: Joe Balogh, Josie Bissett, Fred Bittner, Mel Davis, Charlie Edwards, Fay W. Edwards, Robin Fox, Julia Howards, Michael Lewis, Todd Livingston, Thomas Mitchell, Gary Wade Morton, Sandra Parker, Oralee Sanders, Sashin Sardot, Jason Saucier, Tom Schultheis, Dan Smith and Erika Smith
AKA: *Camper*; *Hitcher 2*; *Hitcher in the Dark*
Approximately 92m; Color
VHS2: *Hitcher in the Dark* [CNC; 90(92)m; Dutch subtitles]

A spoiled rich kid with an oedipal complex and a camper picks up a hitchhiker, and before long she's lying on his bed, naked, throat slashed, with our buggy antagonist perched over her with a knife and taking pictures of the corpse. He disposes of her body (with the assistance of a hungry croc) and heads out to another campground rife with fodder. This time he abducts a young woman who—despite being intent on pissing off the young psycho—manages to stay in his good graces, but she has a brother who is determined to track down his now missing sibling.

Although pretty standard stalk 'n' slash fare, this is one of Umberto Lenzi's more competent, more interesting thrillers. There is not only some intense bloodshed, but a few tense scenes as well. Performances are mostly palatable, and the location shooting (Florida) actually benefits the story. (Not only is it a step up from much of his earlier efforts, *Paura nel Buio* is better than the abysmally homogenized *La Spiaggia del Terrore*, made the year before in similar surroundings.)

As if I haven't said it enough, he's done worse.

Paura nella Città dei Morti Viventi [Fear in the City of the Living Dead] (1980)

Dania Film [It], National Cinematografica [It], Medusa Distribuzione [It]
DIR: Lucio Fulci; PRO: Giovanni Masini; SCR: Lucio Fulci and Dardano Sacchetti; DOP: Sergio Salvati; EXP: Robert E. Warner; SFX: Gino de Rossi; MUS: Fabio Frizzi [Soundtrack from Beat Records]
STR: Janet Agren, Adelhaide Aste, Enzo d'Ausilio, Carlo de Mejo, Daniela Doria, Lucio Fulci, Michael Gaunt, Christopher George, Antonella Interlenghi, Fabrizio Jovine, Katriona MacColl, Luca Paisner, Perry Pirkanen, Giovanni Lombardo Radice, Luciano Ross, Robert Sampson, Michele Soavi, Martin Sorrentino and Venantino Venantini
AKA: *City of the Living Dead*; *Frayeurs* [Frights]; *The Gates of Hell*; *Miedo en la Ciudad de los Muertos Vivientes* [Fear in the City of the Living Dead]; *La Paura* [The Fear]; *Twilight of the Dead*
Approximately 93m; Color
DVD1: *City of the Living Dead* [ABE; 93m; LBX]; VHS1: *City of the Living Dead* [ABE; 93m; LBX]; *The Gates of Hell* [PAR; 90(92)m]; VHS2: *City of the Living Dead* [VIP; 88m]
ADL: *The Dead Shall Rise and Walk the Earth.*

In the perpetually foggy town of Dunwich a priest hangs himself, his death precipitating a series of strange and brutal deaths. Meanwhile, a woman is pronounced dead after participating in a rather eventful séance, and is saved from being buried alive by a journalist. (Don't ask how she got past the embalmer, because the screenwriter never brings up this oversight.) She tells of seven gates to Hell, one of which resides in the aforementioned city that—if not shut up promptly—will cause the world to be overrun by the living dead, who are pretty pissed off and have voracious appetites. Imagine that.

More *Zombi 2*-style mayhem from that film's selfsame director, this offering dishes up more of the same, but with a larger side order of supernatural hokum. Utilizing staples from H.P. Lovecraft's enduring Cthulhu mythos, Fulci attempts to expand the boundaries of the gut-munching genre. There are a few effective moments of gothicism amidst the buckets of hardcore gore, but it is rarely anything more than a catalyst for the outlandish violence. One of the film's highlights—made famous by word of mouth—involves a bewitched young woman throwing up her entire intestinal tract and other, many unidentifiable, organs. Quite grueling at first, the sequence quickly takes on a cartoonish edge as she becomes nothing more than an offal-spewing fire hose. (This scene sparked a tenacious urban legend that the original title of the film was to be *You Can't Keep Your Mouth Shut*, although I seriously doubt the validity of this claim.) The other infamous scene, which has graced many a book devoted to splatter films, involves Giovanni Lombardo Radice getting a drill press through his noggin.

Technically, the film is a few notches above Fulci's earlier efforts,

"THE DEAD SHALL RISE AND WALK THE EARTH"

This film contains scenes which may be considered shocking. No one under 18 should be present.

THE GATES OF HELL

PARAGON
VIDEO PRODUCTIONS

JERRY ZIMMERMAN - MICHAEL FRANZESE PRESENT "THE GATES OF HELL" Starring CHRISTOPHER GEORGE · KATHERINE MACCOLL · ROBERT SAMPSON · Story and Screenplay by LUCIO FULCI & DARDANO SACCETTI · Directed by LUCIO FULCI · Color by MGM LABORATORIES · AN MPM Release · 1983

Video box art for *Paura nella Città dei Morti Viventi* (1980), Paragon Video Productions.

and is graced by an intense—albeit derivative—soundtrack that sounds like a collection of *Dawn of the Dead* outtakes, with a theme inspired by *Profondo Rosso*'s distinctive score. Most of the hokum works, although it is hindered by the low budget. (The disappearing objects and teleporting zombies would have been more effective had they used fades instead of jarring editing.) Luckily, Fulci upped the production values for his sequel, *L'Aldilà* [The Beyond; 1983]; he also sacrificed some of his trademarked brutality for atmosphere, a boon or a bane, depending on your outlook.

As for the really important stuff, the gore is beyond gratuitous. Although the resident dead have no problem with eviscerating their victims, they prefer performing a little hands-on trepanning first, tearing out large chunks of the persons' head before proceeding. Worm infested corpses litter the sets, and the viewers are even treated to a shower of maggots that outdoes anything Fulci or Argento had done previously. Obviously, one can't help but recommend this film to the more jaded splatterpunks, even though it is probably a given that the more jaded fans have *become* jaded by having already endured the bulk of Fulci's work.

Los Perros de la Muerte [*The Hounds of the Dead*] (1985)

Continental Motion Pictures Inc. [Sp/US]

DIR: Carlos Aured Alonso and Claudio Fragasso; PRO: Carlos Aured Alonso and Clark Tyrrel; SCR: Carlos Aured Alonso and Claudio Fragasso; DOP: Jose Garcia Galisteo; EXP: Eduard Sarlui and Helen Sarlui; SFX: Carlo de Marchis; MUS: Grupo Dichotomy

STR: Fernando Baeza, Barta Barri, Nino Bastida, Charly Bravo, Fernando Conde, Alice Cooper, Pepita James, Emilio Linder, Luis Maluenda, Ricardo Palacios, Carlos Santurio, Jose Sarsa and Victoria Vera

AKA: *Leviatán* [Leviathan]; *Monster Dog*; *Il Signore dei Cani* [The Lord of the Dogs]

Approximately 84m; Color

VHS1: *Monster Dog* [TWE; 88(84)m]

ADL: *The Fear ... The Terror ... The Nightmare ... They Will Never Forget It!!!*

Rock star Vincent Raven (Alice Cooper) returns to his ancestral home to shoot a music video. His timing couldn't be better, as the surrounding countryside is plagued by a pack of man-eating wild dogs. Some of the superstitious townsfolk (the same ones who killed Vincent's father for

The Fear...The Terror...The Nightmare...
They Will Never Forget It!!!

ALICE COOPER · VICTORIA VERA in

MONSTER DOG

EXECUTIVE PRODUCER EDUARD SARLUI PRODUCED BY CLARK TYRREL
SCREENPLAY BY C. FRACASSO SPECIAL MAKE-UP EFFECTS BY C. DE MARCHIS
DIRECTED BY CLYDE ANDERSON EASTMANCOLOR

Video box art for *Los Perros de la Muerte* (1985), TransWorld Entertainment.

being a werewolf twenty years previous) have decided that Vincent is somehow behind the murders, and decide to deal with him the same way they dealt with dear old dad.

Treading similar territory as *Howling V—The Rebirth* (1989), *Los Perros de la Muerte* is a Podunk werewolf flick that could've been an entry in *that* series without anyone being the wiser. Despite some nice sets and okay gore effects, this film suffers on almost all counts. The direction is rather homogenized (with no indication that it was helmed by one of the directors who worked with Paul Naschy on the "El Hombre Lobo" series during the '70s), the acting stiff (even Cooper has difficulty showing any range), and the script abysmal (ly-

canthropy is a "heart disease?"). The werewolf is one of the saddest specimens to ever grace a monster movie, and the transformation effects are a grade-school take on *The Howling*. Worst of all—I was saving this for last—is the downright grating music video footage that can be found eating up about fifteen minutes of the total running time. (Even MTV wouldn't dare show anything this inept. Geez. It's hard to fathom that Alice Cooper—not one of my favorite performers to begin with—actually wrote and performed the music herein.)

Hey, if you've wasted your hard earnings on surfing the entire *The Howling* series, why not see it through and rent this flea-bitten sucker as well?

**Pesadilla en Elm Street 2—
La Venganza de Freddy** *see* **A Nightmare on Elm Street 2—Freddy's Revenge**

Pesadilla en Elm Street 3—Dream Warriors *see* **A Nightmare on Elm Street 3—Dream Warriors**

Pesadilla en la Calle del Infierno *see* **A Nightmare on Elm Street**

Pet Sematary (1989)

Paramount Pictures [US]
DIR: Mary Lambert; PRO: Richard P. Rubenstein; SCR: Stephen King; DOP: Peter Stein; EXP: Tim Zinnemann; MFX: David Anderson and Lance Anderson; VFX: Fantasy II Film Effects Inc.; MUS: Elliot Goldenthal [Soundtrack from Varèse Sarabande]

STR: Beau Berdahl, Blaze Berdahl, Susan Blommaert, Mara Clark, Richard Collier, Eleanor Grace Courtemanche, Chuck Courtney, Denise Crosby, Kara Dalke, Liz Davies, Lila Duffy, Matthew Au-

gust Ferrell, Donnie Greene, Brad Greenquist, Fred Gwynne, Andrew Hubatsek, Mary R. Hughes, Miko Hughes, Stephen King, Michael Lombard, Dorothy McCabe, Dale Midkiff, John David Moore, Kavi Raz, Chuck Shaw, Peter Stader, Lisa Stathoplos, Elizabeth Ureneck and Mary Louise Wilson
AKA: *El Cementerio Maldito* [The Cursed Cemetery]; *Friedhof der Kuscheltiere* [Pet Cemetery]
Approximately 103m; Color
DVD1: *Pet Sematary* [PHV; 103m; LBX]; VHS1: *Pet Sematary* [PHV; 103m]; VHS2: *Pet Sematary* [PHV; 98m]
ADL: *Sometimes Dead Is Better.*

A family moves to the country where the father sets up a small veterinary business. After losing their cat to the hazards of living near a highway, he discovers an old Indian burial ground that re-animates anything buried therein. Before long, kitty's back, complete with a nasty temper and glowing eyes. When their young son Gage suffers a similar fate, the desperate father pulls another Lazarus, and finds out the hard way that "sometimes dead is better."

Although not an exceptional film, *Pet Sematary* is better than most of the King adaptations perpetrated in the wake of more successful attempts such as *Carrie* (1976), *The Shining* (1980), and *The Dead Zone* (1983). It's *The Monkey's Paw* proceedings are carried not by a good script, but by believable performances and atmosphere. (Of particular interest is Fred Gwynne, of Herman Munster fame; although a talented actor, it's the novelty of seeing him in a different role that will interest those raised on *The Munsters*.)

The make-up effects are fairly effective (a woman suffering from cerebrospinal meningitis is extremely unnerving, thanks to some top-notch

prosthetic work), but elsewhere the effects falter. Several scenes involve a noticeably fake Gage puppet on a string replacing the child actor, and another pyrotechnic-laden scene involving a manifestation of an evil spirit during a trek to the burial ground, is completely unnecessary.

As an added bonus, the godfathers of punk, the Ramones, contribute the theme song, although it is heard only over the end credits. As in the novel, one of their songs can also be heard playing over the radio during a pivotal scene.

Even if you like *Pet Sematary*, though, I suggest you avoid the sequel. It may have also been directed by Mary Lambert, but the less said about it, the better.

Pezadas *see* **Mil Gritos en la Noche**

Phantasm II (1988)

Spacegate Corporation [US]
DIR: Don Coscarelli; PRO: Roberto A. Quezada; SCR: Don Coscarelli; DOP: Daryn Okada; EXP: Dac Coscarelli; MFX: Mark Shostrom; SFX: Wayne Beauchamp; VFX: Dream Quest Images; MUS: Fredy Myrow and Christopher L. Stone
STR: A. Michael Baldwin, Reggie Bannister, Ruth C. Engel, Lawrence Rory Guy, Paula Irvine, Rubin Kushner, James le Gros, Mark Anthony Major, J. Patrick McNamara, Samantha Phillips, Kenneth Tigar and Stacey Travis
AKA: *Das Böse 2—Phantasm II* [The Evil 2—Phantasm II]; *Phantasm II—The Never Dead Part Two*
Approximately 97m; Color
DVD2: *Phantasm II* [DIG; 93m]; VHS1: *Phantasm II* [MCA; 97m]; *Phantasm II* [UNI; 97m]
ADL: *The Ball Is Back!*

Seven years after the events in *Phantasm*, Mike (now played by James le Gros) is released from an institution, having convinced doctors that his delusions of a tall man and his undead horde are just that. Reunited with Reggie, he eventually convinces his friend that there is some truth to his stories when he predicts the death of Reggie's family. They begin a cross country trek, following a trail of pilfered graveyards and fresh ghost towns, all the while looking for a girl with whom Mike shares a psychic link, someone who is also privy to the tall man's insidious plans.

Picking up where the first film left off, *Phantasm II* fills in the gap by combining old footage with new (careful, of course, not to show Mike's face; even if actor Baldwin was available to reprise his role, the elapsed time would have shown). Despite its insistence on continuity, *Phantasm II* is a slick, almost reiterative sequel that lacks much of the humor and intensity of the original. The make-up effects have improved greatly, but it still has its fair share of cheesiness; with this kind of budget, though, there's no excuse for such shortcomings. Although the initial film was not overtly gory, *Phantasm II* suffers from having most of its bloodshed removed by the ratings board prior to its theatrical release. Highlights include a whole battalion of spheres (referred to as "flying Cuisinarts" at one point), a chainsaw duel (been there, done that), and shopping cart–cam.

It's okay and all, but it will probably appeal to modern filmgoers raised on Freddy Krueger more than it will to fans of the original.

Phantasm II—The Never Dead Part II *see* **Phantasm II**

Das Phantom der Oper *see* **The Phantom of the Opera**

Phantom of Death *see* **Un Delitto Poco Commune**

The Phantom of the Opera (1989)

21st Century Film Corp. [US], Breton Film Productions Ltd. [US]

DIR: Dwight H. Little; PRO: Harry Alan Towers; SCR: Duke Sandefur [Based on the novel *The Phantom of the Opera* by Gaston Leroux]; DOP: Elemer Ragalyi; EXP: Menahem Golan; MFX: John Vulich and Kevin Yagher; SFX: Michael S. Deak; MUS: Misha Segal

STR: Laszlo Baranyi, Terence Beesley, Ottilia Borbath, Patrick Burke, Peter Clapham, Lajos Dobák, Yehuda Efroni, Robert Englund, Mickey Epps, Virginia Fiol, John Ghavan, Andre Thornton Grimes, Terence Harvey, Robin Hunter, Alex Hyde-White, Ray Jewers, Stephanie Lawrence, Nathan Lewis, Jonathan Linsley, Jaclyn Mendoza, Cathy Murphy, Bill Nighy, Emma Rawson, Mark Ryan, Jill Schoelen, Molly Shannon, László Szili and Tommy Wright

AKA: *Das Phantom der Oper* [The Phantom of the Opera]; *Phantom of the Opera—The Motion Picture*

Approximately 92m; Color

VHS1: *Phantom of the Opera—The Motion Picture* [RCA; 93(92)m]

Even though this film was obviously made to cash in on the then-popular musical of the same name, this is still a fairly engaging updating of Leroux' classic. The script's only real downfall is the writer's insistence on spicing up this timeless classic with unnecessary supernatural elements, especially in reference to the phantom's Faustian origin. Otherwise, it is a slick and bloody retelling of what is (to my knowledge) the first piece of fiction to concern stalking, by now a fairly common criminal act.

(Back then I'm sure it was probably referred to in terms more romantic.) Most fans of the original might find exception to the insertion of graphic violence and gore (our deluded antagonist is now an obsessed fan who likes to skin those unlucky enough to stand in the way of his impetus' stardom), but the original story was already particularly lurid, so the inclusion of such doesn't seem too out of place. Some of the make-up effects that highlight these scenes (particularly the phantom's self-applied cosmetic surgery) are extremely effective and nasty enough to appease even the more hardened gorehounds. (A similar MO was employed by Tibor Takács a year previous in *I, Madman*.) Englund does well in the role of Erik Gestler, but, unfortunately, the character often becomes a caricature of Englund's more famous alter ego, Freddy Krueger, with the shameful one-liners and scarred face. The remainder of the cast is at least as adept, even pulling off the fake British accents for long stretches at a time (no Kevin Costner syndrome here).

Phantom of the Opera—The Motion Picture *see* **The Phantom of the Opera**

Phenomena (1984)
DAC Film [It]
DIR: Dario Argento; PRO: Dario Argento; SCR: Dario Argento and Franco Ferrini; DOP: Romano Albani; EXP: Angelo Jacono; MFX: Sergio Stivaletti; SFX: Sergio Stivaletti; MUS: Claudio Simonetti and Various Artists [Soundtrack from Enigma Records]
STR: Fiore Argento, Fausta Avelli, Patrick Bauchau, Marta Biuso, Sophie Bourchier, Jennifer Connelly, Dalila di Lazzaro, Mario Donatone, Paolo Gropper,

Ninke Hielkema, Frederica Mastroianni, Fulvio Mingozzi, Daria Nicolodi, Mitzy Orsini, Francescha Ottaviano, Donald Pleasence, Michele Soavi, Fiorenza Tessari, Geraldine Thomas and Franco Trevisi
AKA: *Creepers*
Approximately 110m; Color
DVD1: *Phenomena* [ABE; 110m; LBX];
DVD2: *Phenomena* [PMD; 111(110)m];
VHS1: *Creepers* [MHE; 82m]; *Phenomena* [ABE; 110m; LBX]
ADL: *It Will Make Your Skin Crawl.*

A young girl (Jennifer Connelly) goes to stay at an all girls' school where some of the students are being knocked off by a brutal serial killer. Luckily for her, she has friends wherever she goes—namely the six-to-eight legged variety—who not only help protect her, but lead her to the killer's lair. Of course, she also has a little help from a wheelchair-bound entomologist (Donald Pleasence) and his chimpanzee assistant.

Whatever you do, don't judge the film's merits by the American print released on video as *Creepers*, for even the most diehard Argento fans are sure to be disappointed with this travesty of nature. Not only was a substantial amount of footage cut—about twenty-eight minutes worth, including all of the gore—the remainder was re-edited, and its soundtrack greatly altered. Any of the inspired moments that remain are quickly swallowed up in the mire that was once a stunning (although uneven) film.

Performances are excellent, despite the oft-stilted dialogue, and the production values are some of the best Argento has had at his disposal. The story combines elements from Argento's two mainstays: the *giallo* thriller (with which his name has become nearly synonymous) and the supernatural mystery that frames his first two films in the unfinished "Three Mothers" trilogy (namely *Suspiria* and *Inferno*, 1977 and 1980, respectively). The photography—as always—is the real star, though; Argento's innovative staging and camerawork once again attest to why he has accrued such a loyal fan following.

Unfortunately, *Phenomena* is also his first work to incorporate heavy metal music into the mix. Although it actually complements the action quite well at times, it more often than not distracts from and cheapens the intensity presented onscreen. (Not a stranger to pounding scores, Argento is usually associated with '70s progrockers Goblin, who only make a token contribution to this film.)

Michele Soavi was assistant director.

Pieces *see* **Mil Gritos en la Noche**

The Pig *see* **El Carnaval de las Bestias**

Piranha Part Two—The Spawning (1981)

Brouwersgracht Investments [Ne], Chako Film Company [It], Columbia Pictures [US]

DIR: Ovidio Gabriele Assonitis and James Cameron; PRO: Jeffrey Schechtman and Chako van Leuwen; SCR: H.A. Milton; DOP: Roberto d'Ettorre Piazzoli; EXP: Ovidio Gabriele Assonitis; MFX: Giannetto de Rossi; SFX: Gilberto Carbonaro, Antonio Corridori, Giannetto de Rossi and Gino de Rossi; MUS: Steve Powder

STR: Tracy Berg, Kidd Brewer, Jr., Phil Colby, Dorothy Cunningham, Carole Davis, Gaetano del Grande, Paul Drummond, Ancil Gloudon, Ricky Paull Goldin, Leslie Graves, Connie Lynn Hadden, Lance Henriksen, Paul Issa, Lee Krug, Hildy Mag-nasun, Jan Eisner Mannon, Steve Marachuk, Tricia O'Neil, Jim Pair, Anne Pollack, Johnny Ralston, Sally Ricca, Ted Richert, Arnie Ross, Albert Sanders, Myra Weisler, Ward White and Aston S. Young

AKA: *Lentávát Tappajat*; *Piranha II—Flying Killers*; *Piranha II—Les Terreurs Volants* [Piranha II—The Flying Terrors]; *Piranha II, o Peixe Vampiro* [Piranha II, the Vampire Fish]; *Piranha Paura* [Piranha Fear]; *Piranha II—The Spawning*

Approximately 84m; Color

VHS1: *Piranha II—The Spawning* [EMB; 88(84)m]; VHS2: *Piranha II—Flying Killers* [MIA; 91(84)m]

ADL: *Guess Who's Coming to Dinner?*

Although some of the contrivances are pretty outrageous (if not

Video box art for *Piranha Part Two—The Spawning* (1981), **Embassy Home Entertainment.**

downright ludicrous), *The Spawning* is a hell of a lot better than one would expect from a sequel such as this. Credit not only goes to first-time director Cameron (yes, that guy who made a couple of bucks off of *Titanic*), but to a top-notch cast that includes the likes of Lance (*Millennium*) Henriksen. Even the heroine (modeled a little too close after Adrienne Barbeau's character from Carpenter's *The Fog*, methinks) and her precocious son are ingratiating.

Some of the deaths are fairly nasty, but—except for the fact that these little suckers responsible for them now fly and breathe air—there's nothing here that wasn't seen in its predecessor. At least it's not left open for a sequel, although that didn't stop executive producer Assonitis from directing a follow-up ten years later all by his lonesome.

Piranha Paura *see* **Piranha Part 2— The Spawning**

Piranha II—Flying Killers *see* **Piranha Part 2—The Spawning**

Piranha II—Les Tueures Volantes *see* **Piranha Part 2—The Spawning**

Piranha II, O Peixe Vampiro *see* **Piranha Part II—The Spawning**

Piranha II—The Spawning *see* **Piranha Part 2—The Spawning**

Planet of Horrors *see* **Galaxy of Terror**

Planeta del Terror *see* **Galaxy of Terror**

Porno Holocaust *see* **Delizie Erotiche**

The Possessed *see* **L'Occhio del Male**

Possession—Until Death Do You Part (1987)

North American Pictures Ltd. [Ca] DIR: Michael Mazo and Lloyd A. Simandl; PRO: John A. Curtis and Lloyd A. Simandl; SCR: Lyne J. Grantham; DOP: Nathaniel Massey; SFX: Jeff Butterworth; MUS: Rick Kilburn and Tom Lavin

STR: April Alkins, Barney, Bob Berger, Shane Carlsson, Geoff Couch, Richard Dale, Geraldine Farrell, Jano Frandsen, Rupert Grant, Angela Harvey, Annie Henderson, James-Dean Hirschfeld, Brad Hutchinson, Leanne Jaheny, John Robert Johnston, Jocelyne Lavoie, Monica Marko, Melissa Martin, Michael Metcalfe, Sally Ogis, Al Robinson, Mark Ruthledge, Debbie Shyers, Cat Williams and Samra Wolfin

Approximately 92m; Color

VHS1: *Possession—Until Death Do You Part* [MAR; 88(92)m]

ADL: *The Mind Snaps ... the Blood Flows.*

The body of a partially nude woman is dragged across someone's front lawn and buried in their rock garden, and the killer is off abducting another young plaything for his amusement before anyone is the wiser. His mother doesn't seem too put off by his odd habits, or the new victim he keeps in his bedroom. The young woman escapes, and her abductor goes buggy and does a number on his mom that is sure to get his chiropractor's license revoked. (That's okay, because all it takes is a little mascara and mommy's back, Norman Bates–style.) Intent on silencing his escaped playmate before she can lead the police to his doorstep, the killer goes after her and a bunch of her friends, who have conveniently decided to get away for a weekend retreat in the isolated countryside.

Everything herein is about what one can expect from a typical stalk 'n' slash pic. The gore is generic and the T&A gratuitous. (Even all of the corpses he keeps stockpiled in his room are in various stages of undress.) The Norman Bates–style antics are committed by a completely unconvincing second-rate actor ranting and raving and mugging for the camera. ("If my mother used to let me do this to her..." he laments.) There's also some extended car chase sequences and gratuitous male stripping, just to ensure that the ninety-plus minutes seem like an eternity.

The Pottsville Horror *see* **The Being**

Pranks *see* **Death Dorm**

Les Prédateurs de la Nuit [The Predators of the Night] (1988)

René Château Productions [Fr]
DIR: Jesús Franco Manera; PRO: René Château; SCR: René Château and Jesús Franco Manera; DOP: Maurice Fellous; MFX: Jacques Gastineau; MUS: Romano Musumarra [Soundtrack from Ariola Records]
STR: Stéphane Audran, Tony Awak, Daniel Beretta, Amélie Chevalier, Mony d'Almen, Anton Diffring, Daniel Grimm, Florence Guérin, Christiane Jean, Christopher Mitchum, Caroline Munro, Marcel Philippot, Henri Poirier, Lina Romay, Laure Sabardin, Telly Savalas, Tilda Thamar, Doris Thomas, Brigitte van Meerhaegue, Howard Vernon and Gérard Zalcberg
AKA: *Los Depredadores de la Noche* [The Predators of the Night]; *Faceless*; *I Predatori della Notte* [The Predators of the Night]; *I Violentatori della Notte* [The Violators of the Night]
Approximately 97m; Color

VHS2: *Faceless* [LUM; 97m; Danish subtitles]; *Faceless* [VIV; 95m]; *Les Prédateurs de la Nuit* [RCV; 97m; French]
ADL: *If There Is but One Life, There Are Several Ways to End It...*

Let me say, first and foremost, that this *is* a Jesse Franco film, but ... Hey! Wait a minute. Where's everyone going? Let me finish, all right?

A plastic surgeon's sister is disfigured (with acid, of course) by the recipient of a bum face tuck. The doctor's wife (Rollin regular Brigitte Lahaie *née* van Meerhaegue) then assists him in a series of very illegal operations involving unwilling donors in an effort to fix sis' ugly puss *à la Les Yeux sans Visage* (1959). (Just what every horror fan lives for ... another mad doctor who takes the term "face lift" just a little *too* seriously.) Also present to lend a hand is the sadistic henchman, who—with his shaved eyebrows—reminds one of Borowczyk's twisted take on Mr. Hyde from *Dr. Jekyll et les Femmes* (1981). It turns out that the surgeon is an ex–Nazi doctor, and thus really doesn't need much provocation in making a mess out of everyone's faces.

Easily being the slickest Franco production I've seen to date, there are still a few telltale signs pointing to the man responsible for this splatterfest. (Surprisingly, Franco's penchant for zooms is not only kept in check, but completely discarded in favor of more professional-looking camerawork.) Franco regular Howard Vernon has a small part as—who else?— the infamous Dr. Orloff. For people unfamiliar with Franco's work, this fictional character has been written into nearly every one of that wacky Spaniard's horror films. Even Franco himself has portrayed the character in a few of these no-budget wonders. Just forget the fact that the character has been killed off almost as many times.

Unfortunately, the gore effects aren't nearly as impressive as the rest of the production values, but then again, Franco has never fared well with effects-laden scenes. (Going by much of his output, he'd rather be stuffing his zoom lens into some poor woman's crotch than into a pile of pig viscera. Go figure.)

Now if only we could eliminate that damn disco theme song from the score, one wouldn't have to use one's mute button so much (I tallied no less than six uses during the film; anyone who might've otherwise rushed out to buy the soundtrack was probably sick to death of this song by the time the end credits rolled).

Predator (1987)

20th Century Fox [US]
DIR: John McTiernan; PRO: John Davis, Lawrence Gordon and Joel Silver; SCR: Jim Thomas and John Thomas [Novelization from Jove Books]; DOP: Donald McAlpine; EXP: Lawrence Pereira and Jim Thomas; SFX: Stan Winston; VFX: R. Greenberg; MUS: Alan Silvestri
STR: R.G. Armstrong, Shane Black, Elpidia Carrillo, Richard Chaves, Bill Duke, Kevin Peter Hall, Sonny Landham, Arnold Schwarzenegger, Sven-le Thorsen, Jesse Ventura and Carl Weathers
Approximately 107m; Color
DVD1: *Predator* [TCF; 107m; LBX]; VHS1: *Predator* [TCF; 107m; LBX]; *Predator* [CBS; 107m]; VHS2: *Predator* [TCF; 102m]

It seems that, for some extraterrestrials, Earth is a great place for big game hunting. Unfortunately for Hollywood ass-kicker Schwarzeneg-

ger and his group of motley mercenaries, man is the most revered game thereon.

Essentially, *Predator* is a big-budgeted retake of the almost forgotten *Without Warning* (1980), which, coincidentally, also starred Kevin Peter Hall as a trophy-minded BEM. Despite its science fiction/horror staples, *Predator* is ultimately little more than an action packed vehicle for Arnold and his blue-collar one-liners. Regardless, the film offers almost two hours worth of gory, mindless fun that plays like an *Outer Limits* episode with too much damn money at its disposal. (And, hey, it's got some of Stan Winston's most impressive effects work this side of *Aliens*, especially in respect to the titular crustacean-like beastie.)

Popular enough to spawn both an equally exhilarating sequel and a butt load of comic book mini-series from Dark Horse.

I Predatori della Notte *see* **Les Prédateurs de la Nuit**

The Presence *see* **L'Altro Inferno**

The Prey (1980)

Essex Distributing [US]
DIR: Edwin Scott Brown; PRO: Summer Brown; SCR: Edwin Scott Brown and Summer Brown; DOP: Teru Hayashi; EXP: Joe Steinman; MFX: John Carl Buechler; SFX: John Carl Buechler; MUS: Don Peake
STR: Steve Bond, Jackson Bostwick, Jackie Coogan, Gayle Gannes, Garry Goodrow, Ted Hayden, Connie Hunter, Lori Lethin, Carel Struycken, Debbie Thureson, Robert Wald and Philip Wenckus
Approximately 80m; Color
VHS1: *The Prey* [EMI; 80m]
ADL: *It's Not Human, and It's Got an Axe!*

A group of teens on a hiking trip is accosted by a killer who was horribly disfigured by a forest fire thirty-two years earlier. (Boy, you can tell the scriptwriters put a lot of overtime into this one.)

No surprises here, folks. You've seen it all before, and undoubtedly you've seen it done with much more finesse. The gore is standard, but the monster make-up is shoddy. (Maybe I'm just disappointed because it didn't meet my expectations; I was under the distinct impression that the perpetrator of the murders was a homicidal Smokey the Bear. The least they could've done was throw a ranger's hat on him.)

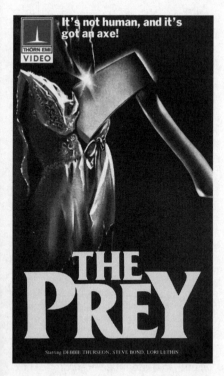

Video box art for *The Prey* (1980), Thorn EMI Video.

The highlights (be as they may) are some impressive National Geographic–style nature photography. In fact, there's so much of the stock footage (did I just hear someone shout "padding?") that the person responsible was given co-cinematographer's credit, and deserved it.

As for all of the "hunter/prey" analogies about which the script waxes so ineloquently, were they so afraid the viewers would miss them (thus justifying their flogging of a particularly ripe dead horse)? Geez ... do they think we're all a bunch of idiots? (Oh, wait ... I did rent this movie, so maybe I should just shut up while I'm ahead.) But, hey, it's got one of my favorite adlines of all time. C'mon ... "It's not human, *and* it's got an axe." At least we know where the screenwriters' inspiration was spent. And well spent it was.

The director went on to do a string of forgettable sexploitation pics.

Prince of Darkness (1987)

Alive Films [US]

DIR: John Carpenter; PRO: Larry J. Franco; SCR: John Carpenter; DOP: Gary B. Kibbe; EXP: Andre Blay and Shep Gordon; MFX: Frank Carrisosa; SFX: Kevin Quibell; MUS: John Carpenter and Alan Howarth

STR: Susan Blanchard, Dirk Blocker, Lisa Blount, Thom Bray, Alice Cooper, Dennis Dun, Jessie Lawrence Ferguson, Robert Grasmere, Anne Howard, Peter Jason, Joanna Merlin, Jameson Parker, Donald Pleasence, Betty Ramey, Victor Wong, Ken Wright and Ann Yen

AKA: *Die Fürsten der Dunkelheit* [The Prince of the Darkness]

Approximately 102m; Color

DVD1: *Prince of Darkness* [IMG; 102m; LBX]; VHS1: *Prince of Darkness* [MCA; 102m]; *Prince of Darkness* [UNI;

102m]; VHS2: *Prince of Darkness* [FFV; 101m]
ADL: *Before Man Walked the Earth ... It Slept for Centuries. It Is Evil. It Is Real. It Is Awakening.*

A priest dies, inadvertently passing a key and a cryptic diary on to one of his peers (Donald Pleasence). Upon discovering an enigma of cosmic significance, he enlists the aid of a friend, a quantum physics professor (Victor Wong). The teacher picks a handful of his best students to help him investigate the discovery, which—as it turns out—is the transubstantiation of pure evil.

This was Carpenter's valiant— albeit highly flawed—attempt to regain the foothold he had in the early days of his auspicious genre-oriented career. (Beginning with his third film, the groundbreaking *Halloween* (1978), and culminating with *The Thing* four years later in 1982.) Sadly, *Prince of Darkness* is not only his last worthwhile horror film, but also the last gasp of a once notable filmmaker.

Tenuously based on some of the much-misunderstood theories of quantum physics, *Prince of Darkness* makes an ultimately fatal attempt to reconcile Christian mythology with modern scientific theory. (Fifteen years earlier, *The Creeping Flesh* made a similar attempt to scientifically explain the abstract concept of primordial evil.) The first half of this film sticks to these unsettling themes, creating an extremely taut atmosphere that evokes Lovecraft at his best. Unfortunately, it then degenerates into cheap *Démoni*-style antics, with the physics students being hunted down and "zombified" by a liquefied antichrist. (Granted, these proceedings

actually bear a great similarly to Carpenter's second film, *Assault on Precinct 13*, but here the gratuitous hokum strips it of any and all suspense.)

Production values are good (save for some tacky make-up effects), and the performances are excellent. The gore is typically subdued for Carpenter, so don't expect anything on the level of *The Thing* (with which this film also bears many similarities). But we do get to see shock-rocker Alice Cooper as an unwashed, zombie-like vagrant, which goes to show that he was still able to obtain roles after contributing his talents to *Los Perros de la Muerte* (1985), aka *Monster Dog*.

Disappointing, but it has its moments.

Prison (1987)

Eden Ltd. [US], Empire Pictures [US] DIR: Renny Harlin; PRO: Irwin Yablans; SCR: Renny Harlin and C. Courtney Joyner; DOP: Mac Ahlberg; EXP: Charles Band; MFX: Mechanical & Make-Up Imageries; MUS: Richard Band and Christopher L. Stone
STR: Luciano Capozzoli, Andres de Shields, Jeff L. Desit, Tom Everett, Chelsea Field, Kane Hodder, Larry Flash Jenkins, Ivan Kane, Matt Kanen, Lyle D. Kelsey, Lincoln Kilpatrick, Hal Landon, Jr., Tom Lister, Jr., Stephen E. Little, Rod Lockman, Viggo Mortensen, Pat Noonan, Lane Smith, Arlen Dean Snyder, Duke Spencer, George D. Wallace and Mickey Yablans
Approximately 102m; Color
VHS1: *Prison* [NWV; 102m]
ADL: *Horror Has a New Home.*

Charles Forsyth is wrongly accused of a crime and sent to the chair without dinner. Almost twenty years later, when a prison reform program is put on hold, the Wyoming State Penitentiary is back in business, having been closed down in the interim.

A clean-up crew of three hundred prisoners is sent over to tidy things up, chaperoned by a hard-as-nails warden. ("Chain gangs and tommy guns is all he knows," one reformer quips.)

A well-meaning but shallow diatribe against the traditional prison system, *Prison* is an engaging and well-made thriller. Although the proceedings get a little hokey at times— no doubt influenced by the popularity of Freddy Krueger and the innumerable entries in the *A Nightmare on Elm Street* series—it never falls back on stale jokes or corny oneliners. Furthermore, the gore is probably a notch above those aforementioned films as well, both in quality and quantity. (Ironically, the director would helm *A Nightmare on Elm Street 4—The Dream Master* the very next year.)

It is obvious from his American debut that Finnish director Renny Harlin (born Lauri Mauritz Harjola) had what it takes to make it as a big Hollywood filmmaker: Characters are cardboard archetypes, the action formulaic, and the production values spit-shined to a fault. (If those weren't telling enough, the fact that there is no shortage of explosions should have tipped everyone off.) He soon followed this with *Die Hard 2* (1990) and a handful of other expensive action flicks.

La Profecia Satanica *see* **Démoni 2—L'Incubo Ritorna**

Profonde Tenebre *see* **Die Säge des Todes**

Prom Night (1980)

Prom Night Productions Inc. [Ca]
DIR: Paul Lynch; PRO: Peter Simpson; SCR: William Gray; DOP: Robert C. New; MFX: Warren Keillor; SFX: Al Cotter; MUS: Paul Zaza and Carl Zittrer
STR: Beth Amos, Ardon Bess, David Bolt, Dean Bosacki, Tammy Bourne, Antoinette Bower, Jamie Lee Curtis, Karen Forbes, David Gardner, Rob Garrison, Debbie Greenfield, Pam Henry, Joyce Kite, Melanie Morse MacQuarrie, Anne Marie Martin, Sylvia Martin, David Mucci, Leslie Nielsen, Pita Oliver, Marybeth Rubens, Sheldon Rybowski, Leslie Scott, Robert Silverman, Brock Simpson, Liz Stalker-Mason, Casey Stevens, Joy Thompson, Michael Tough, George Touliatos, Lee Wildgen, Leff Wincott and Sonia Zimmer
Approximately 91m; Color
DVD0: *Prom Night* [ABE; 91m; LBX];
VHS1: *Prom Night* [ABE; 91m]; *Prom Night* [MCA; 91m]
ADL: ...*Some Will Be Crowned, Others Will Lose Their Heads*

A young girl is killed while a group of friends are playing "killer" (a glorified version of hide and seek) in an abandoned school. The police's only suspect is horribly burned in an accident while they are in pursuit, and promptly institutionalized. Six years later, while preparing for the high school prom, the selfsame peers present during the girl's accident find themselves stalked by someone in a glittered ski mask and bellbottoms who prefers to finish off his victims with a rather nasty shard of glass. One of the targeted just so happens to be the king of the prom, and the queen (Jamie Lee Curtis, go figure) just so happens to be the dead girl's older sister.

Not only does this early slasher film suffer from completely generic execution, the viewer is asked to buy into far too many coincidences and inconsistencies. (When one's suspension of disbelief becomes a piñata just begging for a stick, you know it's time to question the screenwriter's credentials.) Gore is minimal, and—most surprising—there is none of the obligatory T&A one would expect to find in such a production. (And it isn't because they used actual teenagers to play the roles; in fact, I'd be surprised if any of them were even under twenty-one.) We also have to suffer through gratuitous disco dancing (who raided John Travolta's wardrobe, anyway?) and innumerable red herrings, transparent one and all.

The film's only highlights are the presence of Leslie Nielsen (back when he was still plying his trade as a "serious" actor) and early Cronenberg regular Jonathan Silverman. Oh, and let's not forget the ingratiating disco theme song that will have even the headbangers in the audience humming along.

Prom Night III—The Last Kiss (1989)

Comweb Productions Inc. [US], Norstar Entertainment Inc. [US]

DIR: Ron Oliver and Peter Simpson; PRO: Ray Sager and Peter Simpson; SCR: Ron Oliver; DOP: Rhett Morita; EXP: Olana Frank and Dan Johnson; MFX: Nancy Howe; SFX: The Light & Motion Corporation; VFX: Al Magliochetti; MUS: Paul Zaza

STR: Sabrina Boudot, George Chuvalo, Juno Mills Cockell, Robert Collins, Tim Conlon, Suzanne Cyr, Heather Dick, Martin Donlevy, Terry Doyle, Roger Dunn, Nicole Evans, Richard Fitch, June Garba, Laurie Hibberd, Lesley Kelly, Robert Morelli, Eric Murphy, Dylan Neal, Tom Nursall, Cynthia Preston, Tim Progosh, Jeremy Ratchford, Brock Simpson, Colin Simpson, David Stratton, Courtney Taylor and John Vallis

Approximately 95m; Color
VHS1: *Prom Night III—The Last Kiss* [IVE; 97(95)m]
ADL: *Dying for a Good Time? Call Mary Lou.*

Mary Lou Maloney (the antagonist of *Hello, Mary Lou—Prom Night II*) is back to wreak havoc on Hamilton High, armed with the powers of Hell and an unlimited supply of bad puns. (Watch out Freddy.) She falls for a completely average student and begins to knock off anyone standing in the way of his medical career and their relationship.

This intentional comedy (whether it's actually funny or not is debatable) is obviously aimed at indiscriminate splatterpunks raised on '80s trash. There is a lot of gore and low-rent effects, but none of it impressive. Most of the more successful humor involves incidental background happenings (intercom announcements, etc.), thus reminding one of an Abraham/Zucker production (*Airplane*, *The Naked Gun*, etc.).

Worth checking out if you stumble across it on cable, but not worth the trip to a video store.

The Prowler (1981)

Sandhurst [US]

DIR: Joseph Zito; PRO: David Streit and Joseph Zito; SCR: Neal F. Barbera and Glenn Leopold; DOP: Raul Lomas; EXP: James Bochis; MFX: Tom Savini; SFX: Tom Savini; MUS: Richard Einhorn

STR: Steven Bock, Thom Bray, Carlton Carpenter, John Christian, Richard Colligan, Bill Hugh Collins, Donna Davis, Vicky Dawson, Lisa Dunsheath, Bryon Englund, Joy Glaccum, Christopher Goutman, Farley Granger, Matthew Iddings, Dan Lounsbery, Susan Monts, Bill Nunnery, Diane Rode, David Sederholm, John Seitz, Douglas Stevenson, Lawrence Tierney, Timothy Wahrer and Cindy Weintraub

© 1981 VC II INCORPORATED

Video box art for *The Prowler* (1981), VCII.

AKA: *El Asesino de Rosemary* [Rosemary's Killer]; *The Graduation*; *Rosemary's Killer*

Approximately 88m; Color
VHS1: *The Prowler* [DIR; 92(88)m]; *The Prowler* [VII; 92(88)m]

ADL: *The Human Exterminator ... He Has His Own Way of Killing!*

1945: A GI stationed in Europe receives a Dear John letter from his sweetheart Rosemary. On the night of the graduation dance, she and her new squeeze are mistaken for a bail of hay while bumping uglies in a gazebo. The brutal double-murder forces Avalon Bay to discontinue the dance for forty-five years. Obviously, the pissed off GI is still around and none too pleased that the town plans to continue the tradition, so he picks up where he left off, although he doesn't restrict himself to using a pitchfork anymore (a bayonet and a sawed-off shotgun offer him a little room to expand).

Despite the formulaic slasher proceedings, *The Prowler* manages to be more watchable than most of its peers. First, it boasts some impressive gore effects from Tom Savini (with a slit throat and exploding head that almost rivals similar scenes in *Maniac*); and, second, it manages to create some tension by keeping a dark tone throughout. And despite the cheap tactic the filmmakers employ, the shock ending is actually quite jolting.

File with *My Bloody Valentine* and *Hell Night*.

Psicópata see Schizoid

Psicosis II see Psycho II

Psicosis III see Psycho III

Psycho II (1983)

Oak Industries [US], Universal Pictures [US]

DIR: Richard Franklin; PRO: Hilton A. Green; SCR: Tom Holland; DOP: Dean Cundey; EXP: Bernard Schwartz; MFX: Albert Whitlock; SFX: Melbourne Arnold; MUS: Jerry Goldsmith [Soundtrack from MCA Records]

STR: Sheila K. Adams, Victoria Brown, Robert Alan Browne, Claudia Bryar, Jill Carroll, Robert Destri, George Dickerson, Dennis Franz, Ben Frommer, Lee Garlington, Hugh Gillin, Ben Hartigan, Chris Hendrie, Tom Holland, Robert Loggia, Michael Lomazow, Tim Maier, Vera Miles, Anthony Perkins, Osgood Perkins, Thaddeus Smith, Meg Tilly, Robert Traynor and Gene Whittington

AKA: *Psicosis II* [Psychosis II]

Approximately 113m; Color

VHS1: *Psycho II* [MCA; 113m]

ADL: *It's 22 Years Later, and Norman Bates Is Coming Home.*

After being institutionalized for over two decades, everyone's favorite mama's boy is rehabilitated and given a second shot at leading a normal life. He gets a part time job at a diner, but eventually decides to reopen the infamous Bates Motel, cleaning up the joint and firing the sleazy manager. A young woman without a place to stay moves in with him, and everything seems to be going pretty well until Norman starts getting letters and phone calls from his dear old mum.

This is an admirable follow-up to the granddaddy of all slasher flicks, not only in that it's in tune with Hitchcock's original, but by its refusal

Video box art for *Psycho II* (1983), MCA Home Video.

to pander to modern-day filmgoers and lay the gore on thick. (It *is* bloody, but far from gratuitous, and not nearly as gory as the *Friday the 13th* clones popular at the time.) The production values are solid, the performances top-notch. (Perkins is as edgy as ever, and Meg Tilly shows she has some chops as his tenuous love interest.) Best of all, though, is the credible, unpredictable script that keeps it from being a half-baked remake of the first.

A worthy sequel on all counts.

Psycho III (1986)
Universal Pictures [US]
DIR: Anthony Perkins; PRO: Hilton A. Green; SCR: Charles Edward Pogue; DOP: Bruce Surtees; MFX: Michael Westmore; SFX: Louis R. Cooper, Dan Lester and Karl G. Miller; VFX: Illusion Arts Inc.; MUS: Carter Burwell
STR: Gary Bayer, Robert Alan Browne, Patience Cleveland, Juliette Cummins, Jeff Fahey, Lee Garlington, Hugh Gillin, Steve Guevara, Kay Heberle, Karen Hensel, Lisa Ives, Roberta Maxwell, Jack Murdock, Anthony Perkins, Angele Ritter, Diane Rodriguez, Katt Shea Ruben, Diana Scarwid, Donovan Scott and Hugo L. Stanger
AKA: *Psicosis III* [Psychosis III]
Approximately 92m; Color
VHS1: *Psycho III* [MCA; 93(92)m]
ADL: *The Most Shocking of Them All.*

An excommunicated nun winds up taking a room at the Bates Motel, barely a month after a new slew of murders (chronicled in *Psycho II*). Disillusioned by her waning faith, she attempts suicide but is saved by the Mother Theresa of homicidal psychopaths, Norman Bates. Before long, though, the old swamp where Norman once disposed of his victims' corpses starts getting a little cramped, and it seems everyone but Norm's new love interest knows the score.

Video box art for *Psycho III* (1986), MCA Home Video.

Everyone's favorite voyeuristic, cross-dressing taxidermist is back, twitchy as ever, sporting his trademarked tics, his nervous smile intact, and armed with some great retorts. (When, in response to a bloody scene, he claims, "I've seen worse," one can't help but get goose bumps.) And still, the film can't quite get it up.

Okay, so what went wrong?

First, *Psycho III* wallows in gratuity, something the first two avoided. (The first because, well, it was 1960, and the second by choice.) The gore is more representative of a *Friday the 13th* sequel, as is the nudity and general sleaze factor. Second, there is no mystery. We know from square one

who's doing the killing, *why* he's doing the killing, and *who* will die. All of the clever twists and turns have been replaced with paint by numbers stalk 'n' slash.

The film's only saving grace—and its downfall—is Perkins' direction. Norman Bates' character is fleshed out to some degree, making him even more of a sympathetic figure than in the previous installments. There are some truly inspired touches, from the surreal bridges between scenes to the predominantly religious imagery that is the keynote of this film. But, alas, these are not enough to carry what is otherwise a lousy script.

Followed by a forgettable made-for-cable television sequel.

Psycho Cop (1988)

Smoking Gun Pictures [US]
DIR: Wallace Potts; PRO: Jessica Rains; SCR: Wallace Potts; DOP: Mark Walton; MFX: Dawn Bradford, Kevin Conklin, Ray Greer and Roy Kynrim; SFX: Mark Williams; MUS: Alex Parker, Keyth Pisani and Jeff Watkins
STR: Julie Araskog, Dan Campbell, Cynthia Guyer, Denise Hartman, Greg Joujon-Roche, Bruce Melena, Jeff Qualle, Bobby Ray Shafer, Gleen Steelman, Palmer Lee Todd, Linda West and David L. Zeisler
Approximately 87m; Color
VHS1: *Psycho Cop* [SGE; 87m]
ADL: *He's the Last Cop You'll Ever Meet.*

You see, there's this cop and, well, he's a little buggy. And he's a booga booga Satanist to boot!

Psycho Cop is completely lifeless, homogenized fare that I wouldn't even recommend to the truly desperate. Billy Ray Shafer (as the title killer) is completely grating, but somehow he was able to talk someone into doing a sequel.

Another half-witted poster child for my ongoing "Save the Celluloid" campaign.

Psycho Ripper *see* **Lo Squartatore di New York**

Psychos in Love (1986)

Generic Films Inc. [US]
DIR: Gorman Bechard; PRO: Gorman Bechard; SCR: Gorman Bechard and Carmine Capobianco; DOP: Gorman Bechard; EXP: Gary Bechard; MFX: Jennifer Aspinall and Tom Molinelli; SFX: Matt Brooks, Carmine Capobianco, H. Shep Pamplin, Ian Pedis, Nina Port and Jan Radder; MUS: Gorman Bechard and Carmine Capobianco
STR: Lee Ann Baker, Mike Brady, Carla Bragoli, Matt Brooks, Carmine Capobianco, Shawn Cashman, Patti Chambers, Frank Christopher, Michael Citriniti, Barry Clark, Ruth Collins, Donna Davidge, Loren Freeman, Carrie Gordon, Peach Gribauskas, Wally Gribauskas, Herb Klinger, Shawn Light, Chang Pang Lum, Eric Lutes, Big Marty, Kate McCamy, Kathy Milani, Professor Morone, Joe Murphy, Angela Nicholas, Danny Noyes, Ed Powers, Jan Radder, Jerry Rakow, Irma St. Paule, Scott Sears, Frank Stewart, Linda Strouth, Robert Suttile, Debi Thibeault, Cecilia Wilde and Tressa Zannino
Approximately 86m; B&W and Color
VHS1: *Psychos in Love* [WIZ; 88(86)m]
ADL: *Love Hurts...*

The owner of a seedy bar falls for a young manicurist who—like himself—is a psychopathic killer. Even more importantly, they both share a pathological hatred for grapes. Things are going pretty well until they run into a plumber-turned-cannibal who decides to take advantage of their predilections.

Despite the fact that this film's humor is completely hit and miss, and the fact that much of the yucks are reminiscent of many a Troma film,

Psychos in Love is a charming splatstick comedy. It is obvious that the filmmakers' greatest inspiration was the defunct *Monty Python's Flying Circus*; even had the scriptwriters not flagrantly ripped off several lines from *Monty Python and the Holy Grail*, one could have easily determined this influence. There are also some swipes from the Marx Brothers, if any of you out there are old enough to remember them. (At least they stole from *capable* comedians.) There's also a great nod to "the killer never dies" staple in slasher films, although it was done with even greater success in Trey Parker and Matt Stone's *Cannibal! The Musical* (1993).

The film is a chaotic assemblage of mock-documentary footage, outtakes, and the like, refusing to fully adhere to an orthodox approach. *Psychos in Love* is technically competent, if only because one is not sure when they're intentionally *trying* to be campy or when it's the product of limited finances.

And, yes, it's particularly gory, although this also takes a tongue-in-cheek approach, so anyone looking for impressive effects work will need to look elsewhere. If you like your movies gratuitous, *Psychos in Love* comes through in the skin department as well, offering enough shower scenes and striptease acts to please Joe Shmoe Pervo. Whatever you do, though, avoid Bechard's other films (*Cemetery High*, *Galactic Gigolo*, etc.), because—unlike *Psychos in Love*—the humor found therein simply is not funny.

Pumpkinhead (1988)

Lion Films [US]
DIR: Stan Winston; PRO: Howard Smith and Richard C. Weinman; SCR: Mark Patrick Carducci and Gary Gerani; DOP: Bojan Bazelli; EXP: Alex de Benedetti; SFX: Alec Gillis, Richard Landon, Shane Patrick Mahan, John Rosengrant and Tom Woodruff, Jr.; MUS: Richard Stone

STR: Cynthia Bain, Mayim Bialik, Mary Boessow, Brian Bremer, Chance Corbitt, Jr., Lee de Broux, John di Aquino, Jeff East, George Flower, Robert Fredrickson, Lance Henriksen, Joel Hoffman, Madeleine Taylor Holmes, Matthew Hurley, Greg Michaels, Mushroom, Devon Odessa, Joseph Piro, Kerry Remsen, Kimberly Ross, Florence Schauffler, Jandi Swanson, Peggy Walton Walker, Richard Warlock and Tom Woodruff, Jr.

AKA: Vengeance—The Demon
Approximately 86m; Color
DVD1: Pumpkinhead [MUA; 86m];
VHS1: Pumpkinhead [MUA; 87(86)m];
VHS2: Pumpkinhead [TAR; 82m]

While on vacation with a group of his friends, a teen on a dirt bike accidentally kills the young son of a gas station owner (Lance Henriksen). The boy's father evokes an ancient curse in order to take vengeance on the kids, unaware of the repercussions it has on all those involved.

Despite the seemingly simplistic story, this is a thoroughly effective monster flick that proves that—with a little innovation—some truly interesting things can be done with seemingly tired conventions.

Although the hayseed setting is a little forced—probably due to production values being a little too slick for its own good—the atmosphere is consistently creepy. Henriksen is great as the distraught father bent on revenge at all costs (a performance at least as intense as his work in Stuart

Gordon's 1990 updating of The Pit and the Pendulum). The monster effects are no less than extraordinary ... not surprising when one realizes that effects wizard Stan Winston helmed the project.

By far, one of the best creature features to come out of the 1980s.

Q see Q—The Winged Serpent

Q—The Winged Serpent (1982)

Larco Productions Inc. [US]
DIR: Larry Cohen; PRO: Larry Cohen; SCR: Larry Cohen; DOP: Fred Murphy; EXP: Richard de Bona and Dan Sandburg; MFX: Dennis Eger; VFX: Lost Arts Inc.; MUS: Robert O. Ragland

STR: Bobbi Burns, John Capodice, Bruce Carradine, David Carradine, Ron Cey, Candy Clark, Shelly Desai, James Dixon, Richard Duggan, Larkin Ford, Perry Genovese, Peter Hock, Jennifer Howard, Eddie Jones, Ed Kovens, Lee Louis, Malachy McCount, Michael Moriarty, Fred Morsell, Tony Page, Larry Pine, Richard Roundtree, Fred J. Scollay, Larry Silvestri, David Snell, Nancy Stafford, Mary Louise Weller and Gabriel Wohl

AKA: Q; The Winged Serpent
Approximately 92m; Color
DVD0: Q—The Winged Serpent [ABE; 92m; LBX]; VHS1: Q—The Winged Serpent [ABE; 92m; LBX]; Q [MCA; 92m]
ADL:It's Name Is Quetzalcoatl ... Just Call It "Q" ... That's All You'll Have Time to Say Before It Tears You Apart!

While trying to elude police, a bumbling getaway driver for a bank heist (Moriarty) stumbles across an oversized nest in an unfinished skyscraper. Having lost the money, he is later confronted by his cohorts in crime, and lures them to the nest on the pretense that it is where he hid the loot. Meanwhile, people are being sacrificed—flayed alive and/or their hearts ripped out—to an ancient Aztec god.

Video box art for *Q—The Winged Serpent* (1982), Anchor Bay Entertainment.

Q—The Winged Serpent is an enjoyable creature feature that exhibits all of the nuances of an early Cohen production. Unlike *It's Alive!* (1974), though, a balance is struck between tongue-in-cheek humor and its darker, more disturbing moments. Not only does this make it an endearing film, it also helps to distract the viewer from the abundance of implausibilities that riddles the script. For example, the thread holding aloft the viewer's suspension of disbelief is stretched considerably taut by the fact no one seems to notice that a giant airborne lizard has made New York its home. (One character reasons that no one sees the creature flying around during the day-

time because it keeps between the people and the sun when out and about. Now if you don't see the errors in *this* logic, it's time for you to go back to school.) It is also unlikely that a seasoned detective quickly accepts the existence of a mythological creature when offered only the most circumstantial of evidence.

Production values are decent, although its debt to '50s giant creature flicks is paid off with some unimpressive stop-animation effects and a few scenes painfully reminiscent of such tacky films as *The Giant Claw* (1957). There is some nasty gore to be had, including an unnerving scene with one of the sacrificial victims being skinned alive, and a particularly tasty cadaver. Cohen regular Michael Moriarty is a lot of fun to watch as well, and is at his twitchiest. David (*Kung Fu*) Carradine is less convincing as the cop on his tail, but this gem still benefits from his presence.

Quando Alice Ruppe lo Specchio [When Alice Broke the Looking Glass] (1988)

Distribuzione Alpha Cinematografica [It]

DIR: Lucio Fulci; PRO: Antonio Lucidi and Luigi Mannerini; SCR: Lucio Fulci; DOP: Silvano Tessicini; SFX: Angelo Mattei; MUS: Carlo Maria Cordio

STR: Pier Luigi Conti, Sasha Darwin, Rita de Simone, Marco di Stefano, Charles Oliver Hand, Zora Ulla Kesler and Maurice Poli

AKA: *Soupçon de Mort* [Suspicion of Death]

Approximately 84m; Color

After sitting down to dinner, Lester Parson—an older gentleman—retreats to his basement where he pursues one of the finer things in life: taking a chainsaw to the fresh corpse of a young woman and feeding the ground remains to his pigs. As it turns out, he's a chronic gambler who seduces rich widows, cons them out of their life savings, then disposes of them in whatever fashion seems fit. Things are going smoothly until a copycat killer makes the headlines, with all of that wannabe's crimes pointing to poor misunderstood Lester.

Quando Alice Ruppe lo Specchio is an odd outing for Fulci. Not that it doesn't showcase the sort of gratuity with which the director's name has become synonymous; it definitely fills most expectations there. (Once again, most of the gore is so over-the-top, and to such a degree that it is not only unrealistic and ineffective, but also quite laughable in spots.) What's odd about this film is its focus on humor, especially on dated comedy of errors routines. Much of it works, if only because of Brett Halsey's reaction shots; when he *can't* save the material, though, the pratfalls are sure to elicit groans of disapproval from the viewer.

The story is threadbare, albeit engaging, even when it turns out to be nothing more than an extended note from "Me and My Shadow." One is surprised that Fulci was able to carry this out over the entirety of a full-length film without it becoming utterly droll, so the film stands as a testament to the late director's talents, however one may define them.

Quella Villa Accanto al Cimitero
[The House by the Cemetery]
(1981)

Fulvia Film S.r.L. [It]
DIR: Lucio Fulci; PRO: Fabrizio de

Angelis; SCR: Lucio Fulci, Giorgio Mariuzzo, and Dardano Sacchetti; DOP: Sergio Salvati; MFX: Giannetto de Rossi and Maurizio Trani; SFX: Gino de Rossi; MUS: Romano Rizzati [Soundtrack from Beat Records and Graveside Entertainment]

STR: Silvia Collatina, Carlo de Mejo, Giovanni de Nava, Daniela Doria, Ranieri Ferrara, Giovanni Frezza, Lucio Fulci, Elmer Johnson, Dagmar Lassander, Katriona MacColl, Paolo Malco, John Olson, Teresa Rossi Passante, Ania Pieroni and Gianpaolo Saccarola

AKA: *Aquella Casa al Lado del Cementerio* [The House by the Cemetery]; *A Casa do Cemitério* [The Cemetery House]; *Das Haus an der Friedhofsmauer* [The House by the Cemetery Wall]; *The House Outside the Cemetery*; *Het Huis bij het Kerkhof* [The House by the Cemetery]; *La Maison près du Cimitière* [The House by the Cemetery]; *La Mansion cerca del Cementerio* [The Mansion

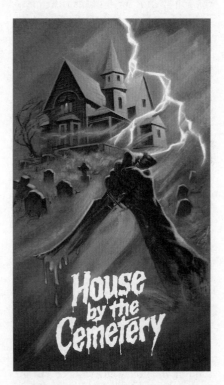

Video box art for *Quella Villa Accanto al Cimitero* (1981), Vestron Video.

by the Cemetery]; *Slagtehuset ved Kirkegar-*
den [House by the Cemetery]
Approximately 87m; Color
DVD1: *The House by the Cemetery*
[ABE; 87m; LBX]; VHS1: *The House by the*
Cemetery [ABE; 87m; LBX]; *The House by*
the Cemetery [VES; 84(78)m]; VHS2: *The*
House by the Cemetery [VIP; 81m]

A family temporarily moves from
New York to Boston so the husband
can finish his research of a man who
hung himself. Unbeknownst to them,
the house (by a cemetery, natch.) was
once owned by a Dr. Freudstein, a
physician who was banned from practicing medicine because of "illegal experiments." If this isn't enough, the
wife is already a little off-kilter, and
the son spends most of his time playing with a little girl (with whom he
apparently shares a psychic rapport)
that no one but he can see. All the
while, someone is making short work
of anyone who dares to venture down
into the basement.

Yes, Fulci is up to his old tricks
again, although the limited body
count keeps him from going full tilt
boogie like he did in *Zombi 2* and
Paura nella Città dei Morti Viventi.
Still, the high-voltage gore is enough
to please the more jaded fans. (Let's
see ... we got zombies, we got pig gut,
we got lots of sharp pokey things, we
got maggots—lots of maggots, yes indeed. Hey ... we got ourselves a Fulci
film!)

As in his "Gates of Hell" series—
as well as many of his splatter offerings—most of the excessive grue is
precipitated by the supernatural; unlike the aforementioned offerings,
though, the hokey elements herein are
kept fairly subdued, making for a
much more effective story and actu-

ally generating some atmosphere. Unfortunately, the barely competent
production values are marked by gratuitous close-ups and some truly awkward edits. (Oh, and let's not forget
the really cheesy fake bat attack.)

If you have any interest in Fulci's
more extreme work, than don't hesitate to put *Quella Villa Accanto al*
Cimitero on your list.

Quella Villa in Fondo al Parco [The House on the Edge of the Park] (1987)

Fulvia Film S.r.L. [It]
DIR: Giuliano Carmineo; PRO: Mau-
rice Matthew; SCR: David Parker, Jr.;
DOP: Robert Garder; MFX: Franco Gian-
nini; MUS: Stefano Mainetti
STR: Janet Agren, Nelson de la Rosa,
Franklin Dominguez, Eva Grimaldi, Ana
Silvia Gruylion, Pepito Guerra, Luisa
Menon, Werner Pochath, Victor Pujols, Jose
Reles and David Warbeck
AKA: *La Casa al Fondo del Parco* [The
House on the Edge of the Park]; *El Hombre*
Rata [The Rat Man]; *The Rat Man*
Approximately 78m; Color
VHS1: *The Rat Man* [CAR; 90(78)m]
ADL: *He Is the Terror*

Here's an odd one for you. *La*
Casa al Fondo del Parco revolves around
a genetically engineered aberration: a
bloodthirsty, psychologically imbal-
anced cross between a rat and a monkey that—to add insult to injury—has
poison claws! The film is a meandering mess, to be sure, but we are treated
to the very politically incorrect sight
of the world's smallest man (Nelson
de la Rosa), made up to look like a
rat, molesting and killing half naked
women. (Only in the Big Boot could
a film like this get made. Many Asian
countries, though, probably wouldn't
have shied away from it, had they
come up with the novel idea first.)

Spanish lobby card for *Quella Villa in Fondo al Parco* (1987).

The production values are typical of mid–'80s Italian fare (save for the particularly muddled script), but who really cares? The scene with the mutant lab rat crawling out of a toilet has to mark one of cinema's grandest moments. (Sorry, but the similar scene in *Ghoulies* just doesn't cut it.) Being an Italian effort, there's no shortage of the red stuff, but even most splatterpunks will be too overawed by the film's audacity to pay it any nevermind.

Unbelievably exploitive, but—as far as geek value is concerned—it's worth its weight in gold.

Quest *see* Galaxy of Terror

Die Rache der Kannibalen *see* Mondo Cannibale (1981)

Die Rache der Mumie *see* Dawn of the Mummy

The Rape After *see* Yin Zhong

Raptors *see* Uccelli Assassini

The Rat Man *see* Quella Villa in Fondo al Parco

Las Ratas Asesinas *see* Deadly Eyes

The Rats *see* Deadly Eyes

Rawhead Rex (1986)

Alpine Pictures [US], Green Man Pictures [UK]
DIR: George Pavlou; PRO: Kevin Attew and Don Hawkins; SCR: Clive Barker [Based on the short story "Rawhead Rex" by Clive Barker]; DOP: John Metcalfe; EXP: Al Burgess and Paul Gwynn; MFX: Coast to Coast Ltd. and Peter Litten; SFX: Gerry Johnston; MUS: Colin Towns
STR: Robert Byrne, Dave Carey, Bob Carlile, Bairbre Ni Chaoimh, Liv Clausen, Bob Coyle, Patrick Dawson, Peter Donovan, David Dukes, Madelyn Erskine, Eleanor Feely, Sheila Flitton, Michael Ford, Maeve Germaine, Derek Halligan, Julie Hamilton, Simon Kelly, Tom Lawlor, Cora Lunny, Barry Lynch, Donald McCann, Lana McDonald, Frank Melia, David Nolan, Niall O'Brien, Hugh O'Conor, Noel O'Donovan, John Olohan, Kelly Piper, Derry Power, Mary Ryan, Gladyl Sheehan, Vincent Smith, Niall Toibin, Heinrich von Shellendorf, Gerry Walsh and Ronan Wilmot
AKA: *Sacristan del Diablo* [Sacristan of the Devil]
Approximately 89m; Color
DVD1: *Rawhead Rex* [PIO; 89m];
VHS1: *Rawhead Rex* [VES; 89m]
ADL: *He's Pure Evil. Pure Power. Pure Terror.*

A farmer removes a monolith from his cow pasture, inadvertently reviving a presumably mythological creature that once terrorized Ireland. Coincidentally, an American writer has come to the area with his family in tow to do research on Neolithic sites and primitive, pre–Christian cults. The church in which he is doing his studies is run by an embittered priest who not only guards the only thing that can destroy the aforementioned rubber-faced beastie, but is in the process of renouncing his faith in favor of—quite literally—becoming the monster's pissboy.

What was once an excellent short story has been reduced to a cheesy monster movie, plain and simple. (Director Pavlou did a similar number on *Transmutations* [1985], another low-budget junker based on Clive Barker's work.) The script makes nods to other stories by Barker, especially "Cabal," which was later filmed as *Night Breed*; there is not only a character named Dekker, there is a priest who renounces his faith, pledges his allegiance to a supernatural being, and who is horribly burned in the process.

Gore is plentiful, although passable at best in its execution, as well as some hokey pyrotechnics that punctuate the silly finale. Whereas the story focuses on primitive, more tangible horrors, the movie attempts to make it a supernatural spectacle, doing away with any tension the film may have yielded.

Read it, don't rent it.

Re-Animator (1985)

Empire Pictures [US], Re-Animator Pictures [US]
DIR: Stuart Gordon; PRO: Charles Band and Brian Yuzna; SCR: Stuart Gordon, William J. Norris and Dennis Paoli [Based on the short story "Herbert West, Re-Animator" by Howard Phillips Lovecraft; novelization by Jeff Rovin from Pocket Books]; DOP: Mac Ahlberg; EXP: Michael Avery and Bruce William Curtis; MFX: John Carl Buechler, Everett Burrell, Anthony Doublin and John Naulin; SFX: Bret Culpepper; MUS: Richard H. Band [Soundtrack from Varèse Sarabande]
STR: Bruce Abbott, Al Berry, Gerry Black, James Earl Cathay, Jeffrey Combs, Barbara Crampton, Velvet Debois, Jack Draheim, James Ellis, Mike Filloon, David Gale, Robert Holcomb, Annyce Holzman, Peter Kent, Lawrence Lowe, Derek Pendleton, Barbara Pieters, Robert Pitzele, Carolyn Purdy-Gordon, Greg Reid, Robert Sampson, Gene Scherer, Bunny Summers and Ian Patrick Williams
AKA: *Resurreccion Satánica* [Satanic Resurrection]; *Zombio* [Zombie]
Approximately 95m; Color
DVD1: *Re-Animator* [VEN; 95m; LBX]; VHS1: *Re-Animator* [VES; 86m]; VHS2: *Re-Animator* [TAR; 81m]
ADL: *Herbert West Has a Very Good Head on His Shoulders—And Another One in a Dish on His Desk!*

After the strange death of his mentor, Dr. Herbert West (Combs) shows up at the Miskatonic University in Arkham, Massachusetts, to continue his teacher's unorthodox experiments. He ends up sharing a house with a medical student who just so happens to be dating the dean's daughter. Even worse, a rival doctor who wants to discredit West also has an obsessive crush on the aforementioned girlfriend. It all seems like a sticky soap opera situation—until, that is, the rival doctor is inadvertently killed and re-animated by West.

Although previous films had used the work of pulp writer H.P. Lovecraft as a springboard—*The Haunted Palace* (1963) and *The Dunwich Horror* (1970), to name but two—this is the first to gain a strong following. This is sad in that it pretty much dispenses with everything that makes this writer's work so appealing. Not to say that *Re-Animator* isn't a worthwhile effort—heck, it's one of the most enjoyable films capitalizing on Lovecraft's name—but it makes a sad statement about the state of the genre. At least this film exposed Lovecraft to a whole generation of horror fans (many of whom wouldn't

Top: **Japanese one-sheet for** *Re-Animator* (1985). *Bottom:* **Mexican lobby card for** *Re-Animator* (1985).

know quality if it bit them in the nards), and thus revived the trend of Lovecraft-inspired films, most of which are at least enjoyable horror offerings.

The film debut of Stuart Gordon and Brian Yuzna, *Re-Animator* is a tongue-in-cheek, over-the-top gore-fest that avoids the pandering tone of similar exercises. The direction is adept, and the performances are excellent, especially Jeffrey Combs, who—as Herbert West—is able to carry every scene in which he appears with his condescending wit and obsessive charm. The film's only real shortcomings are some sorry effects and awkward dialogue. (Thankfully, much of the latter was left out of the unrated version, and used as padding in the R-rated release. Unfortunately, the same can't be said for some of the former.) The gore is definitely "meaty," and is even taken to surreal—albeit hokey—extremes as the film careens towards a downbeat ending.

Highly recommended, as is the sequel, *Bride of Re-Animator*, made four years later.

Re-Animator 2 *see* **Bride of Re-Animator**

Redneck Zombies (1987)

ColorCast Productions Inc. [US], Full Moon Pictures [US]

DIR: Pericles Lewnes; PRO: Pericles Lewnes and George Scott; SCR: Fester Smellman; DOP: Ken Davis; EXP: Edward Bishop; MFX: Edward Bishop, Pericles Lewnes and George Scott; MUS: Adrian Bond and Various Artists

STR: J. Nick Albero, Jim Bellistri, Joe Benson, William E. Benson, Berd, Jr., Sandy Bishop, Anthony Burlington-Smith, Anthony M. Carr, Jed Clemson, Ken Davis, Lisa M. de Haven, Darla Deans, William—

Livingston Dekkar, Benjamin K. Goldberg, Matthew A. Goldberg, Allan Hogg, Ben Horney, James H. Housely, Keith Johnson, Peter Kief, Frank Lantz, Alex Lewnes, Jan Luffman, Jeffrey D. McKinstry, Steve Messick, Stan Morrow, Joan Murphy, E.W. Nesneb, P. Floyd Piranha, Michael Poole, Bucky Santini Shmerd, Jr., Steve Sooy, Alice Fay Stanley, Tyrone Taylor, Boo Teasedale, Brent Thurston-Rogers, Martin J. Wolfman, Zoofeet and others.

Approximately 90m; Color
DVD1: *Redneck Zombies* [TRO; 90m]; VHS1: *Redneck Zombies* [TWE; 83m]; *Redneck Zombies* [TRO; 90m]
ADL: *They're Tobacco Chewin', Cannibal Kinfolk from Hell!*

A barrel of toxic waste (what else?) is responsible for turning a bunch of bad actors into, well, redneck zombies. You figure out the rest. Though *Redneck Zombies* was made by fans who may have actually seen *Dawn of the Dead* more times than Yours Truly, it is unfortunate for the viewer that they didn't actually learn anything about filmmaking from Romero's film. The primary focus of *Redneck Zombies* is gore and bad humor (which can be easily construed from its silly moniker). I'm not sure which were more abused: the bladder effects or the viewer's sensibilities. Regardless, I was not amused.

I know everyone has to start *somewhere*, but the fact that ninety-eight percent of the people behind these homegrown efforts never amount to anything—thus, they are never able to justify our having to suffer through their vanity productions in the first place—makes it difficult for me to offer an encouraging word. (Director Lewnes went on to become an effects technician for Troma; though whether this is a step up in rank or not, I can't really say.)

Regenerator *see* DNA Formula Letale

Rest in Pieces *see* Descanse en Piezas

Resurreccion Satánica *see* Re-Animator

El Retorno del Hombre Lobo
[The Return of the Wolfman]
(1980)
Dálmata Films S.A. [Sp]
DIR: Jacinto Molina Alvarez; PRO: Modesto Pérez Redondo; SCR: Jacinto Molina Alvarez; DOP: Alejandro Ulloa; MUS: CAM
STR: Silvia Aguilar, Pilar Alcón, Jacinto Molina Alvarez, Beatriz Elorieta, Tito García, Azucena Hernández, Narciso Ibañez Menta, Ricardo Palacios, Mauro Rivera, José Ruiz and Julia Salinero
AKA: *The Craving*; La Noche del Hombre Lobo [The Night of the Wolfman]
Approximately 97m; Color
VHS1: *The Craving* [VES; 93m]
ADL: *Two Centuries Later—The Feast Continues!*

Hungarian countess Elisabeth de Báthory is condemned for "witchcraft, vampirism, and dealings with the devil" and promptly buried alive. Her faithful servant, Waldemar Daninsky, has a silver dagger plunged into his heart and is interred alongside her, only to be revived by two hired grave robbers four-hundred years later. Having discovered Báthory's burial site in the Carpathian mountains, an archeologist and her two friends come a calling, all the while everyone's favorite neck-chewing, drool-spewing werewolf is terrorizing the nearby villagers.

Instead of picking up where the last installment of the "El Hombre Lobo" series left off, this entry—

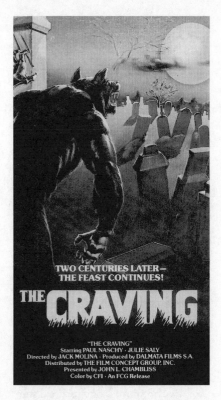

TWO CENTURIES LATER—
THE FEAST CONTINUES!

THE CRAVING

"THE CRAVING"
Starring PAUL NASCHY · JULIE SALY
Directed by JACK MOLINA · Produced by DALMATA FILMS S.A.
Distributed by THE FILM CONCEPT GROUP, INC.
Presented by JOHN L. CHAMBLISS
Color by CFI · An FCG Release

Video box art for *El Retorno del Hombre Lobo* (1980), Vestron Video.

helmed by Naschy himself—is a remake of the third outing, *La Noche de Walpurgis* (1970). Surprisingly, it isn't that much more impressive than the original, and the sleaze quotient tantamount to it as well. (Geez, even the make-up barely qualifies as an upgrade; it's hard to believe that this film was made and released the same year as *An American Werewolf in London* and *The Howling*. Granted, they had much larger budgets, but c'mon…)

The flashback sequences *do* benefit from the higher budget, and the script isn't nearly as chauvinistic as the earlier films in the series (except for the inference that intelligent and driven women are potentially dangerous), but it seems a pointless endeavor to remake a film if it doesn't improve on it to a considerable degree. Regardless, many of us will always be pleased to see Naschy strutting his stuff as El Hombre Lobo once again, and not put off by such cinematic reiterations.

Highlights include music "borrowed" from *L'Ossessa* [The Possessed; 1974], a rather wimpy Blind Dead–like zombie, and the following quote (in reference to how to cure a town's vampiric infestation). "Garlic. A lot of garlic. Garlic up to your ass."

Return of the Alien's Deadly Spawn
see **Return of the Aliens—The Deadly Spawn**

Return of the Aliens—The Deadly Spawn (1981)

Filmline Communications [US]
DIR: Douglas McKeown; PRO: Ted A. Bohus, Sr.; SCR: Douglas McKeown; DOP: Harvey Birnbaum; EXP: Tim Hildebrandt; MFX: Arnold Gargiulo; SFX: John Dods; MUS: Michael Perilstein
STR: John Arndt, Gabriel Bartalos, Diane Bohus, Robert Bohus, Ted A. Bohus, Sr., Ted A. Bohus, Jr., James Brewster, Ken Burge, Jon Cavaluzzo, Madeline Charanis, Michael Robert Coleman, Gary de Franco, Tom de Franco, Joseph Haggerty, Eric C. Hammarstrom, Jonathan Neil Harris, Susan Harris, Charles George Hildebrandt, Rita Hildebrandt, Tim Hildebrandt, Joe Kanarek, Darlene Kenley, Michael Mastrobattista, Judith Mayes, Jean McPherson, Andrew Michaels, Ethyl Michelson, Elissa Neil, Jack Piccuro, Richard Lee Porter, John Riley, Lucile Riley, Cliff Rubin, John Schmerling, William Sorgi, David Steck, Diane Stevens, Jean Tafler, John Tiger, Margaret Truit and Skip Williamson
AKA: *Alien's Deadly Spawn*; *The Deadly Spawn*; *Return of the Alien's Deadly Spawn*

Approximately 90m; Color
DVD2: *The Deadly Spawn* [VIP; 78m]; VHS1: *The Deadly Spawn* [ARR; 90m]; *Return of the Alien's Deadly Spawn* [CON; 90m]; VHS2: *The Deadly Spawn* [VIP; 78m]
ADL: *Survival of the Fittest—Man Vs. the Ultimate Eating Machine*

Unabashedly, I like this *really* low budget alien flick, probably in part because it reminds me of Don Dohler's work: poverty-stricken but innovative science-fiction/horror fare that is obviously made by fans with a lot of drive and just enough talent to back it up. Unlike most of Dohler's output, *The Deadly Spawn* wallows in the gore, be it from children or little old ladies. The splatter effects aren't exactly the best, but the toothsome beasties responsible for the carnage more than make up for it. They're just so damn cute. (I mean, how one can *not* enjoy a film that depicts a gathering of housewives at their own vegetarian luncheon getting eaten alive by a slew of these pesky buggers is beyond me.)

The film is fairly well scripted, offering a few surprises along the way (the biggest being the ludicrous shock ending—a sharp contrast to the pervading dark tone that scores the film—which may or may not be a nod to the Japanese *kaiju eiga* "epics" of the 1960s and 1970s).

Cool stuff if you haven't been completely spoiled by big-budget fare.

Return of the Living Dead (1984)

Fox Films Ltd. [US]
DIR: Dan O'Bannon; PRO: Tom Fox; SCR: Dan O'Bannon; DOP: Jules Brenner; EXP: John Daly and Derek Gibson; MFX:

Bill Mumms; VFX: Fantasy II Film Effects Inc.; MUS: Matt Clifford and Various Artists [Soundtrack from Enigma Records]
STR: David Bond, Derrick Brice, Don Calfa, Paul Cloud, Cathleen Cordell, Michael Crabtree, Robert Craighead, James Dalesandro, Drew Deighan, Leigh Drake, John Durbin, Clu Gulager, James Karen, Ed Krieger, Bob Libman, Thom Mathews, Miguel Núñez, Jr., Brian Peck, John Philbin, Linnea Quigley, Beverly Randolph, Jewel Shepard, Jonathan Terry, Allan Trautman, Mark Venturini and John Stuart West
Approximately 91m; Color
VHS1: *Return of the Living Dead* [EMI; 91m]; *Return of the Living Dead* [HBO; 91m]; VHS2: *Return of the Living Dead* [TAR; 86m; LBX]

"The events portrayed in this film are all true. The names are real names of real people and real organizations." Okay, so maybe *The Texas Chain Saw Massacre* can get away with such a claim, but this ... oh, wait, this is supposed to be a joke, right?

Two employees of a medical supply warehouse are exposed to a chemical that was supposedly responsible for an actual event that inspired the film *Night of the Living Dead*, as were some of the cadavers they keep in stock. Although they manage to destroy the resuscitated remains, they inadvertently expose the tenants of a nearby graveyard ... just in time, it seems, as a group of stereotypical punkers have decided to party on the premises.

Although *some* of the humor works, *Return of the Living Dead* is a sophomoric attempt to hop on the zombie bandwagon, and is obviously aimed at the more adolescent readers of *Fangoria* magazine. All sense of logic is sacrificed for cheap laughs. The effects range from passable to lousy, and the Hollywood-style punk rockers are painfully obnoxious. (Like everyone else, they couldn't even get the music right, although they did settle on cheesy rock music instead of glam metal like most.)

Since no one involved with the making of the original *Night of the Living Dead* ever made any money from their endeavors (due to copyright problems), John Russo and Russell Streiner decided to have a go at it by penning what would be this film. Even though Romero had already made his own sequel, namely *Dawn of the Dead*, Russo was given the legal right to use the "Living Dead" moniker however he saw fit. Unlike Romero, though, Russo didn't play it straight. Nor did he play it well.

Almost enjoyable, if only for the few good shticks and the downbeat ending. (But, hey, it's an opus compared to the sequel.)

The Return of the Living Dead—Part II *(1988)*

Greenfox Productions [US]
DIR: Ken Wiederhorn; PRO: Tom Fox; SCR: Ken Wiederhorn; DOP: Robert Elswit; EXP: Eugene C. Cashman; MFX: Kenny Myers; SFX: Terry Frazee, Geno Crum and Gene Grigg; MUS: J. Peter Robinson [Soundtrack from Island Records] STR: Forrest J Ackerman, Dana Ashbrook, Douglas Benson, Arturo Bonilla, Philip Bruns, Reynold Cindrich, Marsha Dietlein, David Eby, Nicholas Hernandez, James Karen, Michael Kenworthy, Derek Loughran, Annie Marshall, Thom Mathews, Don Maxwell, James McIntire, Richard Moore, Steve Neuvenheim, Larry Nicholas, Brian Peck, Mitch Pileggi, Terrence Riggins, Sally Smythe, Suzanne Snyder, Suzan Stadner, Jonathan Terry, Allan Trautman and Thor van Lingen
AKA: *Battalion 2*
Approximately 89m; Color

VHS1: *Return of the Living Dead—Part II* [KLV; 89m]
ADL: *If Nightmare on Elm Street Made You Scream and Creepshow Split Your Sides, Then ... Return of the Living Dead—Part II Will Scare Your Brains Out!*

A not so coveted "Flogging a Dead Horse" award goes out to this lifeless retread. Not only is it quite reiterative, it even has two of the actors—James Karen and Thom Mathews—reprise what is essentially their same roles from the first film. The effects are lousy and the jokes as clueless as the protagonists. The third entry was better, but considering how bad *that* installment was, one should realize just how important it is to stay away from the franchise altogether.

Definitely a skeleton in Mitch Pileggi's closet. (I wonder if he mentioned this on his résumé when he auditioned for *The X-Files*?)

Return to Horror High *(1987)*

Balcor Film Investors [US], New World Pictures [US]
DIR: Bill Froehlich; PRO: Mark Lisson; SCR: Dana Escalante, Bill Froehlich, Mark Lisson and Greg H. Sims; DOP: Roy H. Wagner; EXP: Greg H. Sims; MFX: Make-Up & Effects Labs Inc.; SFX: James Wayne Beauchamp; MUS: Stacy Widelitz
STR: Richard Brestoff, George Clooney, Darcy DeMoss, Vince Edwards, Cliff Emmich, Will Etra, Al Fann, George Fisher, Panchito Gomez, Dexter Hamlett, Joy Heston, Brendan Hughes, Scott Jacoby, Frank Kniest, Michael Eric Kramer, Lori Lethin, Pepper Martin, Maureen McCormick, Marvin J. McIntyre, Philip McKeon, John Mueller, Alison Noble, Remy O'Neil, Alex Rocco, Andy Romano, Kristi Somers and Larry Spinak
Approximately 95m; Color
DVD1: *Return to Horror High* [ABE; 94(95)m; LBX]; VHS1: *Return to Horror High* [NWV; 95m]

"In 1982, a series of brutal murders rocked Crippen High School. The killer was never apprehended. Three months ago, Cosmic Pictures went to the town of Crippen to film the story of what actually happened—making the movie in the very halls of the now abandoned school. They were not alone."

Okay, I'm sure everyone out there knows where *this* is going, right? Granted, this slasher outing tries for something of a tongue-in-cheek approach, but even with the jokes, *Return to Horror High* promises the viewer nothing in the way of real entertainment. *Nothing*. Well, except Maureen (*The Brady Bunch*) McCormick grabbing her blood-soaked bosom and cooing "Ohhh ... there's blood ... everywhere. Slippery. Just feel." *This* is the stuff of which sick little dreams are made.

Assistant director Rachel Talalay went on to a fairly big Hollywood career, as did a young actor herein by the name of George Clooney.

La Revanche des Mortes Vivantes [The Revenge of the Living Dead Girls] (1988)

Samourai Films [Fr]
DIR: Pierre B. Rheinhard; SCR: Philip Berger and John King; DOP: Henry Froger; MUS: Christopher Ried STR: Véronique Catanzaro, Kathryn Charly, Patrick Guillemin, Laurence Mercier, Sylvie Novak, Gábor Rassov, Christina Schmidt, Cornélia Wilms and Anthea Wyler
Approximately 82m; Color

A truck driver picks up a horny hitchhiker and—while the two are "waylaid"—somebody dumps some nasty pesticide into the tank of milk he's carrying on the back of his rig.

Shortly thereafter, a young woman falls over dead after eating a bowl of cereal. (I wonder if it was Life? Ouch.) Two more deaths quickly follow suit. The vindictive wife of the corporation's boss is behind the foul play, which unwittingly leads to, well, the dead girls coming back to life and going after anything that walks on two legs. If things aren't bad enough for everyone involved, it seems the pesticide also has a fairly unpleasant side effect on anyone even coming in contact with it.

What quickly builds itself up to be typical zombie fare actually turns out to be something entirely different. Not only are there numerous twists and turns, the twist ending is sure to please the stalwart skeptics in the audience.

As for what really matters, a lot of work was put into the effects; unfortunately, the make-up on our undead residents is rather cheesy (justified as that may be). The bloodshed itself is a little better, with some surprisingly gruesome scenes. (For example, I think this is the first—maybe *only*—zombie film where someone gets their penis bitten off by a zombie.) At one point, the cavorting cadavers also take time to get butt naked for a lesbian gang rape. (At least the rest of their bodies aren't decomposed like their heads and hands, otherwise it would be *really* icky.) Oh, and did I mention the sword rape? Maybe it's best that I don't.

Probably even more so than the gore, sex is plentiful, with more gratuitous nudity than one might expect in a genre movie. Well, it *is* a French film, after all, and was helmed by the gentleman who made *French Lolita*

(1993) and *Outrages Transsexuels des Petites Filles Violées et Sodomisées* (1985), a title that transcends any language barriers. Fans of Euro-sleaze shan't be disappointed by the overall seediness of the film, and will probably relish its dated '70s feel.

All in all, *La Revanche des Mortes Vivantes* is worth checking out if you chance upon a copy. (Unfortunately, plunking down $20 for a bootleg is your only option, as I doubt it will be released here any time soon; sword rape or no sword rape, the MPAA would have a field day with this sick little puppy.)

Revenge (1986)

United Entertainment Pictures Inc. [US]

DIR: Christopher Lewis; PRO: Linda Lewis; SCR: Christopher Lewis; DOP: Steve McWilliams; EXP: Bill F. Blair; MFX: DFX Studios; SFX: Robert Brewer, Randy Ditmore, Rod Eaton, Becky Edwards, Doug Edwards, Richard Pittman, David Powell and Donna Powell; MUS: Rod Slane

STR: Andrea Adams, Skipper Baines, John Bliss, Beth Bruntzel, John Carradine, Tony Cox, Charles Ellis, Jerry Franks, Fred Graves, Josef Hardt, Linda Hess, Jimmy Killion, Stephanie Knopke, Bennie Lee McGowan, Don Morrison, Allison O'Meilia, James Potts, Samantha, David Brent Stice, Tinka, Wade Tower, Patrick Wayne and Karen Morgan Williams

AKA: *Blood Cult 2*

Approximately 100m; Color

DVD1: *Revenge* [VCI; 104(100)m]; VHS1: *Revenge* [UHV; 104(100)m]; *Revenge* [VCI; 104(100)m]

ADL: *They Want Your Body ... or Just a Part of It.*

Just in case *Blood Cult* didn't tide you over, this sequel picks up where that film left off with an investigation of the death of the police chief's daughter (the murderess in the first film). Two months later, everything starts up again when a stubborn farmer—unwilling to sell his property to the cultists—gets an axe in the head by a dirt bike–riding, meat cleaver–wielding killer. All the while, turbulence arises within the cult of Caninus over the legitimacy of their beliefs.

Whereas its predecessor is pretty much a straightforward slasher film, *Revenge* introduces numerous supernatural elements, including the inevitable appearance of Caninus himself. As if it needs to be said, their devil god is laughable and not at all deserving of anyone's awe. It can be said that the supernatural is best left to the realm of literature, as one's imagination is far more evocative than anything filmmakers or their effects artists could conceive for the screen. Even classics such as Jacques Tourneur's *Night of the Demon* (1958) can only carry so much weight, so an uninspired no-budget shocker like *Revenge*, with its sad make-up effects, has little chance of success.

Thankfully, the producers decided to spring for film this time out instead of shooting the sequel on videotape. The production values are also a notch above *Blood Cult*'s dimestore approach. This doesn't mean that *Revenge* is much better than its predecessor; only its façade is more palatable. Unfortunately, in its attempt to make the film more accessible, the gore has been tamed down, and skin is nonexistent.

Revenge of the Boogeyman *see* **Boogeyman II**

Revenge of the Living Zombies *see* **Flesh Eater**

The Ripper (1985)

United Entertainment Pictures Inc. [US]

DIR: Christopher Lewis; PRO: Linda Lewis; SCR: Bill Groves; DOP: Paul Mac-Farlane; EXP: Bill F. Blair; MFX: Robert Brewer and David Powell; SFX: DFX Studios; MUS: Rod Slane

STR: Patti Beth Abbott, Andrea Adams, Kimberly Banks, Nicholson Billey, Edward Compos, Rusty Cook, Wilma Cummins, Clayton Farmer, Jeffrey Fontana, Elizabeth Govaerts, Monica Jackson, Shawn Johnson, Teddy Johnson, Georgia Knight, Dennis MacDonnell, Eddie Majors, Marilyn Marloff, Mark Massey, Robert McCall, Bennie Lee McGowan, Derrick Miinter, Todd Neice, Vicki Pemberton-Thomson, Steve Rush, Samantha, Tom Savini, Tom Schreier, Vic Seals, Kim Stephens, Amy Stice, Betsy Stice, Alicia Todd, Wade Tower, Mona van Pernis, C. Scott Walton, Randall White, Karen Morgan Williams, Pamela Williams and Raymond Woodson

Approximately 102m; Color [Shot on video]

VHS1: *The Ripper* [UHV; 104(102)m]

While perusing through an antique store, a college professor who teaches a class on "Famous Crimes on Film" perchances across a ring that—according to a book he owns—was found at the site of Jack the Ripper's last murder in 1888. Coincidentally, similar slashings have just started popping up in the teacher's hometown, attributed to a copycat killer. Within days, one of his students is murdered, and her boyfriend becomes intent on finding out just who is responsible.

In all fairness, *The Ripper* bears more resemblance to a professionally made teleplay than other cheap shot on video productions. The production values are passable, considering, and the performances are better than what we've come to expect from homegrown fare. Unfortunately, the film is a bit overlong and predictable from square one. (Even worse is the gratuitous dance rehearsal footage—smoke machines and all—and the jokes, all of which fall flat.)

Although he receives top billing, effects artist extraordinaire Tom Savini is only on hand for the last ten minutes as the infamous killer himself—an obvious stand-in is used for the remainder of the film—whereupon he tries to make up for lost screen time by hamming it up for the camera. Unfortunately, he had nothing to do with the effects; they are really graphic (mostly throat slashings and eviscerations), but their execution is passable at best.

Almost interesting, even if it is

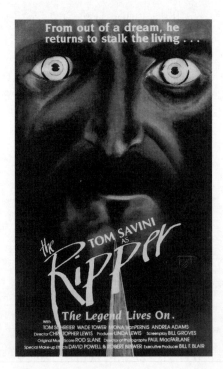

From out of a dream, he returns to stalk the living . . .

The TOM SAVINI AS *Ripper*

The Legend Lives On.

with TOM SCHREIER WADE TOWER MONA VanPERNIS ANDREA ADAMS Director CHRISTOPHER LEWIS Producer LINDA LEWIS Screenplay BILL GROVES Original Music Score ROD SLANE Director of Photography PAUL MacFARLANE Special Make-up Effects DAVID POWELL & ROBERT BREWER Executive Producer BILL F. BLAIR

Video box art for *The Ripper* (1985), United Home Video.

paint by numbers splatter fare. Fans of *Blood Cult*, another Christopher Lewis production—which, by no coincidence, can be seen playing on television in *The Ripper*—should find this to their liking as well.

Rock 'n' Roll Nightmare (1987)

Thunder Films Inc. [Ca]
DIR: John Fasano; PRO: Jon-Mikl Thor; SCR: Jon-Mikl Thor; DOP: Mark Mackay; EXP: Jerry Landesman and Cynthia Sorrell; MFX: Fascination Film Effects, Arnold Garguilo and others; MUS: The Tritonz
STR: Liane Abel, Nancy Bush, Jim Cirile, Jesse d'Angelo, Layra Daans, Denise di Candia, Frank Dietz, Chris Finkel, Adam Fried, Rusty Hamilton, Gene Kroth, Dave Lane, Tralle O'Farrell, Clara Pater, Jillian Peri, Carrie Schiffler, Teresa Simpson and Jon-Mikl Thor
AKA: *Edge of Hell*
Approximately 89m; Color
VHS1: *Rock 'n' Roll Nightmare* [AHE; 89m]
ADL: *When You Raise Hell ... the Devil Must Be Paid—In Full!*

Another Jon-Mikl Thor film? Does it get any worse than that? Yeah, when it turns out to be a rock horror film as well.

A group of big-haired '80s glam rockers with double-digit IQs (led by sensitive Thor, the Alan Alda of crappy rockers) raise hell—quite literally—in this pointless load of horse pucky geared towards alcohol-ridden wannabe metalheads who think Motley Crüe and the WWF are the pinnacles of American culture.

Suffice it to say, this film has absolutely *nothing* going for it. Horrible acting and even worse effects work predominates. Hey, but we get to see a recording studio made by shit-for-brains stagehands who have never stepped foot into a *real* studio but

have definitely sat through their fair share of MTV videos. And speaking of MTV, the ending is comprised of the worst elements of music videos, wrestling, and Jon-Mikl Thor ... the worst elements of the latter being squeezed into a studded jockstrap. And while we're on *that* subject, what's up with the penis monster and his half-pint friends? Maybe this was intended as a sequel to *Ghoulies*, but was retitled so as not to give *that* franchise a bad name.

Gratuitous sex? Sure, there's enough of that, but even with all of the silicone present, Thor still has the biggest tits of the lot. Gratuitous violence? I haven't seen such rubbery gore effects since Andy Milligan was strutting his stuff in the early seventies, but at least he had the sense to douse his dimestore carnage with a few pints of fake blood. Gratuitous dialogue? "You wanna do it right here ... on the grass with all the twigs and mud and things?" That'll work.

Please, no more big hair! No more rockers! No more Jon-Mikl Thor! Someone revoke Fasano's union membership before he films again! Aaaggghhhhhhhhh...

Rocktober Blood (1984)

Sebastian International Pictures [US]
DIR: Beverly Sebastian; PRO: Beverly Sebastian and Ferdinand Sebastian; SCR: Beverly Sebastian and Ferdinand Sebastian; DOP: Ferdinand Sebastian; SFX: Ben Sebastian; MUS: Nigel Benjamin, Richard Onori and Patrick Regan
STR: Nigel Benjamin, Cana Cockrell, Lon Cohen, Mark Durbin, Kevin Eddy, Scott Fisher, Sherry Flowers, Kathleen Griffin, Rene Hubbard, Rich King, Tray Loren, David Mables, Perry Morris, Cindy Pryharski, Tony Rista, Donna Scoggins, Ben Sebastian, Richard Taylor, Les Wagner and Mary Well

Approximately 88m; Color
VHS1: *Rocktober Blood* [VES; 88m]
ADL.: *He's Back from the Dead with a Message from Hell!*

Billy, a rock singer, goes berserk and purportedly kills twenty-five people ... well, not exactly people, but rockers. (Unfortunately, we only see him off two.) A year later, Billy is yesterday's news, and the surviving band members reform with his ex-girlfriend in his stead. They retreat to a summer cabin, and suddenly his ugly mug starts popping up everywhere, but only for her benefit. Nobody believes her, but they humor her by digging up Billy's corpse (a plastic skeleton complete with rubber eyeballs and a live snake). One day she doesn't show up for rehearsal, replaced by a guy in a mask who sounds like Billy; even when he begins offing their stage dancers, nobody seems to think much of it.

Just what the world needs ... more Z-grade stalk 'n' slash choreographed to bad metal music. Unfortunately, this pathetic attempt at exploitation was conceived by the Sebastians, a husband and wife outfit whose low-rent oeuvre was—up until this point—rather charming.

With a somnambulistic performance from one of the punks from *Suburbia* (1983) and the most unconvincing lip-synching this side of Milli Vanilli.

Rosemary's Killer *see* **The Prowler**

Rosso Sangue [Red Blood] (1981)

Filmirage [It], Metaxa Corporation [It]
DIR: Aristide Massaccesi; PRO: Donatella Donati and Aristide Massaccesi; SCR: Aristide Massaccesi; DOP: Aristide Massaccesi; MUS: Carlo Maria Cordio

STR: Annie Belle, Kasimir Berger, Katja Berger, Cristiano Borromel, Manlio Certosino, Ian Danby, Dirce Funari, Hanja Kochansky, Luigi Montefiori, Edmund Purdom, Ted Rusoff, Michele Soavi and Freddy Unger
AKA: *Absurd*; *Ausgeburt der Hölle* [Spawn of Hell]; *The Grim Reaper II*; *Horrible*; *Maldición Satanica*; *Monster Hunter*; *Terror sin Limite* [Terror without Limits]; *Zombie 6—Monster Hunter*
Approximately 94m; Color
VHS1: *Monster Hunter* [WIZ; 91(94)m]; *Zombie 6—Monster Hunter* [EDE; 90 (94)m]; VHS2: *Absurd* [Medusa Video; 90(93)m]
ADL: *Pray You Survive the Hunt.*

"Into a seemingly tranquil village comes a priest with a secret mission— to hunt and destroy inhuman beasts and demonic spirits. The priest finds more than he bargained for—a witch who cruelly blinds her victims, a sinister fog of doom, mutated creatures bent on revenge. The priest's monster

French one-sheet for *Rosso Sangue* (1981).

Mexican lobby card for *Rosso Sangue* (1981), with the Spanish title *Maldición Satanica*.

hunt leads him to the dreaded villa of Dr. Kramer, hidden deep in the shrouded forests where no villagers dare to go. And here lurks an unspeakable trap, a web of supernatural terror that crushes the souls of its victims." Get ready to hear me scream bloody murder, folks.

Now that you've read the wonderful synopsis above, wouldn't it be nice to find out that such a film *actually exists?* This is—hands down—the most misleading and erroneous video box description I've *ever* had the displeasure of discovering. (A "boo, hiss" goes out to the now defunct Wizard Video label, and to Edde Entertainment, who reprinted the selfsame load of hooey after buying the rights to Wizard's prints.) There *is* a priest, but here the similarities end. There is *no*

witch, *no* sinister fog of doom, and *no* dreaded villa of Dr. Kramer. In their stead we get a psychopathic killer, an experiment conducted by the aforementioned priest, and not much else.

Although *Rosso Sangue* is essentially another *Halloween*-inspired slasher flick, Massaccesi does manage to avoid being *too* terribly reiterative. Ignore the sequel-connoting alternate titles, though; not only does this *not* have anything to do with *Anthropophagus* (aka *The Grim Reaper*), there are no incidences of cannibalism. Okay, so one kid in the film claims that the killer wants to eat him, but that doesn't count. And it is much to the viewer's chagrin that the killer is not a man of his word.

Technically, the movie is superior to its predecessor, and the typical

Italian-sounding score is much less distracting than the orchestral hell that befell the previous outing. Not that any of this would make a damn bit of difference to its intended audience. *Rosso Sangue* is—simply put—an unrepentant gorefest. The viewer is accosted by band saws through heads, handfuls of excavated viscera, and other unpleasantries; with so much blood spattering the lens, even I find it difficult to see if the producer's money was spent wisely, or to see if the crewmembers were slacking off. (The similarities to this and some of Lucio Fulci's more celebrated outings are overwhelming.)

Future filmmaker Michele Soavi functioned as an assistant director.

Die Säge des Todes [The Saw of Death] (1980)

Lisa Film [WG], Metro Film [WG], Rapid Film [WG]
DIR: Jesús Franco Manera; PRO: Wolf C. Hartwig; SCR: Rayo Casablanca; DOP: Juan Soler; EXP: Otto W. Retzer; SFX: Juan Ramón Molina; MUS: Frank Duval and Gerhard Heinz
STR: Ann-Beate Engelke, Peter Exacoustos, Antonio García, Nadja Gerganoff, Corinna Gillwald, Jasmin Losensky, Jesús Franco Manera, Christoph Moosbrugger, Sancho Nieto, Olivia Pascal, Otto W. Retzer, María Rubio and Alexander Waechter
AKA: *Bloody Moon*; *Colegialas Violadas* [Violated College Girls]; *Lune de Sang* [Moon of Blood]; *Orgias Sangrienta* [Bloody Orgies]; *Profonde Tenebre* [Deep Darkness]; *Sexmord Pä Pigeskolen* [Girlschool Sex Murders]
Approximately 85m; Color 🔪🔪🔪
VHS1: *Bloody Moon* [TWE; 84m]; VHS2: *Bloody Moon* [ILV; 83m]; *Profonde Tenebre* [AVO; 80m; In Italian]

A scarred young man in a Mickey Mouse mask stabs a woman to death with a pair of scissors when

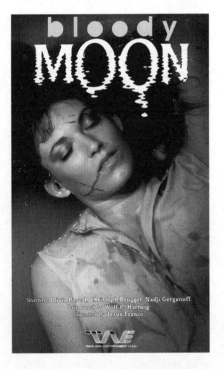

Video box art for *Die Säge des Todes* (1980), TransWorld Entertainment.

she resists his advances. Although put away for five years, he is eventually released and put in the care of his sister. This would seem a reasonable proposition except that she and her aunt run a boarding school for girls. Sure enough, nubile bodies begin piling up in no time.

Although a pretty slick production by Franco's usually less-than-perfectionist standards, *Die Säge des Todes* is far from inspired. Sure, the proceedings are lurid enough, but they aren't reflective of his own sadosexual predilections—cinematically speaking, of course. When imbued with his own obsessions, Franco's films can be artistic, or—at the very least—interesting. *Die Säge des Todes* instead relies on stale slasher conventions, so the end product has about as much depth as Lucio Fulci's *Lo Squartatore di New York*. (The overwhelming misogynist nature of the crimes begs comparisons to this film as well.) The only aspect of Säge that seems at all driven is the incestuous relationship between the siblings, but even this is forgotten amidst the glut of gory, low-rent murders and gratuitous disco dancing.

The murder mystery elements seem unfocused as well. In the hands of an established *giallo* filmmaker, *Die Säge des Todes* may have been engaging; in the hands of Franco, it is convoluted at best. In light of everything, it is fairly obvious that this was the director's attempt to cash in on the then-burgeoning slasher film phenomenon, a decision that was probably prompted by his producers. It is also fairly obvious why he kept his distance thereafter.

Franco's wife and cohort Lina Romay functioned as assistant director on this film.

Santa Sangre [Holy Blood] (1989)

Produzioni Intersound [Sp]
DIR: Alejandro Jodorowsky; PRO: Claudio Argento; SCR: Claudio Argento, Alejandro Jodorowsky and Roberto Leoni; DOP: Daniele Nannuzzi; EXP: René Cardona, Jr., and Angelo Jacono; SFX: Marcelino Pacheco Guzman; MUS: Simon Boswell [Soundtrack from Cinevox Records]
STR: Guadalupe Aguilar, Oscar Serafin Alvarez, Maria de Jesus Aranzabal, Roger Fayard Arroyo, Borolas, Sergio Bustamante, Arturo Contreras, Gloria Contreras, Valerie Crouzet, Sabrina Dennison, Hector Ortega Gomez, Blanca Guerra, Adan Jodorowsky, Axel Jodorowsky, Brontis Jodorowsky, Teo Jodorowsky, Jesus Juarez, Jacobo Lieberman, Zonia Rangel Mora, Billy Motton, Edgar E. Jimenez Nava, S. Rodriguez, Guy Stockwell, Faviola Elenka Tapia, Teo Tapia, Gustavo Aguilar Tejada, Thelma Tixou and Hilario Vargas
Approximately 123m; Color
VHS1: *Santa Sangre* [RPV; 123m]

A boy raised in a circus witnesses his father cutting off his mother's arms after she catches him with the tattooed lady and emasculates him with acid. Interestingly enough, the vengeful mother is the head of a Christian splinter group that has bestowed sainthood on a young girl that was raped and dismembered some years before. Her son winds up in a mental institution (he thinks he's a bird), but eventually escapes, only to start a stage show act with his armless and obviously demented mother.

So, what if Dario Argento and Frederico Fellini pooled their directorial talents just long enough to remake Alfred Hitchcock's *Psycho*? The end product surely couldn't be far from *Santa Sangre*. Surrealist filmmaker Alejandro Jodorowsky—director of cult favorites *El Topo* (1970) and *La Montana Sagrada* (1973)—has managed to create something a little more accessible than his earlier films without sacrificing his trademarked madness. Production values are slick, and—despite some clumsy English dialogue—there are some strong performances to help ground the hallucinatory proceedings, in particular Jodorowsky's talented son in the leading role.

Like most of Jodorowsky's efforts, though, there are some awkward moments, although *Santa Sangre* is by far his most consistent film (if only because this effort doesn't try to inject metaphysical philosophizing into the down-to-earth satire). An entire sequence involving the hero's obsession with a strongwoman—obviously a man in the barest of drag—could have been, and *should* have been, left on the cutting room floor, as it cheapens the otherwise serious proceedings. Also, the film's presumably anti-religious stance could almost instead be construed as a volatile attack on feminism rather than the church, as it was intended. (This latter could be overlooked, though, as it is the director's ambiguity that makes his films so intellectually stimulating.)

The violence itself, too, seems a little forced, never rising far above typical giallo mayhem. It seems odd that Jodorowsky would even bother with the gratuity, except that producers Claudio Argento and René Cardona, Jr., had a hand in this film getting made.

Whether *Santa Sangre* is Jodorowsky's best film is a matter for debate; regardless, it is a statement as to the heights that both horror and splatter films can attain. If other genre films were even half as thought provoking or innovative, people wouldn't be nearly as quick to write the genre off as a whole.

Satan's Altar *see* **L'Ossessione Che Uccide**

Satan's Blade (1982)

M.C. Productions [US]
DIR: L. Scott Castillo, Jr.; SCR: Thomas Cue; DOP: Terry Kempf; EXP: L. Scott Castillo, Jr.; SFX: Paul Batson; MUS: Martin Jaquish
STR: Ramona Andrada, Fred Armond, Paul Batson, Susan Bennet, Tom Bongiorno, L. Scott Castillo, Jr., Carol Cot-

ton, Thomas Cue, Ski Mark Ford, Meg Greene, Rick Hardin, Jean Harshman, Martin Jaquish, Janeen Lowe, Elisa R. Malinovitz, Marti Neal, Jennifer Nelson, Nathalia Quirk, Mary Seamen, Stephanie Leigh Steel, Richard Taecker and Diane Taylor

Approximately 83m; Color
VHS1: *Satan's Blade* [TVC; 87(83)m]; *Satan's Blade* [PRI; 87(83)m]
ADL: *An Unholy Talisman of Murder and Madness*

Two female bank robbers hightail it for the mountains after killing two tellers; one of them gets greedy, hiding the money and offing her accomplice. Unfortunately for her, she is dispatched before she can spend her newly acquired wealth by someone

Video box art for *Satan's Blade* (1982), Trend Video Concepts.

who may or may not be the pissed off spirit of a mountain man who was bequeathed the titular implement by old Scratch himself. Lucky for the opportunistic scriptwriters, the mountain resort where the loot is stashed is doing peak business, despite the murders.

Despite cut-rate acting, stilted dialogue, and sometimes-tedious direction, *Satan's Blade* is surprisingly engaging. Although it should be completely predictable, there is enough character development to distract the viewer, as well as liberal helpings of sex and violence, and a fairly nihilistic ending. Overall, *Satan's Blade* is pretty typical B-grade slasher fare, even though it is more representative of '70s horror than '80s fare.

Savage Apocalypse *see* **Apocalisse Domani**

Savage Lust *see* **Deadly Manor**

Savage Slaughterers *see* **Apocalisse Domani**

Scalps (1983)

American Panther Productions Inc. [US]

DIR: Fred Olen Ray; PRO: The Eel; SCR: Fred Olen Ray; DOP: Larry P. van Loon and Brett Webster; MFX: R. Christopher Biggs, Jon McCallum and Bart J. Mixon; MUS: Drew Neumann and Eric Rasmussen

STR: Forrest J Ackerman, Kirk Alyn, Carroll Borland, Jesus de Luigi, Carol Sue Flockhart, Cynthia Hartline, Richard Hench, Barbara Magnusson, Roger Maycock, Frank McDonald, Pepi, George Randall, Jo Ann Robinson, Romeo Rodriguis, Frank Scott and Jay Walker

Approximately 74; Color

VHS1: *Scalps* [CON; 75(74)m]; *Scalps* [MRQ; 75(74)m]

ADL: *A Hair-Raising Experience*

An archeology professor sends his students out on a dig at an ancient Indian burial ground. It's cursed, of course, a notion subtly introduced to them by an aging Native American who tells them to stay away from "the Black Trees," so, invariably, that's where they dig. A pissed off and downright ugly spirit possesses one of the young men, who almost immediately goes on a killing spree, accumulating a few of the titular fetishes along the way.

This—one of Fred Olen Ray's earlier efforts—is still one of his most engaging films, if only because it some of the harried ingenuity common to '70s genre fare, but lost on much of '80s horror. Sure, the story is simpleminded and derivative, and the production values barely competent, but there is a fair amount of nasty gore (mostly throat slashings and, of course, scalpings) and some surprisingly atmospheric moments to keep it from being completely written off.

Kirk (*Superman*) Alyn stars as the professor, and Forrest J Ackerman (progenitor of *Famous Monsters of Filmland* magazine) makes a cameo. At the end of the film, producers threaten the viewer with: "Next Summer watch for *Scalps II—The Return of D.J.*" Fortunately, Ray didn't follow through with this threat and instead made *Biohazard* (1984), another fun—albeit crappy—splatter flick.

Scanners (1981)

Filmplan International Productions [Ca]

DIR: David Cronenberg; PRO: Claude Héroux; SCR: David Cronenberg; DOP: Mark Irwin; EXP: Pierre David and Victor Solnicki; MFX: Stephan Dupuis, Tom Schwartz, Dick Smith and Chris

Walas; SFX: Dennis Pike and Gary Zeller; MUS: Howard Shore
STR: Neil Affleck, Anne Anglin, Graham Batchelor, Robert Boyd, Jock Brandis, Lee Broker, Don Buchsbaum, Terrance P. Coady, Lawrence Dane, Louis del Grande, Victor Desy, Fred Doederlein, Sony Forbes, Karen Fullerton, Margaret Gadbois, Dean Hagopian, Michael Ironside, Nicholas Kilbertus, Victor Knight, Geza Kovacs, Stephen Lack, Denis Lacroix, Adam Ludwig, Patrick McGoohan, Kimberly McKeever, Jack Messinger, Steve Michaels, Mavor Moore, Elizabeth Mudry, Lee Murray, Malcolm Nelthorpe, Rolland Nincheri, Jennifer O'Neill, Tony Sherwood, Robert Silverman, Alex Stevens, Sam Stone, Jérôme Tiberghien and Ken Umland
   AKA: *Telepathy 2000*
   Approximately 103m; Color
   DVD1: *Scanners* [MGM; 103m; LBX]; DVD2: *Scanners* [AFD; 103m]; VHS1: *Scanners* [TCF; 104(103)m]; *Scanners* [EMB; 104(103)m]; *Scanners* [MGM; 103m]; VHS2: *Scanners* [FFV; 103m]
   ADL: *10 Seconds: The Pain Begins. 15 Seconds: You Can't Breathe. 20 Seconds: You Explode.*

Cameron Vale, a derelict and "telepathic curiosity," is picked up by Consec, a covert government organization. Meanwhile, the group is putting on a demonstration of their "scanner" program in order to gain support, but it winds up with numerous casualties due to the infiltration of a scanner-cum-assassin, Darryl Revok (Ironside), who also heads a scanner underground with plans for world domination. Consec is forced to play their only card, namely Mr. Vale, a powerful but undisciplined scanner who is asked to infiltrate Revok's underground.

Despite the fact that *Scanners* is, technically, quite rough around the edges (even compared to director Cronenberg's earlier outings), the film has proven to be one of his most pop-

ular, most accessible genre offerings. (To date, it has spawned no less than four sequels, with no end in sight.) Dialogue is stilted and the acting is stiff, even on the part of such impressive performers as Michael Ironside, who plays the reserved but highly disturbed antagonist. There are also numerous breeches in the film's logic, yet it does little to detract from the story's nightmarish comic book escapades. (The material was handled in a cleaner but much less interesting fashion by Brian de Palma in *The Fury* two years earlier.)

Of course, this franchise has become synonymous with a single scene—that of one poor sap's head exploding from the power of a scanner's thought waves. (This infamous scenario became, it seems, the sole impetus for the numerable sequels.) The gore is not relegated to this one act, but it is this image that will stay with the viewer when everything else has faded.

Scarecrows (1988)

Effigy Films [US]
DIR: William Wesley; PRO: William Wesley and Cami Winikoff; SCR: Richard Jefferies and William Wesley; DOP: Peter Deming; EXP: Ted Vernon; MFX: Norman Cabrera; SFX: J.B. Jones; VFX: Hollywood Optical Systems Inc.; MUS: Terry Plumeri
   STR: Mike Balog, David James Campbell, Victoria Christian, Marcus Crowder, Dyanne Dirosario, Stephen Gerard, Howard E. Haller, Don Herbert, Kristina Sanborn, Tony Santory, Michael Simms, Larry Stamper, B.J. Turner, Dax Vernon, Ted Vernon, Richard Vidan and Phil Zenderland
   Approximately 88m; Color
   VHS1: *Scarecrows* [FHV; 88m]
   ADL: *Trespassers Will Be Violated.*

A group of renegade commandos heist 3.5 million and hightail it for the border with two hostages. They get sidetracked, and one of them decides that there isn't enough to go around so he tries to take down the others. Having failed to eliminate the competition, he grabs the cash and runs, the others tracking him down to an isolated farmhouse. As can be ascertained from the title, some local strawbags aren't content with just hanging around, and descend upon the criminals.

Scarecrows is an accomplished horror film, just slick enough to avoid the pitfalls of low-budget filmmaking, but not so homogenized as to become patronizing Hollywood fodder. The inanimate scarecrows look spooky as hell, and even the accompanying spook show antics work remarkably well. (Sure, the hokum stretches logic to its limits, but it's kept fairly low-key and doesn't rely on the cheesy visual effects that most supernatural horror films do.)

The gore effects are commendable, and some of the murders are original without being contrived. Granted, *Scarecrows* is little more than an interesting twist on the modern day zombie movie, but it is far more innovative than just about every like film made since George A. Romero's groundbreaking *Dawn of the Dead* (1978).

Both an unrated and a severely cut R-rated version are available.

Scared to Death (1980)

Lone Star Pictures International Inc. [US], Malone Productions Ltd. [US]
DIR: William Malone; PRO: Rand Marlis and Gil Shilton; SCR: William Malone; DOP: Patrick Prince; EXP: William Malone; MFX: William Malone; SFX: Tom Russo; MUS: Tom Chase and Ardell Hake

STR: Pamela Brown, Evan Cole, Johnny Creer, Joseph Daniels, Diana Davidson, Freddie Dawson, Walker Edmiston, Kermit Eller, Stephen Fenning, Michael Griswold, Toni Jannotta, Greer Justin, William Malone, Jonathan David Moses, John Moskel, Jr., Michael Muscat, Joleen Porcaro, Robert Short, John Stinson and Tracy Weddle
AKA: *The Aberdeen Experiment*; *Grito de Panico* [Scream of Panic]; *The Terror Factor*
Approximately 93m; Color
VHS1: *Scared to Death* [MHE; 93m]

Something slimy is slumming around the sewers, making short work of the populace, and it's up to an investigator-turned-hack writer to figure out who—or what—is responsible for the carnage.

Although riding the wave of *Alien* knock-offs, *Scared to Death* is an old fashioned monster-on-the-loose pic, here taking the form of another man in a suit, but this one boasting a rubber tongue that drains the spinal fluid from its prey. (The creature design is okay, but that tongue is something else; maybe they should've just had the monster use a straw, as it wouldn't have seemed nearly as silly.) There is some mild gore, but the abundance of splashy bloodletting helps make up for the lack of torn flesh.

Strictly for fans of gory monster flicks.

Schizo *see* **Nightmare**

Schizoid (1980)

Cannon Films Inc. [US]
DIR: David Paulsen; PRO: Yoram Globus and Menahem Golan; SCR: David Paulsen; DOP: Norman Leigh; SFX: Joe Quinlivan; MUS: Craig Hundley
STR: David Assael, Richard Balin, Fredric Cook, Cindy Donlan, Claude Du-

vernoy, Kathy Garrick, Flo Gerrish, Jon Greene, Richard Herd, Marianna Hill, Kimberly Jensen, Klaus Kinski, Kiva Lawrence, Gracia Lee, Christopher Lloyd, Jay May, Tobar Mayo, Jonathan Millner, Frances Neally, Joe Regalbuto, Craig Wasson and Donna Wilkes

AKA: *Murder by Mail*; *Psicópata* [Psychopath]; *Schizoïd* [Schizoid]

Approximately 91m; Color

VHS1: *Schizoid* [CAN; 89m]; *Schizoid* [MCA; 91m]

ADL: *There's No Cure for What This Maniac Has in Mind...*

A chain-smoking psychiatrist (Kinski) gets a little perturbed when those under his care are knocked off one by one. One of his patients decides to do a little investigation of her own in the hopes of unmasking the killer before she herself becomes a statistic.

This American-style *giallo* thriller tries but never succeeds in surpassing most of the routine slasher fare prevalent at the time. Even Kinski's presence can't salvage the uninteresting script; despite the sleazy goings-on, it is fairly obvious that he is completely uninspired by the material. (Aside from the fact it supplied him with a paycheck, I don't think even Kinski could justify his participation.) The viewer can easily sympathize: Not only does it *not* seem worth it to stick around just to figure out who the culprit is, neither is it worth sitting through for the unimaginative gore. Whodunit? Who cares?

Schizoïd *see* **Schizoid**

Screamers (1980)

Dania Film [It], Medusa Distribuzione [It], United Productions Organization [US]

DIR: Miller Drake and Sergio Martino; PRO: Luciano Martino; SCR: Sergio Donati, Miller Drake, Cesare Frugoni and Sergio Martino; DOP: Giancarlo Ferrando and Gary Graver; MFX: Chris Walas; MUS: Sandy Berman and Luciano Michelini

STR: James Alquist, Barbara Bach, Eunice Bolt, Charles Cass, Claudio Cassinelli, Giuseppe Castellano, Joseph Cotten, Beryl Cunningham, Tom J. Delaney, Mel Ferrer, Franco Iavarone, Richard Johnson, Francesco Mazzieri, Cameron Mitchell, Roberto Posse and Robby Rhodes

AKA: *Something Waits in the Dark*

Approximately 89m; Color

VHS1: *Screamers* [EMB; 83(89)m]

ADL: *They're Men Turned Inside Out! And Worse ... They're Still Alive!*

On an uncharted island in the Caribbean, circa 1891, a group of people is looking for treasure in the "Cave of the Dead" where local natives are said to perform human sacrifices. Before they manage to haul off their booty, though, they are unpleasantly dispatched by some *Humanoids from the Deep* knock-offs. Sometime thereafter, a doctor and a boatload of prisoners—the only survivors of a sunken prison ship—wash ashore, their lifeboat accosted by the aforementioned fishmen. Before you can say "Blood Island," the dwindling survivors are taken in by a sleazy landowner who is financing a series of unethical experiments.

Originally released as *L'Isola degli Uomini Pesce* [The Isle of the Fishmen] in 1978, American distributors felt that the film did not contain sufficient violence to appease modern day filmgoers and decided to insert some gory footage to make it more marketable. (This new footage—directed by Miller Drake and photographed by Gary Graver—is relegated to the intro, and boasts Cameron Mitchell with a very sloppy accent,

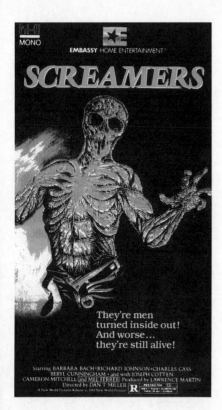

They're men
turned inside out!
And worse...
they're still alive!

Starring BARBARA BACH • RICHARD JOHNSON • CHARLES CASS
BERYL CUNNINGHAM • and with JOSEPH COTTEN
CAMERON MITCHELL and MEL FERRER Produced by LAWRENCE MARTIN
Directed by DAN T MILLER

Video box art for *Screamers* **(1980), Embassy Home Entertainment.**

and some really nasty looking corpses.) In essence, the alterations are very similar to what befell Barbara Peter's *Monster* (1980), more commonly known under the aforementioned moniker of *Humanoids from the Deep*, and the film is made all the more enjoyable because of the tailoring.

Screamers is an oddly contrived genre effort that is one part Jules Verne, one part Eddie Romero, and one part, well, *Humanoids from the Deep*. (The fishmen here may be fairly convincing, but are *not* scary, and evoke none of the *frissons* that Rob Bottin's creations did.) Genetic mu-

tations, voodoo, Atlantis ... it's all here, folks. Except the bullshit about "seeing a man turned inside out before your very eyes," as the adlines claim.

Not to be confused with the fairly lame '90s sci-fi shocker of the same name.

Seeding of a Ghost *see* **Zhong Gui**

As Sete Portas do Inferno *see* **L'Aldilá**

Seven Doors of Death *see* **L'Aldilá**

Seven Doors to Death *see* **L'Aldilá**

Seven Sisters *see* **The House on Sorority Row**

The Seventh Curse *see* **Yuan Zhen-Xia yu Wei Si-Li**

Sexmord Pä Pigeskolen *see* **Die Säge des Todes**

Sexo Caníbal *see* **Mondo Cannibale**

Shadow *see* **Tenebre**

Shiryo No Wana [Trap of the Dead Ghost] (1988)

Joy Pack Film [Ja]
DIR: Toshiharu Ikeda; SCR: Takeshi Ishii; DOP: Masaki Tamura; MUS: Tomohiko Kira
STR: Fumi Katsuragi, Hitomi Kobyashi, Eriko Nakagawa and Miyuki Ono
AKA: *Evil Dead Trap*; *Formation of a Ghost*
Approximately 102m; Color
DVD0: *Evil Dead Trap* [IMG; 102m; LBX]; VHS1: *Shiryo No Wana* [JAP; 102m; LBX; Japanese]

A newscaster receives a video in the mail that depicts what appears to be authentic snuff footage. Using clues intentionally left on the tape, she tracks down the murders to an abandoned and nearly isolated industrial complex, accompanied by a small film crew. Once on the premises, mayhem quickly ensues as they find themselves not only trapped, but also stalked by a hooded killer who takes great pride in the innovative manner in which he metes out their sentences.

Early on, this film establishes a solid foothold with some striking and powerful imagery that make some thought-provoking statements on the ties between voyeurism and the media. Even when it plunges into slasher film territory, the filmmakers make the incisive decision to emulate Dario Argento and his adept Italian peers instead of following the path left by the innumerable American *Friday the 13th* clones. The stylish, often surreal murders single-handedly carry what would be otherwise rote proceedings. (The Goblin-esque score—the main theme being particularly reminiscent of *Profondo Rosso*'s—doesn't hurt either).

Having become accustomed to the inherently contrived nature of most Asian films, it does not come as a surprise that *Shiryo No Wana* inevitably shifts gears as it nears the end. The supernaturally driven finale then makes use of *Tetsuo*-like camerawork and equally innovative editing to give it a hallucinatory quality that is necessary to make the hokey wrap-up work; maybe it doesn't make much sense, but at least it's visually exciting.

And, yes, there is some extreme gore, including a "violence to the eye" scene that would make Lucio Fulci wince. Suffice it to say, *Shiryo No Wana* is not for milquetoasts.

Shiver *see* **Night Train to Terror**

Shock! Shock! Shock! (1987)

Production company unknown [US]
DIR: Arm McConnell and Todd Rutt;
PRO: Arm McConnell and Todd Rutt;
SCR: Todd Rutt; DOP: Todd Rutt; MUS: The Cyphers and Bruce Gordon
STR: Timothy Allen, Cynthia Baker, Marilyn Barclay, David Blair, Bill Brunkhurst, Mike Chirichelli, Robert Fair, Michael Ferguson, Carole Fleishman, Brian Fuorry, Jim Gandolfini, Sonny Greenberg, Marie Grossette, Brad Isaac, Kathleen Laziza, Leonardo Laziza, William Laziza, Marcus Lieberman, Craven Lovelace, Sandra Mandelbaum, Judy Marriott, Kirk McConnell, Cyndy McCrossen, Orc O'Rourke, Allen Rickman, Mike Roberts, Kelly Ross, David Steinberg, Laurie Sullivan, Henry Williams and Linda Wissmath
Approximately 53m; Black & White
VHS1: *Shock! Shock! Shock!* [RHI; 60(53)m]

A man who saw his parents brutally murdered as a child escapes from an institution and picks up a girl running from a crime lord. She is in possession of a rather large diamond ("the mystic Star of Bartos") that she has somehow squeezed into a Rolex. The two are quickly apprehended; he is thrown into a river, left for dead, but is—conveniently enough—found by the young woman's father while out on his morning walk. From here on out, things start getting wiggy.

The criminals, you see, are actually aliens called "Stigmatons" who have super powers and skullcaps a few sizes too big. Using the jewel, our unlikely hero becomes "Spaceman," being given powers just in time to fight a stop-animated creature that is vaguely reminiscent of the Abominable Snowman from Rankin and Bass' Rudolph claymation specials. And, yes, it does qualify as a splatter

Video box art for *Shock! Shock! Shock!* (1987), Rhino Video.

film, although I'm sure you're aware by now that this isn't your everyday blood and guts flick.

Somehow, this amateurish, Super 8mm oddity successfully captures the feel of the pre–'60s films it attempts to both emulate and spoof. (Of course, the grainy B&W footage and post-synch narration has much to do with this.) Knowing its limitations, it embraces such no-budget tricks as celluloid-scratching effects and a goofy, animated credits sequence. And—as I mentioned earlier—there is gore to be had. The opening butchery aside, the lead aliens find themselves meeting no more pleasant a

fate: A running fan blade is shoved in one's face, whilst another suffers from a similarly messy decap.

Not groundbreaking by anyone's standards, but an interesting home-grown effort nonetheless. It's a shame these guys never did anything else.

Shocker (1989)

Universal Pictures [US]
DIR: Wes Craven; PRO: Barin Kumar; SCR: Wes Craven; DOP: Jacques Haitkin; EXP: Wes Craven and Shep Gordon; MFX: Lance Anderson; SFX: Larry Fioritto and Special Effects Services; VFX: Available Light Ltd.; MUS: William Goldstein and Various Artists [Soundtrack from Varèse Sarabande]
STR: Keith Anthony, Lubow Bellamy, Peter Berg, Richard Brooks, Eugene Chadbourne, Camille Cooper, Jessica Craver, Marvin Elkins, Richard J. Gasparian, Vincent Guastaferro, Sue Ann Harris, Stephen Held, Jack Hoal, Linda Kaye, Christopher Kriesa, Heather Langenkamp, Virginia Morris, Michael Murphy, Joseph Roy O'Flynn, Timothy O'Leary, Jeanne K. Peters, Mitch Pileggi, Theodore Raimi, Bingham Ray, Kane Roberts, Emily Samuel, Sam Scarber, Brent Spiner, John Tesh, Peter Tilden and Bruce Wagner
Approximately 110m; Color
DVD1: *Shocker* [UNI; 110m; LBX]; VHS1: *Shocker* [MCA; 111(110)m]; *Shocker* [UNI; 110m]; VHS2: *Shocker* [FFV; 105m]
ADL: *No More Mr. Nice Guy.*

Initially taking its cue from *The Eyes of Laura Mars* (and countless others), *Shocker*'s story features a high school jock having nightmares in which he sees through a serial killer's eyes, and so is able to lead police to Horace Pinker (played by *The X-Files'* Mitch Pileggi). Then, the film taking its cue from *The Horror Show*, the killer is electrocuted, but that doesn't put him down for the count as he's now an electrically charged poltergeist. Then—as if it could be avoided—the movie spends the remainder of its running time taking its cues from Craven's own *A Nightmare on Elm Street* and the series it precipitated, with the teen hero being accosted by the glorified ghost and his painful one-liners. (The fact that Heather Langenkamp makes an appearance only makes the feeling of *déjà vu* that much stronger.)

Shocker is completely generic Hollywood fodder, even though Craven takes a *few* chances during the proceedings: The first half of the movie boasts some death scenes that are pretty brutal, and some of the most visceral stuff Craven had done in years. Of course, once the hokum ensues, the film loses any *frissons* it may have achieved early on. The execution (the movie's, not just Pinker's) is adequately carried out, but lacks the style of Craven's earlier fare. So, if you like your horror reiterative and innocuous, then you're in luck; for any of you who cannot stomach pabulum, this film is the equivalent of strained beets. To make things worse is an unsympathetic hero (unless, of course, you have a thing for halfbacks *and* throwbacks) and an unbelievably long and tedious chase scene.

Brent (*Star Trek—The Next Generation*) Spiner makes an uncredited appearance as a talk show guest.

The title is the biggest misnomer of all.

Il Signore dei Cani *see* **Los Perros de la Muerte**

Le Silence Qui Tue *see* **The Silent Scream**

Silent Madness (1984)

Mag Enterprises [US]
DIR: Simon Nuchtern; PRO: William P. Milling and Simon Nuchtern; SCR: William P. Milling and Robert Zimmerman; DOP: Gerald Feil; EXP: Gregory Earls; MFX: Makeup EFX Labs; MUS: Barry Salmon

STR: Rick Aiello, Marjorie Apollo, John Bentley, Jeffrey Bingham, Conni Brunner, Katie Bull, Noreen Collins, Roderick Cook, Paul de Angelo, Michaelene Donati, Lori-Nan Engler, Kathleen Ferguson, William Gibberson, Shelly Gibson, James Glenn, David Greenan, Tori Hartman, Henry Hayward, Dennis Helfend, Elizabeth Kaitan, Katherine Kamhi, Sydney Lassick, Philip Levy, Viveca Lindfors, Cindy Lloyd, Stanja Lowe, Solly Marx, Lauren McCann, Belinda Montgomery, Susan Mordfin, Chara Peacock, Kim Plumridge, Paige Lyn Price, Sloane Shelton, Bill Shuman, Stacey Simms, Ed van Nuys, Daisy White and Laurie Wilson

AKA: *Beautiful Screamers*; *The Nightkillers*

Approximately 92m; B&W and Color [3-D]

DVD2: *Silent Madness* [PMD; 90m]; VHS1: *Silent Madness* [VTR; 93(92)m]

ADL: *There Is a Sound You Will Hear When the Screaming Stops...*

Due to a clerical error, an overcrowded sanitarium accidentally releases an extremely dangerous inmate. He foots his way to a college campus and makes life difficult for a house full of sorority schoolgirls. (The reason for this can be spotted from miles away by even the most half-witted viewer.)

Silent Madness never rises above the low standards set by early '80s slasher fare; it's obvious even from the flat video release that the film's main impetus was to cash in on the return of the 3-D process. (With movies like this being responsible for the comeback of 3-D, it's no wonder the trend was short-lived.). Sharp instruments are thrust at the viewer at every given opportunity by our resident madman, these effects standing in for subtler, more traditional shocks.

Gorewise, the film's only highlight is a scene involving a drill press to the head; *The Gates of Hell* it isn't, but it's not bad. The viewer is affronted by the lamest excuse for a killer in the making (parents who spank their kids beware), and the most improbable network of maintenance tunnels to be found beneath a simple sorority house. So much for the suspension of disbelief.

Even though *Silent Madness* was directed by the man who shot the additional footage for the infamous *Snuff* (1976), if one film were needed to define "rote," this just may be it.

Silent Night, Deadly Night (1984)

Slayride Inc. [US]
DIR: Charles E. Sellier, Jr.; PRO: Ira Richard Barmak; SCR: Michael Hickey; DOP: Henning Schellerup; EXP: Scott J. Schneid and Dennis Whitehead; MFX: Karl Wesson; SFX: Rick Josephson; MUS: Perry Botkin
STR: John Michael Alvarez, Jonethan Best, John Bishop, Tip Boxell, Tara Buckman, Mollie Cameron, Lilyan Chauvin, Richard D. Clark, Charles Direkop, Joan S. Forster, Leo Geter, Geoff Hansen, Will Hare, Eric Hart, Britt Leach, Jayne Luke, Vince Massa, Gilmer McCormick, Angela Montoya, Paul Mulder, Toni Nero, Linnea Quigley, H.E.D. Redford, Max Robinson, Oscar Rowland, A. Madeline Smith, Barbara Stafford, Randy Stumpf, Amy Stuyvesant, Richard C. Terry, Danny Wagner and Robert Brian Wilson
AKA: *Slayride*
Approximately 92m; Color
VHS1: *Silent Night, Deadly Night* [USA; 92m]
ADL: *Santa's Here.*

I still can't recall all of the hullabaloo that surrounded this film upon its initial theatrical release, or if any of it actually had any basis in fact. Rumors have it, anyway, that a lady took her son to see this flick, under the impression that it was a kid's film. By the time she realized the extent of her folly, it was too late for the little tike. Claiming that her son had been severely traumatized by having seen Saint Nick dismembering a bunch of teens with an axe, she contacted a number of women's groups who thusly began picketing theaters showing the film. Of course, this only gave undeserved recognition to what is otherwise a Podunk slasher film, and gave it enough credentials in order for it to spawn no less than four sequels.

Although pretty typical in execution, *Silent Night, Deadly Night* does deserve credit for putting its low budget to good use, even fostering a slick veneer that belies its spendthrift origins. There are some good performances, although the lead piles it on a bit thick during his psychotic episodes. (Does he really need to shout "punish" before meting out his victims' sentences? Methinks not.) The script is oft times a notch above the norm, and even attributes the killer's psychotic fixations not to a single factor but to a series of events. The gore is nothing special, though, and will only satisfy those who haven't already immersed themselves in the splatter genre.

And, yes, this is one of the films that helped to establish Linnea Quigley as reigning scream queen of the '80s, even though her role herein is relegated to being impaled—while topless, natch—on a pair of antlers. And, no, they weren't Rudolph's.

At least it's not the worst killer

Santa Claus flick to come our way; the next two sequels have the honor of vying for *that* honor.

Silent Night, Deadly Night— Part 2 (1987)

Silent Night Releasing Corp. [US]
DIR: Lee Harry; PRO: Lawrence Appelbaum; SCR: Joseph H. Earle and Lee Harry; DOP: Harvey Genkins; MFX: R. Christopher Biggs; MUS: Michael Armstrong
STR: O.J. Ackson, Jill K. Allen, Stephanie Babbitt, Randy Baughman, Sally Bedding, Janice Carlberg, Lilyan Chauvin, Michael Combatti, Brian Davini, Erin Davini, Lara Davini, John Fitzgibbons, Eric Freeman, Corinne Gelfan, Harvey Genkins, Fred Griggs, Darrel Guilbeau, Amy Hamovitz, Brian Michael Henley, J. Aubrey Island, Kenneth Bryan James, Elizabeth Kaiton, Larry Kelman, Kent Kopasse, Richard Levine, Delia Lombardo, Erika Lundquist, Michael Marloe, Kenneth McCabe, Jean Miller, Ron Moriarty, James L. Newman, Frank Novak, Traci Odom, Stephen L. Parks, Spud Plugman, Randy Post, Linnea Quigley, Lenny Rose, Donald L. Shanks, Scottie Simpkender, Jher Turner, Jennie Webb, Dianne C. Weed, Joanne White, Robert Brian Wilson, Nadya Wynd and others.
Approximately 88m; Color
VHS1: *Silent Night, Deadly Night— Part 2* [IVE; 88m]

Speaking of crappy killer Santa Claus flicks...

First and foremost, about forty minutes of the film's ninety minute running time is nothing more than footage recycled from its predecessor. (And this isn't even counting the movie playing in a theater during the course of the film, as that bit is culled from *Silent Night, Deadly Night* as well.) The footage is easily discernible, as the flashbacks are the only good thing about the film; you'd think one would have to go out of their way to make a movie look so damnably cheap. (Considering how much money they saved with their recycling, the final product should've been pretty gosh darn impressive.)

The performances are overbearing, in particular our current killer Claus. (It is quickly revealed that the younger brother of the first film's antagonist is back to carry on the family tradition, although he prefers the catch phrase of "naughty" in the stead of his late sibling's trademarked "punish.") There are a few funny scenes (intentional? you tell me), but they are not worth the price of admission.

Silent Night, Deadly Night III—Better Watch Out! (1988)

Quiet Films Inc. [US]
DIR: Monte Hellman; PRO: Arthur H. Gorson; SCR: Carlos Laszlo; DOP: Josep M. Civit; EXP: Richard N. Gladstein and Ronna Wallace; MFX: Nina Kraft; MUS: Steven Soles
STR: Richard C. Adams, Michael Ameen, Natalie Anderson, Lauren Becker, Tomczek Bednarek, Alan Benjamin, Richard Beymer, Suzette Boucher, Isabel Cooley, Robert Culp, Erica da Re, Ila Dane, Marc Dietrich, Adam Friedson, Trissa Gabay, Bunnie Gaisford, Richard N. Gladstein, Corrie Gorson, Melissa Hellman, Thomas Herod, Jr., Laura Herring, Carole Hill, Elizabeth Hoffman, Jim Ladd, Leonard Mann, Patty Matlen, Bill Moseley, David Mount, Sheri Mount, Carlos Palomino, Samantha Scully, Stuart Snyder, Tamela Song, Carol Thompson, Joe Torina, David Umstadter and Cheryl Ventura
Approximately 89m; Color
VHS1: *Silent Night, Deadly Night III— Better Watch Out!* [IVE; 90(89)m]
ADL: *When Your Nightmare Ends, the Real Terror Begins.*

A psychiatrist tries to reach a comatose psycho with the help of a spoon-bending girl with a bitchy attitude. (Uri Geller on the rag? There's a protagonist. Geez.) Just in time for Christmas, they succeed, and he's up and about, wandering the city aimlessly. (Apparently, no one sees anything strange about a man in a white gown sporting a see-through Plexiglas skullcap making the rounds.)

A somnambulistic excursion at best, this lame slasher flick spends at least a third of its running time showing people doing nothing more than spouting inane dialogue. (The anti-scientific sentiments are sure to offend anyone with even half a brain.) As could be expected, *Silent Night, Deadly Night III* also pads itself with footage recycled from previous films. Really, how many times do we need to see Santa rape the killer's mother? C'mon...

There is some after the fact gore, as the murders are all committed off screen, but the proceedings are otherwise quite dry. The only "highlights" are a serial killer who looks like he stepped right out of a trashy '50s science fiction flick, and clips from *The Terror* (1963), another Monte Hellman venture. Luckily, this entry is the last of the "old wave" *Silent Night, Deadly Night* flicks. They do get better after this. Really.

The Silent Scream (1980)

Denny Harris Inc. of California [US]
DIR: Denny Harris; PRO: Jim Wheat and Ken Wheat; SCR: Wallace C. Bennett, Jim Wheat and Ken Wheat; DOP: Michael D. Murphy and David Shore; EXP: Denny Harris and Joan Harris; SFX: Steve Karkus; MUS: Roger Kellaway
STR: Juli Andelman, Rebecca Balding, Rachel Bard, Yvonne de Carlo, Steve Doubet, Ina Gould, Joan Lemmo, Cameron Mitchell, Thelma Pelish, Ernie Potvin, Annabella Price, Joe Pront, Brad Rearden,

Virginia Rose, Avery Schreiber, Barbara Steele, Jack Stryker, Tina Taylor, John Widelock and Jason Zahler
AKA: *El Grito Silencioso* [The Silent Scream]; *Le Silence Qui Tue* [The Silence That Kills]
Approximately 86m; Color
VHS1: *The Silent Scream* [MHE; 87(86)m]; *The Silent Scream* [VTR; 87(86)m]
ADL: *Terror So Sudden There Is No Time to Scream.*

A desperate college student rents a room from widower Yvonne de Carlo and her geeky son, who run a boarding house in order to make ends meet. Unbeknownst to them, the old woman is hiding a "secret" in a shuttered attic room. Unfortunately for the new

Video box for *The Silent Scream* (1980), Media Home Entertainment.

boarder—among others—the "secret" has found a way out.

This is one of the more charming slasher films to come out of the '80s, thanks to the presence of '60s B-queen Barbara Steele, and a preferably dated approach to the material. (Give me a "shuttered room" mystery over a *Friday the 13th*–style wood-side massacre any day of the week.) The story is somewhat threadbare, but the pacing, above average performances, and some interesting visuals keep things moving along nicely.

The gore is relegated to numerous slashings; although nothing we haven't seen before, the fact that the damage is inflicted by a mute, bug-eyed Ms. Steele makes it all worthwhile. (It is disappointing that she never had much of an opportunity to display her talents outside of genre fare, as she is quite a capable actress in every respect. We should feel ourselves lucky, though, as only someone with her abilities could pull off a role like this effectively, despite the fact she gives nary a line of speech.)

Hey, even Cameron Mitchell isn't so bad in this flick, so it may be worth checking out if only for *that* novelty value.

Silver Bullet (1985)

Famous Films B.V. [US], International Film Corp. [US]
DIR: Daniel Attias; PRO: Martha Schumacher; SCR: Stephen King [Based on the novella *Cycle of the Werewolf* by Stephen King]; DOP: Armando Nannuzzi; MFX: Carlo Rambaldi; MUS: Jay Chattaway
STR: Roxanne Aalam, James A. Baffico, Kent Broadhurst, William H. Brown, Gary Busey, Paul Butler, Cassidy Eckert, Tovah Feldshuh, Crystal Field, Rebecca Fleming, Megan Follows, James Gammon, Robin Groves, Corey Haim, David Hart, Herb Harton, Ish Jones, Jr., Pearl Jones, Michael Lague, Julius Leflore, Myra Mailloux, Everett McGill, Conrad McLaren, Lonnie Moore, William Newman, Terry O'Quinn, Rick Pasotto, Leon Russom, Heather Simmons, Graham Smith, Bill Smitrovich, Sam Stoneburner, Lawrence Tierney, Wendy Walker, Steven White and Joe Wright
Approximately 95m; Color
DVD1: *Silver Bullet* [PHV; 95m; LBX]; VHS1: *Silver Bullet* [PHV; 95m]; VHS2: *Silver Bullet* [FFV; 90m]

Being little more than an updating of *The Boy Who Cried Werewolf* (1973), *Silver Bullet* concerns a young wheelchair-bound boy who has a heck of a time convincing friends and family alike that the local preacher man is a bloodthirsty lycanthrope.

Despite the sometimes-nasty gore, *Silver Bullet* is second-rate splatter, and depends on too many Hollywood staples to be a truly effective horror film. There are also too many Spielbergian touches, making this seem to be little more than a blood-soaked kiddies matinee film. Also inexcusable is the make-up and transformation sequences which are—despite the budget—no better than what one would find in any number of *Howling* sequels. Everything else about the film is as homogenized as it gets.

As one might expect, there is a focus on small town politics—a penchant of writer Stephen King, as most of his work is inevitably staged in such locales—and an emphasis on character interaction, even though much of it is shallow at best. Suffice it to say, these are about as uninteresting as the horror elements.

Finally, I will be the first to give kudos to any film that casts a handicapped or debilitated individual as the hero, who is shown to have the determination to function "normally" despite their limitations ... as long as it isn't patronizing. *Silver Bullet* tries *sooo* hard to show that Haim's character is "just like everyone else" that it becomes condescending not only to the viewer, but also to the character. (The neon signs pointing out his normality do not garner sympathy from the viewer, nor does the lack of subtlety that accompanies any inspirational messages it attempts to convey.) Oh, and by the way, the title not only refers to the tried-and-true method of dispatching werewolves, but also to the motorized wheelchair employed by the boy. Please beat me over the head some more with your profound wit, Mr. King.

On hand for the proceedings are Everett (*Twin Peaks*) McGill as the angst-ridden killer, Gary Busey as the boy's alcoholic—but kind-hearted—uncle, and Lawrence Tierney as a bartender (no surprise there).

I'd say just to wait until it shows up on TV, but then you'd be missing out on the film's few interesting moments.

Skinned Alive (1989)

The Suburban Tempe Company [US]
DIR: Jon Killough; PRO: J.R. Bookwalter; SCR: Jon Killough; DOP: Michael Tolochko, Jr.; EXP: David de Coteau; MFX: David Lange and Bill Morrison; MUS: J.R. Bookwalter
STR: J.R. Bookwalter, Lester Clark, James L. Edwards, Floyd Ewing, Jr., Mary Jackson, Barbara Katz-Norrod, Jon Killough, Jennifer Mullen, Mike Render, Susan Rothacker, Mike Shea, Scott Spiegel and Michael Tolochko, Jr.
Approximately 90m; Color
VHS1: *Skinned Alive* [CGV; 90m]

ADL: *Unhinged! Insane! Totally Out of Control!*

Despite the fact that *Skinned Alive* was not shot on video, it isn't much better than said productions. (The computer generated opening credits sequence belies the fact that the filmmakers are fairly well versed in the ways of videotaped fare, and have had most of their training through this abhorrent medium.) Most of the production values are on par with most homegrown efforts, although—all things considered—the editing and continuity is surprisingly competent. As if to dash any hopes the viewer may have had of this being a watchable film, one is then forced to suffer through awful dubbing, embarrassing sound effects, and some painfully over-the-top performances.

The story is too derivative of *Texas Chainsaw Massacre 2*, but for those who may be interested, it is at least as messy. The graphic gore effects ("gratuitous" can't begin to describe them) are pretty poorly executed, but it's so overwhelming that indiscriminate splatterpunks should be quite pleased. In keeping with the tone of its obvious inspiration, there are plenty of forced guffaws; although hit and miss, a few truly funny jokes sneak through. (When asked if there "are any motels in this rathole of a town?" a gas station attendant replies, "There was the Bates place out by the old highway ... that closed down years ago.") Much of the humor, though, never rises above "I think I've died and gone to Mayberry."

It's your Friday night; you can waste it however you see fit.

De Slachter van New York *see* Lo Squartatore di New York

Slagtehuset ved Kirkegarden *see* Quella Villa Accanto al Cimitero

Slaughter in the South Bronx *see* Tenement

The Slaughterers *see* Apocalisse Domani

Slaughterhouse (1987)

American Artists Inc. [US], Slaughterhouse Associates [US]

DIR: Rick Roessler; PRO: Ron Matonak; SCR: Rick Roessler; DOP: Richard J. Benda; EXP: Jerry Encoe; MFX: Barney Burman and Mark Lane; SFX: Rob Hinderstein, Tim Larsen and Mike Wowzcuk; MUS: Joe Garrison and Vantage Point

STR: Don Barrett, Joe Barton, Sherry Bendorf, Bill Brinsfield, Jason Collier, Dave Fogel, Jeff Grossi, Hank Gum, Linda Harris, Jane Higginson, Joel Hoffman, William Houck, Courtney Lercara, Tom Normand, Herb Pender, Lee Robinson, Jeanette Saylor, Eric Schwartz, Donna Stevens and Jeff Wright

Approximately 85m; Color 🜲 🜲 🜲

DVD1: *Slaughterhouse* [NAV; 82m]; VHS1: *Slaughterhouse* [CHA; 85m]

ADL: *Buddy Has an Axe to Grind. A Big Axe.*

A meat packing plant tries to buy property from a small-time farmer ("Bacon & Sons Hog Slaughtering") before the county forecloses and puts it up for auction. The old man is none too happy about the whole thing and sics his overweight, retarded son Buddy on them. (He snorts like a pig and has a meat cleaver to match his girth.) A group of teens working on a horror movie also manage to get involved when they decide to film part of their epic on the dilapidated property. (Not surprisingly, they have no

clue as to how to make them ... which means they're sure to make it in Hollywood by the time they're thirty.) Despite evocative sets and decent performances from some of the veterans herein, *Slaughterhouse* is a generic slasher film with homogenized elements from *The Texas Chain Saw Massacre* thrown in for good measure. Gore is standard (although there's a nice scene with a car running over the head of one poor sap), and the shock "guess who's hiding in the back seat" ending is utterly predictable, although I don't think Buddy could fit in the back of a patrol car even if he tried.

The Slayer (1981)

International Picture Show Company [US]

DIR: J.S. Cardone; PRO: William R. Ewing; SCR: J.S. Cardone and William R. Ewing; DOP: Karen Grossman; MFX: Robert Short; SFX: Robert Babb and Spectacular FX; MUS: Robert Folk

STR: Newell Alexander, Frederick Flynn, Jennifer Gaffin, Paul Gandolfo, Michael Holmes, Ivy Jones, Sarah Kendall, Carol Kottenbrook, Carl Kraines, Alan McRae, Sandy Simpson and Richard van Brakel

AKA: *El Malefico Satanico* [The Satanic Evil]; *Nightmare Island*

Approximately 75m; Color

VHS1: *The Slayer* [CON; 75m]; *The Slayer* [PLV; 75m]

An artist suffering from recurring nightmares goes to an island retreat with her hubby and two friends. They haven't even had the chance to get settled in when the toothy antagonist from her dreams begins making mincemeat of anyone within spitting distance, saving her for last, of course. *The Slayer* is a low budget but competently made shocker that makes the best of its limited resources, even instilling a sense of claustrophobia sorely missing from similar films. There are only a handful of deaths, but they are fairly gruesome and even well executed. (*The Slayer* boasts one of the most convincing pitchfork deaths ever committed to screen.) Unfortunately, the bloodthirsty boogeyman—thankfully shown only in the finale—is typical of '80s man-in-a-mask monsters, and the script is extremely ambiguous; no explanations are given, and the tired "hey, it was only a dream" ending is a pathetic attempt to cover up the holes in its logic.

Worth checking out, especially if you can get it on the two-for-one label with *Scalps*.

Slayride *see* Silent Night, Deadly Night

Sledgehammer (1984)

I&I Productions [US]
DIR: David A. Prior; PRO: Nicholas Imaz; SCR: David A. Prior; DOP: Salim Kimaz; EXP: Abdalla Itani and Chuck Malouf; MFX: Blood & Guts; MUS: Marc Adams, Ted Prior and Philip G. Slate
STR: Tim Aguilar, Sandy Brooke, John Eastman, Justin Greer, Ray Lawrence, Doug Matley, Linda McGill, Maria Mendez, Ted Prior, Jeanine Scheer, Michael Shanahan and Steve Wright
Approximately 90m; Color [Shot on video]

Sledgehammer is a nearly pointless exercise in filmmaking that spotlights a gaggle of drunk, muscle-bound jocks that no one will miss once they are knocked off by a psychopathic killer and his titular weapon of choice. (One doesn't feel much sympathy for their girlfriends either, for that matter.) The abysmal production values (bad even by home-grown standards) compliment the sophomoric script and rote proceedings. And—as if the movie wasn't painful enough an experience—this shot on video dreck is liberally padded with recycled footage, still frames, and slow motion photography. There is some graphic skull crushing to be had, but the few bloody highlights that *Sledgehammer* offers do not justify the viewing experience.

The cinematic equivalent of beating *yourself* upside the head with a sledgehammer.

Sleepaway Camp (1983)

American Eagle Film Corp. [US]
DIR: Robert Hiltzik; PRO: Jerry Silva and Michele Tatosian; SCR: Robert Hiltzik; DOP: Benjamin Davis; EXP: Robert Hiltzik; MFX: Edward French; MUS: Edward Bilous
STR: Allen Breton, Lisa Buckler, John Churchill, Christopher Collet, Colette Lee Corcoran, Paul de Angelo, Julie Delisio, John Dunn, Rick Edrich, Karen Fields, Brad Frankel, Dee Dee Friedman, Susan Glaze, Desiree Gould, Fred Greene, Bram Hand, Owen Hughes, Robert Earl Jones, Katherine Kamhi, Mike Kellin, Willy Kuskin, Michael Lerman, Mike Mahon, Alyson Mord, James Paradise, Paul Poland, Carol Robinson, Felissa Rose, Frank Trent Saladino, Loris Sallahian, Frank Sorrentino, Jonathan Tierston, Dan Tursi and Tom van Dell
AKA: *Nightmare Vacation*
Approximately 84m; Color
DVD1: *Sleepaway Camp* [ABE; 84m; LBX]; VHS1: *Sleepaway Camp* [ABE; 84m; LBX]; *Sleepaway Camp* [MHE; 90(84)m]

A boating accident at Camp Arawak leaves at least one dead. Eight years later, someone begins knocking off the patrons of the summer camp. Sounds familiar, doesn't it? (Thank-

A Nice Place For Summer Vacation.
A Perfect Place To Die!

HORROR

Video box art for *Sleepaway Camp* **(1983), Media Home Entertainment.**

fully, there's not a hockey mask in sight.) Who is it? The mousy survivor of the aforementioned incident? Her overprotective cousin with a penchant for violence and potty mouth? The pedophiliac cook? (Hint: The scriptwriter decided to make it really tough for the viewer by going for the obvious. Even then, he's got an ace up his sleeve.)

This *Friday the 13th* knock-off just barely qualifies as a splatter film, and could easily be mistaken for a made-for-TV special were it not for the fact that the kiddies are dispatched left and right. Despite a pretty homogenized approach, *Sleep-*

away Camp stands out for two reasons, the least of which is that all of the kids and teens are played by real honest to goodness kids and teens, and furthermore, they act their age to boot. The main reason, though, to check out this entry in the slasher film genre is the shock ending; despite the fact that it is a bit overdone, it is effective. (The exposed killer comes across as, well, particularly *demonic*, although I don't think this was the director's intention. Geez, it's impressively spooky, if only because it's so damn surreal.)

A guilty pleasure for many a poor soul, Yours Truly included.

Sleepaway Camp 2—Unhappy Campers (1988)

Double Helix Films Inc. [US]
DIR: Michael A. Simpson; PRO: Jerry Silva and Michael A. Simpson; SCR: Fritz Gordon; DOP: Bill Mills; EXP: Stan Wakefield; MFX: Bill Johnson; MUS: James Oliviero
STR: Kendall Bean, Heather Binion, Carol Chambers, Brian Patrick Clarke, Jill Jane Clements, Jason Ehrlich, Renée Estevez, Amy Fields, Walter Franks III, Walter Gotell, Tricia Grant, Valerie Hartman, Tony Higgins, Terry Hobbs, Julie Murphy, Justin Nowell, Susan Marie Snyder, Pamela Springsteen, Carol Martin Vines and Benji Wilhoite
AKA: *Nightmare Vacation II*
Approximately 80m; Color
VHS1: *Sleepaway Camp 2—Unhappy Campers* [NEL; 81(80)m]
ADL: *When You Go Camping Just Take the Essentials.*

Six years after the murder spree at Camp Arawak, Angela is back in business, now a counselor at Camp Rolling Hills and killing off anyone who doesn't fit her image of the good girl/good boy archetypes.

Any charm *Sleepaway Camp* had

is long since gone in this simple-minded pastiche of the stalk 'n' slash genre. (The video box cover depicting odes to *Friday the 13th* and *A Nightmare on Elm Street* should clue one in to the mindset here.) The execution is generic, and the gore doesn't really kick in until towards the end, and even then it's all after the fact. Really, why bother?

Sleepaway Camp II—Unhappy Campers *see* **Sleepaway Camp 2—Unhappy Campers**

Sleepaway Camp 3—Teenage Wasteland (1988)

Double Helix Films Inc. [US]
DIR: Michael A. Simpson; PRO: Jerry Silva and Michael A. Simpson; SCR: Fritz Gordon; DOP: Bill Mills; EXP: Stan Wakefield; MFX: Bill Johnson; MUS: James Oliviero
    STR: Cliff Brand, Haynes Brooke, Yen Tsay Chung, Jerry Griffin, Tracy Griffith, Kyle Holman, Kashina Kessler, Stacie Lambert, Charles Lawlor, Randi Layne, Sonya Maddox, Mike Nagel, Mark Oliver, Michael J. Pollard, Jarrett Seal, Pamela Springsteen, Jill Terashita, Kim Wall and Daryl Wilcher
    AKA: *Nightmare Vacation III*
    Approximately 80m; Color
    VHS1: *Sleepaway Camp III—Teenage Wasteland* [NEL; 80m]
    ADL: *She's Back to Slash Last Year's Record!*

Yes, Angela is back, apparently unsatisfied with the carnage that punctuated the first two entries in a series even more pointless than Jason's infamous kill-a-thon.
    Sleepaway Camp III makes some admirable pokes at slasher flicks, but these are rare occurrences as most of its humor relies on reiterating the stale conventions of the genre while offering a "wink, wink, nudge, nudge"

to the viewer, just so everyone *knows* it's all a joke. (This seems to me to be a pointless endeavor since slasher films are little more than parodies of themselves *anyway*.)
    Production values are mediocre, so the only thing to recommend it for is the humor. It's sophomoric, to be sure, but it will inevitably elicit a chuckle from the viewer, if only because of the screenwriter's perseverance.
    Made back to back with the similarly lackluster *Sleepaway Camp 2—Unhappy Campers*.

Sleepaway Camp III—Teenage Wasteland *see* **Sleepaway Camp 3—Teenage Wasteland**

Sleepless Nights *see* **The Slumber Party Massacre**

The Slumber Party Massacre (1982)

Santa Fe Productions Inc. [US]
DIR: Amy Holden Jones; PRO: Amy Holden Jones; SCR: Rita Mae Brown; DOP: Stephen L. Posey; SFX: Larry S. Carr and Rick Lazzarini; MUS: Ralph Jones
    STR: Jim Boyce, Pam Canzano, Debra Deliso, Andree Honore, Joe Johnson, Ryan Kennedy, Aaron Lipstadt, Gina Mari, Francis Menendez, Jennifer Meyers, Michele Michaels, David Millbern, Anna Patton, Howard Purgason, Pamela Roylance, Brinke Stevens, Robin Stille, Jean Vargas and Michael Villella
    AKA: *Masacre en la Fiesta* [Massacre at the Party]; *Sleepless Nights*
    Approximately 77m; Color
    DVD1: *The Slumber Party Massacre* [NCV; 77m; LBX]; VHS1: *The Slumber Party Massacre* [EMB; 77m]; *The Slumber Party Massacre* [NCV; 77m]
    ADL: *The Ultimate Driller Killer Thriller!*

Okay, so the title says it all. It's hard to believe that this film was helmed almost entirely by women; and I thought only men made hack-neyed sexploitive dreck this bad. Geez.

Although not nearly as obnox-ious as its follow-ups, *The Slumber Party Massacre* is the archetype of generic slasher flicks. There is a *lot* of blood (although we're slighted any real gore) and an abundance of T&A. There are a few moments that could almost be construed as humorous, but even this inspiration is lost amidst the slew of tired conventions. I have a gut feeling that this was intended as a pastiche of slasher films, but—as I've stated many, *many* times before—this becomes moot when the source ma-terial is already a parody of itself.

It only gets worse from here on out, as if that's conceivable.

Slumber Party Massacre II (1987)

Concorde Pictures [US]
DIR: Deborah Brock; PRO: Deborah Brock and Don Daniel; SCR: Deborah Brock; DOP: Thomas L. Callaway; MFX: James Cummins; MUS: Richard Cox
STR: Crystal Bernard, Juliette Cum-mins, Don Daniel, Michael de Lano, Cyn-thia Eilbacher, Joel Hoffman, Atanas Ilitch, Heidi Kozak, Marshall la Plante, Patrick Lowe, Kimberly McArthur, Hamilton Mitchell, Jennifer Rhodes and Scott West-moreland
Approximately 90m; Color
DVD1: *Slumber Party Massacre II* [New Concorde Home Video; 90m]; VHS1: *Slum-ber Party Massacre II* [Embassy Home En-tertainment; 90m]; *Slumber Party Massacre II* [Nelson Entertainment; 90m]; *Slumber Party Massacre II* [New Concorde Home Video; 90m]
ADL: *The Party Begins When the Lights Go Out!*

You just can't get much more insufferable a viewing experience than

this slasher flick-cum-musical. (Yes … it's a musical.) A Freddy Krueger–inspired rocker besets a group of lo-botomized teens staying the weekend in one of their rich parents' condos. None too coincidentally, one is a sur-vivor from the previous film's mas-sacre. The killer sports a '50s greaser look and wields a guitar with a large drill built into it. Prior to several killings, he lip-synchs entire musical numbers (yes … there's musical num-bers) and winks at the audience while filtered lights and a portable smoke machine put in some overtime.

The gore is piled on thick, but any splatterpunk with even an ounce of self-respect will miss the bloody proceedings, as they will inevitably be covering their faces in embarrassment for having rented this film in the first place.

Something Waits in the Dark *see* **Screamers**

Sorority Babes in the Slimeball Bowl-O-Rama *see* **The Imp**

Sotto gli Occhi dell'Assassino *see* **Tenebre**

Sotto il Vestito Niente [Nothing Underneath the Clothes] (1983)

Faso Film [It]
DIR: Carlo Vanzina; PRO: Achille Manzotti; SCR: Franco Ferrini, Carlo Vanz-ina, and Enrico Vanzina [Based on the novel *Sotto il Vestito Niente* by Marco Parma]; DOP: Beppe Maccari; EXP: Raffaello Saragò; SFX: Corridori; MUS: Pino Don-aggio
STR: Cyrus Elias, Anna Galiena, Big Laura, Maria McDonald, Bruce McGuire, Catherine Noyes, Nicola Perring, Donald Pleasence, Sonia Raule, Tom Schanley,

279   **Sotto**

Mimmo Sepe, Renée Simonsen and Paolo Tomei
AKA: *Nothing Underneath*
Approximately 94m; Color

An up and coming model working in Italy mysteriously disappears. Her twin brother, a Yellowstone National Park ranger, "senses" that something has happened to her, and arrives in Europe the very next day. His sister is nowhere to be found, so the concerned sibling goes to the police, and a retiring detective (Donald Pleasence) reluctantly offers his assistance. All the while, murders are being committed in the area by someone wielding a rather ominous pair of scissors. *Obviously*, the model's disappearance and the rash of killings are somehow related.

This is a painfully generic, predictable *giallo* thriller that exhibits none of Italy's trademarked style, and instead could be mistaken for American slasher dreck. Besides the stale conventions, the script also suffers from innumerable breeches in logic, most tied to the silly supernatural pretenses they wish to pawn off on the viewer. (Having a psychic link that stretches halfway across the globe is one thing, but to simultaneously be able to look through the killer's eyes is another matter altogether.)

There's also a tacky slo-mo finale that makes a desperate attempt to evoke Dario Argento, but fails none too surprisingly, and some distressing politics that imply that lesbians are inherently obsessive, evil creatures. *Nothing Underneath* is a pretty accurate retitle, yes indeed.

Sotto il Vestito Niente 2 [Nothing Underneath the Clothes 2] (1988)

Gruppo Bema S.r.L. [It], Reteitalia [It]
DIR: Dario di Piana; PRO: Achille Manzotti; SCR: Claudio Mancini, Achille Manzotti and Dario di Piana; DOP: Alan Jones; EXP: Raffaello Saragò; MFX: Studio Maschera d'Apollo; SFX: Fabio Massimo Traversa; MUS: Roberto Cacciapaglia
STR: Norphana Arrifan, Raffaele Biondi, Stefano Capaccioli, Carlo Carli, François Eric-Gendron, Narco Giorgetti, Enzo Giraldo, Florence Guérin, Randi Ingermann, Helena Jesus, Stefano Lisicki, Francois Marthouret, Roy John Palmer, Ilza Prestinari, Maurizio Ratti, Maurizio Rocchi, Gioa Maria Scola, Sergio Stefanini and Giovanni Tamberi
AKA: *Too Beautiful to Die*
Approximately 95m; Color
VHS2: *Too Beautiful to Die* [CNC; 95m; LBX; Dutch subtitles]

Even shallower than its predecessor, *Sotto il Vestito Niente 2* involves a group of models-slash-dancers (performing in an MTV-style video for a song called "Blades") who start getting knocked off after one of them is raped—with a little assistance from her co-stars—and found dead the next day in a car accident.

This unrelated sequel reiterates its predecessor in many ways, using fashion models as the primary source for fodder, and with a gang rape standing in for an impromptu game of Russian roulette. *Sotto il Vestito Niente 2* is undeniably more stylish (the Italian crew remembered their heritage this time out) but a heck of a lot less engaging than the first film (which is saying something, in light of my review of *Sotto il Vestito Niente*). The characters are all sleazy and undeserving of anyone's sympathy, and the murders quite rote, to boot. Pass.

Sound Stage Massacre *see* **Deliria**

Soupçon de Mort *see* **Quando Alice Ruppe lo Specchio**

La Spiaggia del Terrore [The Beach of Terror] (1988)

Elpico S.A. [It], Laguna Entertainment [US]

DIR: Umberto Lenzi; PRO: William J. Immerman; SCR: Umberto Lenzi; DOP: Antonio Climati; EXP: Josi W. Konski; MFX: Vittorio Rambaldi; SFX: Gary Bentley; MUS: Claudio Simonetti and Various Artists

STR: Jay Amor, John Baldwin, Greg Gerard Bernet, Tom Boykin, Fred Buck, Sarah Buxton, Jennifer Coleman, Gregg Todd Davis, Nicolas de Toth, Joe del Campo, James di Cuia, Dan Fitzgerald, Debra Gallagher, Turk Harley, Yamilet Hidalgo, Jennifer Hingel, Christina Kier, Kristy Lachance, Lance le Gault, Donna Lee, Mitzi Lively, Frank Logan, Michelle Lee Nahm, Ferdie Pacheco, Michael Parks, Shana Rodman, Theresa Maria Rojas, John Saxon, Barry Schreiber, Earl L. Simpson III, Ben Stotes, Luis Valderama, Rawley Valverde, Lisa Vidal and William Wohrman

Approximately 90m; Color

AKA: *Nightmare Beach*; *Welcome to Spring Break*

VHS1: *Welcome to Spring Break* [IVE; 92(90)m]

A biker is framed and sent to the chair, and within a few weeks after the execution someone begins making short work of the tourists, using whatever's handy but obviously exhibiting a penchant for electrocuting his prey.

All of the slasher conventions are present and accounted for. Throw in a wet T-shirt contest (the only titillation herein), a soundtrack littered with lousy '80s pop and metal acts (save for ex–Goblin member Simonetti's contribution, which is little more than an oft-recycled riff that accom-panies each and every murder), and a few (almost successful) running gags. "Welcome to Spring Break ... annual migration of the idiot," one character quips. I couldn't have said it better myself, although it begs the question of why anyone would want to make a film around such people in the first place.

The Spider Labyrinth *see* **Il Nido del Ragno**

Spine (1986)

Xeon Ltd. [US]

DIR: John Howard and Justin Simonds; PRO: John Howard and Justin Simonds; SCR: John Howard and Justin Simonds; MFX: Lori Laverde; SFX: Lori Laverde; MUS: Don Chilcott

STR: Janus Blythe, Brenda Brandon, Marie Dowling, Bill Eberwein, Jason Eberwein, Carl Elliot, Antoine Herzog, Ray Hicks, R. Eric Huxley, Larry Nielson, Lisa Romanoff, Kathy Rose, Donna Sayles, James Simonds, Terry Simonds, Abby Sved and Dan Watson

Approximately 90m; Color [Shot on video]

VHS1: *Spine* [STS; 90m]

ADL: *He Is Looking for Linda ... and That Could Be Anybody!*

This justifiably obscure splatter flick may be better than some of its shot on video peers, but only a handful come to mind. (*Sledgehammer* and *Re-Animator Academy* are two safe bets, anyway.) *Spine* is bottom of the barrel homegrown horror that focuses on a killer who likes to remove the spinal cords of half-naked women. The accompanying effects usually aren't much more impressive than red paint smeared on someone's less than violated backbone. How Janus Blythe—one of the stars from *The Hills Have Eyes* and its sequel—wound up in *this* turkey, I'd rather not know.

Having now seen it, I can honestly say it's one less turd to which I have to look forward stepping in.

Splatter *see* **Futurekill**

Splatter University (1983)

Richard W. Haines Productions Inc. [US]

DIR: Richard W. Haines; PRO: Richard W. Haines and John Michaels; SCR: Michael Cunningham, Richard W. Haines and John Michaels; DOP: Fred Cohen and Jim Grib; MFX: Amodio Giordano; SFX: Amodio Giordano; MUS: Christopher Burke

STR: Paul Bianca, Dick Biel, Charles Brukardt, Suzy Collins, Gloria Cooper, Ralph Cordero, Don Costello, Michael Cunningham, Ron Darrier, Mary Ellen David, Don Eaton, Francine Forbes, Aki Fujiyoshi, Steve Galos, Ken Gerson, Sue Graef, Richard W. Haines, Donna Hartman, Terri Horak, Kathy Lacommare, Sal Lumetta, Alice Martin, Jim Martin, Dennis Michaels, John Michaels, Joanna Mihalakis, Joe Rain, Ric Randig, Jane Doniger Reibel, Jonathan Schwartz, George Seminara, Noel Stilphen, Denise Texera and Clifford Warren

AKA: *Campus Killings*; *Terror en la Prepa* [Terror in the College]

Approximately 78m; Color

VHS1: *Splatter University* [VES; 79(78)m]

ADL: *Where the School Colors Are Blood Red!*

Paranoid schizophrenic William Grayham walks out of the loony bin where he's been locked away for God-knows-how-long and shows up at St. Trinians College three years later to wreak havoc. There, a fledgling teacher reluctantly accepts a position after an instructor is brutally murdered, and thus finds herself in the killer's sights. This low-rent slasher flick proves *almost* engaging, if only for the melodrama involved. Unfortunately, there is no mystery as to the killer's identity, unless you're one of the poor souls who are sidetracked by the fact that the screenwriters made it *too* obvious. The finale holds at least one surprise, if only because the selfsame writers purposefully broke one of the unwritten laws in horror cinema. (Hey, *I'm* not telling. I give away enough spoilers as it is.)

Otherwise, *Splatter University* is completely generic. The victims are mostly obnoxious, stereotypical college students sporting the latest in rubbery slashed throat applications. (Granted, there are gallons of blood, and even some offal thrown in for good measure, but it's still not enough to make the grades.)

It scores higher than *The Dorm That Dripped Blood*, but heck, what doesn't?

Spookies *see* **Twisted Souls**

Lo Squartatore di New York [The Chopper of New York] (1982)

Fulvia Films S.r.L. [It]

DIR: Lucio Fulci; PRO: Fabrizio de Angelis; SCR: Gianfranco Clerici, Lucio Fulci, Vincenzo Mannino and Dardano Sacchetti; DOP: Luigi Kuveiller; MFX: Germano Natali; MUS: Francesco de Masi [Soundtrack from Beat Records]

STR: Elisa Cervi, Cosimo Cinieri, Jobs Cruze, Barbara Cupisti, Cinzia de Ponti, Alexandra delli Colli, Cesare di Vito, Daniela Doria, Giordano Falzoni, Chiara Ferrari, Lucio Fulci, Paul Guskin, Jack Hedley, Violetta Jean, Anthony Kagan, Zora Kerova, Marsha MacBride, Paolo Malco, Babette New, Andrea Occhipinti, Renato Rossini, Rita Silva, Martin Sorrentino and Almanta Suska

AKA: *El Descuartizador de New York* [The Chopper of New York]; *De Doder van New York* [The Killer of New York]; *L'Even-*

Promotional still for *Lo Squartatore di New York* (1982).

treur de New York [The Disemboweler of New York]; *New York Ripper; Psycho Ripper; De Slachter van New York* [The Ripper of New York]
Approximately 93m Color
DVD1: *New York Ripper* [ABE; 93m; LBX]; VHS1: *New York Ripper* [ABE; 93m; LBX]; *New York Ripper* [VID; 88m]; VHS2: *De Doder van New York* [VVV; 93m]; *New York Ripper* [PCM; 90m]
ADL: *Someone's Taking a Big Slice Out of the Big Apple...*

A modern day Jack the Ripper is slicing up young, sexually active women in NY: pros, models, whoever. The only lead police have is that the killer likes to call and taunt the authorities using a Donald Duck voice. Really ... I'm not making this up.

Technically, this is not one of Fulci's better films, although it is easy to see why so little effort was put into it. Even more so than his infamous

zombie pics, *Lo Squartatore di New York* exists solely to accommodate the gore, or—more specifically—to depict sado-sexual violence in the most graphic detail imaginable. Everything is sacrificed for the sake of the "penetration shot," making this the splatter equivalent of porn. Had they been used to convey something besides vicarious thrills, the film's contents would have been truly disturbing; as it stands, *Lo Squartatore di New York* is simply a misogynistic fantasy of the lowest order. It is no surprise that many critics revile this film, whether or not they claim to be fans of the director in question.

Besides its abhorrent single-mindedness, the film is plagued by the alluded to technical incompetence. (The innumerable zooms would inevitably give Jesse Franco a migraine,

Video box art for *Lo Squartatore di New York* **(1982), Vidmark Entertainment.**

for crying out loud.) The script—which barely qualifies as *giallo*—seems to have been hammered out on the spot, again to accommodate the graphic murders. The jazzy soundtrack isn't half bad, and some of the effects are fairly convincing, but the film's mean-spirited nature makes it nearly unwatchable.

A turning point (for the worst, I assure you) in Lucio Fulci's already spotty career.

Stage Fright *see* **Deliria**

Stirba the Werewolf Bitch *see* **Howling II—Your Sister Is a Werewolf**

Strangers *see* **Alien 2 Sulla Terra**

Street Trash (1986)

The Street Trash Joint Venture Inc. [US]

DIR: James Muro, Jr.; PRO: Roy Frumkes; SCR: Roy Frumkes; DOP: David Sperling; EXP: Edward Muro, Sr., and James Muro, Sr.; SFX: Jennifer Aspinall and Mike Lackey; MUS: Rick Ulfik

STR: Glenn Andreiev, Jane Arakawa, Gary Auerbach, Eddie Bay, Sam Blasco, Bill Bondanza, Bill Chepil, Tony Darrow, Julian Davis, Colin Derouin, Craig Edwards, Franco Fantasia, Roy Frumkes, Nadine Garcia, Peter Iasillo, Jr., Clarenze Jarmon, Robert Jonathan, Kristin Kirkconnell, Marilyn Kray, M. D'Jango Krunch, Victoria Lacas, Mike Lackey, Jeanne Laporta, James Lorinz, Allan Lozito, Nora Maher, Julie McQuain, Gina Menza, Vic Noto, Stephen Patterson, Bernard Perlman, Nicole Potter, Carmel Pugh, R.L. Ryan, Stephen Joseph Santiago, Fred Schomaker, Karl Schröder, Marc Sferrazza, Kevin Simmons, Morty Storm, Bruce Torbet, Robynne White, Roman Zack and Miriam Zucker

Approximately 91m; Color

VHS1: *Street Trash* [LIG; 91m]

What passes as a story involves a bargain rotgut found stuffed away in a basement corner; those who drink it do a Technicolor take on *The Incredible Melting Man*. (Having not seen that classic piece of exploitation, one poor sap instead does his best Mr. Creosote impersonation. Think *Monty Python's The Meaning of Life*.) Throw in a subplot about a junkyard hierarchy run by a crazed Vietnam vet, and something about the Mafia, and you have one strange film.

One's first impression of *Street Trash* is: What if Troma films were actually as enjoyable as they would lead you to believe? The humor is usually juvenile, but even then it manages to be ingratiating. Violence is over-the-top, with more traditional gore intermixed with the aforementioned Technicolor variety. (It's no surprise that effects artist Jennifer Aspinall also worked on Troma's *The Toxic Avenger* a few years previous.) There is a cadre of eccentric characters, including the guy who later played the lovelorn doctor in *Frankenhooker*. (As for the actors who portray the homeless people, some of them are extremely convincing; most, though, are little more than cartoonish representations of street people.) On the upside, the film boasts some wonderful Raimi-like photography. On the down, *Street Trash* can get downright misogynistic at times.

Of course, the scene from this film that is most often remembered involves a game of keep-away utilizing a freshly dismembered penis. And it is fairly amusing.

A tasteless but endearing film produced by the director of *Document of the Dead* (1989).

Streghe [Witches] (1989)

United Entertainment Corp. [It/US]
DIR: Alessandro Capone; PRO: Alessandro Capone, Mauro Morigi and Giuseppe Pedersoli; SCR: Alessandro Capone and Rosario Galli; DOP: Roberto Girometti; EXP: Claudio Bonivento; MFX: Rick Gonzales; SFX: Vince Montefusco; MUS: Carlo Maria Cordio
STR: Amy Adams, Jeff Bankert, Ian Bannen, Brock Bips, Bob Bouchard, John Boyd, Charon Butler, Todd Conner, John Freda, Jim Gibson, Peter Gold, Kirk Green, Cecil Hawkins, Elise Hirby, Gary Kerr, Kevin Kirton, Suzanne Law, Jason M. Lefkowitz, Deanna Lund, Mario Millo, Christopher Peacock, Stewart Penn, Richard Powell, Fred Price, Nancie Sanderson and Michelle Vannucchi
AKA: *Superstition 2*; *Witch Story*
Approximately 93m; Color

A group of obnoxious twentysomethings vacationing in Florida stay at an abandoned house where— fifty-seven years earlier—a witch was lynched by the local townsfolk. Something begins possessing the females of the group, who take little time in dispatching the others.

Despite fairly slick production values, this is a rather sad horror film. The actors are hopeless, and the hokum almost as grating as the characters portrayed therein. (And I thought the stereotype of witches as cackling old hags was left to adolescent Halloween fears; in today's day and age, they are simply *not* scary.) It is a reasonably bloody offering, to be sure, but its only real claim to infamy is that it offers the most dubious chainsaw scene in recent history.

Yes, Italy can churn out dreck just as bad as our own if given the opportunity.

Suiito Homu [Sweet Home] (1988)

Toho Company Ltd. [Ja]
DIR: Kiyoshi Kurosawa; EXP: Juzio Itami; MFX: Dick Smith
STR: Juzio Itami, Nobuko Miyamoto, Nokko, Shingo Yamashiro and Tsutomu Yamazaki
Approximately 101; Color

A news crew decides to investigate an old haunted house. Their initial discovery is an ornate mural that seems to scare the bejeezus out of them. Following their find, one of the crew members becomes possessed and then wastes no time in unearthing the corpse of a half-burnt baby (shown earlier in the mural). If that isn't weird enough, the house then coughs up a demonic shadow whose touch ignites whatever it comes in contact with. As could be expected, this Japanese variation of *The Legend of Hell House* offers up an onslaught of paranormal nastiness with which to besiege the uninvited guests. Now if only someone would release a subtitled or English language version of this film, maybe I could make heads or tails out of the proceedings.

The photography is quite nice, exhibiting the same plush atmosphere common to better Japanese horror films of the last two decades. (Blame that on the influence of Argento and his ilk on their cinematic culture.) The visual effects are above average, and there is enough unrestrained grue to interest most splatterpunks. As for the actual script, well, I can't tell you much except I doubt it is anything exceptional, as *Suiito Homu* is apparently based on a popular video game in Japan. (Ads for it immediately precede the film.)

With Nokko, star of the wonderfully politically incorrect live-action *Kekkô Kamen* (1993).

Sundown *see* **Sundown—The Vampire in Retreat**

Sundown—The Vampire in Retreat (1989)

Vestron Pictures Inc. [US]
DIR: Anthony Hickox; PRO: Jefferson Richard; SCR: John Burgess and Anthony Hickox; DOP: Levie Isaacks; EXP: Dan Ireland and Jack Lorenz; MFX: Tony Gardner and Larry Hamlin; SFX: The Physical Effects Group; VFX: Anthony Doublin and Modern Moving Images; MUS: Richard Stone
STR: Dana Ashbrook, Jay Bernard, Christopher Bradley, Morgan Brittany, Bruce Campbell, Christopher Caputo, David Carradine, Helena Carroll, Maxwell Caulfield, Dean Cleverdon, Stuart Cohn, Marion Eaton, Jack Eiseman, Phil Esposito, George Flower, Deborah Foreman, Erin Gourlay, Elizabeth Gracen, Dabbs Greer, John Hancock, Brendan Hughes, John Ireland, Kathy McQuarrie Martin, Gerardo Mejia, Jim Metzler, Mike Najjar, Sunshine Parker, Vanessa Pierson, Burt Remsen, Phillip Simon and M. Emmet Walsh
AKA: *Sundown*
Approximately 104m; Color
VHS1: *Sundown* [VES; 104m]
ADL: *There's Two Kinds of Folks in the Town of Purgatory. Vampires. And Lunch.*

Combining updated vampire mythology with staging culled from old western films, this charming little horror comedy is not only fun, but boasts a surprising amount of gore. Thankfully, the action isn't nearly as patronizing as that which is found in most "gore-omedies." Bruce (*The Evil Dead*) Campbell has a supporting role as Van Helsing's great-grandson, a screw-up who futilely tries following in his ancestor's footsteps. (Campbell's performance is a little more restrained than what one may expect, which actually works on his—and the film's—behalf.) Also on hand for the fun is David (*Kung Fu*) Carradine and everyone's favorite supporting character actor, George "Buck" Flower (who probably has more films to his credit than David's late dad John Carradine).

In spite of numerous shortcomings (the low-rent stop-motion animation comes immediately to mind), this is by far Hickox' best film. Regardless, nothing he does will ever redeem him—in my eyes, anyway—for the 1992 atrocity *Hellraiser III—Hell on Earth*.

Superstition (1982)

Penaria Corp. [US]
DIR: James W. Roberson; PRO: Ed Carlin; SCR: Donald Galen Thompson; DOP: Leon Blank; EXP: Mario Kassar and Andrew G. Vajna; MFX: Steve Laforte and David B. Miller; MUS: David Gibney
STR: John Alderman, Nova Ball, Heidi Bohay, Joshua Cadman, Lynn Carlin, Michael Cornelison, Johnny Doran, Carole Goldman, James Houghton, Jacquelyn Hyde, Billy Jacoby, Stacey Keach, Casey King, Bennett Liss, Kim Marie, Maylo McCaslin, Earl Montgomery, Larry Pennell, Bret Thompson Plate, Albert Salmi, Morgan Strickland and Robert Symonds
AKA: Superstición [Superstition]
Approximately 85m; Color
VHS1: Superstition [LIG; 85m]
ADL: You Should Have Believed!

The haunted house on Mill Road doesn't take kindly to trespassers, "ingeniously" and brutally knocking off anyone loitering about the premises. The authorities insist that the proud owners—the church—do something with the property before they take action and have it razed to the ground. An unorthodox young priest has the responsibility thrown in his lap, and he decides to look into it. Not only does he have to deal with the creepy caretaker and his mute son, he also has to come to grips with the fact that there's something "unnatural" living in a nearby pond.

Superstition is fairly slick but ultimately silly hokum that should whet the appetites of most gorehounds. Points of interest include a head exploding in a microwave, a window pane cutting one young man in half, a dislodged saw blade bouncing across the room and giving a priest a severe case of heartburn ... and these are all in the first twenty minutes. The execution of the gore is passable, although we do have to suffer through some tacky bladder effects at one point. Superstition also boasts some nice sets, which grant the film some creepy atmosphere. (Had a more adept filmmaker taken advantage of the location shooting, the film could have been a truly effective horror movie.)

Enjoyable spook show fare, if only because of the gratuity and nihilistic ending.

Telepathy 2000 see Scanners

Tenebre [Darkness] (1982)

Sigma Cinematografica [It]
DIR: Dario Argento; PRO: Claudio Argento; SCR: Dario Argento and George Kemp; DOP: Luciano Tovoli; EXP: Salvatore Argento; SFX: Giovanni Corridori; MUS: Goblin
STR: Isabella Amadeo, Mirella Banti, Lamberto Bava, Christian Borromeo, Mirella d'Angelo, Anthony Franciosa, Giuliano Gemma, Ennio Girolami, Veronica Lario, Monica Maisani, Marino Masé, Fulvio Mingozzi, Daria Nicolodi, Ania Pieroni, Eva Robins, Gianpaolo Saccarola, Ippolita Santarelli, John Saxon, Michele Soavi, Carola Stagnaro, John Steiner, Francesca Viscardi and Lara Wendel
AKA: El Placer del Miedo [The Pleasure of Fear]; Sotto gli Occhi dell'Assassino [Beneath the Eyes of the Murderer]; Tenebrae [Darkness]; Tenebres [Darkness]; Unsane
Approximately 101m; Color
DVD0: Tenebre [ABE; 101m; LBX]; DVD2: Tenebrae [NOU; 105(101)m]; VHS1: Tenebre [ABE; 101m; LBX]; Tenebrae [COL; 101m; LBX; Japanese subtitles]; Unsane [FOV; 91m]

While visiting Rome, a mystery writer (Anthony Franciosa), both hailed and lambasted for his violent work, has to confront the fact that a madman is using his latest book, Tenebre, as a blueprint to commit a series of brutal murders.

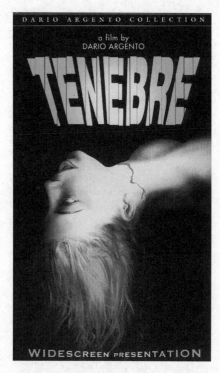

DARIO ARGENTO COLLECTION
a film by
DARIO ARGENTO

TENEBRE

WIDESCREEN PRESENTATION

Video box art for *Tenebre* (1982), Anchor Bay Entertainment.

Having directed two style-laden supernatural shockers (*Suspiria* and *Inferno*, 1977 and 1980, respectively), Argento returned to his roots and created one of the best, most complex giallo thrillers that Italian cinema has to offer. (Just try to ignore the fact that it makes creators of violent material out to be inherently homicidal, and that the killer's impetus is the silliest justification offered in such a film, if you can.) Stylish, gory, and unpredictable, *Tenebrae* is a successful effort in a genre overwrought with pretentious direction, rote brutality, and convoluted storylines, and is surpassed only by the director's own *Profondo Rosso* [Deep Red; 1975].

Due to contractual rights, the film credits the soundtrack to "Simonetti, Pignatelli, and Morante" instead of their group name of Goblin. Also of note, future filmmakers Lamberto Bava and Michele Soavi functioned as assistant directors.

Be wary that earlier American prints (released under the rather silly name of *Unsane*) were butchered by the MPAA, leaving them not only goreless but almost incomprehensible as well.

Tenebres *see* **Tenebre**

La Terreur des Zombies *see* **La Regina dei Cannibali**

Terror at Tenkiller (1987)

United Entertainment Pictures [US]
DIR: Ken Meyer; PRO: Ken Meyer; SCR: Claudia Meyer; DOP: Steve Wacks; EXP: Bill F. Blair; MUS: Bob Farrar
STR: Dale Buckmaster, Jill Holmes, Debbie Killian, Dean Lewis, Stacy Logan, Michele Merchant, Kevin Meyer, Mike Wiles and Freeman Williams
Approximately 87m; Color
VHS1: *Terror at Tenkiller* [UHV; 87m]
ADL: *Just When You Thought It Was Safe to Go on Vacation.*

Yawn. This humdrum melodrama finally kicks in with some slasher elements thirty minutes into the tired proceedings, but these are just as lifeless as the rest of the godforsaken film. There's a fair amount of titillation, but—of course—this doesn't make the film. The only thing to separate this from every other crappy stalk 'n' slasher is the abundance of rubber "Look, Ma ... no bones!" prosthetics, and a soundtrack which consists almost entirely of a looped high-hat cymbal. Truly, truly droll.

Terror at the Opera *see* **Opera**

Terror en el Convento *see* **L'Altro Inferno**

Terror en la Prepa *see* **Splatter University**

The Terror Factor *see* **Scared to Death**

Terror in the Forest *see* **The Forest**

Terror in Toyland *see* **Christmas Evil**

Terror sin Limite *see* **Rosso Sangue**

The Terror Within (1988)

Concorde Pictures [US]
DIR: Thierry Notz; PRO: Roger Corman; SCR: Thomas McKelvey Cleaver; DOP: Ronn Schmidt; MFX: Sara Deal, Nancy Fallace, Bill Forche, Dean Gates, Faron Johnson, Dean Jones, Starr Jones, Ken Lamplugh and Scott Wheeler; SFX: Gregory C. Langerer, Larry Roberts and Steven Wolke; MUS: Richard Conrad
STR: Starr Andreeff, Joal Corso, Al Guarino, Joseph Hardin, Tommy Hinchley, George Kennedy, John la Fayette, Yvonne Saa, Andrew Stevens, Butch Stevens, Roren Sumner and Terri Treas
Approximately 89m; Color
DVD1: *The Terror Within* [NCV; 90(89)m]; VHS1: *The Terror Within* [MUA; 89m]

I'm not going to waste my time with a synopsis; although the setting is a research laboratory in the Mojave Dessert, and the antagonist is a genetic mutation instead of a blood-thirsty extraterrestrial, *The Terror Within* is a shameless retread of *Alien*. Not only are the claustrophobic chases and keynote birth scene reiterated, but, most noticeably, the characters are carbon copies of the players in

Ridley Scott's film, even going so far as to filching mannerisms and entire lines of dialogue from them. (The presence of a token black man and his parroting, mentally deficient sidekick are the most obvious swipes.) In fact, there is *nothing* in the film that *does not* evoke some sense of *déjà vu* in the viewer. (A strobe-lit finale, a similarly staged climax, etc.)

Oh, and the toothy monster is bad even as far as man-in-a-rubber-suit beasties go, and the gore is similarly shoddy, so unless you can't get enough of cut-rate chest-bursters, avoid *The Terror Within* and its sequel.

Tetsuo [Iron Man] (1989)

Kijyu Theatre [Ja]
DIR: Shinya Tsukamoto; PRO: Shinya Tsukamoto; SCR: Shinya Tsukamoto; DOP: Kei Fujiwara and Shinya Tsukamoto; MUS: Chu Ishikawa
STR: Kei Fujiwara, Renji Ishibashi, Nobu Kanaoko, Tomoro Taguchi, and Shinya Tsukamoto
AKA: *Tetsuo—The Iron Man*
Approximately 67m; B&W
DVD0: *Tetsuo—The Iron Man* [IMG; 92(67)m; In Japanese w/English subtitles]; VHS1: *Tetsuo—The Iron Man* [FLV; 67m; In Japanese w/English subtitles]

Tetsuo has been described as everything from "*Terminator* meets *Eraserhead*" to a "low-budget, live-action rip-off of *Akira*." Regardless of its inspiration(s), *Tetsuo* is an entity unto itself, culling together aspects of Transgressive Cinema, cyberpunk and splatterpunk culture, surrealism, and even Kabuki theatre.

The story has *something* to do with a long distance runner who becomes a victim in a hit and run, of sorts, after he performs some disturbing home-style surgery on himself. The couple responsible for the accident tosses his body in a ravine and find themselves inexplicably hot and bothered by the turn of events. Before long, the husband discovers that he has been infected by some sort of bio-mechanical disease, eventually turning into a junkyard version of Marvel Comics' *Iron Man*. His nemesis is the resuscitated runner, who suffers from a similar contagion but is much more in control of his new-found powers.

The film's themes revolve around the ties between sex and violence, alluding to child abuse and—in general—desensitization as probable causes. A cautionary tale, *Tetsuo* does not shy away from nightmarish and disturbing scenes of sexual violence, avoiding the literal for the hallucinatory. Unfortunately, much of this is discarded or trivialized as it careens towards the climax, sacrificing the claustrophobic feel for grander Toho-style escapades. (The finale is so painfully overplayed—the phallic imagery is sure to reach even the most addle-minded viewers—that it comes across as patronizing.)

The budget appears to be both detrimental and its saving grace. Although some of the effects fail miserably because of an underprivileged effects department, ingenuity abounds. One becomes distracted from the not-so-special effects by the sheer power of the camerawork, staging, and editing. As with the works of the most stylized filmmakers, the camera literally comes alive and becomes integral to the material. And let's not forget Ishikawa's score that runs the gamut from free-spirited jazz to pounding,

clanging industrial rhythms (*à la* Einstürzende Neubauten) that is also indivisible from the action.

A truly amazing piece of work.

Tetsuo—The Iron Man *see* **Tetsuo**

Texas Chainsaw 2 *see* **The Texas Chainsaw Massacre 2**

The Texas Chainsaw Massacre 2 (1986)

Cannon Film Group Inc. [US]
DIR: Tobe Hooper; PRO: Yoram Globus and Menahem Golan; SCR: L.M. Kit Carson; DOP: Richard Kooris; EXP: Henry Holmes and James Jorgensen; MFX: Tom Savini; MUS: Tobe Hooper and Jerry Lambert [Soundtrack from I.R.S. Records]
STR: John I. Bloom, Wirt Cain, Chris Douridas, Ken Evert, Kinky Friedman, James N. Harrell, Dennis Hopper, John Martin Ivey, Dan Jenkins, Bill Johnson, Harlan Jordan, Judy Kelly, Barry Kinyon, Bill Moseley, Lou Perry, Jim Siedow, Kirk Sisco and Caroline Williams
AKA: *Masacre en el Infierno* [Massacre in Hell]; *Masacre en Texas 2* [Massacre in Texas 2]; *Texas Chainsaw 2; The Texas Chainsaw Massacre Part 2*
Approximately 100m; Color
DVD1: *The Texas Chainsaw Massacre 2* [MUA; 100m; LBX]; VHS1: *The Texas Chainsaw Massacre 2* [ABE; 95m; LBX]; *The Texas Chainsaw Massacre 2* [MUA; 95m]; *The Texas Chainsaw Massacre Part 2* [MHE; 101(100)m]
ADL: *After 10 Years of Silence, the "Buzz" Is Back!*

Thirteen years after the events in *The Texas Chain Saw Massacre*, the Sawyer family is back, making life hell for Stretch, a DJ who inadvertently records the murder of two college students by the cannibals during a call-in request. Meanwhile, a deranged Texas marshall (Dennis Hopper), armed with saws of his own, is hot on their trail.

AFTER TEN YEARS OF SILENCE, THE "BUZZ" IS BACK!

CANNON

.TOBE HOOPER..

THE TEXAS CHAINSAW MASSACRE PART 2

THE CANNON GROUP, INC. PRESENTS
A GOLAN-GLOBUS PRODUCTION A TOBE HOOPER FILM THE TEXAS CHAINSAW MASSACRE PART 2 STARRING DENNIS HOPPER
MUSIC BY TOBE HOOPER AND JERRY LAMBERT CO-PRODUCER TOBE HOOPER EXECUTIVE PRODUCERS HENRY HOLMES AND JAMES JORGENSEN
WRITTEN BY L.M. KIT CARSON PRODUCED BY MENAHEM GOLAN AND YORAM GLOBUS DIRECTED BY TOBE HOOPER
COPYRIGHT © MCMLXXXVI CANNON FILMS, INC. AND CANNON INTERNATIONAL, B.V.

© CANNON

HORROR

Video box art for *The Texas Chainsaw Massacre 2* (1986), Cannon Video.

Instead of reiterating the previous film, director Hooper makes the wise decision to take an entirely different approach, turning the inevitable sequel into an over-the-top black comedy. Granted, some of the jokes are a bit stale by this point in time—many of them swiped from such films as *Motel Hell* (1980), which were caricatures of *The Texas Chain Saw Massacre* to begin with—but Hooper still manages to scrape up enough verve to make them funny. Unfortunately, one still pines over the decision, even in light of the sequels' failure to capture the initial film's success.

Jim Siedow is the only actor from the first film to reprise his role the second time out (as the Cook, now referred to by his given name of Drayton Sawyer), and—as the most coherent of the lot—is given the chore of running the family business ("the Last Round-Up Rolling Grill," which is recognized statewide for their chili). Bill Johnson replaces Gunnar Hansen as Leatherface, whose brutal veneer has been softened by viewer sympathy, thanks to his "interest" in Stretch (Caroline Williams). The Hitchhiker's character has been replaced by his similarly buggy sibling (Bill Moseley), a Vietnam vet who apparently was stationed overseas while the incidents in *The Texas Chain Saw Massacre* were taking place. And last but not least, Grandpa is back, looking a little less peaked than he did before, and a little more eager to bash in some heads.

Gore is gratuitous and ranges from excellent to downright shoddy. (One wonders if Savini's heart was really in it by this point in time.) The addition of some sexual tension—due to late bloomer Leatherface and his crush on the harassed DJ—makes for some disturbing moments, and contributed to its limited theatrical run, being jerked from national release after opening in Los Angeles and New York. Although unsubstantiated, many feel that it would have received an X rating had it been submitted to the MPAA because of certain cinematic taboos, and that its unrated status hindered it from being financially successful. (One local newspaper cited the film as being "irresponsible and morally corrupt," stating "that it may be the single best argument for censorship," and even erroneously claiming that Williams is "raped with a chain saw." So much for objective reporting.)

Also of interest, film reviewer-cum-trash film icon Joe Bob Briggs (*né* John I. Bloom) made a cameo as a victim, but his scenes were left on the cutting room floor. Better luck next time, Joe Bob.

Again, disappointing, but a worthy film in its own right. (If only they'd cut out the silly-ass finale. Geez.)

The Texas Chainsaw Massacre III
see **Leatherface—The Texas Chainsaw Massacre III**

The Texas Chainsaw Massacre—A Family Portrait (1988)

Doornail Films [US]
DIR: Brad Shellady; PRO: Brad Shellady; SCR: Brad Shellady
STR: Forrest J Ackerman, Chas Balun, John Dugan, Gunnar Hansen, Edwin Neal and Jim Siedow
Approximately 70m; Color [Shot on video]
VHS1: *The Texas Chainsaw Massacre—A Family Portrait* [MTI Home Video; 70m]

"In 1974 Tobe Hooper unleashed a film that was an intense study of homicidal madness and psychological horror. It has since become a cult phenomenon and the most successful independent horror film ever made. This is the first-ever comprehensive documentary on the making of this landmark film. It includes in-depth interviews with Gunnar (Leatherface) Hansen, Edwin (the Hitchhiker) Neal, John (Grandpa) Dugan and Jim (the Cook) Siedow. Including footage from the film and never

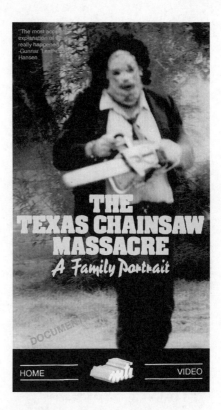

Video box art for *The Texas Chainsaw Massacre—A Family Portrait* (1988), MTI Home Video.

before seen production photos, so sit back and experience the making of a nightmare..."

Needless to say, anyone with an interest in *The Texas Chain Saw Massacre* should track down a copy of this insightful documentary. The recounting of the film's harried production by those who were there make it easy to see why the film captures an intangible intensity that few other movies do, due to the hellish ordeals that the cast and crew had to endure in order to finish the film. (Much of the fear, animosity, and desperation that made it onscreen is little more than a reflection of real emotions prevalent on the plagued set, it seems.) Additionally, it is interesting to discover how the picture ultimately affected the actors' careers, and the amusing anecdotes offered by the cast—especially those told by comedian-at-heart Edwin Neal—should keep the casual viewer from losing interest.

There Was a Little Girl (1981)

Chesham [It/US]
DIR: Ovidio Gabriele Assonitis; PRO: Ovidio Gabriele Assonitis and Peter Shepherd; SCR: Ovidio Gabriel Assonitis, Stephen Blakley, Robert Gandus and Peter Shepherd; DOP: Roberto d'Ettorre Piazzoli; MUS: Riz Ortolani
STR: Janie Baker, Richard Baker, Allison Biggers, Joe Camp, Don Devendorf, Doug Dillingham, Trish Everly, Jerry Fujikawa, Morgan Hart, Edith Ivey, Michael McRae, Dennis Robertson and Huxsie Scott
AKA: *And When She Was Bad*; *Flesh and the Beast*; *Hullujenhuone*; *Madhouse*
Approximately 94m; Color
VHS1: *Madhouse* [MHE; 90(93)m]
ADL: *Many People Visit ... No One Ever Leaves.*

A teacher reluctantly visits her hospitalized twin sister (suffering from sclerosis, neurofibromitosis, and some serious mental problems, to boot) who had tortured her unmercifully while growing up together. Shortly thereafter, and only days before their mutual birthday, the crazed and disfigured woman escapes, eager to pick up where she left off before being put away. With a little help from her trusty rottweiler, of course.
   Despite the fact that *There Was a little Girl* is a US production, it's quite obvious from square one that it was helmed by a predominantly Italian crew. (The spaghetti stains are unmistakable.) Production values are

good, with an emphasis on style, and there are a few unexpected, *giallo*-like twists thrown in for good measure. Characterization is adept, save for a few unsightly stereotypes and some overacting on the part of the film's psychopaths. The gore is passably executed, although the fake dog effects are particularly bad.
   Even with a scene blatantly lifted from *Happy Birthday to Me* (among others), and a scenery-chewing maniac who needs to give it a rest with the nursery rhymes, this is by far one of Assonitis' better efforts, and helps boost his rather weak track record.

The Thing (1982)

Universal Pictures [US]
DIR: John Carpenter; PRO: David Foster and Lawrence Turman; SCR: Bill Lancaster [Based on the short story "Who Goes There?" by John W. Campbell, Jr.; movie novelization, by Alan Dean Foster, from Bantam Books]; DOP: Dean Cundey; EXP: Wilbur Stark; MFX: Rob Bottin; SFX: Roy Arbogast; VFX: Albert Whitlock; MUS: Ennio Morricone
STR: A. Wilford Brimley, T.K. Carter, Anthony Cecere, David Clennon, Keith David, Richard A. Dysart, Larry J. Franco, Charles Hallahan, Kent Hays, Larry Holt, Nate Irwin, Melvin Jones, Peter Maloney, Eric Mansker, Richard Masur, Denver Mattson, Donald Moffat, Joel Polis, Clint Rowe, Kurt Russell, Ken Strain, Thomas G. Waites, Rock Walker, Robert Weisser, Jerry Wills and William Zeman
AKA: *Das Ding aus ein Anderen Welt* [The Thing from Another World]
Approximately 108m; Color
DVD1: *The Thing* [CTS; 108m; LBX]; *The Thing* [UNI; 108m; LBX]; VHS1: *The Thing* [MCA; 108m]; *The Thing* [UNI; 108m; LBX]; VHS2: *The Thing* [FFV; 103m]
ADL: *The Ultimate in Alien Terror.*

An outpost in the Antarctic discovers the remains of an alien crash buried in the ice. Most unfortunate for them is that this remake of Christian Nyby's 1951 film is fairly true to the source material, so instead of a giant bloodthirsty carrot played by James (*Gunsmoke*) Arness, the critter they must fight is essentially a parasitic contagion which eventually absorbs its hosts and has the ability to mimic their properties at any given time.

Screw Leonard Maltin and every other mainstream film critic who sum up this film as being a simple display of gross-out effects. Sure the script has its fair share of holes, and the cast has—on occasion—difficulty with the awkward dialogue; but *The Thing* stands as not only Carpenter's most ambitious film, but also one of those few horror movies that gets to the very root of the genre's namesake. The themes encompass xenophobia (re: *Alien*), paranoia (re: *Invasion of the Body Snatchers*), humankind's tenuous relationship with the flesh (re: any number of David Cronenberg films), disease (re: *The Andromeda Strain*), and the list goes on. (One can even look at it as a heavily veiled play on infidelity, if they'd like.) Even more specific, there's the fear of isolation, of the unknown, of ... well, you name it. *The Thing* manages to strike so many chords that it is bound to disturb even the most phobia free individual at some point.

Of course, many people may be distracted by the effects, some of the best ever conceived by Rob Bottin. Sure, they falter at times, but when one takes into consideration the scope of the film, how imaginative (and surreal) the images are, and just how extensive the effects work was, *The*

Thing is almost beyond reproach. (Unfortunately, innumerable films have since copped the amorphic monster formula, but without the talent or imagination of a Bottin backing them up, they simply become the type of fare Leonard Maltin ballyhooed this as.)

On hand for the fun is Kurt Russell, A. Wilford Brimley (that guy from the voluminous Quaker Oats commercials), and Carpenter's wife Barbeau donating her vocal talents as a chess-playing computer.

Das Tier *see* **The Howling**

Titan Find (1984)

Titan Productions Inc. [US]
DIR: William Malone; PRO: William G. Dunn, Jr., and William Malone; SCR: William Malone and Alan Reed; DOP: Harry Mathias; EXP: Moshe Diamant and Ronnie Hadar; MFX: Bruce Zahlava; SFX: Michael McCracken; VFX: The L.A. Effects Group Inc.; MUS: Thomas Chase and Steve Rucker
STR: Earle Dugan, Michael Griswold, Stan Ivar, Robert Jaffe, Thomas C. James, Klaus Kinski, Marie Laurin, Annette McCarthy, Jim McKeny, David Moses, Buckley Norris, Diane Salinger, Wendy Schaal, Eileen Seeley, Ashit Shah, Jeff Solomon, John Stinson, Bud Walker and Lyman Ward
AKA: *Creature*; *Créature* [Creature]
Approximately 94m; Color
DVD1: *Creature* [DIA; 94m]; VHS1: *Creature* [MHE; 100(94)m]

"In a competition for new materials and advance manufacturing techniques, two multi-national corporations have invested heavily in space. The rival firms of Richter Dynamics (West Germany) and NTI (USA) are locked in a fierce race for commercial supremacy." With this out of the way, the film cuts to Titan, where two astronauts have discovered

Nominated as
Best Horror Film of 1984
by the Academy of Science Fiction,
Fantasy and Horror Films.
CREATURE features stunning
special effects by Doug Beswick
(STAR WARS, THE EMPIRE STRIKES BACK).

Video box art for *Titan Find* (1984), Media Home Entertainment.

a structure that dates back at least 200,000 years. They inadvertently wake up a none-too-happy critter, which makes short work of them with its innumerable teeth. A search team is sent to find the "missing" explorers, and they find themselves not only dealing with a hungry extraterrestrial but a buggy German competitor (Klaus Kinski) as well.

Besides lots of grue (most of it not half bad), *Titan Find* is obviously yet another *Alien* knock-off that shamelessly lifts as many plot devices as copyright laws will allow. Even the toothy alien bears a striking resemblance—more so than most—to H.R. Giger's groundbreaking creation, al-

though *Titan Find*'s unimaginative foam rubber beastie doesn't have anything on Gigcr's progeny.

The film's only other point of interest is the presence of Kinski offering yet another on-edge performance. It's a long way from Werner Herzog's *Aguirre—The Wrath of God* (1972), to be sure, but it's no less fun watching him chew the scenery. Otherwise, *Titan Find* will only interest fans of second-rate xenophobia fare.

The film was nominated as Best Horror Film of 1984 by the Academy of Science Fiction, Fantasy and Horror Films, for what it's worth.

Der Todesking [The Deathking] (1989)

JB Films [WG]
DIR: Jörg Buttgereit; PRO: Manfred O. Jelinski; SCR: Jörg Buttgereit and Franz Rodenkirchen; DOP: Manfred O. Jelinski; MUS: The Angelus, Hermann Kopp, Daktari Lorenz and John Boy Walton
STR: Susanne Betz, Gerd Breitung, Ingo Büsing, Jörg Buttgereit, Andreas Döhler, Heinrich Ebber, Dirk Felsenheimer, Daniela Geburtig, Angelika Hoch, Manfred O. Jelinski, Bärbel Jütte, Alexander Kiersch, Hermann Kopp, Michael Krause, Gudrun Kromrey, Eva M. Kurz, Harald Lundt, Nicholas Petche, Mark Reeder, Franz Rodenkirchen, Hille Saul, Simone Spörl, Ades Zabel and Eddi Zacharias
Approximately 72m; B&W and Color
ꙮ ꙮ ꙮ
VHS1: *Der Todesking* [FTV; 74(72)m; In German w/English subtitles]; VHS2: *Der Todesking* [SCR; 72m; In German w/ English subtitles]

A chain letter encouraging people to commit suicide is the keynote linking together a series of unrelated vignettes, all dealing with mortality and—more specifically—taking one's own life. To add something akin to chronology, these segments are la-

DER TODESKING

A MANFRED O. JELINSKI PRESENTATION
A JÖRG BUTTGEREIT FILM
DER TODESKING (THE DEATHKING)
WITH: HERMANN KOPP, HEINRICH EBBER, MICHAEL KRAUSE, EVA KURZ, ANGELIKA HOCH, NICHOLAS
PETSCHE · DIRECTOR: JÖRG BUTTGEREIT · STORY: FRANZ RODENKIRCHEN & J. BUTTGEREIT
ASST. DIRECTOR: FRANZ RODENKIRCHEN · CAMERA: MANFRED O. JELINSKI · MUSIC: DAKTARI
LORENZ, JOHN BOY WALTON, HERMAN KOOP

Video box art for *Der Todesking* (1989),
Film Threat Video.

beled as different days of the week, although time itself is completely disregarded except as a means to an end.

This under appreciated film walks a fine line between art and exploitation, even more so than the necrophilic epics which garnered German filmmaker Buttgereit a cult following. *Nekromantik* and—especially—*Nekromantik 2* could claim to being much more than simple gross-out horror films, but they are not nearly as thought-provoking or evocative as *Der Todesking*, and the cinematic transgressions that this movie dishes up are more easily justified. To accompany the unsettling material, Buttgereit and his cohorts Jelinski and Rodenkirchen extend their proclivities for experimental camera-

work, and capitalize on a stream of consciousness–style approach that is only hinted at in their earlier work. (This imbues the film with a dreamlike essence, and is essential in capturing the abstractions that a more traditional approach would have forfeited.) The picture is also graced with one of the most evocative scores ever conceived, powerful despite its sometimes-minimalist approach, which helps to capture the naïve, almost child-like perception of death that punctuates the proceedings.

And, yes, there's gore. Although not as over the top as his other efforts, Buttgereit does exercise his penchant for excess herein. The most amazing shot is the time-lapse disintegration of a corpse, the remains being stripped by maggots, that is used to bridge the aforementioned vignettes. Although not entirely realistic, it is quite convincing in spots, and sparked a rumor that a real corpse was used to accomplish the sequence. (How the effects were achieved can be seen in *Corpse Fucking Art*, a documentary that is further recommended to anyone interested in the director's oeuvre.) There are other scenes that will command the attention of gorehounds everywhere as well—one of the more unsettling instances being an emasculation performed by an Ilsa-clone and a handy pair of hedge trimmers—but these are all secondary to the material itself.

If you are at all interested in transgressive cinema, or intelligently written post-modern horror, I suggest you seek out *Der Todesking* (as well as any of Buttgereit's other full-length feature films). You won't be disappointed.

Toxic

Too Beautiful to Die *see* Sotto il
Vestito Niente 2

The Toxic Avenger (1984)

Troma Inc. [US]

DIR: Michael Herz and Lloyd Kaufman; PRO: Michael Herz and Lloyd Kaufman; SCR: Joe Ritter; DOP: Lloyd Kaufman and James A. Lebovitz; MFX: Jennifer Aspinall and Tom Lauten; MUS: Delmar Brown and Various Artists

STR: Jennifer Baptist, Mitchell Cohen, Andrew Craig, Reuben Guss, Doug Isbecque, Patrick Kilpatrick, Charles Lee, Jr., Sarabel Levinson, Chris Liano, Cindy Manion, Andree Maranda, Dick Martinsen, Al Pia, Norma Pratt, Robert Prichard, Michael Russo, Pat Ryan, Jr., Gary Schneider, Ryan Sexton, Dan Snow, Larry Sutton, Marisa Tomei, Mark Torgl, David Weiss and others.

AKA: *El Vengador Toxic* [The Toxic Avenger]

Approximately 82m; Color

DVD1: *The Toxic Avenger* [TRO; 90(82)m]; DVD2: *The Toxic Avenger* [TRO; 76m]; VHS1: *The Toxic Avenger* [MHE; (90)82m]; *The Toxic Avenger* [TRO; 90(82)m]; VHS2: *The Toxic Avenger* [TRO; 76m]

ADL: *Warning! Explosively Funny. May Cause Irritation to the Excessively Serious.*

Kickdog Melvin, a geeky janitor at a gym, is exposed to toxic chemicals during a vicious practical joke and mutates into an egg-faced muscle-bound superhero that—quite literally—rends bad guys limb from limb.

Unfortunately, *The Toxic Avenger* is the pinnacle of Troma's trademarked humor; pretty sad considering that this is the first in a *looong* catalog of titles to their credit. It has its moments, but most of it is painfully sophomoric, including the over the top but often comical gore. Be warned, though, that *The Toxic Avenger* is

available in both uncut and cut R-rated editions.

Much easier to appreciate once one has had the displeasure of sitting through the inevitable sequels. With Oscar nominee Marisa Tomei in an uncredited cameo as a health club extra.

The Toxic Avenger—Part II (1988)

Troma Inc. [US]

DIR: Michael Herz and Lloyd Kaufman; PRO: Michael Herz and Lloyd Kaufman; SCR: Lloyd Kaufman and Gay Partington Terry; DOP: James A. Lebovitz; MFX: Kelly Gleason, Joel Harlow and Roy Knyrim; SFX: Pericles Lewnes; MUS: Barrie Guard

STR: Eric Alan, Keith Allen, John Altamura, Fernando Antonio, W.E. Benson, Paul Borgese, Rick Collins, Jack Cooper, Felix Cortes, Sylvester Covin, Alex Cserhart, Paul Davis, William Decker, Michael Drummer, Theresa Faw, Ron Fazio, Bill Ferris, Joe Fleishaker, Marc Fusile, Bonnie Garvin, Lisa Gaye, Marc Allan Ginsberg, Florence Gummersbach, Thomas Harding, Sloane Herz, Arthur Jolly, Mayako Katsuragi, Charlotte Kaufman, Lily Hayes Kaufman, Lisbeth Kaufman, Patricia Kaufman, Karen King, Frank Kramer, Phoebe Legere, Michael Leoce, Sal Lioni, Didi Mancuso, Traci Mann, Carol Mazzei, Doug McDonald, Emmy Meyer, Matt Miller, John Mollica, Benny Nieves, Melissa Osborne, Bryan Perkins, Kariim Ratcliff, Phil Rivo, Erika Schickel, Tsutomu Sekine, Shinoburyo, Raven Skye, Dan Snow, Irene Scase Summerville, Roy Sundance, Elliot Weiss, Helen Wheels, Michael White, Susan Whitty, Andrew Wolk, Doug Wright, Rikiya Yasuoka, Jeremiah Yates and others.

Approximately 96m; Color

DVD1: *The Toxic Avenger—Part II* [TRO; 96m]; DVD2: *The Toxic Avenger— Part II* [DIG; 80m]; VHS1: *The Toxic Avenger—Part II* [WAR; 96m]; *The Toxic Avenger—Part II* [TRO; 96m]

I don't think I can properly verbalize just how dang bad this sequel

Japanese one-sheet for *The Toxic Avenger—Part II* (1988).

is. Any wit that the original film managed to scrape up (a proven scarcity in Troma films in general) is long gone. It is difficult to see how any viewer with their faculties intact could *not* be offended by the affront to their sensibilities, or how anyone with any self respect could keep down the condescending gags (a fitting term in this case) shoved down their throats by the screenwriters.

Me? I stopped the tape about a third of the way in and fast-forwarded to the end, so I may not be the best person to critique it. (Had I actually sat through it in its entirety, I might've been more inclined to say something less than flattering.)

Tasteless juvenilia, at best.

The Toxic Avenger Part III— The Last Temptation of Toxie (1989)

Troma Inc. [US]
DIR: Michael Herz and Lloyd Kaufman; PRO: Michael Herz and Lloyd Kaufman; SCR: Lloyd Kaufman and Gay Partington Terry; DOP: James A. Lebovitz; MFX: Kelly Gleason, Joel Harlow and Roy Knyrim; SFX: Pericles Lewnes; MUS: Christopher Demarco
STR: Eric Alan, Orentha Alava, Keith Allen, John Altamura, Fernando Antonio, W.E. Benson, Paul Borgese, Edward Burrows, Rick Collins, Sylvester Covin, Paul Davis, William L. Decker, Sophia Domoulin, Jessica Dublin, Paul Eagle, Ron Fazio, Joe Fleishaker, Kathleen Foster, Marc Fusile, Bonnie Garvin, Lisa Gaye, Marc Allan Ginsberg, Florence Gummersbach, Sandra Hataley, Arthur Jolly, Michael J. Kaplan, Karen King, Phoebe Legere, Michael Leoce, Pericles Lewnes, Sal Lioni, Dee Dee Mancuso, Traci Mann, Jim McCluskey, Doug McDonald, Matt Miller, Benny Nieves, Melissa Osborne, Bryan Perkins, Joey Pisoni, Kariim Ratcliff, Phil Rivo, Ara Romanoff, Brian Sanet, Raymond Seiden, Tsutomu Sekine, Raven Skye, Dan Snow, Roy Sundance, Jerry Valle, Helen Wheels, Michael White, Susan Whitty, Ichiro Yamanak, Jeremiah Yates and others.
Approximately 103m; Color
DVD1: *The Toxic Avenger Part III— The Last Temptation of Toxie* [TRO; 86m]; DVD2: *The Toxic Avenger Part III— The Last Temptation of Toxie* [DIG; 98m]; VHS1: *The Toxic Avenger Part III— The Last Temptation of Toxie* [VES; 103m]; *The Toxic Avenger Part III— The Last Temptation of Toxie* [WAR; 103m]

Since the films were made back to back, refer to my review for *The Toxic Avenger—Part II*. (I've already wasted more than enough space just giving everyone involved their "dues.")

Toxic Spawn *see* **Alien Contamination**

Toxic Zombies *see* **The Blood Eaters**

Treasure of the Living Dead *see* La Tumba de los Muertes Vivientes

Le Trésor des Morts Vivants *see* L'Abime des Morts-Vivants

Truth or Dare? (1986)

Gaff Productions [US], Peerless Films [US], Twisted Illusions Inc. [US]

DIR: Yale Wilson; PRO: Yale Wilson; SCR: Tim Ritter; DOP: Christopher M. Burritt and Ned Miller; EXP: Geoffrey L. Miller and Steven R. Weitzman; MFX: Steve Prouty; SFX: Bob Shelley and Special Effects International; MUS: Johnny Britt and Ken Karlson

STR: Terrence Andreucci, Jere Beery, Michael Bellefeuille, Christopher Bontempo, John Brace, Margaret Carbone, Raymond Carbone, Jon Creamer, Richard K. Day, Kelly Dreber, Baby Duff, Christine Duff, Jennifer Duff, Priscilla Duff, Christine Efstathion, Edward L. Elliott II, Therese C. Elliott, Mary Fanaro, Asbestos Felt, Cynthia Frisch, Jim Frisch, Ted Frisch, Robert Gann, Valerie Gobos, Dash Goff, Bruce Gold, Mona Jones, Lydia Krino, Alexander J. McLean, Geoffrey L. Miller, Rick Paige, Bruce Paquette, Wendy Ritter, Angelina Rodell, Norm Rosenbaum, Rachel Rutz, Joe Scheurer, Tami Smith, Si Stillerman, Anthony T. Townes, Kerry Ellen Walker, Pam Weitzman, Scott Weitzman, Timothy Wellman and Joel D. Wynkoop

AKA: *Truth or Dare? A Critical Madness*

Approximately 87m; Color

VHS1: *Truth or Dare? A Critical Madness* [PEE; 90(87)m]

A man prone to nervous breakdowns finds his wife cheating on him with his best friend. While running from his problems, he hooks up with a hitchhiker who engages him in a rather brutal game of "Truth or Dare?" Turns out, she's just a figment of his imagination, and he's thrown away for a year. Due to overcrowding at the institution, he's released, whereupon he takes his revenge. Put

away for a second time, he decides to stick around long enough so as to excel in metal shop, forging himself a rather cheesy copper mask. An opportunity to escape comes his way, and it's *Halloween* revisited.

This is a pointless exercise in derivative filmmaking that boasts abysmal editing, sub-par acting, and similarly lacking effects. The repetitive synth score (Philip Glass has nothing on these guys) is occasionally broken by some nice piano work, but the end theme ("Critical Madness") will make you wish you had muted the film altogether.

But, hey, it's fun just to see people wearing underwear while in the full throes of sexual intercourse. (Avoiding gratuitous nudity is one thing, but c'mon people...)

Yet another "Save the Celluloid" nomination.

Truth or Dare? A Critical Madness *see* Truth or Dare?

La Tueur de la Pleine Lune *see* Un Delitto Poco Comune

La Tumba de los Muertos Vivientes [The Tomb of the Living Dead] (1981)

Marte Films Internacionale S.A. [Sp]

DIR: Jesús Franco Manera; PRO: Miguel Tudela; SCR: Marius Lesœur; DOP: Juan Soler Cozar; SFX: Richard Green; MUS: Fabio Vill

STR: Miguel Aristu, Juan Soler Cozar, Eduardo Fajardo, Manuel Gélin, Albino Graziana, France Jordan, Javier Malza, Antonio Mayans, Doris Regina and Lina Romay

AKA: *El Desierto de los Zombies* [The Desert of the Zombies]; *Treasure of the Living Dead*

Approximately 84m; Color

Before continuing, you need to read my review for *L'Abîme des Morts-Vivants*. Why? Technically, they're different films, but both were shot simultaneously, utilizing the same script, same sets, and recycling the same crappy zombie footage (though they do boast different sets of actors in the starring roles). Otherwise, it's the same gosh darn film. Even comparing the two back to back, I had difficulty differentiating the two. The only noticeable deviation is that *L'Abîme des Morts-Vivants* has a *little* more gore and *some* nudity (which doesn't even add up to a minute's worth of footage in and of itself).

So, unless you want to see the same damn movie twice (and are extremely masochistic to boot), I suggest you avoid this mess altogether. (Luckily, the film is so scarce that your chances of stumbling upon it are nil.)

Twilight of the Dead *see* **Paura nella Città dei Morti Viventi**

Twisted Issues (1988)

Twisted Films [US]
DIR: Charles Pinion; PRO: Charles Pinion; SCR: Steve Antczak, Hawk and Charles Pinion; DOP: Charles Pinion and Lisa Soto; SFX: David Peck; MUS: Various Artists
STR: Debra Althea, Steve Antczak, Pete Brightman, Jennifer Canal, Jorge Cervera, Coop, Pam Gauthier, Robyn Goodkind, Sam Gough, Michelle Gould, Rachel Guinan, Hawk, Ross Jones, Paige Kelly, Robert Marvin, Clif Nelson, Tom Nordlie, K.P., David Peck, Bill Perry, Lausanne Phillips, Walt Pressley, Karin Roach, Lisa Soto, Paul Soto, Chuck Speta and Vic Wilkinson
Approximately 84m; Color [Shot on video] ʞ ʞ ʞ

Some kid with a video camera got all of his skateboarding friends together to make a horror film about a loser whose TV tells him to kill people. (Another gets his faced all mussed up, and is so distraught that he nails his feet to his trusted skateboard, unsuccessfully.) Somehow, the filmmakers manage to drag out this ballyhoo for over an hour, if only because much of the film focuses on the aforementioned pinheads either sitting in a car and getting drunk, or sitting on a couch and getting stoned.

This has to be the most incompetent, no-talent shot on video production I've seen to date. (Even the people behind such dreck as *Re-Animator Academy* had *some* grasp of Filmmaking 101.) The photography, editing, sound ... *everything* is utterly abysmal. The gore effects are about as shocking as runny eggs, and the actors are convincing as skateboarding losers only because, well, they are. The director *did* manage to improve his "craft" with such later efforts like *Red Spirit Lake*, but if you've seen *Twisted Issues*, you'll know just how moot a point that is.

Twisted Souls (1985)

Twisted Souls Inc. [US]
DIR: Thomas Doran, Brendan Faulkner and Eugenie Joseph; PRO: Thomas Doran, Franco Fantasia, Brendan Faulkner and Eugenie Joseph; SCR: Thomas Doran, Franco Fantasia and Brendan Faulkner; DOP: Robert Chappel, C.W. Cressler, Franco Fantasia and Ken Kelsch; MFX: Jennifer Aspinall, Gabriel Bartalos, Arnold Gargiulo, Jr., and Vincent J. Guastini; SFX: John Dods; MUS: James Calabrese and Kenneth Higgins
STR: Gabriel Bartalos, John Beatty, Pat Wesley Bryan, Peter Dain, Joan Ellen Delaney, Peter Delynn, Robert Epstein, Lisa

Friede, Nick Gionta, James M. Glenn, Peter Iasillo, Jr., A.J. Lowenthal, Al Magliochetti, Kim Merrill, Alec Nemser, Soo Paek, Maria Pechukas, Dan Scott, Charlotte Seely, Anthony Valbiro, Felix Ward and others.
AKA: *Spookies*
Approximately 85m; Color
VHS1: *Spookies* [SON; 85m]
ADL: *A Demonic Game of Hide-and-Seek ... a Night of Unrelenting Terror...*

Twisted Souls amounts to little more than some nonsense about an old house superintended by a sorcerer and a variety of ghosties and ghoulies who do their best to make life a living heck for a bunch of inept actors who—thanks to a hackneyed script—stumble upon the whole frigging mess.

Evoking all the subtlety of Michael Jackson's *Thriller*, the only redeeming feature of this contrived horror flick (which a friend of mine refers to as a "live-action D&D movie," thanks to an endless supply of rooms, each containing a different monster) is the none-so-serious listing of "Zombie Wrangler" in the end credits. Had the innumerable filmmakers (too many cooks spoil the broth, they say) left out the tits and gore, they could have easily passed off this sucker to the *Goosebumps* generation as an entry in that popular book-inspired series. (I'd say R.L. Stine didn't deserve such a crack, but I'd be lying.)

A lame synth score, tacky optical effects, awful stop-motion animation, hideous make-up effects and an abundance of rubbery critters ... how in the hell can I recommend this one? Apparently, *someone* liked it, as it won the 1986 Delirium Award from the International Science Fiction & Film Society at their annual Film Festival.

Oh, wait, did I forget to mention the farting tar monsters?

Über dem Jenseits *see* **L'Aldilá**

Uccelli Assassini [Killer Birds] (1987)

Filmirage [It], Flora Film [It]
DIR: Claudio Lattanzi and Aristide Massaccesi; PRO: Claudio Lattanzi and Aristide Massaccesi; SCR: Daniele Stroppa; DOP: Aristide Massaccesi; SFX: Robert Gould, Harry Harris III and Martin Schwerk; MUS: Carlo Maria Cordio
STR: Leslie Cummins, Lin Gathright, John H. Green, Sal Maggiore, Jr., Brigitte Paillet, Ellis Paillet, Nona Paillet, James Sutterfield, Robert Vaughn, James Villemaire, Timothy W. Watts and Lara Wendel
AKA: *Dark Eyes of the Zombie; Killing Birds; Raptors*
Approximately 92m; Color

A GI returns home to find his wife in bed with another man. Predictably, he is none too happy and knocks off the two of them. A couple with a baby makes the mistake of showing up unannounced, and they too—save for the young child—are slaughtered. Immediately thereafter, the killer is mauled by his own aviary, leaving him a sightless, adoptive father. Years later, a group of college students are given a grant for a study of the ivory-billed woodpecker. Heading the team, of course, is the aforementioned child, all grown up, and their host is none other than Mister Birdman himself. (The young killer's identity is kept secret early on, but only because the casting department didn't want to have to track down a young Robert Vaughn lookalike, I assume.)

Raptors is—bar none—probably the most contrived slasher film I've seen to date. Having realized just how stale all of the stalk 'n' slash conventions really are (despite having already borrowed from other genres, most notably "man vs. nature"), it switches gears two-thirds in and becomes a generic zombie film. (Don't worry ... this revelation had me doing a double-take as well.) The schizoid approach is fleshed out with the help of painfully stilted dialogue, sub-par actors, and the like. (*Raptors* does boast a typically loud Italian score, but—alas—it isn't Goblin.)

The gore is mostly comprised of slashed throats and a particularly messy scene involving one poor sap getting his head and hand caught in a running generator. This scene in itself is worthy of note, but not worth the effort to suffer through the other ninety-one minutes of the film.

The Unborn (1989)

Califilm [US]
DIR: Rodman Flender; PRO: Rodman Flender; SCR: Henry Dominic; DOP: Wally Pfister; EXP: Mike Elliot; MFX: Joe Podnar; MUS: Gary Numan and Michael R. Smith
STR: Brooke Adams, Brad Blaisdell, Elizabeth Burrelle, K. Callan, Jane Cameron, Michael Castagnola, Jerome Coleman, Francis Smalls Collier, Rick Dean, Jonathan Emerson, Angela Estrada, Kathy Griffin, Daryl Haney, Elizabeth Harnett, Jeff Hayenga, Wendy Kamenoff, James Karen, Janice Kent, Lisa Kudrow, Rick Podell, Matt Roe, Adam Simon, Laura Stockman and Jessica Zingali
Approximately 85m; Color
DVD1: *The Unborn* [NCV; 85m]; VHS1: *The Unborn* [CTS; 85m]; *The Unborn* [NCV; 85m]; *The Unborn* [RCA; 85m]

A woman prone to miscarriages is recommended to a doctor who— unbeknownst to his mostly infertile patients—is a genetic engineer whose work is understandably controversial.

This pre-natal *It's Alive!* meets the *Children of the Damned* flick is a passable enough shocker, slick but with just enough gratuitous gore to interest splatterpunks. (The exploding fetuses are almost worth the price of admission alone.) As with similar films, the monster baby effects are poor, making what should have been fairly horrific laughable at best.

Many critics seem to read more into this film than what was probably intended (not that I don't do enough of that myself), but it's still a fairly enjoyable horror movie that at least tries to create some tension without relying entirely on stock shocks.

With Lisa (*Friends*) Kudrow in a small role.

Unhinged (1982)

Anavisio Productions Ltd. [US]
DIR: Don Gronquist; PRO: Don Gronquist; SCR: Don Gronquist and Reagan Ramsey; DOP: Richard Blakeslee; EXP: Dale Farr; MUS: Jonathan Newton
STR: Sara Ansley, Dave Hood, Barbara Lusch, Francine Molter, John Morrison, Laurel Munson, J.E. Penner, Virginia Settle and Bill Simmonds
Approximately 74m; Color
VHS1: *Unhinged* [Lighthouse Home Video; 74m]
ADL: *The Nightmare Begins When You Wake Up...*

Three college girls put their car in a ditch en route to a rock concert, and—rather reluctantly—they find themselves the houseguests of a spinster and her domineering mother. In addition to being wheelchair-bound, the latter is as nutty as a fruitcake. Both women claim that the man of the house was put away in an institution years before, but the girls seem to think otherwise.

Although not a bad film, *Unhinged* is exceptionally slow; the abundance of talking heads actually slackens much of the suspense and tension the film strives to generate. And despite some wonderful plot twists—the above average shock ending being a pleasant surprise—the scriptwriting rarely rises above that of pulp horror, derivative of such films as *Three on a Meathook* (1973). (In the hands of actors any less capable, it might have come across as little more than an H.G. Lewis flick.) As far as production values are concerned, *Unhinged* is average, although the fact that the synth score isn't nearly as grating as most should please even the more discriminate fans.

Surprisingly, the grue—specifically, the staging of the bloodshed—is probably the one thing worth noting above all others. Even as the girls are being picked off (a scythe and a hatchet being the killer's weapons of choice), *Unhinged* is able to keep the rest of the proceedings subdued. This—the fact that the viewer doesn't expect such brutal scenes in a low-key shocker like this—is what makes the gore particularly effective. (The slo-mo abattoir scene is especially nasty, and manages to stand out in an over saturated genre.)

Unfortunately, director Gronquist only made one other film thirteen years later, *The Devil's Keep* (1995), which is disappointing in that *Unhinged* showed so much promise for a debut.

The Unholy (1987)

Team Effort Productions [US]
DIR: Camilo Vila; PRO: Matthew Hayden; SCR: Fernando Fonseca and Philip Yordan; DOP: Henry Vargas; EXP: Wanda S. Rayle, Duke Siotkas and Frank D. Tolin; MFX: Isabel Harkins and Jerry Macaluso; SFX: Christopher Anderson and Movie Magic Emporium; VFX: Bob Keen; MUS: Roger Bellon

STR: Frank Barnes, Xavier Barquet, Susan Bearden, Ned Beatty, Phil Becker, John Boyland, Earleen Carey, Jill Carroll, Ellen Cody, Ben Cross, Jeff d'Onofrio, Anthony Deans, Sr., Anthony Deans, Jr., Norma Donaldson, Nicole Fortier, Peter Frechette, Steven Hadley, Martha Hester, Hal Holbrook, Trevor Howard, Selma Jones, Laur Pivacco, Sandy Queen, Willemina Riley, Claudia Robinson, William Russ, David Sanderson, Joshua Sussman, Alan Warhaftig and Lari White

AKA: *El Anticristo II* [The Antichrist II]

Approximately 102m; Color
VHS1: *The Unholy* [VES; 105(102)m]
ADL: *You Haven't Got a Prayer.*

Ben (*Dark Shadows*) Cross plays Father Michael, a priest who is targeted by demons but survives being pulled through a window and falling twenty-some stories. For his troubles, the archbishop gives him his own parish; ironically, it was previously run by a priest who was murdered by a seductive demon on his own altar. Shortly after settling in, Father Michael hooks up with a girl who works at a "Satanic" club, and who was also somehow involved with his predecessor's demise.

The Unholy has an excellent cast but suffers from lax scriptwriting and lousy effects work (more on that shortly). The script deals not with the struggle between good and evil, as one might surmise, but the contentions between science (psychiatry) and religion (blind faith). Of course, it's a silly supernatural horror flick, so religion wins out as per usual.

Considering the budget this film

obviously had, there is no excuse for the downright shoddy effects the hokum falls back upon. The gore is okay, but the monsters consist of a demon kingshit who looks like a third-rate rip-off of *Prophecy*'s mutant bear, and dwarves in padded suits as his pathetic little minions. Due to the cheesy effects, the "much anticipated" final battle comes across as little more than glorified Coffin Joe shtick.

Engaging, but ultimately disappointing.

Uninvited *(1987)*

Greydon Clark Productions Inc. [US] DIR: Greydon Clark; PRO: Greydon Clark; SCR: Greydon Clark; DOP: Nicholas von Sternberg; EXP: Douglas C. Witkins; MFX: Make-Up & Effects Laboratories Inc.; SFX: A&A Special Effects; MUS: Dan Slider

STR: Cecile Callan, Clare Carey, Greydon Clark, Trevor Clark, Alex Cord, Beau Dremann, Rob Estes, Clu Gulager, Jack Heller, Michael Holden, Toni Hudson, George Kennedy, Eric Larson, Paul Martin, Ron Presson, Gina Schinasi, Shari Shattuck and Austin Stoker

Approximately 90m; color VHS1: *Uninvited* [BMV; 92(90)m] ADL: *Cats Have Nine Lives ... You Only Have One!*

A pussycat escapes from a high security laboratory and is taken in by two women who get hooked up with the mafia through a Wall Street broker. Before long, the adopted kitty is coughing up a fur ball with teeth and poisoned claws that threatens to make short work of the lot of them on an ocean-bound yacht.

Sure, maybe George Kennedy is in top form here as a teen-hating heavy, but this film will forever remain a blight on his acting résumé. *Uninvited* is a ludicrously silly mon-

ster flick whose only charm is in the fact it is so bad, even for exploitation mogul Greydon Clark. (Give me *Satan's Cheerleaders* and *Without Warning* any day, thank you.) This film suffers from abysmal continuity (especially in regards to the creature's size at any given moment), an awful hand puppet–style critter, shoddy gore and abused bladder effects, model in a bathtub miniatures, and the worst overdubbing of cat noises to grace a bad horror film. (Even with its mouth shut the cat never ceases with it's incessant meowing, reminding one of similar *faux pas* made in many adults-only films.)

Viewers should take heed of the title and keep themselves from getting on the guest list.

The Unnamable *(1987)*

K.P. Productions Inc. [US], Yankee Classic Pictures [US]

DIR: Jean-Paul Ouellette; PRO: Jean-Paul Ouellette and Dean Ramser; SCR: Jean-Paul Ouellette [Based on the short story "The Unnamable" by Howard Phillips Lovecraft]; DOP: Tom Fraser; EXP: Paul White; MFX: Art & Magic and R. Christopher Biggs; MUS: David Bergeaud

STR: Laura Albert, Katrin Alexandre, Colin Cox, Alexandra Durrell, Paul Farmer, Eben Ham, Charles King, Nancy Kreisel, Marcel Lussier, Paul Pajor, Mark Parra, Delbert Spain, Mark Kinsey Stephenson, Blane Wheatley and Lisa Wilson

Approximately 87m; Color VHS1: *The Unnamable* [SHV; 87m]; *The Unnamable* [VID; 87m] ADL: *There Are Things on God's Earth That We Can't Explain and We Can't Describe.*

The Unnamable is an adeptly made, but predictable and unsuspenseful, shuttered house horror based loosely on an H.P. Lovecraft story of the same name. Gone are the wonderfully gothic trademarks of the master, having been mostly replaced by the staples of the innumerable teens-in-peril horror flicks. (No amount of in-jokes—references to other Lovecraft stories and characters—can make up for the tired proceedings.)

Technically, *The Unnamable* is reminiscent of Full Moon's semi-gloss fare. Similarly, the gore is pretty average, but occasionally messy enough to catch one's interest. The monster is vaguely interesting; as impressive as the suit may be, though, the actor within should have taken a few minutes to look up the word "subtlety" in the dictionary.

Disappointing considering the source.

The Unsane *see* **Tenebrae**

Vendredi 13 *see* **Friday the 13th**

Vengeance—The Demon *see* **Pumpkinhead**

The Video Dead (1987)

California Limited Partnership [US], Highlight Productions [US], Interstate 5 [US]

DIR: Robert Scott; PRO: Robert Scott; SCR: Robert Scott; DOP: Greg Becker; VFX: Dale Hall Jr.; MUS: Leonard Marcel, Kevin McMahon and Stuart Rabinowitsh

STR: Roxanna Augesen, Bachelor, Vickie Bastel, Douglas Bell, Stephen Bianchi, Don Clelland, Maurice Diller, Garrett Dressler, Rocky Duvall, Anthony Ferrante, Cliff Gardener, Walter Garrett, Thaddeus Golas, Muffie Greco, Diane Hadley, Joanne Jarvis, George Kernan, Melissa Martin, San David McClelland, Al Millan, Jennifer Miro, Jo Ann Peterson, Lory Ringuette, Mark Rosseau, Libby Russler, Michael St. Michaels, Carl Solomon, Jack Stellman, Patrick Treadway and Cliff Watts

Approximately 90m; Color
VHS1: *The Video Dead* [EMB; 90m]

Ludicrous story about ghouls emerging from a TV set (which is always playing the film *Zombie Blood Nightmare*) that is shipped to the wrong address. Yes, that's all, folks.

Although not nearly as condescending as it could have been, *The Video Dead* is still pretty much unwatchable. Bad acting abounds, as does below par production values. There are a few unpredictable turns, and some messy gore, but it's just not worth the hassle. (One funny exchange, though, following the disappearance of Chocolate the poodle, goes something like: "Why don't you calm down... he couldn't have gotten far." "You don't understand. He likes to chase skunks in the woods, and when he finds them he tries to mate with them, only skunks don't like to mate with poodles, so they spray him, and then he *really* gets turned on.")

Definitely fast-forward material, if you're naïve enough to rent it in the first place. In retrospect, I'm beginning to wonder if it was worth George Romero making three of the greatest horror films in recent history; without the "Living Dead" trilogy kick-starting the flesh-eating zombie trend, we might never have been accosted by so much dreck.

Video Violence—When Renting Is Not Enough (1986)

Little Zach Productions [US]
DIR: Gary P. Cohen; PRO: Ray Clark; SCR: Gary P. Cohen and Paul Kaye; DOP: Philip Gary; EXP: James Golff and Salvatore Richichi; MFX: Mark A.S. Dolson, Jodi Halifko and Mark Kwiatek; MUS: Gordon Osview

305   Videodrome

STR: Lori Andres, Bill Biach, Cara Biach, Jennifer Biach, Barbara Brunnquell, Bob Brunnquell, David Christopher, Ray Clark, Lisa Cohen, Ellen Dreyer, Marci Garfinkel, Richard Haig, Kevin Haver, Linda Herman, Richard Johnson, Chick Kaplan, Jerry Kopf, Joseph Kordos, Ricky Kotch, Robin Leeds, Art Neill, Jackie Neill, Karen Oujo, Jo Ann Poll, Paige Price, Bonnie Schedin, Madison Schedin, Gary Schwartz, Judy Seplowin, Susan Speidel, Susan Stern, O. Selig Stokes, Bart Sumner, William Toddie, Uke, Christopher Williams and Mike Yvonne
Approximately 90m; Color [Shot on video]
VHS1: *Video Violence—When Renting Is Not Enough* [CAM; 90m]

Another unnecessary shot-on-video production, this one about "down home" snuff films produced and circulated in a small Midwestern town. (Think *Two Thousand Maniacs,* armed with camcorders.) Production values are standard for '80s home-grown fare; although unwatchable on these terms alone, some of the snuff footage is unnervingly misogynistic, making it even harder to stomach.

Funny, though, that if you replace the violence with hardcore sex, the politics surrounding these snuff films seem to foreshadow the entire amateur XXX video trend that has since become the standard in the adult film industry.

It's *your* brain cells.

Video Violence Part 2—The Exploitation! *see* **Video Violence Two**

Video Violence Two (1988)

Little Zach Productions [US]
DIR: Gary P. Cohen; PRO: Ray Clark; SCR: Gary P. Cohen; DOP: Steven Grossman; EXP: James Golff and Salvatore Richichi; MFX: Mark A.S. Dolson and Mark Kwiatek; MUS: Gordon Osview

STR: Robert F. Amico, Tammy Bowen, Bill Bowers, Barbara Brunnquell, Neil Cerbone, Vivian Chiaramonte, David Christopher, Ray Clark, Lisa Cohen, Michael Dundon, Debbie Forte, Joey Forte, Steven Grossman, Richard Haig, Mavis Harris, Sue Kalitan, Roger Kennedy, David C. Lewis, Robin Lilly, Chris McGarry, Tim McKanic, Elizabeth Lee Miller, Carol Moloney, Paul Morer, Gail Mueller, Art Neill, Jackie Neill, Gordon Osview, Judy Panaccione, Suzanne Schrenell, Mitchell Speert, Susan Speidel, Tom Straffi, Bart Sumner, William Toddie, Uke, Don Weber and Wilbur
AKA: *Video Violence Part 2—The Exploitation!*
Approximately 90m; Color [Shot on video]
VHS1: *Video Violence Part 2—The Exploitation!* [CAM; 90m]

If you thought the original was rank, I strongly suggest you keep upwind from this sucker. Granted, *Part 2* makes a valiant attempt to not cover the exact same ground as *Video Violence,* but it is ultimately nothing more than an extended spoof of talk shows, relying on half-baked satire. Furthermore, the twist ending is unexpected, and the gore is plentiful, but—again—don't mistake my observations as recommendations.

The video box cover claims that this film's predecessor was nominated for Best Drama by the American Film Institute and Billboard in 1987. Maybe if the entire town that was involved in the making of these films cast ballots, it's conceivable; otherwise, methinks some palms were greased.

Videodrome (1982)

Filmplan International II [Ca]
DIR: David Cronenberg; PRO: Claude Héroux; SCR: David Cronenberg; DOP: Mark Irwin; EXP: Pierre David and Victor

Solnicki; MFX: Rick Baker; SFX: Frank Carere; MUS: Howard Shore [Soundtrack from Varèse Sarabande]

STR: David Bolt, Lally Cadeau, Leslie Carlson, Harvey Chao, Bob Church, Jack Creley, Peter Dvorsky, Jayne Eastwood, Henry Gomez, Lynne Gorman, Deborah Harry, Kay Hawtrey, Franciszka Hedland, Julie Khaner, Sam Malkin, Reiner Schwarz, Sonja Smits, David Tsubouchi and James Woods

Approximately 88m; Color

DVD1: *Videodrome* [UNI; 87(88)m; LBX]; VHS1: *Videodrome* [MCA; 89(88)m]; VHS2: *Videodrome* [FFV; 85m]

ADL: *First It Controls Your Mind. Then It Destroys Your Body.*

The executive of a TV station (James Woods) that specializes in "softcore pornography and hardcore violence" discovers a pirate broadcast that transmits on-the-air live snuff footage, and sets out tracking down the source in order to obtain the rights. He soon finds out that the transmissions contain a subliminal signal that provokes the growth of brain tumors upon repeated viewings, leaving the victims suffering from acute hallucinations that wreak havoc with their perception of reality.

By far one of Cronenberg's most complex and experimental works, *Videodrome* was his last film before moving on to more mainstream fare (*The Fly, Dead Ringers*, etc.). The mélange of concepts (snuff films, subliminal messages, conspiracy theories, etc.) works, despite their contrived nature, and helps contribute to the general theme of desensitization. All the while, the escalating dream-like

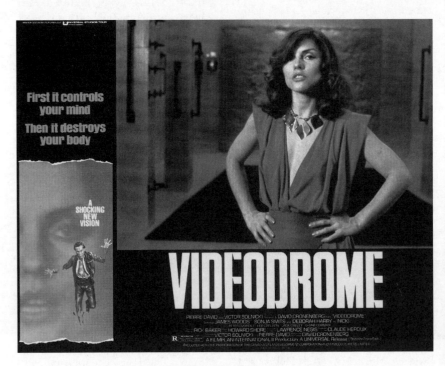

American lobby card for *Videodrome* (1982).

structure of the film blurs the line between reality and "reality" as seen
through the camera's eye, making this
one of the better films to examine the
subject.

The production values are slick,
the performances adept (even from
Blondie vocalist Deborah Harry, who
plays a radio announcer and James
Woods' "lust" interest), and the staging superb. The special effects (supplied mostly by Rick Baker) falter at
times, if only because they're given
too much screen time. The finale—as
nihilistic as one can possibly get—
packs a wallop, and is sure to stick
with the viewer for some time.

One of Cronenberg's most ambitious films... and it shows.

Viernes 13 *see* **Friday the 13th**

Violent Shit (1989)

Blood Pictures [WG], Reel Gore Pro-
ductions [WG]
DIR: Andreas Schnaas; PRO: Andreas
Schnaas; SCR: Andreas Schnaas; DOP:
Stephan Aquilina; SFX: Andreas Schnaas;
MUS: Micky Engels
STR: Stephan Aquilina, Gabi Bäzner,
Christian Biallas, Uwe Boldt, Marco Heg-
ele, Wolfgang Hinz, Werner Knifke, Volker
Mechter, Andreas Schnaas, Lars Warncke,
Bettina X, Maren Y, Beate Z and others.
AKA: *Violent Trash*
Approximately 72m; Color [Shot on
Video]
VHS1: *Violent Shit* [TEM; 75(72)m;
In German]

Well... the name says it all, with
an equal emphasis on both words.

Yes, there is an unbelievable
amount of gore; the viewer can't turn
a corner without having a slop bucket
of fake blood thrown in his/her face.
Is it worth it? One of the more
graphic scenes—amusing for all of the

wrong reasons—depicts a poor chap
who is cut in half, revealing the fact
that he was apparently born with no
internal organs. At least the effects
crew could have stuffed something,
anything into the hollow abdomen;
with all of the blood, viewers would-
n't have been able to differentiate between pig gut and a garden hose, so
even the most rudimentary viscera
would have sufficed. But then again,
had they used the real thing, they
would have taken great pains to make
it as unconvincing as possible.

As for the film's "technical com-
petency," well, shoot... where do I
begin? Whoever was behind the camera took full advantage of the many
obnoxious video effects at their disposal. Apparently, though, they spent
so much time playing with the bells
and whistles that they never had time
to learn how to focus the damn thing.
The editing appears to have been
done on the spot with the selfsame
camera; I'd be surprised if *any* post-
production work was done on the film
besides the credits. And then there's
the script. Referring to the story as
"threadbare" would be a gross understatement. And... the list goes on.
Suffice it to say, it is films like this
that make me truly ashamed to be a
splatterpunk.

Violent Shit. Yes indeed.

Violent Trash *see* **Violent Shit**

I Violentatori della Notte *see*
Prédateurs de la Nuit

Virus (1981) *see* **Inferno dei**
Morti-Viventi

Virus (1982) *see* **Apocalisse Domani**

Vrijdag de 13de *see* Friday the 13th

The Wailing *see* L'Ossessione Che Uccide

Ward 13 *see* Hospital Massacre

Waxwork (1988)

Vestron Pictures Inc. [US]
DIR: Anthony Hickox; PRO: Steffan Ahrenberg; SCR: Anthony Hickox; DOP: Gerry Lively; EXP: Gregory Cascante, Dan Ireland, William J. Quigley and Mario Sotela; MFX: Image Animation; MUS: Roger Bellon
STR: Steffan Ahrenberg, Dana Ashbrook, Edward Ashley, Paul Badger, Joe Baker, Jennifer Bassey, Gary Bettman, Christopher Bradley, Carolyn Bray, Eric Brown, J. Kenneth Campbell, Candy, Clare Carey, Kendall Conrad, Gabriella Dufwa, Dave Elsey, Hilary English, Henrietta Folkeson, Julian Forbes, Deborah Foreman, Zach Galligan, Micah Grant, Kim Henderson, Anthony Hickox, James Hickox, Dan Ireland, Michelle Johnson, James Lincoln, Gerry Lively, Irene Olga Lopez, Patrick Macnee, Thomas McGreevey, Mhaly Meszaros, Ann Sophie Nobley, Buckley Norris, Miles O'Keefe, Leonard Pollack, John Rhys-Davies, Eyal Rimmon, Joanne Russell, Steven Santamaria, Karen Schaffer, Nicole Seguin, Merle Stronck, Cliff Wallace, David Warner, Jack David Warner and Nelson Welch
AKA: *Reise Zurück in die Zeit* [Journey Back in Time]
Approximately 100m; Color
VHS1: *Waxwork* [VES; 100m]
ADL: *More Fun Than a Barrel of Mummies*

A spoiled rich kid and his cardboard cutout buddies are invited to a "private showing" at a waxwork that suddenly appears in a quiet suburban neighborhood. Showing up at midnight, they are ushered in by a midget and one of Lurch's kin, and waste no time in being sucked into the various exhibits. (Let's see, we've got a were-

wolf-plagued countryside, a vampire's castle abode, the tomb of an Egyptian mummy, the Marquis de Sade's infamous boudoir, and a zombie-infested graveyard, the latter being in black and white. Of course, before film's end, a slew of other stock movie monsters are shamelessly abused by the filmmakers as well.)

Straight to the point (as if it actually had one), this contrived offering wastes no time in dishing out dimestore monsters, gore, and even some gratuitous T&A. Highlights include a silly-looking lycanthrope with mechanized ears, a vampire lord who *really* likes to say the words "steak tartar," a mummy that would make Al Adamson proud, an abysmal and painfully inaccurate depiction of de Sade and his infamous "crimes," and an insulting pastiche of Romero's groundbreaking zombie film.

"They'll make a movie about anything nowadays," the waxwork's owner exclaims, a statement that is much more profound than I'm sure even the screenwriter intended.

Although it isn't surprising that the perpetrator of this mess is the director of *Hellraiser III—Hell on Earth*, I can say that *Waxwork* is, at the very least, watchable.

Nightmare in Wax meets *The Monster Club*.

The Weirdo *see* The Weirdo—The Beginning

The Weirdo—The Beginning (1988)

Green Tiger Pictures Inc. [US]
DIR: Andy Milligan; PRO: Neva Friedenn and Kenneth Haker; SCR: Andy Milligan; DOP: Andy Milligan; EXP: Paul

Maslak; MFX: Rodd Matsui; MUS: Michael Meros and Jeff Peters
STR: Lynne Angus, Steve Burington, Nick Butterfield, Lynne Caryl, Kim Clark, Jeff Davidson, Melanie Ewbank, Richard C. Forrest, Bill Grey, Mary Locke, Shari Michaels, Jennifer Erin Morse, Carroll Oden, Robert Peck, Shawn Player, John Rand, Anthony Rinaldi, Dennis Robbins, Janet Roberts, Naomi Sherwood, Jessica Straus, John Taylor, Patrick Thomas, Scot Vandergrift and Julie Winchester
AKA: *The Weirdo*
Approximately 91m; Color
VHS1: *The Weirdo* [RAE; 91m]
ADL: *Not Just Another Love Story…*

Donny is a mentally deficient young man who gets harassed and bullied by just about everyone in town … everyone, that is, except a young crippled girl with whom he falls in love. Even with her at his side, he is inevitably pushed over the edge by, again, just about everyone in town, and ends up killing (mostly out of self defense), uhm, just about everyone in town. Touching, really.

The Weirdo—The Beginning is the only film by trash film auteur Andy Milligan (1929–1991) made after *Carnage* (1983) that has been released on video. Suffice it to say, this is the only one made after Carnage that deserves a proper release. (Having seen them, we should count our blessings that *Surgikill* and *Monstrosity*, 1988 and 1990 respectively, were never made available.)

Technically, *The Weirdo* is quite competent, and by far the pinnacle of a very long, very inauspicious career. Although it is comparable to low end independent fare, it is a testament to a man who spent over twenty years making movies on the most shoestring of budgets. Some of his films are unwatchable, yes, but many sur-

pass their limited resources, and all of them reflected his love for filmmaking.

Twenty years after his first genre film, gore is still a prerequisite. Unlike his other efforts, though, *The Weirdo* seems more a personal statement than an exploitation film. One can't help think that the lead character is a reflection of his creator: a lonely, alienated individual with limited means, and a product of abuse, futilely trying to find acceptance. Milligan's obvious fetishism for period pieces suggests that he already felt out of place, out of synch with the times, and it is probably safe to assume that his homosexuality and abusive upbringing only made him disassociate further. Yet all of this is placed within the confines of exploitation cinema, possibly as a defense mechanism.

Hey, it's a hell of a lot better than *The Ghastly Ones*. Really it is.

Welcome to Spring Break *see* **La Spiaggia del Terrore**

We're Going to Eat You *see* **Diyu Wu-Men**

The Werewolf and the Magic Sword *see* **La Bestia y la Espada Mágica**

White Cannibal Queen *see* **Mondo Cannibale**

Whodunit (1982)
SRN [US]
DIR: William T. Naud; PRO: William T. Naud, Sally Roddy and Tom Spalding; SCR: William T. Naud; DOP: Tom Spalding; MFX: Make-Up Effects Lab; SFX: Image Engineering Inc.; MUS: Joel Goldsmith
STR: Marie Alise, Rick Dean, Ron Gardner, Terry Goodman, Richard Helm,

Video box art for *Whodunit* (1982), Applause Productions Inc.

Jeanine Marie, Red McVay, Gary Phillips, Jim Piper, Dean Richards, Michael Stroka, Bari Suber, Steven Tash and Jim Williams
AKA: *Island of Blood*
Approximately 82m; Color
VHS1: *Island of Blood* [API; 84(82)m]
ADL: *They Come Seeking Fame and Fortune! What They Found Was a Blood Bath!*

A group of struggling actors and musicians (they're struggling *for a reason*, I assure you) are gathered together on an isolated island retreat to make an uplifting film about—*egads*—what's right with the world. Before anyone can belt out a line from "We Are the World," some maniac who takes the lyrics of rock music a little too seriously begins knocking them off in a predictably bloody fashion.

Whodunit is none too exciting, but just different enough to be pass-

ably engaging slasher dreck. The screenwriter tries really hard to flesh out the players, but character devel opment just doesn't seem to be his strong suit. (Apparently, killing off low-rent actors in a perfunctory fashion is, though.) The finale is surprising, but not so much a *whodunit* as a *why*dunit.

Since I've used the "Whodunit? Who cares?" bit on films much more deserving, I'll refrain from reiterating it here, despite the fact that the title itself cries out for such abuse.

The Winged Serpent *see* Q—The Winged Serpent

Witch Story *see* Streghe

Wolf Devil Woman (1982)

Production company unknown [HK]
DIR: Ling Chang; PRO: Tin-Tsu Chang and Tsai-Lai Hsu; SCR: Ling Chang; EXP: I-Shiang Chang
STR: Fung Shek, Ling Chang and Ying Shek
Approximately 92m; Color ❅❅❅
VHS1: *Wolf Devil Woman* [OCS; 92m]

Okay, listen up, because this one's a doozy. *Wolf Devil Woman* opens with a weird ceremony involving a gold statuette, a crucified man, a voodoo doll, a horde of robed beastmen, and—last but not least—a high priest wearing long clip-on nails and a Merlinesque hat (complete with gold sequins and a tacked on felt skull and crossbones). The man is sacrificed via the aforementioned doll and some cheesy effects, christening a newborn girl. The concerned parents decide to grab the kid and leave the isolated temple, but are accosted by the priest's ninja monster squad while making their way down the mountain. Being the good parents they are, they promptly commit suicide, but not before covering the newborn in their own blood (to keep it warm) and head-butting the snow-covered hillside until it causes an avalanche. Wolves perchance upon the scene, eating the parents' corpses but sparing the child. One of the wolves raises the kid as its own, and if you're not already overwhelmed by the film's "complexities," being hit with the realization that you're only ten minutes into this outrageous flick should do the trick.

The child grows up into a feral woman who takes to wearing heavy eyeliner and a stuffed dog on her head. To make things even more outrageous, whenever she gets ticked off, she—quite literally—wigs out, spinning around like TV's *Wonder Woman* until her hair turns white. She runs into two travelers looking for the thousand-year ginseng, and is eventually coaxed into joining them against the aforementioned wizard and his undead legion.

Where do I start? *Wolf Devil Woman* has darn near everything. Stock music from American films (they're especially fond of the same piece used during the helicopter scene in the US edit of *Dawn of the Dead*). Unconvincing chop-socky action with the actors forced to fly through nearly every scene on visible wires. Horrendous dubbing which is the epitome of, well, horrendous dubbing. Animated hocus-pocus. Headache-inducing zooms, and ... what? You don't consider these high points? How about hopping vampires? Human skin lanterns? There's loads of Asian gore: Blood spews, heads and limbs

are ripped from their bodies, faces split open, etc. (Of course, none of it is the least bit convincing, but it's the *thought* that counts.) The attempts at intentional humor are remarkably sad, but once the film puts on a straight face, it's one laugh after the next. (How any of the actors kept a straight face throughout production, I'll never know.) On the down-side, there is geeking galore, so if you're not fond of animal cruelty, I suggest you either have your scan button ready or avoid this film altogether.

Wolf Devil Woman is a trash fiend's wet dream, especially if you like your fare both over-the-top *and* bottom-of-the-barrel.

Woman from Deep River *see* **Cannibal Ferox**

X-Ray *see* **Hospital Massacre**

X-Tro *see* **Xtro**

Xin Tiao Yi Bai *(1987)*

Cheng's Film Production Co. Ltd. [HK]

DIR: Juk-Si Cheng and Lo Kin; PRO: Wan Ka Man and Pak-Man Wong; SCR: Bak-Ming Wong; DOP: James Chan; EXP: Wan Ka Man

STR: Ho-Nam Cheng, Juk-Si Cheng, Philip Cheng, Man-Yuk Cheung, Bonnie Law, Fong Lui, Man Fai Ng, Fui-On Shing, Bak Ming Wong, Ching Wong and Fung Woo

AKA: *Heartbeat 100*
Approximately 88m; Color
VHS1: *Heartbeat 100* [RAI; 88m; In Chinese w/ English subtitles]

A woman kills a bank robbery suspect with a hunting knife while screwing the poor sap, but she's dispatched immediately thereafter by whoever arranged the set-up to begin with. Meanwhile, a TV writer and her two girlfriends take a trip to the small village where the remaining suspects of the bank heist are presumed to be hiding out. A young go-getting cop comes to town looking for the criminals, and hooks up with the girls.

Heartbeat 100 is a consistently interesting crime film that is punctuated by engaging melodrama, some well orchestrated humor, and—at least in the second half—a slew of gory axe murders. The mystery aspects are handled quite well, promising numerous surprises along the way. Production values are slick, so those turned off by low-rent Asian fare will be pleasantly surprised.

Highly recommended for fans of Asian crime and splatter cinema.

Xiong Bang (1981)

Century Motion Picture & Distribution Co. Ltd. [HK]
DIR: Yun Kong Yu; PRO: Chan-Sin Wong; SCR: Kam-Moon Cheung, Ping-Hing Kam and Lee Ten; DOP: Bob Thompson
STR: Juk-Si Cheng, Chin Cheun-Lam, Wah Ngok, Ching Wong and Yu Yi-Ha
AKA: *The Imp*
Approximately 98m; Color
VHS1: *Xiong Bang* [CCC; 98m; In Chinese w/English subtitles]

An out-of-work father-to-be becomes a security officer working graveyard at a high-rise building that may just be haunted. Shortly after finding himself the center of supernatural activity, his few co-workers begin showing up dead, victims of inexplicable accidents. He enlists the aid of a priest (who performs a failed exorcism on the building itself), and discovers that an evil spirit is attempting to reincarnate itself in his unborn child.

Xiong Bang is an engaging drama that loses its foothold once the hokum ensues; from there on out it's fairly traditional Chinese spook show fare with some striking visuals to help carry it through to its conclusion. (The scene where our hero quite literally takes an elevator ride to Hell is creepy, evoking the finale of Lucio Fulci's *L'Aldilá*.) The film isn't nearly as gratuitous as many Hong Kong genre offerings, but it proffers a few explicit scenes (including some very nasty staged surgery footage), as well as some obligatory zombie-like ghosts.

Suggested viewing for Hong Kong horror enthusiasts.

Xtro (1982)

Ashley Productions [UK]
DIR: Harry Bromley-Davenport; PRO: Mark Forstater; SCR: Iain Cassie and Robert Smith; DOP: John Metcalfe; EXP: Robert Shaye; MFX: Francis Coates; SFX: Tom Harris; MUS: Harry Bromley Davenport
STR: Robert Austin, Katherine Best, Danny Brainin, David Cardy, Maryam d'Abo, Robert Fyfe, David Henry, Robert Longdon, Peter Mandell, Anna Mottram, Simon Nash, Philip Pereno, Philip Sayer, Vanya Seager, Susie Silvey, Bernice Stegers, Tik, Tok, James Walker, Arthur Whybrow and Anna Wing
AKA: *X-Tro*
Approximately 83m; Color
VHS1: *Xtro* [EMI; 82(83)m]
ADL: *Some Extra-Terrestials Aren't Friendly.*

A family man is abducted by aliens while lounging around one day; unfortunately for him, they've never seen *Close Encounters of the Third Kind* (1977). Three years later, one of the same BEMs crash lands on Earth and rapes a woman now living in the man's country house, orally-impregnating her. Lucky for her, her term is condensed down to a few short hours, but—not so favorably—she gives birth to a full-grown man, namely the missing father. (That one *had* to hurt.) Eventually, the angst-ridden dad makes his way back to his family, now living in the city, and things start getting *really* funky.

Made in the wake of *Alien* and its innumerable clones, *Xtro* actually avoids most of the staples established by said films. This xenophilic shocker instead trades in the alien cat and mouse antics for hallucinatory shocks, sacrificing logic and reason for the same. Accepting the presence of aliens is one thing, but inexplicable phenomenon like toys coming to life—and becoming full-size—is a little harder to swallow. (One may almost find it worthwhile just to see a homicidal dwarf clown, though.)

Production values are pretty standard for British horror at the time, save for the low-rent make-up and visual effects; there are a few innovative scenes that work to dramatic effect, but most are painfully second-rate. Thankfully, the synth score—as cheesy as it is—compliments the film, and is heads and tails above the sort that usually accompanies most shot on video fare.

Evidently, the British theatrical release of *Xtro* contains a different ending than the one that was offered to American audiences. I'm guessing they've seen enough American fare to know that we can't watch a film unless it has a crappy shock ending to spoil it.

Xtro may not be very good, but at least it *is* something completely different.

Yin Zhong (1986)

Production company unknown [HK]
DIR: Meng-Hua Ho
STR: Ching-Tu Chang and Tsui Sui
AKA: *The Rape After*
Approximately 88m; Color
VHS1: *The Rape After* [OCS; 88m; In Chinese w/English subtitles]

A sleazy photographer steals a cursed statuette, inadvertently letting loose a demon. It rapes and impregnates a young model. (As if she didn't already have enough problems of her own: Her brother suffers from leprosy, and her mother killed her father after he contracted syphilis while sleeping around, stuffing his corpse in a closet in a pathetic attempt to cover up her crime.) Thinking he's the child's father, the photographer takes the model to a back-street abortionist, and the real daddy shows up. Then things get a little messy.

As could be construed from the above synopsis, *Yin Zhong* doesn't shy away from the excesses of Chinese horror fare. Gore is in abundance, and most of it is fairly well executed. (A pregnant corpse is one of the more unnerving props used.) The demon and baby monster effects, though, leave much to be desired. Overall, the production values are decent, with an engaging script to keep the film from losing its focus.

With flesh-eating zombies, frog regurgitation, and Chinese-style brain surgery.

One of the better Hong Kong supernatural shockers.

You Better Watch Out *see* **Christmas Evil**

Yuan Zhen-Xia yu Wei Si-Li [Dr. Yuen and Wisely] (1986)

Golden Harvest [HK]
DIR: Wei-Tsang Lan; PRO: Raymond Chow and Ngai Kai Lam; SCR: I Kuang STR: Ken Boyle, Man-Yuk Cheung, Nina Li Chi, Siu-Hou Chin, Yuen Chor, Yun-Fat Chow, Hu Hui Chung, Joyce Godenzi, Ying-Hung Hui, Yasuaki Kurata, Kam-Kong Tsui, Sau-Lai Tsui, Lung Wei Wang, Dick Wei, Jing Wong and Tung-Shing Yee
AKA: *The Seventh Curse*
Approximately 81m; Color
DVD0: *The Seventh Curse* [TAI; 81m; LBX; In Chinese w/English subtitles]; VHS1: *The Seventh Curse* [TAI; 81m; In Chinese w/English subtitles]; VHS2: *The Seventh Curse* [MIA; 93(81)m]

A medical team goes to Thailand in search of heretofore-unknown medicinal herbs, and perchance upon a tribe that still practices ritual sacrifice. Anyone disputing the high priest's wishes is chewed up by a gooey fetus beastie hiding in his cape. (The critter must've seen *Alien* one too many times, as he obviously enjoys reenacting the infamous chestbursting scene ... the only problem is finding a way to get *inside* the victim in order to pull it off.) Their god is a lich-like creature who has a penchant for—sure enough!—virgins. Once his blood thirst is sated, it metamorphoses into a steroid-ridden, batwinged *Alien* clone. One of the explorers is cursed, but is temporarily cured by a native woman who feeds him part of her breast! He escapes, but a year later the adverse effects of the malady returns, and it's off to Thailand again in order to release him from the spell.

Okay, so where do we start? There's gore galore: One person performs a self evisceration, while another is torn in half like a wishbone by a booby trap; heads are lopped off, others are squashed; young children are crushed to death; and lots of other people are generally mangled by whatever means available. There's chop socky action (with a particularly impressive fight scene staged atop a giant stone Buddha), tacky visual effects, and—the cornerstone of Asian horror—worms. Lots and lots of worms.

Although the gore effects are pretty dang good, the monster effects that punctuate the finale—despite the slick production values—are sad. On the upside, *Yuan Zhen-Xia yu Wei Si-Li* adamantly shies away from the geek show gore that usually sullies Chinese genre fare.

Truly wild stuff.

Het Zaad van Mars see **Alien Contamination**

Zhong Gui (1986)

Shaw Brothers [HK]
DIR: Yang Chuan; PRO: Mona Fong and Ka Hee Wong; EXP: Run Run Shaw STR: Siu-Keung Chiu, Fai Ko and Wong Yun
Approximately 90m; Color
VHS1: *Seeding of a Ghost* [WOR; 90m; In Chinese w/English subtitles]

A grave robbing sorcerer is saved from a lynch mob by a taxi driver; in return for the service, the magician eventually aids the man in taking revenge on not only his wife's lover, but two hooligans who later rape and kill her.

The story may sound pretty typical as far as Asian supernatural revenge films go, but the exceptional characterization—as well as the fact that it surpasses the already extreme limits set by its predecessors—make it easier to recommend than its peers. Not only do we get the prerequisite regurgitation of live insects (mostly worms, in this case) and tacky visual effects (optical, stop-motion animation, etc.), *Zhong Gui* eventually evolves into a brutal monster flick that owes more to Western fare, in particular films like *Alien*. (It is probably no coincidence, then, that some of the soundtrack was flagrantly stolen from that selfsame film.) It also boasts a fair amount of full-frontal nudity—a rarity for Chinese films at the time—just to up the overall sleaze quotient.

Production values are surprisingly good, and there is some nice photography to help offset the sometimes-primitive effects and hokey horror staples.

Originally designed as the third entry in the infamous *Black Magic* series, *Zhong Gui* was released as an unrelated film due to censorship problems its predecessors faced.

An often repulsive, sometimes funny, but always interesting shocker that is sure to please fans of Asian splatter.

Zombi 3 (1988)

Flora Film [It]
DIR: Lucio Fulci and Bruno Mattei; PRO: Franco Gaudenzi; SCR: Claudio Fragasso; DOP: Riccardo Grassetti; MFX: Franco di Girolami; SFX: Tony Ceyl and Joseph Ross; MUS: Stefano Mainetti [Soundtrack from Beat Records]
STR: Deborah Bergamini, Alan Collins, Ottaviano dell'Acqua, Marina Loi, Mike Monty, Ulli Reinthaler, Beatrice Ring, Deran Serafian and Massimo Vanni
AKA: *Zombie 3*; *Zombie Flesh Eaters 2*
Approximately 95m; Color

VHS1: *Zombi 3* [TJV; 90(95)m; LBX; Japanese subtitles]

A scientific experiment yields the "Death-One Compound," a biological weapon that has an interesting side effect. (Okay, so maybe it's not all *that* interesting, in retrospect.) A scientist is exposed to the nasty substance whilst trying to escape the top secret compound where it was created, and winds up being cremated for his troubles, along with several others who made the mistake of coming in contact with him. In a plot device obviously swiped from *Return of the Living Dead*, birds exposed to the now airborne virus die but return as flesh-eating zombies. Of course, it becomes an epidemic, and before too long a small group of survivors find themselves trying to escape the clutches of the walking dead (which shouldn't be too difficult, considering one could probably smell the suckers coming from a mile away).

Started as a pseudo-sequel to *Zombi 2* by Lucio Fulci, but finished by Mattei due to Fulci's failing health, this Italian gut-muncher is a completely derivative affair. Everything has been done before—and better—by both of the filmmakers involved. (There's Fulci's aforementioned contribution, of course, and Mattei was responsible for *Inferno dei Morti-Viventi* [1981], to which this film is obviously indebted.) The make-up is, overall, quite shoddy, and everything else is sacrificed for shock effect: logic, common sense, *whatever*. (An unborn zombie baby, as well as a bad, bad, *bad* flying zombie head—are you sure this isn't an Indonesian effort?—are sure to make even the most indiscriminate splatterpunk cry uncle.) There is a cool hyperactive, machete-wielding zombie, but it's still a zombie and— deep breath—I'm *sick to death of zombies!*

I've had enough ... how about you?

Zombie 4—After Death *see* **Oltre la Morte**

Zombie 6—Monster Hunter *see* **Rosso Sangue**

Zombie Creeping Flesh *see* **Inferno dei Morti-Viventi**

Zombie Flesh Eaters 2 *see* **Zombi 3**

Ein Zombie Hing am Glockenseil *see* **L'Aldilá**

Zombie Inferno *see* **Inferno dei Morti-Viventi**

Zombie Island Massacre (1983)

Picnic Productions [US]
DIR: John N. Carter; PRO: David Broadnax; SCR: Logan O'Neil and William Stoddard; DOP: Robert M. Baldwin; EXP: Abraham Dabdoub and Michael Malagiero; MFX: Dennis Eger; SFX: Steve Kirshoff; MUS: Harry Manfredini
STR: David Broadnax, Tom Cantrell, Debbie Ewing, Christopher Ferris, Tom Fitzsimmons, Diane Clayre Holub, Deborah Jason, Rita Jenrette, Oscar Lawson, Mignon Lowe, Ian McMillian, Ralph Monaco, Emmett Murphy, George Peters, Luba Pinus, Harriet Rawlings, Trevor Reid, Dennis Stephenson, Bruce Sterman and Kristina Wetzel
Approximately 89m; Color
VHS1: *Zombie Island Massacre* [MHE; 89m]; VHS2: *Zombie Island Massacre* [TRO; 85m]
ADL: *Have a Fun-Filled Vacation! Toe-Tapping Machete Head Dances! Glamorous Zombie-Style Cosmetic Surgery! Fabulous Air-Condition Tiger Pits!*

A bunch of idiot vacationers get knocked off one by one by what they assume to be zombies—or, at the very least, cannibals—after witnessing an obviously staged voodoo ritual.

Bland production values highlight this forgettable mock-horror flick that, for numerous reasons, will probably remind the viewer of a *Scooby Doo* episode. (Where's Casey Casum when you need him?) Performances are okay, as is the gore, but neither is anything to hoop and holler about. (Most of the action takes place at night, so much of the violence— maybe thankfully—is underexposed.) The viewer is also subjected to an unnecessary shower scene (with a "native" replacing Norman Bates) and some gratuitous timpani music. There are a few surprises, though, and despite all of its faults, the film is not wholly unengaging.

Zombie Nosh *see* **Flesh Eater**

Zombie of the Savanna *see* **Inferno dei Morti-Viventi**

Zombies Atomicos *see* **Incubo sulla Città Contaminata**

Zombies unter Kannibalen *see* **La Regina dei Cannibal**

Zombiethon (1986)

Taryn Productions Inc. [US]
DIR: Ken Dixon; PRO: Ken Dixon; EXP: Charles Band; MFX: Joe Reader
STR: Tracy Burton, K. Janyll Caudle, Laura Lady, Janessa Lester, Janelle Lewis, Frank Olechnicki, Dante Renta, Randolph Roehbling, Paula Singleton, Chuck Spera and Guy Thorpe
Approximately 90m; Color
VHS1: *Zombiethon* [WIZ; 90m]

"Just when you thought it was safe to go back into the graveyard, *Zombiethon* puts more dead bodies back into action than Frankenstein ever dreamed of as one zombie gem after another creeps across your screen. From the classic cornerstone of the undead, *Zombie*, through the wet look of *Zombie Lake* and the dry look of *Oasis of the Zombies*, any real horror fan will relish this smorgasbord of zombie fare. *Revenge of the Zombies*, *Return of the Zombies*—we've got them coming and going. *White Zombie*, *Space Zombies*, zombies from all walks of death. *The Invisible Dead* appear by popular demand. The hysterical midnight matinee clearly shows, 'Death is never having to say you're not coming back.' The living dead are the living end in *Zombiethon*."

Say ... you think there are any zombies in this film? Much to my chagrin, there were.

I let the tacky video box synopsis do all the work for me. (Hey, I've put a lot of time into this book, and it's the last entry, so cut me some slack, all right?) If you like crappy zombie flicks, you've probably seen most of the productions from which this compilation culls their "highlights," so why pay a video company just so they can advertise their back catalog? Okay, so Wizard Video is long since dead, and most of these flicks were later made available from Edde Entertainment, but I don't like compilation tapes. I don't think it's fair that *you* can cheat and watch the few interesting scenes these films have to offer, whereas Yours Truly has the abominable chore of having to sit through each and every one of them in their entirety just so I can tell you the obvious.

Zombiethon also has a really obnoxious, almost incoherent wraparound sequence, but if you rent this sucker instead of suffering as I have, you deserve to have to sit through it. So there.

Oh, and contrary to what the box claims, clips for *Revenge of the Zombies*, *Return of the Zombies*, and *White Zombie* are nowhere to be found. (Having been repeatedly exposed to the consummate ineptitude that was Wizard Video, it doesn't surprise me that they didn't stick around for very long, pretty display boxes or no pretty display boxes.)

Zombio *see* **Re-Animator**

Sources for DVDs and Videocassettes

The following are legitimate video companies:

A-Pix Entertainment, 500 Fifth Avenue, New York, NY, 10110, *www.un apixent.com*

Anchor Bay Entertainment, 500 Kirts Blvd., Troy, MI, 48084, *www.anchor bayentertainment.com*

Arrow Films, *www.arrowfilms.co.uk*

Artisan Entertainment, *www.artisan ent.com*

Avalanche Home Entertainment, 578 Post Road East, Suite 712, Westport, CT, 06880

Barrel Entertainment, PO Box 182035, Shelby Township, MI, 48318, *www.barrel-entertainment.com*

Columbia/TriStar Home Video, 10202 West Washington Blvd., Culver City, CA, 90232-3195, *www. cthv.com*

Dead-Alive Productions, 111 West Main Street, Mesa, AZ, 85201

Diamond Entertainment, 800 Tucker Lane, Walnut, CA, 91789, (909) 839-1989

Elite Entertainment, *www.elitedisc. com*

Entertainment Programs International, 4230 Del Rey Avenue, Suite 507, Marina Del Rey, CA, 90292

Fantoma, *www.fantoma.com*

Film Threat Video, PO Box 3170, Los Angeles, CA, 90078-3170, *www. filmthreat.com*

Fox Lorber Home Video, 419 Park Avenue South, New York, NY, 10016, *www.foxlorber.com*

Full Moon Home Video, 3030 Andrita Street, Los Angeles, CA, 90065, (323) 468-0599, *www.fullmoonpictures.com*

Image Entertainment, 9333 Oso Avenue, Chatsworth, CA, 91311, *www. image-entertainment.com*

Japan Shock, PO Box 12117, 3501 AC Utrecht, the Netherlands, *www. japanshock.com*

Live Entertainment, Inc., 15400 Sherman Way, Van Nuys, CA, 91406

Madacy Entertainment, Inc., PO Box 1445, St. Laurent, Quebec, Canada, H4L 421, *www.madacyvideo.com*

Manga Entertainment, (212) 777-8056, *www.manga.com*

MGM Home Video, 2500 Broadway, Santa Monica Blvd., CA, 90404-3061, *www.mgm.com*

MPI Media Group, 16101 S. 108th Avenue, Orlando Park, IL, 60467, *www.mpimedia.com*

New Line Cinema Home Video, *www.newline.com*

Paramount Home Video, 5555 Melrose Avenue, Hollywood, CA, 90038, *www.paramount.com*

Program Power Entertainment, 190 Pomona Avenue, Long Beach, CA, 90803, (562) 621-9090, *www.programpower.com*

Republic Pictures Home Video, 12636 Beatrice Street, Los Angeles, CA, 90066-0930

Rhino Home Video, 10635 Santa Monica Blvd., Los Angeles, CA, 90025-4900, 1-800-432-0020, *www.rhino.com*

Salvation Films, Ltd., BCM PO Box 9235, London, WC1N 3XX, UK, *www.salvation-films.com*

Something Weird Video, PO Box 33664, Seattle, WA, 98133, (206) 361-3759, *www.somethingweird.com*

Synapse Films, PO Box 1860, Bloomington, IL, 61702, (309) 661-9201, *www.synapse-films.com*

Tai Seng Video Marketing, 170 South Spruce Avenue, Suite 200, South San Francisco, CA, 94080, 1-800-888-3836, *www.taisengentertainment.com*

Tempe Video, 3727 West Magnolia Blvd., #241, Burbank, CA, 91510-7711, *www.tempevideo.com*

Troma Inc., Radio City Station, PO Box 486, New York, NY, 10101-0486, *www.troma.com*

20th Century–Fox, *www.foxhome.com*

Universal Home Video, *www.universal.com*

VCI Entertainment, 11333 East 60th Place, Tulsa, OK, 74146, *www.vcientertainment.com*

Vipco, *www.horrorvideo.com*

Warner Home Video, 4000 Warner Blvd., Burbank, CA, 91522, *www.warnerbros.com*

World Artists Home Video, PO Box 36788, Los Angeles, CA, 90036-0788

The following are legitimate outfits who specialize in new or out of print factory-made videos:

Asian Cult Cinema, PO Box 16-1919, Miami, FL 331166, (305) 386-2227, *www.asiancult.com*

Cinema Classics, PO Box 174, Village Station, New York, NY, 10014, (212) 677-6309, *www.cinemaclassics.com*

Draculina, PO Box 587, Glen Carbon, IL, 62034, (800) 358-2755, *www.draculina.com*

EI Independent Cinema, PO Box 371, Glenwood, NJ, 07418, (973) 509-9352, *www.eicinema.com*

Scarlet Street Video, PO Box 604, Glen Rock, NJ, 07452, *www.scarletstreet.com*

Science Fiction Continuum, 1701 East Second Street, Scotch Plains, NJ, 07076, (908) 322-2010, *www.sfcontinuum.com*

The Trash Collector, PO Box 5273, Everett, WA, 98206-5273, *www.thetrashcollector.com*

Trash Palace, PO Box 1972, Frederick, MD, 21702-0972, (301) 681-4625, *www.trashpalace.com*

Video Wasteland, PO Box 81551, Cleveland, OH, 44181-1551, (440) 891-1920, *www.videowasteland.com*

Water Bearer Films, 48 West 21st Street, Suite 301, New York, NY, 10010, (212) 242-8686, *www.waterbearer.com*

Although every attempt has been made to ensure that this list is up to date, some contact information and URLs may have changed by the time this book is published.

Index

343 *Index*